16-BIT MODERN MICROCOMPUTERS
The Intel I8086 Family

GEORGE W. GORSLINE

Virginia Polytechnic Institute & State University
Blacksburg, Virginia

PRENTICE-HALL, INC., Englewood Cliffs, New Jersey 07632

Library of Congress Cataloging in Publication Data

Gorsline, G. W. (date)
16-bit modern microcomputers.

Bibliography: p.
Includes index.
1. Microcomputers. 2. Intel 8086 (Microprocessor)
I. Title. II. Title: Sixteen-bit modern microcomputers.
QA76.5.G645 1985 001.64'2 84—9991
ISBN 0-13-811415-3

Editorial/production supervision: *Lynn Frankel*
Cover design: *Diane Saxe*
Manufacturing buyer: *Gordon Osbourne*

Printed in the United States of America

10 9 8 7 6 5 4 3 2

ISBN 0-13-811415-3 01

Prentice-Hall International, Inc., *London*
Prentice-Hall of Australia Pty. Limited, *Sydney*
Editora Prentice-Hall do Brasil, Ltda., *Rio de Janeiro*
Prentice-Hall Canada Inc., *Toronto*
Prentice-Hall of India Private Limited, *New Delhi*
Prentice-Hall of Japan, Inc., *Tokyo*
Prentice-Hall of Southeast Asia Pte. Ltd., *Singapore*
Whitehall Books Limited, *Wellington, New Zealand*

Contents

Preface

During the 1980 through 1982 period I was privileged to discuss the different 16-bit microcomputers with students, faculty, and programmers at scattered colleges and universities across the United States. In most of these discussions there were a surprising number of very knowledgeable high school students as well as their parents and teachers. The questions from these groups made it clear that an integrated presentation of the software system aspects of a popular 16-bit machine was badly needed. At that time I was also teaching an upper-division college course covering the area of microcomputer software design and implementation. This book is the direct result of my unsuccessful search for a satisfactory text for that course coupled with the expressed need of practitioners for such materials.

Most colleges and universities are offering an upper-division course treating some aspect of microcomputers in some depth. At Virginia Tech, we have at least four such offerings: a hardware-oriented course in Electrical Engineering, an interfacing-instrumentation course in Chemistry, an educational techniques course in Education, and a systems-software-oriented course in Computer Science. The latter course serves students possessing a fairly rigorous background in procedural-level language programming as well as a good introduction to basic computer hardware, to an assembly language, to translator design, and to operating systems, including concurrent process synchronization. A text that concentrated on the software systems aspects of a popular modern microcomputer system was not available.

This book was conceived as a response to the need for a text emphasizing the 16-bit microcomputer system—the combination of system software integrated with the hardware to adequately support modern applications. It is designed to be used in a college-level course treating microcomputers for software-oriented students as well as for the growing numbers of computer-oriented superior high school students, their ambitious teachers, and their frustrated parents. It will also be valuable to practicing programmers who need or desire additional background in modern microcomputer systems.

Even though the field of computational systems is extremely dynamic, it is possible to defend the gross generalization that several different markets exist, although overlap is also evident. Thus there is the "number-crunching market" for a relatively small number of supercomputers characterized by the CRAY 1 system; there is the "maxicomputer market" typified by the IBM 3081 system; there is the "midicomputer market" typified by the DEC VAX 780 and the IBM 4341; there is the "minicomputer market" dominated by the DEC PDP 11 family and being invaded by the newer, more capable 16-bit microcomputer systems; and there is the "microcomputer market," which has been characterized by the Radio Shack TRS 80 based on the 8-bit ZILOG 80 and the Apple based on the 8-bit Motorola 6502 but which is also being invaded by the 16-bit microcomputer systems. It is almost certain that the small business, the word processing, the educational, and personal/home computer market will be dominated by 16-bit microcomputers.

The September 1982 issue of *BYTE* magazine reported that the 1981 shipment of 16-bit microprocessors was just under 1-million units. The Intel I8086 family dominated the market with 78%—718,000 units in the year. At the same time, prices for these microcomputer systems have been steadily decreasing at both the wholesale and the retail level. The Intel prices of the 16-bit processor-based systems are fully comparable to the prices of 8-bit systems, with similar memory sizes and peripherals. Additionally, whereas most 8-bit systems are near or at their expansion/upgrade ceiling, the 16-bit systems can easily be expanded. Quality software is available, including operating systems, language translators, and applications programs. Prices for minimal systems currently range from about $750 to $3500, depending on the peripherals. Small business and professional office systems can be purchased in the range $4000 to $10,000, with customized software applications systems requiring at least an equal or greater investment. Multiaccess systems supporting up to eight terminals for educational, business records, or word processing are available at a cost from $8000 to $20,000 or more, with customized software often doubling or tripling the initial investment.

GEORGE W. GORSLINE

1

The Classical Microcomputer

A VIEWPOINT

THE ABILITY–COST–SIZE TREND

Over the past century and half there have been many innovative developments and trends in implementing and programming arithmetic-logic machines. Considering hardware, computers have progressed from the original mechanical logic "engine" of Charles Babbage in the second third of the nineteenth century, through the electromagnetic relay machines of the first third of the twentieth century, to the vacuum tube/acoustic memory of the first electronic stored digital program computer of the mid-1940s. These were followed by the discrete transistor/coincident current core memory computers of the 1950s through the initial small-scale integrated-circuit computers of the early 1970s to the very large scale integrated circuit (VLSI) microcomputers of the early 1980s. The trend has been: simplified assembly and repair; smaller physical size and reduced operating energy; greater reliability and lower cost; increased speed, logical complexity, and ability; as well as more registers with increased abilities together with faster and logically much larger memories.

Similarly, the programming of digital computers—that is, the design and implementation of the ordered set of instructions that constitute the program—originally required expressing the data manipulation process (the algorithm) in the absolute address machine language (a series of binary 1's and 0's). A progression over time occurred through the incorporation of "shop-standardized" input/output sections of absolute machine language code; through the invention of one-to-one symbolic programming systems, that is, assembly languages; to the development of macro assemblers, conditional assembly, relocating linking loaders, and libraries of subprograms; as well as procedural-level compiler languages such as FORTRAN. Included was the development of monitors that led to operating systems with such current common features as multiprogramming, interactive processing, virtual memory, data base management systems, and job control languages. The trend has been to allow the applications program designer/problem solver to pay less and less attention to the details of the computer while depending on systems of software produced by technical "experts" and thus to approach and solve larger and more complex problems. Programmers have become almost addicted to compiler languages, to libraries of useful procedures, to the services of an operating system, and to expert consultation help. This trend may eventually develop into professionalism when the current large, intense research efforts produce results that finally permeate the education of new generations of computer personnel. This will force the presently practicing personnel to "lift themselves by their own bootstraps" into the world of the near future.

Economically, these past, present, and probable near-future developments have resulted in the establishment, proliferation, and growth of a data processing industry whose gross dollar worth is measured in the several tens of billions and whose operations permeate the daily life of each and every person in "developed countries." The industry is presently vital and absolutely essential to the functioning of Western civilization, that is, the finding, production, and distribution of the human necessities of food, shelter, clothing, and so on. For the computer professional, the most important economic trends are of *three* kinds:

1. A steady, long-term, and drastic reduction (a dramatic and revolutionary reduction) in the cost of the hardware necessary for performing a data manipulation or transformation
2. A steady, long-term increase in the cost of the personnel necessary to determine the problem specifications and solution strategies; to design the solution tactics and implement the computer procedures; to collect and build the requisite data bases; to acquire and operate the computer equipment; and to manage the personnel, equipment, and supplies
3. A steady, long-term, but relatively slow reduction in the cost of computing and outputting a quantum of information

A consequence of these trends is the relative decrease in cost of the computer itself (produced in non-labor-intensive environment) compared to the systems software and applications programs (produced in a labor-intensive environment). An approximate graphical presentation of this relationship is shown in Figure 1.1.

Additionally, economists enunciate the *economy-of-scale* "law." In terms of computer technology it is stated as follows:

> A larger and/or faster computational system will produce applications problem output at a lower cost per quantum than a smaller and/or slower computational system until

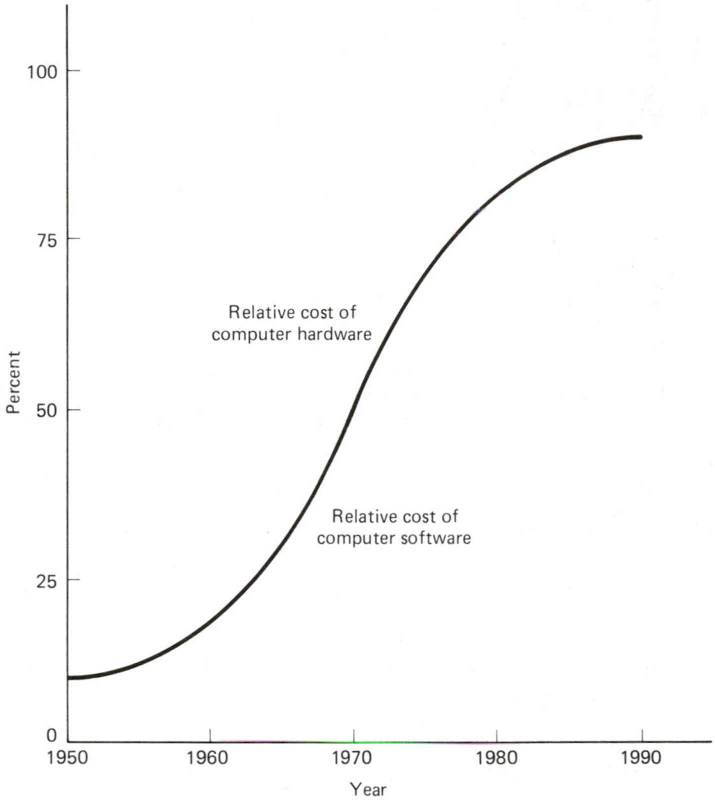

Figure 1.1 Long-term trend in the relative costs of hardware and software.

the expense of coping with the volume of input/output or the overhead of the more complex and larger operating system overcomes the economies of scale.

A graphical representation of this relationship is shown in Figure 1.2. Many years ago, Herbert Grosch formulated the empirical relationship between the price of computational systems and the ability of the same systems:

$$\text{price} \times 2 = (\text{ability})^2$$

Note that *Grosch's law* can be derived from the law of economy of scale if only the left side is considered, that is, if the area of positive economy-of-scale effects is considered. This is illustrated in Figure 1.2.

There are subjective reasons to believe that the introduction of a radical new technology will cause discontinuities in the law of economy of scale and in that portion of it known as Grosch's law. Among these effects, the following seem important:

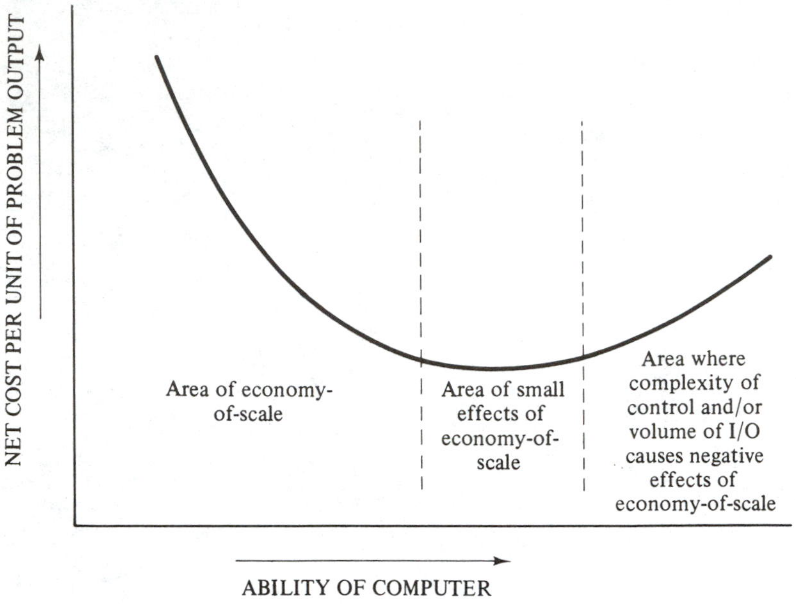

Figure 1.2 Rough diagrammatic illustration of the economy-of-scale relationship as it applies to computers within a single technological base. (Reprinted with permission from G.W. Gorsline, *Computer Organization: Hardware/Software,* Prentice-Hall, Inc., Englewood Cliffs, N.J., 1980.)

Symbolic assembly languages in wide use	1950 approx.
Discrete transistors in computers	1954 approx.
Coincident core memory	1957 approx.
First integrated circuits	1958–1959 approx.
Procedural-level languages in wide use	1960 approx.
Minicomputers	1963 approx.
Families of compatible computers	1964 approx.
Practical transistor memories	1965 approx.
Microprocessor-on-a-chip-based microcomputers	1968 approx.
Microcomputer-on-a-chip-based microcomputers with high ability	1978 approx.

Some of these long-term gross cost effects are illustrated in Figure 1.3.

It is strongly suggested that the traditional minicomputer will rapidly disappear over the next very few years from the cost-ability pressure of the 16/32-bit microcomputer. Early examples of this class of microcomputer are the Intel 8086, the Zilog Z8000, the Digital Equipment Corporation (DEC) LSI 11, the Texas In-

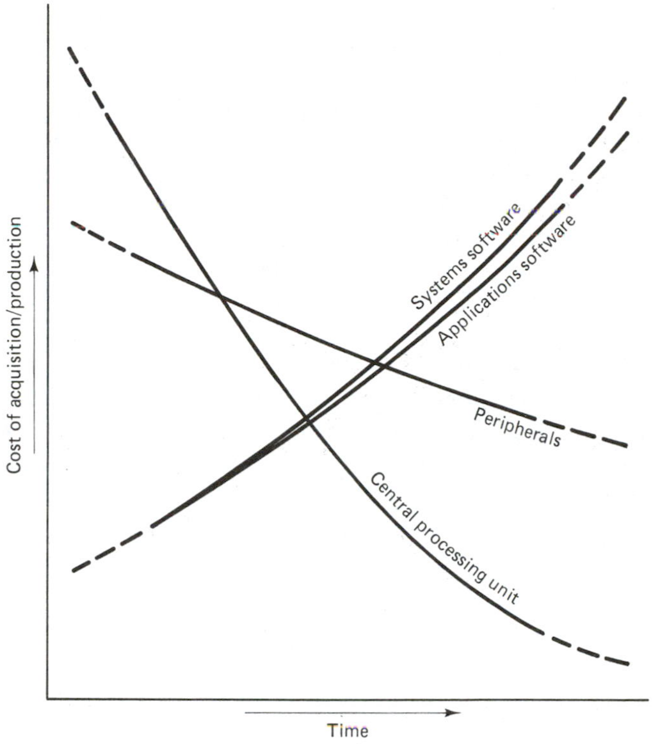

Figure 1.3 Relationship of trends in the costs of the CPU, peripheral devices, systems software (operating system, etc.), and applications programs.

struments TI 99/4, the Motorola MCS68000, and the Intel iAJX 432. It is also very probable that the low-ability end of maxicomputer families will also rapidly disappear (a process now well under way) due to the cost/ability pressure from the midicomputer. Examples of this class of midicomputer are the DEC VAX 780, the P.E 32XO, the Prime 750, the IBM 43X1, the IBM System 38, and others.

HISTORICAL PERSPECTIVE

The most volatile technological developments of the contemporary industrial age are in the electronics industry. Since the introduction of the transistor in 1948 and its incorporation into computers in 1954, the physical size of electronic devices has been reduced by an average factor of 2 every year. Until the advent of the transistor, each type of component in an electronic circuit was fashioned from one or more materials possessing the needed electrical characteristics. For example, carbon was used for resistors, ceramics and a dielectric for capacitors, tungsten for the emitters in vacuum tubes, and so on. Such components, with characteristics defined by their composition and construction, were used in creating a circuit with specified characteristics and responses. Circuits were then combined into systems.

The transistor was the first electronic component in which materials with different electrical characteristics were not interconnected but were physically fabricated in one structure. Thus the transistor obviated the need for separate materials (carbon, tungsten, ceramics, etc.) used in fabricating the circuit components. Nevertheless, the discrete transistor did little to alter the requirement for connecting the individual components—and electronics is a technology of complex interconnections.

The preferred transistor raw material was a single crystal of silicon sliced into round wafers. By suitable masking and "doping" techniques, which selectively altered the electrical behavior of small regions, many transistors could be fabricated on each wafer slice. Each such transistor was sealed into a three-connection canlike package about 0.25 inch in diameter. The problem of combining these discrete transistors into a complex circuit with many interconnections remained.

A series of standard circuit modules on plastic boards, each with a specific function, were developed and used as logical building blocks for creating subsystems that could be plugged together as needed. As systems became larger and more complex, the fabrication of the complex wiring interconnection networks between boards became very costly as well as a signal speed limit for the system. Thus as transistor technology increased the switching speed of the circuits, it became increasingly important to decrease both the size of the components and the length of the interconnections.

In October 1958, Jack Kilby of Texas Instruments, Inc., created what is considered the first integrated circuit (IC) by manually connecting in a predetermined pattern, using very fine wires, the many transistors on a single wafer of silicon. This process not only did not reduce the problem of complex interconnections but, as can be imagined, it was not very practical. In April 1959, Robert Noyce of Fairchild Semiconductor perfected a method of depositing (evaporating) aluminum as planed interconnections between the many transistors on a silicon wafer. This "planar process" resulted in the first practical integrated circuit and thus was the breakthrough that has "solved" the long-standing electronics problem of complex interconnections. The special properties needed for the various circuit elements were achieved by selectively diffusing traces of impurities into the silicon or oxidizing it to silicon dioxide. The principles of photolithography were used to expose selected regions of the silicon to diffusion while protecting other regions.

Continued development has raised the number of "components" contained in such an integrated circuit from about 5 to 20 (small-scale integration, SSI), through several hundred components (medium-scale integration, MSI) to thousands of components (large-scale integration, LSI), and finally to hundreds of thousands of components (very-large-scale integration, VLSI). Point faults in the semiconductor crystal cause faulty circuits and thus reduce the yield of acceptable units. Such crystal faults are randomly distributed over the surface of the silicon wafer and thus of the chip. Different technologies have different characteristics and costs. An exploration of this subject is beyond the scope of this book. An excellent tutorial, presented at the university student level, is given in Clark (1980).* Figure 1.4 traces the developmental trends.

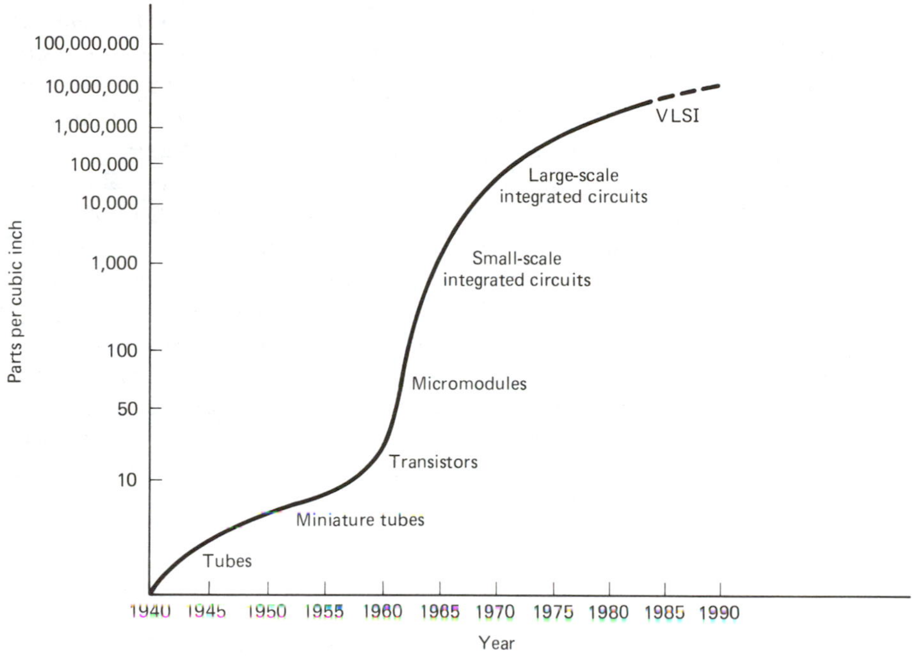

Figure 1.4 Electronics miniaturization trends. (From E. Braun and S. MacDonald, *Revolution in Miniature,* Cambridge University Press, New York, 1978.)

In 1967, a patent was issued for an experimental four-function pocket calculator based on a single integrated circuit (McWhorter, 1976). By 1970 it was practical to market such a device for less than \$100, and in 1976 several mass-produced models were available for less than \$10. Sophisticated multifunction models that include a wide selection of trigonometric functions and are user programmable have also become available at higher prices.

The steady increase in integrated-circuit component density, complexity, and organization led to the microcomputer, a full-fledged general-purpose machine whose logic and memory circuits could be mounted on a single plastic card. In 1971, the Intel Corporation developed a versatile, programmable, single-chip

*Complete information for all references cited is given in the Bibliography.

microprocessor, the Intel 4004 (see Figure 1.5). Logically a central processing unit (CPU), the I4004 manipulated data that were 4 bits wide and had instructions for both binary- and decimal-mode data manipulations. The I4004 had 2250 transistors on a silicon substrate measuring 0.117 by 0.159 in. Combined with a master clock, a primary memory, and a control memory (for microinstructions), it would be a minimal general-purpose microcomputer priced below $100 (current prices).

A few months later, Intel introduced a microprocessor chip designed to manipulate 8-bit data, the I8008, that had more computing power and flexibility and thus was more suitable for data handling and control applications. Two other early models were designed and manufactured by Rockwell International and National Semiconductor. These microprocessors were quickly incorporated into a wide range of applications, from laboratory/industrial instruments to sales terminals and electronic games. It should be noted that the first known commercial use of an integrated circuit occurred with miniaturized hearing aids in December 1963.

Companies such as Rockwell, National Semiconductor, and Fairchild introduced microprocessors to the market and these gained sufficient acceptance to encourage further activity. In 1973, the modern microprocessor era began when Intel announced the 8080 microcomputer, which had more capability than prior microcomputers. It was followed a year later by Motorola's 6800, which had such features as index registers, two accumulators, and an input–output system that programmatically looked like memory. The next step, the entry by other semiconductor companies with their microcomputer designs, was quite predictable. The microcomputer had arrived!

Year	Company	Development
1964	Viatron Computer	Developed first 8-bit LSI microprocessor used to control data terminal
1969	Viatron Computer	Developed first 8-bit LSI microprocessor used as basic element in a minicomputer
1971	Intel	Developed 4-bit 4004 for commercial sales
1972	Rockwell	PPS-4 microprocessor
	Fairchild	PPS-25 microprocessor
	Intel	8008
1973	National Semiconductor	IMP
	Intel	8080
1974	Motorola	6800
	Monolithic Memories	Bit-slice introduction
1975	Texas Instruments	4-bit slice
	Fairchild	F-8

Figure 1.5 Early historical development of the microprocessor.

THE MICROCOMPUTER

The microcomputer as a system has as its basis the microprocessor chip. These chips come in various sizes and are implemented in various technologies. When the microprocessor chips are combined with other integrated circuits, a microcomputer system can be constructed. The majority of these have been 8-bit data oriented, although the number of 16-bit devices is increasing, and a few 32-bit devices have been announced. The evolution of the microcomputer is summarized in Figure 1.6.

One of the continually evolving aspects of the physical microcomputer system topology is the number of functions centered on a single chip. Most VLSI chips now available are really microprocessors. For a microprocessor to qualify as a microcomputer requires the addition of enough circuits to allow basic computer functions to take place—usually a basic arithmetic processor that can interact with

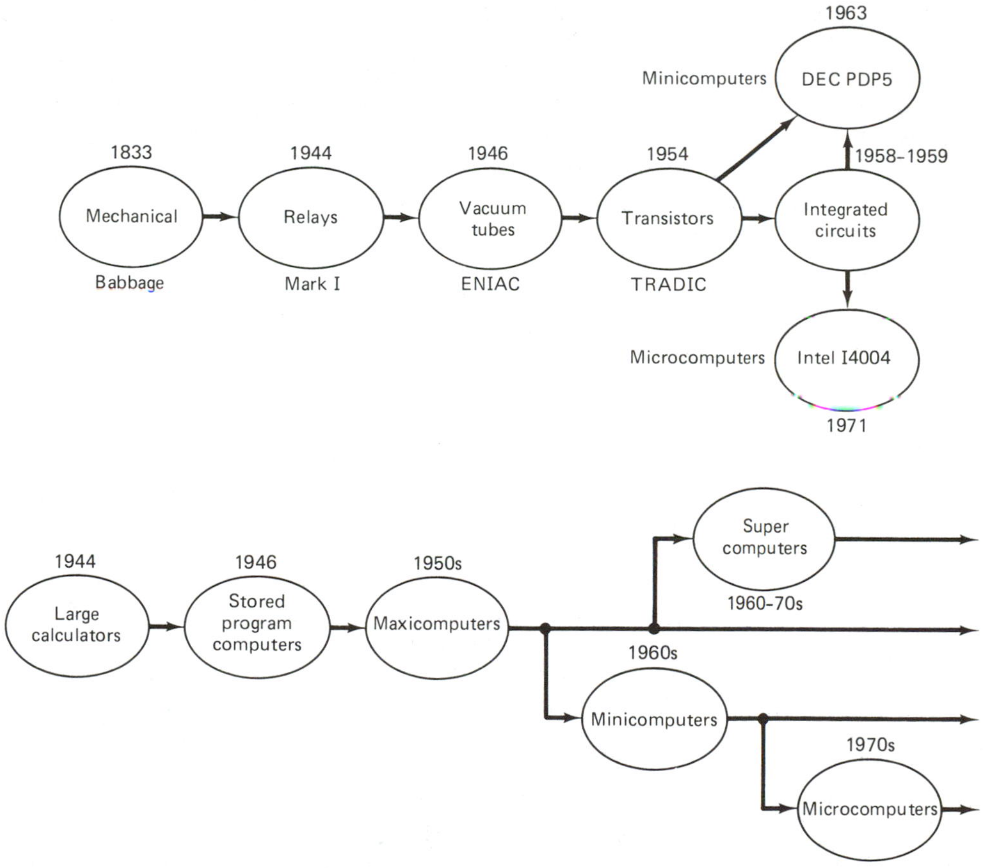

Figure 1.6 Microcomputer evolution.

a memory and also control the input and output of data. Some microcomputers for limited applications, such as carburetion control of an automobile, are self-contained on a single chip.

ALU

The arithmetic-logic unit is the central element of the entire microcomputer. A typical implementation of the ALU function includes primitive arithmetic operations such as the addition and subtraction of data words. The unit also performs logic operations such as "and," "or," and "exclusive or." Quite often, the majority of the miscellaneous processor operations, such as counting, will all be centralized here. This is advantageous, because the ALU already contains the basic logic pieces used to perform most such operations.

Interfacing

This is a key problem area in a microprocessor. Interfacing must solve the question of how to handle the interaction between functions on different chips and, more specifically, the connection of the processor functions with the memory and the input/output. An obvious answer to one aspect, the interaction of processor functions, is the emergence of true single-chip processors.

In the first-generation chips (such as the Intel 4004), additional logic was required to interface the various microprocessor pieces, such as the timing and the interfaces to memory and input/output (Figure 1.7*a*). Because of the problems in adjusting timing circuits, it was quite common to have an external clock. In some of the later microprocessors the timing was placed on the chip itself. The only external connection required was to a crystal oscillator. As the chips evolved, memory addressing was assigned to separate pins so as to eliminate some of the memory interface requirements. This had certain limitations because of the number of memory circuits that could be electrically driven was small. If the memory requirements were extensive, additional "driving" circuits were still required.

Control

Microcontrol is the sequencing of primitive operations within the CPU. Thus the sequence of steps that constitute the fetching of an instruction from program memory and its subsequent execution is initiated and controlled by this subsystem. The control function may be directly implemented in hard circuits with a permanent information path and step logic. Alternatively, this function may be implemented employing a lower-level micro-control function and control-program memory that is microprogrammed to implement (to emulate) each step of fetching and executing every instruction of the microcomputer as seen by the applications and systems programmer. An early and excellent tutorial on implementing the control function of computers through microprogramming was published in *Computer Surveys* (Rosin,

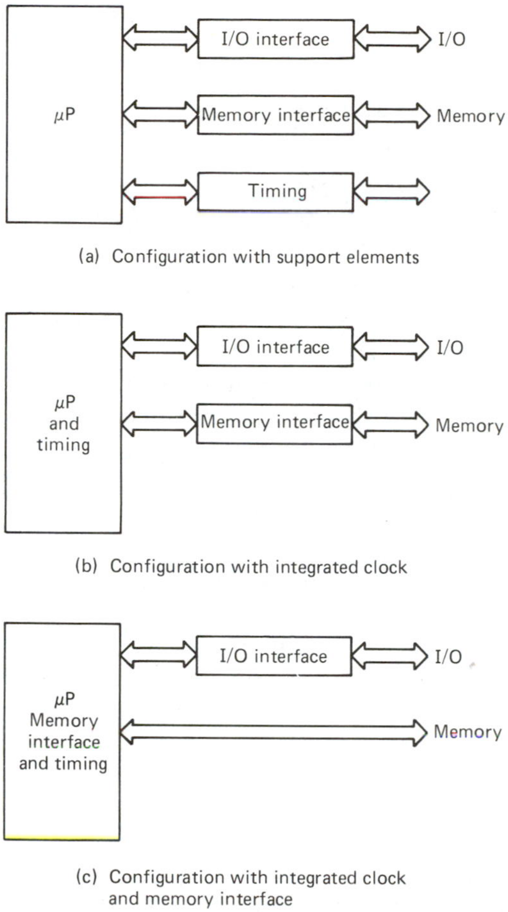

(c) Configuration with integrated clock and memory interface

Figure 1.7 Trends in microcomputer configurations.

1969). Some microprocessors use random logic and place the control on the same chip as the ALU (I8080, M6800), which, of course, requires more logic functions on the chip. The decision on how best to partition the functions is significantly dependent on how the control function is implemented.

It is often desirable to separate the control function from the other processor functions. This is because read-only memory (ROM) can now be implemented using any standard commercial ROM chip, and thus the CPU chip becomes less dense with a potentially higher yield (Figure 1.8). This technique is used in the DEC LSI-11. It results in additional chips which are used to microprogram the microprocessor. The flexibility of added functions obtained from the microprogramming technique will quite often offset the cost of the additional control chips. In fact, the additional chips necessary to add functions to nonmicroprogrammed processors will often add more chips to the system than would be required for microprogrammed control.

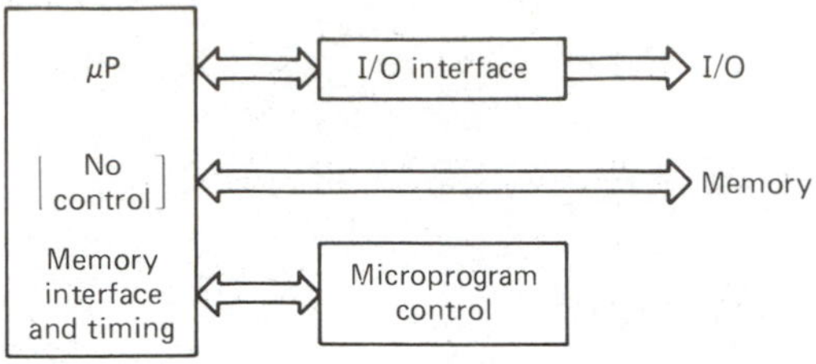

Figure 1.8 Microprogrammed control.

This fact indicates that the assignment of functions to a chip is not always done with total system minimization as a goal. Further, there is a preoccupation by the manufacturer to market the one-chip microprocessor. This is, of course, quite desirable for controller applications. When used in a systems applicaton, the resulting large chip count often comes as a shock and is a reminder of the meaning of *caveat emptor.*

Registers

The register section of the CPU varies considerably from processor to processor. The number of registers may vary from one to eight or more. Some of the possible uses of the registers are for address modification, for saving subroutine addresses, for the program counter, for auxiliary accumulators, or as a small scratch-pad memory. Of course, various combinations of these uses depend on the architectural plan.

Memory

The interfacing of the processor with memory requires some amount of read/write memory, which is usually random-access memory (RAM). Portions of this can be replaced by a fixed program in read-only memory (ROM). For systems with large amounts of memory, a memory address register must be added. Some processor chips do not have sufficient logic to handle the expansion of memory, so that additional external control circuitry may be necessary.

Input/Output

The I/O control section is always the most difficult portion of the computer to standardize. But in general, buffering of data and of control is almost always required between I/O devices and the computer. The effort to place as much of this buffering as possible on the processor chip is a continuing effort. The proper sequencing of I/O data to and from the processor demands that some of this control be incorporated into the micro control of the processor. However, this may not be sufficient if there is any expansion of I/O functions so that additional control with additional circuits will probably be needed.

When all the pieces are put together to form a usable microcomputer, no matter how the manufacturer partitioned the computer, it has become a computer-on-a-board (Figure 1.9). How well the pieces intermesh to form a smoothly functioning computer structure will determine the success of the architectural plan.

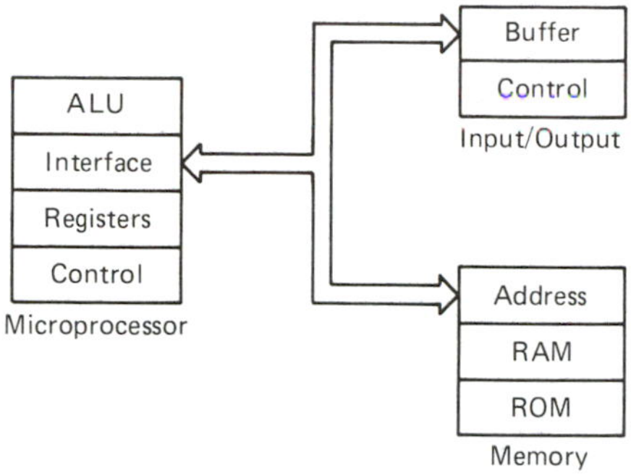

Figure 1.9 Main elements of a microprocessor.

MICROCOMPUTER CHARACTERISTICS

Microcomputers, in a very generalized sense, have some characteristics in common, although exceptions exist in almost every case. These characteristics for 8-bit machines can be summarized as follows:

1. Relatively narrow data paths, memory cells, and registers. Memory cells and data paths tend to be 8 bits wide with simultaneous parallel information transmission. Registers tend to be 8 bits and 16 bits wide. Address paths tend to be 16 bits wide. The 16-bit microcomputers do not possess these limitations.
2. Arithmetic and logic instructions tend to be register-to-register and register-to-memory binary operations with an instruction to cause decimal-digit correction as an anachronism dating to the origin of the microprocessor in the calculator industry. Fairly nice bit-manipulation instructions are often available.
3. The size of primary memory is often limited to 64K (K = 1024) as a result of the 16-bit address lines. An index register may be available, although not universally. The 16-bit microcomputer often can support memory sizes of 1 million bytes or more.
4. Stack-pointer instructions are generally available to support primary-memory-resident subprocedure return-address stacks.
5. Privileged instructions are not generally available. The 16-bit microcomputers employ various design strategies to accomplish the desired protection feature.
6. The instructions supporting hardware interrupts and software interrupts (supervisor calls) usually interfere with each other in ways that prevent both types of interrupts from being used in the same software system. The 16-bit microcomputers avoid this restriction.

7. I/O is often of the memory-mapped type, although the Intel 8080 and related systems have I/O instructions.

THE INSTRUCTION CYCLE

Consider the somewhat generalized microcomputer whose organizational structure is shown in Figure 1-10. The memory subassembly of this, and all other conventional computers, consists of consecutively numbered cells each one of which can contain one byte of information. This information can represent (1) a portion of a program, (2) a portion of the data that the aforementioned program is designed to manipulate, or (3) undefined or noise contents of a memory cell that has not been deliberately filled with either data or program.

A program for all conventional microcomputers is a fully ordered set of instructions that will be executed in sequential order (except for those instructions that specifically change this execution order—jumps or branches). The address in memory of the instruction currently being executed is contained in the program counter (PC)—one of the addressing registers illustrated in Figure 1.10 (often the

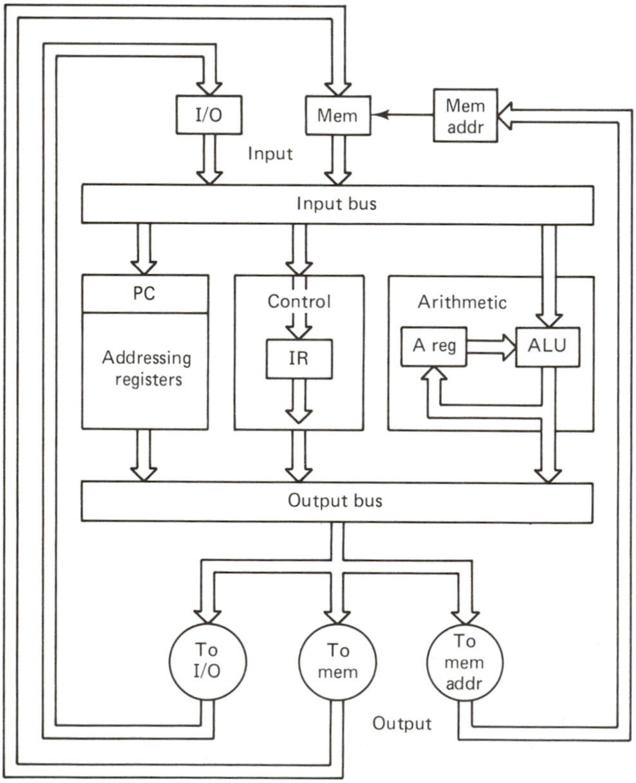

Figure 1.10 Generalized microcomputer structure.

only one). To reiterate, the PC contains the address in memory of the instruction currently being executed.

An instruction of all conventional microcomputers consists of two portions: an operations code that specifies the action, and an operand address or addresses, each of which explicitly specifies the address in memory of a datum on which the action specified in the operations code (opcode) is to be carried out. In general, microcomputers are designed with the following instruction types: (1) data manipulation, (2) input/out, and (3) program control flow.

1. Data manipulation instructions:

MOV	X,Y	[Register (X)]	←	[Register (Y)]
MOV	X,MemAddr	[Register (X)]	←	[Memory (Z)]
MOV	MemAddr,X	[Memory (Z)]	←	[Register (X)]
MOV	X, = '17'	[Register (X)]	←	Datum
MOV	MemAddr, = '17'	[Memory (Z)]	←	Datum
ADD	X,Y	[Register (X)]	←	[Register (X)] + [Register (Y)]
ADD	X,MemAddr	[Register (X)]	←	[Register (X)] + [Memory (Z)]
ADD	X, = '17'	[Register (X)]	←	[Register (X)] + Datum

2. Data input/output instruction:

IN	X,Device#3	[Register (X)]	←	[Device (3)]

3. Program control flow instructions:

JMP THERE	[PC] ← MemAddr THERE
JMPZ THERE	IF < last result = 0 >
	Then [PC] ← MemAddr THERE
	Else [PC] ← [PC] + 1

In accomplishing the instructions listed above, as well as numerous additional instructions, conventional computers, including microcomputers, must first obtain the instruction from memory and then execute it. As this process is repeated for every instruction in a program, a repetitive process or loop is indicated:

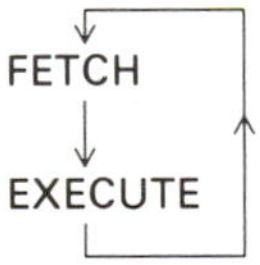

We will illustrate this *instruction cycle* through tracing the details of executing an instruction commonly known as ADD IMMEDIATE. This instruction is often indicated in an assembly language program as

ADD #17 [Register] ← [Register] + Datum

and resides in the memory locations whose address is currently contained in the program counter (PC) and in the next consecutive location. Referring to Figure 1.11, it should be realized that our example hypothetical microcomputer possesses only one accumulator register, and therefore its identification is implied in the instruction.

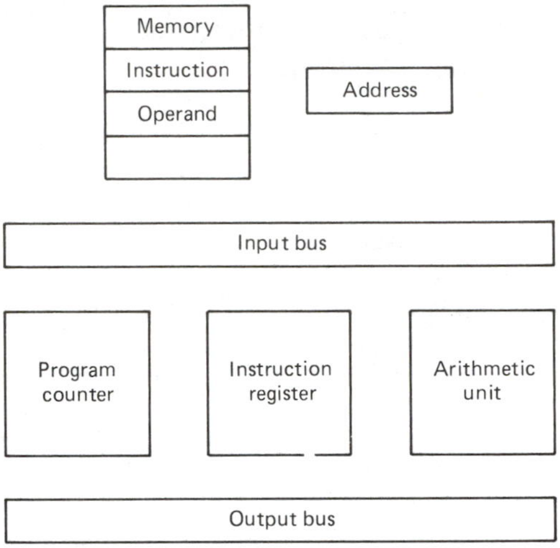

Figure 1.11 Subassemblies of the microcomputer diagrammed in Figure 1.12. Using this structure of subassemblies, Figure 1.12 illustrates the instruction cycle for the Move Immediate Instruction ADD #17, where the operation code is contained in the memory location whose address is contained in the program counter, the data are contained in the next sequential memory location, and the next sequential instruction is the memory location following.

The instruction cycle for this instruction of our hypothetical microcomputer consists of four instruction steps, as illustrated in Figure 1.12. A flowchart of the instruction cycle is given in Figure 1.13. Figure 1.14 illustrates some alternative microcomputer organizational schemes that would affect the details of the instruction cycle.

PROGRAM FLOW-OF-CONTROL INSTRUCTIONS

The actions of the execute phase of the instruction cycle of various instructions are illustrated in Figure 1.15. Particular attention should be given to the method of accomplishing a branch, as shown in Figure 1.16. Recall that the normal flow of program execution is the sequential execution of instructions in the order of their occurrence in memory. Also recall that this is accomplished by incrementing the program counter during the fetch phase of the instruction cycle (and also in the execute phase of many instructions). The typical branch instruction of microcomputers has the form

```
JMP THERE
```

where the symbolic operand represents an address within the program in memory. The branch is accomplished by replacing the contents of the program counter with this address, after which the sequential nature of the microcomputer is again in

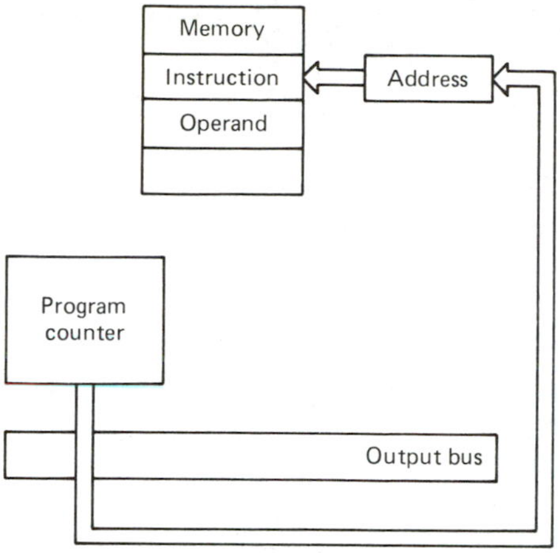

(a) Instruction Cycle – Fetch Phase – Step 1:

[MAR] ← [PC]

Send the contents of the Program Counter to the Memory Address Register.

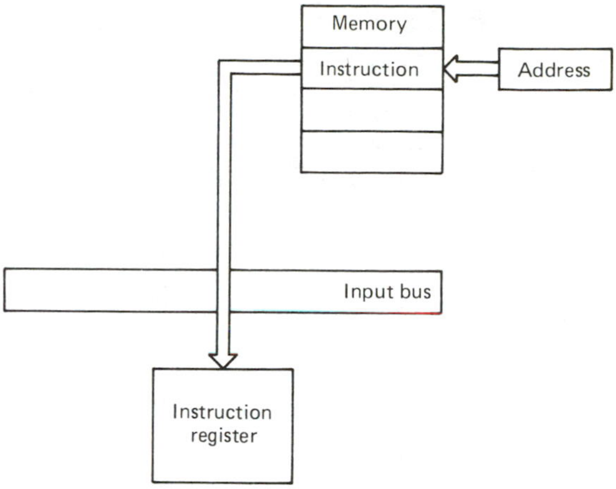

(b) Instruction Cycle – Fetch Phase – Step 2:

[IR] ← [Memory (MAR)]
[PC] ← [PC] + 1

Get the operation code from memory and send it to the Instruction Register (IR). Simultaneously increment the Program Counter so that it points at the next sequential memory location.

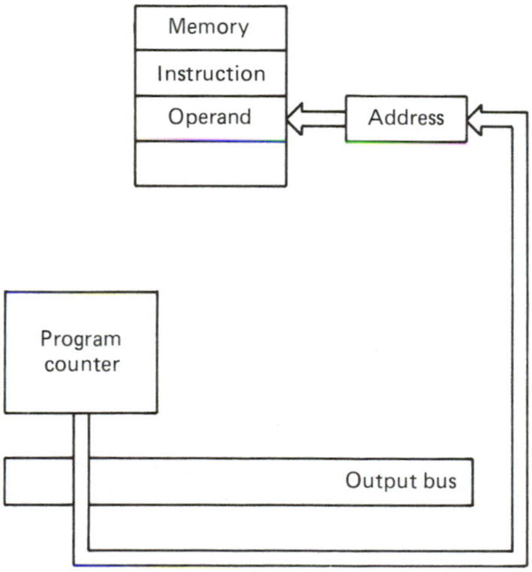

(c) Instruction Cycle -- Execute Phase – Step 3:

Decode Operation Code
[MAR] ← [PC]

After determining, by the bit pattern of the contents of the Instruction Register, that this is an Add Immediate instruction (the data is implied as the contents of the next memory location); contents of the Program Counter are sent to the Memory Address Register.

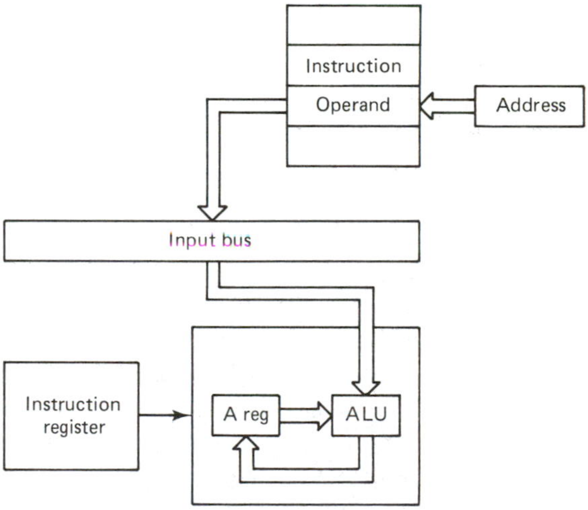

(d) Instruction Cycle – Execute Phase – Step 4:

[A] ← [A] + [Memory (MAR)]
[PC] ← [PC] + 1

Get immediate data from memory and send it to adder-circuits in Arithmetic/Logic Unit; also send contents of Accumulator Register to adder circuits and deliver sum from adder circuits to Accumulator Register. Simultaneously, increment the Program Counter so that it prints to the next memory location – the next sequential instruction. Start Fetch Phase.

Figure 1.12 Execute cycle of an ADD Immediate instruction.

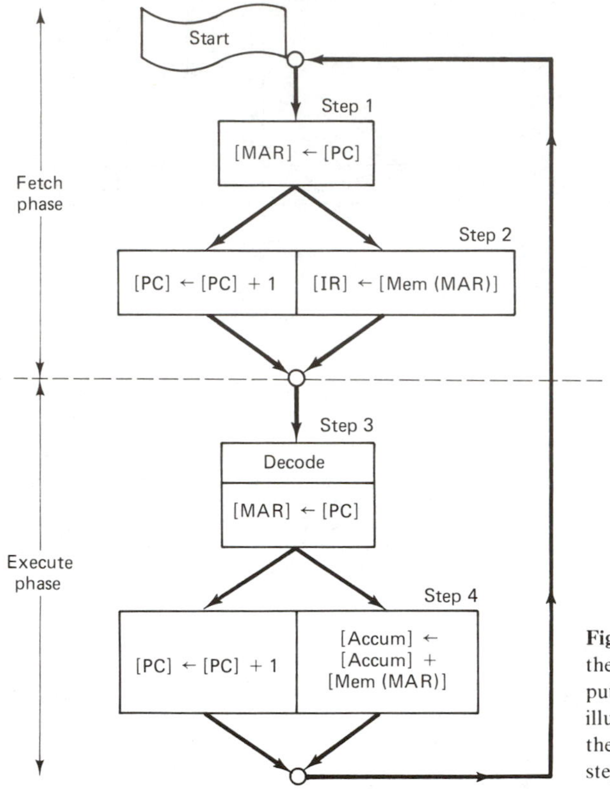

Figure 1.13 Graphical representation of the instruction cycle for the microcomputer instruction ADD Immediate, also illustrated in Figures 1.11 and 1.12. Note the parallelism achieved in instruction steps 3 and 4.

force through incrementing the program counter during the fetch phase (and during the execution phase, if indicated) of subsequent instructions.

The conditional branch instruction is accomplished, as illustrated on the bottom of Figure 1.16, by first testing the specified condition flag—overflow, for example—and then either executing the branch in the identical manner described above or by incrementing the program counter so as to point to the next sequential instruction just beyond the operand address of the conditional branch instruction.

Although it is not certain exactly who invented the closed subprogram, it is a matter of record that Maurice Wilkes made extensive use of this concept in programming the first operational stored program electronic digital computer, the EDSAC, at Cambridge University in Great Britain during 1948 or slightly earlier. Essentially, a closed subprogram is a logically *and* physically separate entity that is invoked by an instruction such as

```
JMPSUB    ANYSUB
```

or

```
CALL      ANYSUB
```

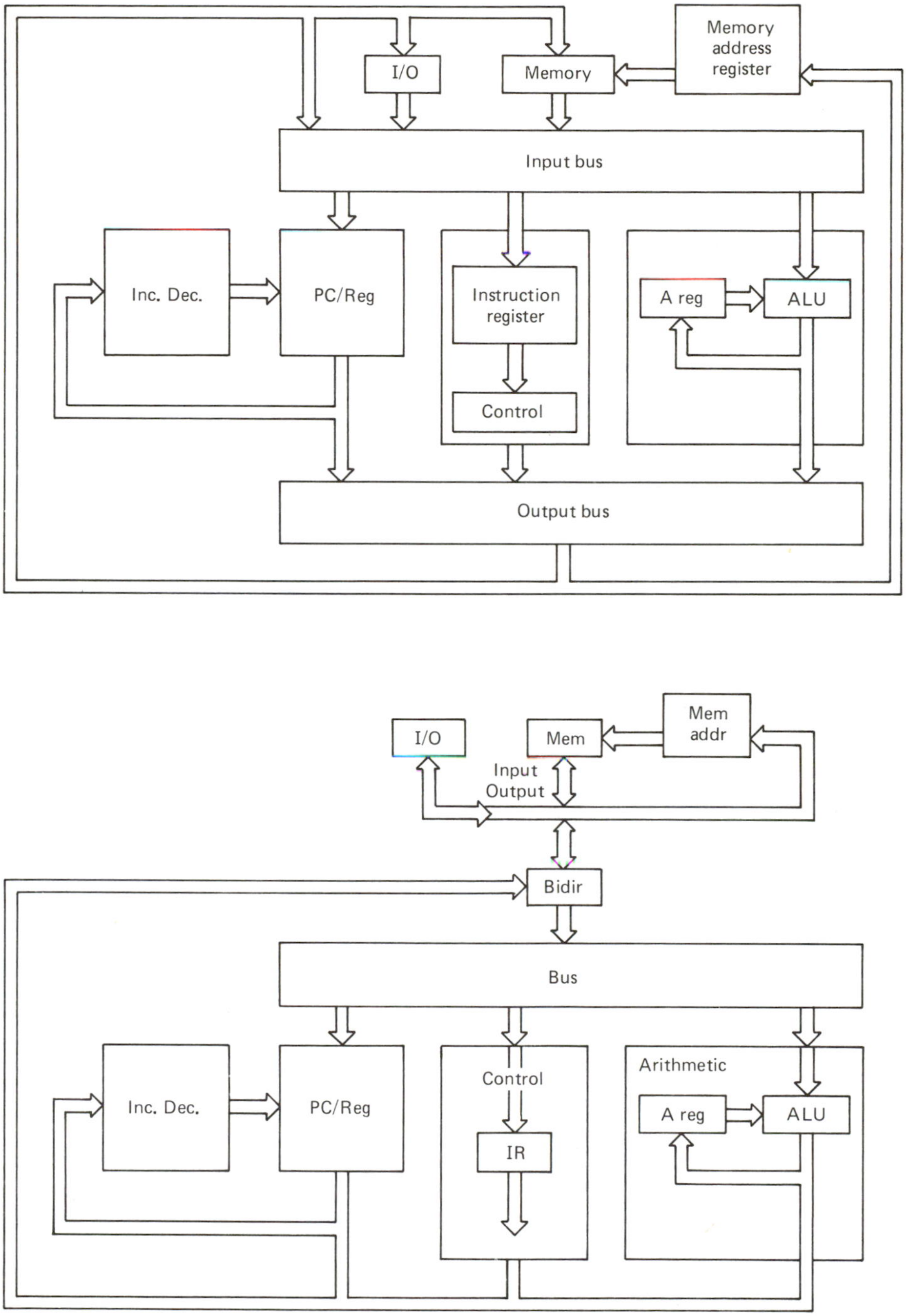

Figure 1.14 Alternative microcomputer organizational scheme examples. Although the details of the instruction cycle would change, the overall principle would remain constant.

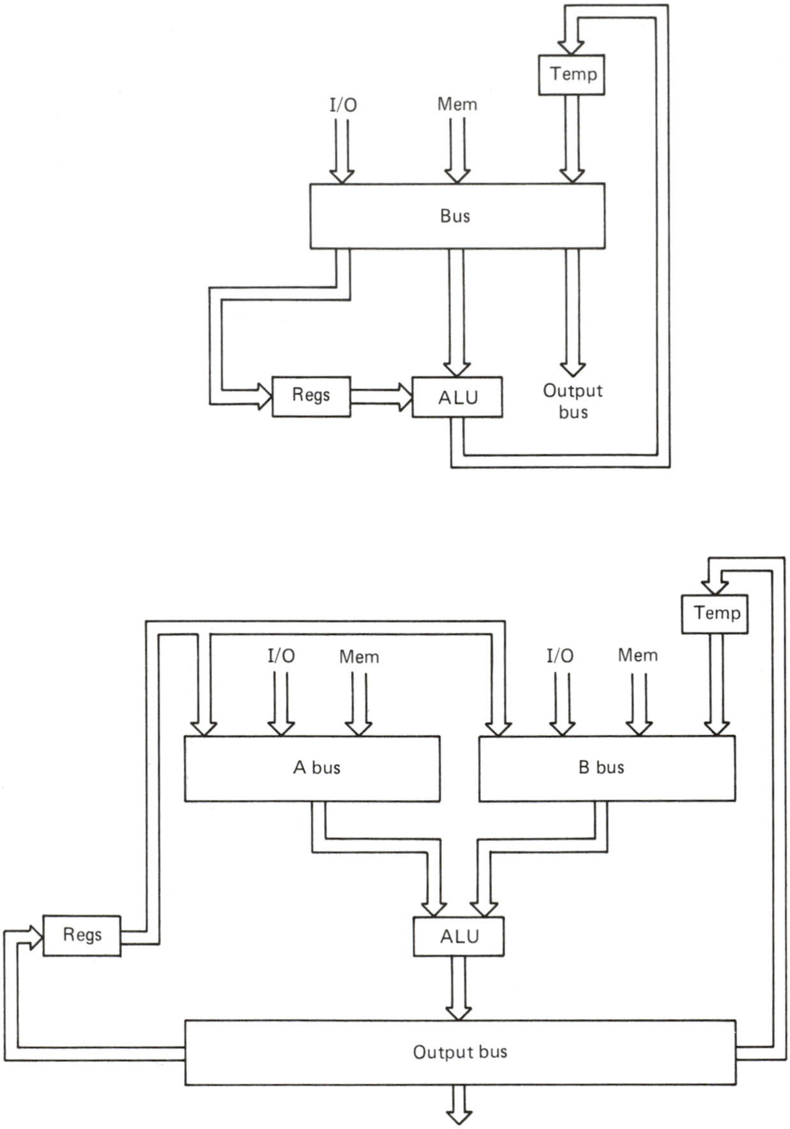

Figure 1.14 *(continued)*

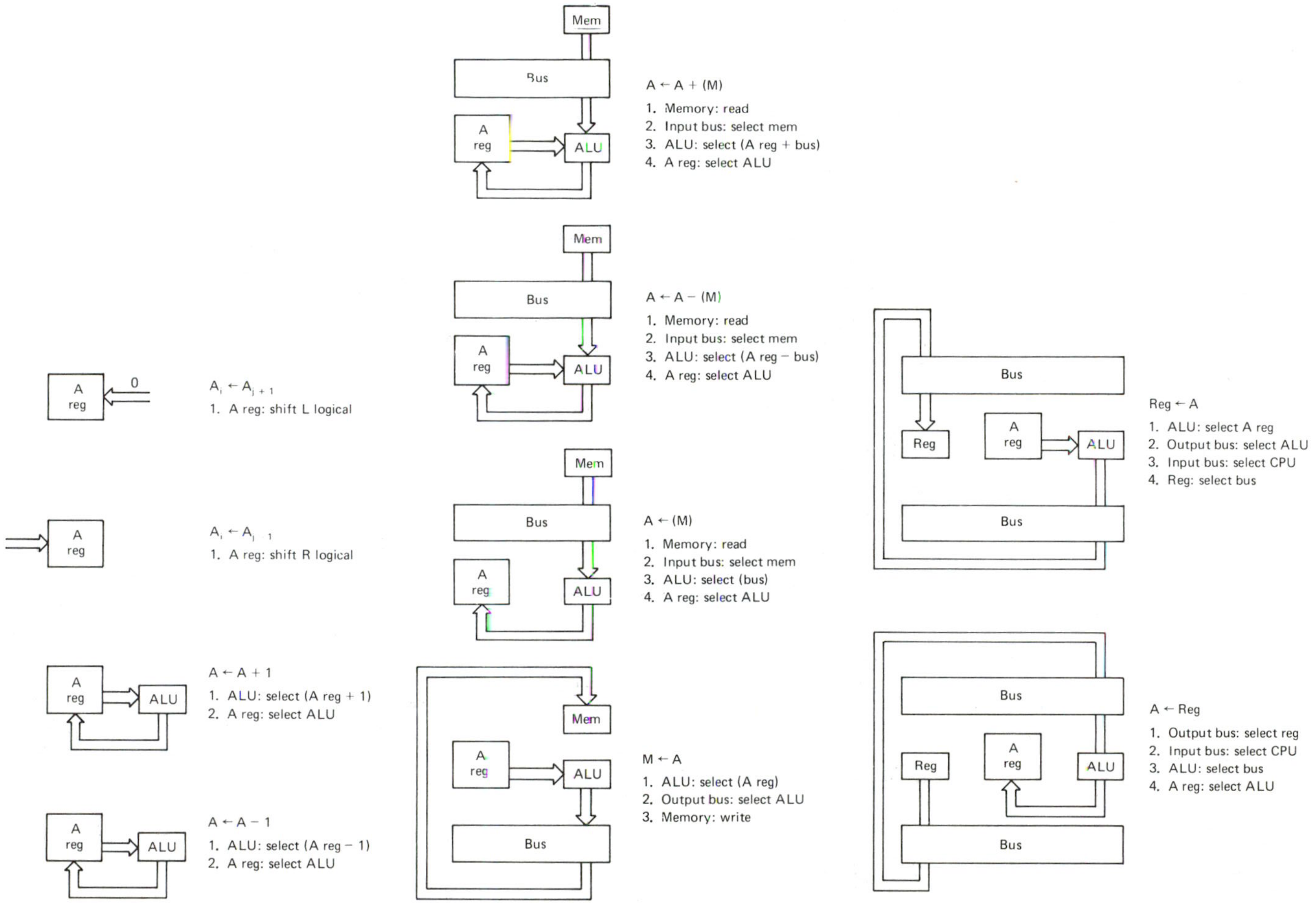

(a) Action of the execute phase of instruction cycle of four one operand – the accumulator – instructions. The bits involved in representing a datum are numbered from zero on the left to the bit capacity on the right.

(b) Action of the execute phase of the instruction cycle of four instructions that access memory.

(c) Action of the execute phase of the instruction cycle of two register-to-register microcomputer instructions.

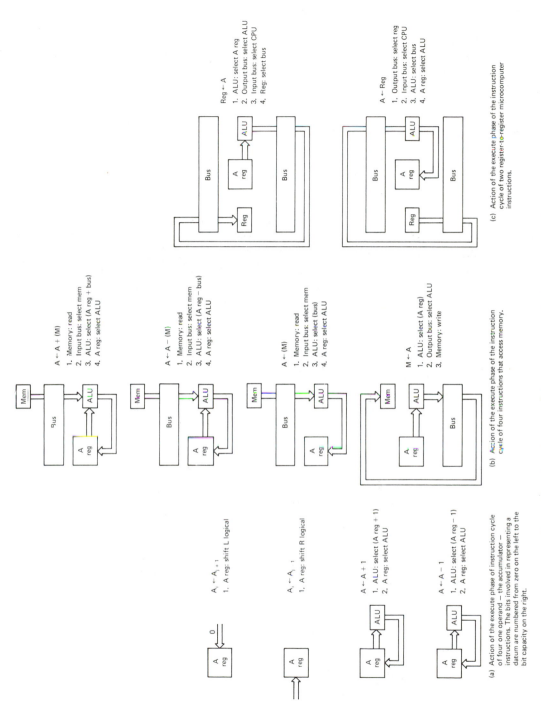

Figure 1.15 Execute phase of the instruction cycle of various instructions.

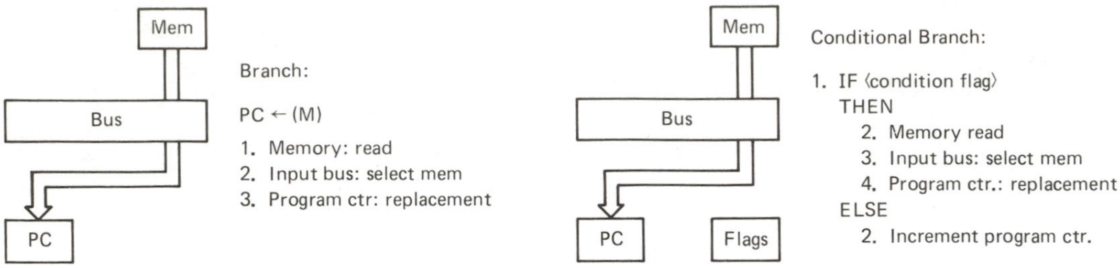

Figure 1.16 Action of the execute phase of the instruction cycle of two microcomputer instructions that change the program flow from sequential to a jump or a branch.

After execution of the instructions constituting the closed subprogram, control must revert to the instruction sequentially following the invoking instruction (JMPSUB or CALL) of the calling routine. Thus it is necessary that the *return address* be available for placement into the program counter at the execution conclusion of the subprogram. The return address must be preserved by the invoking program in a place known to the subprogram. Figure 1.17 illustrates the three common methods that have been used to solve this problem.

The historically earliest method is shown at the top of Figure 1.17. Note that the return address is placed in the first memory location of the subprogram and that execution starts at the location following this return address. The coding of the subprogram might be

```
ANYSUB    JMP     RETURN ADDRESS IN CALLING PROGRAM
START      -
           -
           -
           -
           -
ENDSUB    JMP     ANYSUB
          END
```

with execution starting at the instruction at memory address START. This scheme necessitates placing the return address in the subprogram. Thus the subprogram is altered, does not consist of pure code, and cannot execute from ROM. Note that if the subprogram invokes itself, the original return address is covered up and destroyed so that a return to the original calling program is impossible. In effect, the program loses itself. Thus recursive subprocedure calls are not possible. Nevertheless, subprograms may call—invoke—other subprograms to an arbitrary depth as long as self-calling or calling in circles (recursion or pseudorecursion) are not allowed. This somewhat antiquated method of subprocedure return address preservation is powerful and adequate for all situations not requiring pure code (ROM or PROM memory) or recursive calls. This method is not employed in conventional microcomputers.

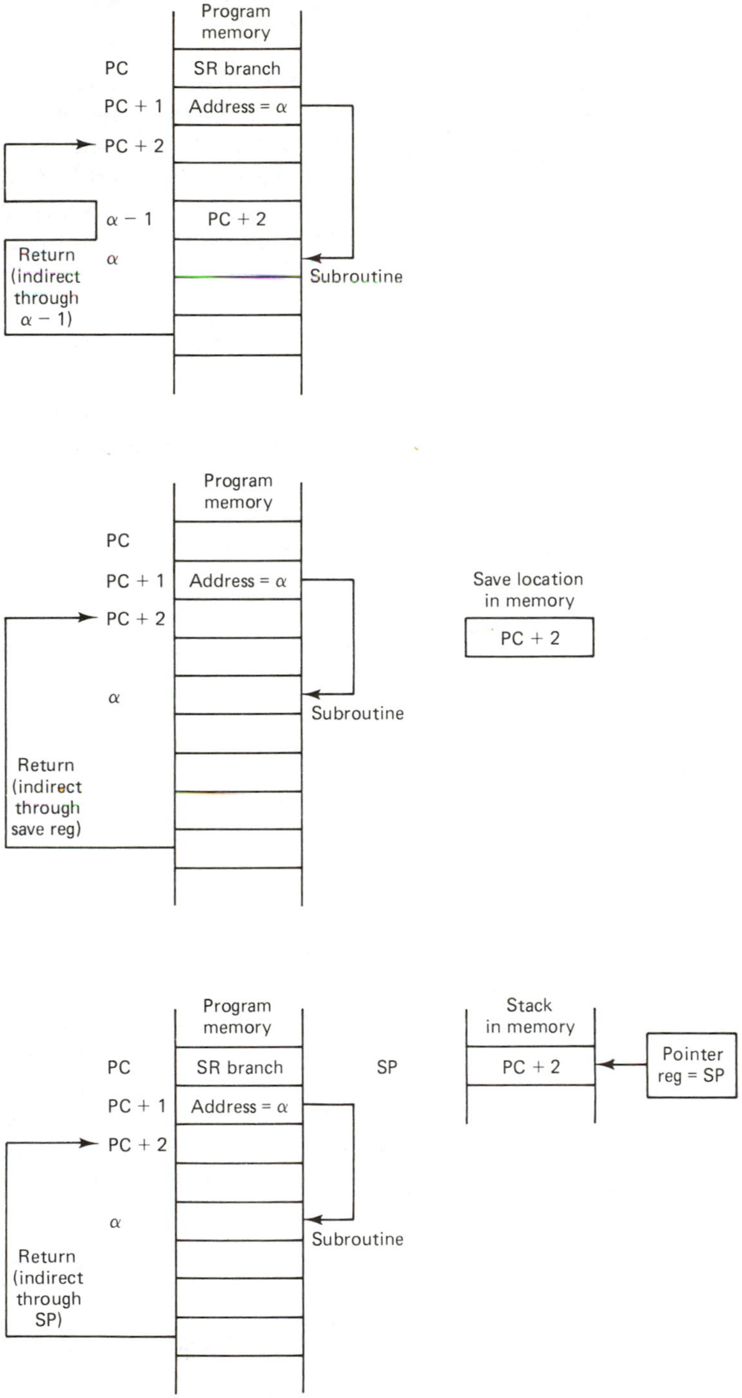

Figure 1.17 Three commonly implemented methods of subprogram invocation and return.

A method commonly employed in maxicomputers (IBM/360–IBM/370–IBM 303X extended family) and used in the Texas Instruments microcomputer 99/4 is illustrated in the middle portion of Figure 1.17. In this scheme the software system assumes that the return address has been placed in a particular register by the calling program (register 14 in both the IBM and the TI conventions). Thus a return is accomplished by branching to the address in register 14. In the IBM case this could be

```
BR      14          *BRANCH TO ADDRESS IN REGISTER 14
```

It is further assumed that if a call to a subprogram subservient to the subprogram is made, the called subprogram will save the return address of the calling program in a known place in memory before placing its own return address in register 14. Thus provisions for calling subprograms to any depth are provided. Additionally, as the code of the subprogram is not altered, pure code is achieved. As a last, and most important point, the return address is not destroyed (at least not intentionally), and thus recursive and circular subprogram calls are allowed.

The bottom portion of Figure 1.17 illustrates the more usual call/return scheme employed with conventional microcomputers as well as with some mini-, midi-, and maxicomputers (examples: HP3000, B6700, etc.). All conventional microcomputers are designed and implemented with an address register—the *stack pointer* (SP)—which has special execution characteristics when one of the inverse-twin instructions JMPSUB and RET is executed.

For an understanding of this subprogram scheme, it is necessary first to understand the action of a stack. A stack of return addresses, of data, of playing cards, or of dishes all behave identically—an item may only be placed on top of the stack and an item may only be taken from the top of the stack. Thus only the last item (or card, or dish) placed on the stack is available for retrieval from the stack. The discipline is *last in–first out* (LIFO). With a stack of information in computer memory we universally term the two complementary actions as PUSH and POP and use the terminology "push onto" and "pop from." Also, with a stack of information in contiguous locations in memory, it is necessary to maintain the address of the top of the stack—the address of the place to PUSH to and the place to POP from. In conventional microcomputers, a special *stack pointer* register is devoted to this task and thus contains the memory address of the top of the stack. The action of the complementary instructions PUSH and POP are:

```
PUSH    DATUM     1. Store DATUM at a location in memory whose
                     address is in SP.
                  2. Increment SP contents to point to one place
                     beyond the new stack top (the next empty loca-
                     tion).
POP     DATUM     1. Decrement SP contents to point to current
```

nonempty stack top (which will be new empty location after POPping).
2. Retrieve DATUM from stack top.

Note that these actions are complementary and inverse. An examination of Figure 1.17*c* should make clear the use of a stack of return addresses:

CALL	ANY	1. PUSH return address to stack from PC.
		2. Increment SP.
		3. Load address of start of subprogram ANY into PC.
		4. Resume normal instruction fetch.
RET		1. Decrement SP.
		2. POP return address from stack to PC.
		3. Resume normal instruction fetch.

This scheme allows

1. Calling subprograms to any depth
2. Pure code subprograms
3. Recursive and circular subprogram invocation

MEMORY

Memory in a computational system is any entity that has the ability to retain information over time. As a generality, memory reacts to two instructions:

STORE	Datum at address
RETRIEVE	Datum from address

It must be emphasized that memory is a passive device that preserves information over time but does not change or transform it in any way. Memory may logically be classified in several ways. Among these are those storage locations accessible as operand addresses of simple arithmetic statements such as ADD. There are two kinds: registers and primary memory.

Registers are temporary data and address storage entities. Usually, there are a relatively few registers with numeric or alphabetic identifiers. Some registers may be reserved by hardware or by software conventions for special purposes.

Primary memory, often called *main memory,* consists of program and data storage entities. The amount of primary memory is usually (always) a power of 2, with the maximum number of locations depending on the number of bits available as an operand address. Memory sizes for microcomputers with data entities of length 4 bits (a nibble) tend to have byte-length addresses and thus have a maximum memory size of 256 = 2^8 = 1/4K nibbles; 8-bit microcomputers tend to use two bytes for operand addresses and thus can access up to 65,536 = 2^{16} = 64K bytes; 16-bit microcomputers often employ a 16-bit operand address, although the use of additional addressing techniques allows up to 48 million bytes of primary memory with one design. In current conventional microcomputers, primary memory is implemented as random address integrated circuits. Memory for variable data storage must be read/write and is often referred to as RAM, memory for programs and constants of a permanent nature is often implemented as read-only memory (ROM), and semipermanent programs are often stored in programmable (alterable) read-only memory (PROM). Figure 1.18 may be helpful. The term "*random-access memory*" means that any address may be accessed next and that any address may be accessed in an equal amount of time—that is, access time for RAM is constant. In some microcomputer designs, memory is logically treated as an external device; in other microcomputer designs, external devices are logically and programmatically treated as memory locations. Figure 1.19 helps to explain this.

INPUT/OUTPUT

Those storage locations accessible as addresses on external devices through the use of input/output instructions and not available as operand addresses of simple arithmetic instructions are known as *secondary memory.* Although RAM secondary memory exists, it is not employed with conventional microcomputers.

The action of the execute phase of the instruction cycle of simple input/output instructions of microcomputers that require I/O through the ALU is illustrated in Figure 1.20. This scheme is enlarged on and given additional detail in Figure 1.21. The top portion of Figure 1.21 can be interpreted as I/O through the accumulator, as in the Intel 8080/8085, in which the device address is the number of an I/O port that connects with the I/O device. Its control and data buffer are shown in the middle portion of Figure 1.21. Alternatively, the middle portion of Figure 1.21 can be interpreted as memory-mapped I/O, as in the Motorola 6800 and DEC LSI 11, in which each device is associated with a double-word of memory. In this scheme, the device data buffer is an address in memory and the control/status information is the next sequential address in memory. Thus the Intel 8080/8085 has a separate READ and a separate WRITE instruction, while the Motorola 6800 and the DEC LSI 11 use memory MOVE instructions to accomplish I/O.

INTERRUPTS

An interrupt is a signal that something has happened. An interrupt will result in some reactive program action (possibly null) in the future. An interrupt usually is posted by some event that is time-unexpected; that is, it is expected but the exact time of its happening is unknown. The posting of an interrupt will result in the in-

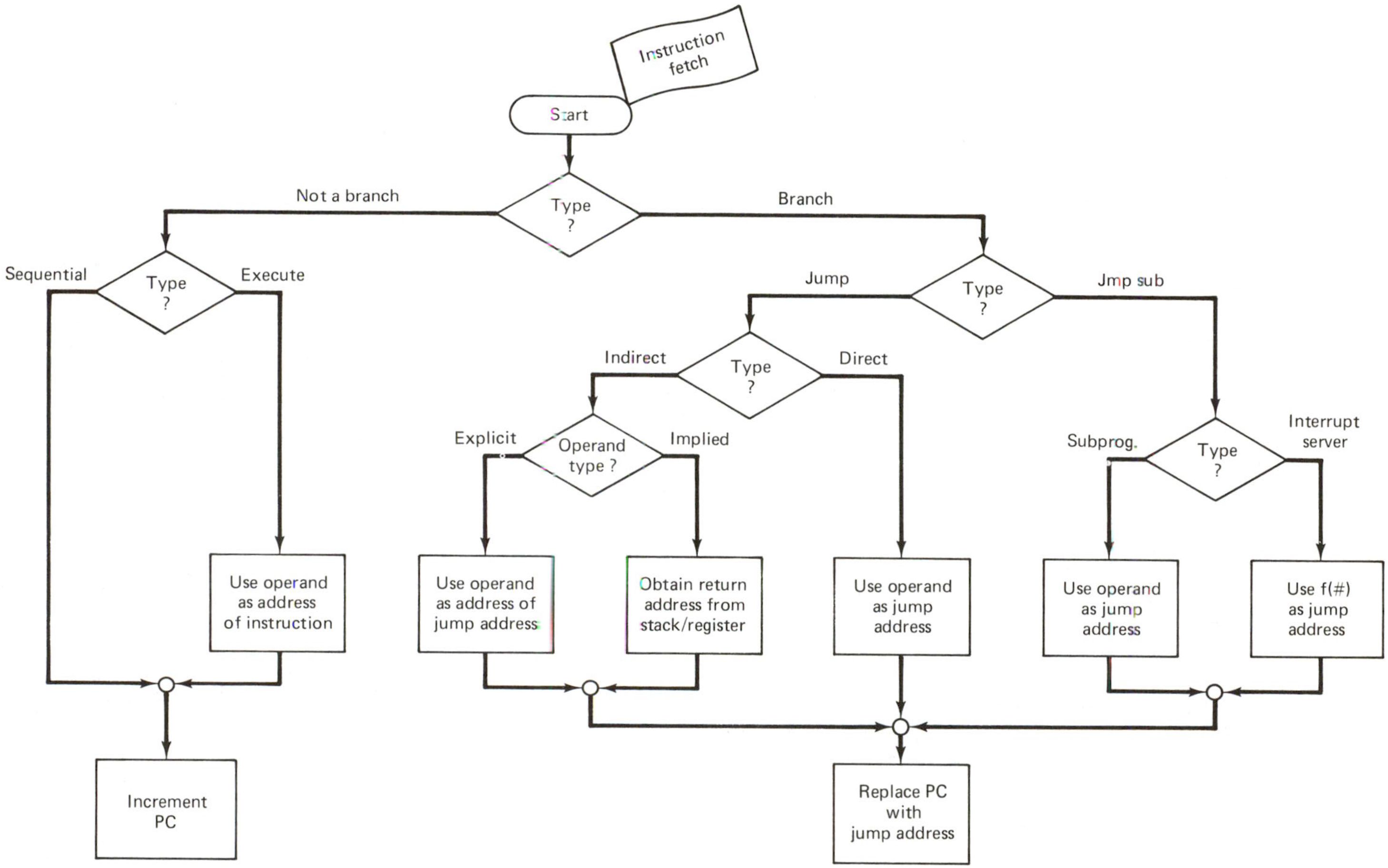

Figure 1.18 Generalized schemata of instruction acquisition, emphasizing the program counter (PC) register changes.

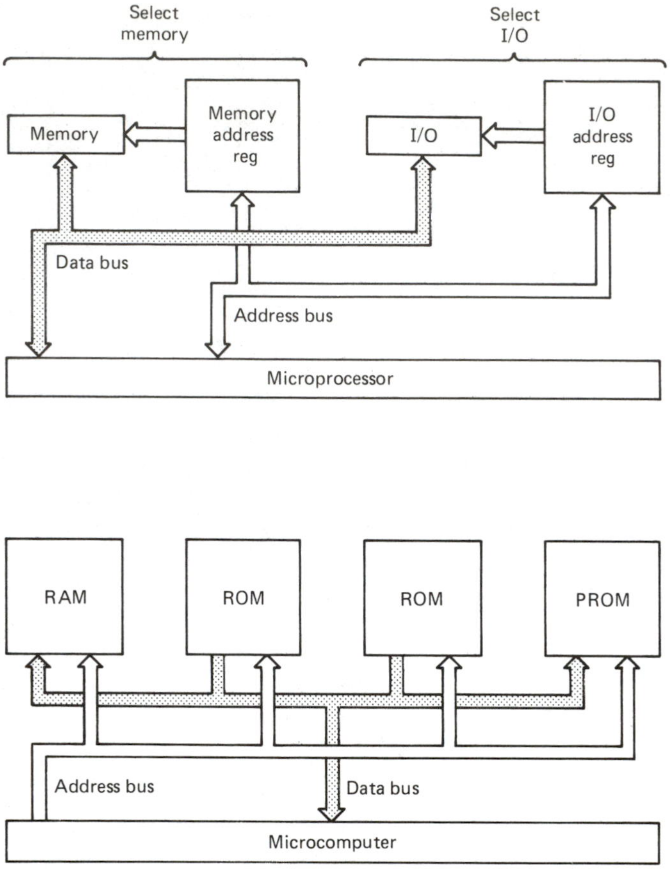

Figure 1.19 Two differing aspects of memory.

vocation of a software *interrupt servicing routine* at some time in the future (usually very soon). This is accomplished by the hardware forcing the known absolute address of the appropriate interrupt service routine to replace the contents of the program counter and the saving of the original contents of the PC for an eventual return to the previously executing program at the point of interruption. Note the very close similarity to a subprocedure invocation, with the obvious differences that the interrupt branch is externally (not program) caused and that the interrupt branch address is event controlled. With additional logic external to the conventional microcomputer it is possible to implement a priority scheme for interrupt servicing. Figure 1.22 may be helpful. Interrupts allow many programs to execute much faster and may allow the attachment of various I/O devices without alteration to the applications programs using the devices.

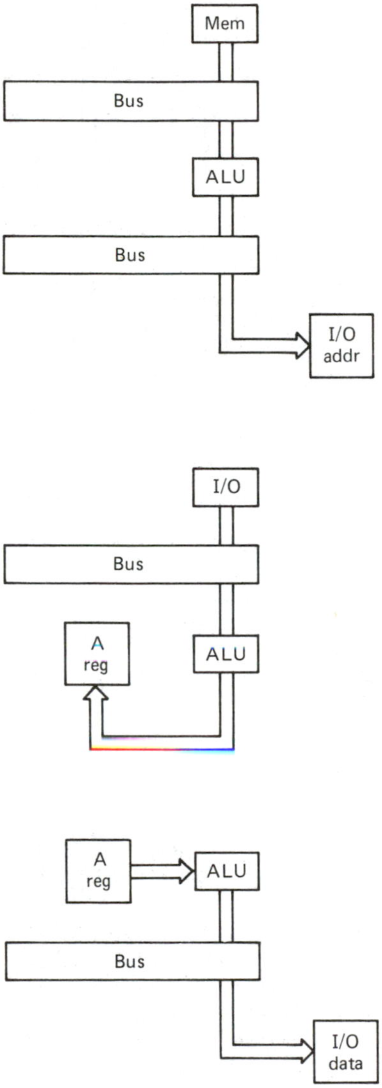

I/O addr ← M

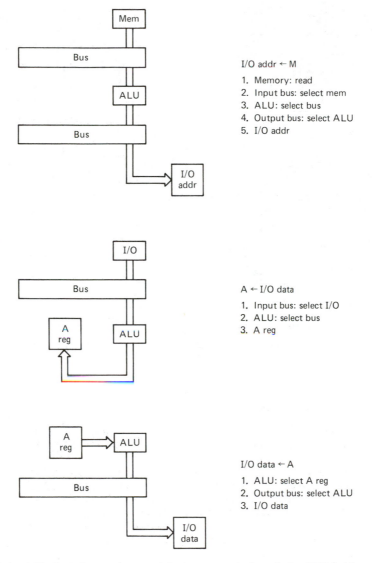

1. Memory: read
2. Input bus: select mem
3. ALU: select bus
4. Output bus: select ALU
5. I/O addr

A ← I/O data

1. Input bus: select I/O
2. ALU: select bus
3. A reg

I/O data ← A

1. ALU: select A reg
2. Output bus: select ALU
3. I/O data

Figure 1.20 Input/output in many microcomputers is through the ALU (arithmetic-logic unit) and effectively prevents simultaneous compute and I/O. The action of the execute phase of the instruction cycle of three I/O instruction is illustrated.

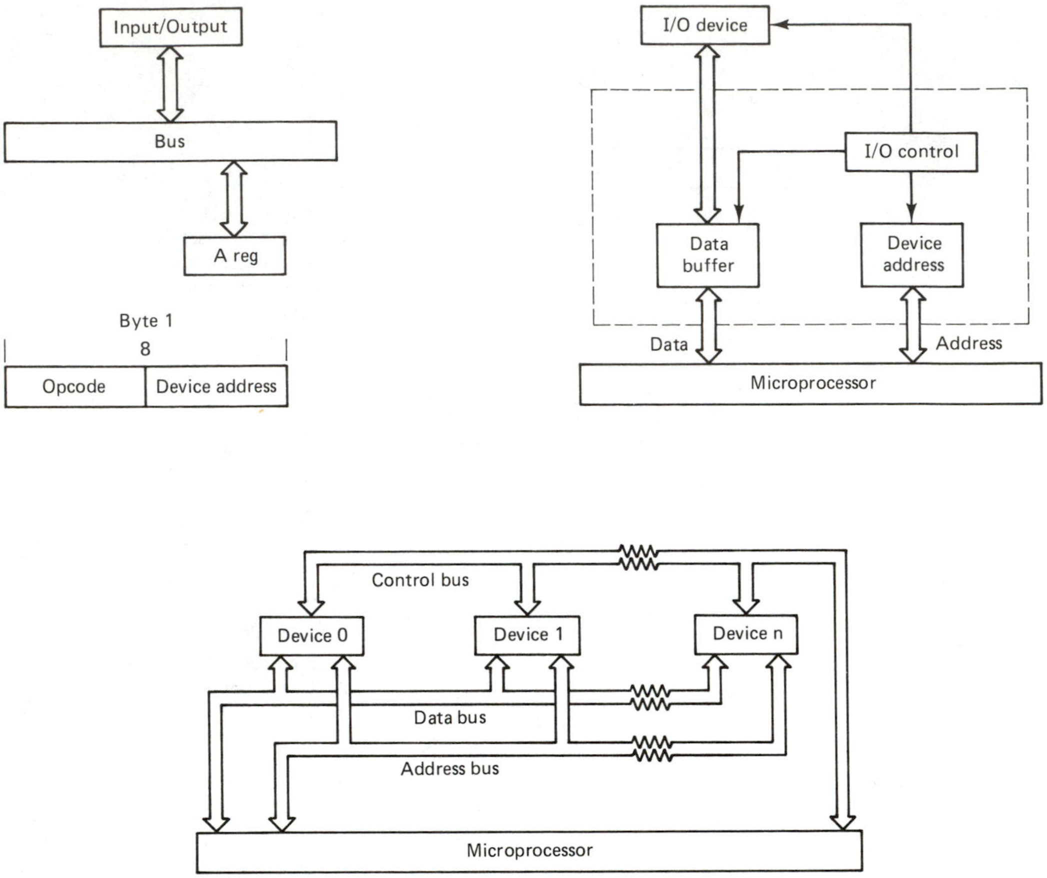

Figure 1.21 The two types of I/O schemes can be interpreted from these diagrams. In those microcomputers with I/O instructions such as the Intel 8080/8085, I/O is required to be to or from the accumulator, from or to an I/O device. In those microcomputers without separate I/O instructions, the devices are assigned non-existent memory "addresses" and I/O is accomplished by memory MOVE instructions. This "memory-mapped I/O" scheme was pioneered with the DEC PDP 11 and is quite common in microcomputers, including the Motorola 6800. The middle diagram hives additional I/O detail for a single device. In memory-mapped I/O, the data buffer would occupy one memory "address" and the control would occupy the next. The bottom diagram illustrates the use of multiple I/O devices.

MEMORY ADDRESSING TECHNIQUES

The *short-word problem* is characterized by a need to specify more information in a computer instruction than there are bits available with which to do so. Figure 1.23 illustrates some aspects of the short-word problem. Although one of the basic characteristics of stored program computers is the ability of the computer to change or alter its own instructions, long experience by thousands of programmers strongly

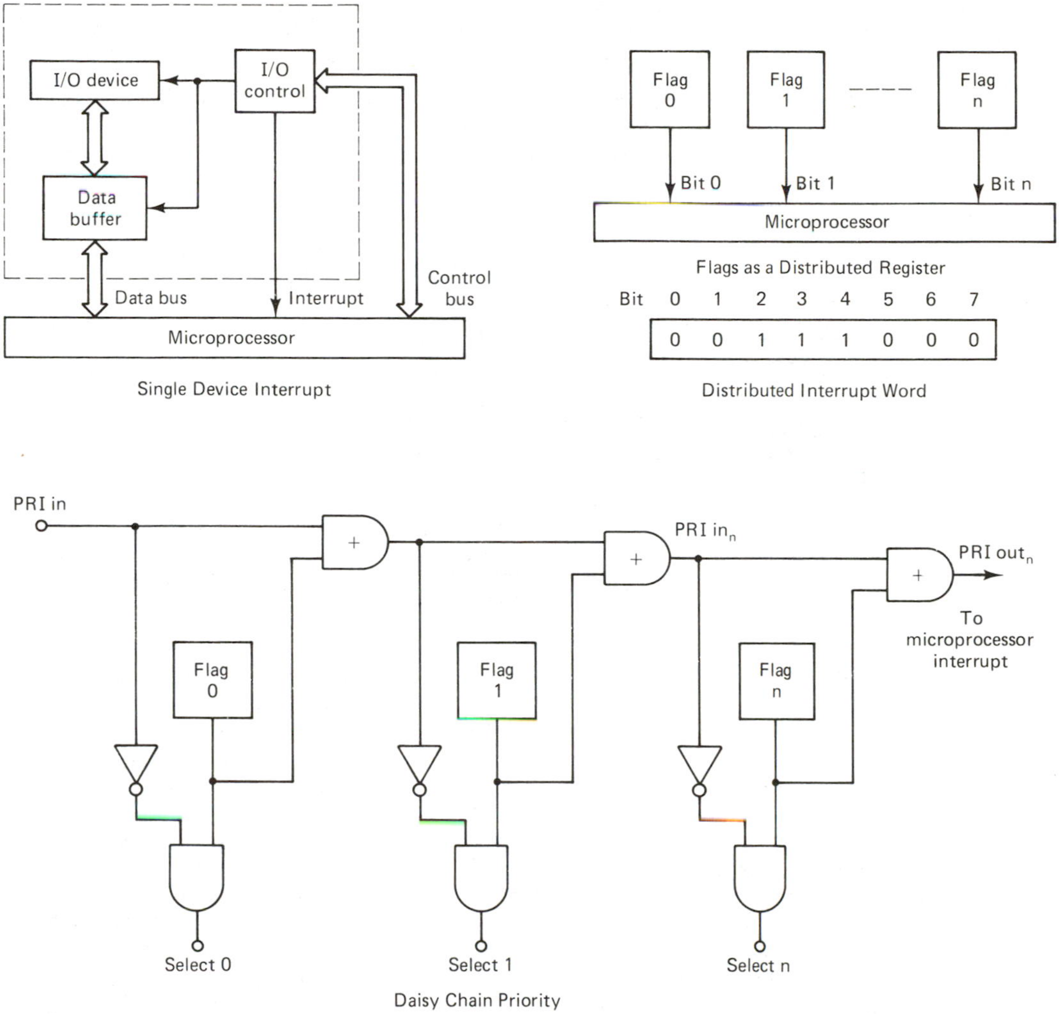

Figure 1.22 An interrupt is a signal that an unexpected event (at least time-expected) has occurred that requires some action (possible null). Thus an interrupt will result in the invocation of a software service routine at a specific memory location and an eventual return to the original program at the point of interruption. Interrupts may have a priority.

suggests that self-modifying programs are difficult to understand, almost impossible to debug, and all in all are a very bad programming technique. Thus we may claim that there are two kinds of information available to the computer during execution of a program: *instructions* and *data.* The instruction contains two types of information: the operation code (opcode) or what to do, and the operand address(es), or where the datum is that is to be transformed.

With modern conventional microcomputers, data registers and memory are

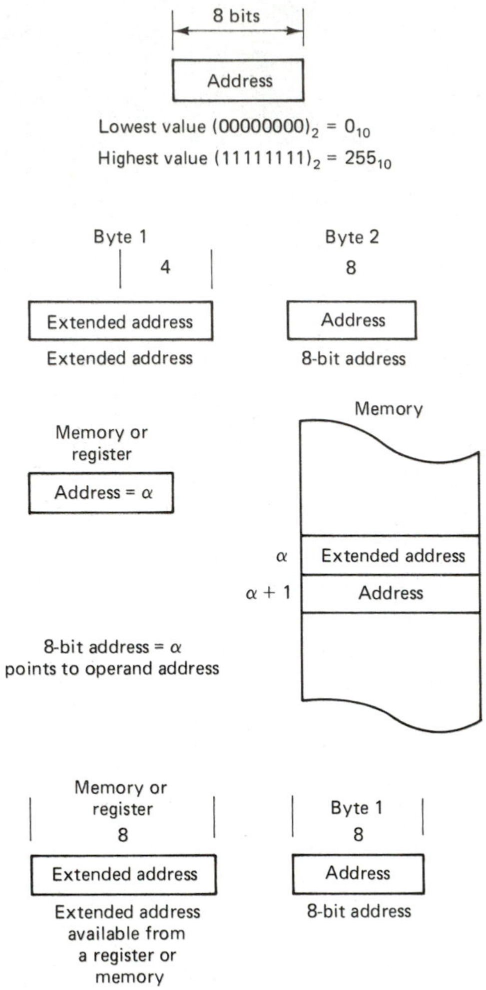

Figure 1.23 The "short-word problem" is exemplified in the top diagram by an 8-bit address that allows a memory size much too small for many applications. Although the second diagram allows for a memory size of 4096 cells, only 16 opcodes are possible—not an attractive solution. The bottom diagram illustrates two methods of providing a 16-bit address to address 64K. The next to bottom address illustrates one form of indirect addressing.

usually organized and addressable as 8-bit bytes, although a few microcomputers exist with data registers and memory organized and addressable as 4-bit nibbles. The relatively new 16-bit microcomputers that we will discuss later in this book have memory organized as 8-bit bytes but addressable as 8-bit, 16-bit, 32-bit, or longer entities. While discussing the problem of incorporating the information necessary to specify a practical number of opcodes, at the same time incorporating the information necessary to specify a memory location of data in a memory large enough to be practical, we will use the very common 8-bit Intel 8080 microcomputer as an example.

Even if all 8 bits of a byte were used as a memory address, allowing a memory with 256 locations, program implementers would have great difficulty in fitting practical problem solutions into the available memory space. Thus the designers of the Intel 8080 decided to allow for 16-bit memory addresses or a maximum memory size of 65,536 = 64K bytes. They also decided to provide six 8-bit data registers and one accumulator as well as referring to the use of memory as being the use of the nonexistent eighth register (with the address of the data being placed at some other known place). Additionally, they provided a group of 16-bit address registers (some of which consist of combining two of the data registers). Their scheme for specifying a usable number of instructions (72), a usable numbers of data registers (seven), and a usable-size memory (64K) is not only interesting in its own right but is instructive as an illustration of an intelligent practical alleviation of the short-word problem.

Instructions in the Intel 8080 are of length one byte, two bytes, or three bytes, depending on the need for information content. Without attempting to be complete, some of the one-byte instructions are of the following form:

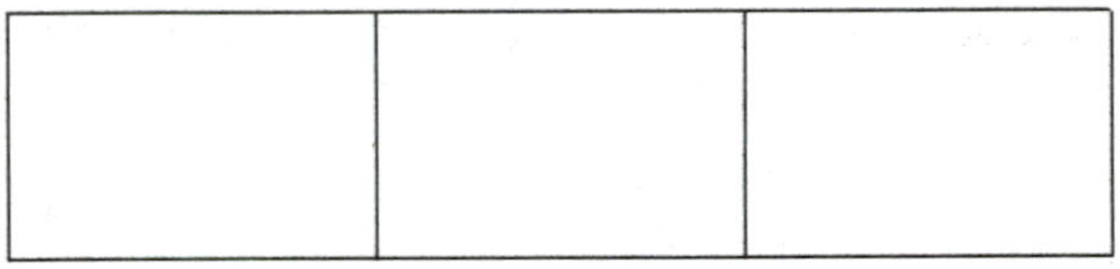

Data register to data register

2-bit opcode	3-bit register ID	3-bit register ID
01	010	011

Example: MOV C,D

Meaning: [C] ← [D], or replace current contents of register C with contents of register D; do not change contents of register D.

This type of addressing is generically known as *register addressing*. In the Intel 8080, the registers have the following symbolic names and corresponding numerical designation:

B	0	H	4
C	1	L	5
D	2	M	6 (memory)
E	3	A	7 (accumulator)

If one of the registers is specified as M or 6, the 16-bit contents of the address register H (physically the data registers H and L or the HL pair) is used as an address in memory. This type of memory addressing is generically known as *indirect addressing through a register* and is fairly common in microcomputers. As the hardware facilities to allow memory moves do not exist in the Intel 8080, the memory-to-memory move instruction (01110110) is illegal; this bit pattern is interpreted as a HALT instruction.

As further examples of the instruction formats, consider the following two-byte I/O instruction:

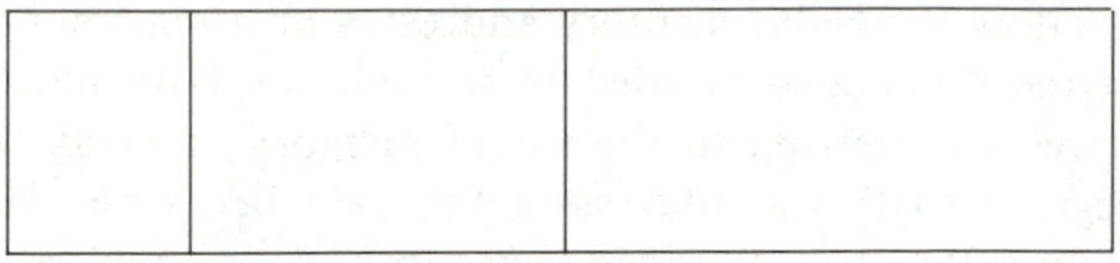

Register to output device

11
therefore, 8-bit opcode | output device number
11010011 00010001
Example: OUT 17
Meaning: [17] ← [A], or, place contents of register A on output device 17 while preserving contents of register A.

Another two-byte instruction is

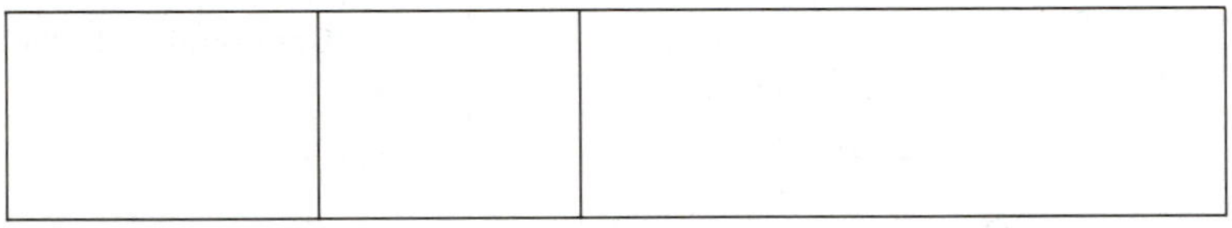

Constant datum to data register

5-bit primary opcode | 3-bit datum register ID
00 000 110 00010001
Example: MVI B, 17
Meaning: (B) ← 17, or, place a 17 in register B

This type of addressing is known as *immediate addressing.* Note that the datum itself is a portion of the instruction. From another standpoint, this type can be called program counter *relative addressing.*

As a last example, consider the three-byte memory-to-register A instructions:

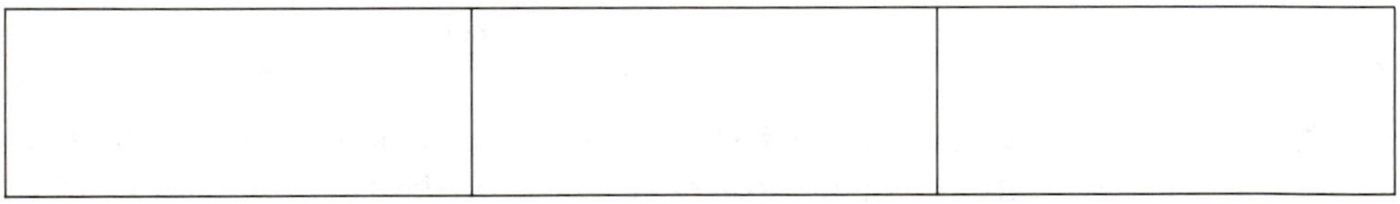

5-bit primary opcode | 3-bit register ID | 16-bit memory address
00 111 110 LDA IT Memory to register A
00 110 111 STA IT register A to memory
[A] ← [Mem(IT)]
[Mem(IT)] ← [A]

This type of addressing is known as *direct addressing.*

The object of this entire discussion is to give an understanding of the derivation or calculation of the location of the data—be it in a register, in a location in memory, or on an I/O device. If an address in memory must be derived by some calculation or by using the contents of a register pair or two memory locations as an address, such an operation is referred to as *finding the effective operand address* (EOA). Figure 1.24 is a summary of this process.

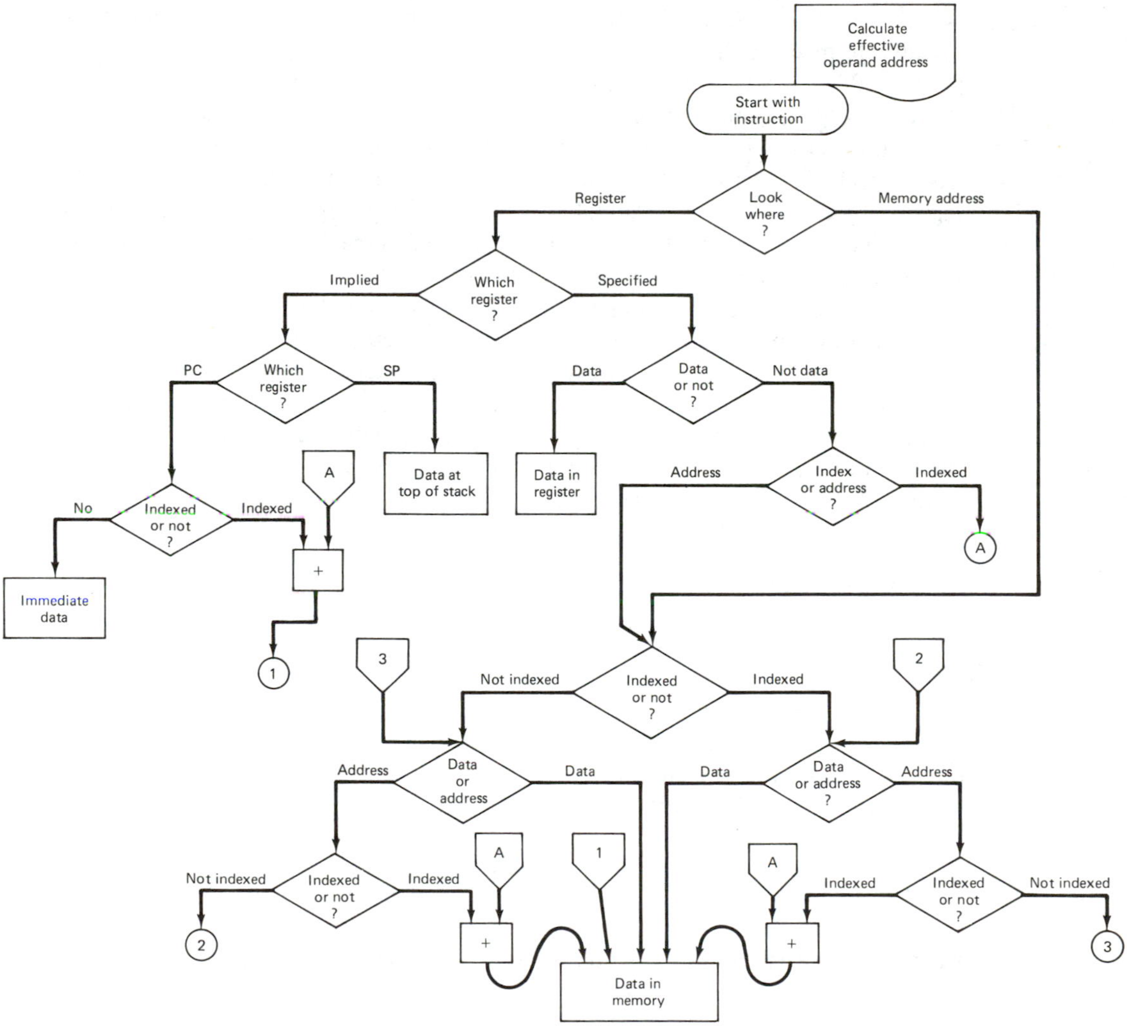

Figure 1.24 Generalized schemata for calculating the effective operand address of data. Note that the EOA may be an offset from the PC (PC relative) or from another register (array base relative), that indirect addressing can be to any depth, and that indexing may be pre- or post-indirect.

Most conventional microcomputers provide hardware assistance for maintaining data in a STACK. Recall that a stack is similar to a cafeteria plate holder. The topmost item is the only one available. If an item is added, the stack drops down, with the new item on top. If the topmost item is removed, the next item pops up. The discipline is *last in–first out* (LIFO).

A possible implementation of a stack would employ a contiguous area in primary memory as the stack receptacle and a register as an address pointer to the current top of the stack. The process of placing a datum on the stack is almost universally termed PUSH and must be preceded by an incrementation of the stack pointer (SP) register. Care must be taken to avoid PUSHing a datum onto a full stack, that is, beyond the upper limits of the stack area in primary memory, lest other information be overwritten and destroyed. The process of removing a datum from the stack is termed POP and must be followed by a decrementation of the SP register. Again, care must be taken to avoid POPping a datum from an empty stack, that is, below the lower limit of the stack area in primary memory, lest an unwanted datum be used in an incorrect context.

As discussed earlier, and shown in the bottom diagram of Figure 1.17, the subprocedure invocation instruction places the return address on the top of the stack as pointed to by the address in the SP register. Similarly, the return instruction uses the top of the stack as the return address. Figure 1.18 illustrates the logic of deriving the new value of the program counter (PC), and Figure 1.24 illustrates the logic of determining that the operand is in a memory location whose address is in the SP register. The Intel 8080 provides two one-byte instructions:

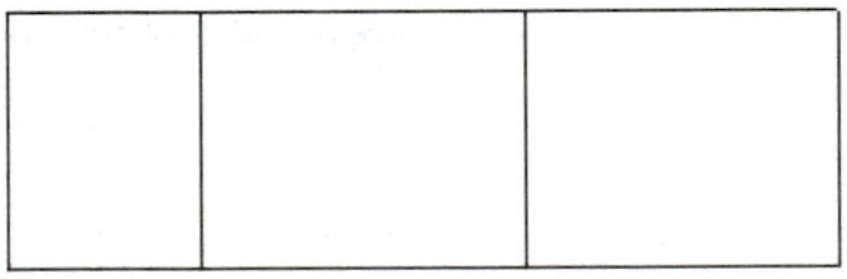

2-bit primary opcode	3-bit register ID	3-bit secondary opcode

11	ID	101	PUSH	register pair
11	ID	001	POP	register pair

where the register pairs are identified by the number of their first register:

BC	000	0
DE	010	2
HL	100	4
A status	110	6

Figure 1.25 should be helpful in understanding the action of these instructions:

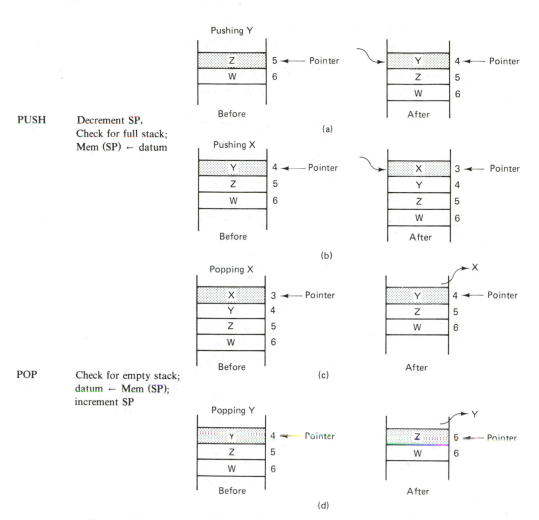

PUSH Decrement SP,
Check for full stack;
Mem (SP) ← datum

POP Check for empty stack;
datum ← Mem (SP);
increment SP

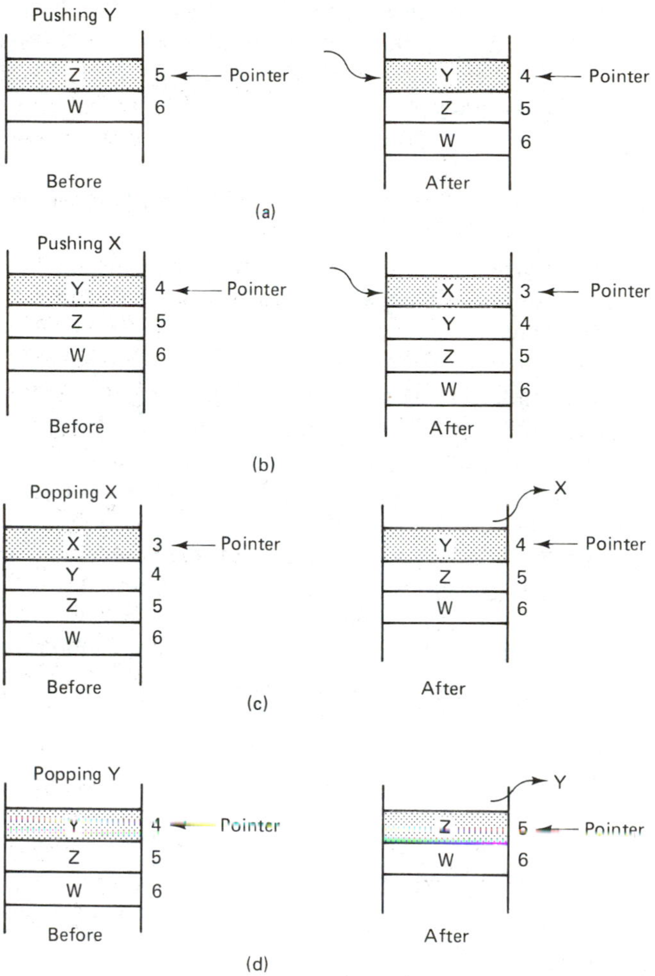

Figure 1.25 A stack acts like a stack of plates with a datum being able to be "pushed" onto the top or a datum being able to be "popped" from the top. Conventional microcomputers contain a stack pointer (SP) register that contains the address in memory of the current stack top. Note that a stack in a conventional microcomputer has the addresses in reverse order. The access discipline of a stack is first in-last out (FILO) or last in-first out (LIFO). After defining storage space for the stack, the stack pointer register must be initialized to the high address of the stack area.

	Push H	Pop H
Step 1	Decrement SP	Load register L from top of stack
Step 2	Store register H at top of stack	Increment SP
Step 3	Decrement SP	Load register H from top of stack
Step 4	Store register L at top of stack	Increment SP

Note that the stack in the Intel 8080/8085 is backward, with the first item at the highest address, and that 16-bit addresses are involved. The programmer is responsible for being sure that the program does not PUSH to a full stack or POP from an empty stack.

ACCESSING DATA

The purpose of a computer is to manipulate information; that is, a microcomputer is an information-manipulating machine. Human beings create things. Although it is probable that some things are created idly with absolutely no purpose in mind, most human creations have a purpose. This purpose may be aesthetic, with the created thing serving the purpose of pleasing the senses; or this purpose may be practical, with the created entity alleviating a felt need by serving a useful purpose. Without a doubt, there is an aesthetic quality—a beauty—in the logical interrelationships of the functional parts of a microcomputer as a mechanism for alleviating the practical problem of rapidly and accurately manipulating symbolic information. Nevertheless, most microcomputers are secured and used as tools in solving the very practical problems of acquiring, storing, transforming, transmitting, comparing, or otherwise massaging information. Without denigrating the aesthetics, we will concentrate on the practical information-manipulating aspects of microcomputers.

Information in a modern microcomputer is represented using one or more of a series of flip-flops, each able to be either on or off. The setting of a single flip-flop may encode the information that is interpreted by the human computer user as a numeric 0 or 1 or, alternatively, as a logical true or false. That is, the meaning of bit patterns within a microcomputer is entirely arbitrary. In a more formal sense, the semantic meaning of a particular bit pattern is arbitrary and determined by the context of the usage.

DATA TYPES

By convention, microcomputers are designed and implemented with the ability to manipulate correctly groups of bits whose settings are interpreted as one of the data types listed below.

Logical Data

The setting of each bit is interpreted as "true" or as "false" or as "on" or "off." In some circumstances, it is advantageous to have a single flip-flop known as a *flag;* in other circumstances, it is advantageous to group flags together into a register. The transformations allowed to logical data normally include AND, OR, XOR, NOT, SET, and CLEAR.

Integer Data

A group of bits that are interpreted as a number. The Institute of Electrical and Electronics Engineers (IEEE) standard interpretation in microcomputers involves the base 2 number system, with the sign being indicated by the leftmost bit. Negative numbers are coded in the two's-complement notation. Figure 1.26 illustrates the bit patterns and their interpretation is this notation. Some standardization of data sizes has occurred within the microcomputer industry:

Nibble: 4-bit item; range unsigned is +0 to +15, two's-complement range is +7 to −8.

Byte: 8-bit item; range unsigned is +0 to +255, two's-complement range is +127 to −128.

Word: 16-bit item; two's-complement range is +32,191 to −32,192, unsigned range is +0 to +65,383.

Double-word: 32-bit item; two's-complement range is +2,147,483,647 to −2,147,483,648.

Quad-word: 64-bit item; where the two's-complement range is +9,223,372,038,854,775,807 to −9,223,372,038,854,775,808.

Base 2	Base 10	Unsigned	Two's complement	Base 16
0000	0	0	0	0
0001	1	1	1	1
0010	2	2	2	2
0011	3	3	3	3
0100	4	4	4	4
0101	5	5	5	5
0110	6	6	6	6
0111	7	7	7	7
1000	8	8	−8	8
1001	9	9	−7	9
1010	—	10	−6	A
1011	—	11	−5	B
1100	—	12	−4	C
1101	—	13	−3	D
1110	—	14	−2	E
1111	—	15	−1	F

Figure 1.26 Common semantic interpretations of 4-bit integer data items in microcomputers, illustrating both the unsigned integer (assumed positive) interpretation and the two's-complement interpretation. Note particularly that the range is from +7 through 0 to −8 utilizing the two's-complement notation.

While working with numbers represented in base 2, human comprehension tends to be overwhelmed by the mere length of the bit pattern, and mental translation to base 10 is normally impractical. For these reasons many computer workers have developed the habit of mentally manipulating base 2 numbers in groups of 4 bits, that is, as base 16 numbers. Figure 1.26 illustrates this concept. The use of octal is a historical anachronism and should be discontinued when working with microcomputers.

It is sometimes convenient and advantageous to represent base 10 numbers directly in a microcomputer. Such a notation has become known as *binary-coded decimal* (BCD). BCD numbers normally have the sign (if a sign exits) designated in a separate nibble and employ the signed-magnitude number representation. Many microcomputers possess an operation to convert unsigned binary representation to the equivalent BCD representation.

Character Data

Almost all microcomputers employ the American Standard Code for Information Interchange (ASCII) for encoding character or alphanumeric data. Being very exact, we are referring to Standard No. X3.4-1968 of the American National Standards Institute (ANSI X3.4-1968). ASCII is a 7-bit code with each character occupying an 8-bit byte, with the leftmost bit (the most significant bit) set to zero. Thus 128 characters may be encoded using ASCII. Programmers should be aware that the leftmost bit (the sign bit) of ASCII characters may be employed for various purposes during data transmission and thus may not be a zero upon receipt and input into a microcomputer. Conservative programming practice would include zeroing out the leftmost bit before using the data, on the philosophy that it is better to be safe than sorry. Figure 1.27 illustrates the encoding pattern of the 7-bit ANSI X3.4-1968 ASCII encoding scheme.

Certain characteristics of the ASCII encoding scheme are worth noting:

1. The numerical difference between corresponding uppercase and lowercase letters is 00100000 (20 base 16), enabling programmatically simple conversions.
2. The uppercase letters start with 01000001 (41 base 16), representing an A, and have a uniform encoding space of one between letters such that 01011010 (5A base 16) represents a Z, while the lowercase letters start with 61 base 16 representing an a and 7A base 16 representing a z.
3. The alphanumeric numerals start with 00110000 (30 base 16) representing a zero and have a uniform encoding space of one such that 00111001 (39 base 16) represents a nine. It must be emphasized that these symbols have no associated numeric semantics in the microcomputer design. Arithmetic operations are meaningless.
4. A single alphanumeric numeral may be converted to BCD encoding by subtracting 00110000 (30 base 16). The conversion of a string of ASCII nu-

First hexadecimal digit	Second hexadecimal digit															
	0	1	2	3	4	5	6	7	8	9	A	B	C	D	E	F
0	NUL[a]	SOH	STX	ETX	EOT	ENQ	ACK	BEL	BS	HT	LF	VT	FF	CR	CO	SI[a]
1	DLE[a]	DC1	DC2	DC3	DC4	NAK	SYN	ETB	CAN	EM	SUB	ESC	FS	GS	ES	US[a]
2	SP	!	"	#	$	%	&	'	(	)	*	+	,	-	.	/
3	0	1	2	3	4	5	6	7	8	9	:	;	<	=	>	?
4	@	A	B	C	D	E	F	G	H	I	J	K	L	M	N	O
5	P	Q	R	S	T	U	V	W	X	Y	Z	[	\	]	|	—
6	\	a	b	c	d	e	f	g	h	i	j	k	l	m	n	o
7	p	q	r	s	t	u	v	w	x	y	z	{	|	}	~	DEL

Notes:

1. To find the ASCII binary code for a given symbol: (a) Find the symbol on the chart. (b) Read the first hexadecimal digit on the same horizontal line at the left edge of the chart. (c) Read the second hexadecimal digit on the same vertical line at the top of the chart. (d) Convert the two-digit hexadecimal number to binary.

2. To find the symbol for a given binary code: (a) Add a leading zero if necessary and convert the 8-bit binary number into the equivalent two-digit hexadecimal code. (b) Find the first hexadecimal digit on the left edge of the chart. (c) Find the second hexadecimal digit at the top of the chart. (d) The desired ASCII symbol is at the intersection of the first digit row and the second digit column.

[a] Teletype control characters.

Figure 1.27 Seven-bit ANSI X3.4-1968 ASCII encoding scheme used for character data in most microcomputers.

merals to BCD and then to binary, or the reverse, requires somewhat complicated but straightforward algorithms that will be presented later in a more appropriate section.

Floating-Point Numbers

It is sometimes necessary and often extremely convenient to be able to represent numeric values that include a fractional portion or whose value exceeds the range representable employing integer encoding. In such circumstances an encoding scheme known as *floating point,* which is based on scientific notation, is employed in microcomputers. The recently adopted IEEE Floating-Point Standard for Microcomputers has largely been implemented on the Intel 8087 auxiliary numeric data processor described later in this text. This standard provides that a value be interpreted from the syntax

$$\pm \text{significand} \times \text{base}^{\pm \text{exrad}}$$

Note that four pieces of information must be available for correct interpretation of the significand and of the exrad (a total of eight pieces of information). The IEEE standard provides that the significand be expressed as a base 2 fraction with the implied radix point on the extreme left and with no leading-zero bits. The sign of the significand shall be the leftmost bit of the floating-point datum and thus corresponds in position to the sign bit of an integer datum. The magnitude of the significand (the precision) consists of a binary fraction of length 23 bits for single precision, 52 bits for double precision, and at least 63 bits for double extended precision. The latter precision is employed for all temporary intermediate calculation values. The IEEE standard also provides that the exrad be expressed as a base 2 integer and thus the implied radix point is on the extreme right. The magnitude of the exrad consists of 8 bits for single precision, 11 bits for double precision, and at least 15 bits for double extended precision. Values of the exrad above the midpoint are interpreted as positive by the amount of deviation from the midpoint; values of the exrad below the midpoint are interpreted as negative by the amount of deviation from the midpoint. Note that the terms *significand* and *exrad* are employed to specify the bit patterns or syntax, and the terms *mantissa* and *exponent* are used to specify the interpretation, meaning, or semantics of the components of the floating-point data type.

The IEEE Floating-Point Standard specifies that a floating-point overflow results from an attempt to develop an exponent whose magnitude is too large for the bit pattern of the exrad to represent. An appropriate flag will be set "on" and a special bit pattern signifying either infinity or "not a number" will replace the inappropriate value. An underflow results from an attempt to develop an exponent whose magnitude is less than that allowed for by the bit pattern of the exrad while the binary fractional significand is all zeros. Again, an appropriate flag will be set "on" and a special bit pattern signifying either infinity or "not a number" will replace the inappropriate value. Subsequent arithmetic operation involving an operand whose value is either infinity or "not a number" results in an operand with a similar value. Figure 1.28 illustrates the syntax and specifies the semantic interpretation of the IEEE Floating-Point Standard.

Instructions

The fully ordered sequence of operation code and operand pointer(s) that constitute a program are also data—data of a special kind, but data all the same. The only firm rules for the bit patterns that are interpreted as instructions by microcomputers are:

1. Each instruction must have a unique bit pattern with a unique interpretation. Thus each bit pattern must have one and only one meaning, and each meaning must have one and only one bit pattern.
2. The operations code must be placed to the left of the operand address pointer(s).

Data within a microcomputer must exist as bit patterns within a memory physically and logically as a portion of the microcomputer system. Again, it must be emphasized that memory is passive; that is, memory can preserve bit patterns representing information, but memory cannot cause the change of that bit pattern (barring a rare error). Memory reacts to versions of a single order from logically adjacent portions of a microcomputer:

Move datum to here from there

with no change in the bit pattern (syntax) of the datum. Memory exists in microcomputer systems as several logically distinct entities.

Flags

Flags are single-bit flip-flops with an explicit name used to record the occurrence of an event. Thus they record "on" or "off" or, alternatively, "true" or "false." Groups of flags may or may not be grouped together into indicator or condition registers. Instructions are provided to test the setting of flags or condition registers as well as to set or clear them.

Registers

Registers are specially named groups of flip-flops with the ability to retain information. Often certain registers of microcomputers are associated with certain operations, while certain instructions may access specific registers through implication. The registers of certain microcomputers are materially faster than program or data

Single. A 32-bit format for a binary floating-point number X is divided as shown below. The component fields of X are the 1-bit sign s, the 8-bit biased exponent e, and the 23-bit fraction f. The value v of X is as follows:

a. If $e = 255$ and $f \neq 0$, then $v = \text{NaN}$.
b. If $e = 255$ and $f = 0$, then $v = (-1)^S \infty$.
c. If $0 < e < 255$, then $v = (-1)^S 2^{C - 127}(1.f)$.
d. If $e = 0$ and $f \neq 0$, then $v = (-1)^S 2^{-126}(0.f)$.
e. If $e = 0$ and $f = 0$, then $v = (-1)^S 0$ (zero).

Single-Precision Format

s	e	f
0	8	31

Double. A 64-bit format for a binary floating-point number X is divided as shown below. The component fields of X are the 1-bit sign s, the 11-bit biased exponent e, and the 52-bit fraction f. The value of X is as follows:

a. If $e = 2047$ and $f \neq 0$, then $v = \text{NaN}$.
b. If $e = 2047$ and $f = 0$, then $v = (-1)^S \infty$.
c. If $0 < e < 2047$, then $v = (-1)^S 2^{C - 1023}(1.f)$.
d. If $e = 0$ and $f \neq 0$, then $v = (-1)^S 2^{-1022}(0.f)$.
e. If $e = 0$ and $f = 0$, then $v = (-1)^S 0$ (zero).

Double-Precision Format

s	e	f
0	11	63

Single extended. Extended is an implementation-dependent format. An extended binary floating-point number X has four components: a 1-bit sign s, an exponent e of specified range combined with a bias which might be zero, a 1-bit integer part j, and a fraction f with at least 31 bits. The exponent must range between a minimum value $m \leq -1023$ and a maximum value $M \geq +1024$. The value of X is as follows:

a. If $e = M$ and $f \neq 0$, then $v = \text{NaN}$.
b. If $e = M$ and $f = 0$, then $v = (-1)^S \infty$.
c. If $m < e < M$, then $v = (-1)^S 2^e(j.f)$.
d. If $e = m$ and $j = f = 0$, then $v = (-1)^S 0$ (this is normal zero).

Double extended. The double extended format is the same as single extended, except that the exponent must range between $m \leq -16383$ and $M \geq +16384$ and the fraction must have at least 63 bits.

Figure 1.28 Basic formats of the IEEE proposed standard for binary floating-point data.

memory, while the registers of other microcomputers may not possess this access-speed advantage. Even if the registers of a microcomputer have no speed advantage, their existence (or pseudoexistence) is an advantage in that they exist in lower numbers than the cells of program or data memory; therefore, fewer bits are needed in an instruction to refer to a register. The main use of registers is to save data or addresses before and between data transformations or address manipulations.

Main memory

Although this author prefers the term *primary memory,* many microcomputer venders employ the term *main memory.* In either case, the term refers to that memory whose addresses occur as operand pointers in ordinary arithmetic-logic instructions such as ADD or AND. Most modern microcomputers have main (primary) memory implemented as random-access memory (RAM) whose addressable quantum of information is the byte with a numeric identifier (address) ranging from zero to (usually) some power of 2 minus 1. The term RAM means that access to any address may be next and that the time to access the data at that address is the same as the time to access any other address—a constant. A very few special-purpose microcomputers have their main (primary) memory in two separately addressed logical and physical spaces both starting at address zero. In all cases, this situation implies that program memory is not alterable during normal program execution—it is read-only memory (ROM) that is also RAM. Programs stored in ROM cannot alter themselves, cannot contain any variable data areas, and are known as *pure code.*

Auxiliary memory

Many forms of relatively large storage capacity auxiliary memory devices exist which are accessed by microcomputers as if they were input/output devices. Among these devices are "hard" disks, floppy disks, cassette and cartridge magnetic tapes, magnetic bubble memory (MBM), charge-coupled devices (CCD), as well as other storage media. We will delay our discussion of these secondary memories until later when we treat microcomputer I/O.

MAIN MEMORY ADDRESSING MODES

As discussed earlier, a microcomputer program is an ordered set of instructions designed and implemented to manipulate data to satisfy a need. Each of the data manipulation instructions must consist of (1) a specification of what manipulation is to be carried out (the opcode) utilizing (2) data residing at some location in main memory, in some register, or on some auxiliary memory device the designation of which is a pointer [the *operand address*(es)]. The operand address in the instruction often points directly to the location of the datum; alternatively, the operand address must be modified in one or several ways to point to the location of the datum. This process of operand address pointer modification is often referred to as calculating or deriving the *effective operand address* and can be illustrated in general as

effective address ← operand address + modifier + - - - + modifier

where the + stands for any functional operation, including substitution, and the term *modifier* implies the contents of any register or location in main memory. Very often the different methods of deriving the effective address of a datum are termed *addressing modes.*

The various addressing modes and their associated methods of effective operand address calculation can be understood from several considerations.

Direct Addressing

The unmodifiable address of the datum is given by the operand address in the instruction. This address can be the identifier (name) of a flag, a register, or an address in main memory. Thus there is *flag direct, register direct,* and *memory direct* addressing, where the location of the datum is explicitly or implicitly given in the instruction.

Indirect Addressing

The unmodified address of the datum in main memory is contained in the register or main memory address pointed to by the operand address in the instruction. Thus there is *register indirect* and *memory indirect* addressing, where the location of the datum in main memory is explicitly contained in the register or memory location pointed to explicitly or implicitly in the instruction. Some microcomputers provide automatic incrementing or decrementing of the address register either before or after use. Thus there can be automatic postincrement register indirect, automatic predecrement register indirect, and so on. Included in this group is *stack addressing,* in which the datum is contained in the memory location at the current top of the stack whose address is always contained in the stack pointer (SP) register.

Relative Addressing

The operand (a displacement) in the instruction is added to the starting address of a section of memory contained in a register designated explicitly or implicitly in the instruction. Thus there is *base address relative* and *program counter relative* addressing, where the location of the datum is derived as the sum of the starting address of a memory area in a register and the displacement in the instruction. The common *immediate data* addressing mode can be considered as program counter relative zero addressing, in that the datum follows the opcode and therefore is pointed to by the PC.

Indexed Addressing

The address of the datum in main memory is modified by the contents of an index register. It is common to combine indexing with the other addressing modes, resulting in *indexed memory direct, preindexed register indirect, postindexed register indirect, preindexed memory indirect, postindexed memory indirect,* and *indexed base address relative* addressing. Note that the combination of indexing with indirectness can specify that the indexing be performed before or after the indirectness is accomplished.

A Classification of Addressing Modes

The Intel 8086/8088 assembly language uses the following terminology and syntax to specify the semantics of deriving the effective operand address (addressing mode) of both the source and destination operands. Normally, instructions must contain two operands, as follows:

MOV X,Y; [X] ← [Y], or replace the current value at location X with the value at location Y while preserving the value at location Y

ADD X,Y; [X] ← [X] + [Y], or replace the current value at location X with the sum of the value at location X and the value at location Y while preserving the value at location Y

The standard for microcomputer assembly language provides for at least 19 different methods of calculating the effective address of both the destination and the source data operands. For convenience in grasping the concepts, we have classifed these 19 addressing modes into 5 groups. Figures 1.29 through 1.35 should be helpful in studying these 5 groups of addressing modes. A summary of the addressing modes follows.

Direct addressing

- **Register Direct:** the contents of register AX. Example:

```
AX
```

- **Memory Direct:** the contents of the main memory location designated by the identifier THERE with or without displacement. It can be indexed. Examples:

```
THERE
THERE + 17
```

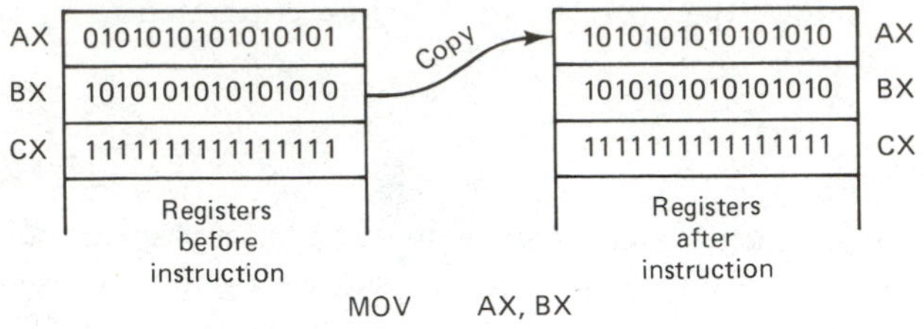

(a) Register direct addressing mode

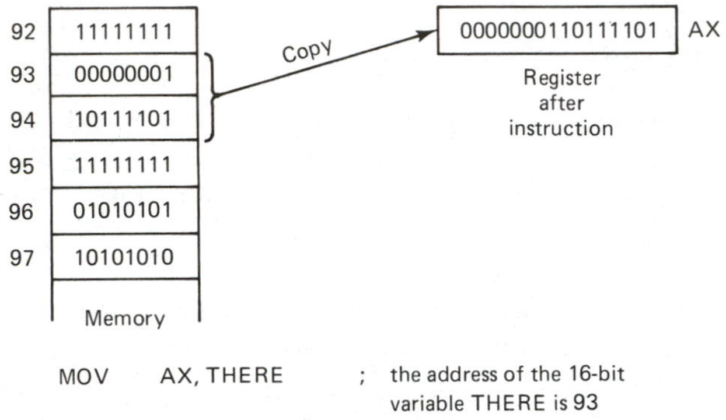

(b) Memory direct addressing mode

Figure 1.29 Direct addressing modes.

Indirect addressing

- **Register Indirect:** the contents of the main memory location whose address is contained in register SI (restricted to index and base registers on I8086; can have displacement). Examples:

(SI)	I8086
@SI	IEEE

- **Memory Indirect** (not available on I8086): the contents of the main memory location whose address is contained in the main memory location designated by the operand identifier. Displacement is often allowed.

Relative addressing

- **Base Address Relative:** the contents of the main memory location whose address is derived as the sum of the address in the base address register plus the

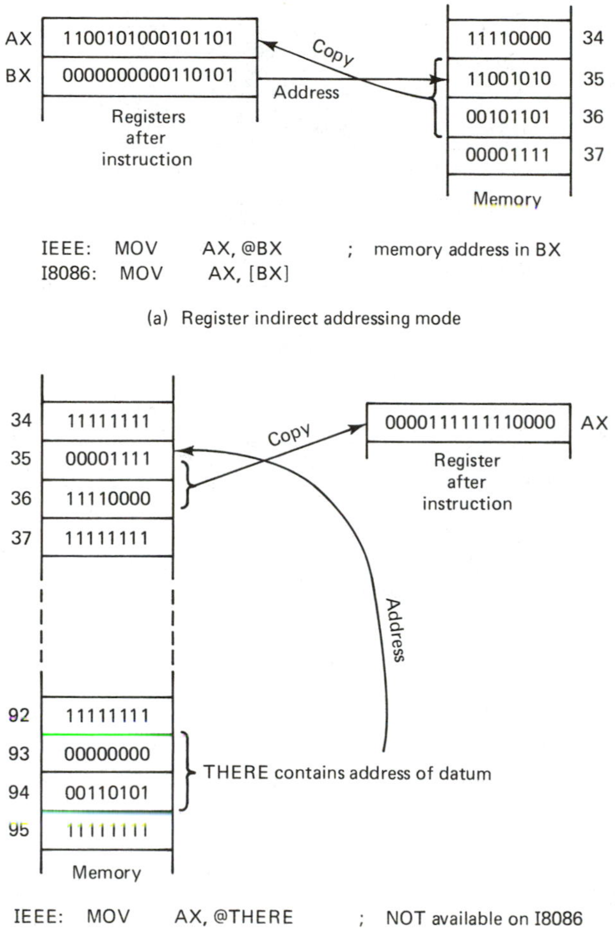

(b) Memory indirect addressing mode

Figure 1.30 Indirect addressing modes.

displacement or offset given as the operand in the instruction. Can have absolute displacement or structure displacement. Examples:

$BX	IEEE
(BX)	I8086
(BP+3)	I8086
(BP)– ANY	I8086

- **Program Counter Relative** (not available on I8086): the contents of the main memory location whose address is derived as the sum of the address in the PC (the address of the current instruction) plus the displacement or offset given as

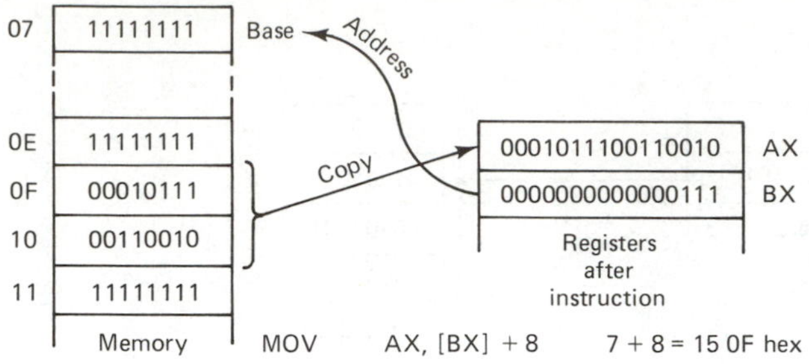

(a) Base address relative addressing mode: $Reg ± offset

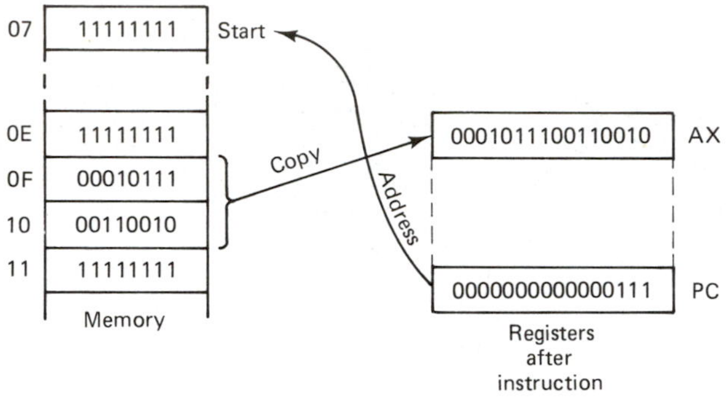

MOV AX, $PC + 8 ; not available on I8086

(b) Program counter relative addressing mode: $PC ± offset

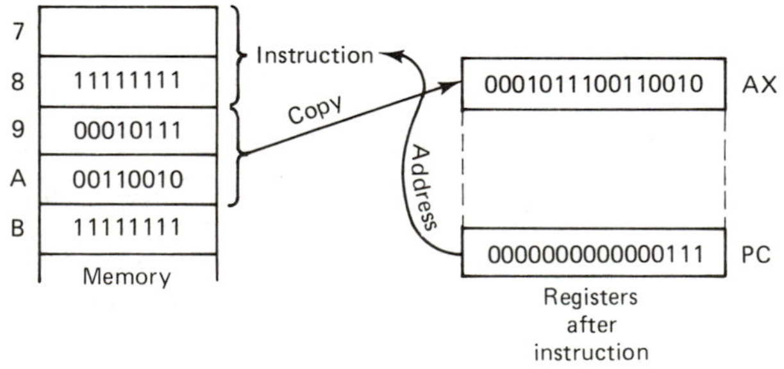

MOV AX, 1732h

(c) Immediate addressing mode: #Value

```
IT:  MOV    DX, THERE
     MOV    AX, 1732h
     MOV    BX, CX
     JMP    * -3              ;  go to statement IT
```

(d) Current statement relative branch addressing

Figure 1.31 Relative addressing modes.

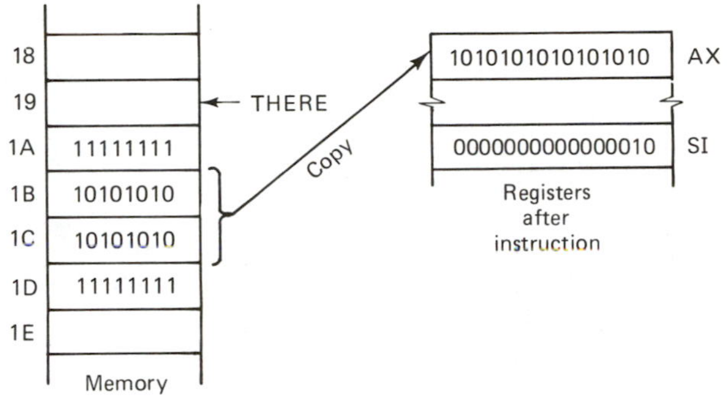


```
MOV     AX, THERE[SI]     ; address of THERE = 19
                          ; address of datum =
                          ; THERE + SI
                          ; 19 + 02 = 1B hex
```

Figure 1.32 Indexed direct memory addressing modes.

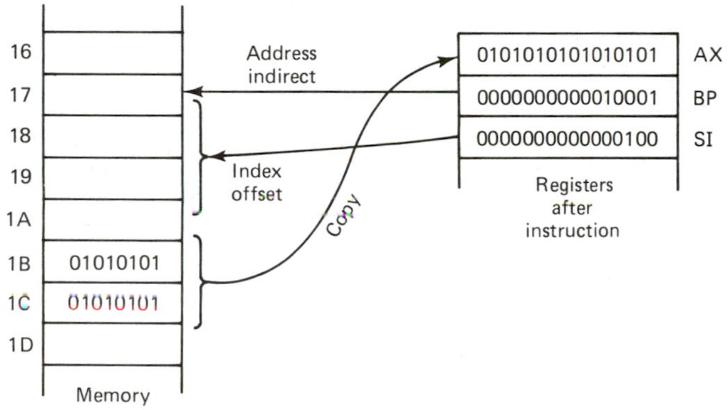


```
MOV     AX, [BP] [SI]     ; BP = 17, SI = 04
                          ; datum at 1B hex
```

Figure 1.33 Indexed base register indirect memory addressing mode.

the operand in the instruction. Note the resemblance to base address relative addressing.

- **Immediate:** the value of the operand field is to be used as the datum. In effect, the datum is pointed to by the PC and the offset is zero. Note that the value cannot start with a hexadecimal A through F. Examples:

```
123h    I8086
OA1h    I8086
```

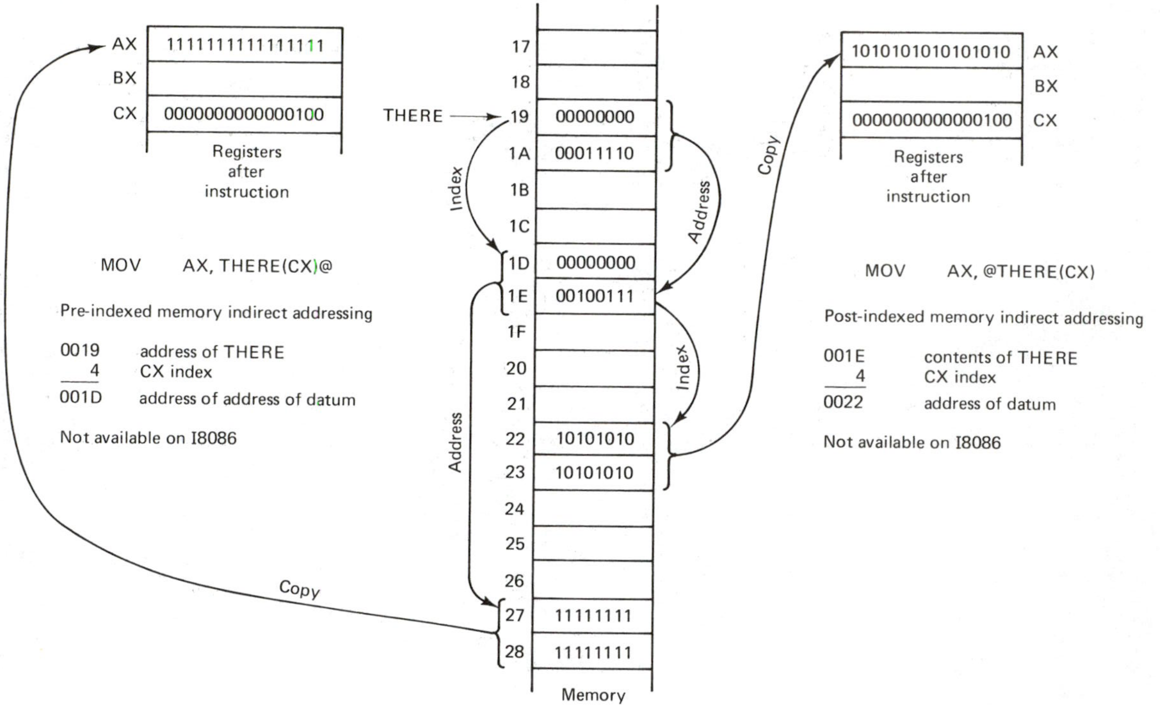

Figure 1.34 Indexed memory indirect addressing modes. Not available on I8086.

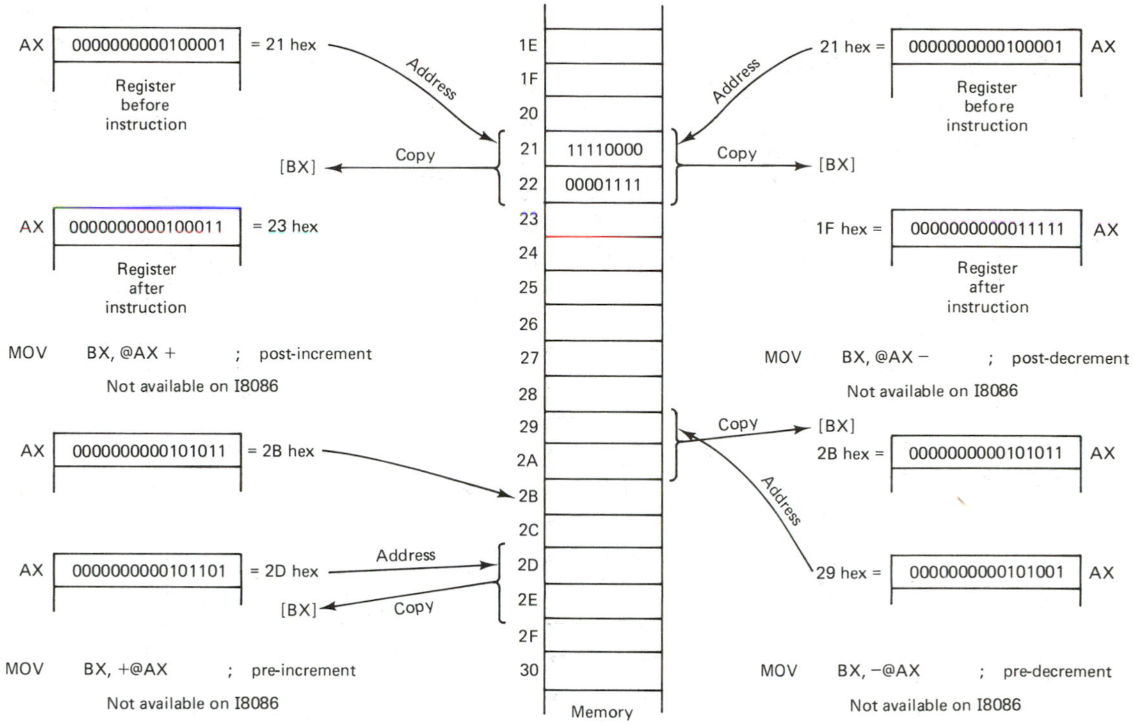

Figure 1.35 Automatic post-increment and post-decrement as well as pre-increment and pre-decrement register indirect addressing modes. Not available on I8086.

```
#123h   IEEE
#A1h    IEEE
```

- **Current Statement Relative:** used in JUMP statements (program flow-of-control statements) to indicate that the next statement to be executed is plus or minus the number of statements from the current jump statement. This form of programming is not recommended, in that later addition or deletion of statements during debugging or maintenance may not always include a correction of the JUMP offset amount, with subsequent disastrous results. Examples:

```
*+7
*–7
```

Absolute addressing

Not normally used on I8086, absolute addressing means that the value of the operand is used directly as an address in main memory to obtain the desired datum.

In effect, an absolute address is an offset from the beginning of main memory and thus is computed as zero + offset. The segment register organization of the I8086 (described in Chapter 2) makes this addressing mode unnecessary.

Indexed addressing

- **Indexed Memory Direct:** the contents of the main memory location designated by the sum of the address of the identifier THERE and the contents of the index register SI, with or without a displacement. The Intel and IEEE syntax are identical. Examples:

```
THERE (SI)
THERE (SI + 3)
THERE (SI) + 3
```

- **Indexed Indirect**
  1. *Indexed Base Register Indirect:* the contents of the main memory location pointed to by the base register BX modified by the contents of index register SI. The last example below gives the displacement as the number of bytes into a defined structure of the substructure identifier ANY. Examples:

```
(BX) (SI)         I8086
$BX (SI)          IEEE
(BP).ANY (SI)     I8086
```

  2. *Indexed Memory Indirect*
     a. *Postindexed Memory Indirect* (not available on I8086): uses the contents of the main memory location pointed to the contents of the location THERE modified by the contents of the index register SI.
     b. *Preindexed Memory Indirect* (not available on I8086): modifies the address of the identifier THERE by the contents of the index register SI and uses the contents of this location as the address in main memory of the datum.

Automatic increment/decrement register indirect addressing

Auto-Postincrement Register Indirect (not available on I8086): the contents of the main memory location whose address is contained in a register whose contents are automatically incremented by the width of the datum in bytes after each access.

Auto-Postdecrement Register Indirect (not available on I8086): the contents of the main memory location whose address is contained in a register whose contents are automatically decremented by the width of the datum in bytes after each access.

Auto-Preincrement Register Indirect (not available on I8086): the contents of the main memory location whose address is contained in a register that has been automatically incremented before use by the width of the datum.

Auto-Predecrement Register Indirect (not available on I8086): the contents of the main memory location whose address is contained in register AX, which has been automatically decremented before use by the width of the datum.

2

The Intel 8086/8088

The Intel 8086/8088 microcomputer possesses an organization centered around an information bus that is used to communicate both address information (memory location and I/O port identity) and data from various subassemblies to other subassemblies. Figure 2.1 illustrates the clean separation of the information-processing unit from memory and from the input/output portions. This separation is typical of modern microcomputers. In the terminology being employed, the information-processing unit acquires an instruction, decodes and executes it, calculates the effective address of the datum in memory or on an I/O device, and finally, updates the address of the next instruction in memory.

Employing Figure 2.2, we will first concentrate in some detail on the execution cycle of an instruction. We will employ an ADD instruction as our example. The Intel 8086/8088 microcomputer has several different ADD instructions involving signed integer data with variations involving the possible magnitude as well as the location of the data. In all cases, the ADD instruction involves acquiring two source, or input, data and results in the production of one destination, or result, datum. This may be illustrated as

$$[D] \leftarrow [S1] + [S2]$$

where the brackets signify the signed numeric value of the data contained in the memory location or register with this identifier (or name). The wording above was used for complete accuracy and has the relatively simple meaning: the contents of a named memory location or register. The design of the I8086/8088 microcomputer specifies that the instructions to accomplish diadic arithmetic-logic operations must explicitly specify two operand addresses or values and that only one of these

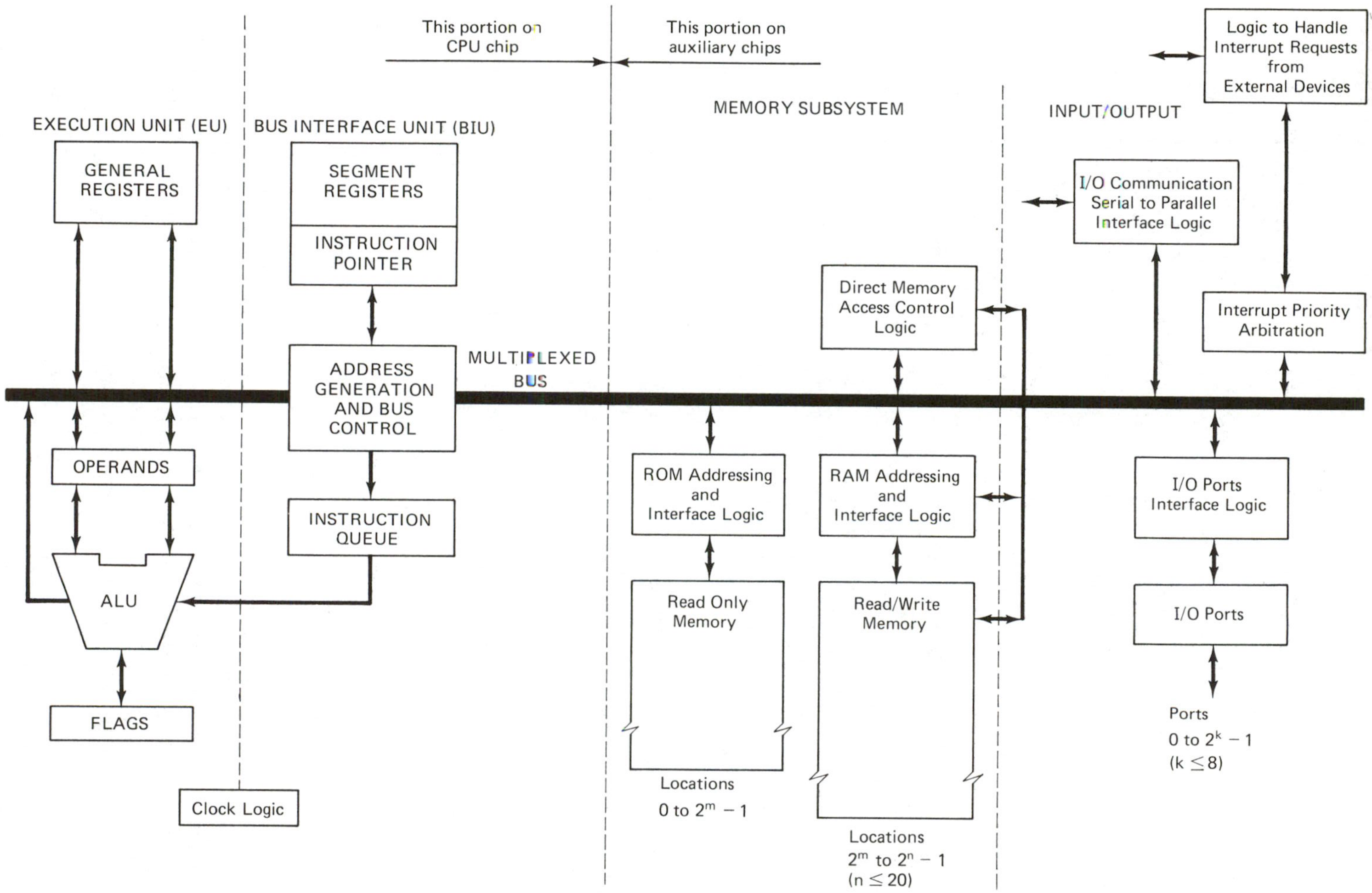

Figure 2.1 Diagrammatic representation of Intel 8086/8088 microcomputer organization. (Reprinted by permission of Intel Corporation. Copyright 1980.)

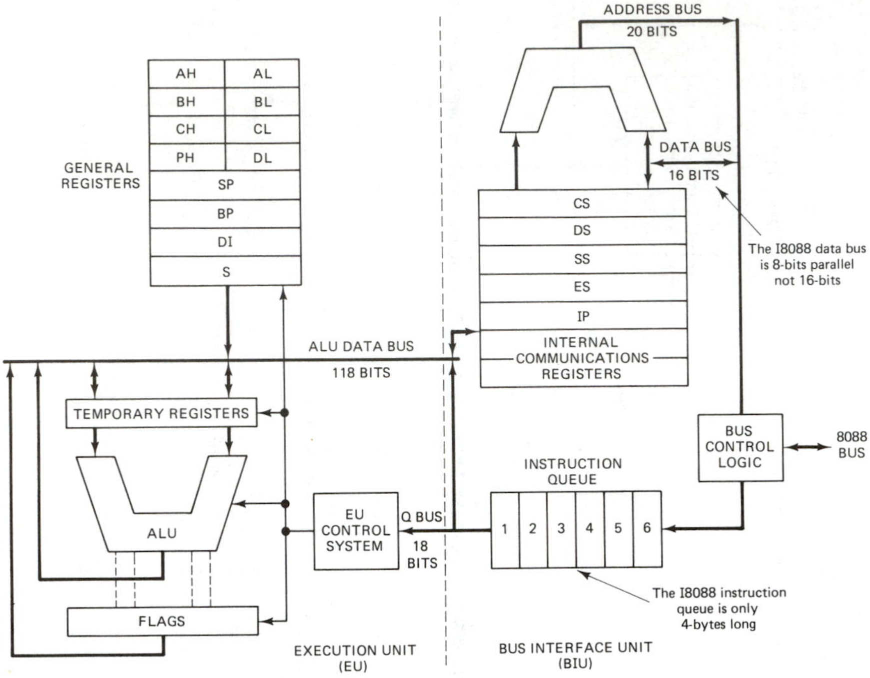

Figure 2.2 I8086/block diagram. Note that the I8088 is almost identical physically and is identical from a programmatic viewpoint. (Reprinted by permission of Intel Corporation. Copyright 1980.)

addresses can be in main memory, with the other being a register or an immediate datum. This is accomplished by implicitly specifying the third operand address. Thus the ADD instructions have the following symbolic format with designated meaning:

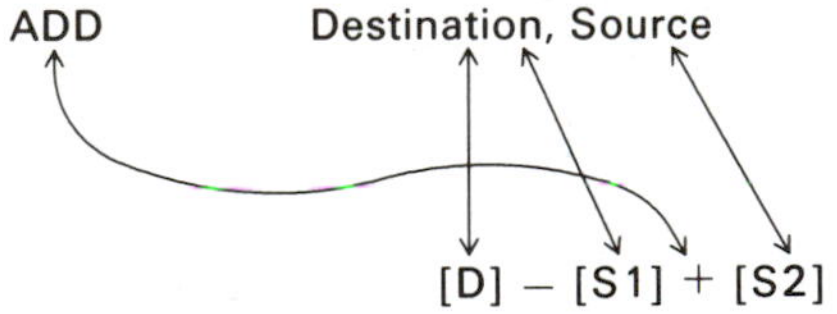

where the destination/source 1 operand identifier may refer to any location in read/write (RAM) main memory or to a register and where the source 2 operand identifier may refer to any location in main memory, to a register, or alternatively, may be the actual datum value (an immediate).

Thus the register-to-register word instruction

```
ADD        CX,DX
```

is interpreted as: replace the contents of the 16-bit register CX with the sum of the contents of the 16-bit registers CX and DX while leaving the contents of the 16-bit register DX unaltered. The overflow flag will be set ON if the value of the sum exceeds the capacity of the register, the sign flag will be set ON if the sum is negative, the zero flag will be set ON if the sum is zero, and the carry flag will be set ON if the sum exceeds the capacity of the register considered unsigned (useful for multiprecision arithmetic). Note that a word instruction is implied by the use of word operands.

Similarly, the register-to-register byte instruction

```
ADD     CH,DL
```

is interpreted as: replace the contents of the 8-bit register CH with the sum of the contents of the 8-bit registers CH and DL while leaving the contents of the 8-bit register DL unaltered. The flags will be set as specified above. Again, a byte execution is implied by the use of byte operands. The mixture of word with byte operands is not legal.

Referring to Figure 2.2, note that registers CX and CH overlap, as do other similarly named registers. Thus the register designations refer to nonunique data containers. Register AX refers to a 16-bit data container that completely overlaps the two 8-bit data containers designated as AH and AL, as shown in Figure 2.3.

It must be emphasized that changing the contents of register AL changes the contents of register AX, changing AH changes AX, changing AX changes AH and AL, but changing AH does not affect AL, or vice versa. Thus corresponding byte registers completely overlap word registers. In effect, the programmer has available eight byte-size registers, four word-size registers, or noninterfering combinations as follows:

Byte		Word
8	and	0
6	and	1
4	and	2
2	and	3
0	and	4

This table emphasizes that the I8086/8088 microcomputer is not "rich" in registers.

Consider the following memory-to-register word instruction and the corresponding register-to-memory word instruction employing the direct memory addressing mode:

```
ADD     AX,TEMP
ADD     TEMP,CX
```

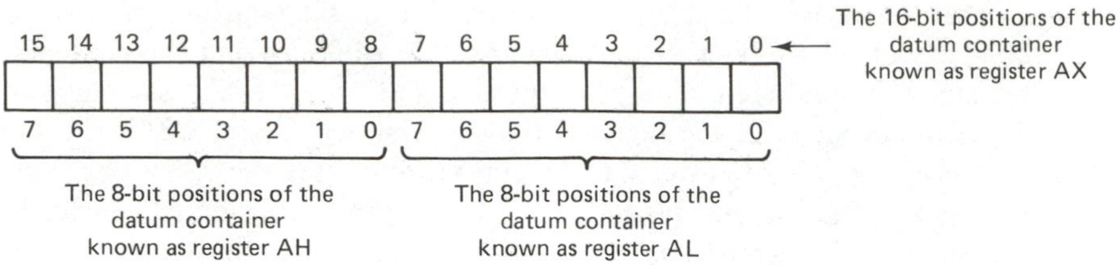

Figure 2.3 The word and byte registers of the I8086/8088 completely overlap.

It must be emphasized that all the memory addressing modes are available for use with both the ADD word and ADD byte instructions. Employing the add memory word-to-register instruction, examples would be

ADD	AX,TEMP	memory direct
ADD	AX,(SI)	register indirect
ADD	AX,(BP) (SI)	indexed base relative register indirect
ADD	AX,TEMP (SI)	indexed memory direct

The source datum value may occupy the space usually used by the source operand address in instructions known as *immediates.* The following four instructions are examples in which D means decimal or base 10 and H means hexadecimal or base 16:

ADD	CL,2D	byte register immediate
ADD	BTEMP,2D	byte memory immediate
ADD	CX,16A9H	word register immediate
ADD	WTEMP,16A9H	word memory immediate

It should be noted that, if the register is the accumulator—that is, the AL register or AX register—a short, fast form of the add register immediate instruction can be employed. It should also be noted that all modes of memory addressing are available with the add memory immediate instruction.

MEMORY SEGMENTATION

Referring to Figure 2.4, note that all of the address registers are 16 bits in length and thus are able to specify any location within a 64K area of memory (a segment). Also note that the data path or bus to memory and I/O has the ability to carry a 20-bit address and thus is able to specify any location within a 1024K = 1M memory. The method employed to calculate the physical address of an instruction will clarify the design solution strategy used to overcome this anomaly.

All program instructions must be located in main memory in one or more *code segments.* The instruction sequence currently being executed must have its

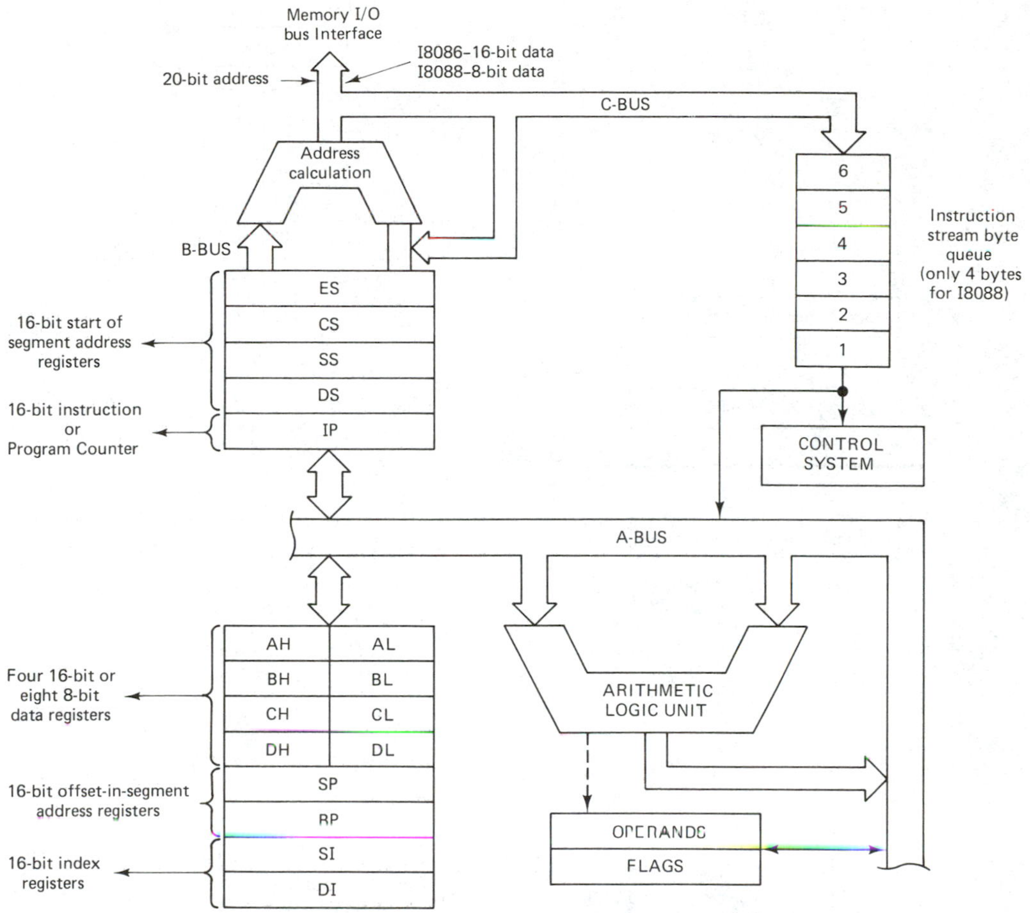

Figure 2.4 Intel 8086 detailed functional block diagram. (Reprinted by permission of Intel Corporation. Copyright 1980.)

starting address as the contents of the CS register (code segment register). Note that only 16 bits are available to specify 20 bits of address information. By definition the CS register will contain the 16 most significant bits of the start-of-segment address, while the four least significant bits are assumed to be zeros. Thus a segment of code (of program) can start in location 0, or 16, or 32, or 48, or . . . , but cannot start in locations whose addresses are not evenly divisible in base 16. The exact instruction currently being executed is offset from the beginning of its code segment by the contents of the IP register (instruction pointer or program counter). As an example, using hexadecimal (base 16) notation,

AAABO	contents CS × 16—start of code segment
+0 0 6 6 9	contents of IP—offset of instruction
AB 1 1 9	physical address of instruction

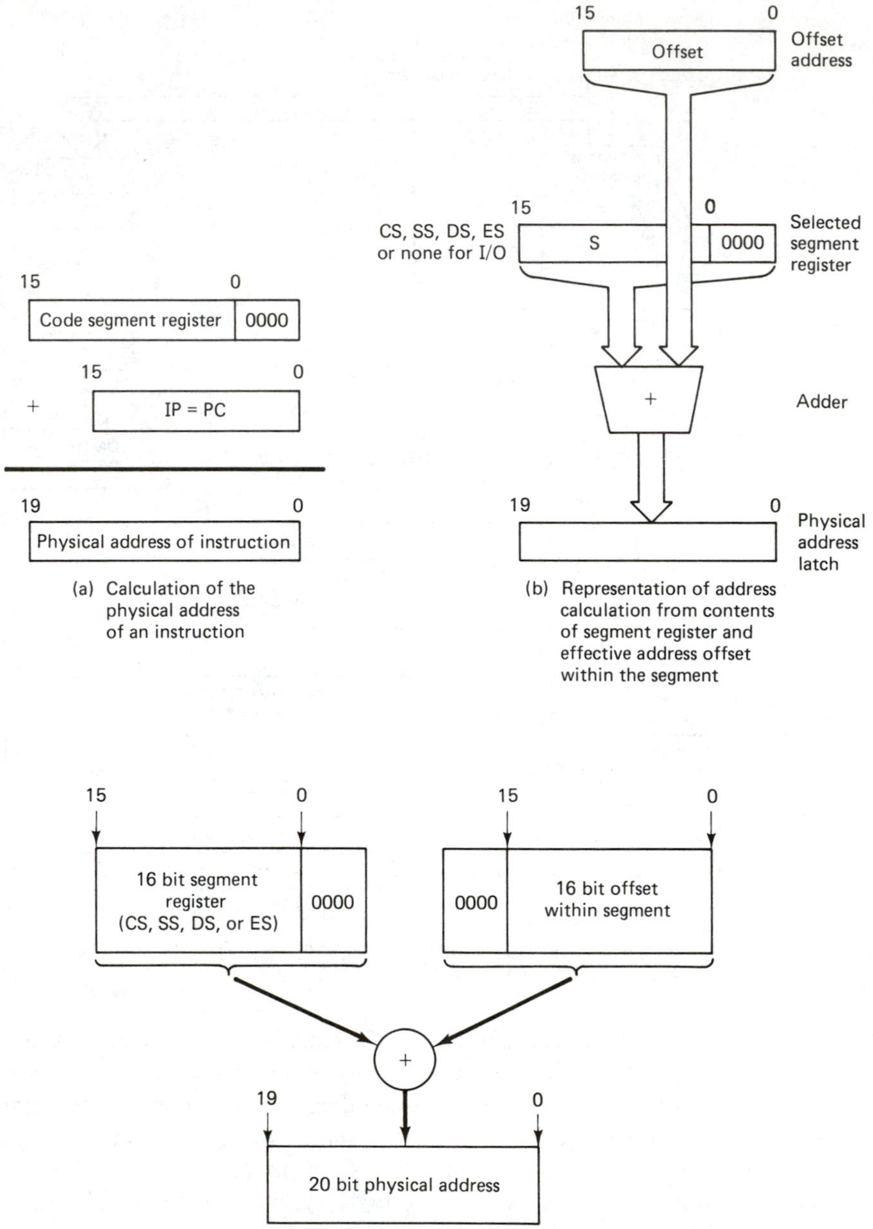

(a) Calculation of the physical address of an instruction

(b) Representation of address calculation from contents of segment register and effective address offset within the segment

Figure 2.5 Intel 8086/8088 20-bit physical memory address calculation, allowing access of any location in a 1-mega byte memory (1024K) employing a 16-bit register. Note that the address bus to memory would be 20-bits wide. Reprinted by permisssion of Intel Corporation. Copyright 1980.)

Figure 2.5 illustrates the process, and the resulting memory segmentation is shown in Figure 2.6.

The default usage of the segment registers during physical address calculation is as follows:

Code segment (CS) register: All instructions of a program are relative to the contents of the CS register × 16 as offset by the contents of the IP (or PC). Note that the datum given within an immediate instruction is relative to the CS register. Also note that programs are pure code (read-only) unless the code segment is overlaid by a data segment so that a portion of the program can be accessed as data. Such dynamic self-alteration of programs is both difficult to accomplish correctly and almost impossible to debug. Therefore, self-altering programs are considered poor programs.

Data segment (DS) register: All data references to memory are relative to the contents of the DS register × 16 as offset by the effective operand address. Exceptions are those references involving the SS or the ES registers, as noted below.

Stack segment (SS) register: All memory references involving the contents of the stack pointer (SP) register as an offset are relative to the contents of the

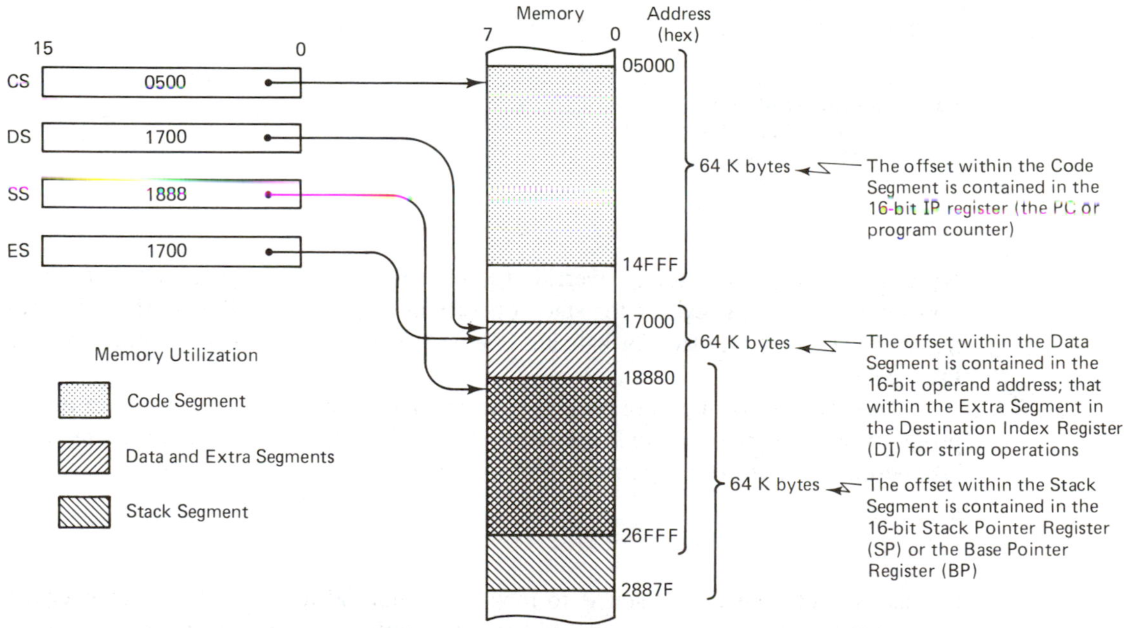

Figure 2.6 One of N possible segment-to-memory assignments possible within the Intel 8086/8088. Note that segments may overlap or may be discontiguous in physical memory. (Reprinted by permission of Intel Corporation. Copyright 1980.)

SS register × 16. Additionally, all memory references involving the contents of the base pointer register (BP) as an offset are also relative to the contents of the SS register × 16.

Extra segment (ES) register: All memory references during string operations, which use the contents of the destination index (DI) register for string effective address calculation, are relative to the contents of the ES register × 16.

The segment register that is to be employed to transform an offset within the segment to a physical memory address is typically implied by the instruction. On the other hand, it is possible to override this implicit segment register default designation in most instances and thus to designate explicitly a nonstandard segment register. The method available for this substitution of a segment register involves prefixing the individual instruction with a *segment override byte.* Thus the substitution, or override, of the default segment register is effective for only a single instruction. The format of the segment default override prefix byte is

bit 7							bit 0
0	0	1	r	r	1	1	0

Segment register identifier, where:

00	ES register
01	CS register
10	SS register
11	DS register

Note that it is not possible to override the use of (1) the CS register for an instruction fetch, (2) the SS register for stack operations implicitly employing the SP register, and (3) the ES register for a string operand destination implicitly employing the DI register.

One method of incorporating this segment default override prefix byte into a program is to specify a constant using the define byte (DB) assembly pseudoinstruction just before the instruction in question:

```
DB      00101110B      ; DB = define byte
```

In this example, the CS register is to replace the normal default segment register for the instruction following the override byte (and only for that instruction). An alternative method, probably preferable, is to employ the assembler pseudoinstruction

```
SEGMENT     CS
```

which will result in an identical action. Figure 2.7 summarizes the default and the permissible override segment register assignments.

Reference type	Segment register	Alternates	Logical address
Instruction fetch	CS (code segment)	None	IP
Stack operation	SS (stack segment)	None	SP
Variable (except below)	DS (data segment)	CS,ES,SS	Effective address
BP used as base register	SS (stack segment)	CS,ES,DS	Effective address
String source	DS (data segment)	CS,ES,SS	SI
String destination	ES (extra segment)	None	DI

Figure 2.7 Default and override segment registers for memory reference types. (Reprinted by permission of Intel Corporation. Copyright 1980.)

INSTRUCTIONS

We will continue to employ the generic ADD instruction as our example while discussing the bit patterns of Intel 8086/8088 instructions. Let us first consider

```
ADD     CX,DX
```

which places the 16-bit sum of the 16-bit contents of registers CX and DX into register CX, and

```
ADD     CH,DL
```

which places the 8-bit sum of the 8-bit contents of registers CH and DL into register CH. The format of these register-to-register instructions is given in Figure 2.8.

It is possible to generalize the ADD instruction of the I8086/8088 with the variations provided by the instruction format fields provided by the designer. These variations include:

W: Word- or byte-length operands.

D: Result in memory or in register.

MOD: Both operands in registers, or one operand in memory and no displacement, or signed byte displacement, or unsigned word displacement.

REG: One of eight word or byte registers contains operand.

R/M: If R, operand location is one of eight word or byte registers. If M, effective operand address calculated using one of eight methods.

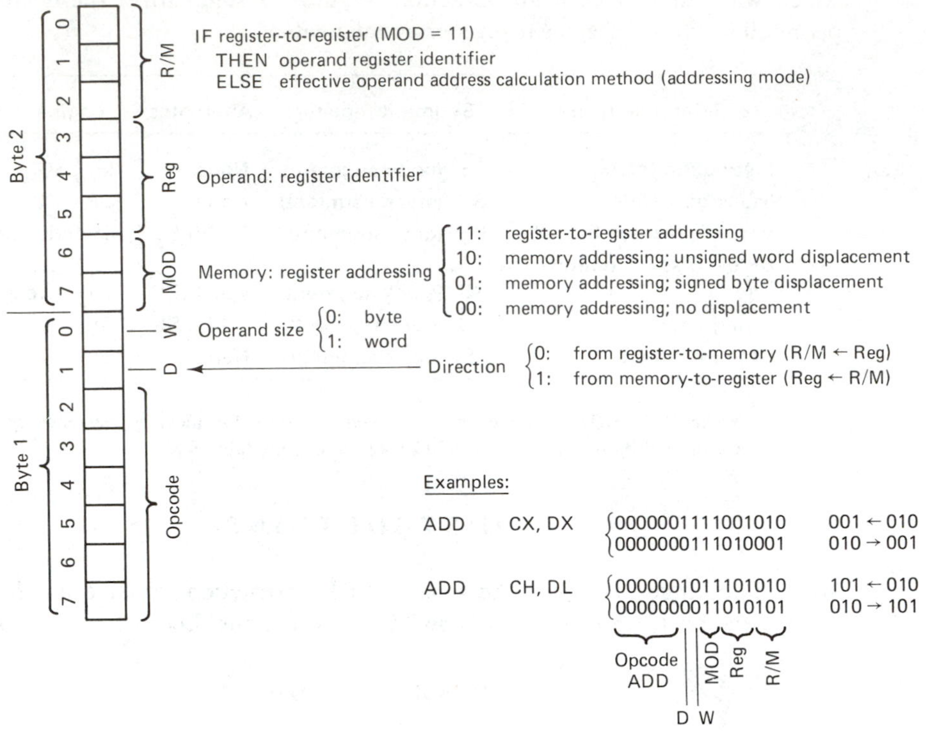

Figure 2.8 The format and corresponding semantics of the I8086/8088 ADD register-to-register instructions for both 16-bit and 8-bit data. Note that the direction bit allows two equivalent forms of both instructions with identical speeds.

Thus there are at least 2 (B/W) × 3 (displacement) × 8 (addressing modes) × 3 (mem ← reg/reg ← mem/reg ← reg) = 144 different instructions encompassed within the single generic ADD instruction.

It is important to understand that the two-explicit operand instructions, such as the ADD of the I8086/8088, are of the following three types only:

[register 1] ← [register 1] + [register 2]
[register] ← [register] + [memory location]
[memory location] ← [memory location] + [register]

Note particularly that memory-to-memory instructions are not allowed in the design of the I8086/8088. The designation of the 72 variations of the ADD word instruction and the 72 variations of the ADD byte instruction can be derived from Figure 2.9.

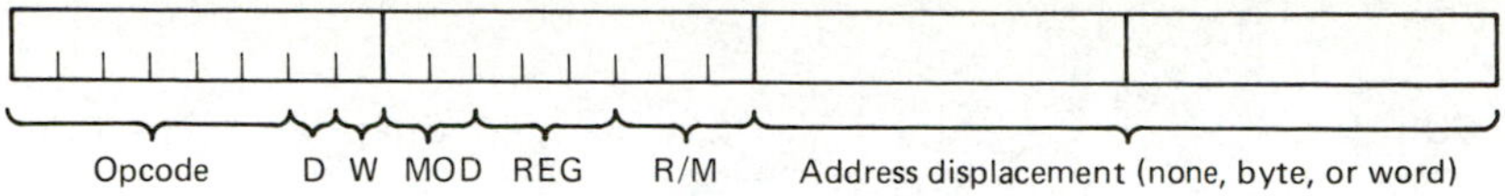

Intel 8086 instruction format.

Direction bit (D) = 1 signifies register is destination
Word bit (W) = 1 signifies word length operand values

Identifier Designation of Register Fields	
Word Operation (W = 1)	
000	AX
001	CX
010	DX
011	BX
100	SP
101	BP
110	SI
111	DI
Byte Operation (W = 0)	
000	AL
001	CL
010	DL
011	BL
100	AH
101	CH
110	DH
111	BH

Memory addressing modes

	no displacement	signed byte displacement	unsigned word displacement	no memory reference
r/m =	mode = 00	mode = 01	mode = 10	mode = 11
000	Base Relative Indexed BX + SI	Base Relative Indexed BX + SI + DISP	Base Relative Direct Indexed BX + SI + DISP	Register Identification in R/M field for Register-to-Register Instructions
001	Base Relative Indexed BX + DI	Base Relative Direct Indexed BX + DI + DISP	Base Relative Direct Indexed BX + DI + DISP	
010	Base Relative Indexed Stack BP + SI	Base Relative Direct Indexed Stack BP + SI + DISP	Base Relative Direct Indexed Stack BP + SI + DISP	
011	Base Relative Indexed Stack BP + DI	Base Relative Direct Indexed Stack BP + DI + DISP	Base Relative Direct Indexed Stack BP + DI + DISP	
100	Implied SI	Direct Indexed SI + DISP	Direct Indexed SI + DISP	
101	Implied DI	Direct Indexed DI + DISP	Direct Indexed DI + DISP	
110	Direct Direct Address	Base Relative Direct Stack BP + DISP	Base Relative Direct Stack BP + DISP	
111	Base Relative BX	Base Relative Direct BX + DISP	Base Relative Direct BX + DISP	

Figure 2.9 Format of the I8086/8088 two-operand instruction such as ADD with variations. Memory-to-memory instructions are not provided. Note that the instruction can occupy two, three, or four bytes. (Reprinted by permission of Intel Corporation. Copyright 1980.)

The format of the ADD immediate to register or to memory variations of this instruction are given in Figure 2.10. The designation of the additional 51 variations of the ADD immediate byte instruction and the additional 26 variations of the ADD immediate word instruction can be derived from this figure. Note that these 77 variations given a total of 221 variations of the generic ADD instruction. For complete accuracy, it must be noted that there are an additional 221 variations involving the *carry bit* that are useful in programming extended precision arithmetic. Thus it is possible to maintain that there are 442 variations of the generic ADD instruction.

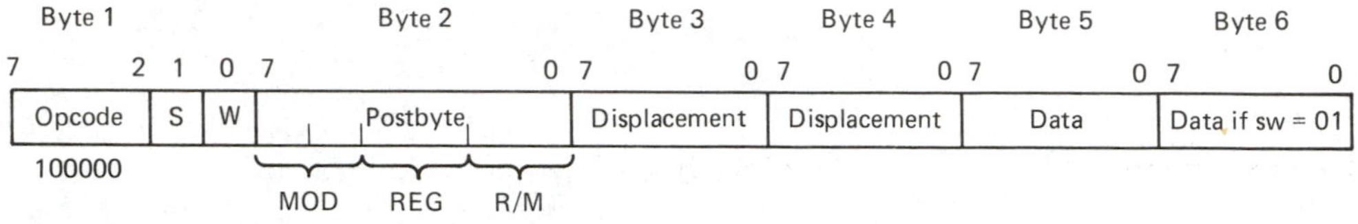

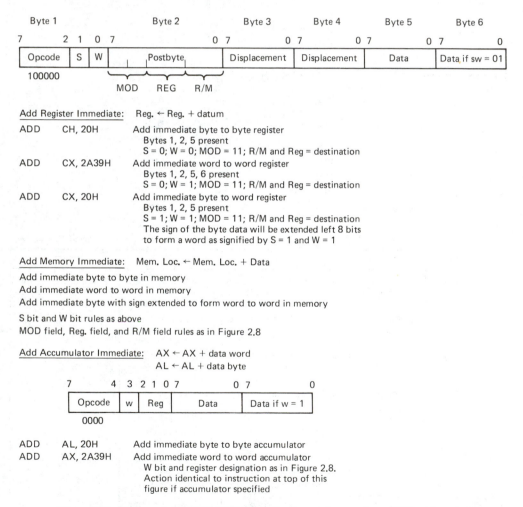

Add Register Immediate: Reg. ← Reg. + datum

ADD	CH, 20H	Add immediate byte to byte register Bytes 1, 2, 5 present S = 0; W = 0; MOD = 11; R/M and Reg = destination
ADD	CX, 2A39H	Add immediate word to word register Bytes 1, 2, 5, 6 present S = 0; W = 1; MOD = 11; R/M and Reg = destination
ADD	CX, 20H	Add immediate byte to word register Bytes 1, 2, 5 present S = 1; W = 1; MOD = 11; R/M and Reg = destination The sign of the byte data will be extended left 8 bits to form a word as signified by S = 1 and W = 1

Add Memory Immediate: Mem. Loc. ← Mem. Loc. + Data

Add immediate byte to byte in memory
Add immediate word to word in memory
Add immediate byte with sign extended to form word to word in memory

S bit and W bit rules as above
MOD field, Reg. field, and R/M field rules as in Figure 2.8

Add Accumulator Immediate: AX ← AX + data word
AL ← AL + data byte

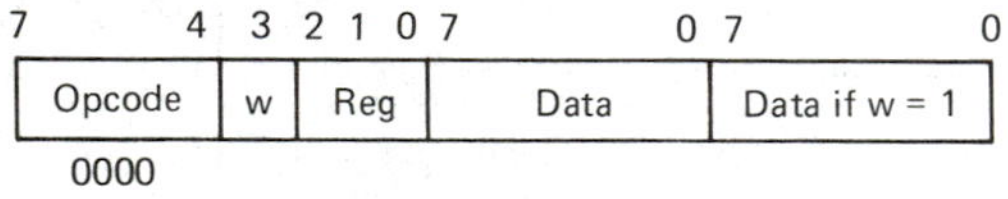

ADD	AL, 20H	Add immediate byte to byte accumulator
ADD	AX, 2A39H	Add immediate word to word accumulator W bit and register designation as in Figure 2.8. Action identical to instruction at top of this figure if accumulator specified

Figure 2.10 Format of the I8086/8088 immediate instructions, such as ADD with variations. Note the short form of the immediate-to-accumulator instruction at the bottom.

INDICATOR-STATUS FLAGS

The reference above to the carry bit requires that we now consider the flag register of the I8086/8088. Figure 2.11 may be helpful. At this time only those flags that can be set by the ADD instruction will be discussed. These are OF, SF, ZF, AF, PF, and CF. The meaning of these flags are:

OF, overflow flag: This bit flag is set ON to signal a magnitude overflow in signed integer binary arithmetic.

SF, sign flag: This bit flag is set to the value of the sign bit in signed integer binary arithmetic (0 = positive; 1 = negative).

ZF, zero flag: This bit flag being set ON signifies a result of zero (0 = nonzero; 1 = zero).

PF, parity flag: This bit flag being set ON signifies an even number of 1 bits in the result of any data operation, while OFF signifies an odd number of 1 bits in the result.

CF, carry flag: This bit flag being set ON signifies a "carry-out" in integer binary arithmetic operations. Thus it can signify a "borrow" during subtraction, as two's-complement arithmetic is employed for this operation.

AF, auxiliary carry flag: This bit flag being set ON signifies a "carry-out" in BCD base 10 (binary-coded decimal) arithmetic of the low-order 4 bits. This can be interpreted as a low-order decimal-digit overflow.

The direction flag (DF), the interrupt flag (IF), and the trap flag (TF) will be discussed in a later section.

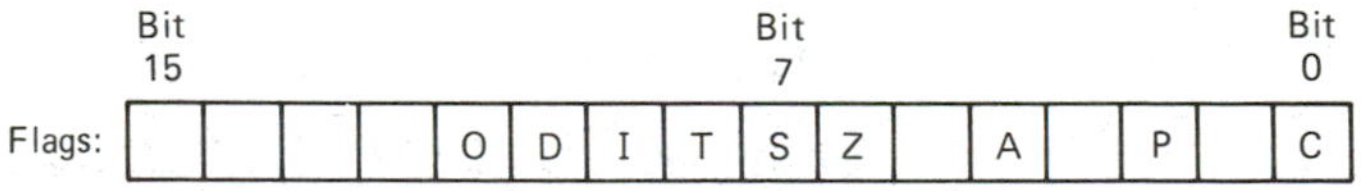

AF: auxiliary carry
CF: carry
DF: direction
IF: interrupt enable
OF: overflow
PF: parity
SF: sign
TF: trap
ZF: zero

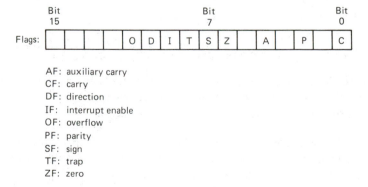

Figure 2.11 Intel 8086 flag register. (Reprinted by permission of Intel Corporation. Copyright 1980.)

CALCULATION OF THE OPERAND ADDRESS

In general, the effective operand address is the address of the location of a datum. Five different classes of effective operand addresses occur in the I8086/8088 microcomputer, with a plethora of subclasses. Figure 2.12 may be helpful while studying this section. Chapter 1 also considered this topic.

Register addressing

The datum (the value of the operand) is contained in the register named. If the operand is of length 16 bits, the datum is contained in register AX, BX, CX, or DX; if the operand is of length 8 bits, the datum is contained in register AL, AH, BL, BH, CL, CH, DL, or DH.

Immediate addressing

The datum (the value of the second source operand) is a portion of the instruction. That is, the datum is contained in the memory locations immediately following the rest of the instruction. The destination operand address may be one of the registers or any location in memory.

Memory addressing

The datum (the value of the operand) is contained in the memory location whose effective address is calculated in various ways.

Direct Memory Addressing. The effective operand address in memory is offset from the segment starting address by the displacement amount specified in the instruction

$$PA \leftarrow [Seg.\ Reg.] * 2^{**}4 + Displac.$$

where PA signifies the physical operand address in the one megabyte memory and [Seg. Reg.] signifies the contents of the appropriate segment register which is multiplied by 16 and thus gives the segment starting address.

Indexed Direct Memory Addressing. The effective operand address in memory is offset from the segment starting address by the displacement amount altered by the contents of the specified index register:

$$PA \leftarrow [Seg.\ Reg.] * 2^{**}4 + Displac. + [Index\ Reg.]$$

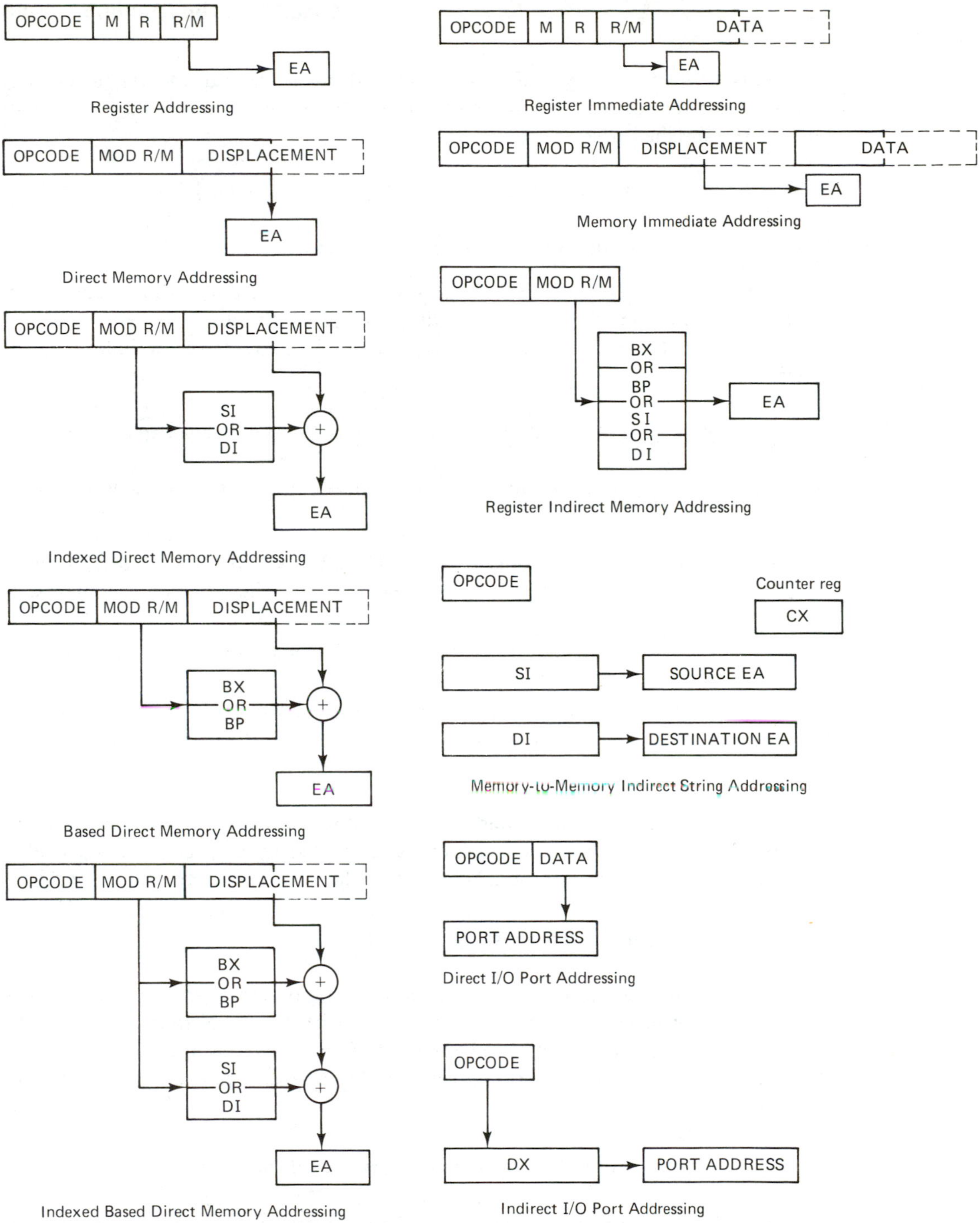

Figure 2.12 Calculation methods for the effective operand address. (Reprinted by permission of Intel Corporation. Copyright 1980.)

Based Direct Memory Addressing. The effective operand address in memory is offset from the segment starting address by the displacement altered by the contents of the specified base register:

PA ← [Seg. Reg.] * 2**4 + Displac. + [Base Reg.]

Note the similarity to indexed direct addressing above.

Indexed Based Direct Memory Addressing. The effective operand address in memory is offset from the segment starting address by the displacement altered by the contents of the specified base register and by the contents of the index register specified:

PA ← [Seg. Reg.] * 2**4 + Displac. + [Base Reg.] + [Index Reg.]

Note the similarity to double indexing as provided by certain computer organizations.

Register Indirect Memory Addressing. The effective operand address in memory is offset from the segment starting address by the specified register's contents:

PA ← [Seg. Reg.] * 2**4 + [Reg.]

The indirect address register is limited to be one of the base or index registers. Accessing different elements of an array is accomplished via instructions that increment or decrement the indirect address register as appropriate either before or after accessing the datum.

Note that based indirect and indexed indirect addressing are not available with the I8086/8088. This lack is somewhat alleviated by a special looping facility and does not usually pose a serious difficulty while solving a programming problem.

Memory-to-memory indirect string addressing

The I8086/8088 microcomputer defines a string datum as the contents of contiguous bytes of memory starting at location X with length N in bytes or words. Although the interpretation of the bit patterns of the individual memory bytes is irrelevant, it is common for ASCII characters to be represented. The typical string instruction is

```
MOVSB        ; byte operands implied indirect
```

which specifies that *one* byte of the string whose address is in the SI register will be moved to memory at the address in the DI register. More important, this string instruction may be prefixed by a "repeat" modifier to accomplish a single instruction loop. For example, the instruction diad

```
MOVW        CX,23D
REP MOVSB
```

will first move the immediate datum 23 base 10 into the default counter register CX and then execute the MOVSB instruction 23 times (or until the counter register equals zero). At each execution, a byte will be moved from the memory address in register SI to the memory address in register DI, these two registers incremented (or decremented), and the counter register decremented. The direction of movement (left to right or right to left) is controlled by presetting the direction flag in the flag register. Thus the physical address of a string in memory is offset from the segment starting address by the contents of the string pointer register:

```
PA ← [Seg. Reg.] * 2**4 + [Reg.]
```

The source string pointer register is the SI register; its default segment register is the data segment (DS) register although this may be overridden. The destination string pointer register is the DI register; its default segment register is the extra segment (ES) register which cannot be overridden. Thus for string operations, the DS and ES registers normally contain the same value (the data and extra segments are identical).

Input/output device addressing

The I8086/8088 has the ability to address directly 256 different ports connected to I/O devices. The direct input instructions and the direct output instructions are as follows:

```
IN      AL,PORTNO
OUT     PORTNO,AL
IN      AX,PORTNO
OUT     PORTNO,AL
```

No segment register is involved, so the port number in the instruction is the physical port designation.

Similarly, the I8086/8088 has the ability to address indirectly up to 64K byte-length ports or up to 32K word-length ports. Indirect port addressing involves the DX register and does not involve a segment register. Thus the port number in the DX register is the physical port designation:

```
IN      AL,DX
OUT     DX,AL
```

```
IN      AX,DX
OUT     DX,AX
```

Direct memory access I/O (DMA) and memory-mapped I/O can both be implemented on the I8086/8088. A discussion of these alternative and probably more efficient forms of input/output is given later in a more appropriate section.

A summary of the calculation of the physical memory address calculation is given in Figure 2.13.

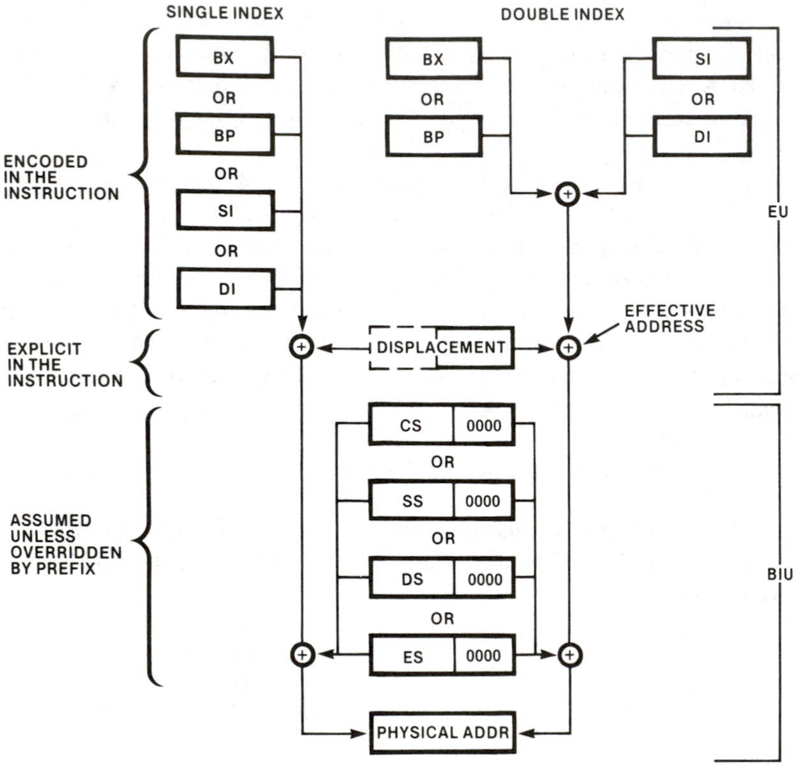

Figure 2.13 Physical memory address computation. (Reprinted by permission of Intel Corporation. Copyright 1980.)

3

Program Flow of Control

It must be heavily emphasized and fully understood that the normal default program flow of control is sequential statement-to-statement execution. The inherent power of a computational system to solve an involved problem stems from the ability of certain instructions to choose alternative processing strategies—to cause a branch or not to cause a branch—depending on the current state of some specified flag, register, or memory location. In higher-level languages, such as Pascal or PL/I, this is commonly expressed as follows:

```
IF A > B
    THEN DO ;
            -
            -/*Execute these statements if A > B */
            -
            END ;
       ELSE DO ;
            -
            -/*Execute these statements if A <= B */
            -
            END ;
NEXT:
```

Diagrammatically, this is the program structure shown in Figure 3.1. In I8086/8088 assembly language, the code section above could be written as follows (assuming that variable A is contained in register AX and B in register BX):

```
IF:        CMP        AX,BX
           JNG        ELSE
```

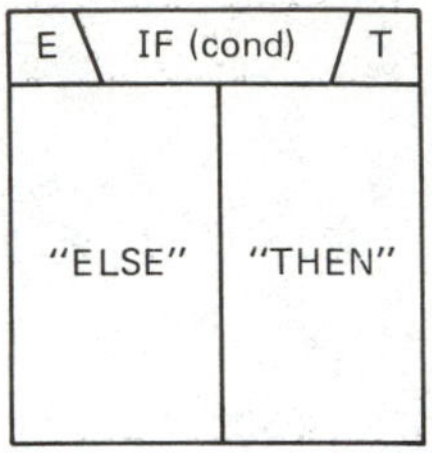

(a) Nassi-Shneiderman chart

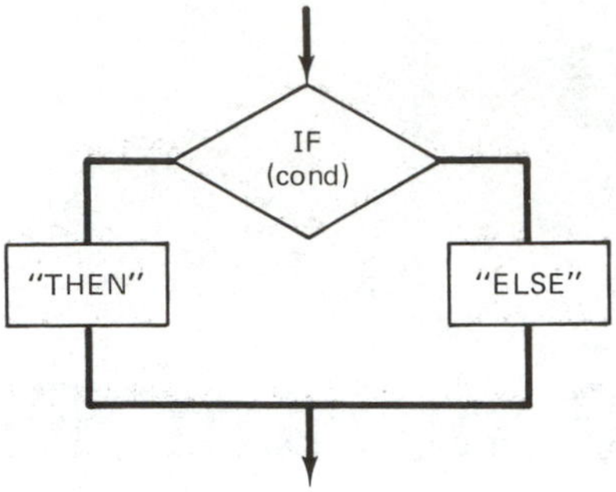

(b) Böhm-Jacopini diagram

```
IF ⟨decision condition⟩
    THEN  begin 'true' action
              .
              .
              .
          end 'true' action;
    ELSE  begin 'false' action
              .
              .
              .
          end 'false' action;
    endif block;
```

Figure 3.1 ALTERATION or IF-THEN-ELSE program flow-of-control structure.

```
THEN:       -
            -         ; Execute these statements if [AX] > [BX]
            -
            JMP       NEXT
ELSE:       -
            -         ; Execute these statements if [AX] <= [BX]
            -
NEXT:       NOP
            -
            -
            -
```

UNCONDITIONAL BRANCHES

The formats of the I8086/8088 program unconditional flow-of-control instructions are given in Figure 3.2. These instructions correspond to the higher-level language construct

GO TO THERE

Modern theories of programming strongly suggest that the "GO TO" be avoided when programming in a higher-level language. The same prohibition is fully

Branch Direct

Jump Direct Short

	Byte 2
Opcode	Displacement

JMP THERE
JMP *±#

Jump to address close by in same segment displacement range, $+127_{10}$ to -128_{10}, may be specified by programmer or calculated by assembler as: Address Target − PC.

Jump Direct Near

Byte 1	Byte 2	Byte 3
Opcode	Displacement	

JMP THERE

Jump to address in same segment displacement range, $+32767_{10}$ to -32768_{10}; calculated by assembler.

Jump Direct Far

Byte 1	Byte 2	Byte 3	Byte 4	Byte 5
Opcode	Displacement		Segment	Address

JMP THERE

Jump to address in different segment displacement and segment address both calculated by assembler (Segment Address altered by linking/loader).

Branch Indirect

Jump Register Indirect Near

	Byte 2		
Opcode	M	R	R/M

JMP @ CX

Jump to address in same segment contained in register specified in instruction.

Jump Memory Indirect Near

Byte 1	Byte 2			Byte 3	Byte 4
Opcode	M	R	R/M	Displacement	

JMP @ THRU_IT

Jump to address in same segment contained in memory location pointed to by instruction.

Jump Memory Indirect Far

Byte 1	Byte 2			Byte 3	Byte 4
Opcode	M	R	R/M	Displacement	

JMP @ THRU_IT

Jump to address in different segment whose offset is contained as first 16-bits and Segment Address as second 16-bits in memory quad pointed to by instruction.

Figure 3.2 Format of the six I8086/8088 unconditional jump or branch instruction variations. All address notation places the low-order 8 bits before the high-order 8 bits. Thus the address 1234 hex is noted in the instruction as 3412 hexadecimal.

justified when coding in assembly language, although it is often impossible fully to avoid the assembly language unconditional jump. An example of the legitimate use of the unconditional branch is shown above in the assembly language version of the IF-THEN-ELSE construct. The use of the unconditional jump instruction is justified only in implementing the assembly language equivalents of the higher-level language structured programming constructs.

It is important to note that the I8086/8088 records its 16-bit address in reverse byte order in the binary instruction form. This address notation peculiarity is a historical artifact derived from the address notation employed on the predecessor Intel computers. Thus the I8086/8088 is an upgrade of the 8-bit I8080/8085, which was developed from the 8-bit I8008, which was an upgrade from the 4-bit I4004/4040. The address in an instruction is noted as (in base 16)

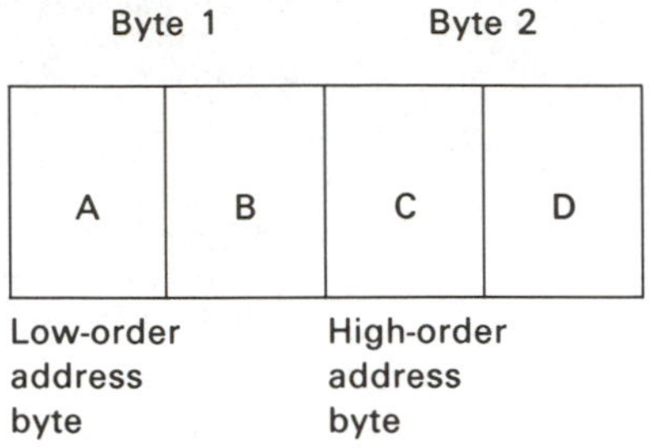

which is interpreted as meaning: CDAB hexadecimal.

CONDITIONAL BRANCH INSTRUCTIONS

All conditional jump or branch instructions are of the *conditional short direct jump* type. Thus they are only able to cause a jump to an instruction at a distance of +127 through −128 bytes. In general, these instructions examine the setting of one of the ALU flags and either branch or not accordingly. As an example, we give the following two Jump on Less Than instructions:

```
JL      *+7       ; jump forward seven statements
JL      THERE     ; jump to label THERE
```

These examples will cause a branch if, and only if, the SF (sign flag) is "ON," which signifies that the immediately preceding arithmetic, compare, or test instruction has generated a negative result. If the SF is "OFF," the next sequential instruction will be executed; that is, a branch will not be taken. The action of these conditional branches is

```
IF <condition true>
    Then PC ← PC + Signed Short Displacement
    Else PC ← PC + 2 (execute next instruction)
```

In the first example above, the amount (the distance) of the branch is expressed in terms of assembly language statements. We emphasize that the branch is to the seventh statement following the branch and not seven bytes. In the second example above, the branch is to a statement with the label THERE. This label must be within 127 bytes following the branch or 128 bytes preceding the branch. The assembler calculates the offset during the assembly process. The bit format of the conditional branch instructions as well as a list of them are given in Figure 3.3.

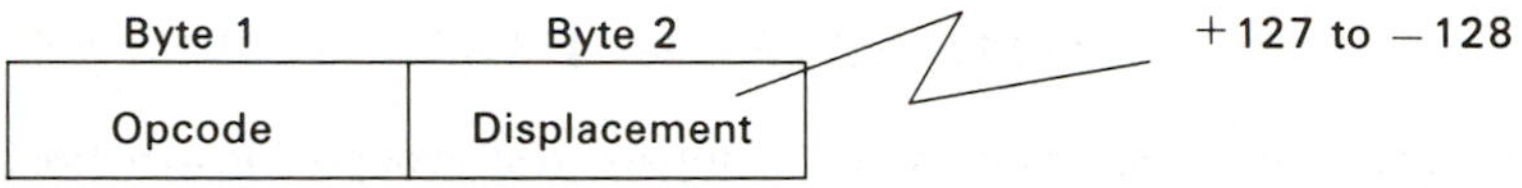

Mnemonic	Opcode	Function		Test condition
JNS	79	JUMP	Positive	SF = 0
JS	78	JUMP	Negative	SF = 1
JE	74	JUMP	Equal	ZF = 1
JNE	75	JUMP	Not equal	ZF = 0
JZ	74	JUMP	Zero	ZF = 1
JNZ	75	JUMP	Nonzero	ZF = 0
JG	7F	JUMP	Greater than	ZF = 0 or SF ⊗ OF = 0
JL	7C	JUMP	Less than	SF = 1; ZF = 0
JGE	7D	JUMP	Greater than or equal	SF = 0
JLE	7E	JUMP	Less than or equal	ZF = 1 or SF ⊗ OF = 1
JB	72	JUMP	Before	CF = 1
JA	77	JUMP	After	CF = 0 or ZF = 0
JBE	76	JUMP	Before or same	CF = 1 or ZF = 1
JAE	73	JUMP	After or same	CF = 0
JC	72	JUMP	On carry	CF = 1
JNC	73	JUMP	On no carry	CF = 0
JO	70	JUMP	On overflow	OF = 1
JNO	71	JUMP	On no overflow	OF = 0
JP	7A	JUMP	On parity (#1 bits) even	PF = 1
JNP	7B	JUMP	On parity (#1 bits) odd	PF = 0
JCXZ	E3	JUMP	On counter register (CX) zero	[CX] = 0

Figure 3.3 I8086/8088 conditional branch instructions are all of the short direct type, allowing only a signed byte displacement or amount of branch. The 21 mnemonics assemble to only 17 instructions, as 4 are identical. (⊗ is XOR.)

The flag bits or certain specific flag bits are affected by the following groups of instructions:

Arithmetic instructions
Logic instructions
Rotate/shift instructions
Load flags from stack top
Return from servicing an interrupt
Compare/test instructions

Thus results of instructions in these groups that precede a conditional jump instruction may result in a branch or may not result in a branch, depending on the result formed.

COMPARISON INSTRUCTIONS

At this time we will examine the compare/test group of instructions because of their intimate relationship to the conditional branch instructions. The compare group of instructions causes the second operand to be subtracted from the first operand with all appropriate flags being set and the result of the subtraction being discarded so that no memory locations or registers are affected (only the appropriate flags are affected). The test group of instructions causes the two operands to be combined using the logical AND operation, with the result being discarded (again, only the appropriate flags are affected). Note in Figure 3.4 (1) that both instruction groups are available using byte or word operations; (2) that the register-to-register, memory-to-register, register-to-memory, immediate-to-register, and immediate-to-memory versions are available with all memory addressing modes; as well as (3) a space- and time-efficient immediate-to-accumulator version. Also note that a string-to-accumulator and a string-to-string compare are available and that these string comparison operations may be combined with the repeat prefix to form a version of a pseudoinstruction that might be termed SEARCH or FIND.

PROGRAM FLOW-OF-CONTROL STRUCTURES

In higher-level procedural-type languages, the three modern decision structures that allow program flow-of-control change are IF-THEN, IF-THEN-ELSE, and CASE. In an attempt to assist understanding, we will illustrate these control structures in I8086/8088 assembly language. In these examples, the procedural-level form will be given first followed by the assembly-level form. In all cases involving numerical variables, we are assuming integer 16-bit data container declarations.

```
                -
                -
IF A > = B
     THEN DO ; /* A >= B */
            -
            -
            END ;
                -/* A < B */
                -
                -
                -
IF:             CMP AX,BX
                JL NEXT
THEN:           -          ; [AX] = > [BX]
                -                ;
                -                ;
NEXT:           -          ; [AX] < [BX]
                -
                -
```

Compare Register-to-Register

Opcode	M	R	R/M

CMP	BL, CH	TEST	BL, CH
CMP	BX, CX	TEST	BX, CX

Compare Memory-to-Register

Opcode	M	R	R/M	Displacement

CMP	BL, THERE	TEST	BL, THERE
CMP	THERE, BX	TEST	THERE, BX

Compare String-to-Accumulator

Opcode

SCASB	REPE	SCASB	(Test string not available)
	REPNE	SCASB	
SCAS	REPE	SCAS	
	REPNE	SCAS	

Compare Strings

Opcode

CMPSB	REPE	CMPSB	(Test string not available)
	REPNE	CMPSB	
CMPS	REPE	CMPS	
	REPNE	CMPS	

Compare Accumulator Immediate

Opcode	Datum

CMP	AL, 20H	TEST	AL, 20H
CMP	AX, 2A39H	TEST	AX, 2A39H

Compare Register Immediate

Opcode	M	R	R/M	Datum

CMP	BL, 20H	TEST	BL, 20H
CMP	CX, 2A39H	TEST	CX, 2A39H

Compare Memory Immediate

Opcode	M	R	R/M	Displacement	Datum

CMP	THERE, 20H	TEST	THERE, 20H
CMP	THERE, 2A39H	TEST	THERE, 2A39H

Figure 3.4 The I8086/8088 compare instructions. All addressing modes to memory are available. The compare instruction acts as a "subtract" while the test instruction acts as "and" with the results discarded.

Note that the statements included in the THEN group (the true branch) are executed only if the condition is true. The IF-THEN construct might be characterized as a "do or skip" construct.

The IF-THEN-ELSE construct, illustrated in Figure 3.1, is a true alternation construct in that either the THEN group of statements or the ELSE group of statements is executed, with the other group being skipped.

```
IF A < B
     THEN DO ;
          -                          /* A < B */
          -
          END ;
     ELSE DO ;
          -                          /* A > = B */
          -
          END ;
     -                               /* collector node */
     -
     -
```

```
IF:             CMP     AX,BX
                JGE     ELSE
THEN:            -                   ; [AX] < [BX]
                 -
                JMP     NEXT
ELSE:            -                   ; [AX] => [BX]
                 -
NEXT:            -                   ; collector node
                 -
                 -
```

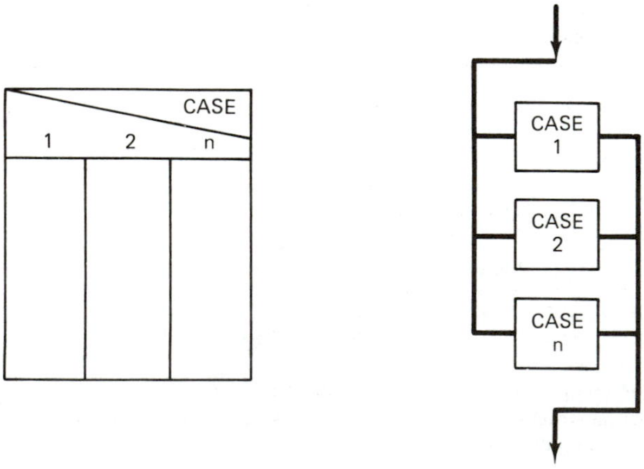

(a) Nassi-Shneiderman chart (b) Flow diagram

```
CASE_of_A,
     A = 17 DO .......... END,
     A =  3 DO .......... END,
     A = 12 DO .......... END,
     .
     .
     .
     OTHERWISE DO .......... END,
     ENDCASE block;
```

Figure 3.5 CASE or multiway branch program flow-of-control structure.

The CASE construct is a generalization of the alternation scheme that allows a branch to one of N unique paths in the flow of control with a single collector node. Our example (see Figure 3.5) illustrates a CASE construct with three specified branches and an "otherwise" to encompass all conditions not specified.

```
        -
        -
CASE_OF_A ;
          CASE_A = 7 DO ;
              -
              -
              END ;
          CASE_A = -2 DO ;
              -
              -
              END ;
          CASE_A = 1 DO ;
              -
              -
              END ;
          OTHERWISE DO ;
              -
              -
              END ;
          END_CASE ;
          -
          -
CASE_OF_A:
;
CASE_7:         CMP     AX,7D
                JNE     CASE_N2
                -                           ; [AX] = 7
                -
                JMP     END_CASE_A
CASE_N2:        CMP     AX,-2D
                JNE     CASE_1              ; [AX] = -2
                -
                -
                JMP     END_CASE_A
CASE_1:         CMP     AX,1D
                JNE     OTHERWISE
                -                           ; [AX] = 1
                -
                JMP     END_CASE_A
OTHERWISE:      -       ; [AX] ≠ 7 ≠ -2 ≠ 1
                -
                -
END_CASE_A:     NOP     ; collector node
```

LOOPING

These same conditional branch instructions may be employed to implement program loops in order to accommodate iterative operations. We will illustrate possible approaches to seven modern and common loop constructs.

The first three illustrations of loop constructs are commonly known as DO COUNT. Because of the wide historical use of this loop construct in FORTRAN, we will follow the IBM practice of placing the test for termination at the loop end (thus the loop is always executed at least once) and provide for the possible use of the loop counter index within the loop (thus we employ the DX register for the counter index).

```
                    -
                    -
            DO I = 1 to 9 step 1 ;             /* loop 1 */
                        -
                        -
                    END ;
                    -
                    -       -
                                -
                         MOV DX,1D
LOOP1:                          -
                                -
                         INC  DX
                         CMP  DX,9D
                         JLE  LOOP1
                                -
                                -

                    -
                    -
            DO I = 1 to 9 step 2;              /* loop 2 */
                    -
                    -

            END ;
                    -
                    -      -
                           -
                         MOV            DX,1D
LOOP2:                                  -
                                        -
                         ADD            DX,2D
                         CMP            DX,9D
```

```
                    JLE            LOOP2
                                   -
                                   -
                    -
                    -
        DO I = 19 to -17 step -1 ;  /* loop 3 */
            -
            -
          END
            -
            -
                                   -
                                   -
                    MOV            DX,19D
LOOP3:                             -
                                   -
                    DEC            DX
                    CMP            DX,-17D
                    JGE            LOOP3
                                   -
                                   -
```

The DO_WHILE (Figure 3.6) and DO_UNTIL (Figure 3.7) constructs continue to loop until a specified condition is satisfied. Although it is not absolutely necessary, the DO_UNTIL version almost always tests the condition at the foot of the loop and thus requires that the loop body be executed at least once. The DO_WHILE version tests at the beginning of the loop and thus does not require any execution of the loop body.

```
            -
            -
        DO_UNTIL I <= J ;          /* loop 4 */
              -
              -
            END ;
            -
            -
                    -
                    -
                MOV DX,I
LOOP4:              -
                    -
                CMP DX,J
                JG  LOOP4
                    -
                    -
            -
            -
```

```
                DO_WHILE I > J                /* loop 5 */
                    -
                    -
                  END ;
                  -
                  -         -
                            -
                          MOVW                          DI,I
LOOP5:                    CMP DX,J
                          JLE  LOOP_END
                            -
                            -
                          JMP       LOOP5
LOOP_END:                   -
                            -
```

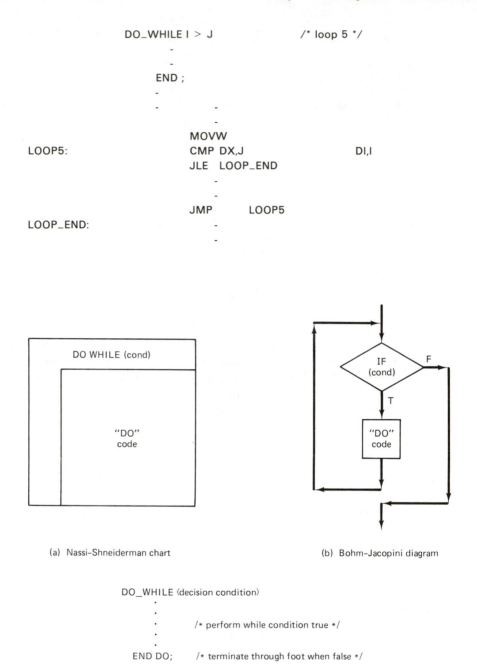

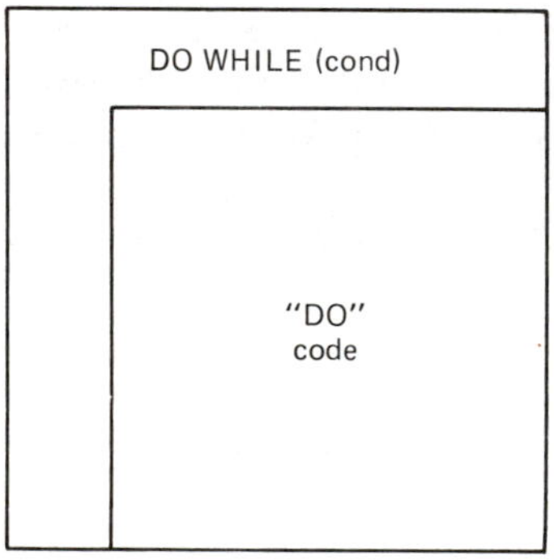

(a) Nassi-Shneiderman chart

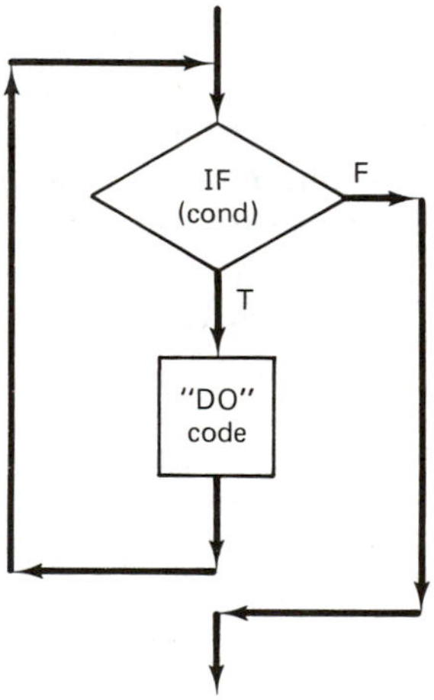

(b) Bohm-Jacopini diagram

```
DO_WHILE ⟨decision condition⟩
   .
   .
   .          /* perform while condition true */
   .
   .
 END DO;      /* terminate through foot when false */
```

Figure 3.6 DO_WHILE looping or repeat program flow-of-control structure.

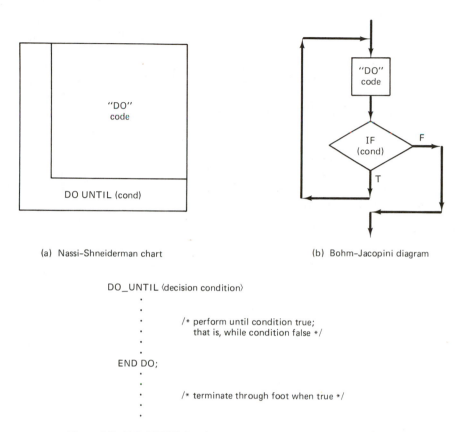

(a) Nassi-Shneiderman chart

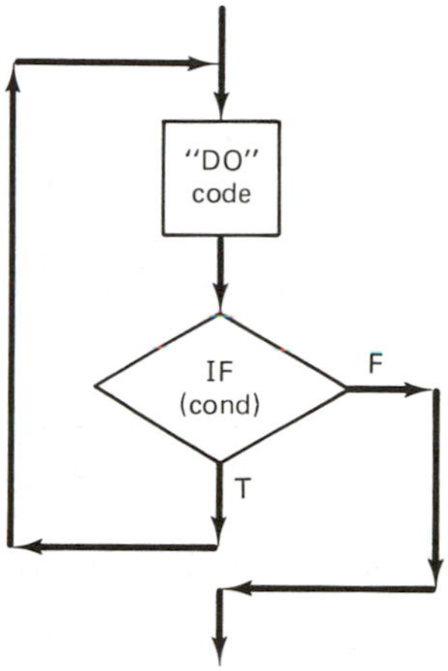

(b) Bohm-Jacopini diagram

```
DO_UNTIL <decision condition>
     .
     .
     .          /* perform until condition true;
     .             that is, while condition false */
     .
     .
  END DO;
     .
     .
     .          /* terminate through foot when true */
     .
     .
```

Figure 3.7 DO_UNTIL looping or repeat program flow-of-control structure.

Some procedural-level languages allow the DO_WHILE and DO_UNTIL to be combined.

```
              -
              -
DO_WHILE I > J UNTIL N >= 17 ; /* loop 6 */
                -
                -
              END ;
              -
              -
                -
                -
              MOV          DX,I
```

```
LOOP6:      CMP     DX,J
            JLE     LOOP_END
             -
             -
            CMP     N,17D
            JL      LOOP6
LOOP_END:            -
             -
```

A few modern procedural-level languages allow the exit of a loop from a place in the loop body other than the foot. The general form of this construct is known as the LEAVE statement. We will illustrate this construct using the DO_FOREVER form of the DO_WHILE.

```
          -
          -
DO_WHILE-TRUE.;        /* loop 7 - LEAVE */
           -
           -
      IF X < 1 LEAVE ;
           -
           -
      END ;
          -
          -
          -
          -
LOOP7:    -
          -
      CMP     X,1D
      JGE     END_LOOP
          -
          -
      JMP     LOOP7
END_LOOP:
          -
          -
```

SPECIALIZED LOOP CONTROL INSTRUCTIONS

As illustrated in Figure 3.8, the I8086/8088 provides four loop control instructions that employ the counter (CX) register as their primary control. It must be emphasized that these loop control instructions were designed to implement the DO_COUNT loop and are almost useless in implementing the DO_UNTIL, the DO_WHILE, and the LEAVE constructs. Even in implementing the DO_COUNT loop,

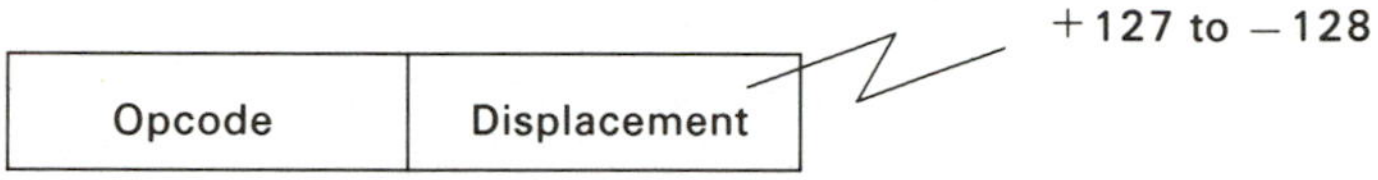

LOOP	LP_STRT	Decrement counter register (CX) without affecting flags IF [CX] = 0 THEN Exit loop through foot ELSE Go to top of loop Suitable to implement Do-Count loops with increment of minus one.
LOOPZ LOOPE	LP_STRT LP_STRT	Decrement counter register (CX) without affecting flags IF [CX] ≠ 0 & [ZF] = 1 THEN Go to top of loop ELSE Exit loop through foot
LOOPNZ LOOPNE	LP_STRT LP_STRT	Decrement counter register (CX) without affecting flags IF [CX] ≠ 0 & [ZF] = 0 THEN Go to top of loop ELSE Exit loop through foot
JCXZ	LP_START	Examine counter register (CX) IF [CX] = 0 THEN Go to top of loop ELSE Exit loop through foot

Figure 3.8 I8086/8088 specialized loop control instructions. Note that the jump is short.

the assumptions are made that the loop index will not be required in the body of the loop and that the index will be stepped by a negative one. It must be concluded that the special loop control instructions of the I8086/8088 are of minimal utility in implementing the common loops of modern "structured" procedural languages.

The loop illustrated earlier as LOOP1 can be implemented as follows:

```
            -
            -
DO I = 1 to 9 step 1 ;        /* loop 8 */
            -
            -
     END ;
            -
            -
     -
     -
     MOV       CX,9D
```

```
LOOP8:      -
            -
            LOOP      LOOP8
            -
            -
```

The fact that the loop counter index is not available within the body of the loop and that the step must be plus one are both important limitations of the implementation of this instruction.

Although the LOOPZ/LOOPE and the LOOPNZ/LOOPNE instructions are not designed to accommodate the normal procedural-level language loop constructs, they do find utility in implementing specialized systems control routines. For example, it is often desired to move the contents of a byte input stream received byte by byte in the AL register to a buffer in memory with the assumptions that the stream is at least one byte and not more than 133 bytes in length with a termination character of 1D hex (carriage return). A pseudolanguage version might be represented as follows with two possible assembly language implementations.

```
DO I = 1 TO 133; /* loop 9 */
     GET CHAR;
     IF CHAR = 1DH /* 29 base 10 */
          THEN LEAVE;
     BUFFER (I) = CHAR;
     END;
          -
          -

          -
          -
            MOV       CX,85h ; 133 decimal
LOOP9A:     MOV       DI,85h
            IN        AL,PORTN
            CMP       AL,1Dh
            JE        THATS_ALL
            SUB       DI,CX
            MOV       BUFFER(DI),AL
            LOOPNE    LOOP9A
THATS_ALL:            -
            -
            MOV       DI,1h
LOOP9B:     IN        AL,PORTN
            CMPB      AL,1DH
            JE        THATS_ALL
            INC       DI
            CMP       DI,85h ; 133 decimal
            JL        LOOP9B
THATS_ALL:
            -
            -
```

In processing strings of character data, a common need is to search for a character, to search for a group of characters, to determine that two strings are different, or to determine the position or address of a character. Our examples will employ a hypothetical higher-level language whose syntax is, hopefully, self-explanatory.

```
                    -
                    -
                    -
FIND FIRST '. '  IN STRG;          /* Find position of period */
                    -
                    -
                    -
                 MOV               AL, '. ' ; ASCII period
                 LEA               DI,STRG_ADDR
                 MOV               CX,STRG_LNGTH
                 CLD               ; Direction is left to right
          REPNE  SCASB
                 JCXZ              NOT_FOUND
FOUND:              -                          ; [CX] = POSITION OF '. '
                    -                          ; from right end
                    -                          ; [DI] = ADDRESS OF '. '
                 JMP               NEXT
NOT_FOUND:          -                          ; [CX] = 0
                    -                          ; [DI] = address of right end
NEXT:               -
                    -
```

The code above obviously requires some explanation. The SCASB instruction (compare a byte of a string to the accumulator) requires an extensive setup:

1. The address of the first byte of the string must be placed in the DI register. The LEA (load effective address) instruction accomplishes this task.
2. The REPNE prefix instruction specifies that the compare will continue employing the succeeding character as long as the compare is not equal. It forms a one-instruction loop.
3. The CLD instruction specifies that the search will proceed from left to right in the string.
4. The number of characters to be searched (the length of the string) before declaring failure must be placed in the CX (counter) register.

The SCASB with the prefix REPxy automatically decrements the counter register (CX) and increments (for direction left to right) the destination index register (DI) each time through the single-instruction loop. Executing the branch if CX zero instruction (JCXZ) signifies that the search has failed for the entire string while a "fall through" signifies success. A successful search will terminate the single-instruction loop, with the contents of the DI register being the effective operand address of the success position and the contents of the CX register being the success position from the right end of the string. The success position from the left end (the start) of the string would be obtainable by subtracting the contents of the CX register from the string length.

```
            FIND    STRG1      NON_MATCH IN STRG2;
                      -
                      -
                    LEA        DI,STRG1_ADDR
                    MOV        CX,STRG_LNGTH
                    CLD                    ; left-to-right direction
               REPE CMPSB
                    JCXZ       MATCH
NON-MATCH:            -                    ; [CX] position of nonmatch
                                           ; from right end
                      -                    ;
                      -                    ;
                      -                    ; [DI] & [SI] Addresses of
                                           ; nonmatch
                      -                    ;
                    JMP        NEXT
MATCH:                -                    ; [CX] = 0
                      -                    ; [DI] & [SI] Addresses of
                                           ; right ends
                      -                    ;
NEXT:                 -
                      -
```

The CMPSB compares from left to right similarly positioned bytes of two strings whose addresses are in the destination index (DI) and the source index (SI) registers and whose length is in the count register (CX). The REPE prefix instruction forms a single-instruction loop whose termination is caused by either [CX] = 0 or a nonequal compare.

```
FIND STRG1 EMBEDDED IN STRG2;
                          -
                          -
                        MOV          AL,STRG1
                        LEA          DI,STRG2_ADDR
                        MOV          CX,STRG2_LNGTH
                        CLD          ; LFT_RT
```

```
TRY_FIRST:      REPNE   SCASB
                        JCXZ    NOT_FOUND
FOUND_FIRST:            CMP     STRG1_LNGTH,CX
                        JG      NOT_FOUND
                        MOV     SAVE,DI
                        MOV     SAVE+2,CX
                        LEA     SI,STRG1_ADDR
                        MOV     CX,STRG1_LNGTH
                        CLD     ; LFT_RT
TRY_INNER:      REPE    CMPSB
                        JCXZ    FOUND
TRY_AGAIN:              MOV     DI,SAVE
                        INC     DI
                        MOV     CX,SAVE+2
                        DEC     CX
                        JMP     TRY_FIRST
NOT_FOUND                 -
                          -
                        JMP     NEXT
FOUND:                    -
                          -
NEXT:                     -
                          -
```

The algorithm illustrated first courses across the second string searching for an occurrence of the lead character of the first string that has been placed in the accumulator. If this initial search is not successful in finding the first character, the entire algorithm is abandoned. If the first character is found, a check is made for sufficient room for the first string to fit into the remainder of the second string. If there is insufficient space, the entire algorithm is abandoned. If space exists, the two strings are compared. Note that this involves saving the DI register (address is string 2) and the CX register (space left in string 2) for possible reuse if the string match fails. The string comparison instruction (CMPSB) requires the address of string 1 in the source index (SI) register and the length in the CX register. If the match is successful, a branch to FOUND is made and the algorithm terminates. If not, registers DI and CX are restored from the save area, respectively incremented and decremented to bypass the previous first character match, and the entire search algorithm restarted from this position in the second string.

SUBPROCEDURES

Almost all computer languages allow a procedure to invoke and use a physically separate block of code with eventual resumption of program flow just beyond the invocation point. Figure 3.9 illustrates the concept while emphasizing that a

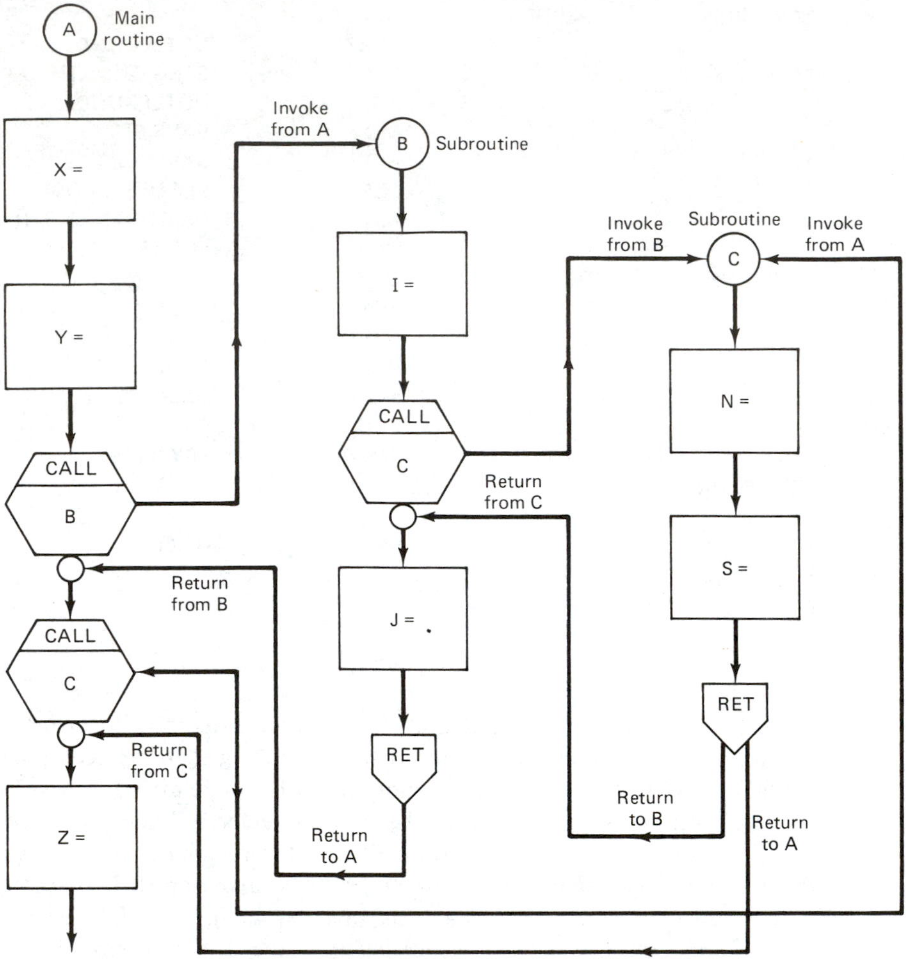

Figure 3.9 Subroutine (out-of-line block) invocation program flow-of-control. Control resumes in-line via a RETURN statement.

subprocedure can be invoked more than once from different calling procedures or from the same one. Recall from Chapter 1 that there are three common methods of saving the return address to allow resumption of processing just beyond the invocation point. The most generalized of these employs a stack with the contents of the program counter being PUSHed during the CALL and POPped back to the program counter during the RETurn. Figure 1.17*c* illustrates this concept, which is used by the I8086/8088 in common with almost all microcomputers (the TI 99/X family of micro- and minicomputers uses a variation of the method of Figure 1.17*b*). The call-return instructions of the I8086/8088 are shown in Figure 3.10.

	Within segment	To different segment
Call Direct		
CALL ANY_PROC	[SP] ← [SP] − 2 [Mem(SP)] ← [PC] [PC] ← $ANY\_PROC_{address}$	[SP] ← [SP] − 2 [Mem(SP)] ← [PC] [SP] ← [SP] − 2 [Mem(SP)] ← [CS] [PC] ← $ANY\_PROC_{address}$ [CS] ← CS_{Any_Proc}
Call Register Indirect		
CALL (AX)	[SP] ← [SP] − 2 [Mem(SP)] ← [PC] [PC] ← [AX]	Not available
Call Indirect via Index into Table of Procedure Addresses		
CALL TABLE(SI)	[SP] ← [SP] − 2 [Mem(SP)] ← [PC] [PC] ← [TABLE(SI)]	Not available
Call Indirect via Index into Based Structure of Procedure/Segment Addresses		
CALL (BX).TASK(SI)	Not available	[SP] ← [SP] − 2 [Mem(SP)] ← [PC] [SP] ← [SP] − 2 [Mem(SP)] ← [CS] [PC] ← [(BX).TASK(SI)] [CS] ← [(BX).TASK(SI + 2)]
Return from Subprocedure		
RET	[PC] ← [Mem(SP)] [SP] ← [SP] + 2	[CS] ← [Mem(SP)] [SP] ← [SP] + 2 [PC] ← [Mem(SP)] [SP] ← [SP] + 2

Figure 3.10 I8086/8088 subprocedure CALL and RETurn instructions.

When considering procedural-level languages, it is useful to distinguish between two types of subprocedure invocation:

1. CALL subroutines in which a keyword such as GOSUB or CALL conveys the order to branch or jump to the named out-of-line block of code, execute it, and eventually return to a point just beyond the invocation. Examples could be

```
GOSUB 127
CALL ANY
```

A CALL subprocedure may, or may not, have arguments to convey information between the caller and callee as well as to return any results. Refer to Figure 3.11.

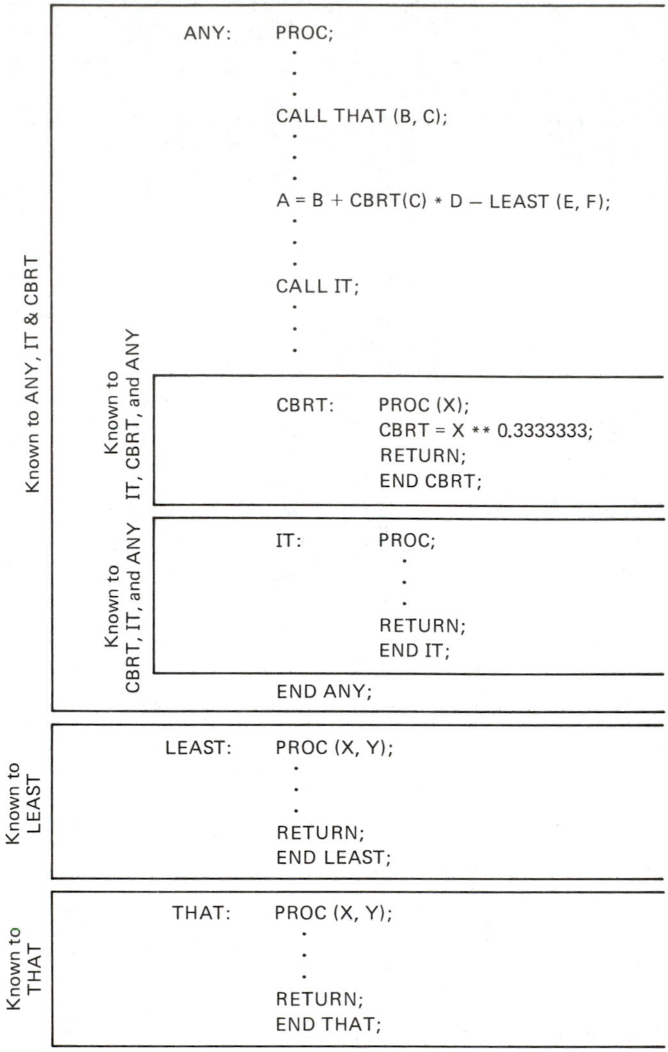

Figure 3.11 Internal vs. external and CALL vs. function subprocedure situations.

2. Function subprocedures in which the use of the subprocedure name in a replacement-assignment statement conveys the order to branch or jump to the named out-of-line block of code, execute it, place the single result in an expected place, and eventually return to a point in the replacement-assignment statement just beyond the invocation. An argument is always required. FORTRAN and BASIC expect the result to be placed in the *default accumulator* (register AX or AL of the I8086/8088), whereas PL/I expects the result to be referred to as an implied extra argument. Again, refer to Figure 3.11.

When considering procedural-level languages, it is also useful to distinguish between two types of subprocedures viewed from a different logical dimension:

1. Internal subprocedures in which the subprocedure block of code is physically within the code of invoking procedure and is translated with it. Thus the translator—the compiler or assembler—"knows" all about the variables and their addresses in both blocks of code. Figure 3.11 shows an example.
2. External subprocedures in which the subprocedure block of code is physically separate and disjoint from the code of the invoking procedure and is translated separately and at a different time. Thus the translator "does not know" anything about the variables or their addresses in the other block of code. Figure 3.11 also shows this situation.

Main procedures can be implemented in a procedural-level language or in assembly language; similarly, subprocedures can be implemented in a procedural-level language or in assembly language. Although it is easiest to implement a subprocedure in the same language as that used for the main procedure, it is possible to mix languages when external subprocedures are involved. It is particularly difficult to implement an assembly language main procedure correctly with a procedural language subprocedure. We will consider only four of the possible situations in two groups.

THE MAIN PROCEDURE: ASSEMBLY LANGUAGE

As complex replacement/assignment procedures, particularly arithmetic, are not usual in programs implemented in assembly language, function subprocedures are not normal. Thus we will consider only CALL subprocedures.

Internal Call Subprocedures: Assembly Language

Because both the invoking procedure and the subprocedure are assembled at the same time employing a common variable names dictionary (symbol table), each procedure "knows" about all of the data container names and addresses. For this reason it is unnecessary, and not usual, to use arguments for communication between procedures. On the other hand, it is vital that the register values of the invoking procedure not be destroyed by the subprocedure. The contents of registers should be stored—"saved"—in a "save area in memory" at the start of the subprocedure and loaded—"restored"—from the save area just before the RETurn. As values can be "returned" in a register, care must be taken not to destroy these values during the register restoration process.

External Call Subprocedures: Assembly Language

Because the invoking procedure is assembled separately from the subprocedure, neither has any knowledge of the other's variable names or their addresses. If communication of variable values or addresses is required, two methods are commonly employed: send/receive the value via an argument, or send/receive the address via an argument. The I8086/8088 provides a stack and associated stack pointer register as a very "handy" place to pass arguments. Thus the argument contents would occur in the stack just below the return address.

THE MAIN PROCEDURE: PROCEDURAL-LEVEL LANGUAGE

As the subprocedures in assembly language must be assembled separately from the compilation of the invoking procedure, only external subprocedures are possible. This necessitates that arguments or global variables be used for interprocedural communication. Although information passage via global variables is possible, this method is not only more involved but is usually considered to be a questionable programming practice. We therefore suggest the use of arguments and discourage global variable communication, particularly in a mixed-language situation. In all cases, the exact methods (value, address, address of address) and location used for argument passage by the particular procedural language must be determined, understood, and meticulously followed, employing documentation that is usually less than ideal.

External Call Subprocedures: Assembly Language

Happily, in most, if not all I8086/8088 compiler implementations, argument values or addresses are pushed onto the stack just prior to the CALL, and thus occur just prior to the return address in reverse order. It is easy for the subprocedure to acquire the arguments and to replace values before returning. Note that the eventual top of the stack must be the return address.

External Function Subprocedure: Assembly Language

Again, I8086/8088 compilers generate code that places the arguments on the stack before the return address. As with CALL subprocedures, the FUNCTION code can retrieve the arguments for use and eventually assure that the top of the stack contains the return address. Recall that the single result of a function is used directly in a procedural language replacement/assignment statement expression. This requires that the rules of the language implementation be carefully followed in order to place the returned function value exactly where it is expected to be. Often this place will be the accumulator (register AX or AL); sometimes this place will be an extra "dummy" argument. "Abnormal functions" change the value of one or more arguments or a global variable. The use of abnormal functions results in difficulties during procedure debugging and maintenance and should be avoided if not prohibited.

A somewhat deeper treatment of procedural-level languages, including the external/internal, the local/global scope of variables, and the run-time support environment situation is given in Chapter 11. It must be emphasized that it is rapidly becoming accepted practice to limit the use of assembly language to short, fast, necessary support subprocedures to higher-level procedural languages. These ASM 86 subprocedures accomplish functions not easily coded or that execute slowly in the higher-level language of the main-line implementation. This is true of both systems and applications problem solutions.

4

Manipulating Data

From both a theoretical and pragmatic viewpoint, a digital computational system is an information-manipulating device. In a sense, it can be maintained that information must be stored before it can be manipulated and that the results must be stored after the manipulation. Thus many workers also emphasize the information storage characteristics of a computer. The long-term and continuing growth and importance of "data banks" as permanent or semipermanent information repositories constitutes justification for this broader viewpoint.

In either case, only three general types of computer instructions are available to directly affect information:

1. *Data movement*: Instructions that cause the movement of data from one place in the computer to another without changing the information in any way.
2. *Transduction*: Instructions that change the physical encoding of the information without affecting the meaning; that is, the syntax is changed while the semantics are retained (example: the magnetic encoding of the character A on a magnetic tape being transformed via transduction to the settings of transistors in memory also encoding the character A).
3. *Data operations*: Instructions that result in the manufacture of new information (example: subtracting 7 from 11 gives the result 4; this result is new and has never existed before, even if many copies have existed).

We are immediately faced with the philosophical and extremely practical question: Above the bit levels, *what is the fundamental unit of information*? Is the number 7 a fundamental unit? The number 78? The matrix A of order 17? The letter Z? The string ZEKE?

In dealing with digital computers, the answer is suprisingly definitive and simple: The fundamental unit of information is a portion of the language definition. It follows directly that the operations available to manipulate this fundamental information unit are also a portion of the language definition.

Some languages, such as BASIC or PL/I provide for data aggregates such as a matrix or a string as one of their fundamental information units. On the other hand, assembly languages are a symbolic encoding of the hardware architectural design and are limited to manipulating those data types directly supported by the hardware, employing instructions provided by the design. This important point bears repeating: assembly language data consist of simple nonaggregate elements, and assembly language instructions provide for manipulating a single simple datum with no provision for aggregated data such as matrices. The I8086/8088 does allow indexing within strings and arrays as well as allowing qualified names in structures.

At the same time it must be realized that some computers possess instructions that deal with multiple data elements. As an example of this, the IBM 360/370/303X/43X1 extended computer family implements an instruction,

```
Load Multiple        LM       0,15,TEMP
```

that moves the contents of memory word location TEMP to register 0, TEMP + 1 to register 1, . . . , TEMP + 15 to register 15 and the reverse for

```
Store Multiple       STM      0,15,TEMP
```

In effect, Load Multiple is a single-instruction loop that moves the contents of successive memory word locations to consecutive registers starting with register I through register J. Specific instructions in other computers could also be cited. As one other specific example, we again draw your attention to the REPE/REPNE instruction prefix discussed in Chapter 3 while examining string processing. Lest I be misunderstood, recall that the art and science of assembly language programming involves translating an algorithm into a series of correct, complete, and legal instructions to manipulate data, data that can be logically organized as simple single elements or organized as aggregates of simple single elements or as aggregates of aggregates.

As computer designers react to justified pressures to support higher-level languages more efficiently and adequately, it should be expected that an increased tendency will be manifested to implement aggregate data types and corresponding manipulation instructions directly into the architectural design. Current technological developmental directions strongly suggest that this will be accomplished by employing microprogramming and/or programmed logic arrays. The relative costs of acquiring hardware versus producing software, as discussed in Chapter 1, are major economic incentives forcing this trend.

DATA MOVEMENT INSTRUCTIONS

WORD AND BYTE DATA MOVEMENT

We are defining data movement instructions as those instructions that cause a datum to be moved from one physical location to another physical location with no change in the bit pattern (syntax) and no implications regarding the meaning of the bit pattern (semantics). In the I8086/8088 the generic data movement instruction is

```
MOV     X,Y     ; [X] ← [Y]
```

where X can be any register or any address in writable memory accessible via any of the various addressing modes as reviewed in Chapter 3, and where Y can be any register or any address in memory accessible via any of the various addressing modes or an immediate datum. None of the flag (status) register bits are affected.

As discussed in Chapter 2, register-to-register, register-to-memory (store), memory-to-register (load), immediate-to-register, and immediate-to-memory datum moves are allowed; but memory-to-memory datum moves are not accommodated by the I8086/8088 design. Additionally, only X or Y, but not both, can be one of the four segment registers (CS, DS, SS, or ES). That is, complete freedom is allowed as to the datum container specified by X and by Y with only the following exceptions:

1. X must be an address in read/write memory or a register.
2. X cannot be an immediate datum.
3. Only one (X or Y) can be a memory address.
4. Only one (X or Y) can be a segment register.

The I8086/8088 provides a data movement instruction that exchanges the contents of two data containers without employing a temporary location:

```
XCHG     X,Y ; [X] ↔ [Y]
```

where X and Y can be any general-purpose register or an address in read/write memory accessible via any of the various addressing modes. Again only one of the operands may be a memory address, as memory-to-memory instructions are not supported by the I8086/8088 design.

In certain circumstances it facilitates the construction of an algorithm to be able to employ an index into a table easily and quickly as a means of replacing a datum with another desired value. This process has become known as *translate* and is a fairly common instruction in computers. As implemented in the I8086/8088 (Figure 4.1), the table in memory must have its address in the BX register and consist of 8-bit (byte) data elements. The index into the table must be in the 8-bit accumulator (AL register), which implies that the table should be of length 256 bytes (i.e., [BX]+0 through [BX]+255) unless special programmatic provisions are provided to prevent out-of-table addressing. The translate instruction has implied operands:

XLAT

and is exactly equivalent to

MOV AL,(BX) (AL)

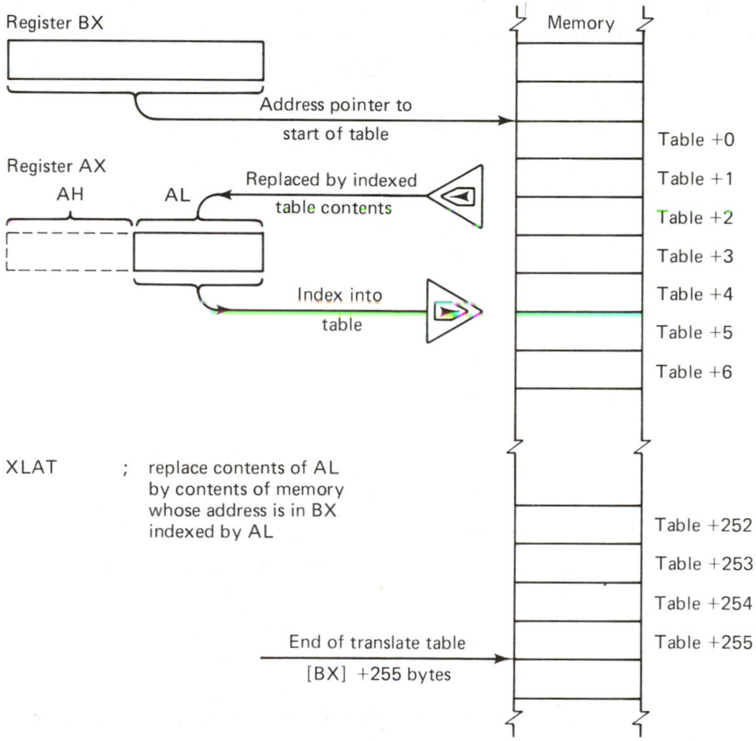

Figure 4.1 The translate instruction of the I8086/8088 acts like

MOV B AL, [BX] [AL]

where AL contains an unsigned (positive) 8 bit index before instruction execution.

To maintain assembly language compatability with the predecessor 8-bit I8080/8085 microcomputer, it is necessary to be able to concatinate the 8080 status flags (the low-order 8 bits of the 8086 status flags) with the AL register (the equivalent of the 8080 accumulator) for PUSHing the AX register to and POPping it from the stack. Thus the following instructions will allow the I8086/8088 to simulate the stacking/unstacking of the 8080 PSW:

```
LAHF        ; MOV AH,FLAG
SAHF        ; MOV FLAG,AH
```

where the operands are implied to be exactly those shown.

ADDRESS MOVEMENT

Both the MOV and XCHG instructions can be employed to move an address from a register to a register, from memory to a register, and from a register to a memory. Although any 16-bit register or memory location may be used as a data container for an address, certain registers have specific uses for addresses in the I8086/8088 design. Four of these, the segment registers (CS, DS, SS, and ES), were discussed in some detail in Chapter 2. The contents of these segment registers may be changed through the use of the MOV instruction, although it is important to recall that the segment register-to-segment register move is not allowed. Four other registers with special indirect addressing characteristics are also available to the assembly language programmer of the I8086/8088:

SP: stack pointer register
BP: base pointer register
SI: source index register
DI: destination index register

Addresses may be moved into and out of these data containers through the use of both the MOV and the XCHG instructions, as described earlier in this section.

Additionally, the I8086/8088 provides three special "load address" instructions (Figure 4.2):

```
LEA     X,Y
```

where X can be any one of the eight 16-bit data/pointer/index registers and Y must be a 16-bit address within a segment. When manipulating string data, it is necessary to place in the SI register the starting address of the source string that is within the DS segment and the starting address of the destination string that is within the ES segment in the DI register. Although the MOV word instruction may be used to ac-

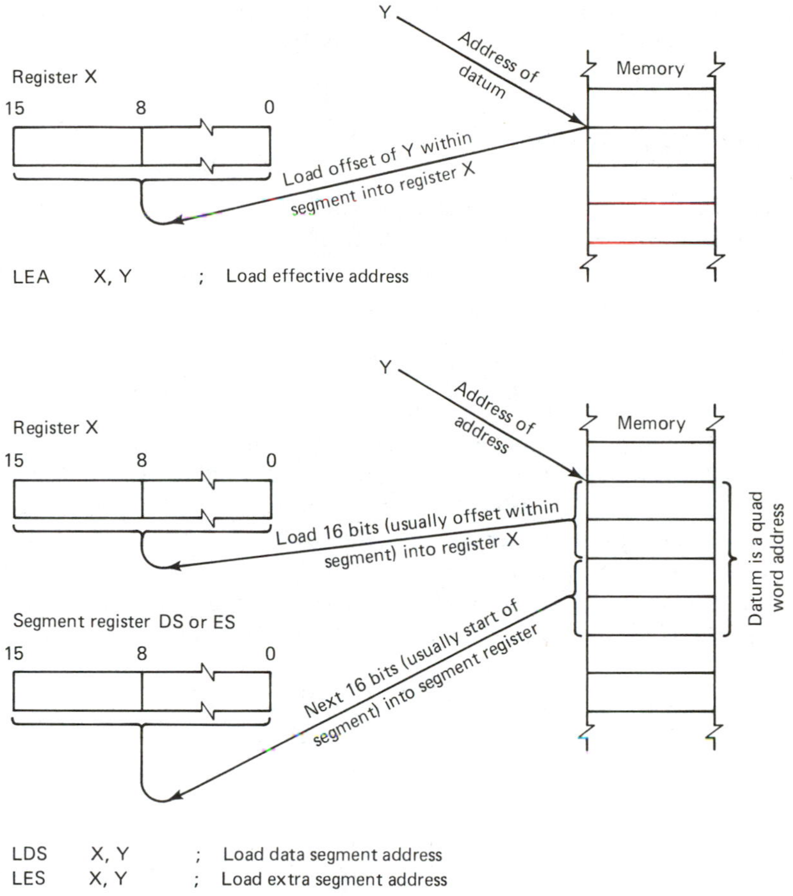

Figure 4.2 The LOAD address instructions of the I8086/8088.

complish the movement of these addresses to the necessary data containers, it is often efficient programmatically to use the following instructions:

```
LDS     X,Y
LES     X,Y
```

where X must be any one of the eight 16-bit data, pointer, or index registers and Y must identify an address in memory accessible via any addressing mode. In both cases the 16-bit contents of the memory location Y is copied into register X (usually the SI register for LDS and the DI register for LES) and the 16-bit contents of the memory location Y + 2 is copied into the segment register (DS for LDS and ES for LES). Employed in this manner, it is assumed that the programmer will have stored the effective address of the string (using the LEA instruction) and the starting address of the segment (using the MOV instruction) in memory at the address of the identifier Y and Y + 2, respectively.

STRING DATA MOVEMENT

A string is defined as a contiguous block of data in memory whose address is contained in the SI or DI register. Although most string processing will involve ASCII character (byte) data, the I8086/8088 allows the same algorithmic constructions involving word data. The primary string data movement instruction is

```
MOVS        (DI), (SI)
```

where the datum at the effective address in the SI register (an offset in the DS segment) is moved to the effective address in the DI register (an offset in the ES segment). Subsequently, the contents of the DI and SI registers are decremented or incremented by the width of the datum. If the direction flag (DF) is set to 1, the DI and SI registers are decremented after the datum is moved; if the direction flag (DF) is set to 0, incremention takes place and the strings are processed left to right. The direction flag is assigned a value by the following instructions:

```
CLD
STD
```

which have no operands. It is normal for the block move instruction to have the prefix instruction REP and thus to employ the CX register as a counter for a one-instruction loop, with the counter register (CX) being decremented by one until it becomes zero, consequently forcing a loop fall through.

It is very important to realize that the block move instruction is among the very few memory-to-memory data movement instructions allowed in the I8086/8088 design. Additionally, note that the instruction format of this computer restricts this memory-to-memory move to indirect through-register-type addressing for both operands. An example of the use of this instruction may help. In our simple example we are illustrating the movement of an ASCII string of length 129 characters (bytes) named SOURCE to a string data container named DESTIN, both in the same physical segment whose address is already contained in both the DS and the ES segment registers (i.e., the data and extra segment exactly overlay each other):

```
-
-
LEA     SI,SOURCE
LDA     DI,DESTIN
```

```
                  MOV      CX,129D
                  CLD
         REP      MOVSB    (DI), (SI)
                  -
                  -
                  -
SOURCE            DSB      129d          ; define byte storage;
DESTIN            DSB      129d          ; length in base 10
                  -
                  -
```

A reciprocal pair of instructions to load to or store from the accumulator (AL or AX register) from or to a string are provided:

```
LODS     AL,(SI)
STOS     (DI),AL
```

The mechanics of these instructions and of the indirect string addressing are exactly as explained for the MOVS string move instruction above.

STACK DATA MOVEMENT

Similarly to most microcomputers and some maxicomputers, the I8086/8088 provides a stack pointer (SP) register whose contents are an address in the stack segment whose starting address is in the stack segment (SS) register. Two instructions are provided to push data to the top of the stack and to pop data from the top of the stack:

```
PUSH    X
POP     X
```

where X can be any 16-bit register (data, pointer, index, flag, or segment) or any location in memory via any of the addressing modes, and the implied other operand is a memory location addressed via the stack pointer indirect—(SP). Recall that, in microcomputers, the stack has its foot or base at high addresses and grows downward to lower addresses. Also recall that the stack has the primary design purpose of holding 16-bit addresses. Thus the stack pointer (SP) register is decremented by 2 before the PUSH and incremented by 2 after the POP. Note that this pair of instructions also allows a memory-to-memory move and that at least one of the operands (the top of the stack) is an implied memory indirect through the stack pointer register.

INPUT/OUTPUT DATA MOVEMENT

These instructions move a datum with no change to the bit pattern to or from the accumulator (AL or AX) from or to an input/output device attached to a specific port numbered from 0 through 255:

```
IN      AL,PORT_NO      ; PORT_NO is immediate
OUT     PORT_NO,AL      ;
```

Alternatively, these same instructions may input data to the accumulator or output data from the accumulator from or to a device attached to the port whose number is contained in the DX register. In effect, I/O is via the port indirectly specified by the DX register and thus these forms of the instructions are

```
IN      AL,(DX)
OUT     (DX),AL
```

DATA TRANSDUCTION INSTRUCTIONS

By definition, data transduction produces a different data syntax without changing the semantics. The traditional example in computers is the transformation of the value of a datum on a punched card encoded as holes (whose position indicates the value) being transduced to the setting of the transistors in the accumulator register whose interpretation (or meaning) is the same. This I/O type of data transduction is performed by the input/output devices of a computational systems.

Our main interests at this time, however, are the data transductions (meaning preserving encoding changes) that are sometimes algorithmically necessary within the computer after input or before output. These transductions are caused by specific instructions or by a series of instructions and essentially are changes in data type. The data types "designed into" the I8086/8088 are:

Addresses

Physical	20-bit unsigned
Offset within Segment	16-bit unsigned
Modifiers	
Word	16-bit unsigned
Byte	8-bit signed or unsigned
Increment/decrement	1-bit signed

Numerical data

Integer

Unsigned	
Binary	16- and 8-bit
Decimal	
Binary-coded decimal	4 bits per digit in pairs
Unpacked (byte) decimal	8 bits per digit
ASCII decimal	8 bits per digit
Signed (two's complement)	
Binary	16- and 8-bit
Floating point (via software or the I8087 auxiliary processor)	32-, 64-, and 80-bit IEEE Standard format

Logical data

Flags	1 bit grouped in a word
Byte	8-bit
Word	16-bit

Character data

Single character (ASCII)	8-bit byte
Strings of characters	0- to 64K-byte aggregates

Additionally, by combining instruction into special algorithms, it is possible to manipulate almost any kind of data with a well-defined syntax and associated semantics. Two examples will suffice as illustrations:

1 *Rational numerical data.* The exact numerical value is expressed as a numerator/denominator pair in lowest form expressed either as two signed binary- or decimal-coded integers of the necessary length. Software routines to manipulate this data type would allow exactly accurate computation, although the manipulation time and storage requirements are often excessively great. [Note: Other formats (syntaxes) for the rational data type are possible, exist, and may be preferable.]

2. *EBCDIC* (Extended Binary-Coded Decimal Interchange Code). An 8-bit code devised by and standard for the IBM 360/370/303X/43X1 extended family of computers. If it is necessary or desirable for an I8086/8088 computational system to communicate with an IBM computer employing the EBCDIC encoding, either the Intel or the IBM system must tranduce ASCII encoded data to equivalent EBCDIC encoded data and the reverse. The translate (XLAT) instruction of the I8086/8088 or the equivalent IBM instruction allows this transduction to be accomplished rapidly and economically.

The I8086/8088 data transduction instructions cause the encoding of a value to be changed to a different encoding; that is, changing the data type of a value is a transduction. Nine instructions of the I8086/8088 allow such changes; eight deal with integer numerical data and the ninth deals with signed byte data with any semantic interpretation. In our present discussion we are completely ignoring floating-point numerical, data addresses per se, and any transduction requiring more than a single instruction.

The translate instruction was discussed earlier in this chapter, as it can also be considered a data movement instruction:

```
XLAT
```

Recall that the byte accumulator register (AL) contains an index into a table of byte data whose starting address is in the BX register. This instruction replaces the contents of the AL register by the contents of the table location indexed by the AL register. In effect, the XLAT instruction is equivalent to

```
MOV     AL,(BX)(AL)
```

where the index is an 8-bit unsigned quantity.

An instruction is provided to transform an 8-bit signed integer datum to a 16-bit signed integer datum:

```
CBW
```

where the source byte must be contained in register AL and the destination is register AX. No flags are affected. Similarly, the

```
CWD
```

instruction has its source as register AX, with the destination being the combined DX:AX 32-bit register pair (useful in division). Both instructions extend, or copy, the sign bit leftward; thus if the source is positive a 0 is extended leftward and the value is preserved; if the source is negative (i.e., two's complement), a 1 is extended leftward and the value is preserved. Admittedly, the identical net result could be achieved otherwise, but not as efficiently or with a single instruction. A principle is involved that is well worth mentioning. Many workers have established the theoretically possible existence of a single-instruction computational device with general abilities. It follows that additional instructions in a computer are not necessary but do facilitate the construction of algorithms that execute faster and occupy less space.

DATA OPERATION INSTRUCTIONS

LOGICAL INSTRUCTIONS

The I8086/8088 provides one single-operand and three two-operand logical instructions:

```
NOT     X       ; one's complement
AND     X,Y     ; and
OR      X,Y     ; inclusive or
XOR     X,Y     ; exclusive or
```

where X can be a register (data, pointer, or index) or any location in read/write memory accessible via any addressing mode and Y can be a register (data, pointer, or index) or any location in memory accessible via any addressing mode or an immediate datum. In all cases both X and Y must be byte length or both X and Y must be word length. As before, memory-to-memory operations are not allowed.

SHIFT/ROTATE INSTRUCTIONS

In computers, a shift instruction pushes bits in the direction of the shift within a data container with bit contents being lost off the end of the data container in the direction of the shift and 0 bits being introduced into the other end of the data container. A rotate, on the other hand, has the bits shifted out in the direction of the rotate introduced at the other end of the data container. Additionally, a shift may include the leftmost bit (logical shift) and thus treat the data container as a logical or unsigned integer value cell, while the arithmetic shift treats the data container as a holder of a signed integer value and thus treats the sign bit as being sacrosanct (see Figure 4.3). The left shift arithmetic instruction shifts bits out around the sign while introducing 0 bits on the right. The right shift arithmetic instruction shifts bits out on the right end while reproducing the sign bit toward the right (thus preserving the legality of two's complement negative and positive integer values). Rotates and shifts in the I8086/8088 are of length N bits and involve the carry flag in one way or another, where the amount of the shift or rotate is the second operand that is placed in the CL register by the programmer if the shift amount is greater than 1 bit. Following are some examples.

1. Shift left logical/shift right logical:

```
SHL     X,amount        ; alternative instruction is SAL
SHR     X,amount
```

where X can be a register (data, pointer, or index) or any location in read/write memory accessed via any of the addressing modes and the CL register contains the amount of the shift in bits. If the amount is negative or 0, the instruction is illegal; if the amount is 1, the shift is relatively fast. In all cases, the last bit shifted out is placed in the CF (carry flag) and the content of the CL register is destroyed.

2. Shift right arithmetic:

```
SAR     X,amount
```

SHL X, amount
SAL X, amount

SHR X, amount

SAR X, amount

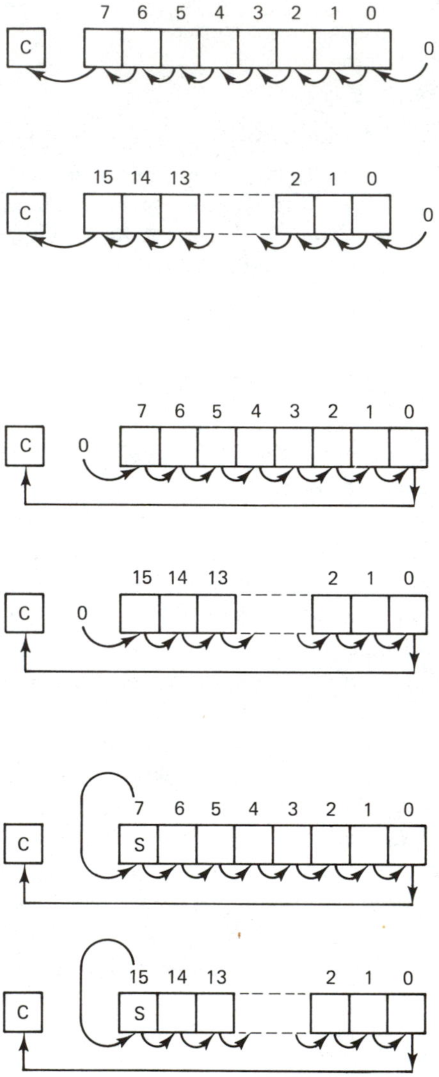

X is { any data, pointer, or index register, or
any read/write memory location (any addressing mode)

Amount in bits: if amount > 1, preload into CL register

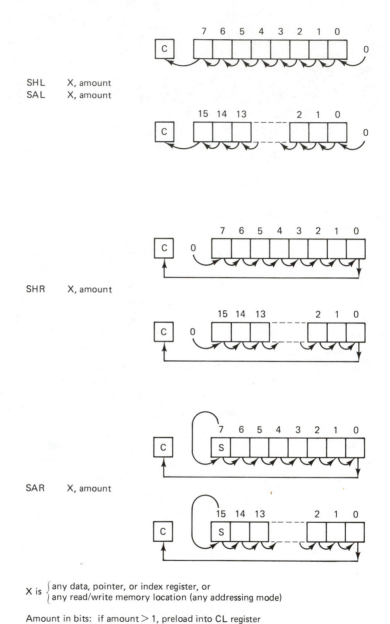

Figure 4.3 The shift logical and shift arithmetic instructions of the I8086/8088. Note that the shift left arithmetic instruction is not available.

where X can again be a register or memory location and "amount" is the amount of the shift. Note particularly that an arithmetic left shift instruction does not exist in the I8086/8088. In those cases where the value of the datum in binary occupies fewer bits than the data container length minus the count length in bits, the logical left shift may be used without danger. In the other cases, the sign bit must be programmatically saved and restored in order to assure that the expected action for an arithmetic left shift actually happens. The shift right arithmetic instruction propagates the sign bit to the right and places the last bit shifted out of the right end of the data container into the carry flag (CF).

3. Rotate left/rotate right:

```
ROL     X,amount
ROR     X,amount
```

where X is a register or memory data container and the CL register is preloaded with the amount of rotate in bits as before. All rotates in the I8086/8088 are logical in character and treat the sign bit in the same manner as any other bit (see Figure 4.4). These instructions rotate the "shifted-out" bit into the first bit position at the opposite end of the data container and copy that bit value into the carry flag (CF).

4. Rotate left through carry/rotate right through carry:

```
RCL     X,amount
RCR     X,amount
```

where X again is a register or memory data container and the CL register is preloaded with the amount of the rotate in bits as before. These rotate instructions treat the carry flag (CF) as an appended (or extra) bit on the left end of the data container to be rotated. Thus a byte rotate with carry involves 9 bits and a word rotate with carry involves 17 bits, formed by concatenating the carry flag with the datum.

ARITHMETIC INSTRUCTIONS

Instructions are provided in the I8086/8088 architectural design for byte- and word-length signed binary integer arithmetic, byte- and word-length unsigned binary arithmetic, and result syntax corrections to accomplish BCD unsigned arithmetic and ASCII-coded addition and subtraction.

Signed Binary Arithmetic

```
ADD     X,Y
SUB     X,Y
IMUL    X,Y ; X must be AL or AX register
```

ROL X, amount

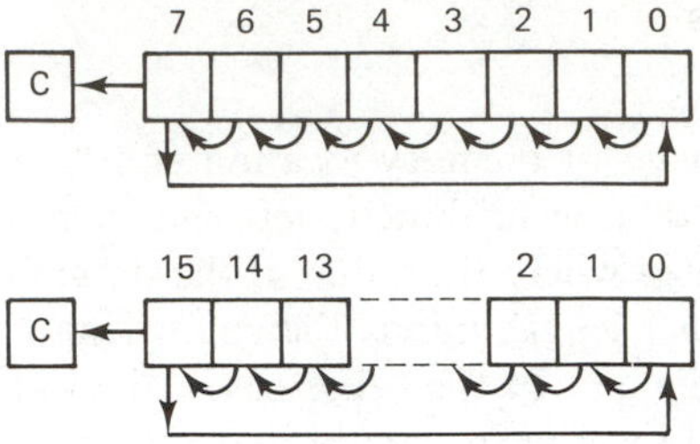

ROR X, amount

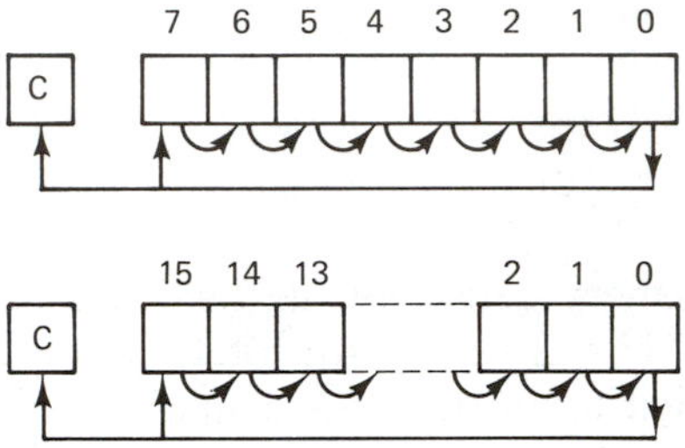

RCL X, amount

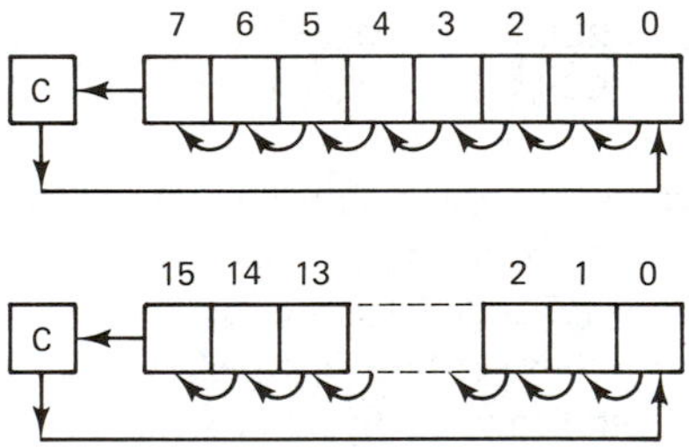

RCR X, amount

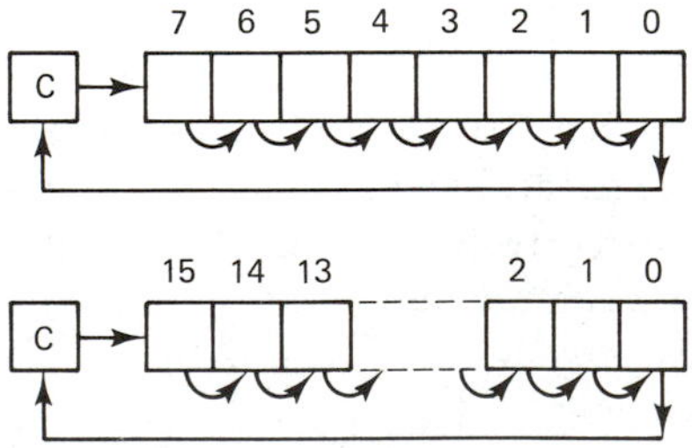

X is { any data, pointer, or index register, or
any read/write memory location (any addressing mode)

Amount in bits: if amount > 1, preload into CL register

Figure 4.4 The rotate instructions of the I8086/8088.

```
IDIV    X,Y ; X must be AX or DX/AX pair register
ADC     X,Y
SBB     X,Y
NEG     X   ; two's complement
INC     X
DEC     X
```

where X can be a register (data, pointer, index) or (with exceptions) a location in read/write memory accessible via any addressing mode and Y can be a register (data, pointer, or index), a location in memory accessible via any addressing mode, or an immediate datum. All status flags except the direction, interrupt, and trap flags, are set; that is, the overflow, sign, zero, nibble carry (auxiliary carry), parity, and carry flags are set. Again, memory-to-memory operations are not allowed.

While the ADD, SUB, ADC, SBB, and NEG instructions perform their data operations as expected; the other instructions demand further explanation. Thus the convert or extend (CBW and CWD) instructions are often useful in converting byte data to word data before word arithmetic and converting word to double-word data before word division. The add with carry implies X ← X + Y + CF and the subtract with carry implies X ← X − Y − CF (i.e., the carry flag is used as a "borrow" source if necessary). These instructions are particularly useful in constructing multiple-precision arithmetic algorithms.

The signed integer multiply instructions (Figure 4.5) act as follows:

Signed byte multiply	AX ← AL * 8-bit datum
Signed word multiple	DX:AX ← AX * 16-bit datum

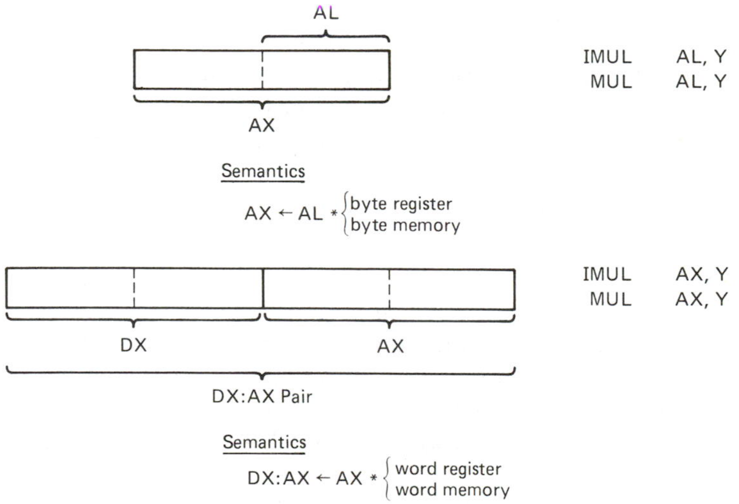

Figure 4.5 The multiply signed integer and multiply unsigned integer instructions of the I8086/8088 give a double-length result.

Note that multiplying two 8-bit source data results in a 16-bit result datum and that multiplying two 16-bit source data results in a 32-bit result datum.

The signed integer divide instructions (Figure 4.6) act as follows:

Signed byte divide	AL ← AX / 8-bit datum
	AH ← remainder
Signed word divide	AX ← DX:AX / 16-bit datum
	DX ← remainder

The extend instruction (CBW) must be used before the divide byte instruction to propagate the sign of the source dividend in the AL through the AX register. Similarly, the extend long instruction (CWD) must be used before the divide word instruction to propagate the sign of the source dividend in the AX through the DX register. Note that this implies that the signed byte divide is really a word/byte divide, whereas the signed word divide is really a quad/word divide.

Unsigned Binary Arithmetic

Only two instructions pairs are specifically provided by the I8086/8088 to perform unsigned binary integer arithmetic using unsigned binary source operands:

```
MUL     X,Y
DIV     X,Y
```

where the restrictions on X and Y are exactly those of the corresponding signed integer instructions, with the additional provision that both X and Y are considered unsigned positive integer values and the result (new X) is also an unsigned positive integer value.

Addition and subtraction of unsigned integer values (assumed positive) involving or not involving the carry flag and including incrementation and decrementation are carried out using the instructions for signed integer data operations.

Binary-Coded-Decimal Arithmetic

The data format of BCD unsigned decimal numerical values (sometimes referred to as *packed decimal*) uses a nibble for each decimal digit and provides for two digits per byte as illustrated on the top of Figure 4.7. All values are assumed positive by the I8086/8088 instructions. Normally, the binary signed integer with carry arithmetic instructions is employed to manipulate these BCD values, with two special instructions to adjust the result to be a legal BCD value:

```
DAA     ; use after an ADD or ADC
DAS     ; use after a SUB or SBB
```

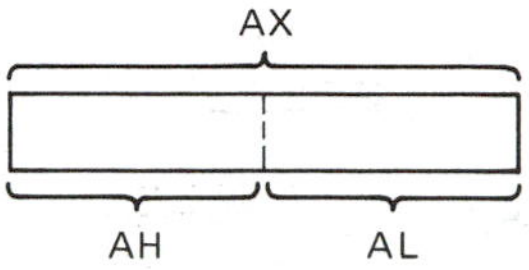

IDIV AL, Y
DIV AL, Y

<u>Semantics</u>

AL ← AX / {byte register, byte memory}

AH ← remainder

<u>Required setup</u>

<u>Signed integer</u>

```
MOV    AL, source
CBW    AL
IDIV   AL, {byte register
            {byte memory
```

<u>Unsigned integer</u>

```
MOV    AL, source
MOV    AH, 00H
DIV    AL, {byte register
            {byte memory
```

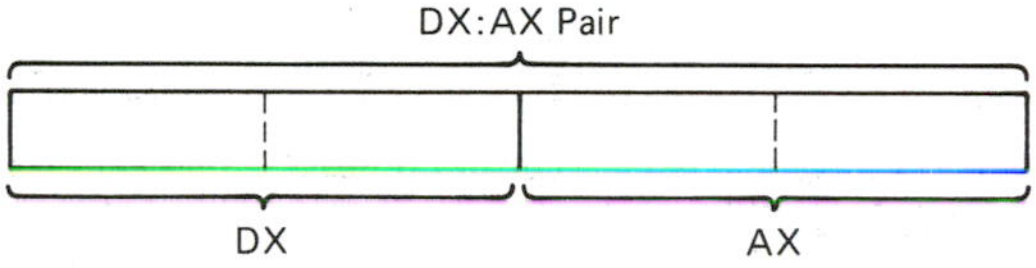

IDIV AX, Y
DIV AX, Y

<u>Semantics</u>

AX ← DX:AX pair / {word register, word memory}

DX ← remainder

<u>Required setup</u>

<u>Signed integer</u>

```
MOV    AX, source
CWD    AX
IDIV   AX, {word register
            {word memory
```

<u>Unsigned integer</u>

```
MOV    AX, source
MOV    DX, 0000H
DIV    AX, {word register
            {word memory
```

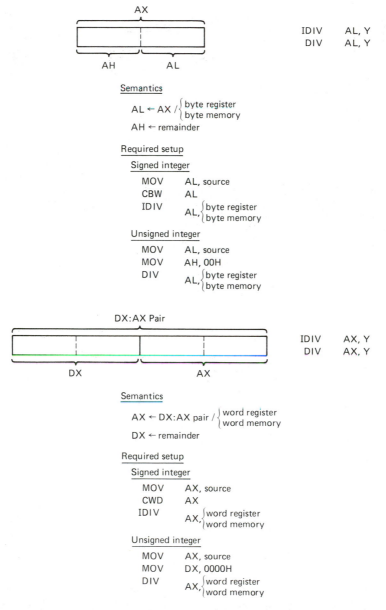

Figure 4.6 The divide signed integer and divide unsigned integer instructions require a setup to extend the sign bit into the high-order portion of the dividend.

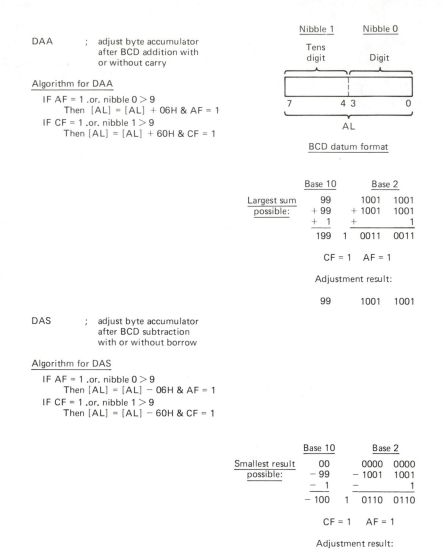

DAA ; adjust byte accumulator after BCD addition with or without carry

Algorithm for DAA

```
IF AF = 1 .or. nibble 0 > 9
    Then [AL] = [AL] + 06H & AF = 1
IF CF = 1 .or. nibble 1 > 9
    Then [AL] = [AL] + 60H & CF = 1
```

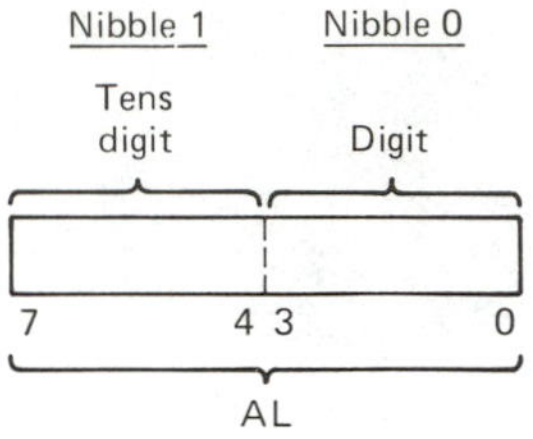

BCD datum format

```
                    Base 10        Base 2
Largest sum           99          1001   1001
possible:           + 99        + 1001   1001
                    +  1        +           1
                     199     1    0011   0011

                       CF = 1   AF = 1

                    Adjustment result:

                      99          1001   1001
```

DAS ; adjust byte accumulator after BCD subtraction with or without borrow

Algorithm for DAS

```
IF AF = 1 .or. nibble 0 > 9
    Then [AL] = [AL] − 06H & AF = 1
IF CF = 1 .or. nibble 1 > 9
    Then [AL] = [AL] − 60H & CF = 1
```

```
                    Base 10        Base 2
Smallest result       00          0000   0000
possible:           − 99        − 1001   1001
                    −  1        −           1
                   − 100     1    0110   0110

                       CF = 1   AF = 1

                    Adjustment result:

                      00          0000   0000
```

Figure 4.7 The BCD adjustment instructions for the I8086/8088.

where the implied operand must be the AL register (the byte accumulator). These instructions both assume that the source operands were legal BCD values in the range 00 through 99. Algorithms for adjusting the results of multiplying or dividing BCD numbers can be devised using the two instructions listed above.

The process of converting a two-digit ASCII number to BCD can be illustrated by

```
3731        ASCII number encoding the meaning 71, requiring two bytes (as-
              sumed to be in register AX)
SUB         AX,3030H        ; results = 0701 hexadecimal in AX
SHL         AH,4d           ; results = 7001 hexadecimal in AX
ADD         AL,AH           ; results = 7071 hexadecimal in AX
SUB         AH,AH           ; results = 0071 hexadecimal in AX = 0071
                            BCD
```

The process of adding two BCD two-digit numbers and subtracting two BCD two-digit numbers with the appropriate postarithmetic decimal adjustment is illustrated in Figure 4.7.

On the other hand, the normal binary-coded-decimal value will consist of a signed string of 4-bit nibbles grouped in contiguous two-nibble pairs per byte with a separate byte on the left end encoding the sign and possibly the length in digits. Addition and subtraction would be accomplished from right to left in the strings with the operation (add/sub) and the sign of the result both being a function of the desired operation, the magnitude of the BCD strings, and their respective signs. The rules of ordinary base 10 arithmetic as learned in elementary school would apply. As a simple example, we will add the two equal-length BCD strings below, giving a third string as the result. The first byte of the strings will contain the length and sign in signed-magnitude form, ranging from plus 127 through minus 127.

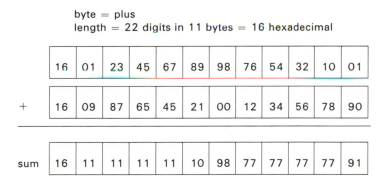

byte = plus
length = 22 digits in 11 bytes = 16 hexadecimal

	16	01	23	45	67	89	98	76	54	32	10	01
+	16	09	87	65	45	21	00	12	34	56	78	90
sum	16	11	11	11	11	10	98	77	77	77	77	91

```
;     ADDRESS OF X IN BP REGISTER
;     ADDRESS OF Y IN SI REGISTER
;     ADDRESS OF SUM IN DI REGISTER
;
;     SEE IF SIGN OR LENGTH ARE DIFFERENT
;
          MOV  CL,(BP)
          CMP  CL,(SI)
          JNE  DO_DIFFERENT
;
```

```
;       SET_UP FOR BCD ADD OF SAME SIGN & LENGTH
;
                MOV (DI),CL      ; SIGN & LENGTH TO SUM
                MOV CH,00h
                AND CL,80h       ; CX HAS LENGTH IN DIGITS
                SHR CX,1d        ; CX HAS LENGTH IN BYTES
                ADD BP,CX        ; RIGHT BYTE ADDRESS OF X
                ADD SI, CX       ; RIGHT BYTE ADDRESS OF Y
                ADD DI, CX       ; RIGHT BYTE ADDRESS OF SUM
;
;       ADD BYTES RIGHT TO LEFT WITH CARRY & DECIMAL ADJUST
;
                CLC              ; CLEAR CARRY FOR FIRST ADD
ADD_LOOP:       MOV AL,(BP)
                ADC AL,(SI)
                DAA
                MOV (DI) ,AL
                DEC BP
                DEC SI
                DEC DI
                LOOP ADD_LOOP
                JC  OVER_FLOW ; CARRY ON LEFT BYTE
                JMP ALL_DONE
;
;       CODE FOR OVERFLOW ERROR WOULD FOLLOW
;       CODE FOR UNEQUAL LENGTHS WOULD FOLLOW
;       CODE FOR DIFFERENT SIGNS WOULD FOLLOW
```

Byte Decimal (Unpacked Decimal) Arithmetic

The data format of unsigned byte decimal numerical values (sometimes referred to as *unpacked decimal*) uses a full byte for each decimal digit and thus only allows for one digit per byte, as illustrated on top of Figure 4.8. All values are assumed positive by the I8086/8088 instructions. Normally, the binary signed integer with or without carry addition and subtraction instructions are employed to manipulate byte decimal values. Decimal adjustment instructions are available for all four arithmetic operations. We will discuss each operation through the use of an example.

Addition of byte decimal quantities

The 16-bit first operand in the AX register may be byte decimal or byte decimal/ASCII numerals combination, whereas the second operand (source) must be an 8-bit byte decimal or ASCII single-digit numeric value. The situations could be (in hexadecimal)

Exp1	0007H + 02H → 0009H	byte decimal
Exp2	3037H + 32H → 3069H	ASCII

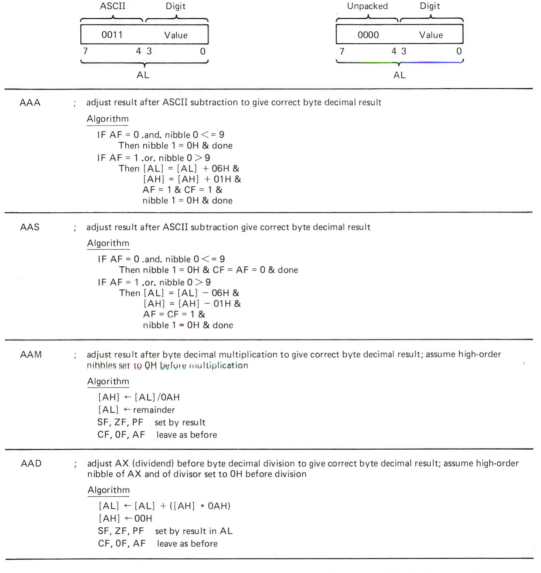

AAA ; adjust result after ASCII subtraction to give correct byte decimal result

Algorithm

```
IF AF = 0 .and. nibble 0 <= 9
     Then nibble 1 = 0H & done
IF AF = 1 .or. nibble 0 > 9
     Then [AL] = [AL] + 06H &
          [AH] = [AH] + 01H &
          AF = 1 & CF = 1 &
          nibble 1 = 0H & done
```

AAS ; adjust result after ASCII subtraction give correct byte decimal result

Algorithm

```
IF AF = 0 .and. nibble 0 <= 9
     Then nibble 1 = 0H & CF = AF = 0 & done
IF AF = 1 .or. nibble 0 > 9
     Then [AL] = [AL] - 06H &
          [AH] = [AH] - 01H &
          AF = CF = 1 &
          nibble 1 = 0H & done
```

AAM ; adjust result after byte decimal multiplication to give correct byte decimal result; assume high-order nibbles set to 0H before multiplication

Algorithm

```
[AH] ← [AL]/0AH
[AL] ← remainder
SF, ZF, PF    set by result
CF, OF, AF    leave as before
```

AAD ; adjust AX (dividend) before byte decimal division to give correct byte decimal result; assume high-order nibble of AX and of divisor set to 0H before division

Algorithm

```
[AL] ← [AL] + ([AH] * 0AH)
[AH] ← 00H
SF, ZF, PF    set by result in AL
CF, OF, AF    leave as before
```

Figure 4.8 The byte decimal adjustment instructions for the I8086/8088. Note the difference between ASCII numerals and byte decimal numerals (often termed unpacked decimal).

Exp3	0007H + 04H → 000BH	byte decimal
Exp4	3037H + 34H → 306BH	ASCII
Exp5	0137H + 32H → 0169H	byte/ASCII
Exp6	0137H + 34H → 016BH	byte/ASCII

Using the adjust byte decimal result of addition instruction

AAA

which assumes that the result will be placed in the AX register, the addition results above would be transformed by the algorithm on Figure 4.8 to

0009H → 0009H	correct
3069H → 3009H	incorrect
000BH → 0101H	correct
306BH → 3101H	incorrect
0169H → 0109H	correct
016BH → 0201H	correct

Note particularly that byte decimal inputs to the addition always adjust correctly, that ASCII byte inputs also work, but that an ASCII numeral in the AH register gives incorrect results. The following code will assure correct results, including the carry:

```
AND     AX,0F0FH
ADD     AL,Y        ; Y IS IN MEMORY OR REGISTER
AAA
```

Subtraction of byte decimal quantities

The 16-bit first operand in the AX register may be a byte decimal or a byte decimal/ASCII numerals combination, whereas the second (source) operand must be a 8-bit byte decimal or ASCII single-digit numeric value. The same rules regarding ASCII values apply as were discussed above for addition. The adjust byte decimal result of the subtraction instruction is

AAS

which also assumes the result to be in the 16-bit AX register. The adjustment algorithm used is given in Figure 4.8.

Multiplication of byte decimal quantities

The 8-bit byte decimal first operand (the multiplicand) must be in the AL register, the 8-bit byte decimal second operand (the multiplier source) must be in a register or in memory, and the double-length result will occupy the 16-bit AX register. ASCII input operands are not allowed. An example of code could be

```
        MOV       AL,THERE
        MUL       AL,MULTIPLIER
        AAM                              ; adjusted result in AX
```

A numeric example, employing the adjustment algorithm in Figure 4.8, is

```
09H * 09H → 0051H
0051H adjust → 0801H
```

Note particularly that this binary-to-byte decimal conversion algorithm is quite general and can be employed for a positive or unsigned numeric integer quantity of any byte length. Recall that if the source byte value is greater than 99 base 10, three bytes will be required for the result. In other words, the AAM instruction gives the byte decimal version of the 8-bit source value in the AL register modulo 100 base 10. An algorithm to accomplish a general unsigned binary byte conversion to a three-digit byte decimal value in the DL:AH:AL triplet could be

```
          MOV     AL,BIN_POS_BYTE
          MOV     DL,AL
          AAM
          SUB     DL,63H        ; 99 base 10
          JG      AGAIN
          MOV     DL,00H        ; two-digit result
          JMP     DONE
AGAIN:    SUB     DL,63H        ; 99 base 10
          JG      FIXIT
          MOV     CL,01H        ; between 100 and 199
          JMP     DONE
FIXIT:    MOV     DL,02H        ; between 200 and 255
DONE:     NOP
```

Division of byte decimal quantities

The 16-bit two-digit byte decimal dividend (range 0 to 99) in the AX register must be converted to binary before division by an 8-bit one-digit byte decimal divisor (range 1 to 9), with the result being in the AL and the remainder in the AH register.

```
          MOV     AX,BYT_DEC_WRD
          AAD
          DIV     AL,DIV_BYT
          MOV     REMAINDER,AH
          AAM
```

Four numeric examples may assist understanding:

71/8 = 8 remainder 7

0110001 – AAD → 01000111/1000 = 1000 R = 0111

1/9 = 0 remainder 1

00000001 – AAD → 00000001/1001 = 0000 R = 0001

90/9 = 10 remainder 0

10010000 – AAD → 01011010/1001 = 1010 R = 0000

99/1 = 99 remainder 0

10011001 – AAD → 0110011/0001 = 01100011 R = 000

Note particularly that the last two examples illustrate the possibility of developing a result greater than 9 base 10 and thus require the saving of the remainder from the AX register and then the conversion of the binary answer (range 10 to 99 base 10) to two-digit byte decimal format occupying the entire AX register through the use of the AAM instruction.

As with BCD numerical values, the normal byte decimal numerical value will consist of a signed string of 8-bit contiguous bytes with a separate byte on the left end encoding the sign and possibly the length in bytes. Algorithms to accomplish addition and division of byte decimal strings are straightforward and proceed from right to left through the source strings in an analogous manner to the example given earlier for BCD data. Algorithms to accomplish multiplication and subtraction of byte decimal strings, although straightforward, are not short, simple, or easy to understand. These algorithms will not be shown but will be left to the reader to devise, implement, document, test, and verify.

STATUS FLAG INSTRUCTIONS

Three instructions are provided that affect the value of the carry flag (CF) as well as two instructions that affect the direction flag (DF). These five status flag instructions each have an implicit operand:

```
CLC        ; set CF to 0
STC        ; set CF to 1
CMC        ; change setting of CF
CLD        ; set DF to 0
STD        ; set DF to 1
```

Recall that the direction flag is employed to indicate the direction of processing of character string data. Thus CLD results in left-to-right string processing with the addressing register(s) being incremented, and STD results in right-to-left string processing with the address register(s) being decremented.

When considering the status flag registers it is important to remember that the following instructions affect these flags:

CMPS	
CMP	
TEST	
POP	
RETI	
Logical data operations	(no effect on DF, IF, or TF)
Shift logical/rotate	(only CF and OF)
Shift arithmetic	(no effect on DF, IF, or TF)
Arithmetic operations	(no effect on DF, IF, or TF)

Programmers should also be aware that a 16-bit data word can be constructed via logical instructions or as a constant and then loaded into the status flag register. One method of doing this is to PUSH the datum to the stack and then POP it to the status flag register.

5

Input/Output

An explosion of computer applications has caused, or is the result of, the availability of the scores of new and different I/O devices that are now a part of computer systems. Despite this proliferation of devices, the techniques employed to connect I/O devices into a computer system are fairly standard. On the other hand, the characteristics of I/O devices vary widely. Nevertheless, a programmer who understands the basic principles of I/O interfacing and programming can rapidly learn the characteristics of any new device and somewhat easily design and code programs to interact correctly with the device.

I/O ORGANIZATION

Figure 5.1 shows a computer consisting of a processor (arithmetic-logic unit and control), with memory connected to the processor by a memory bus, and input/output connected to the processor by an I/O bus. In this scheme provisions exist for identifying the peripheral device (via an I/O address); for initiating, terminating, and otherwise controlling the device action (via the I/O control path), as well as for transferring the data (via the I/O data path). No possibility for interference with memory usage exists, as one bus is provided for memory accesses and a physically separate bus is provided for I/O accesses.

The I/O subsystem in Figure 5.1 contains several sets of I/O devices and interfaces. Whereas the data and control lines between each peripheral device and its specialized interface are unique to that device, the connections between the interface and the I/O bus are generalized and usually exactly alike. Thus the I/O interface (i.e., the device interface) provides uniform control, uniform timing, a uniform ad-

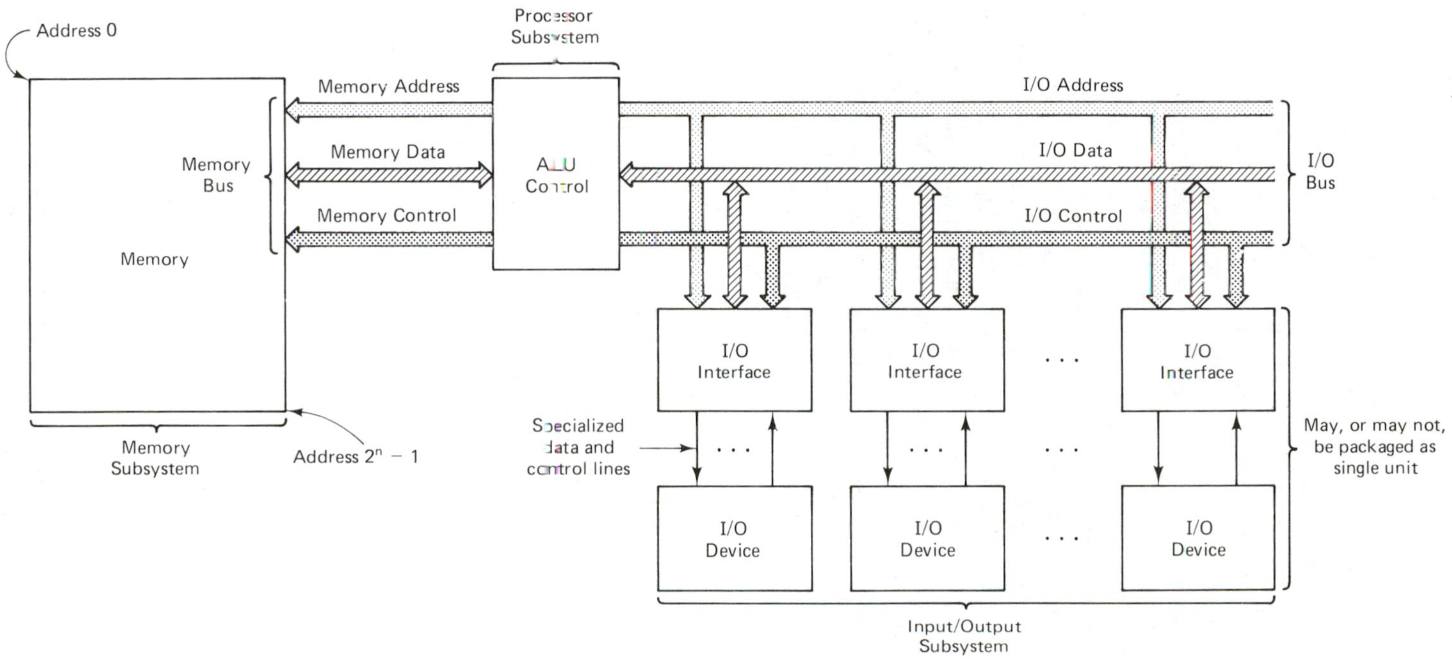

Figure 5.1 Conceptual diagram of a computer with a bus serving the memory subsystem and a separate bus serving the input/output subsystem.

dress, and a uniform data connection between the I/O bus and the peripheral device. It controls the operation of the device according to commands from the processor subsystem and converts data from the bus format to that required by the device, and vice versa, as well as being the physical I/O address (or port).

Additional detail is shown in Figure 5.2 for a keyboard input device (read-only by design) and for a light-emitting diode seven-segment digit display device (write-only by design). In both cases, the bus interface–I/O bus connection is general, while the circuits of the interface itself provide specialized services to the specific device. In the case of the keyboard, the depression of a key causes an electrical pulse to be transmitted to the circuits of the encoder, which generate a key-specific 7-bit ASCII code that is transmitted to the I/O register (or I/O port) of the bus interface. In most cases a high-order 0 bit is appended to make an 8-bit data "package," although some devices may employ this high-order bit for other specific purposes. For this reason, programmers must never assume that bit 7 of ASCII data received from a device is zero. It should always be "masked" out. Thus the I/O register of a keyboard interface will contain the 7-bit ASCII code corresponding to the key being depressed or 00000000 if no key is currently depressed.

To read data from the keyboard, a program executes an instruction that transfers the contents of the I/O register in the bus interface into a register in the proces-

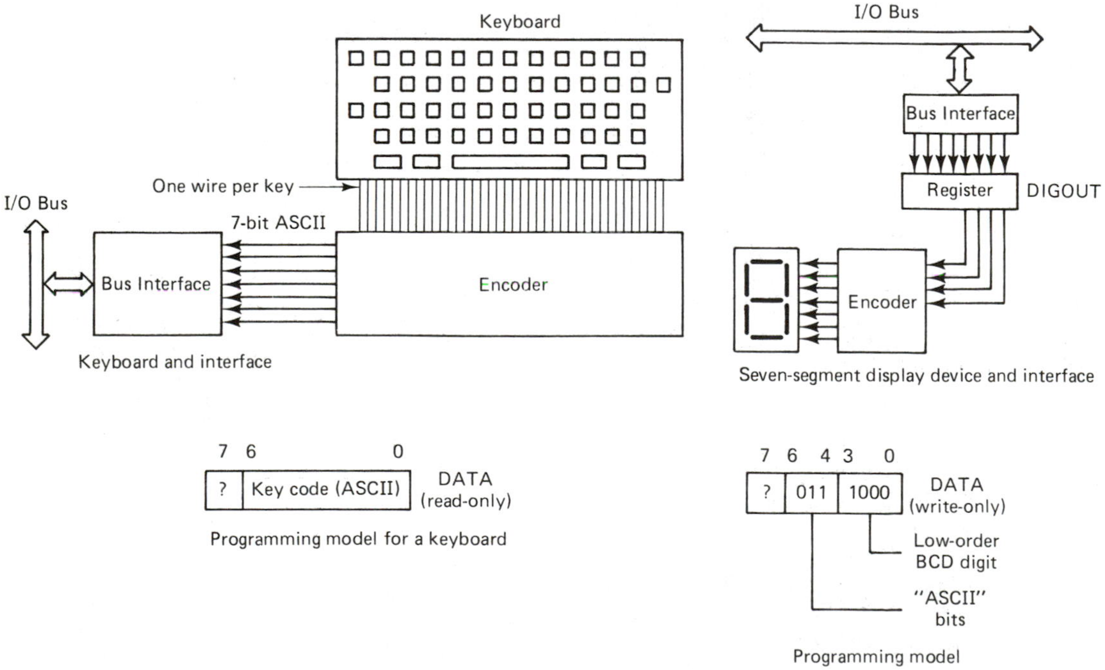

Figure 5.2 Diagram of a keyboard device and associated bus interface as well as a light-emitting diode seven-segment display device and associated bus interface. In both cases the programming model consists of the I/O register (or I/O port).

sor, where it can be manipulated as ordinary data. Any attempt of a program to write data from a processor register to the keyboard interface I/O register will be unsuccessful (and may result in an error condition); therefore, this keyboard device employs an "input port." Also note that the input ASCII character must be transferred from the interface I/O register while the key is depressed, or it will be replaced by 00000000 and lost.

In the case of the diode display, the transmission from a processor register of an ASCII numeric character with control and device address via the I/O bus will be recognized by the display interface and accepted into the I/O register of the interface. The interface will transmit the low-order 4 bits to the diode display encoder, which will interpret them into the correct electrical pulses to energize the appropriate light-emitting diodes of the seven-segment display to represent the value as an arabic numeral. As the I/O register of the display device interface is an output port, it is a true storage register whose value does not change until the next output operation. Thus the light-emitting seven-segment display remains lighted with the correct arabic numeral configuration until it is purposely changed. Any attempt of a program to input data from this output port will be unsuccessful and may result in an error condition or may simply be ignored.

BUS ORGANIZATION

The memory bus and I/O bus of the I8086/8088 are combined into one time-shared (or time-multiplexed) system bus that is used by both subsystems (memory and I/O) as needed to transfer data to and from the processor and memory or I/O ports. Even though the transmission of memory data and of I/O data share address and data lines on a multiplexed basis, they are logically independent. Numerically identical addresses on the bus for memory or for I/O refer to different physical entities because a control signal from the processor distinguishes between memory and I/O operations. Thus I/O address (port) 6 is different and totally independent of memory address (location) 6.

In the top portion of Figure 5.3, note that the multiplexed bus serving both memory and I/O has a maximum capacity for addresses of 20 bits and a maximum capacity for data of 16 bits. While accessing I8086 memory, it is normal for two 8-bit bytes to be transmitted to or from two separate banks (or portions) of memory simultaneously, with one bank containing all the odd-numbered addresses and the other all the even-numbered addresses. Thus two bytes can be delivered or received in one memory cycle by a I8086 with 16-bit external data bus connections. Similarly, 16 bits of I/O data can be transmitted. Eight-bit transmission is also possible.

In the bottom portion of Figure 5.3, note that the multiplexed bus serving both memory and I/O has a maximum capacity for addresses of 20 bits and a maximum capacity for data of 8 bits. Thus only one byte can be transmitted from or to memory per memory cycle. Similarly, only one 8-bit byte of I/O data can be transmitted.

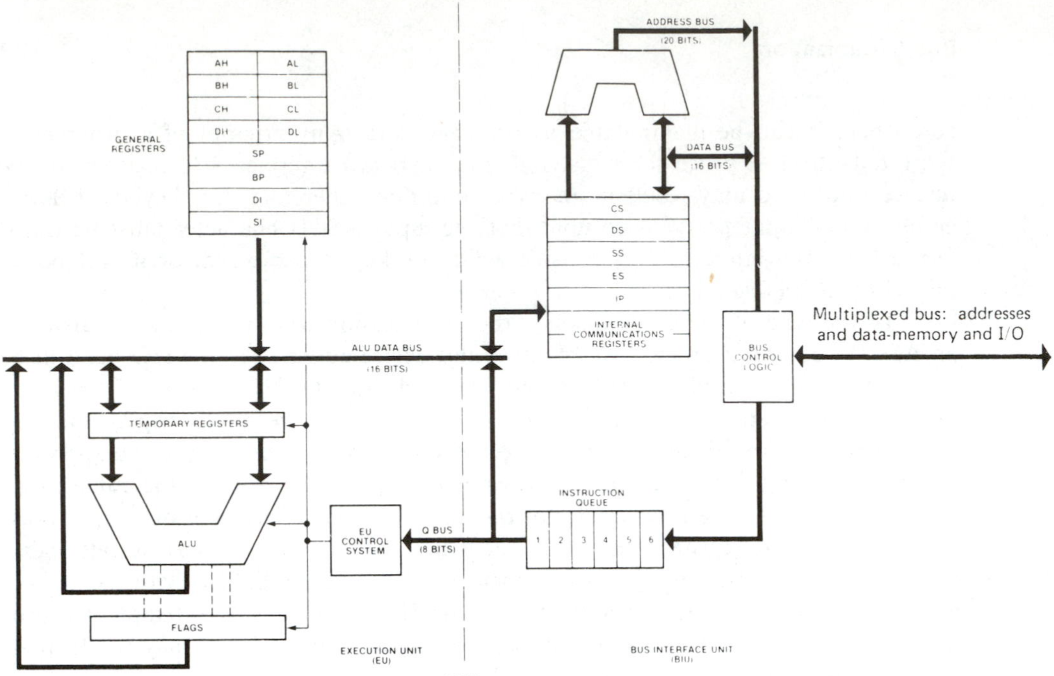

8086

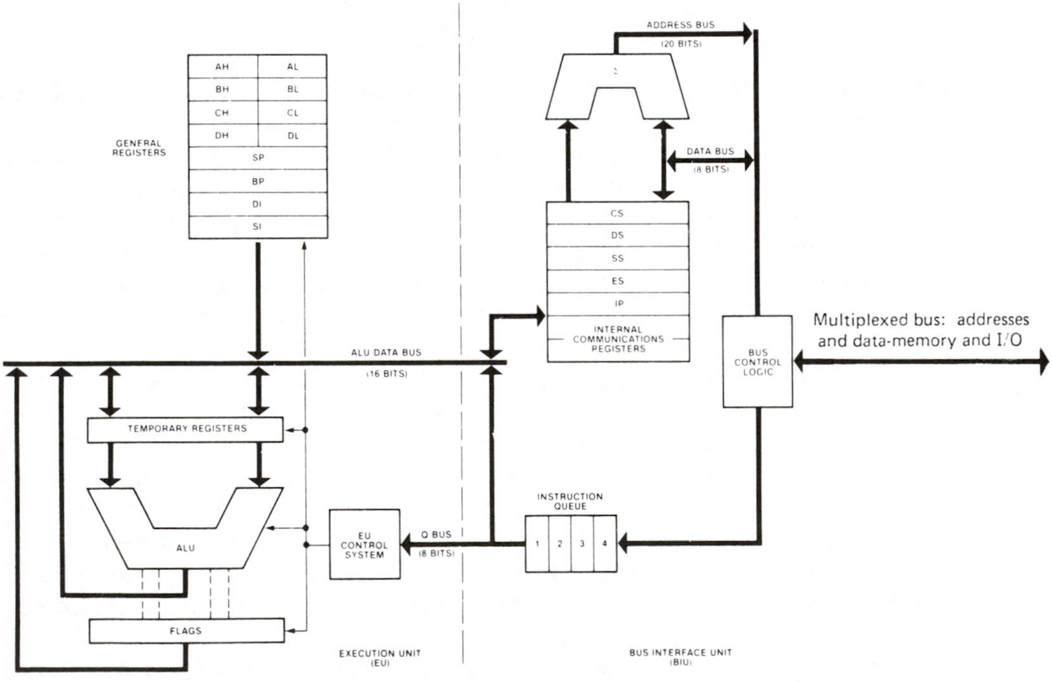

8088

Figure 5.3 Processors of the I8086 (*top*) and the I8088 (*bottom*) illustrating the connection of the time-multiplexed bus to off-chip memory and I/O ports. Note that the I8086 can access two bytes, whereas the I8088 can only access one byte per cycle. (Reprinted by permission of Intel Corporation. Copyright 1980.)

Figure 5.3 allows us again to note that the bus interface unit (BIU) is time-controlled independently from the execution unit (EU) so that memory–I/O accesses can be simultaneous with instruction execution.

Bus Operation

A bus cycle is an asynchronous event with four clock periods in which an address of a memory location or I/O port is presented in the first clock period, followed by either a read control signal (order) to capture the data from the memory bank–I/O port or a write control signal (order) to transmit the data to the memory bank–I/O port. The actual data capture or transmission occurs during the third and fourth clock periods. At the end of the fourth clock period the data transfer is complete. A schematic of this process is shown in Figure 5.4 with the action timed as follows:

Clock cycle "T state"	Action for the: Read bus cycle	Write bus cycle
T1	Processor (BIU) places address on bus	Processor (BIU) places address on bus
T2	Processor (BIU) changes from send address to capture data mode	Processor (BIU) places data on bus
T3	Processor (BIU) accepts data on bus	Data remain on bus
T4	Processor (BIU) accepts data on bus	Data remain on bus; available at clock cycle "fall"

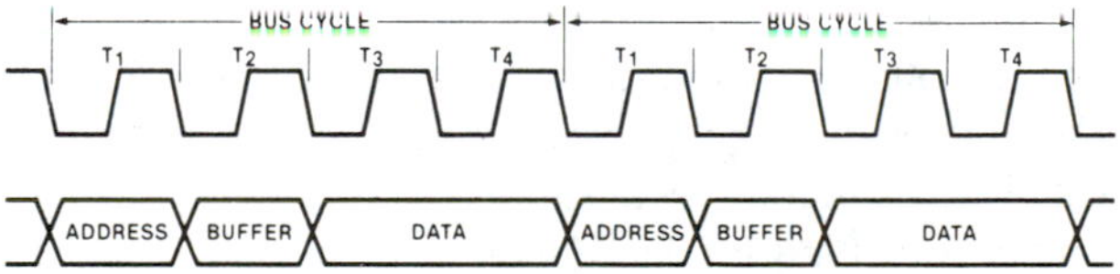

Typical BIU Bus Cycles

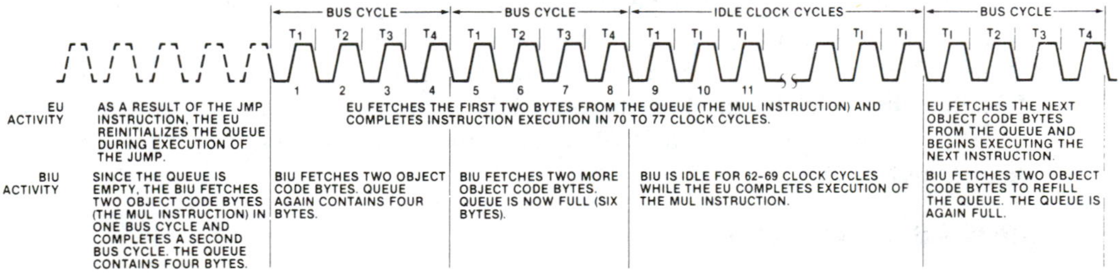

Figure 5.4 Schematic of the clock cycles (T-states) of the bus cycle and of the idle (wait) states of the bus interface unit (BIU) of the I8086/8088. (Reprinted by permission of Intel Corporation. Copyright 1980.)

The BIU (bus interface unit) executes a bus cycle only when

1. The EU (execution unit) requests a bus cycle as a portion of instruction execution, or
2. The BIU must fill the instruction queue.

Consequently, idle periods can occur between BIU and bus cycle activity. Additionally, provision exists for inserting additional "wait" clock cycles (T states) into the bus cycle to compensate for slow devices (memory or I/O) that cannot transfer data at the maximum rate. These wait states are inserted between T3 and T4, with the data on the bus remaining unchanged. This process is illustrated in Figure 5.4.

As shown in Figures 5.5 and 5.6, the bus cycle timing varies between a read (capture) data by the processor and a write (transmit) data to memory or an I/O port. Further, by comparing Figure 5.5 with 5.6, it is apparent that the bus cycle timings for the I8086 that can transmit a 16-bit datum are different from the bus cycle timings for the I8088, which can only transmit an 8-bit datum.

INTERLACING THE MULTIPLEXED BUS CYCLES

Consider what happens when an instruction is executed on the I8088 with an 8-bit (one byte) data path to and from the BIU and memory or I/O.

I8088 Bus Cycle Usage

Note from Figure 5.3 that the instruction queue is four bytes long. Beginning with the simplest case, we will assume that the instruction queue is empty. Therefore, when the execution unit (EU) requests an instruction, the BIU will initiate a bus cycle to fetch the first byte of the instruction. This timing is illustrated in Figure 5.7*a*. Assuming that the instruction occupies two bytes, the BIU will immediately initiate another bus cycle as in Figure 5.7*b*. For our illustration, we will assume that this instruction needs a byte-length datum from memory in order to perform a register-by-memory-to-register arithmetic operation. Continuing our assumptions, we specify that seven clock periods will be needed to compute the effective operand address and convert this to a physical data address in memory and that the arithmetic operation will consume nine clock periods. This resultant timing is illustrated in Figure 5.7*c*. But the I8088, having asynchronous (able to execute independently with simultaneity) operation of the EU and BIU, will actually execute this example instruction as in Figure 5.7*d*.

I8086 Bus Cycle Usage

Note also from Figure 5.3 that the instruction queue is six bytes long. Also note that the data path to or from the BIU and memory or I/O is 16 bits (two bytes) in capacity. For our purposes of illustrating a principle, we will assume that the two-byte in-

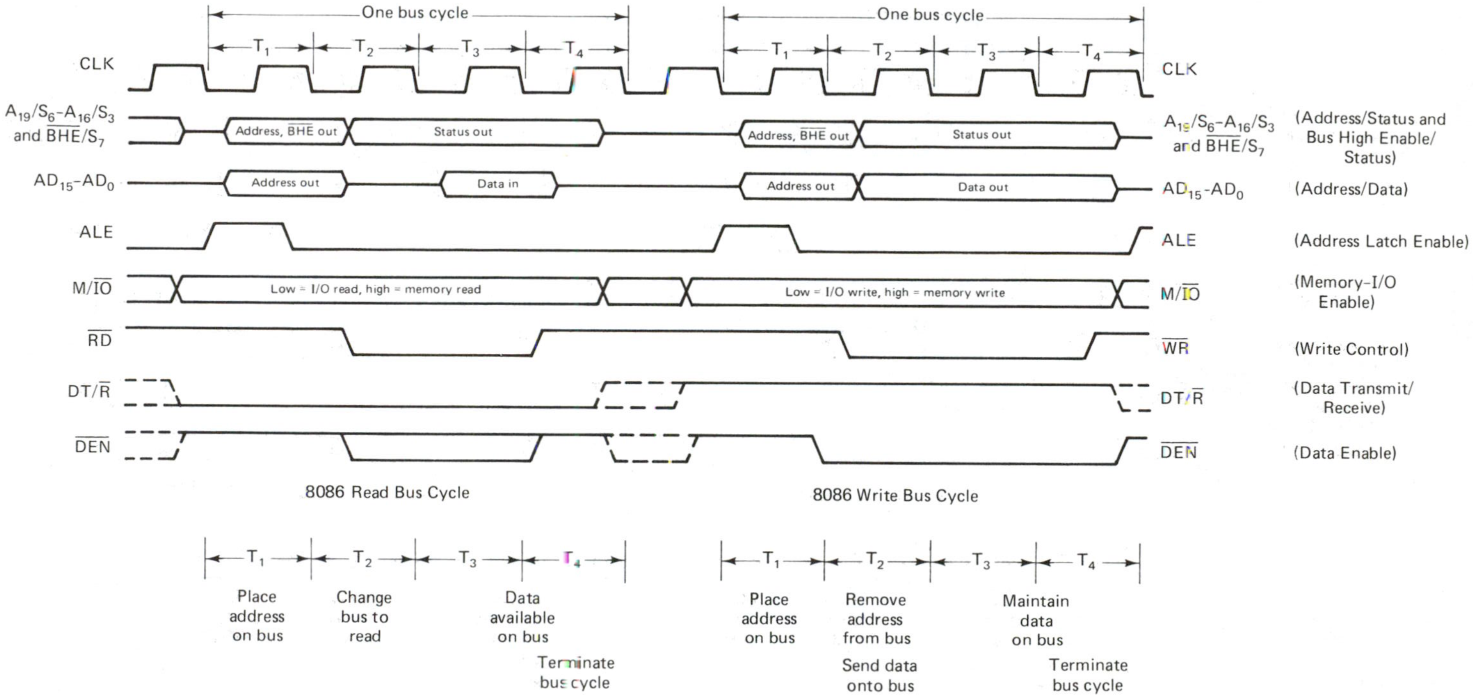

Figure 5.5 Details of the bus cycle for I8086 accessing 16-bit (two-byte) datum or 8-bit (one-byte) datum. (Reprinted by permission of Intel Corporation. Copyright 1980.)

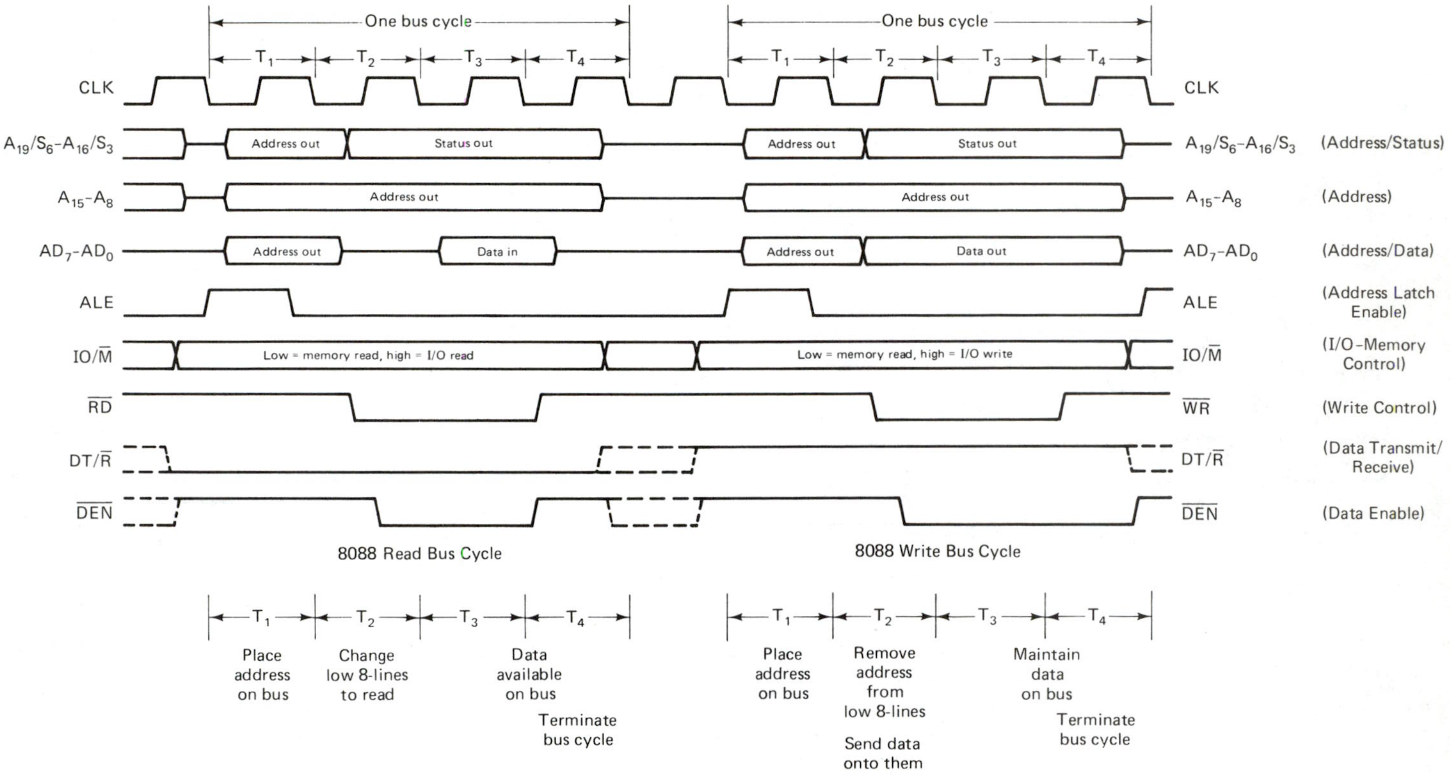

Figure 5.6 Details of the bus cycle for I8088 accessing 8-bit (one-byte) datum only. (Reprinted by permission of Intel Corporation. Copyright 1980.)

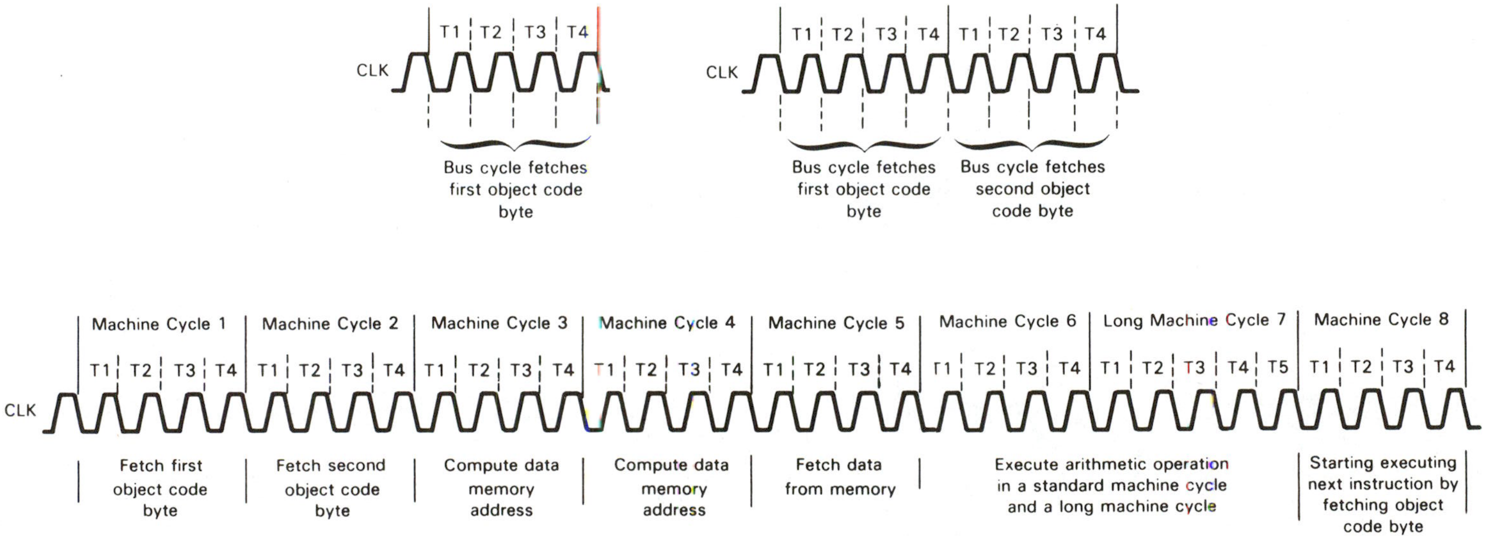

Figure 5.7 Instruction cycle timing for the I8088 and the I8086. Part (d) is realistic for the I8088 and part (e) for the I8086; that is, subsystem overlap is included. (Reprinted with permission from R. Rector and G. Alexy, *The 8086 Book.* Copyright Osborne/McGraw-Hill, 1980.)

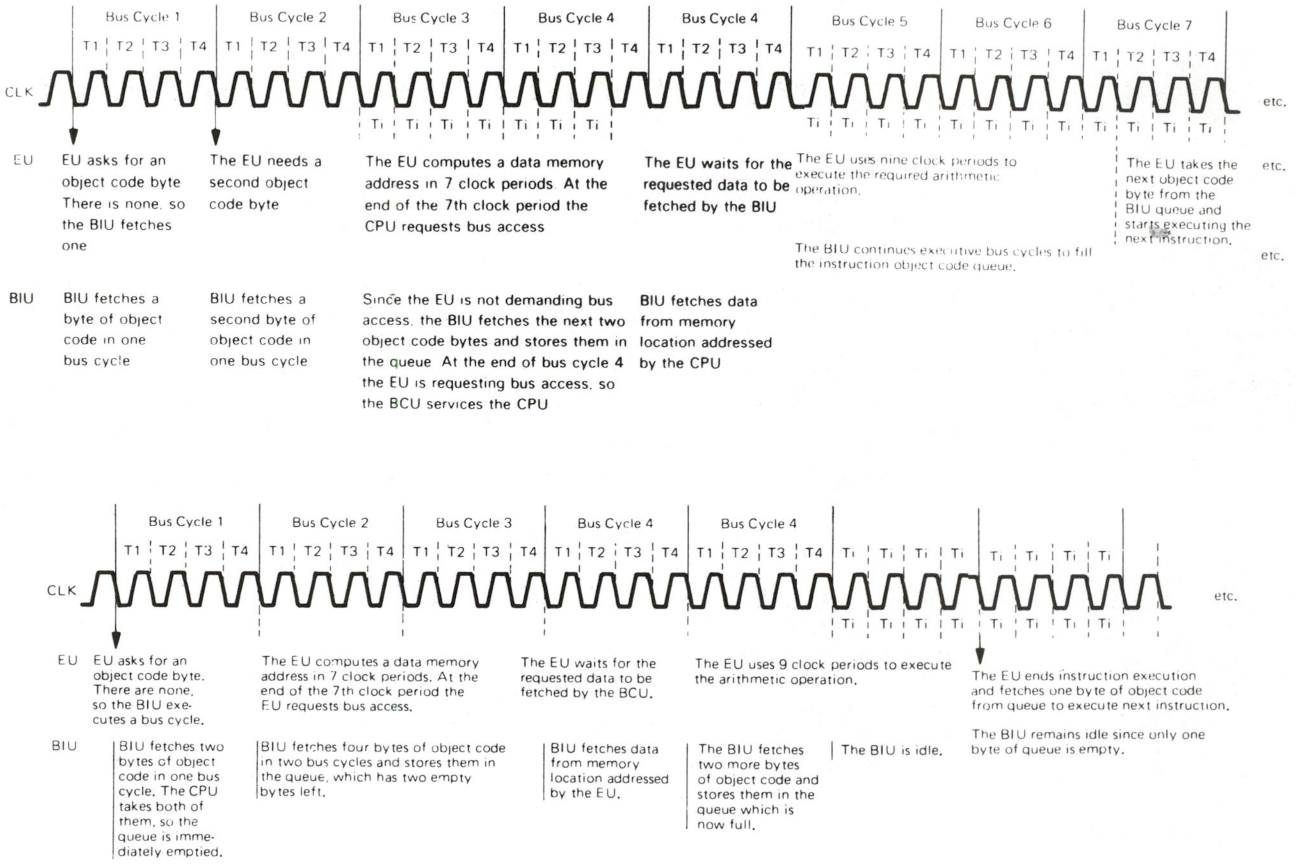

Figure 5.7 *(continued)*

struction and the datum both lie on an even-byte address boundary in memory so that advantage can be taken of the 16-bit data path. We should also note that the I8086 fetches instructions from memory and loads them into the instruction queue only when there are two or more empty bytes in the queue. The I8086, with a 16-bit data path to or from the BIU and asynchronous operation of the EU and BIU, will execute the same example instruction with the timing shown in Figure 5.7*e*.

BUS CYCLE TIMING

It is important to understand that bus cycles are entirely a BIU activity. As far as the EU is concerned, bus cycles do not exist. The EU knows about the BIU, but it does not know about the bus or bus cycles. EU activity is timed by a sequence of clock periods with no special groupings or numeric combinations.

On the other hand, the BIU groups clock periods into bus cycles *only* when data must be transferred to or from the processor. First priority is given to a bus cycle request from the EU. Second priority is given to filling the instruction queue. These priorities are not preemptive. If the EU does not need a bus cycle and the instruction queue is full, the BIU ceases executing bus cycles and a sequence of idle BIU clock periods occur.

The processor may have to wait for access to the bus because a previously initiated bus cycle has not completed. In Figure 5.7*e*, the EU required seven clock periods to compute the physical memory address of the operand datum. At this time the EU issued a data request to the BIU, but the BIU was in the midst of an instruction fetch bus cycle which it first finished and only then honored the EU request to fetch the operand datum. This example emphasizes that the priority for bus cycles is not preemptive.

Because the example we have just discussed is not atypical, it is correct to maintain that the I8086 has essentially eliminated instruction fetch time. About the only times that the EU will be forced to wait while the BIU fetches the next instruction is when a branch or a branch-on-condition instruction causes a branch out of the instruction sequences already in the instruction queue or when the memory accesses are so frequent that the BIU is unable to initiate bus cycles to prefetch instructions into the instruction queue (a second priority activity).

DEMULTIPLEXING THE I/O MEMORY BUS

The information on the time-multiplexed bus controlled by the BIU of the I8086/8088 must be separated into three constituent components: address, data, and control. The Intel Corporation markets both the I8282 chip and the I8283 chip, which accomplish this task for the I8088, with 8-bit data and 20-bit addresses as shown in Figure 5.8.

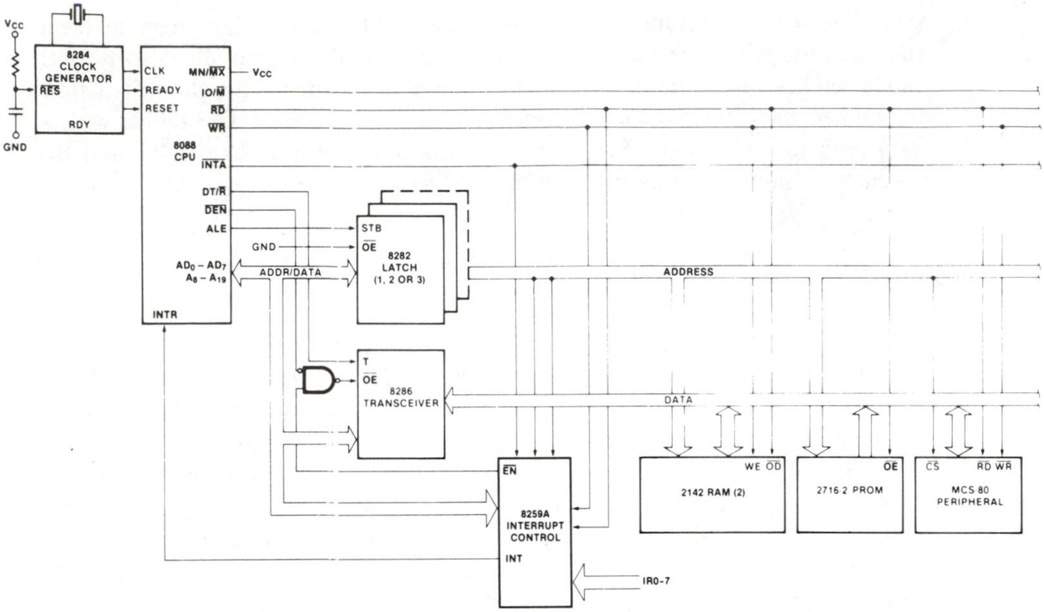

Figure 5.8 The time multiplexed I8088 bus signals can be demultiplexed onto the system's bus via an I8282 or I8283 chip. (Reprinted by permission of Intel Corporation. Copyright 1980.)

The equivalent bus demultiplexing task for the I8086 with a 16-bit data/20-bit address width additionally requires either the I8287 chip or the I8286 chip, which allow simultaneous access of odd–even address low-bit interleaved main memory banks. As shown in Figure 5.9, this allows the BHE and AO control signals to specify that a 16-bit datum is to be transferred to or from memory (a byte for each bank), or an 8-bit datum to be transferred from either single bank, or that no memory data are involved (an I/O operation is involved).

INPUT/OUTPUT TYPES

The design of the Intel 8086/8088 allows input/output through the accumulator, in which case overlap of the I/O function with the compute function is virtually impossible. I/O is also allowed via pseudomemory locations through a scheme that has become known as *memory-mapped* I/O, which will be described and discussed very shortly. Again, overlap of the I/O function with the compute function is virtually impossible. Additionally, I/O direct to or from memory is possible through the use of a second processor (sometimes specialized) that can access memory indepen-

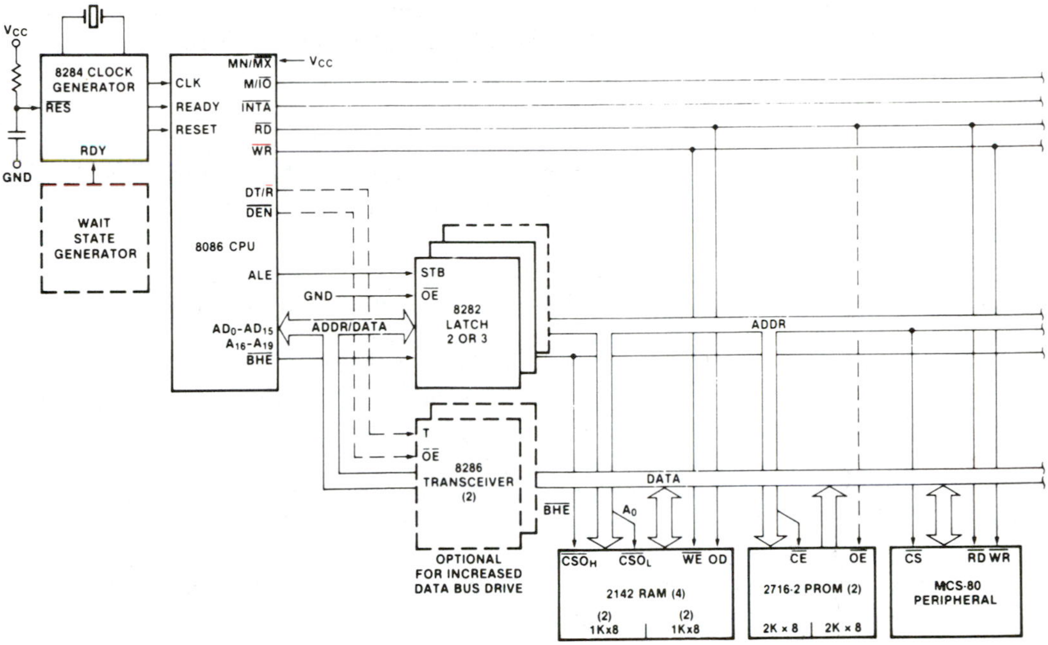

BHE	A0	Byte Transferred
0 (low)	0	Both bytes
0	1	Upper byte to/from odd address
1 (high)	0	Lower byte to/from even address
1	1	None

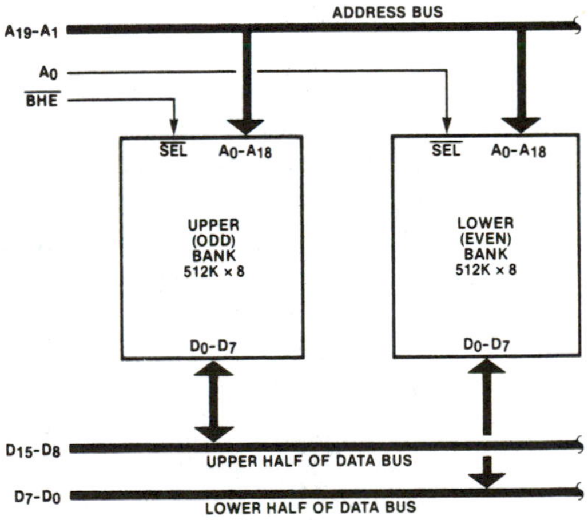

Figure 5.9 The I8086 time multiplexed bus information is demultiplexed onto the system's bus by the I8282 or I8283 chip. The use of the I8286 or I8287 chip to allow access of odd-even low-bit interleaved memory banks is also shown. (Reprinted by permission of Intel Corporation. Copyright 1980.)

dent of the I8086/8088 processor. This scheme is often termed *direct memory access* (DMA) and can be implemented via the I8089 I/O processor (which will be discussed in a subsequent chapter) or via other DMA processor chips.

Accumulator-Based I/O

Eight instructions are available for I/O to or from the AL (one byte) or AX (two bytes) accumulator register. We will discuss them in two groups:

```
IN      AL,PORTNO     (AL) ← (interface register)
OUT     PORTNO,AX     (interface register) ← (AX)
```

These instructions move a byte or a word of data from or to the AL/AX register to or from the I/O register in the interface permanently associated with the port number used as the immediate operand in the instruction.

```
IN      AL,(DX)       (AL) ← [interface register (DX)]
OUT     (DX),AX       [interface register (DX)] ← (AX)
```

These instructions act similarly to the previous instructions except that the port number of the interface I/O register must first be loaded into the DX register.

Memory-Mapped I/O

In this I/O scheme, certain specific memory locations do not exist but are physically wired to the interface of a peripheral device. Thus the I/O register of a device exists as a pseudomemory location and an access of that memory location via a MOV instruction results in device action. Consequently, an input port responds to any processor instruction that moves data from the "memory" location with that address and an output port responds to any processor instruction that moves data to the "memory" location with that address. The control aspects of the device interface must correspond to the control aspects of memory.

Any processor can employ memory-mapped I/O if the system fabricator attaches device interface I/O registers (ports) to the multiplexed bus in such a way that they respond to memory control signals and thus become pseudomemory addresses. The Digital Equipment Corporation pioneered the concept of memory-mapped I/O in small computers with their PDP 11, on which no special I/O instructions exist.

In certain instances it is possible to implement memory-mapped I/O on the I8086/8088 so that a device interface register (I/O port) increments from one "memory" location (address) to the next automatically. Such an arrangement would allow an applications programmer to choose between the following two code segments:

```
                        .
                        .
                MOV     CX,31
PUT_A_BYTE:     MOV     AL,(SI)
                INC     SI
                OUT     PORTNO,AL
                LOOP    PUT_A_BYTE
                        .
                        .
                        .
                        .
                MOV     CX,31
                CLD
        REP     MOVS    (DI),(SI)
                        .
                        .
                        .
                        .
```

This author is not convinced that significant advantages actually exist for memory-mapped I/O using the I8086/8088, compared to direct memory access I/O.

Direct Memory Access I/O

Although we will present a fuller explanation of DMA while discussing the I8089 I/O processor in a later chapter, a brief introduction is justified at this point.

A direct memory access channel is an arrangement of hardware that allows a device interface to transfer data rapidly directly to or from main memory without processor intervention. A DMA channel allows the processor to issue a single high-level command such as

```
READ PORTNO,MEM_ADRS,NO_BYTES
```

to indicate a sequence of low-level I/O events such as transferring individual bytes of data. This is accomplished by transferring data directly between an I/O device interface and memory without any processor work beyond initiating the transfer and noting its completion.

Ordinarily, the BIU (bus interface unit) of the processor is master of the multiplexed bus. The BIU provides the address and control signals for each transfer that takes place. However, a DMA channel has the logic temporarily to become master of the multiplexed bus to control the transfer of I/O data directly between the I/O port register in the peripheral device interface and a series of locations in main memory.

Because a DMA channel transfers data between the device and memory with no processor intervention after initiation, the transfer has no effect on the processor state (assuming that DMA data do not overwrite code or data being used by the executing program). The only effect of DMA operations on program execution is that instructions occasionally take a trifle longer because they must wait for a memory access. For example, suppose that a disk is able to transfer one byte of data every 8 microseconds and that main memory has a cycle time of 1 microsecond. The DMA channel could "steal" one memory cycle out of every eight to transfer disk data when and if the disk needed servicing. Seven memory cycles out of every eight would remain available for the processor to use in the worst of circumstance when the disk–memory data transfer is taking place at its maximum rate. In this example, the processor is slowed down by a maximum of 12.5%. The actual slowdown will probably be much less because of two very likely circumstances:

1. The DMA transfer of data between memory and disk will not occur continuously but will be intermittent.
2. The DMA channel may steal memory cycles that the processor had no use for —it did not need memory at that instant. For example, the processor may have been occupied in executing an instruction not requiring a memory access, such as a register-to-register multiply or divide.

I/O PROTOCOLS

The keyboard and light-emitting seven-segment diode display illustrated previously are very simple devices to control. Most peripheral devices require a more complicated control sequence, including some type of "hand-shake" protocol.

Device interfaces contain three types of information that are typically held in three registers.

1. A *data register* containing the data to be input to the BIU or a receptacle for the data to be output by the BIU
2. A *status register* containing an indication of when data are available to input or when the data register can receive data, whether or not errors have occurred, and other information about the device
3. A *control register* containing information used to initialize the mode of operation and to control the logical and physical characteristics of the date channel

All three registers are not always required or present. In some cases only the data register is present; in some cases the interface is automatically initialized when power is applied, thus rendering the control register unnecessary. A schematic of a typical interface is shown in Figure 5.10.

As an example of a simple I/O process, we will employ a common communications terminal consisting of a keyboard and a cathode ray display tube (CRT) or visual display unit (VDU). The combination input device and output device will employ an Intel 8251A programmable communication interface chip as its transducer to the I8086/8088 multiplexed bus (Figure 5.11). Data will be transmitted indepen-

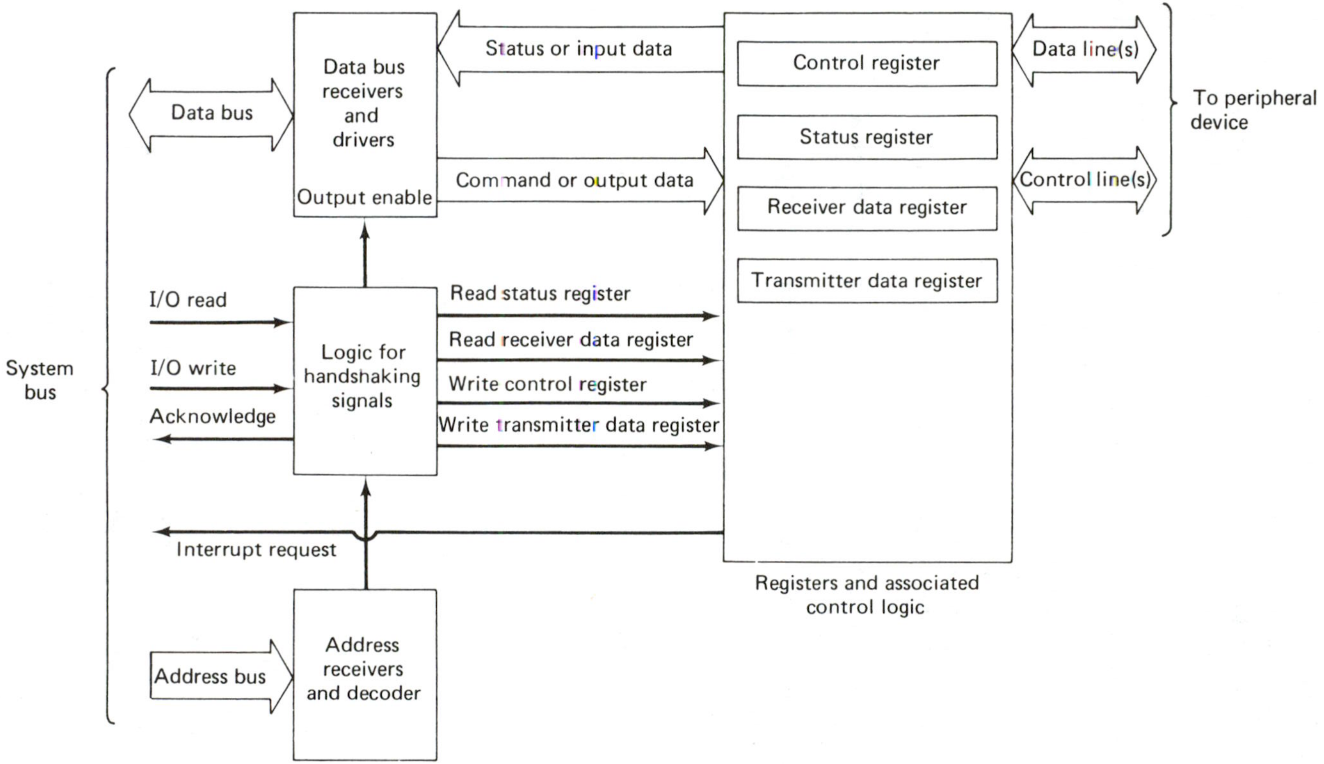

Figure 5.10 Schematic of a typical interface. (Reprinted by permission from G. Gibson and Y. Liu, *Microcomputers for Engineers and Scientists*, Prentice-Hall, Englewood Cliffs, N.J., 1980.)

dently one character at a time and will not be buffered at the keyboard/CRT terminal. This type of data transmission is often referred to a *serial input/output* (SIO). Note that we must be very specific in our example. This specificity is typical, as each device and interface has very specific and often unique transmission characteristics.

The I8251A SIO programmable interface chip requires that I/O commands and data be presented to it by the processor. The processor can use a register(s) for this purpose, or the stack may be used, or an area in memory pointed to by an address in a register or on the stack may be used. The last method is often termed a *task block* and is the common method employed by operating systems. We will keep our example very simple by using a register to contain the datum and another register to contain the command information.

The I8251A SIO requires three different input/output control specifications:

1. *Data path width*: 5-bit, 6-bit, 7-bit, or 8-bit characters are allowed. Our example will use 8-bit characters.
2. *Data transfer speed*: We will specify 9600 characters per second as the maximum rate.
3. *Handshake protocol*: We will have the processor ask the interface if data can be transmitted; that is, we will *poll* the I8251A in our example.

Thus we are implying that a program has certain functions to execute to accomplish the transfer of a character. It is usual to centralize the functions necessary to com-

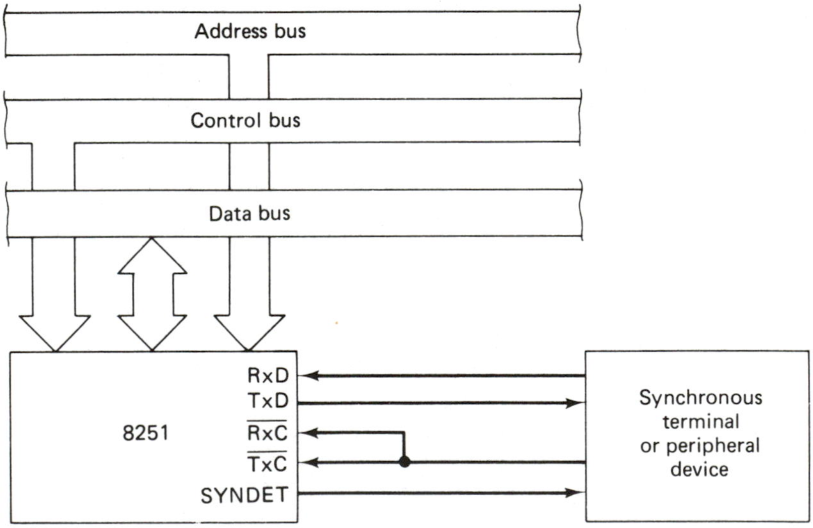

Figure 5.11 Two views of the Intel 8251A programmable communications interface (PCI) used as a bus/device interface. (Reprinted by permission from G. Gibson and Y. Liu, *Microcomputers for Engineers and Scientists*, Prentice-Hall, Englewood Cliffs, N.J., 1980.)

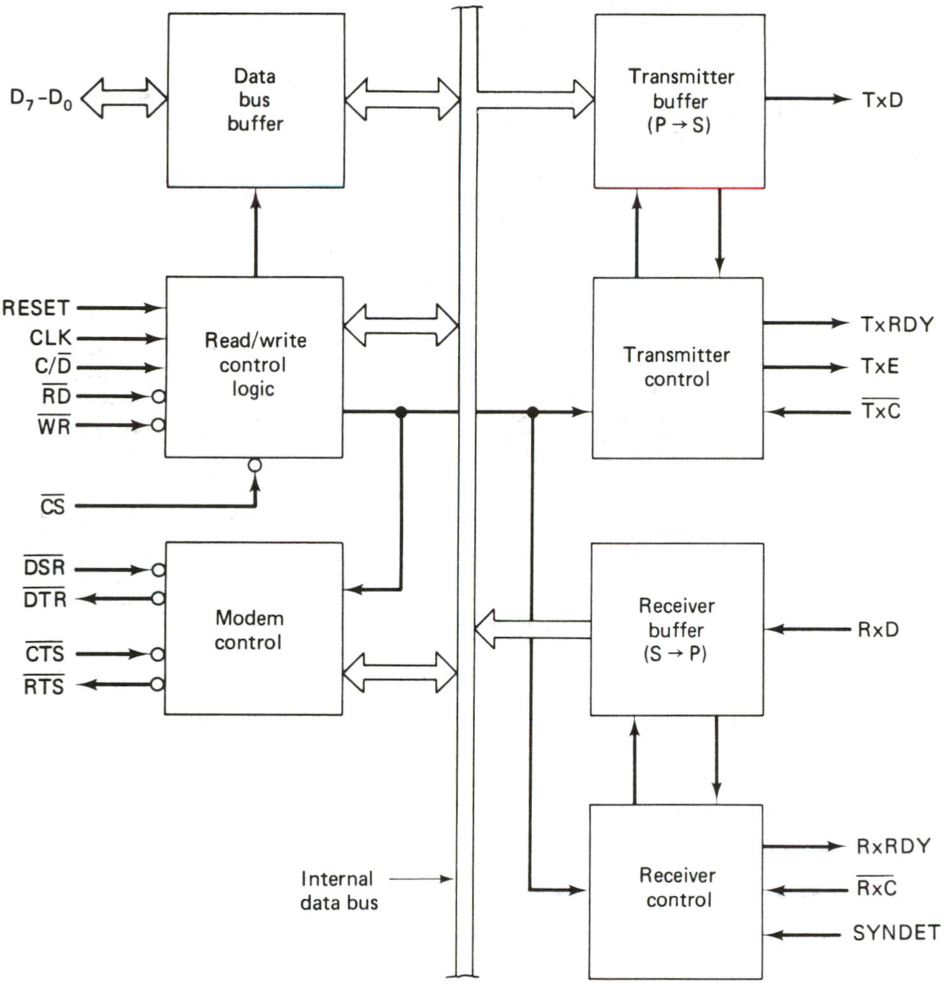

Figure 5.11 *(continued)*

municate with a device/interface pair into an *I/O driver* routine than can be used as needed by an applications program. Our example, therefore, will be directed toward designing and implementing an I/O driver routine for a keyboard-CRT terminal/I8251A SIO interface pair.

Our example terminal driver must first transmit control information to the interface (the I8251A) and receive status information from it before data can be transmitted (either input or output). We will need a two-byte initialization sequence: (1) a mode select byte, and (2) a command select byte. The specifications for these two pieces of information are shown in Figures 5.12 and 5.13. Upon completion of the data transfer, the status register will contain information, as shown in Figure 5.14.

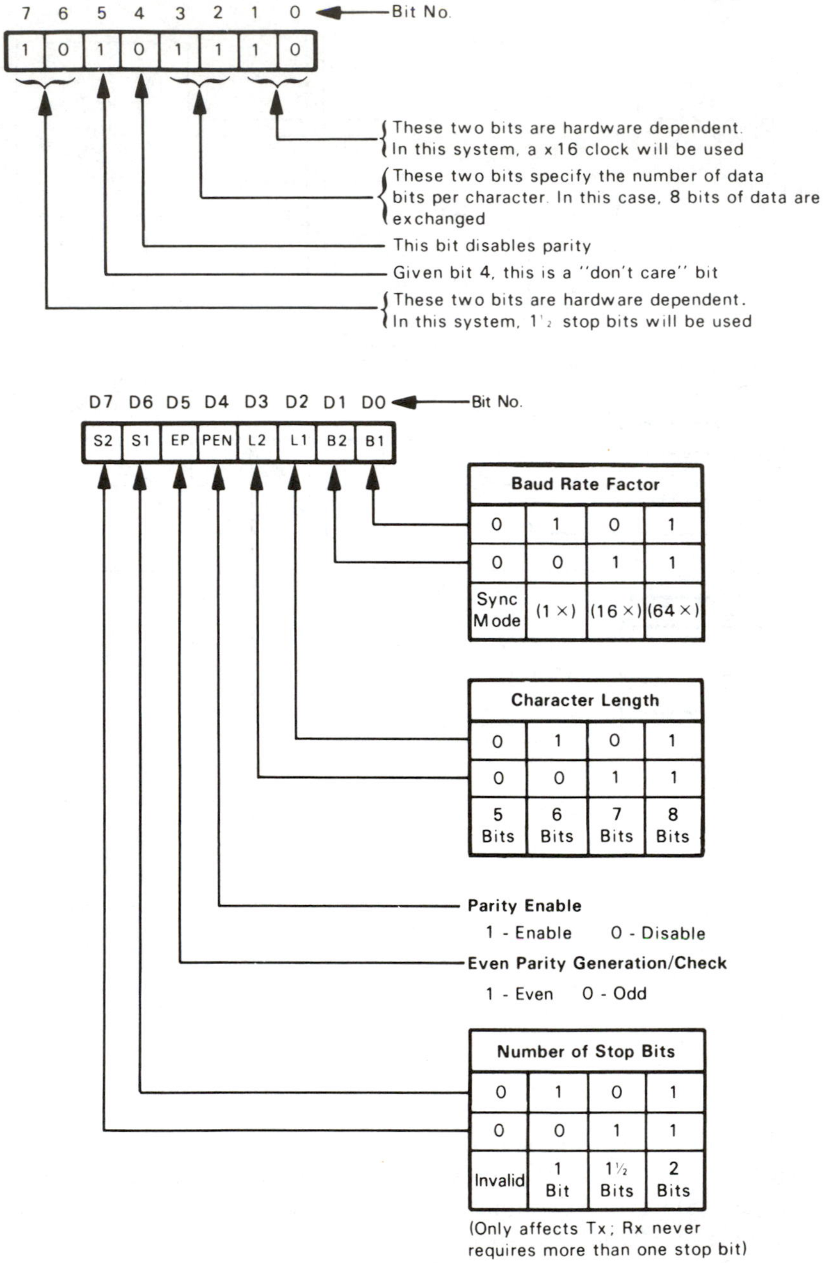

Figure 5.12 I8251A Programmable controller mode select byte. (*Top*) Example settings for input from the terminal keyboard. (*Bottom*) Meanings of bit settings. (Reprinted with permission from R. Rector and G. Alexy, *The 8086 Book.* Copyright Osborne/McGraw-Hill, 1980.)

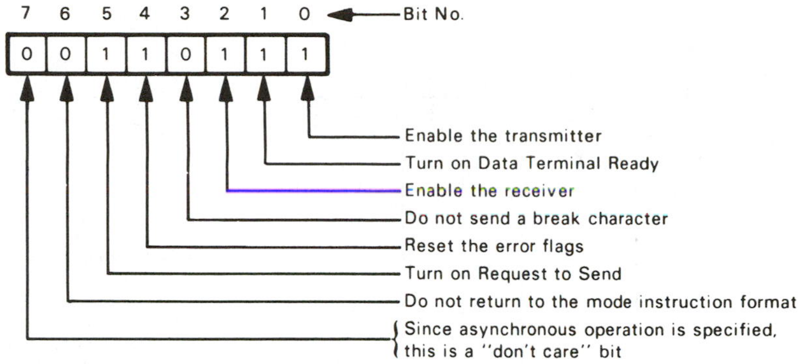

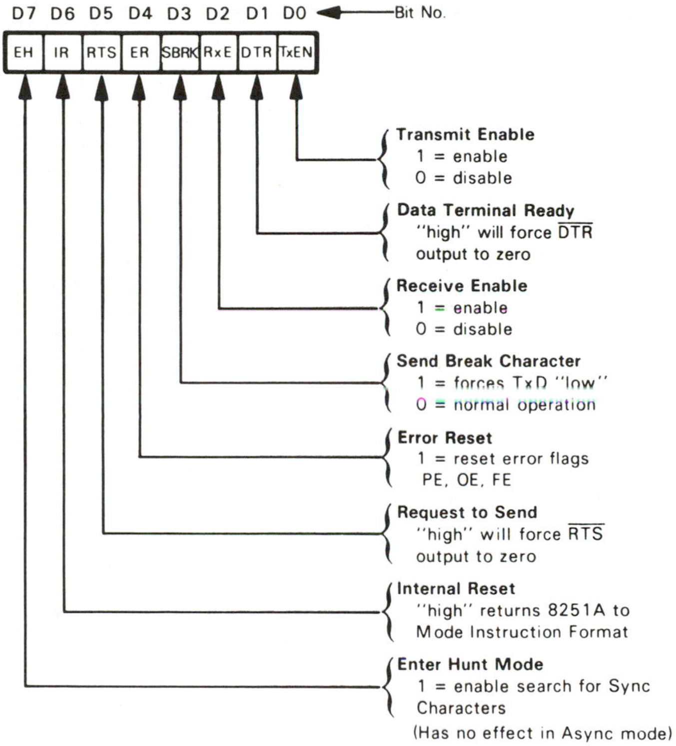

Figure 5.13 I8251A Programmable controller command select byte. (*Top*) Example settings for input from the terminal keyboard. (*Bottom*) Meanings of bit settings. (Reprinted with permission from R. Rector and G. Alexy, *The 8086 Book*. Copyright Osborne/McGraw-Hill, 1980.)

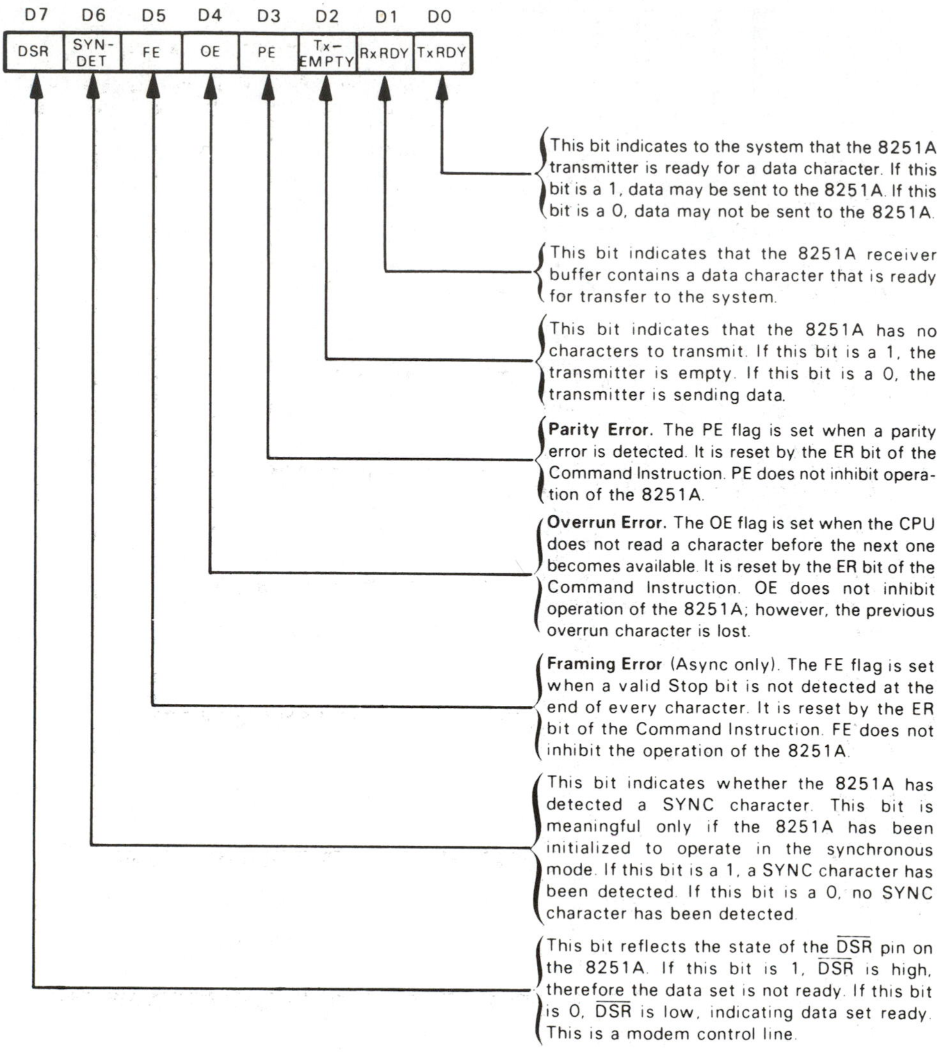

Figure 5.14 When a byte is read from the status port, the information in this figure is transferred to the system. (Reprinted with permission from R. Rector and G. Alexy, *The 8086 Book.* Copyright Osborne/McGraw-Hill, 1980.)

AN EXAMPLE OF A SIMPLE I/O DRIVER

We will first consider the initialization routine. In our example, shown in Figure 5.15, the parameters are made available to the initialization routine (are passed) via registers. Particularly note that the third line from the end defines a four-byte initialization string in order to provide for the possibility that the I8251A programmable controller for the keyboard/CRT terminal was in the command control input or the mode control input stage. The four-byte initialization sequence will correctly initialize the I8251A, regardless of its previous status.

Considering the routine to input a single character, note that a test is made for no character available (time-out return) and for serial input/output (SIO) errors. This routine, which is called by the initialization routine, is shown in Figure 5.16. Figure 5.17 shows the routine to output a single character. Note the close similarity to the input routine.

These primitive I/O driver routines to initialize, to input a single character, and to output a single character are suitable building blocks to construct I/O routines to input a string of characters or to output a string of characters. In these examples, shown in Figures 5.18 and 5.19, we will employ an input string task block

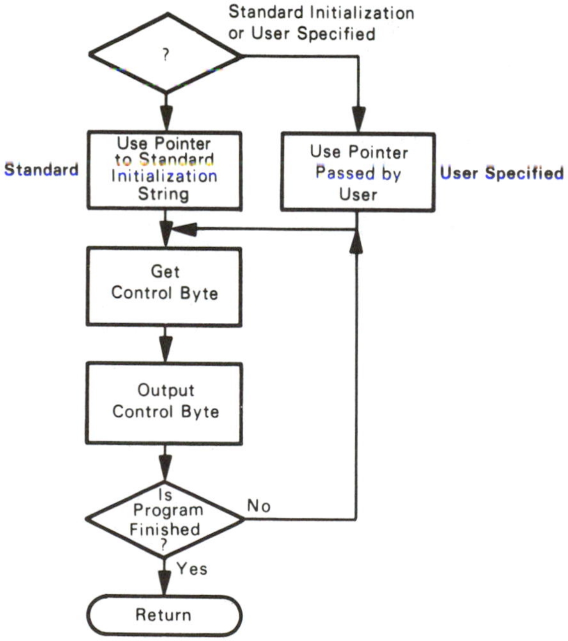

Figure 5.15 Initialization routine for I/O driver routines for an Intel 8251A programmable controller-keyboard/CRT terminal device interface pair for an I8086/8088 microcomputer system. (Reprinted with permission from R. Rector and G. Alexy, *The 8086 Book.* Copyright Osborne/McGraw-Hill, 1980.)

```
CONTROL$PORT                              EQU      12H
STATUS$PORT                               EQU      12H
DATA$PORT                                 EQU      10H

;   IF BIT 0 OF THE AH REGISTER IS 1, THE USER HAS LOADED SI WITH A
;   POINTER TO THE STRING TO BE SENT TO THE CONTROL PORT. IF BIT 0 IS A 0, A
;   STANDARD INITIALIZATION STRING WILL BE SENT
;

USER$INITIALIZATION$BIT                   EQU      01H
TIMEOUT$VALUE                             EQU      0F000H

;   BITS 3, 4, AND 5 OF THE SIO STATUS BYTE ARE ERROR BITS

SIO$ERRORS                                EQU      38H
;   BIT 1 INDICATES WHETHER OR NOT THE RECEIVER IS READY
;   BIT 0 INDICATES WHETHER OR NOT THE TRANSMITTER IS READY

SIO$RECEIVER$READY                        EQU      02H
SIO$TRANNY$READY                          EQU      01H
TIMEOUT$ERROR$FLAG                        EQU      0FFH

;   CARRIAGE RETURN IS TERMINATION CHARACTER FOR READ

CARRIAGE$RETURN                           EQU      0DH

;   '$' IS TERMINATION CHARACTER FOR WRITE

TERMINATION$CHARACTER                     EQU      24H
EXTRN SYSTEM$ERROR:                       FAR
```

```
CODE SEGMENT
  ASSUME CS: CODE

;   THE INITIALIZATION OPERATES BY:
;   1.  TESTING FOR USER SPECIFIED OR
;        SYSTEM INITIALIZATION STRING
;   2.  SENDING THE STRING TO THE CONTROL PORT,
;        TERMINATING WHEN A 0 IS DETECTED
;
;   THIS ROUTINE USES AX AND SI

INITIALIZATION       PROC   NEAR
                     AND    AH,USER$INITIALIZATION$BIT              ;TEST FOR USER INIT
                     JNZ    SI$LOADED$BY$USER
                     MOV    SI,OFFSET PORT$INITIALIZATION$STRING    ;LOAD STANDARD STRING
SI$LOADED$BY$USER:   LODSB
                     OR     AL,AL                                   ;SET FLAGS TO TEST FOR 0
                     JZ     DO$A$RETURN                             ;EXIT IF 0
                     OUT    CONTROL$PORT,AL
                     JMP    SI$LOADED$BY$USER

PORT$INITIALIZATION$STRING  DB       0CEH,40H,0CEH,37H,00H
DO$A$RETURN:                RET
INITIALIZATION              ENDP
```

Figure 5.15 *(continued)*

```
;   SINGLE CHARACTER INPUT OPERATES BY:
;   1.  LOADING TIMEOUT VALUE
;   2.  READING THE STATUS PORT AND TESTING FOR SIO ERRORS
;   3.  CHECKING FOR TIMEOUT ERRORS
;   4.  READING THE DATA
;
;   THIS ROUTINE USES AX AND CX
;
;   IF ZFLAG IS 1 ON RETURN - ERROR CONDITION
;   IF ZFLAG IS 0 ON RETURN - NORMAL OPERATION
;   ERROR CONDITIONS RETURNED IN AH

SINGLE$CHARACTER$INPUT      PROC    NEAR
                            MOV     CX,TIMEOUT$VALUE

TEST$STATUS:                IN      AL,STATUS$PORT              ;READ STATUS
                            TEST    AL,SIO$ERRORS               ;CHECK FOR ERRORS

                            JNZ     INPUT$ERROR$RETURN
                            DEC     CX                          ;CHECK FOR TIMEOUT
                            JZ      INPUT$TIMEOUT$ERROR$RETURN
                            AND     AL,SIO$RECEIVER$READY       ;RECEIVER READY?
                            JZ      TEST$STATUS

                            IN      AL,DATA$PORT                ;GET VALUE
                            RET

INPUT$ERROR$RETURN:         MOV     AH,AL                       ;SAVE STATUS
                            XOR     AL,AL                       ;SET ZERO FLAG
                            RET

INPUT$TIMEOUT$ERROR$
  RETURN:                   MOV     AH,TIMEOUT$ERROR$FLAG       ;FF IS TIMEOUT ERROR
                            RET

SINGLE$CHARACTER$INPUT      ENDP
```

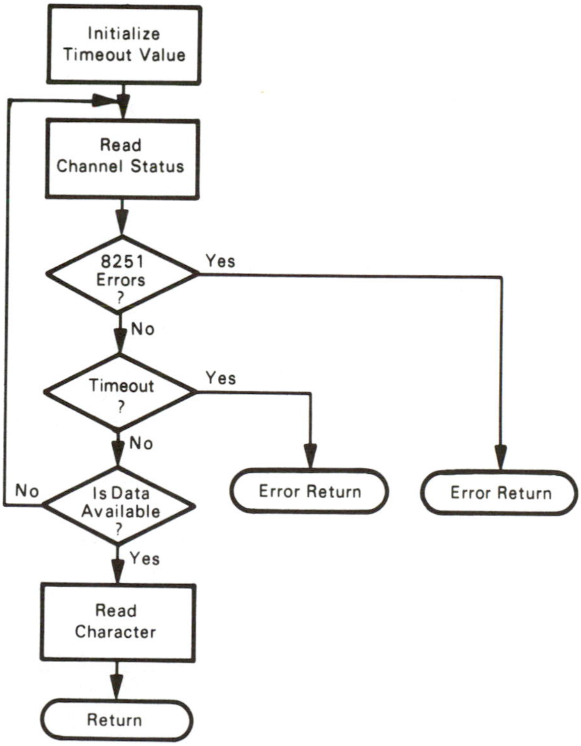

Figure 5.16 I8086/8088 I/O driver routine for inputting one character from an Intel 8252A programmable controller for a keyboard/CRT terminal. (Reprinted with permission from R. Rector and G. Alexy, *The 8086 Book.* Copyright Osborne/McGraw-Hill, 1980.)

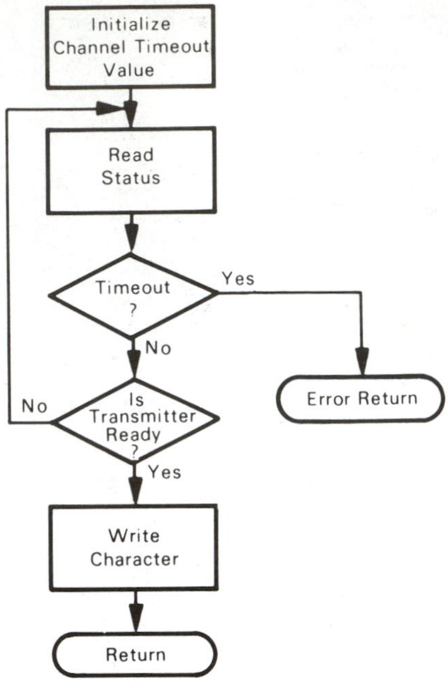

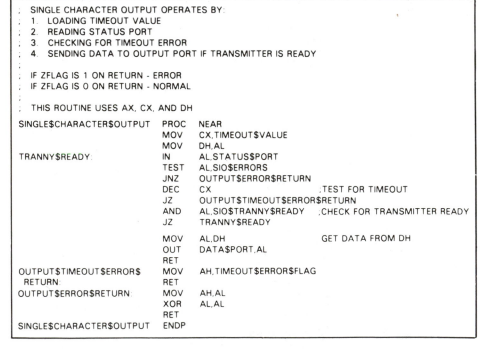

```
;  SINGLE CHARACTER OUTPUT OPERATES BY:
;  1.  LOADING TIMEOUT VALUE
;  2.  READING STATUS PORT
;  3.  CHECKING FOR TIMEOUT ERROR
;  4.  SENDING DATA TO OUTPUT PORT IF TRANSMITTER IS READY
;
;  IF ZFLAG IS 1 ON RETURN - ERROR
;  IF ZFLAG IS 0 ON RETURN - NORMAL
;
;  THIS ROUTINE USES AX, CX, AND DH
SINGLE$CHARACTER$OUTPUT   PROC   NEAR
                          MOV    CX,TIMEOUT$VALUE
                          MOV    DH,AL
TRANNY$READY:             IN     AL,STATUS$PORT
                          TEST   AL,SIO$ERRORS
                          JNZ    OUTPUT$ERROR$RETURN
                          DEC    CX                      ;TEST FOR TIMEOUT
                          JZ     OUTPUT$TIMEOUT$ERROR$RETURN
                          AND    AL,SIO$TRANNY$READY     ;CHECK FOR TRANSMITTER READY
                          JZ     TRANNY$READY

                          MOV    AL,DH                   GET DATA FROM DH
                          OUT    DATA$PORT,AL
                          RET
OUTPUT$TIMEOUT$ERROR$     MOV    AH,TIMEOUT$ERROR$FLAG
 RETURN:                  RET
OUTPUT$ERROR$RETURN:      MOV    AH,AL
                          XOR    AL,AL
                          RET
SINGLE$CHARACTER$OUTPUT   ENDP
```

Figure 5.17 I8086/8088 I/O driver routine for outputting one character to an Intel 8251A programmable controller for a keyboard/CRT terminal. (Reprinted with permission from R. Rector and G. Alexy, *The 8086 Book.* Copyright Osborne/McGraw-Hill, 1980.)

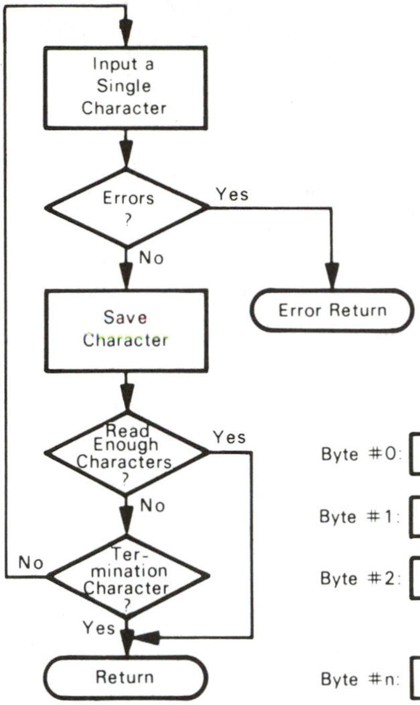

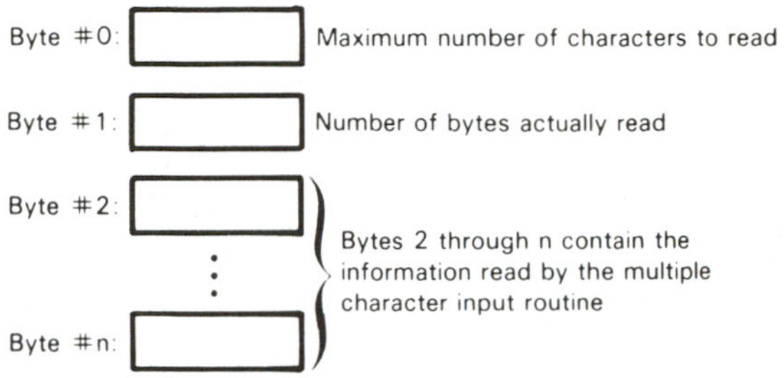

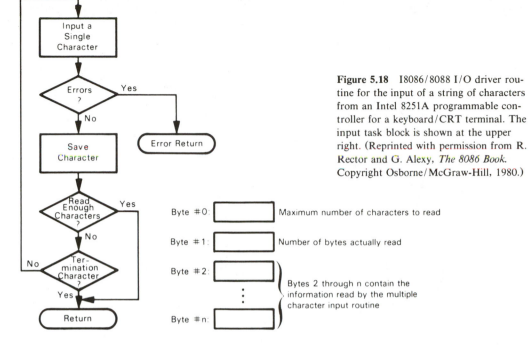

Figure 5.18 I8086/8088 I/O driver routine for the input of a string of characters from an Intel 8251A programmable controller for a keyboard/CRT terminal. The input task block is shown at the upper right. (Reprinted with permission from R. Rector and G. Alexy, *The 8086 Book.* Copyright Osborne/McGraw-Hill, 1980.)

```
CHECK$CHANNEL$STATUS       PROC   NEAR
                           IN     AL,STATUS$PORT             ;READ
                           RET
CHECK$CHANNEL$STATUS       ENDP
```

```
SEND$CONTROL$INFORMATION   PROC   NEAR
                           OUT    AL,CONTROL$PORT            ;WRITE
                           RET
SEND$CONTROL$INFORMATION   ENDP
```

```
;  MULTIPLE CHARACTER INPUT OPERATES BY:
;  1.  GETTING # OF BYTES TO READ
;  2.  CALLING SINGLE CHARACTER INPUT UNTIL
;      •  ERROR FROM SINGLE CHAR
;      •  THE MAXIMUM # OF CHARACTERS HAVE BEEN ENTERED
;      •  A TERMINATION CHARACTER (CARRIAGE RETURN) IS ENTERED
;  THIS ROUTINE IS CALLED WITH SI POINTING AT THE TASK BLOCK
;
;THIS ROUTINE USES SI, DI, AX, CX

MULTIPLE$CHARACTER$INPUT   PROC   NEAR
                           LODSB
                           OR     AL,AL                      ;LOAD MAX # OF BYTES TO READ
                           JZ     ZERO$COUNT$THEN$RETURN
                           MOV    DL,AL                      ;SAVE MAX # IN DL
                           MOV    DI,SI
                           INC    DI                         ;POINT AT BUFFER
GET$A$CHARACTER:           CALL   SINGLE$CHARACTER$INPUT     ;GET CHARACTER
                           JZ     INPUT$ERROR
                           STOSB
                           INC    BYTE PRT [SI]              ;INCREMENT # READ
                           CMP    DL,[SI]                    ;TEST FOR READ MAXIMUM #
                           JZ     ZERO$COUNT$THEN$RETURN

                           CMP    AL,CARRIAGE$RETURN
                           JNZ    GET$A$CHARACTER
ZERO$COUNT$THEN$RETURN:    RET
INPUT$ERROR:               JMP    SYSTEM$ERROR
MULTIPLE$CHARACTER$INPUT   ENDP
```

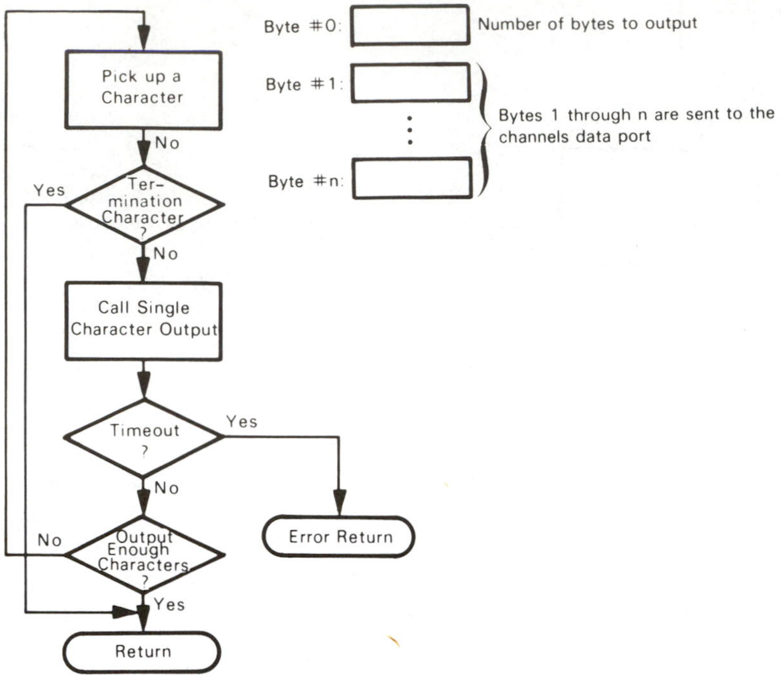


```
; MULTIPLE CHARACTER OUTPUT OPERATES BY:
;  1. GETTING THE NUMBER OF CHARACTERS TO WRITE
;  2. CALLING SINGLE CHARACTER OUTPUT UNTIL
;     • ERROR FROM SINGLE CHARACTER OUTPUT
;     • THE MAXIMUM # OF CHARACTERS HAVE BEEN WRITTEN
;
; THIS ROUTINE IS CALLED WITH SI POINTING AT THE TASK BLOCK
;
; THIS ROUTINE USES AX, SI, DX, AND CX
MULTIPLE$CHARACTER$OUTPUT   PROC    NEAR
                            LODSB
                            OR      AL,AL
                            JZ      DO$RETURN
                            MOV     DL,AL                       ;SAVE # OF BYTES TO
                                                                 OUTPUT
OUTPUT$A$CHARACTER:         LODSB
                            CMP     AL,TERMINATION$CHARACTER
                            JZ      DO$RETURN                   ;TEST FOR TERMINATION
                                                                 CHARACTER
                            CALL    SINGLE$CHARACTER$OUTPUT
                            JZ      OUTPUT$ERROR
                            DEC     DL
                            JNZ     OUTPUT$A$CHARACTER
DO$RETURN:                  RET
OUTPUT$ERROR:               JMP     SYSTEM$ERROR
MULTIPLE$CHARACTER$OUTPUT   ENDP
```

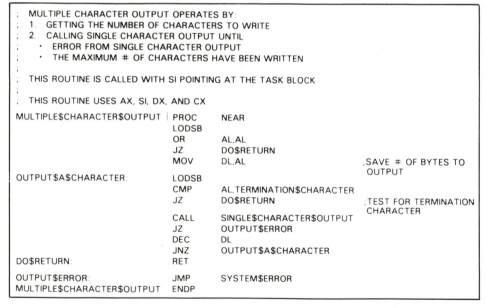

Figure 5.19 I8086/8088 I/O driver routine for the output of a string of characters to an Intel 8251A programmable controller for a keyboard/CRT terminal. The output task block is shown at the upper right. (Reprinted with permission from R. Rector and G. Alexy, *The 8086 Book.* Copyright Osborne/McGraw-Hill, 1980.)

and an output string task block. These routines must be called by the applications program, which must place the address of the task block in the SI register before the call. The input routine uses the SI, DI, AX, and CX registers, and the output routine employs the SI, AX, CX, and DX registers. The applications program should protect these registers (save them) before calling these routines and restore their values after the return.

GENERALIZING I/O DRIVERS

Considerations that must be taken into account when designing and programming an I/O driver include:

1. *Initialize the channel.* When power is applied to the system, the 8251A powers up in an unknown state. The I/O driver will put the channel into a known state.
2. *Input a single character.* When this function is requested, the driver reads the status port and waits until data are available, then the driver reads the data port and passes the information back to the system.
3. *Output a single character.* When this function is requested, the system must pass the character to be output, or a pointer to that character, to the driver. The driver reads the status port and waits until the transmitter is available. When the transmitter is available, the driver will transfer the specified character to the data port.
4. *Check the channel's status.* Perhaps the system does not need to read a character; rather, it needs to know if a character is available. Under such circumstances the system will read the status port contents.
5. *Send control information to the channel.* The system may need to alter the state of the channel, for example, to allow the channel to check for parity errors.
6. *Input a series of characters from the channel.* You may wish to input characters until some terminating condition is detected. For example, a carriage return may constitute a terminating condition, or a fixed number of characters may have to be input. Five numeric characters constitute a ZIP code, for example. The I/O driver will read data from the channel. This involves waiting for data to be available, then reading the information present at the data port while saving the data in a designated place in memory, then testing to determine if the terminating condition has been reached.
7. *Output a series of characters to the channel.* The system may wish to output a series of characters until a terminating condition is detected. Possible termination conditions might include either the detection of a predetermined end-of-string character or the output of a specific number of characters. The I/O

driver will test for the termination condition; if the terminating condition is not detected, the I/O driver will load data from a specified memory location and send the data to the channel.

NOTICING EVENTS WITHIN THE COMPUTER SYSTEM

In general, three types of events can occur in a computational system:

1. Those events whose occurrence is not only expected but whose timing in respect to the sequence of program instructions is known. We refer to these as *synchronous events* or as *time-expected events.* An example would be the input of a character using the example I/O driver shown in Figure 5.14.
2. Those events whose occurrence is expected at some time but the exact time in respect to the sequence of program instruction is unknown. We refer to these as *asynchronous events* or as *time-unexpected events.* An example would be the completion of an I/O via DMA.
3. Those events whose occurrence is not expected and, therefore, are a surprise both in terms of the event and in terms of its time in respect to the sequence of program instructions. We refer to these as *asynchronous events* or as *time-unexpected events.* An example would be a power failure or a divide by zero.

These three types of events are of two kinds: (1) those events that the program itself purposely creates at a known and specific point in the program code, and (2) those events that the program or the software system must react to that occur at an unplanned point in the program code.

Events of the first kind are equivalent to type 1 and will be disregarded for the rest of this chapter. Events of the second kind are equivalent to types 2 and 3 and will be the subject of our attention for the next several pages.

Two methods of detecting time-unexpected events are implemented in computers in two general ways:

1. *Software polling*: In this scheme the program is responsible for examining each possible interesting condition in order that a reactive routine may be invoked if necessary. This implementation technique places the entire responsibility for tracking events on the applications programmer and usually results in excessive overhead. It essentially prevents overlap of I/O and processing except in those cases where device timing is exactly known and the programmer calculates instruction timings and thus can interface the I/O–compute process intelligently. Although programmers were expected to know, be proud of, and use such techniques in the early days, current programmers have no desire, normally do not care about, and rarely program in this fashion. Figure 5.20 illustrates the device polling concept.

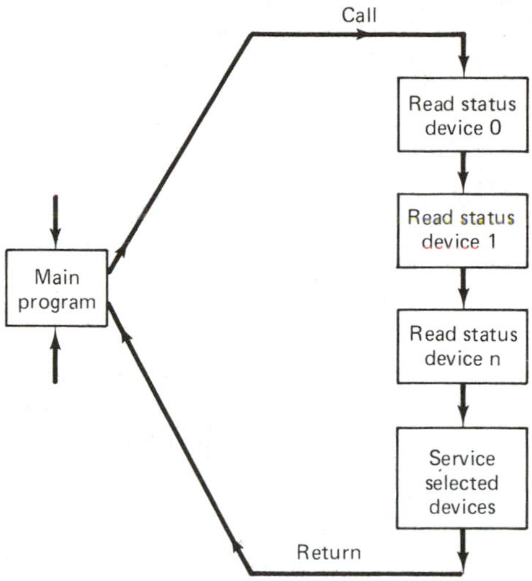

Figure 5.20 General schema for software polling of peripheral devices to determine the need for I/O service.

2. *Interrupt system*: An interrupt is a time-asynchronous hardware notation that an event has happened. This is usually accomplished by the setting of a flag (a flip-flop) by the event and the subsequent recognition of the flag "ON" condition by the control subsystem of the processor. The instruction cycle becomes a three-step loop:
   a. Fetch the instruction and update the program counter.
   b. Execute the instruction.
   c. Check for interrupt indicator.

Figure 5.21 may be helpful.

It should be obvious that an interrupt system simplifies programming, allows more efficient use of computational system resources, and speeds program execution. Interrupts may be serviced from any point in the program, as illustrated in Figure 5.22.

THE INTERRUPT STRUCTURE OF THE I8086/8088

The interrupt structure of the I8086/8088 computational system is based on a table of service routine addresses (the interrupt vector table) stored by the software in the first 1024 bytes of main memory. The purpose of the interrupt vector table is to contain the entry address of the various interrupt service routines. As each address must contain the 16 bits used to define the beginning of the code segment (used to "fill" the CS register) and the 16 bits giving the offset of the service routine from the start of the code segment (used to "fill" the program counter), the interrupt vector address is four-bytes long. Thus the I8086/8088 interrupt vector table allows for 256 distinct interrupts. Figure 5.23 details the structure of this table.

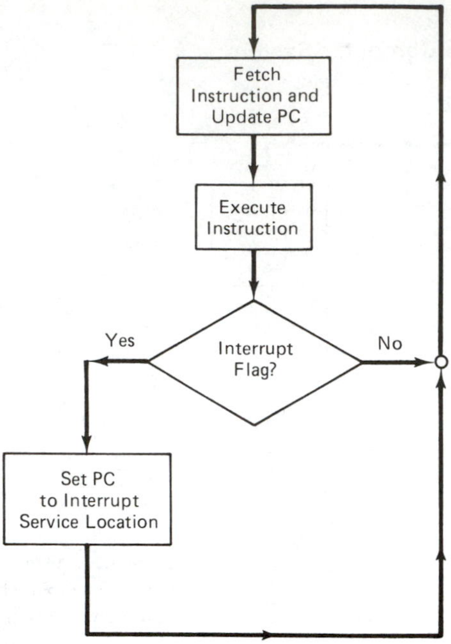

Figure 5.21 Instruction cycle of a processor with an interrupt system. Note that essentially no time is expended checking for an event but that the occurrence of an event forces, through hardware, a "subroutine" branch to a routine to react to the event with an eventual "return" to normal program processing.

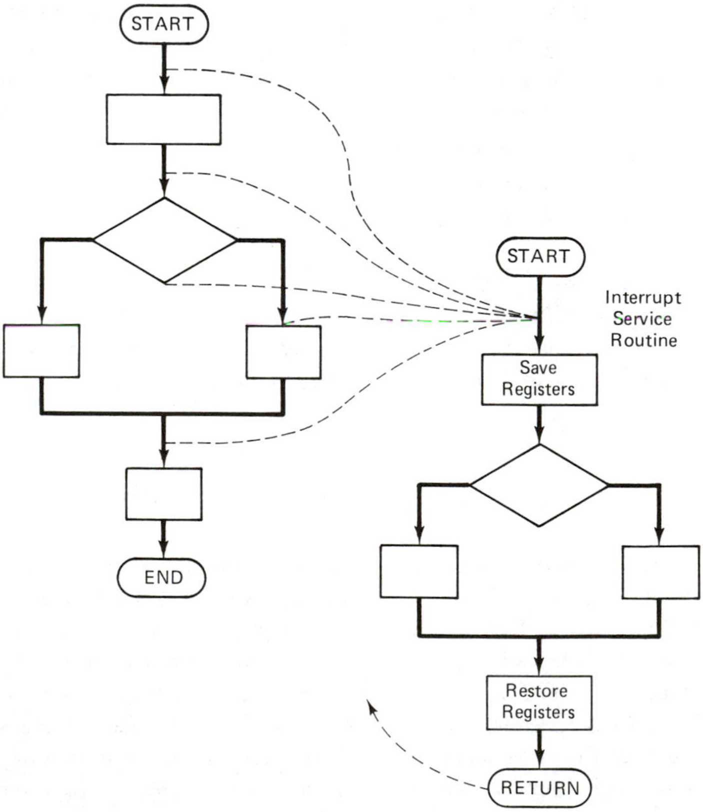

Figure 5.22 A program may be temporarily interrupted to service an interrupt event at many locations.

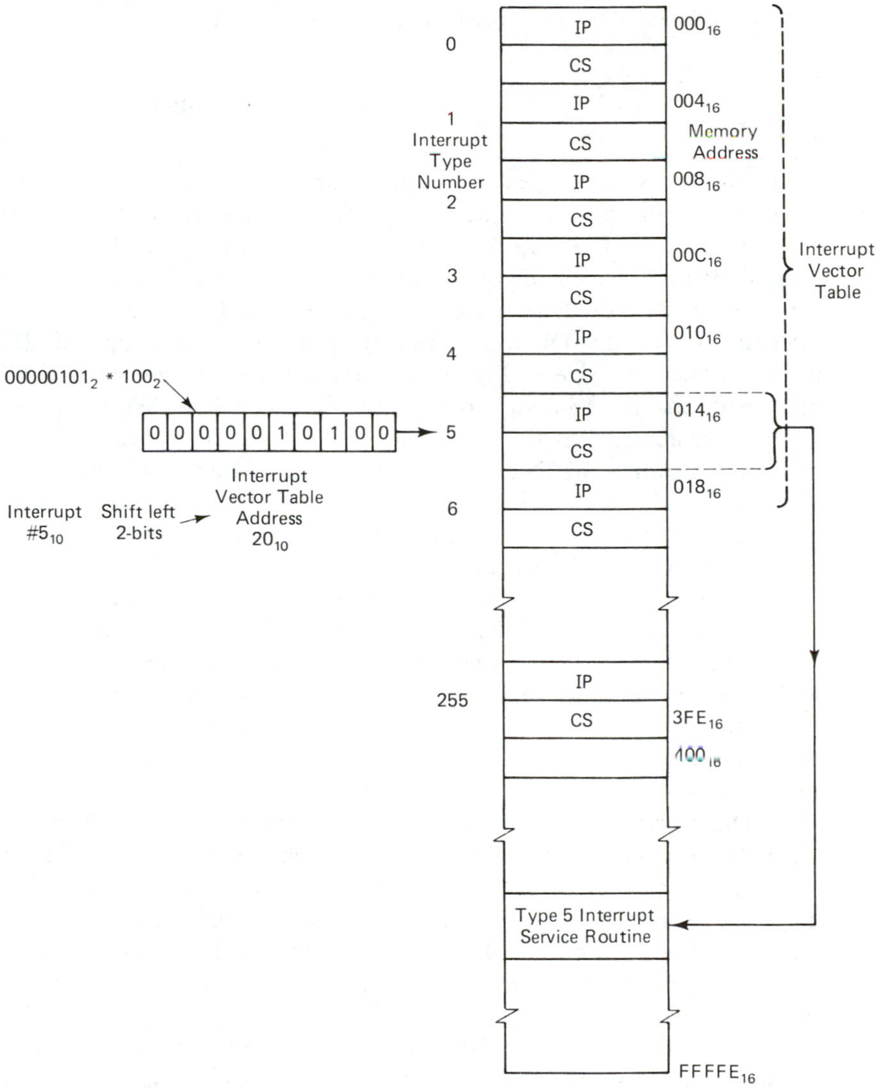

Figure 5.23 I8086/8088 interrupt vector table of 256 interrupt service routines in the first (low-address) 1K of main memory. (Reprinted by permission of Intel Corporation. Copyright 1980.)

We will now describe the interrupt acknowledgment sequence for the general case, that is, for interrupts number 32 through 255. Interrupts number 0 through 4 and software interrupts initiated by the break instruction

```
INT        nnn        ; nnn is interrupt number
```

(and thus an expected event at a known time in respect to the program code) are exceptions to this general sequence, which will be discussed shortly.

At the end of each instruction (with the exceptions of MOV to a segment register, POP to a segment register, and an instruction prefix such as REP), the interrupt request line of the processor (INTR = pin 18) is tested unless the disable interrupt instruction (DI) has previously set the mask interrupt bit (IF). As shown in the instruction cycle in Figure 5.19, the existence of an unmasked interrupt request will force the processor to enter an interrupt acknowledge sequence.

To guarantee that the interrupt request has been recognized, the device interface must maintain the INTR line until an interrupt acknowledge is received (INTA = pin 24 or S0, S1, S2 = pins 26, 27, and 28). The interrupt acknowledge signal may be delayed if an interrupt and a hold are requested while a locked instruction is executing in a multiprocessor system.

The interrupt acknowledge sequence consists of two bus cycles separated by two idle clock periods and thus occupies 10 clock periods. The first INTA bus cycle signals the device interface that an interrupt acknowledge sequence is in progress and allows the interface to prepare its interrupt number for transmittal. The interrupt number is transmitted to the processor during the second INTA bus cycle via the lower 8-bit lines of the data bus (AD0 to AD7) with the same timing as the read bus cycle illustrated in Figures 5.5 and 5.6.

The processor multiples the interrupt number by four (shift left 2 bits) to generate the absolute address of the interrupt vector (the address of the interrupt service routine in the interrupt vector table in low memory). Refer to Figure 5.23 for details. The four bytes of the interrupt vector contain the address of the interrupt service routine: bytes 0 and 1 are the offset within the segment, and bytes 2 and 3 are the beginning address of the code segment containing the interrupt service routine.

Next, the processor PUSHes the program status word onto the stack, resets the trap and interrupt flags, then PUSHes the current code segement register (CS) and program counter register (IP) contents onto the stack. Then the new CS register and (program counter) IP register contents are loaded from the interrupt vector table. The latter accomplishes a branch to the interrupt service routine with the stack holding the current address in the interrupted procedure for an eventual return. Note the resemblance of an interrupt service routine to a subroutine, with the distinct difference that the location is an absolute address determined by hardware design. Figure 5.20 may be helpful.

TYPES OF INTERRUPTS IN THE I8086/8088

Catastrophic Events

Interrupt 2, a nonmaskable interrupt, is reserved for pointing to an interrupt service routine to react to such events as a power failure or an operating system "watch-dog" timer reaching zero. The Intel documentation refers to this vector as being a NMI (nonmaskable interrupt).

Arithmetic Events

Interrupt 0, a nonmaskable interrupt, notes a divide-by-zero condition in the processor arithmetic-logic unit. Specifically, the divide-by-zero interrupt (interrupt 0) is requested as a portion of the standard divide instruction logic if the quotient exceeds the maximum value allowed by that instruction. This service routine normally should disable the interrupt system, replace the quotient with a logical substitute result, and reenable the interrupt system. As division by zero is undefined in arithmetic, determining a suitable substitute quotient is not always straightforward. This author suggests that three possibilities may be justified:

1. If the numerator was also zero, the quotient may logically be assigned a value of one, or
2. If the numerator was nonzero, the quotient may logically be assigned a signed value of the maximum allowable value, or finally
3. The program may be halted with an error condition noted—"divide by zero attempted at location XYZ."

Interrupt 4 occurs if, and only if, the overflow flag (OF) is set and the INTO instruction (trap to an overflow error service routine) is encountered. As this interrupt is specifically requested by the program, it is nonmaskable and is termed a *software interrupt*—that is, an interrupt invoked by the software at a time known in respect to the program code. The service routine should either: (1) substitute the signed maximum value, or (2) halt the program with an appropriate error message.

Device Interface Events

These maskable interrupts [via use of the CLI (disable interrupts) instruction] are generated by the interface chip of a peripheral device with a specific port number ranging from 32 base 10 through 255 base 10. The resultant action was discussed in some detail in the preceding section. The interrupt service routine would be specific for each device and presumably would be suitably reactant to the specific event. The addition of a new peripheral-device interface requires the design and coding of an interrupt service routine specific to that device.

Software Interrupts Supervisory Calls

A programmer may generate an interrupt by executing the instruction

```
INT    nn
```

where nnn is the entry in the interrupt vector table containing the address of the software interrupt service routine that will perform some desired or necessary action for the program. Software interrupts may be numbered from 32 base 10 through 255 base 10 and are maskable by use of the CLI instruction. Note that the device interface event interrupts and the software interrupts employ the same entry numbers in the interrupt vector table; therefore, the system designer should take care not to employ a vector entry number for a software interrupt that is being employed for a peripheral-device interface interrupt.

Software interrupts are extremely useful (almost vital) in constructing an operating system. As the prime example, most operating systems and procedural-level languages prevent the applications programmer from directly using I/O instructions and require that the program request such I/O services from the operating system. Thus the FORTRAN statement "READ (5,10) Variable" would be translated to INT #, where # is the vector entry of the software interrupt service routine that will actually input the value of the variable from the peripheral device interface corresponding to unit 5 according to the format specifications in statement 10. In actuality, the value will probably be transferred from an operating system prefilled buffer corresponding to the device.

Note that the INT nnn instruction contains the interrupt vector number in the instruction stream (acquired from the instruction queue). Thus the processor does not have to acquire this information from an interface via the multiplexed bus, and two bus cycles (10 clock cycles) are not expended for software interrupts that are expended for device interface event interrupts. Also note that software interrupts are specifically requested by the program, are maskable, and are invoked by the software at a time known in respect to the program code.

Breakpoints

The instruction INT 3 invokes the nonmaskable software interrupt 3 that is often employed by programmers during code debugging to locate errors and dump the contents of certain registers as an aid to perfecting a problem solution. As the INT 3 instruction translates into a single-byte instruction, it may be substituted for any other instruction in memory without major program alterations. As no bus cycles are required to acquire the interrupt vector entry number, the timing execution of the program up to the breakpoint is not affected and thus is not a factor for consideration during debugging using this breakpoint method. Presumably, the breakpoint software service routine would display the register contents and invoke a "wait state" that is terminable in some way.

Single-Step Interrupts

This maskable interrupt (1) is invoked by setting the trap flag (TF) in the program status word and is employed during debugging in order to execute a program one instruction at a time. The service routine can provide various diagnostic capabilities, such as display the register contents, and then enter a "wait state" that is terminable in some way, resulting in the next instruction being executed normally or in the single-step state depending on the setting of the trap flag (TF).

To invoke the single-step software interrupt, execute the following instruction sequence to set the trap flag:

```
PUSH    PSW
AND     (SP),0100H    ; set TF
POP     PSW
```

which will set to "ON" the trap flag bit (bit 8) in the program status word and result in a single-step interrupt request at the end of the next instruction's execution.

When the single-step interrupt request is acknowledged by the processor, the trap flag is cleared to "OFF" to ensure that the single-step interrupt service routine is not executed in the single-step mode. TF will remain set to "ON" in the program status word on the stack. If the service routine returns to the invoking code via an IRET (return from interrupt) instruction, the program status word will be restored from the stack and the single-step mode will remain in effect. If the service routine returns to the invoking code via a RET (return from subroutine) instruction, the program status word will not be restored and the single-step mode will be terminated. The single-step service routine should be designed to request directions from the console relative to which return to employ.

Reserved Interrupt Entries

Interrupt vector table entries 5 through 31 are reserved by the Intel Corporation for possible hardware enhancements or for use in their proprietary software. The use of these vector entry numbers is not recommended by the Intel Corporation, as it may result in a system becoming incompatible with possible future hardware and/or software enhancements or new products. For example, the new I186 and I286 systems use interrupt entry 5 to indicate "out-of-bounds" indexing into an array, as described in Chapter 12.

INTERRUPT PRIORITY

Every interrupt service routine should protect the program that was interrupted by saving the contents of any registers that it will use before such contents are destroyed and restoring these registers before returning (usually via an IRET instruction) to the interrupted program. This "protection" scheme is shown in the generalized flow diagram of an interrupt service routine in Figure 5.24. If the interrupt service routine should *not* be interrupted during execution, the interrupts should not be reenabled after the registers are saved and disabled just before they are restored. Of course, the interrupt system must be enabled before returning to the interrupted program.

Interrupt Priorities in the I8086/8088

In the noninterruptible interrupt service routine logic flow shown on Figure 5.24, the interrupt currently being serviced has absolute highest priority—with the exception of the nonmaskable interrupts catastrophic event, 2; divide by zero, 0; overflow

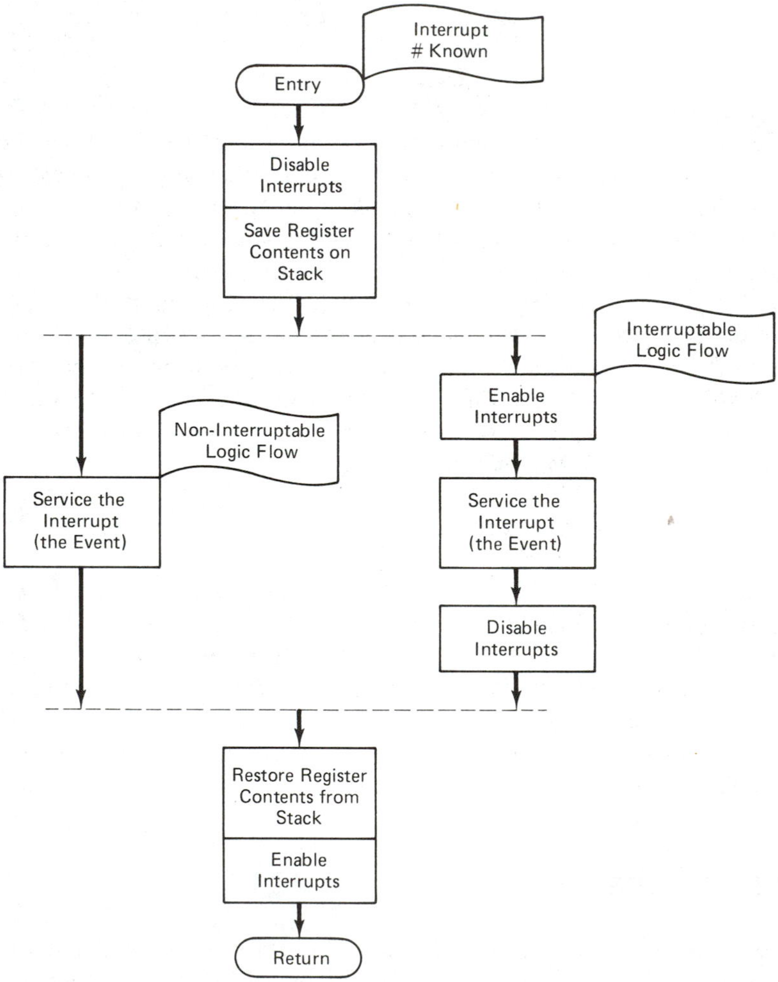

Figure 5.24 Interrupt service routine logic diagram.

4; and breakpoint, 3. At the conclusion of the service routine, the next-occurring interrupt will be serviced (with absolute highest priority).

In the interruptible interrupt service routine logic flow shown in Figure 5.24, an interrupt service routine can be interrupted by the occurrence of another interrupt. In this scheme, the last occurring interrupt will have highest priority. Although there are many situations where this result is perfectly satisfactory, it is easy to imagine other situations where this might seriously degrade system performance. The worst case might occur if a particular condition (interrupt event) continued rapidly to generate an interrupt request and thus caused repeated invocations of an interrupt service routine during the execution of the service routine. The consequent PUSHing of the registers (in order to save their contents and to provide a return address) would rapidly consume the available stack space, cause stack overflow, and result in a system crash. The more common situation presupposes that certain events causing an interrupt are "more important" than other events and thus should be given a higher priority for servicing.

The Intel Corporation markets the I8259A priority interrupt controller, which allows the system designer to define a fully ordered priority scheme for multiple external-device-interface event-generated interrupt requests. Figure 5.25 illustrates the chip and Figure 5.26 shows a possible configuration containing three I8259A chips to prioritize interrupt request signals from more device interfaces than one chip could accomplish. Figure 5.26 also illustrates the use of the I8286 and I8782 chips

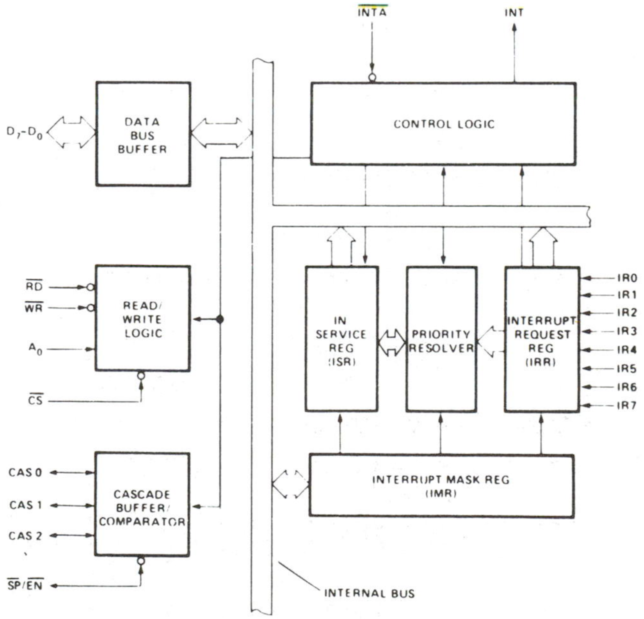

Figure 5.25 Schematic of the I8259A priority interrupt controller. (Reprinted by permission of Intel Corporation. Copyright 1980.)

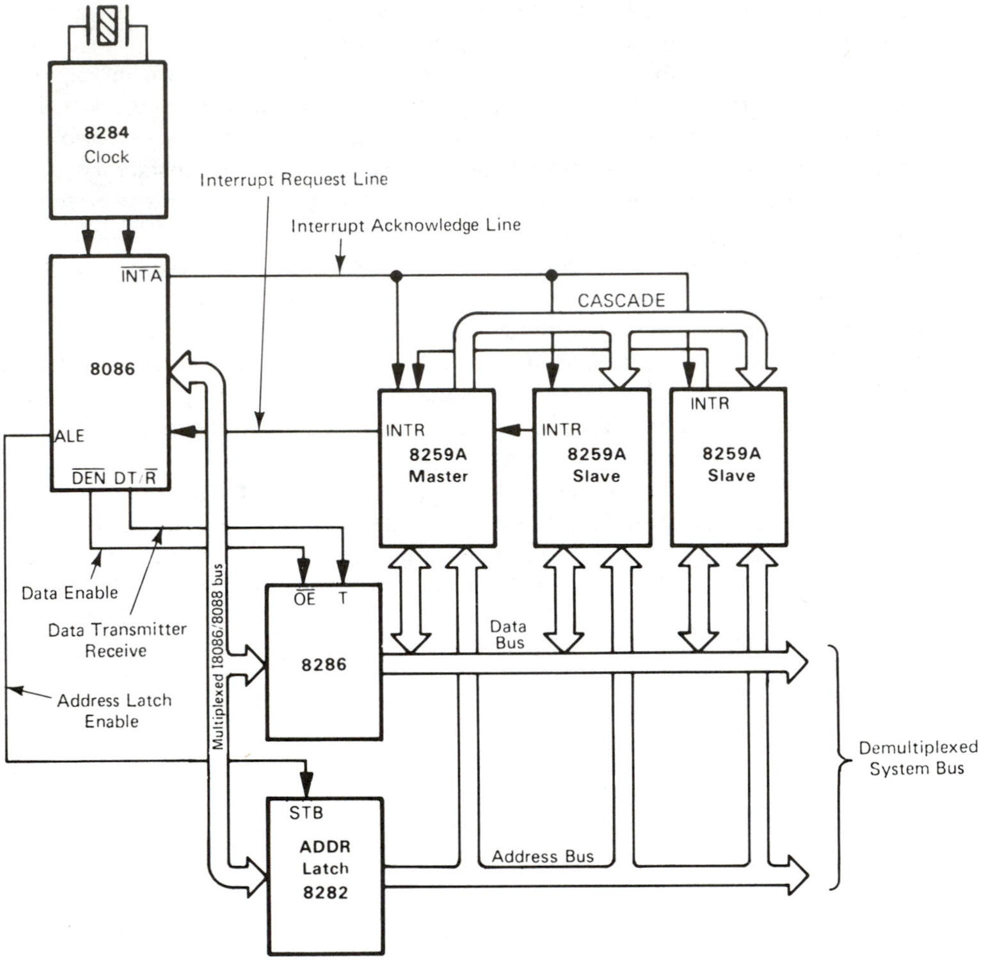

Figure 5.26 Cascade of three I8259A priority interrupt controllers configured on the demultiplexed system bus. (Reprinted with permission from R. Rector and G. Alexy, *The 8086 Book.* Copyright Osborne/McGraw-Hill, 1980.)

to "demultiplex" the data signals from the address signals of the I8086/8088 multiplexed bus onto a demultiplexed system base. The I8284 clock chip is also shown.

DIRECT MEMORY ACCESS

As discussed briefly earlier in this chapter, a DMA channel allows the processor to request an I/O sequence to be accomplished while the processor continues execution of the program. Because the I/O transfer is directly between the device and memory, bypassing the processor, the bus interface unit (BIU) of the processor must relinquish control of the bus to the DMA channel controller intermittently as each byte or word is transferred. Additionally, logic is required to count the number of bytes/words transferred and to appropriately increment the memory address. Finally, the finish of the block transfer must be recognized and the processor notified via an interrupt.

The general arrangement of this DMA control logic within a computational system is illustrated in Figure 5.27, with additional details given in Figure 5.28. Note that the controller accepts I/O action parameters from the executing program, which then continues normal processing. The controller interprets these parameters (device identification, which may include track/sector information, main memory starting address, block length, and word/byte mode) and accomplishes the data transfer by capturing the systems bus for each byte/word movement, after which it relinquishes the bus, increments the main memory address, and decrements the count. At the completion of the block transfer, the processor is notified via an interrupt.

It is necessary to emphasize that the program employing a DMA channel data transfer is proceeding with the execution of its instructions independently of the transfer. Referring to the program schematic on the left of Figure 5.27, it would be disastrous if the program used "data" in calculations before such data had been delivered to memory via the independently executing DMA. Thus the program design-

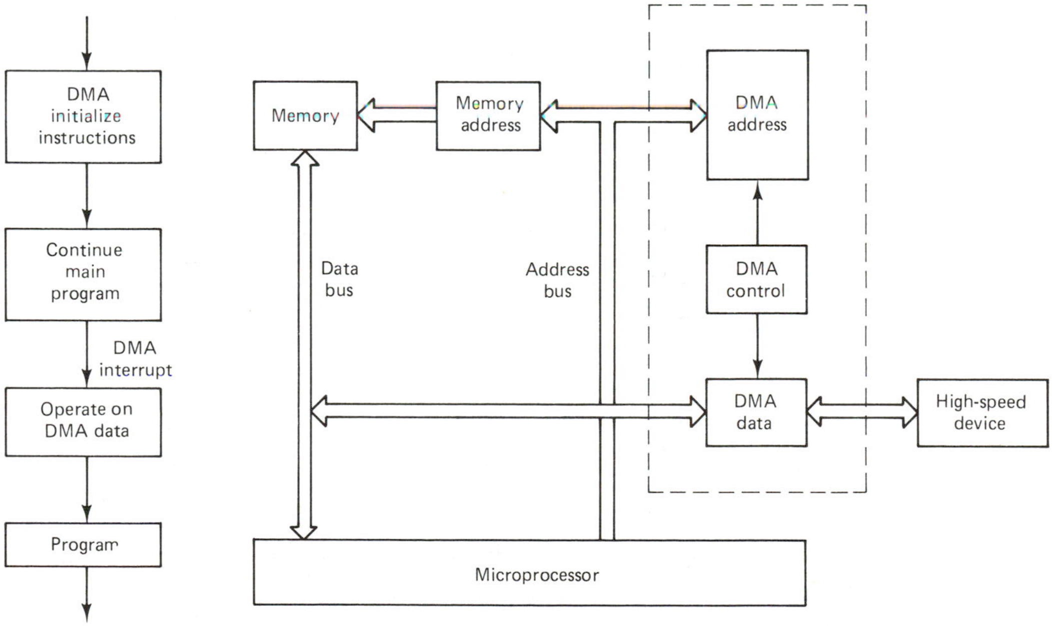

Figure 5.27 Interconnection logic of direct memory access controller (DMA). A short pseudolanguage section of a program employing DMA for input is also shown.

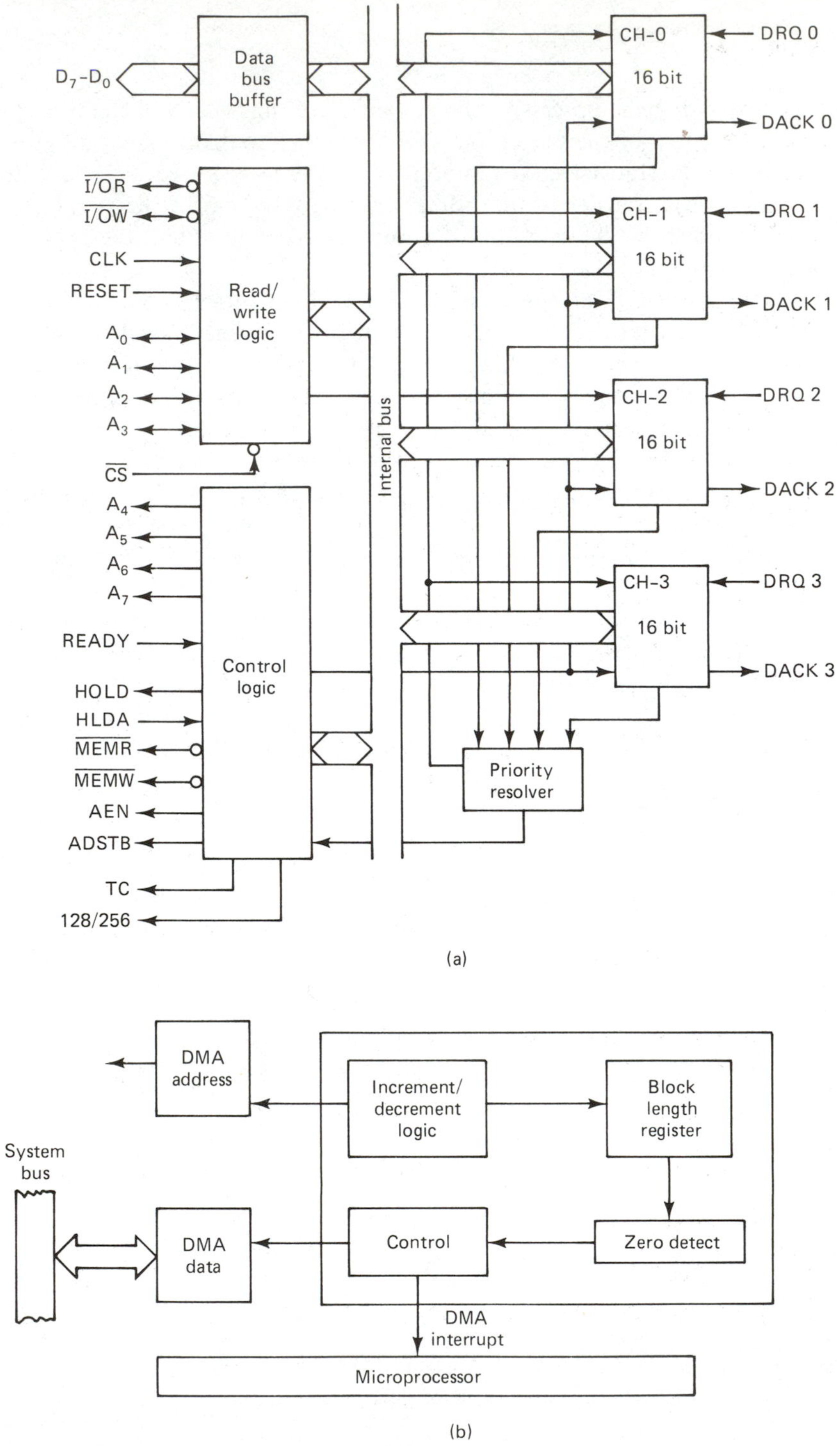

(a)

(b)

Figure 5.28 Block diagram of the I8257A programmable DMA controller (*top*) and a schematic of its placement in a system (*bottom*).

er must be aware of such a possibility and insert a "wait for DMA completion interrupt" at appropriate places in the program. Note that the analogous situation can occur during a DMA output operation. The generic name for this situation of two (or more) independent, but interdependent procedures executing simultaneously is *co-routines.* We will examine this fairly common concept when we discuss the I8089 input/output processor in Chapter 8.

DATA TRANSMISSION

Up to this point, we have considered transferring data in a parallel mode—that is, one line for each bit to be transmitted, as illustrated on the bottom of Figure 5.29. Notice that an entire datum can be transmitted in one time unit but that 4 signal lines are required to transfer a hexadecimal digit, 7 lines for an ASCII character, 8 lines for a byte, and 16 lines for a word.

On the other hand, some I/O devices require that they receive/transmit data in the bit-serial transmission mode. Thus a system of logic must be employed to transform data to/from the parallel transmission mode of the system bus from/to the bit-serial mode often required.

Let us consider a device transmitting a stream of bits to another device that must receive them one bit at a time. Each time the clock of the sending device "beats," a bit is sent; each time the clock of the receiving device beats, a bit is received. If the two clocks "drift" too far out of time synchronization, a bit will be lost. In some cases, the receiving device can adjust its clock to the rate of the sending device clock; in other cases, this is not attempted.

If the transmitting and receiving device clocks are not synchronized, the rate of drift makes it impossible to transfer more than 10 or 15 bits correctly before a bit is "missed." For this reason, asynchronous transmission is one character at a time with a start bit, a stop bit (often two stop bits), and sometimes an error-detecting parity bit. This asynchronous mode of data transmission is illustrated in Figure 5.29. Double-bit errors cannot be detected and error correction is impossible. For this reason, many asynchronous transmission schemes transmit each character back to the sender for comparison and retransmission if the comparison fails—indicating an error.

If the transmitting and receiving device clocks are synchronized, it is possible to transmit correctly a fairly long stream of characters in bit-serial mode. Thus a message or packet can contain many characters, including error-correcting codes. Such messages are preceded by clock synchronizing characters (usually two). Thus synchronous transmission allows multicharacter messages and can allow fairly sophisticated error-correcting techniques.

As would be expected, many corporations market chips to accomplish parallel-to-serial data transduction and bit-serial data receive/transmit in either the asynchronous or the synchronous modes. These are termed the *UART* (universal asynchronous receiver/transmitter), illustrated in Figure 5.30, and *USART* (universal synchronous/asynchronous receiver/transmitter).

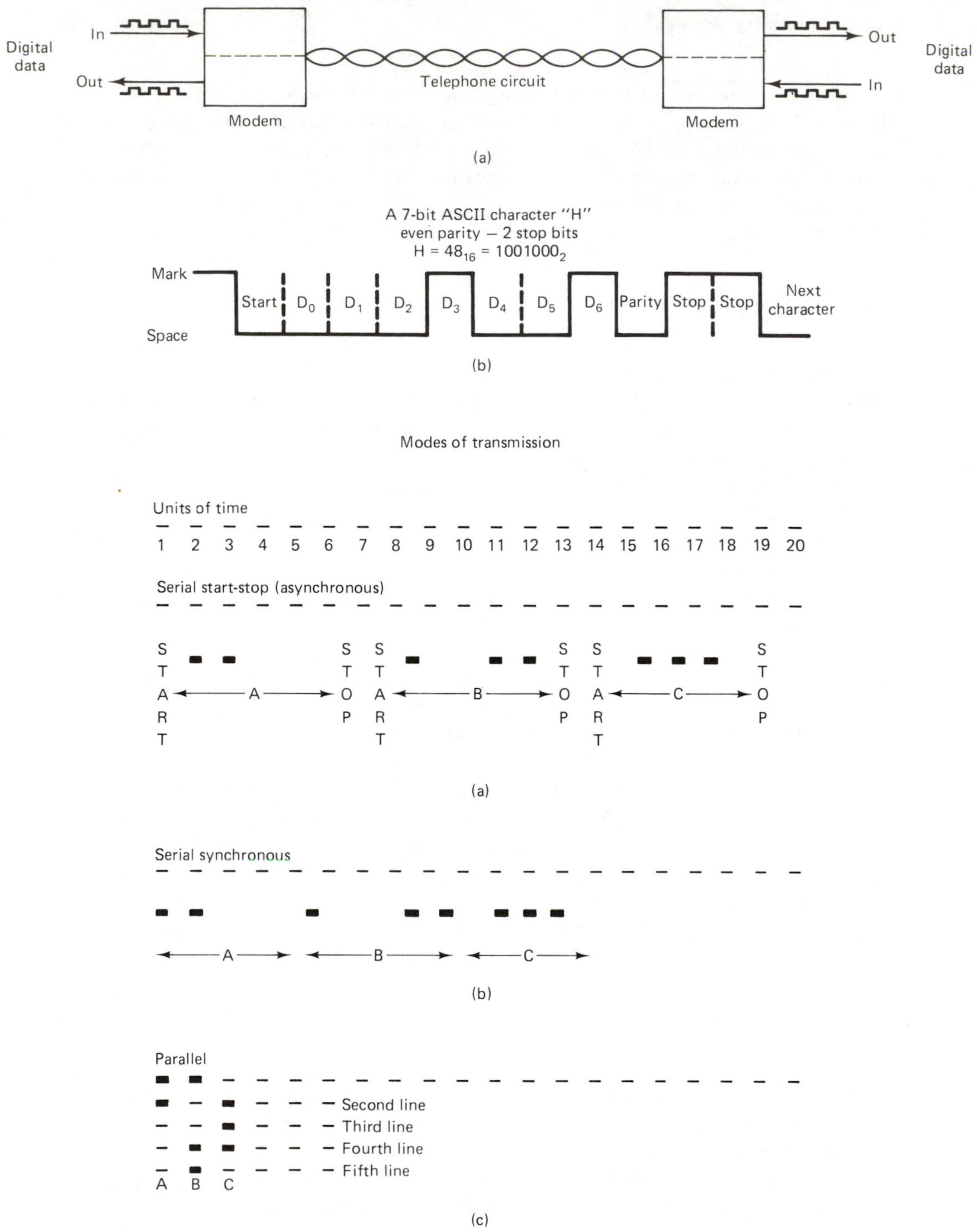

Figure 5.29 Asynchronous bit-serial, synchronous bit-serial, and parallel modes of data transmission.

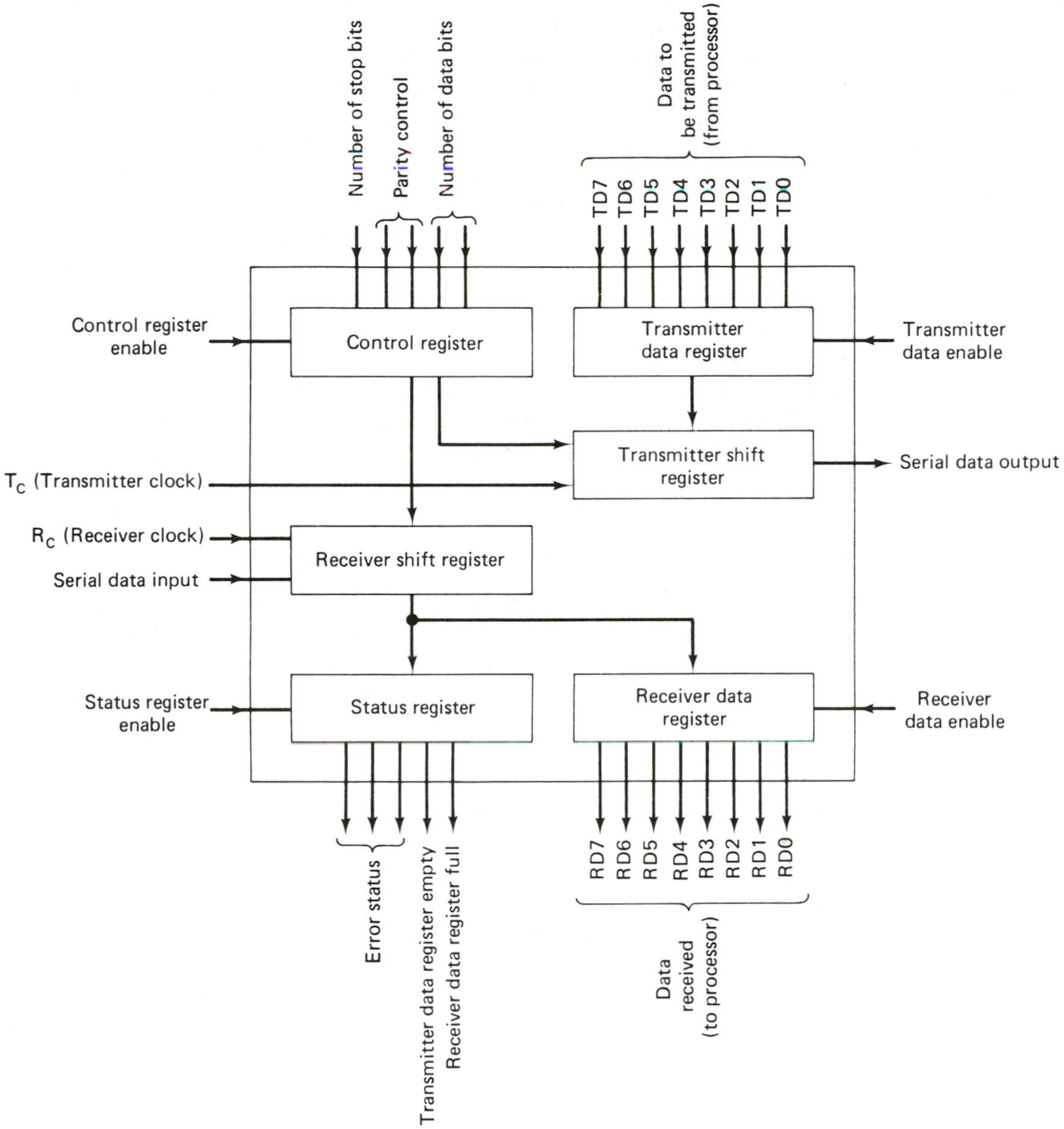

Figure 5.30 Block diagram of a UART (universal asynchronous receiver/transmitter). (Reprinted with permission from G. Gibson and Y. Liu, *Microcomputers for Engineers and Scientists,* Prentice-Hall, Englewood Cliffs, N.J., 1980.)

Although telephone lines are able to transmit data coded digitally, it is more usual to transform them to audible tones, where one tone could signify a binary 1 and another tone a binary 0. More complicated schemes are possible and are commonly employed, but we will delay their discussion until we treat networks in a subsequent chapter. The device employed to transform a bit stream from digital to sound form (analog), and vice versa, is called a *modulator–demodulator* (MODEM). The logical placement of MODEMs in a system is shown in Figures 5.29 and 5.31.

The production and detection of changes in tone encoding a bit stream of information has a physical speed termed *BAUD.* Technically, BAUD specifies the number of changes per second and normally is 100, 150, 300, or 1200. As shown in Figure 5.32, the normal character in asynchronous transmission is usually coded as 11 bits or as 10 bits. Thus a 100-BAUD transmission line can transfer approximately 10 characters per second.

As a last point, transmission lines can be *simplex* (transmission in one direction only), *half-duplex* (transmission in both directions but only one direction a time), and *full duplex* (transmission in both directions simultaneously).

SLOW DEVICES

Although the types of devices that can accept data from or send data to the processor are currently extensive and constantly proliferating, we shall treat briefly only a few of the more common ones. Figure 5.33 illustrates a fairly typical interactive stand-alone small business system eminently suited to the storage and manipulation of inventory, sales, and other records in addition to its fairly nice abilities for word processing. This particular system, marketed by International Business Machines, Incorporated, is built around an I8088 processor and includes a keyboard/CRT terminal, two floppy disk drives, and a printer.

Keyboard/CRT–Keyboard/Hardcopy Devices

It is necessary that a microcomputer possess a keyboard for data, program, and command input. Sometimes these ASCII character keyboards are physically boxed separately, although it probably is more common for them to be associated physically with a CRT output screen or typewriterlike hardcopy output device. Some keyboards involve significant physical key movement to cause a circuit to close, whereas others react to the slightest pressure. The printing mechanism to produce hardcopy may involve a "ball-like" element or may actually "throw" ink at the paper in an ink jet, as shown in Figure 5.34. The choice of an input/output terminal will involve such factors as original cost, reliability, cost and availability of repair, clearness of the final copy, and so on.

The integrated keyboard/CRT terminal concept is illustrated in Figure 5.35. Some of the more economical, less capable screens are only capable of one-color character generation. Other, more expensive screens have true graphics with line-

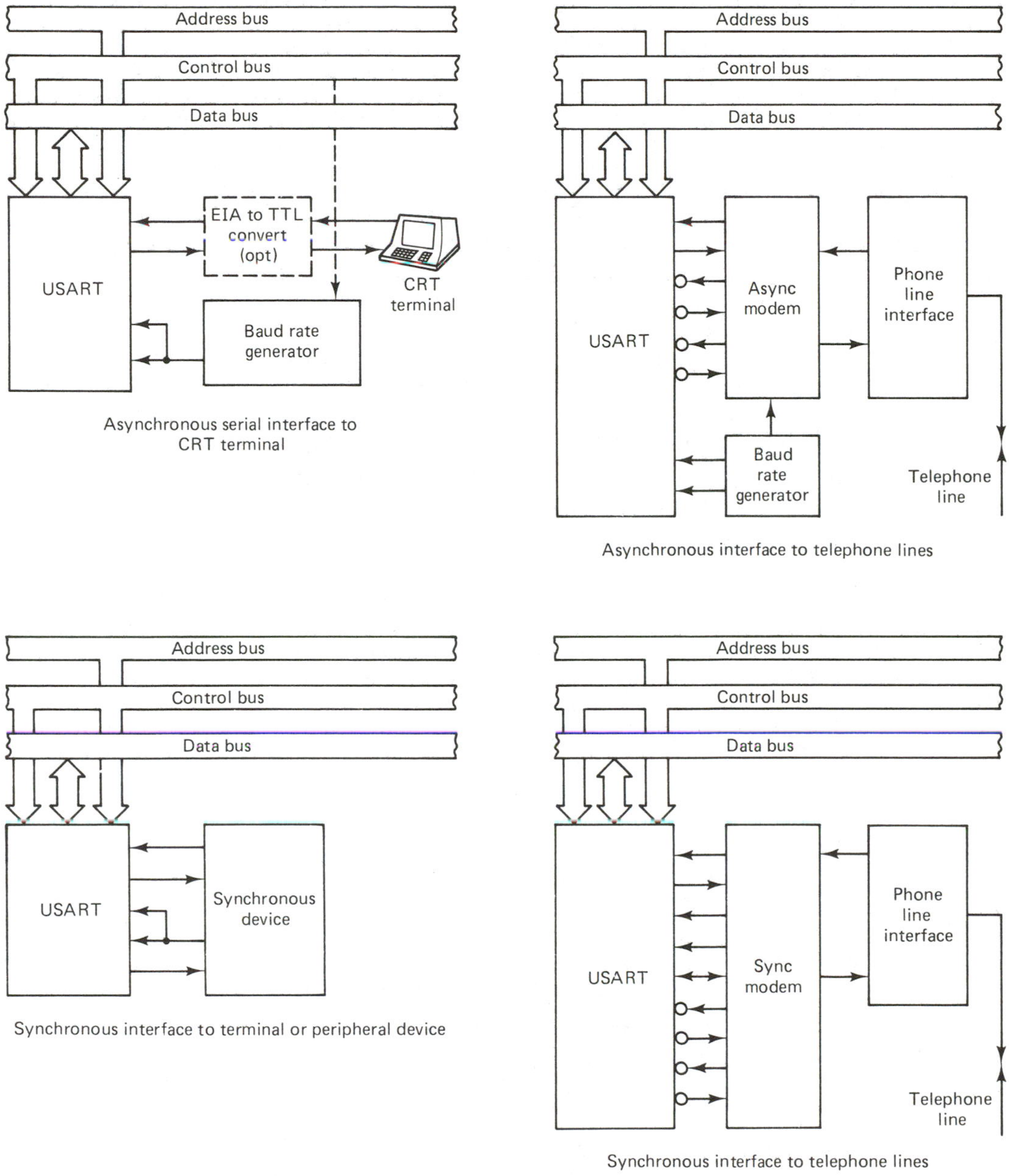

Figure 5.31 Input/output arrangements for common devices. A commonly available integrated-circuit chip to facilitate such communication is a universal synchronous/asynchronous receiver/transmitter (USART). Asynchronous transmission is limited to a single character and requires that the communication line be established before starting transmission. Synchronous transmission allows messages of more than one character and may include device addresses and line-switching information. (Reprinted with permission from S.E. Greenfield, *The Architecture of Microcomputers,* Winthrop, Cambridge, Mass., 1980.)

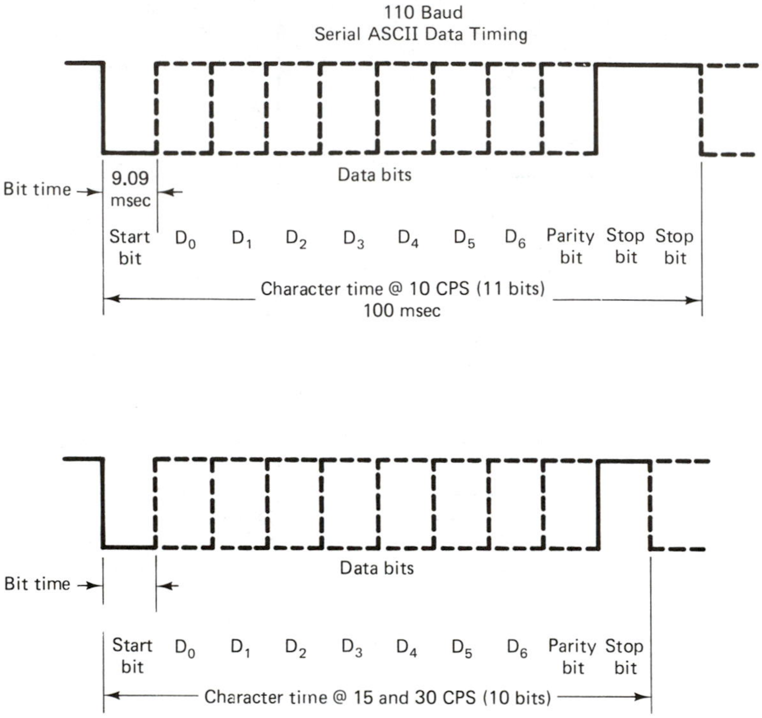

Baud rate	110	150	300
Characters/sec	10	15	30
Bit time (msec)	9.09	6.67	3.33
Character time	100	66.7	33.3

Figure 5.32 ASCII character transmission timing.

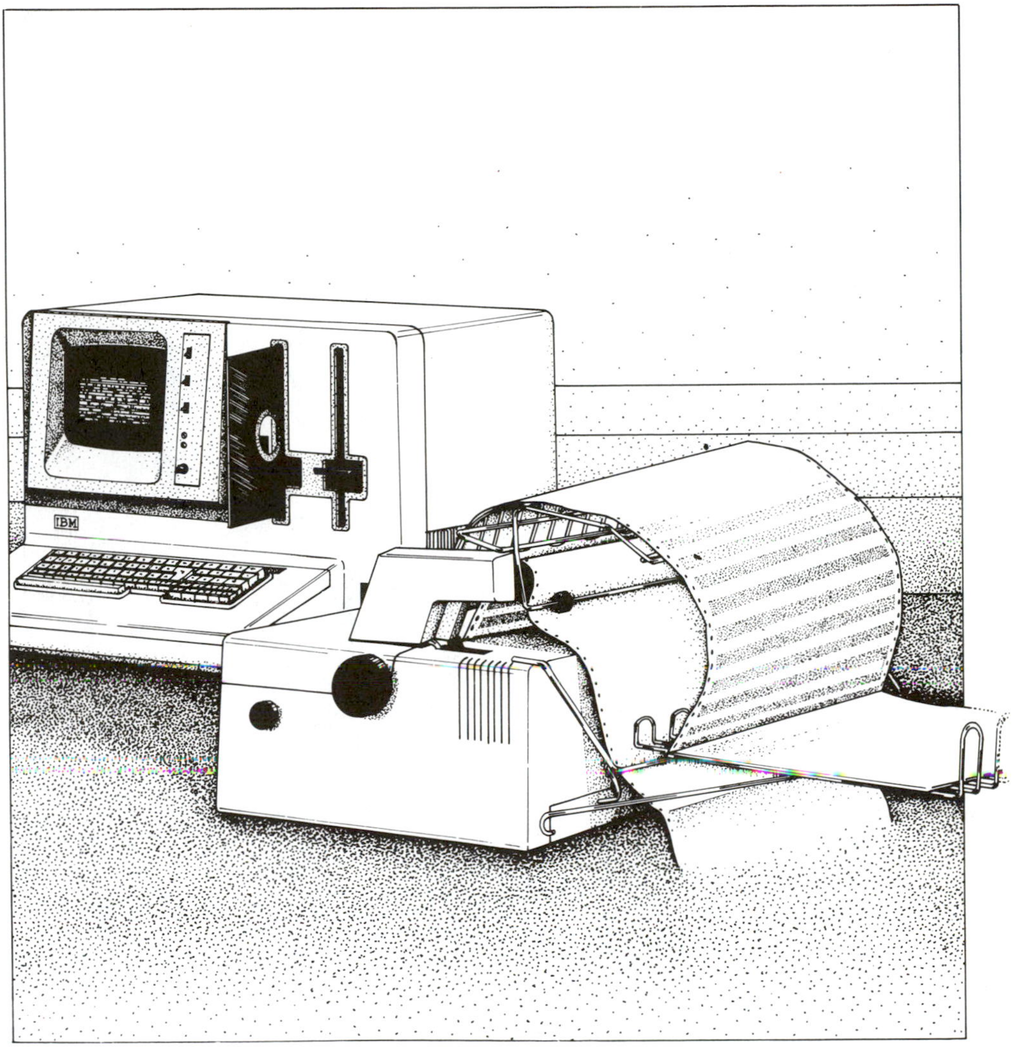

The IBM 5120 computing system

Figure 5.33 Microcomputer-based small business system including a floppy disk, a keyboard/CRT, and a hardcopy printer. (Reprinted with the permission of International Business Machines Corporation.)

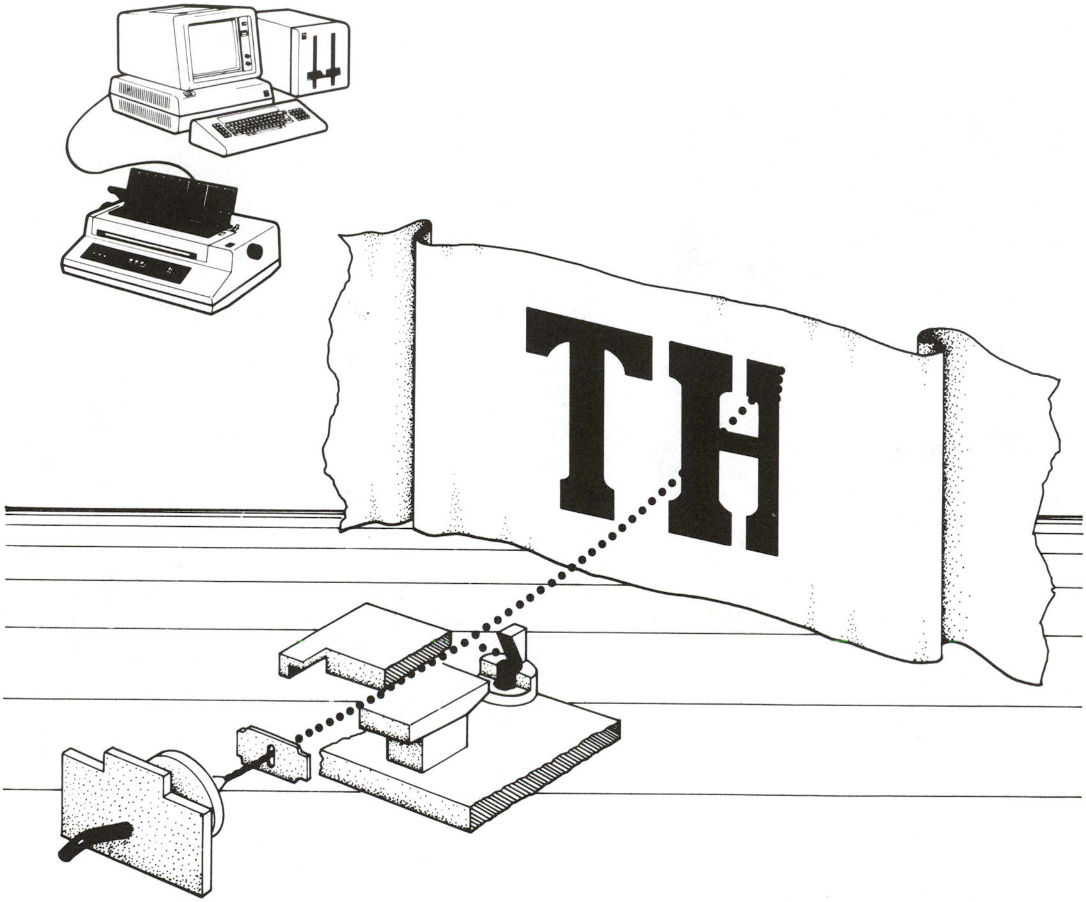

Figure 5.34 Ink-jet printer concept. (Reprinted with the permission of International Business Machines Corporation.)

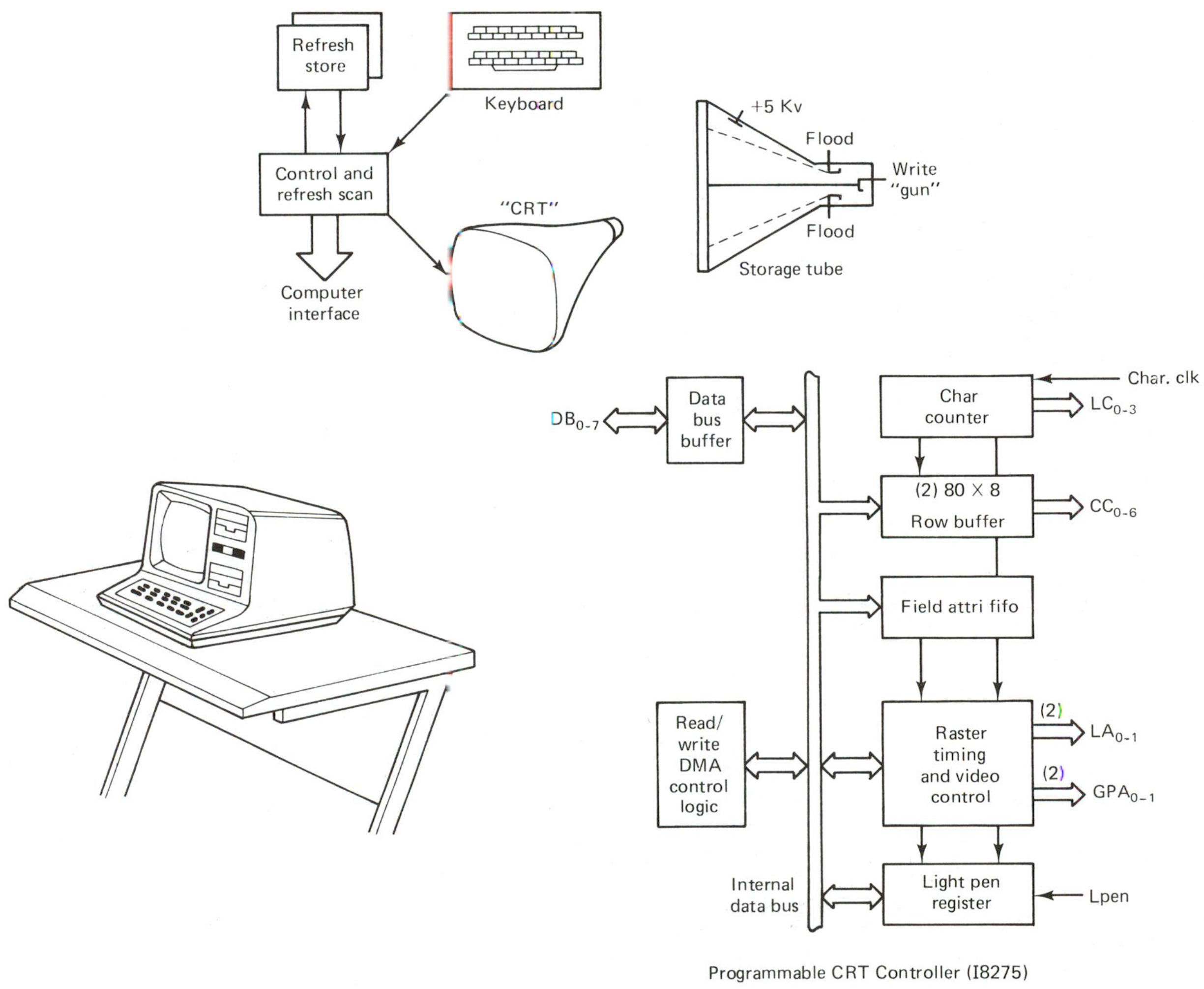

Figure 5.35 Keyboard/CRT computer terminal. (Reprinted by permission of Intel Corporation. Copyright 1980.)

segment-producing ability as well as multiple colors. It is somewhat common to employ the household TV set as the CRT for personal microcomputers.

Printers

The difference between the hardcopy output device with an associated keyboard and the separate hardcopy printer is often small or nonexistent. Alternatively, for microcomputers possessing fairly extensive data storage and manipulating abilities that service a small business or that are employed for extensive word processing, a higher-quality, more durable line printer may be required. One rapidly emerging technology employs a controlled jet of ink, as illustrated in Figure 5.34. The cost, durability, maintainability, print appearance, speed, and overall suitability of hardcopy printers varies immensely.

Small Business Systems for Record Storage and Word Processing

The small business or the branch office of a large firm has need of a system to record transactions, trace inventory, maintain personnel and accounting information, as well as to automate a myriad of other "clerk-based" tasks. Not the least of the prospective office-type candidate tasks for microcomputer-based assistance is word processing, where a system allows the entry of text and assists in its editing and final production.

Usually, a keyboard/CRT, printer, floppy-disk-based system, such as that illustrated in Figure 5.33, is adequate for the relatively small beginning office operation. Care should be exercised in choosing this "starter" installation so that provisions for growth exist, such as specifying a 16-bit processor and an operating system that allows growth.

I8086/8088-based systems are not only commonly available but usually include software that is designed particularly for office automation. Although many of the 8-bit-processor-based systems commonly available have excellent software, it must be noted that the potential for the expansion of their abilities is severely limited. That is, they are almost at the point of being the "top of the line." A 16-bit-processor-based system avoids this restriction. Current pricing trends (1983) indicate that I8086/8088-based systems with comparable or superior software are becoming available at fully competitive prices. If office systems expansion in the future is a possibility, as it usually is, the acquisition of an 8-bit-processor-based system is very questionable.

Process Control

We will not attempt to explore this vitally important and rapidly growing applications area beyond noting two points. For many process control situations, such as the automobile carburetor or the microwave oven, a 4-bit or 8-bit processor is eminently capable and suitable. For other situations, additional ability and/or speed requires the use of a 16-bit processor. The examples of process control shown in Figure 5.36 are typical. It is also probably true that a fairly capable home control microcomputer will become an economically justified feature of many homes almost immediately. The control of lighting, heating, security, and so on, would be involved as well as family financial records, Christmas lists, bills, and entertainment.

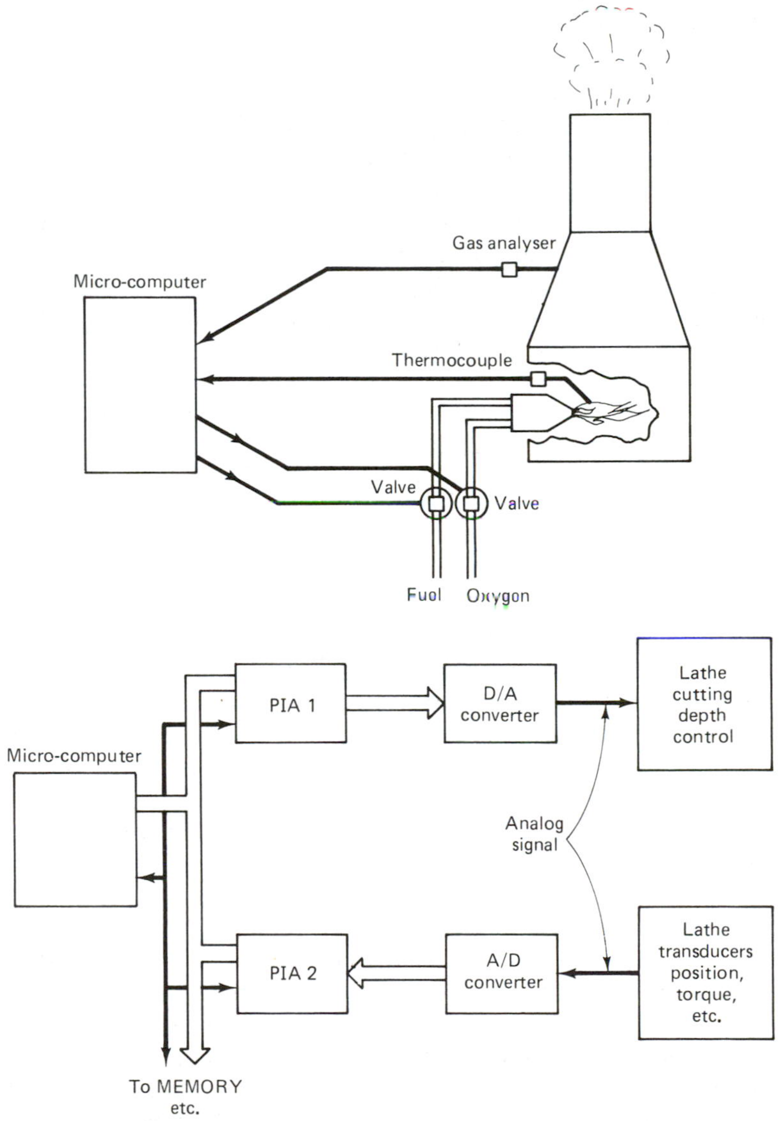

Figure 5.36 The microcomputer is being widely applied in process control situations.

FAST DEVICES

In general, the devices in this group provide mass storage for data beyond the capacity of main memory. These devices are often termed secondary memory and are accessed via I/O commands. Usually, a DMA channel is employed. We will examine three types of devices: disk, magnetic tape, and magnetic bubble memory.

Rotating Memory Devices

The rotating portion of the disk is named for its geometric shape. Information is recorded as magnetic spots in concentric circles, known as tracks, on the flat surface (Figure 5.37). Often both the top and bottom surfaces are used. In the case of an early-model floppy disk, one read/write head for the single surface is located on an extendable-retractable arm whose placement is under programmatic control.

Floppies were introduced in June 1970 as a storage device for the microprograms to control the IBM 3330 disk storage system. They were also used to contain the microcode for the reloadable control storage of the IBM/370 models 115, 125, 135, 145, and 155. A sales possibility has stimulated the development of the floppy disk and its associated drive as an economical direct-access device for microcomputers. A system has from one to eight drives, a controller, a power supply, an interface, interconnecting cables, diagnostics, and software to control the device (a driver).

The IBM 3740 diskette is a magnetic-oxide-coated Mylar computer tape cut as a 7.8-inch disk packaged in an 8-inch-square plastic envelope with apertures for drive-hub mounting, index-mark sensing, and read/write-head access. Because the inside of the envelope has a soft surface, the disk can rotate while the envelope is held stationary. As shown in Figures 5.38, 5.39, and 5.40, the floppy cartridge is slipped into the drive, positioned by the drive hub, and then held against the rotating drive spindle by a hub clamp. Pressure pads hold the read/write head in physical contact with the disk recording medium. A servomotor and feedback mechanism controls track-to-track head movement and track-head positioning. This device has 77 tracks, 3200 bits per inch (bpi), 26 sectors, storage of 242K bytes per track, 360 rpm, 250-kHz transfer rate, and a total capacity of 3.1M bits.

Although standards have not been published, the industry has largely concentrated on 8-, 5.25-, and 3-inch floppy disks. The in-contact read/write head causes diskette wear, although most vendors guarantee 2 million passes per track. All schemes of sectoring have an index hole in the diskette, detectable by a photoelectric cell, to mark the beginning of the tracks to the drive controller. Sectoring divides the diskette into equal-size pie-shaped slices. Thus each track is sectored to form a matrix of track-sector units that are addressable in mailbox fashion—track:sector. After moving the head to the proper track of a "soft-sectored" disk, the controller, on being informed that the index hole has been found by the photoelectric cell, instructs the read/write head to read the track until it finds the desired sector. *Hard sectoring* identifies each sector with a hole in the diskette that is sensed

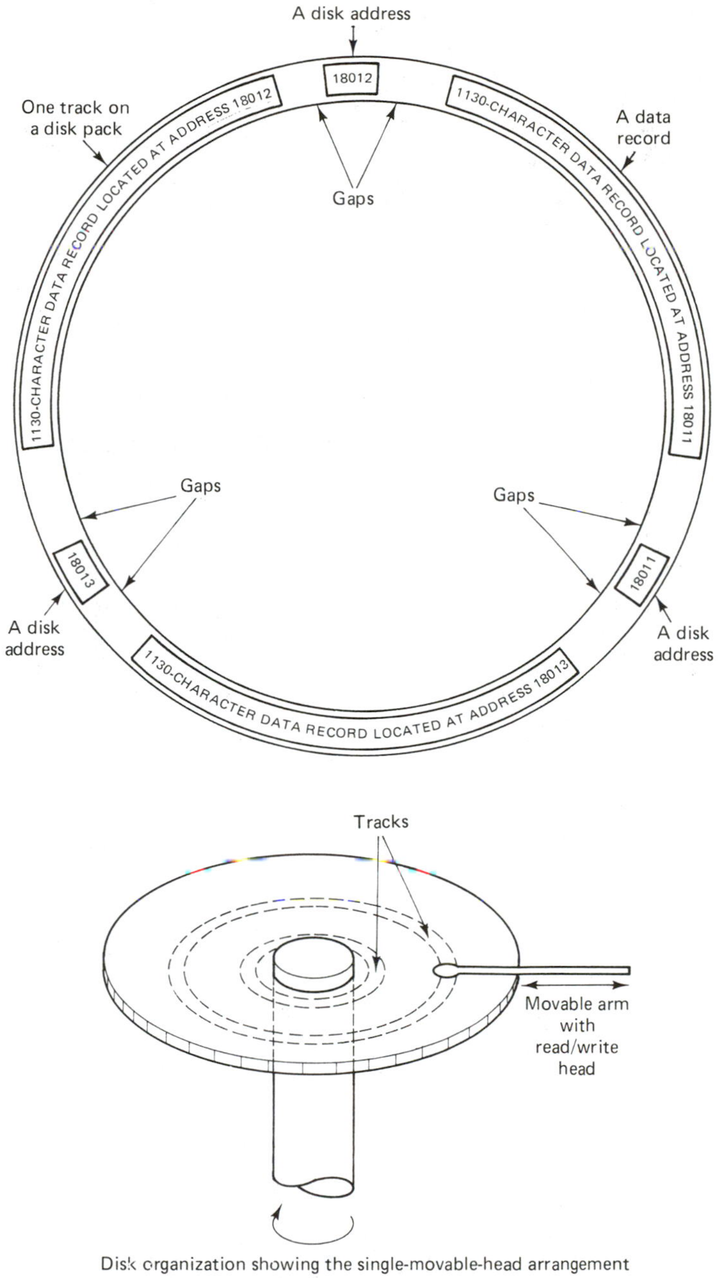

Figure 5.37 Disk organization showing the single movable head and the arrangement of addresses and data on a single track. (Reprinted with permission from G.W. Gorsline, *Computer Organization: Hardware/Software,* Prentice-Hall, Englewood Cliffs, N.J., 1980.)

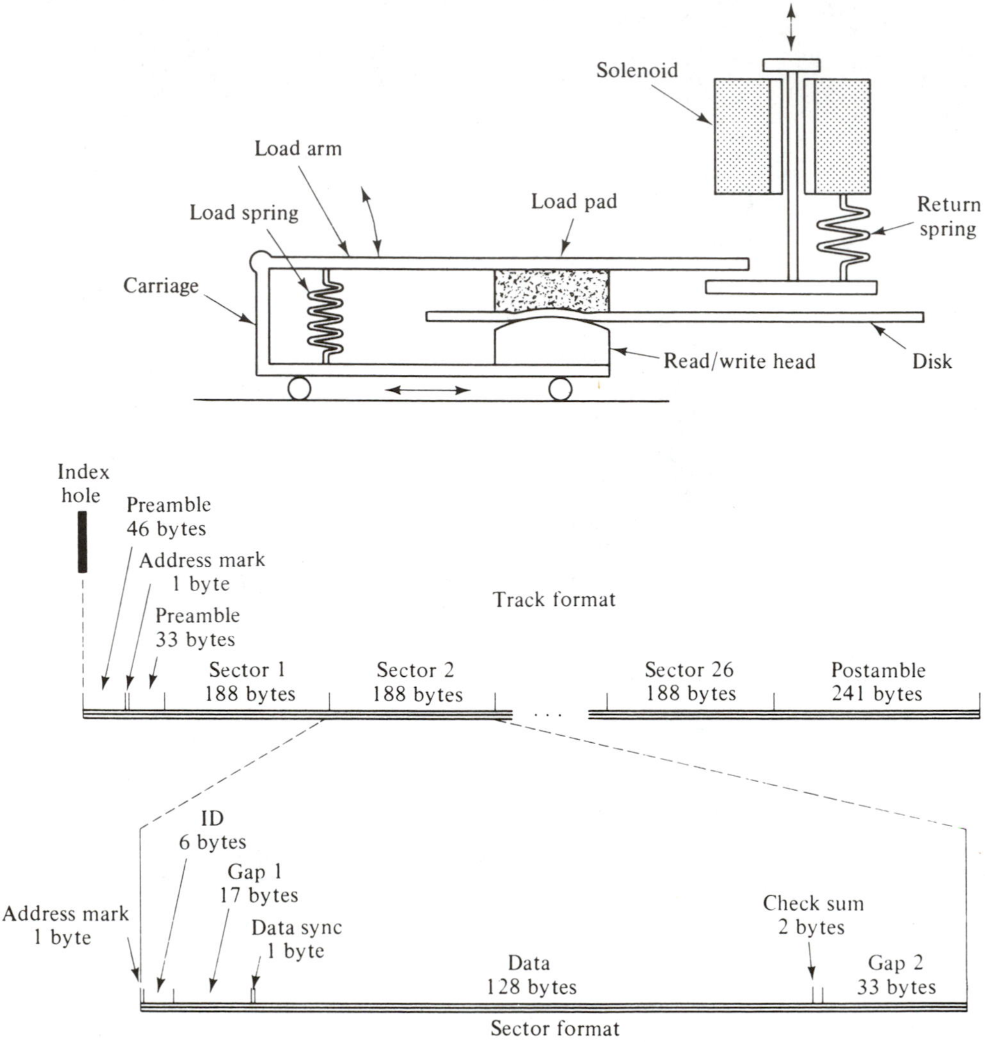

Figure 5.38 IBM 3740-compatible floppy disk drive and diskette soft-sectoring scheme. (Reprinted with permission from G.W. Gorsline, *Computer Organization: Hardware/Software*, Prentice-Hall, Englewood Cliffs, N.J., 1980.)

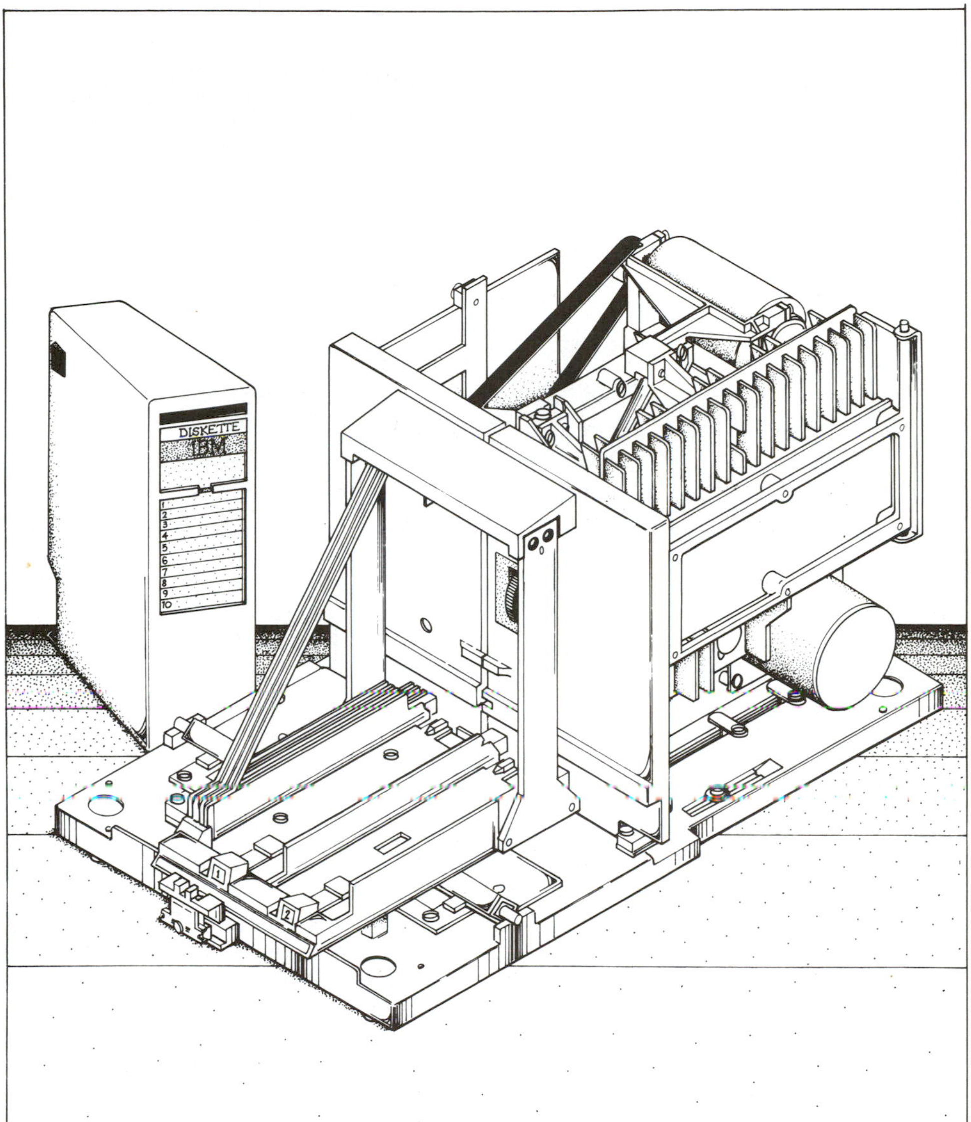

Figure 5.39 Floppy diskette assembly. (Reprinted with permission of International Business Machines Corporation.)

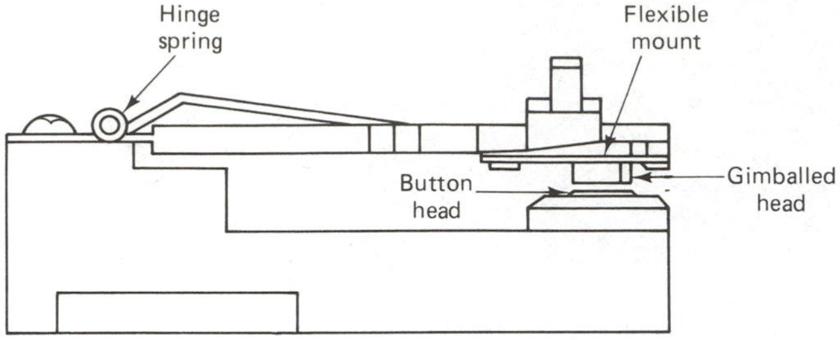

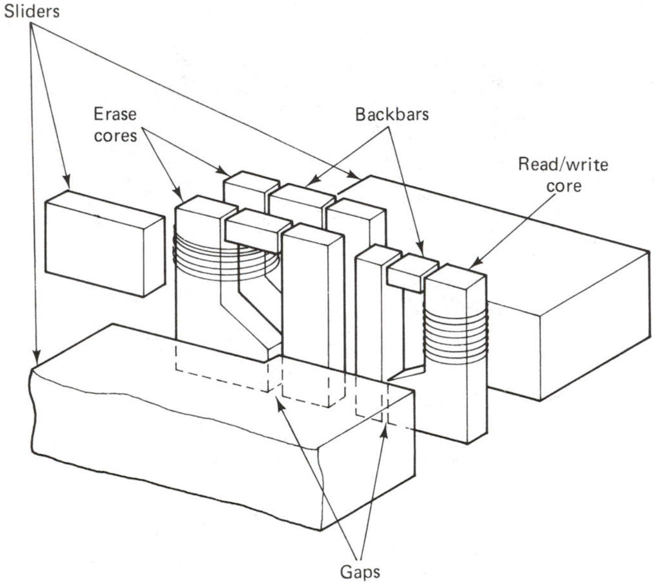

Figure 5.40 Read/write floppy disk head arrangement employed by one vendor of double-sided double-recording density 5¼-inch minifloppy disks.

by a photoelectric cell in the same fashion as the track index hole. The sector hole is sensed and the controller signals the head to read the magnetically encoded sector ID. After the controller receives the sector ID, it counts the number of sector holes that it must pass to find the desired sector.

Floppy disks are presently used as direct-access devices for microcomputers, for keyboard microprocessor-based data-entry devices, and as auxiliary memory for various microprocessor-based keyboard terminals. Standards do not currently exist for floppy disks, so various sizes and configurations are available.

Floppy disks are an example of direct-access memory (DAM). The term *direct-access memory* means that any address may be next, but that the time to access a particular datum is a nonlinear function of the addressing distance. Thus access time for a movable-head disk is composed of three portions:

access time	←	time to move head to desired track	+	time for desired sector to rotate under Head	+	time to read sector

When using disks with movable heads, the arrangement of data on the device can have gross effects on the speed of access. For example, if block 1 is on track 7, block 2 is on track 77, and block 3 is on track 50, a large amount of time will be consumed in head movement. In fact, it would be best to place these three blocks in sectors of the same track. Some devices cannot access a sector without a preceding minimum time that prevents accessing of contiguous sectors. This characteristic would result in large access-time savings if contiguous blocks were placed on the device in every other sector. You can imagine the effects with large files. In many cases, a job will use more than one file; in almost all cases these should be placed on separate devices to minimize head movement.

The *Winchester disk,* as employed with microcomputers, is marketed in both a permanently mounted (fixed) version and in a removable/mountable cartridge version. In at least one case, as illustrated in Figure 5.41, both types are assembled into a single package. The advantages of the Winchester disk include larger capacity, a lower error rate, faster data transfer, and quicker head movement. The initial cost of the drive and of the cartridges is relatively high, although the cost per unit of information storage is usually low.

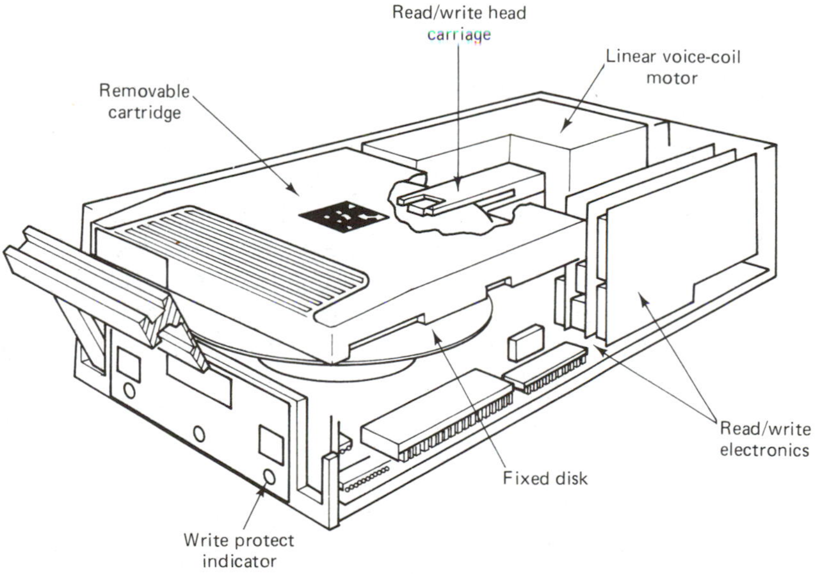

Figure 5.41 Example of Winchester disk technology.

Magnetic Tape

A *serial-access memory* is one in which the time to access a storage cell is a linear function of the address distance between the present position and the desired datum. The cells of serial-access memories, such as a cassette tape, do not have a physically designated address, the programmer must keep track of his or her position within the memory by count. In general, if the start of the desired block is N blocks in distance and the time of access for each block is t, the time required to access that block is t * N.

$$\text{access time} \leftarrow \text{number of blocks to desired datum} \times \text{time to read one block}$$

A magnetic-tape system includes not only the tape and suitable cassette or cartridges, but also a magnetic read/write head, a transport, and electronic circuitry to control tape motion and data transduction. The tape transport (often called a *tape drive*) is linked to the data path of the computer through a DMA channel control unit. This tape control unit provides a data buffer for synchronizing data transfer, executing the tape imperatives (e.g., REWIND, BACKSPACE, etc.), and reporting the status of the transport.

The tape itself is typically Mylar plastic with a thin coating of ferromagnetic material on one side. Information recording is accomplished by applying electromagnetic signals to the tape by a write head. This creates small, very local, magnetically saturated regions in the ferric oxide coating on the tape. During a read operation, this magnetized spot creates a field in the gap between the tape and the read head, inducing a voltage in the output coil as a result of the tape motion. Figure 5.42 illustrates magnetic tape principles.

The inertia involved in mechanically starting and stopping the tape absolutely prevents starting or stopping the tape between characters. Contiguous characters are grouped into blocks separated by blank tape segments called *interblock gaps.* These gaps serve both as a delimiter and as a coasting area for mechanically starting and stopping the tape motion. Programmers will recognize that the buffer in memory and the block on tape are the same size. Logical records are a programming device and are normally a portion of a buffer (and a block). The mechanical accuracy of starting and stopping a tape is not great enough to replace a block in situ. For this work, all record-update work employing tapes is performed tape to tape and involves copying/correcting the entire tape.

Magnetic Bubble Memories

Information is stored in the form of magnetized regions or bubbles in cylindrical domains within a thin layer of magnetic material with magnetization opposite to that of the surrounding area. Figures 5.43 and 5.44 illustrate some of the details and Figure 5.45 illustrates one implementation of a magnetic bubble memory

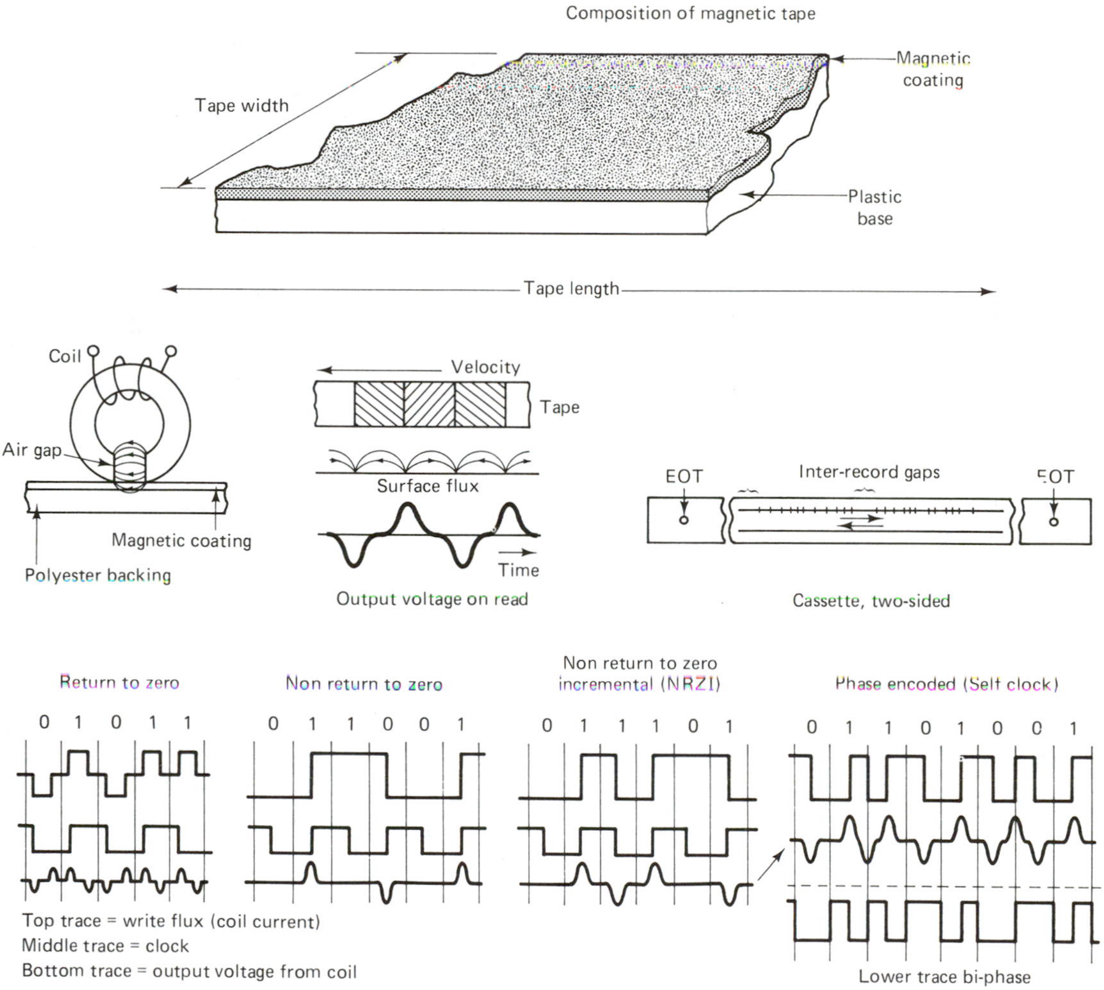

Figure 5.42 Magnetic tape recording principles.

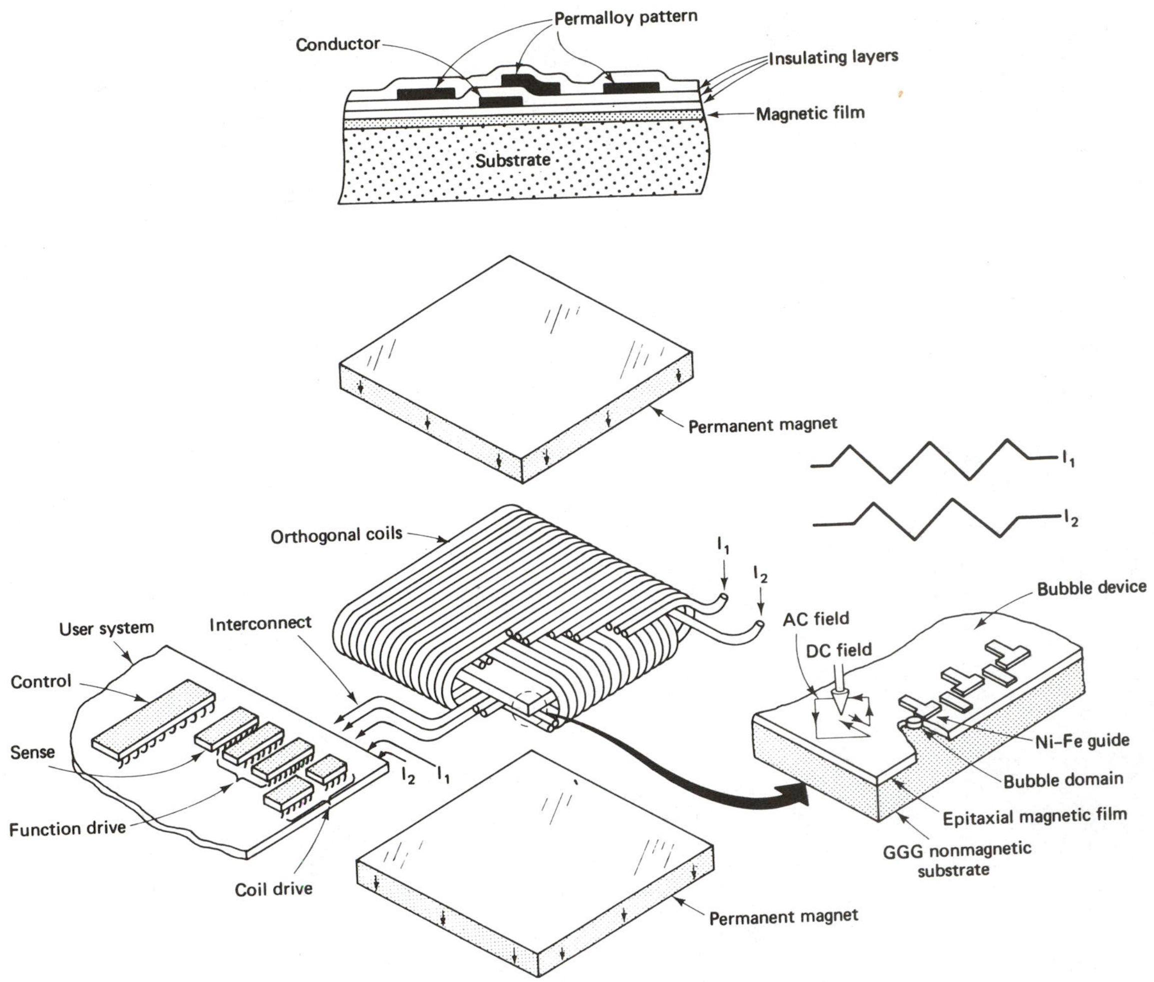

Figure 5.43 Construction of a magnetic bubble memory (MBM) unit. (Reprinted with permission from G. Gibson and Y. Liu, *Microcomputers for Engineers and Scientists,* Prentice-Hall, Englewood Cliffs, N.J., 1980.)

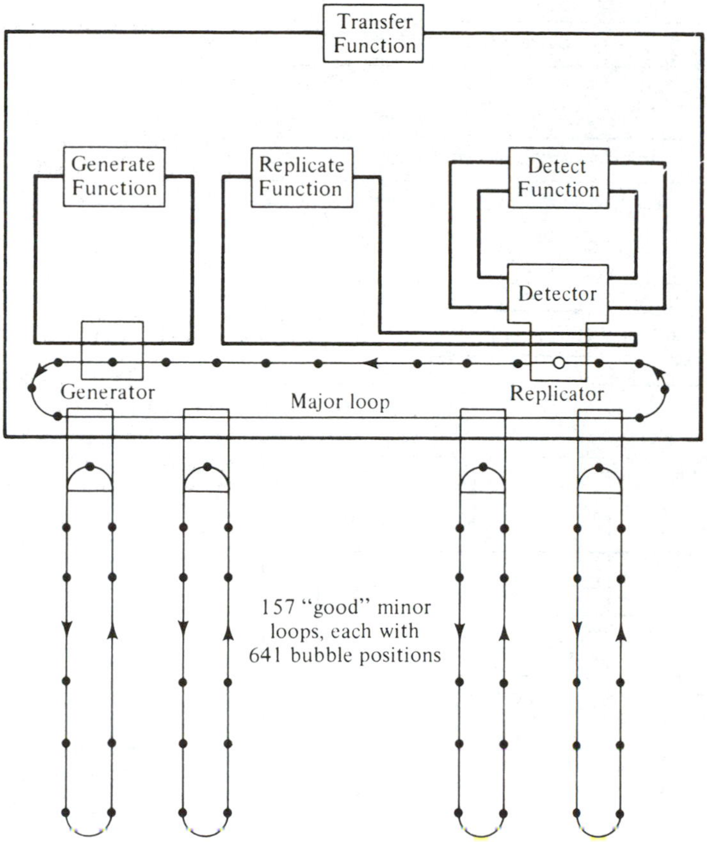

Figure 5.44 Magnetic bubble memory illustrating the usual major and minor loop organization of the 92K LSI chip. (Reprinted with permission from G.W. Gorsline, *Computer Organization: Hardware/Software,* Prentice-Hall, Englewood Cliffs, N.J., 1980.)

(MBM) controller. The presence or absence of a magnetized bubble at a specific location corresponds to a binary digit (on or off) at that location. Bits are made available by moving the bubbles within the solid layer to an access device. The storage material can be either a magnetic garnet grown epitaxially on a nonmagnetic garnet substrate or an amorphous metallic magnetic layer sputtered onto a substrate such as glass.

Four basic functions are required to operate a magnetic bubble memory organized as a single loop of bubbles: propagation, generation, detection, and annihilation. Such an organization possesses serial-access characteristics, with a single bit being followed by a single bit followed . . . . The more usual block organization shown in Figure 5.44 would also need the replication and transfer functions, in addition to the four basic functions. An important characteristic of MBM systems is

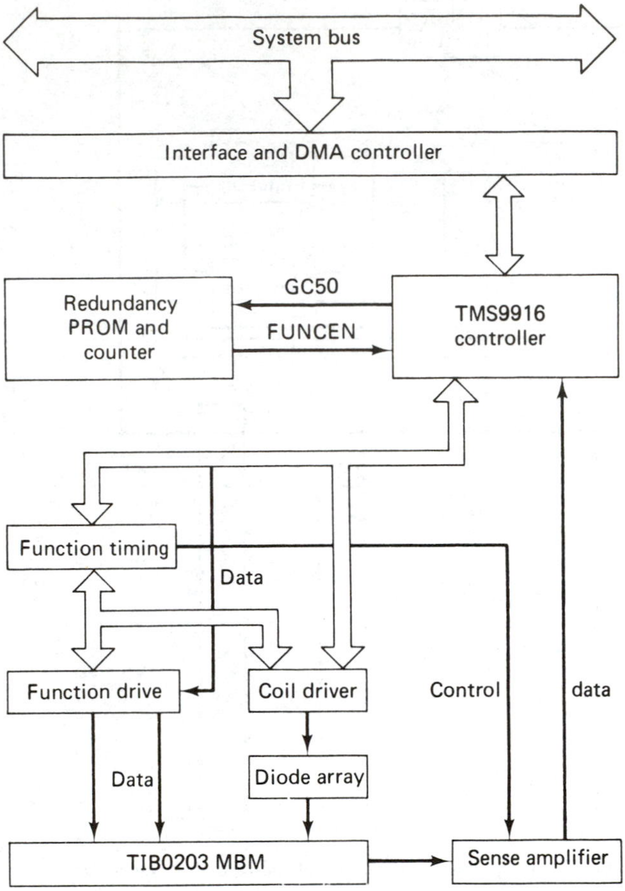

Figure 5.45 Block diagram of a magnetic bubble memory and its control circuiting. (Reprinted with permission from G. Gibson and Y. Liu, *Microcomputers for Engineers and Scientists,* Prentice-Hall, Englewood Cliffs, N.J., 1980.)

that they can be stopped or turned off (no bubble movement) without information loss. Thus they are nonvolatile and static.

1. *Bubble propagation* is required to move the bubbles within the substrate and thus for access to the information on the MBM chip. The usual method at present is to magnetize Permalloy patterns with an in-plane rotating field. These patterns can have any one of several shapes.
2. *Bubble generation* is the process of writing information into the memory, usually with a nucleate generator (a horseshoe-shaped conductor loop that produces a magnetic bubble inside the horseshoe when energized by a current pulse).
3. *Bubble detection* for reading is generally accomplished in a section of the propagation circuit. The magnetic bubbles are stretched into wide strips that cause

a distinct change in the magnetoresistance of the Permalloy equivalent to preamplification. This assures a sense signal of several millivolts when the detector pattern and three bubbleless dummy patterns are interconnected as a bridge.

4. *Bubble annihilation* clears the memory data and is usually combined with a replicator to allow a nondestructive read operation. By duplicating information, one copy of the bubble can be read (and thus destroyed) while a copy of the original bubble is retained. Most replicators stretch the bubble, cut it in half, and send the pieces to different destinations.

The organization of the magnetic bubble memory chips currently (and originally) marketed have the major/minor loop arrangement shown in Figure 5.44. To access data, corresponding bubbles (or the absence of bubbles) in each minor loop are first shifted (rotated) to the position closest to the major loop. Then a bubble or its absence is transferred from all minor loops simultaneously to the major loop. The major loop is then shifted (rotated) to be read, annihilated, or replicated as required, and finally transferred back to the minor loops in the original positions.

A recent existing development in MBM technology is the Intel iPAB (Plug-a-Bubble) memory system, which is a 128K-byte (1 megabit) removable bubble memory cassette. This particular product furnishes automatic error correction, write protection, an average access time of 48 milliseconds, and a burst transfer rate of 12.5K bytes per second (100 kilobits/sec).

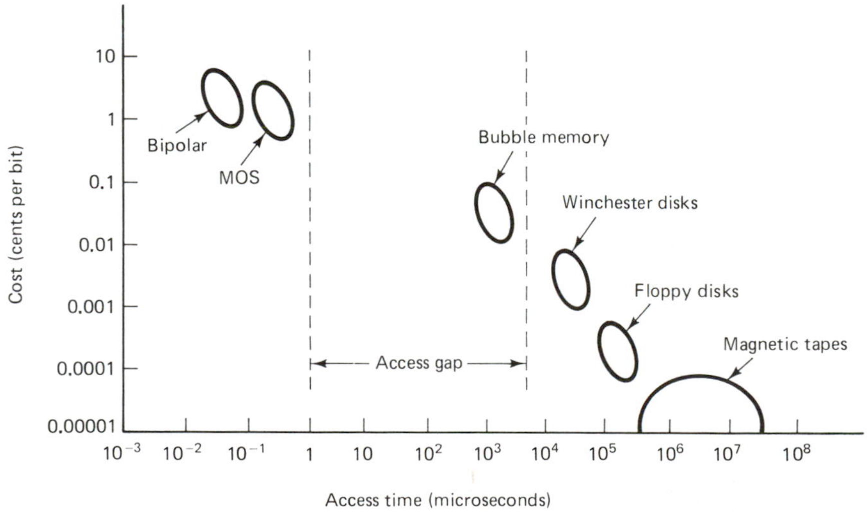

Figure 5.46 Cost versus access time for representative types of memory, illustrating the economics of the speed/cost relationship.

Mass Storage Economics

As illustrated in Figure 5.46, there is a general relationship between the cost of storing a quantum of information and the time required to access that information. An examination of this relationship strongly suggests that MBM fills an "access gap" as illustrated. On the other hand, the rapidly diminishing cost of VLSI RAM chips may shortly remove this cost/speed gap in storage technologies.

6

The I8087 Numeric Data Processor

Very often, while solving an applications problem, it is necessary to deal with numeric quantities involving fractional values. At times it is also necessary to manipulate numbers whose values exceed the range that is provided for with the integer representation of the computer being used. As is usually expected, methods have already been developed for dealing with both of these situations.

THE PROBLEM OF VERY LARGE NUMBERS

Very large numbers are often represented using multiple words in memory and software multiple-precision program packages to accomplish the manipulation. In this manner, complete accuracy is maintained. Multiple-precision addition and subtraction present few problems and are easily programmed using the carry flag (CF) of the I8086/8088. On the other hand, multiplication and division are somewhat difficult and involve rather esoteric solutions in the general case. Nevertheless, multiple-precision arithmetic packages are necessary for those cases where complete accuracy is necessary. As an indication of the methodology, we give a possible implementation of an algorithm for triple-precision integer addition (48-bit).

```
            -
            -
            -
; 48-BIT  INTEGER ADDITION EXAMPLE
;     (MEMORY TO MEMORY - THREE ADDRESS)
;
```

```
;        C ← A + B
;
         CLC
         MOV     AX,A+4      ; 4 = (3 words - 1) *
         ADC     AX,B+4      ; two bytes per word
         MOV     C+4,AX
         MOV     AX,A+2
         ADC     AX,B+2
         MOV     C+2,AX
         MOV     AX,A
         ADC     AX,B
         MOV     C,AX
         JC      OVFLW_ERR
```

If, and only if, complete accuracy is not required, it is possible to scale the numeric quantities by some consistent value and thus perform the calculations using single-precision arithmetic. Thus in dealing with 48-bit values where the least-significant 32 bits are not required (say that they are only rough estimations of the true values), it is sometimes possible to disregard them by scaling. In our example, this method would require the use of only the high-order 16-bit word of each variable. Expressed in a different way, the approximate value of $A = A \times 2^{32}$; $B = B \times 2^{32}$; and $C = C \times 2^{32}$. The scaled arithmetic becomes

$$C \leftarrow A + B$$

The notation $A \times 2^{32}$ is often termed scientific notation and is closely related to logarithms.

Fractional numbers may be exactly represented as numerator–denominator pairs and can be manipulated employing the algebraic rules for operating on fractions. In computer terminology, such manipulations and data representations are known as *rational arithmetic.* In designing algorithms to accomplish symbolic algebra on computers, important operations involve the coefficients of the term (perhaps cancellation) and thus require complete accuracy in their representation. Rational number arithmetic is commonly employed in these applications.

It is important to realize that certain fairly common values are not exactly representable as fractions. Pi (π) and *e* (the base of natural logrithms) are among these values. As these values are usually "carried along" in symbolic form during algebraic manipulations, they do not constitute a major problem in rational arithmetic. On the other hand, fractional values developed during rational arithmetic manipulations often involve an excessively long numerator or denominator even when reduced to lowest form. Thus complicated algorithms for storage will most likely be involved.

Two forms of rational arithmetic and data storage have been, and are, the subject of research and use. The *pure rational* method expresses numeric values as a numerator/denominator diad with either the numerator or the denominator being signed. A report by Thacker (1978) strongly suggests that the length of the two component portions often becomes excessively long. Nevertheless, the pure rational number data format is employed by some algebraic manipulation packages. The *fixed-slash rational* method expresses numeric values as an integral portion:numerator portion:denominator portion triad, where the fractional part is always between zero and one and the integral portion is a signed integer. Kornerup and Matula (1978) have reported research on this data representation that demonstrates its superiority to the pure rational form in most circumstances.

In some applications where a determined accuracy is required, *scaling* of the quantity is perfectly satisfactory. In operations with dollars and cents, it is often perfectly legitimate and extremely easy to accomplish all manipulations in terms of mills (1/10 cent) by scaling all values by 1000 and utilizing integer arithmetic on the mill-scaled equivalents. Thus

$$\$100.93 + \$7.14 = \$108.07$$

becomes

$$100930 + 7140 = 108070$$

A data diad is employed in the *fixed-point* format to express numbers involving a fraction where the integral portion is expressed as one integer value and the fractional portion as a second integed value (scaled to become an integer). Thus 100.93 could be expressed and manipulated as

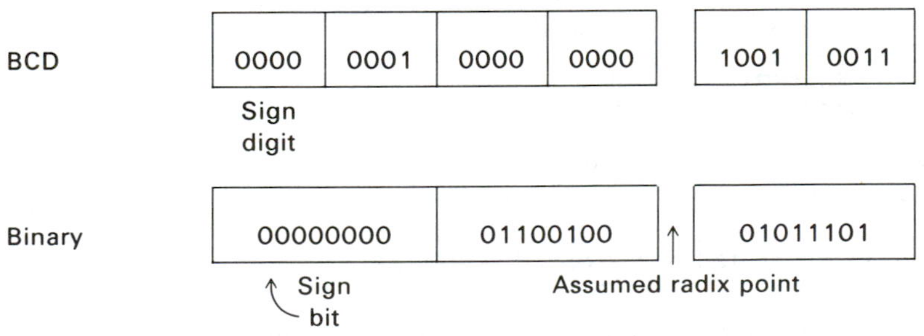

Care must be taken to allow a carry-out from the fractional portion to the integral portion during addition and a borrow from the integral portion to the fractional portion during subtraction. With the BCD format, the sign-magnitude style is suggested, whereas the two's-complement style is satisfactory for the binary format. It must also be realized that multiprecision arithmetic may be required.

THE FLOATING-POINT DATA FORMAT

An adaptation of scientific notation was developed for very early computers used for numerical mathematics that is known as *floating point.* Various styles of this format are used and manipulated by appropriately implemented hardware or software packages on super-, maxi-, midi-, mini-, and microcomputers. In all cases, an adaptation of the two-part scientific notation is used:

$$+0.731 \times 10^1$$

whose interpretation is +7.31. This value is obtained by taking the significand (+0.731) and multiplying it by the base raised to power of the exrad (+1); in this case, $+0.731 \times +10 = +7.31$.

The two portions of a floating-point number *each* must specify four pieces of information for a total of eight pieces of information:

1. The number base
2. The sign
3. The position of the radix point
4. The magnitude

The internal representations (the syntax) of the two portions are known as *significand* and *exrad,* and their interpretations (the semantics) are known respectively as *mantissa* and *exponent.*

With microcomputers it is usual to specify explicitly only a portion of the eight items of information necessary for a valid interpretation while implicitly specifying the rest. In a commonly employed syntax,

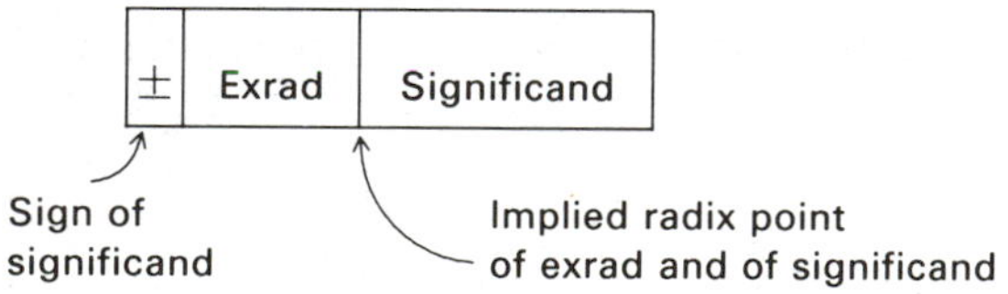

The syntax of the exrad is interpreted as follows:

1. The number base is assumed to be 2, thus the value is binary.
2. The radix point is assumed on the extreme right, thus the value is integral.
3. The sign is interpreted as negative if the value is below the midpoint of the possible magnitude and positive if above that value, thus if the leftmost exrad bit is zero—the exponent is negative—and if the leftmost bit of the exrad is one—the exponent is positive.
4. The magnitude of the exponent is derived as the *deviation* from the midpoint value of the exrad.

The syntax of the significand is interpreted as:

1. The number base is assumed to be 2, thus the value is binary.
2. The sign is the leftmost bit of the floating-point format and occupies the same position as the sign of an integer number.
3. The radix point is assumed on the extreme left, thus the value is always fractional.
4. The magnitude of the mantissa is derived as the signed-magnitude binary fraction as specified by the significand bit pattern.

It is usual for the fractional significand to have no leading zero bits. If such leading zero bits are generated, the significand is shifted left until they are lost while the exrad is appropriately adjusted to preserve the value. This process is termed *normalization* and may involve shifting in zeros from the right.

It should be noted that the *magnitude or range* of a floating-point number is determined largely by the exponent as the value of a floating-point number is the product of the fractional mantissa and the number base raised to the power of the exponent:

$$\text{value} = \text{mantissa} \times 2^{\text{exponent}}$$

It follows that the values that can be exactly represented are more dense (occur closer together) when the exponent is small (as the interpreted values approach zero as a limit) than when the exponent is large (as the interpreted values diverge from zero); or oppositely, the values that can be exactly represented are less dense (occur farther apart) when the interpreted value is large than when it is small. Thus the average absolute error necessarily is greater for a large number than it is for a small number.

It must also be emphasized that the conversion of an external base 10 fractional quantity to an internal base 2 fractional mantissa, and vice versa, generally contains some error. This base conversion error will exist for all fractional mantissas not exactly representable in both cases (.25, .5, .75, etc.). Additionally, the significand contains a finite number of bits (23, 52, or 64 bits with the I8087 Numeric Data Processor). Therefore, the large majority of the desired base 10 mantissa values cannot be exactly represented by the finite fractional binary significand.

Overflow occurs when a floating-point value becomes so large in magnitude that the exrad cannot represent the value of the exponent. *Underflow* occurs when a floating-point value becomes so close to zero magnitude that the exrad is zero and the significand cannot be normalized. In some schemes that allow unnormalized floating-point values, absolute underflow occurs when the exrad is zero and the significand is zero. The I8087 terms this condition *gradual underflow.*

THE IEEE FLOATING-POINT STANDARD AND THE I8087

The I8087 numeric data processor (see Figure 6.1) implements the IEEE Floating-Point Standard (shown in Figure 6.2) as well as additional data types and operations. We will first consider the floating-point aspects and then discuss the extensions.

Three floating-point data formats are supported: real, long real, and extended real. Figure 6.2 illustrates their syntax and semantics. Figure 6.3 presents the syntax and associated meanings of the various flags and pointers that constitute the "environment" of the I8087. The I8087 numerical data processor conforms to, or exceeds, the IEEE Floating-Point Standard in all aspects that this author has been able to verify. In addition, several data types and instructions are included that clearly augment the standard.

The basic architecture of the I8087 is that of a zero-address (stack oriented) arithmetic-logic unit. In this concept the typical arithmetic instruction assumes that the two source operands are the contents of the two top elements of the stack and that they both are replaced by the results as the contents of the top element of the stack. Thus the zero address instruction

```
ADD
```

removes (POPs) the stack top and then also removes (POPs) the new stack top, adds them, and places (PUSHs) the result back as the new stack top. The stack is one element smaller after the instruction is executed. As an illustration, we offer the following program fragment of a mythical zero-address (stack-oriented) processor executing the FORTRAN-like (memory-to-memory) statement

```
        -
A = B + C
        -
        -            ; stack of depth zero
        PUSH C       ; stack of depth one
        PUSH B       ; stack of depth two
        ADD          ; stack of depth one
        POP A        ; stack of depth zero
```

An "adder, complementer, multiplier, etc." is implied that destructively obtains its source operands from the stack and places its result operand on the stack. The stack structure of the I8087 is illustrated in Figure 6.4.

The stack elements of the I8087 can also be considered as registers that are identified as Top(i), where i is a number from zero to seven with the stack top being Top(0). Thus register-to-register arithmetic is possible. Additionally, arithmetic is provided between system main memory and the stack top or the stack element register whose identification is "Top(i)" as above.

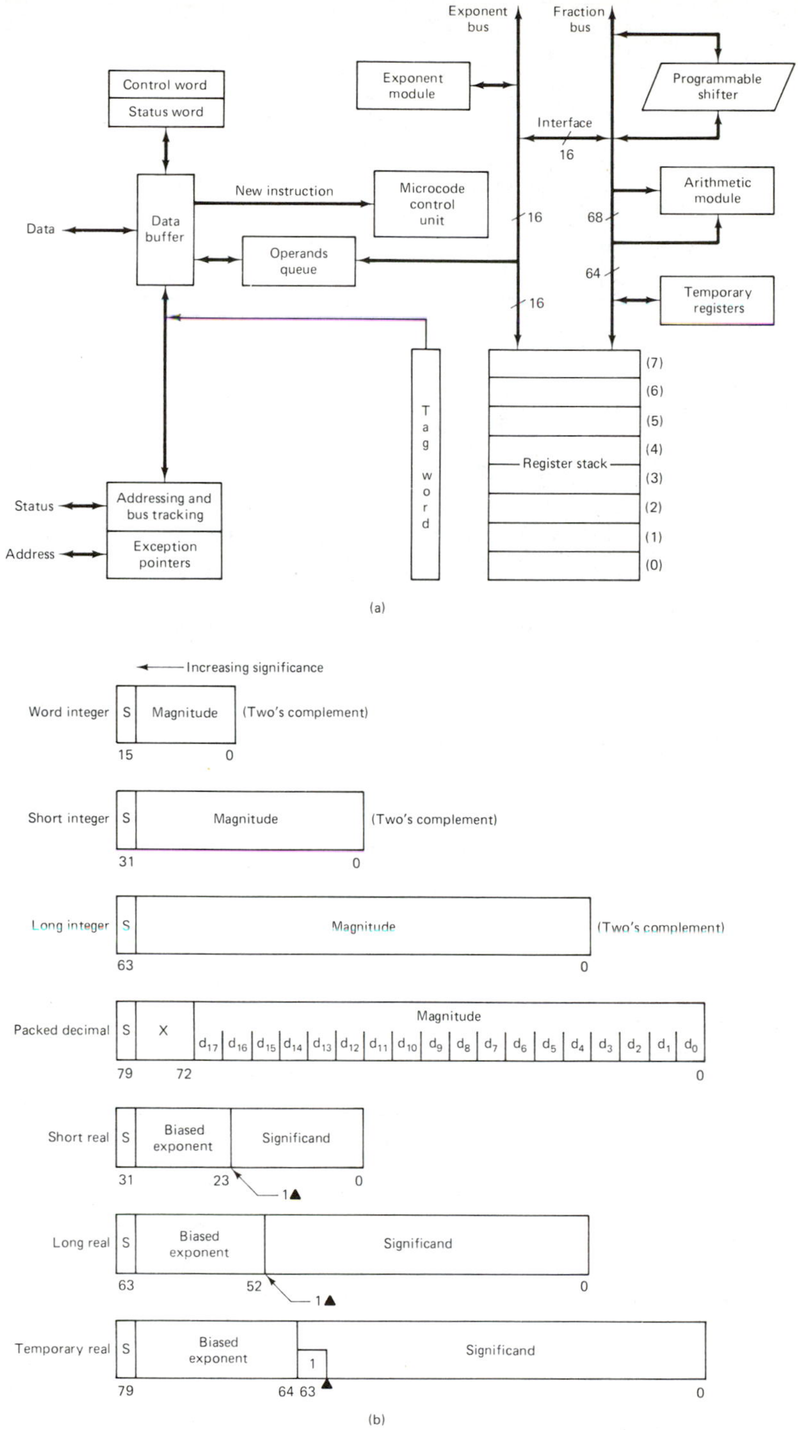

Figure 6.1 (*Top*) Internal structure of the I8087 numeric data processor. (*Bottom*) Formats of the six data types that can be loaded into the stack top and stored from the stack with automatic conversion to or from 80-bit real. (Reprinted by permission of Intel Corporation. Copyright 1980.)

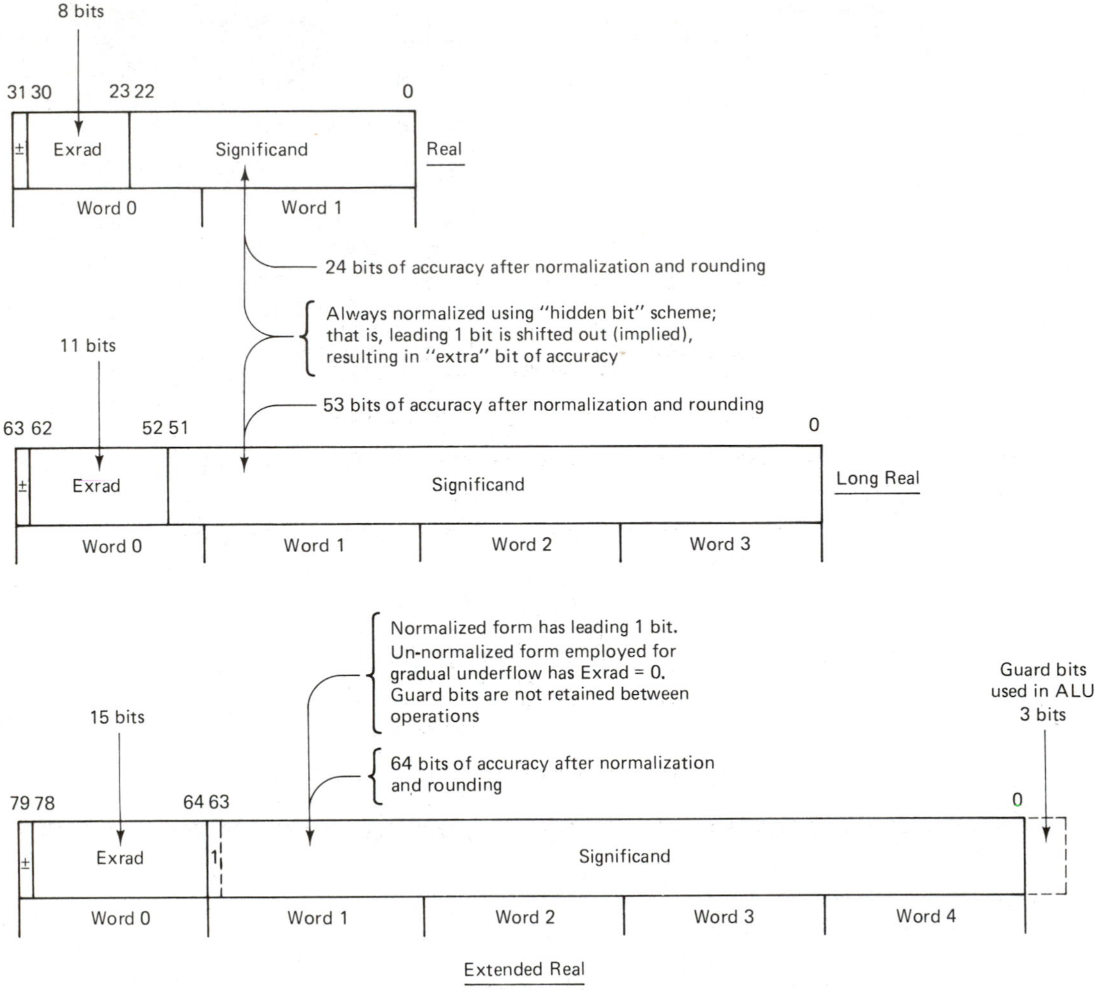

Figure 6.2 Format of the floating-point data types of the I8087. All calculations employ a 67-bit ALU with post arithmetic normalization and programmer-controlled rounding to one of the three formats.

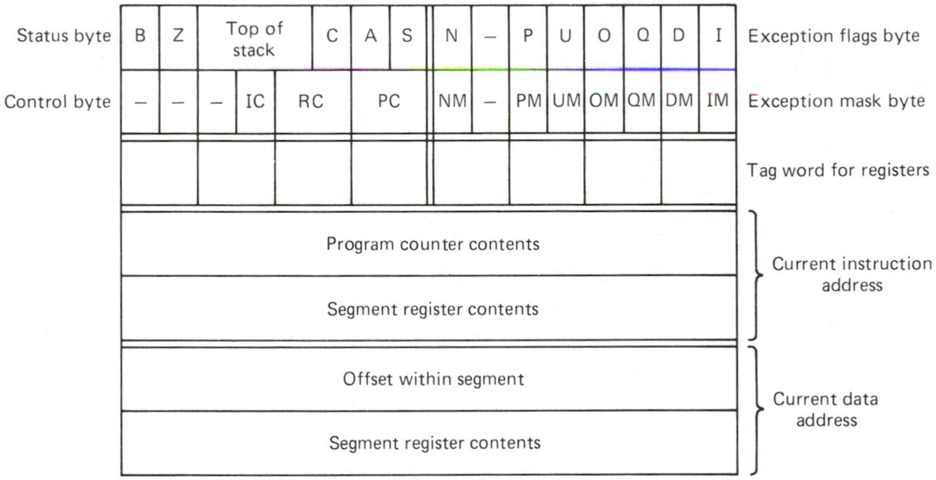

Status byte

B	I8087 Processor busy
Z	Zero result flag
C	Carry flag
A	Auxiliary carry flag
S	Sign flag
Top	Register identifier of current top-of-stack

Exception flags byte

N	Pending interrupt
P	Result with inexact precision
U	Underflow
O	Overflow
Q	Division of nonzero by zero
D	Un-normalized result (gradual underflow)
I	Invalid operation

Control byte

IC	Affine or projective infinity
RC	Round results to: unbiased to nearest, toward $+\infty$, toward $-\infty$, toward zero
PC	Round to precision of: extended real, long real, or real

Mask byte

By use of a mask, any exception flag or flags may be masked out

Figure 6.3 Seven-word I8087 environment register ("—" indicates not currently used).

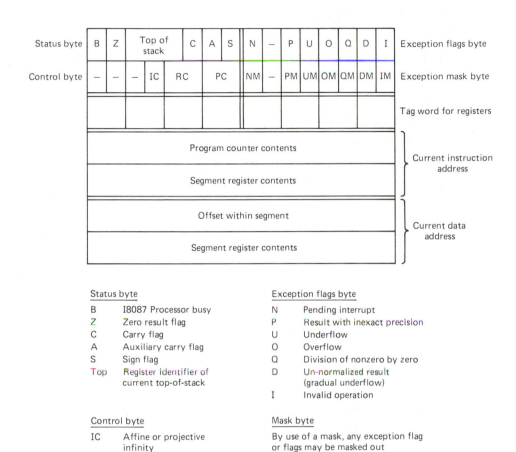

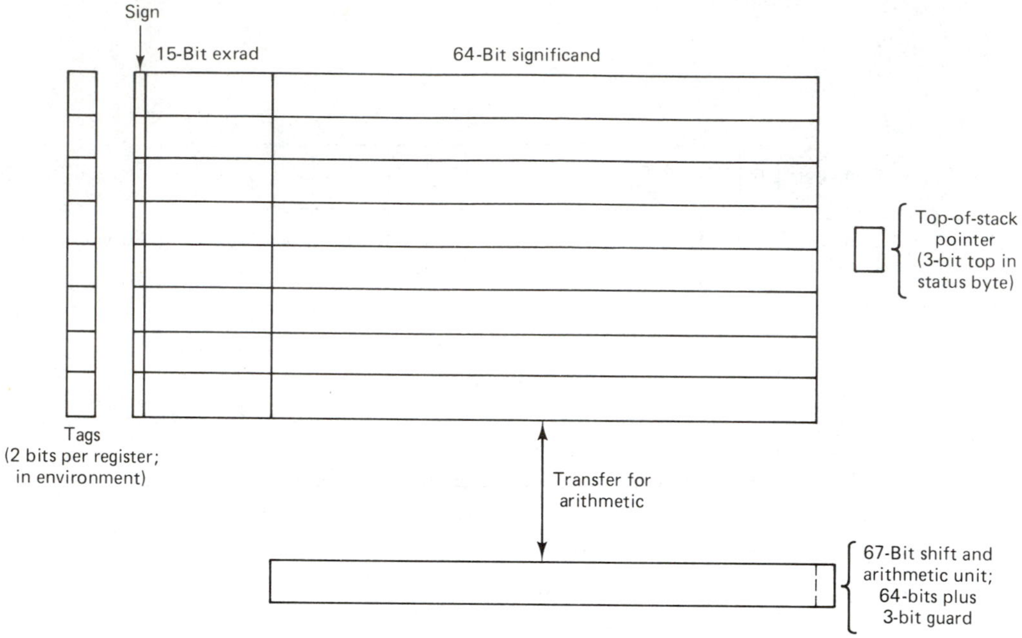

Figure 6.4 I8087 stack.

I8087 INSTRUCTIONS

PUSH/POP–LOAD/STORE

Loading or pushing a datum into the new stack top register always results in the datum being converted to the internal 80-bit extended real format. Transfer of the datum is from a stack register or from the system memory (never from the I8086/8088 data registers). The memory address furnished by the I8086/8088 to the I8087 consists of a 16-bit offset and the 16-bit contents of the segment register. The instructions are:

```
FLD     stack(i) ; newtop = stack(i)
        memory   ; newtop = 32-bit real memory
                 ;        = 64-bit real memory
                 ;        = 80-bit real memory
FILD    memory   ; newtop = 16-bit integer memory
                 ;        = 32-bit integer memory
                 ;        = 64-bit integer memory
                 ;          (converted to real)
FBLD    memory   ; newtop = 18-digit packed decimal
                 ;          memory (converted to real)
```

```
FLDZ      -   ; newtop = real plus zero
FLD1      -   ; newtop = real plus one
FLDPI     -   ; newtop = constant = PI
FLDL2T    -   ; newtop = constant = log2 (10)
FLDLG2    -   ; newtop = constant = log10 (2)
FLDL2E    -   ; newtop = constant = log2 (e)
FLDLN2    -   ; newtop = constant = loge (2)
```

where "Mem" is an offset/segment complete address into system memory. Pushing occurs with no loss of accuracy, as internal extended precision is able to contain the complete converted datum.

Storing or popping a datum from the stack top always results in the datum being converted from the internal 80-bit extended real form to the specified format before storage in system memory. The store/pop instructions are:

```
FST    stack(i)  ; stack(i) = top (copy-top remains)
       memory    ; 32-bit real memory = top (copy-top remains)
                 ; 64-bit real memory = top (copy-top remains)
                 ; 80-bit real memory = top (copy-top remains)
FSTP   stack(i)  ; stack(i) = top (pop top)
       memory    ; 32-bit real memory = top (pop top)
                 ; 64-bit real memory = top (pop top)
                 ; 80-bit real memory = top (pop top)
FIST   memory    ; 16-bit integer memory = top (copy-top remains)
                 ; 32-bit integer memory = top (copy-top remains)
                 ; 64-bit integer memory = top (copy-top remains)
                 ; (converted to integer)
FISTP  memory    ; 16-bit integer memory = top (pop top)
                 ; 32-bit integer memory = top (pop top)
                 ; 64-bit integer memory = top (pop top)
                 ; (converted to integer)
FBSTP  memory    ; 18-digit packed decimal = top (pop top)
                 ; (converted to packed decimal)
```

These instructions all employ the rounding rules specified by the programmer in the I8087 environment (Figure 6.3). These four available types of rounding will be discussed shortly.

Data movement within the stack is accomplished by a load, by a store, and by an exchange instruction:

```
FLD stack(i)    ; newtop = stack(i)
FST stack(i)    ; stack(i) = top (copy-top remains)
FSTP stack(i)   ; stack(i) = top (pop top)
FXCH stack(i)   ; top ⟷ stack(i)
FXCH            ; top ⟷ stack(next)
```

STACK AND STACK-MEMORY ARITHMETIC-LOGIC INSTRUCTIONS

The zero address arithmetic instructions pop the top two elements from the I8087 stack, perform the arithmetic operation, and push the result to the top of the stack. The operands are all internal extended floating-point data type. The arithmetic generic instructions each have variations. In the memory case, they are

top of stack ← top of stack + converted memory

with the memory operand being integer 16-bit word, double-precision 32-bit integer, real (32-bit), or double-precision (64-bit) real.

```
FADD                 ; newtop = oldtop + oldnext (both lost)
FADD    ST,stack(i)  ; top = top + stack(i)
FADD    stack(i),ST  ; stack(i) = stack(i) + top (no pop)
FADDP   stack(i),ST  ; stack(i) = stack(i) + top (pop top)
FADD    memory       ; top = top + 32-bit real memory
                     ; top = top + 64-bit real memory
FIADD   memory       ; top = top + 16-bit integer memory
                     ; top = top + 32-bit integer memory
FSUB                 ; newtop = oldtop - oldnext (both lost)
FSUBR                ; newtop = oldnext - oldtop (both lost)
FSUB    ST,stack(i)  ; top = top - stack(i)
FSUBR   ST,stack(i)  ; top = stack(i) - top
FSUB    stack(i),ST  ; stack(i) = stack(i) - top (no pop)
FSUBR   stack(i),ST  ; stack(i) = top - stack(i) (no pop)
FSUBP   stack(i),ST  ; stack(i) = stack(i) - top (pop top)
FSUBRP  stack(i),ST  ; stack(i) = top - stack(i) (pop top)
FSUB    memory       ; top = top - 32-bit real memory
                     ; top = top - 64-bit real memory
FSUBR   memory       ; top = 32-bit real memory - top
                     ; top = 64-bit real memory - top
FISUB   memory       ; top = top - 16-bit integer memory
                     ; top = top - 32-bit integer memory
FISUBR  memory       ; top = 16-bit integer memory - top
                     ; top = 32-bit integer memory - top
FMUL                 ; newtop = oldtop * oldnext (both lost)
FMUL    ST,stack(i)  ; top = top * stack(i)
FMUL    stack(i),ST  ; stack(i) = stack(i) * top (no pop)
FMULP   stack(i),ST  ; stack(i) = stack(i) * top (pop top)
FMUL    memory       ; top = top * 32-bit real memory
                     ; top = top * 64-bit real memory
FIMUL   memory       ; top = top * 16-bit integer memory
                     ; top = top * 32-bit integer memory
FDIV                 ; newtop = oldnext/oldtop (both lost)
FDIVR                ; newtop = oldtop/oldnext (both lost)
```

```
FDIV      ST,stack(i)  ; top = top/stack(i)
FDIVR     ST,stack(i)  ; top = stack(i)/top
FDIV      stack(i),ST  ; stack(i) = stack(i)/top (no pop)
FDIVR     stack(i),ST  ; stack(i) = top/stack(i) (no pop)
FDIVP     stack(i),ST  ; stack(i) = stack(i)/top (pop top)
FDIVRP    stack(i),ST  ; stack(i) = top/stack(i) (pop top)
FDIV      memory       ; top = top/32-bit real memory
                       ; top = top/64-bit real memory
FDIVR     memory       ; top = 32-bit real memory/top
                       ; top = 64-bit real memory/top
FIDIV     memory       ; top = top/16-bit integer memory
                       ; top = top/32-bit integer memory
FIDIVR    memory       ; top = 16-bit integer memory/top
                       ; top = 32-bit integer memory/top
FABS                   ; top = | top |
FCHS                   ; top = top * (-1)
FSQRT                  ; top = square root (top)
F2XM1                  ; top = (2 ** top) - 1
FRNDINT                ; top = rounded integer (top) as real
FPREM                  ; top = top modulus next-top
FSCALE                 ; top = top ** chopped integer (next-top)
FXTRACT                ; top = exponent (top) as real
                       ; newtop = significand (top) with
                       ;           exponent = 0
FYL2X                  ; top = oldnext * log2 (oldtop)
FYL2XP1                ; top = oldnext * log2 (oldtop +1)
FPTAN                  ; top = Y ; where:
                       ; newtop = X ; Y/X tan(top)
FPATAN                 ; top = arctan (oldnext/oldtop)
```

COMPARISON/TEST INSTRUCTIONS

The comparison instructions subtract the operand value from the stack top, set the I8087 flags, and discard the subtraction result. The test instructions compare the stack top to zero in a similar manner.

```
FCOM                 ; top - stack next
FCOM      stack(i)   ; top - stack(i)
FCOM      memory     ; top - 32-bit real memory
                     ; top - 64-bit real memory
FCOMP                ; top - stack next (pop top)
FCOMP     stack(i)   ; top - stack(i) (pop top)
FCOMP     memory     ; top - 32-bit real memory (pop top)
                     ; top - 64-bit real memory (pop top)
FCOMPP               ; top - stack next (pop both)
FICOM     memory     ; top - 16-bit integer memory
                     ; top - 32-bit integer memory
```

```
FICOMP   memory  ; top − 16-bit integer memory (pop top)
                 ; top − 32-bit integer memory (pop top)
FTST             ; top − 0.0
FXAM             ; set condition codes for: plus/minus,
                 ; NAN/zero/normal/unnormal/
                 ; denormal/empty
```

The comparison/test instructions set the I8087 exception flags in the environment register as follows:

Test	Compare	
top = +	top > operand	C0 = 0, C3 = 0
top = −	top < operand	C0 = 1, C3 = 0
top = 0	top = operand	C0 = 0, C3 = 1
top = ?	top ? operand	C0 = 1, C3 = 1 (NAN & infinity)

It is usually desired to use the result of I8087 comparison/tests to control program flow in the I8086/8088. Thus the I8087 status byte must be transferred to the flag word of the CPU via the following code:

```
FSTSW   STATUS_8087        ; store status word
FWAIT                      ; synchronize
MOV     AH,STATUS_8087+1   ; move to register
SAHF                       ; load to 8086 flags
```

At this time the I8086/8088-8087 program may use the conditional branch instructions:

```
JB    ? ; branch if top < operand or ?
JBE   ? ; branch if top =< operand or ?
JA    ? ; branch if top > operand or ?
JAE   ? ; branch if top => operand or ?
JE    ? ; branch if top = operand or ?
JNE   ? ; branch if top ≠ operand or ?
```

LOAD/STORE ENVIRONMENT INSTRUCTIONS

The following instructions allow an I8086/8088 program to examine and modify the environment registers of the I8087. In a multiprogramming system, the saving of the environment is an absolute necessity when a program loses control of the system. The restoration of the environment is necessary when the program regains control (finishes its time slice and subsequently is granted a new time slice). Referring to Figure 6.3, these instructions store in system memory or load from system memory different positions or all of the I8087 environment registers on a 16-bit word basis.

```
FNOP                              ; no operation (top = top)
FWAIT or WAIT                     ; I8086/8088 is not to proceed
                                  ; until I8087 is finished
                                  ; (synchronize processors).
FINCSTP                           ; stack-ptr = stack-ptr + 1 (mod 8)
FDECSTP                           ; stack-ptr = stack-ptr - 1 (mod 8)
FFREE      stack(i)               ; Mark stack(i) as "empty."
FSAVE      memory                 ; Save I8087 environment and
                                  ; registers in 96-byte memory
                                  ; area and initialize I8087.
                                  ; Assembler generates WAIT before
                                  ; FSAVE. FNSAVE has no WAIT.
FSTOR      memory                 ; Restore I8087 environment and
                                  ; registers from 96-byte memory
                                  ; area. Should be preceded
                                  ; by WAIT.
FDISI                             ; Disable interrupts of I8087
                                  ; after assembler generated
                                  ; WAIT. FNDISI has no WAIT.
FENI                              ; Enable interrupts of I8087
                                  ; after assembler-generated
                                  ; WAIT. FNENI has no WAIT.
FCLEX                             ; Clear I8087 exception flags after
                                  ; assembler-generated WAIT.
                                  ; FNCLEX has no WAIT.
FSTSW      memory                 ; Store I8087 status word after
                                  ; assembler-generated WAIT.
                                  ; FNSTSW has no WAIT.
FSTCW      memory                 ; Store I8087 control word after
                                  ; assembler-generated WAIT.
                                  ; FNSTCW has no WAIT.
FLDCW      memory                 ; Load I8087 control word.
FSTENV     memory                 ; Store I8087 environment in
                                  ; 14-byte memory area after
                                  ; assembler-generated WAIT.
                                  ; FNSTENV has no WAIT.
FLDENV     memory                 ; Load I8087 environment from
                                  ; 14-byte memory area. The
                                  ; next I8087 instruction
                                  ; should be preceded by WAIT.
FINT                              ; Initialize I8087 processor
                                  ; (a Reset) after assembler-
                                  ; generated WAIT.
                                  ; FNINT has no WAIT.
```

THE CO-PROCESSOR CONCEPT

Instructions for the I8087 and for the I8086/8088 are combined into a single program that carries out the desired data manipulations as defined by the programmer to solve the problem at hand. The program is a single unified and ordered sequence of instruction for manipulating data in a single systems memory regardless of whether the instructions are to be executed by the I8086/8088 central processor or by the I8087 floating-point processor. It is obvious that the processors must be able to recognize their own instructions and act only on them, ignoring instructions for the other processor. It is also obvious that some method must exist to prevent one of the processors from attempting to use data produced by the other before it has been delivered and to prevent the issuance of a new I8087 instruction before the present one is finished; that is, the processors must be kept in phase—they must be synchronized. In the scheme employed by the Intel designers, the I8086/8088 and the I8087 are allowed to execute different instructions of the same program simultaneously but under the overall control of the I8086/8088. This programming concept is accomplished via *co-routines.* When implemented on two or more processors, they are termed *co-processors.*

In many ways, the I8087 floating-point co-processor appears as an extension to the instructions of the I8086/8088 that allow particular data manipulations to be accomplished. As a matter of fact, all of the instructions to manipulate floating-point data could be accomplished employing subprocedures or macros executing on the I8086/8088. From this viewpoint, the I8087 is a hardware implementation of an extensive floating-point program library. In support of this viewpoint, such a software library exists and can be obtained from the Intel Corporation.

The implementation of the floating-point data manipulation functions in hardware (the I8087) not only allows increased processing speed, but results in smaller programs (as the software routines do not exist) and allows a modicum of concurrent instruction processing. This concurrency of processing is also true for DMA I/O as introduced in Chapter 5. The I8089 input/output processor, which will be the theme of Chapter 8, also allows concurrent processing of instructions within a computational system.

Instruction execution of the combined I8086/8088–8087 fully ordered instructions (the program) is always initiated by the control portion of the I8086/8088, obtaining an instruction from the instruction queue of its BIU. If the first byte of this two-, three-, or four-byte instruction has the bit pattern

11011XYZ

it is interpreted as an "escape" instruction. That is, it is not an I8086/8088 instruction but rather an instruction for a co-processor (in this example, an instruction for the I8087 numeric data processor). If this pattern is anything else, the I8086/8088 executes the instruction itself. If the pattern is an escape (11011XYZ) the I8086/8088 generates any necessary operand addresses, puts it on the address bus, and ignores the operation code. The I8086/8088 then resumes fetching/executing instructions.

The I8087 continuously monitors the instruction queue status lines (Q/S) of the I8086/8088. When an escape instruction bit pattern is found (11011XYZ), the I8087 begins to execute it. If the instruction involves a memory operand address, the I8087 will obtain it from the bus (recall that the I8086/8088 has generated the necessary 20-bit address and placed it on the bus). A schematic of the necessary communications is shown in Figure 6.5. The I8087 turns on its BUSY signal whenever it is executing an instruction and turns its BUSY signal off when finished with an instruction.

If the I8087 needs to access system memory, it requests the bus via the bidirectional request/grant line (RQ/GT). The I8086/8088 grants the bus to the

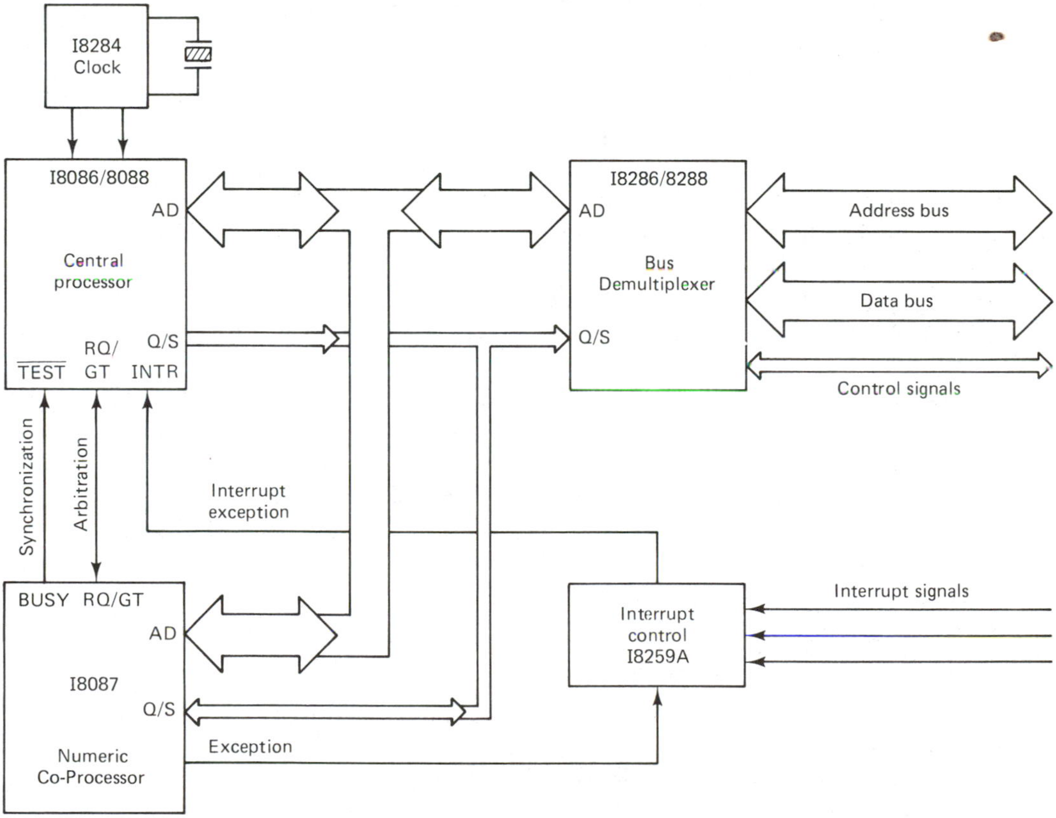

Figure 6.5 System containing an I8086/8088 central processor that fetches all instructions and executes those that it owns. The I8087 numeric co-processor monitors the instruction stream and executes any of its instructions. An I8086/8088 "wait" instruction causes it to wait until the I8087 signals instruction completion; thus, simultaneity can be achieved.

I8087 via this same RQ/GT line and the I8087 notifies the system of the end of its bus need via the same line, whereupon the I8086/8088 again assumes bus control.

Note that the I8086/8088 continues fetching and executing instructions simultaneously with the execution of an escape instruction by the I8087. Thus it is possible, and often probable, that the I8086/8088 could fetch and execute an instruction (possibly one that needs the result of the current I8087 instruction or a second escape instruction) before the finish of the I8087 operation. The result would be an unexpected happening: Either the production of a wrong value (the correct input operand was not yet stored by the I8087) or the ignoring of an escape instruction (the I8087 was currently working and "missed" the new instruction). In either case, an inappropriate result would have been generated because the I8086/8088 got "ahead" of the I8087—they got out of phase, out of proper synchronization. The dual-processor system would not be "deterministic."

The necessary synchronization can be programmer forced, and forced only by the programmer, by placing FWAIT instructions in the program at appropriate synchronization spots. When the I8086/8088 executes a FWAIT instruction, one of two actions will result:

1. If the I8087 BUSY signal is "on" (the I8086/8088 TEST signal is off), the I8086/8088 will wait and do nothing until the BUSY signal is "off" (signifying that the I8087 is finished).
2. If the I8087 BUSY signal is "off," the I8086/8088 treats the FWAIT instruction as a NOP.

Thus the FWAIT instruction is the programmatic mechanism whereby the programmer can force co-processor synchronization and assure that the I8086/8088 and I8087 do not get out of phase. The instruction execution scheme shown in Figure 6.7 for the co-processor situation should be helpful in fully understanding this limited but effective implementation of the more general semaphore control of the coroutine synchronization problem. It must be noted that no mechanism, beyond programmer care, exists to prevent the I8086/8088 from inadvertently overwriting I8087 data, or vice versa.

I8087 INSTRUCTIONS

The five formats of the "escape" instruction group are given in Figure 6.6. Note that one format involves instructions that use only the internal arithmetic stack top or stack registers of the I8087 and do not reference memory. The other four formats involve instructions that reference the stack top and also reference system memory via the addressing modes of the I8086/8088 as specified by the two MODE bits and the three R/M bits. Figure 3.8 summarizes the available addressing modes and should be referred to while studying Figure 6.6. Using this information, the I8086/8088 will generate the correct 20-bit system memory address and place it on

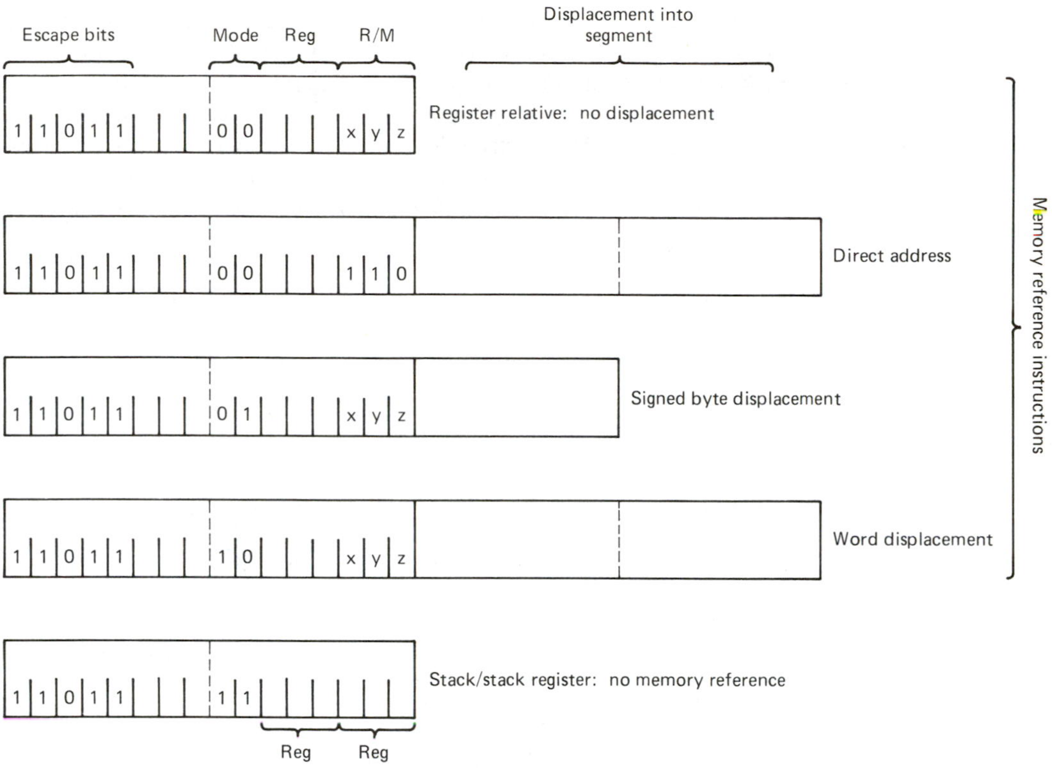

Figure 6.6 Instruction formats for I8086/8088 Escape instructions. These formats, then, are the instruction formats for I8087 instructions. Figure 3.8 gives the details of the memory addressing modalities.

the multiplexed bus for these memory reference escape instructions. The escape instruction operation code (opcode) will be treated as a NOP by the I8086/8088 while it is simultaneously recognized and executed by the I8087.

Because of the instruction queue, the I8086/8088 can fetch an instruction at some unknown and variable length of time before it executes that instruction. Additionally, the host processor (the I8086/8088) does not signal the co-processor (the I8087) whether the instruction it is currently executing is an escape instruction or not. Thus, to identify an escape instruction intended for the co-processor, the co-processor must examine the same instruction stream that the host is executing. To allow instruction examination synchronization of the two processors, the host signals when it fetches an instruction from memory into the instruction queue and when an opcode byte of an instruction is removed from the queue and decoded for execution. Lest the I8087 be busy executing an instruction when another instruction is encountered and thus not recognize it, it is a good idea to precede most escape instructions with a FWAIT.

In different but equivalent words, in order to recognize escape instructions, the co-processor (the I8087) must examine all instructions executed by the host processor (the I8086/8088). When the host obtains an instruction byte from its instruction queue, the co-processor must also, simultaneously, obtain the same instruction byte from its instruction queue. The I8087 follows these actions of the host processor by monitoring the bus status signals, the queue status signals, and the data bus signals of the I8086/8088. Of the eight possible states of the host bus status signals, five affect the I8087 co-processor:

S0	S1	S2	Activity of the host and the co-processor
0	0	1	Code fetch
1	1	0	Halt
1	1	1	Idle
1	0	1	Read data memory
0	1	1	Write data memory

the four queue status states have the following activity meanings:

QS1	QS2	Meaning to the host	Meaning to I8087
0	0	No operation	No queue action
0	1	Empty queue	Empty queue
1	0	Opcode byte-decode	Opcode byte-decode
1	1	Subsequent byte	If opcode was Escape, then decode; else ignore and flush

When the host I8086/8088 encounters an escape instruction, it either

1. Does nothing (treats it as a NOP)—this would correspond to a stack or register/stack I8087 instruction, or
2. Calculates an effective address, converts it to a physical address, reads a value from system memory, and ignores that value—this would correspond to a memory access I8087 instruction. The I8087 will latch this value from the data bus at the end of T3 during the memory read cycle.

If the I8087 co-processor requires a datum longer than one word (I8086) or one byte (I8088) or if it must write information to memory, the co-processor must capture and save the physical memory address for subsequent use and be able to become bus master. Thus the I8087 will latch the physical address from the bus during T1 of the memory cycle and store it. All memory references of the I8087 co-processor are relative to this physical 20-bit memory starting address. As shown in Figures 3.8 and 6.7, an escape memory reference instruction is identified in the second byte (QS1:QS2 = 11) by a MODE value of 00, 01, or 10. The existence of data

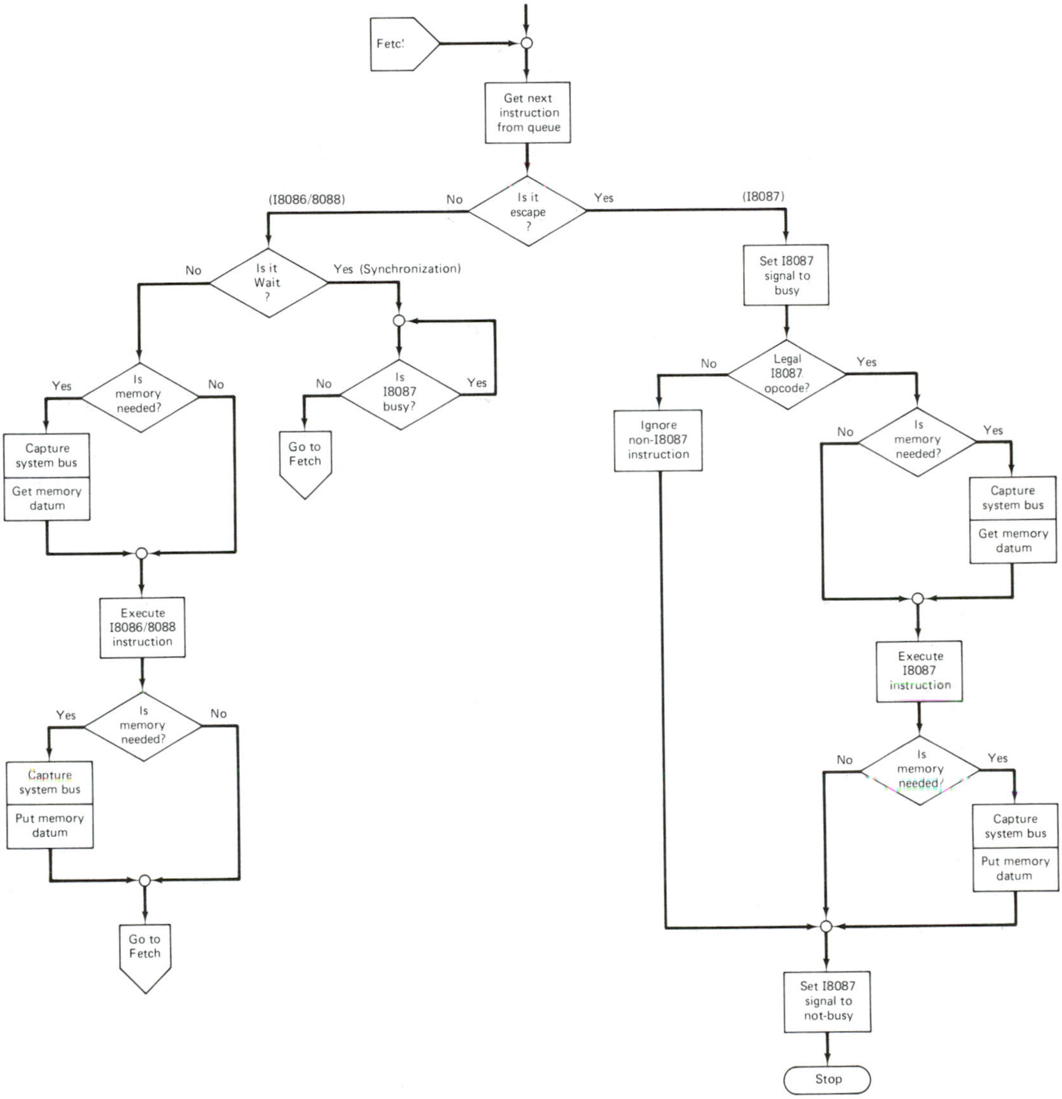

Figure 6.7 Instruction execution scheme for I8086/8087—I8087 co-processor system. Note that the I8086/8088 acquires all instructions and that it performs a synchronization wait only if it encounters a **WAIT** instruction and the I8087 is busy. Also note that the system bus is shared.

on the bus for the I8087 has been indicated to the I8087 by the host processor signaling 101 on the S0/S1/S2 lines and 0 on the S6 line.

When the co-processor I8087 needs to access memory itself, it will capture the bus, increment the physical address it had previously captured and stored, and then perform the memory access. Note that this requires that the I8087 know if the host processor is an I8086 with a 16-bit data transfer or an I8088 with an 8-bit data transfer. The I8087 co-processor identifies the host as an I8086 or as an I8088 by monitoring its pin 34 on the first memory cycle after power up. If the host is an I8086, pin 34 will be the BHE signal and be low; if the host is an I8088, pin 34 will be the SS0 signal and be high. Upon obtaining the low/high pin 34 signal during the first memory cycle after a FINT, the I8087 co-processor will configure its data bus width accordingly.

Incidentally, the I8087 has no memory address alignment restrictions for word operands in memory but will perform a one-byte memory operation for word operands starting at an odd address or word memory operation for word operations starting at an even address. Only execution speed will be affected. Similarly, the memory address alignment of floating-point operands for the I8087 co-processor have no effect on the numeric results. The number of memory accesses and thus the execution speed will be affected. The I8087 will minimize the number of bus cycles, when possible as a co-processor to an I8086 host, by first performing a byte memory access for an operand starting at an odd address and then performing word operation with a final byte operation when necessary.

An I8087 co-processor hosted by an I8088 will perform all memory access operations on a byte basis and thus will execute more slowly. The numeric results will be identical, as will all program control and interrupt actions. Note that all instruction timings for the I8088 and for the I8088 hosted I8087 co-processor are identical regardless of memory address alignment of data. Also, note that an I8088-based system tends to be memory access speed limited to a much greater extent than does an I8086-based system, although the problem solution results are always identical.

FLOATING-POINT NUMBERS

FINITE REPRESENTATION AND ERRORS

The syntax and associated semantics of binary floating-point arithmetic specified in the IEEE Standard as implemented by the I8087 numeric data processor use a fixed number of bits to represent the different portions of numbers in each data format. In the internal extended real format, the biased binary exrad occupies 15 bits, the binary fractional significand occupies 64 bits, and its sign occupies 1 bit. The value is

$$\pm 0.\text{significand} \times 2^{\text{exrad} - 16383}$$

The close affinity of this notation to scientific notation and to logarithms was discussed earlier.

The representable numbers group naturally into intervals of the form

$$2^n, 2^{n+1}, 2^{n+2}, \ldots$$

called *binades* (from the analogous term *decades*). Within each binade representable numbers are uniformly spaced with a separation of 1 bit in their least significant place. As the numbers increase in magnitude via an increase in the magnitude of the exponent, this absolute spacing of exactly representable numbers increases by a value of 2 from binade to binade and the average accuracy of the number becomes correspondingly less. Similarly, as the numbers approach zero, this absolute spacing of exactly representable numbers decreases by a value of 2 from binade to binade and covers half the remaining distance to zero with the average accuracy of the number becoming correspondingly greater. This relationship is shown in Figure 6.8.

Earlier in this chapter we defined a normalized floating-point number as one in which the most significant bit of the fractional mantissa was a 1-bit. If normalization is mandatory, all numbers of less value than allowed would be made zero and an exception flag set indicating "underflow." If nonnormalization is allowed, numbers of smaller value (closer to zero) are allowed, although an exception flag should be set. This is termed *gradual underflow.* Figure 6.9 illustrates these concepts.

A value whose floating-point representation cannot be contained by the largest exrad/significand diad has a magnitude too large for the available format. The development of such a value should set the "overflow" exception flag. The appropriate subsequent action is usually problem dependent and cannot be completely generalized.

Assuming no overflow for mathematically well-defined results, a satisfactory model for floating-point arithmetic is: Compute the results with infinite precision and range and then, if necessary, round to the appropriate representable number (nearest, next higher, next lower). This concept can be represented as

$$\text{finite stored result} = \text{true infinite result} \pm \text{roundoff}$$

where roundoff is no more than $^1/_2$ ulp (unit in the last place) for nearest rounding or no more than 1 ulp for rounding up or rounding down (truncation).

Roundoff errors, then, result from using a finite set of binary fractions to represent an infinitely fine graduation over a range of real numbers. Quantization errors due to format size limitations result from the inexact binary representation for almost all of the numbers. Since two consecutive significand values span an infinity of real numbers, of which only the largest and smallest are represented precisely, roundoff error can be assumed in the floating-point representations of all (very nearly all) numbers.

Using the term *ex* for the roundoff error in the floating-point representation of the true infinite value of X and *xx* for the finite stored result, we can see that

Floating-point quantities

Sign	Exponent	Significand	Quantity
0	MAX	>0	+ NaN
0	MAX	0	+ Infinity
0	0 < E < MAX	>0	+ Real
0	0	>0	+ Denormalized
0	0	0	+ 0
1	0	0	− 0
1	0	>0	− Denormalized
1	0 < E < MAX	>0	− Real
1	MAX	0	− Infinity
1	MAX	>0	− NaN

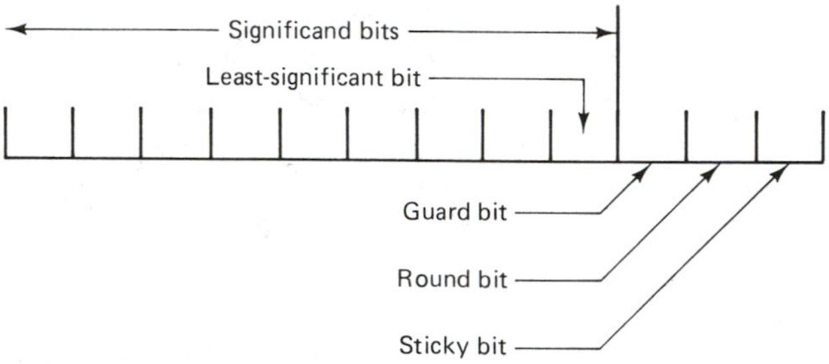

Guard, round and sticky bits ensure accurate unbiased rounding of computed results to within half a unit in the least-significant bit. Two bits are required for perfect rounding; the guard bit is the first bit beyond rounding precision, and the sticky bit is the logical OR of all bits thereafter. To accommodate post-normalization in some operations, the round bit is kept, beyond the guard bit, and the stickly bit is a logical OR of all bits beyond round.

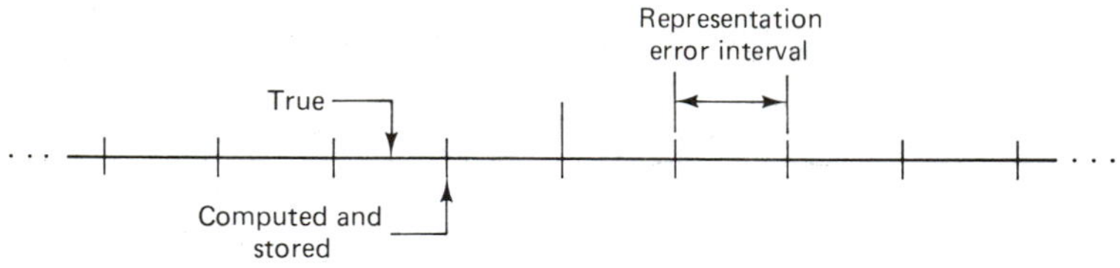

Figure 6.8 The error effects of employing finite representations for infinitely precise quantities necessarily includes roundoff. (Adapted from *SIGNUM (ACM) Newsletter,* October 1979.)

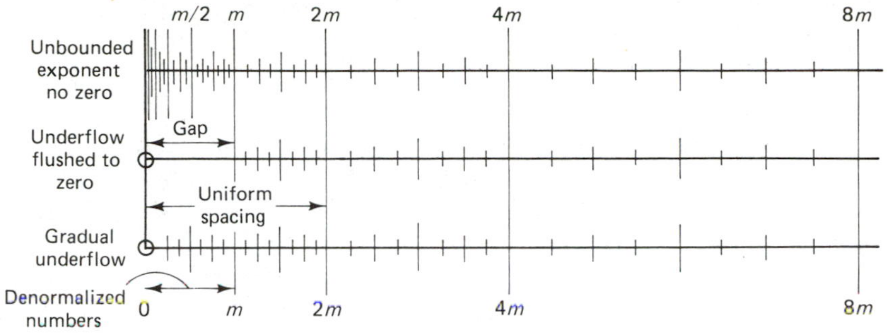

Each vertical tick stands for a 4-bit significand binary floating-point number. The underflow threshold *m* is a power of ½ depending upon the allowed range of exponents; every floating-point number bigger than *m*, but none smaller, is representable as a normalized floating-point number. Flushing underflows to zero introduces a gap between *m* and 0 much wider than between *m* and the next larger number. Gradual underflow fills that gap with denormalized numbers as densely packed between *m* and 0 as are normalized numbers between *m* and 2*m*. Doing so relegates underflow in most computations to a status comparable with roundoff among the normalized numbers.

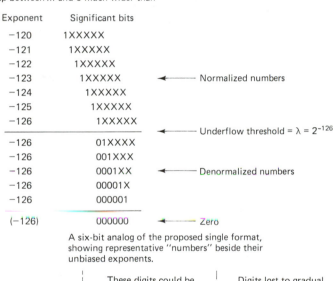

Exponent	Significant bits	
−120	1XXXXX	
−121	1XXXXX	
−122	1XXXXX	
−123	1XXXXX	← Normalized numbers
−124	1XXXXX	
−125	1XXXXX	
−126	1XXXXX	
		← Underflow threshold = $\lambda = 2^{-126}$
−126	01XXXX	
−126	001XXX	
−126	0001XX	← Denormalized numbers
−126	00001X	
−126	000001	
(−126)	000000	← Zero

A six-bit analog of the proposed single format, showing representative "numbers" beside their unbiased exponents.

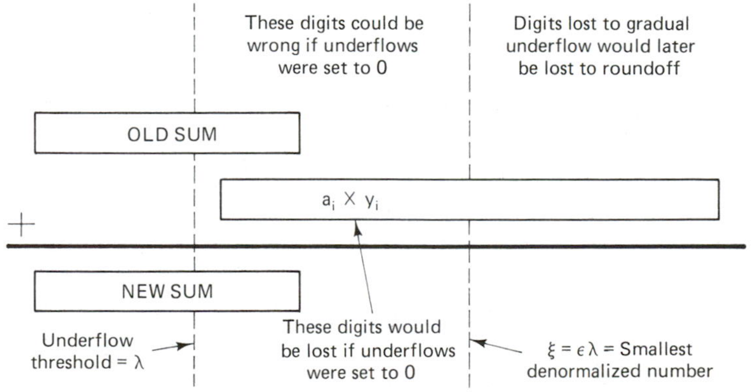

The effect of gradual underflow and store 0 on small sums

Figure 6.9 The gradual underflow effect necessarily increases computational accuracy. (Adapted from *SIGNUM (ACM) Newsletter,* October 1979.)

$$X + Y = (xx + ex) + (yy + ey) = (xx + yy) + (ex + ey)$$

$$X - Y = (xx + ex) - (yy + ey) = (xx - yy) + (ex - ey)$$

$$X \times Y = (xx + ex) * (yy \times ey) = (xx \times yy) + (xx \times ey) + yy \times ex) + (ex \times ey)$$ (last term is so small that it can be ignored)

$$X = \quad (xx + ex) - xx + ex - (X \times ey)$$ (where = means approximately equal)

$$Y = \quad (yy + ey) = yy + ey - (Y \times eY)$$

Unfortunately, absolute error expressions are not really appropriate for floating-point roundoff error analysis. Instead, it is the relative error that is really important. The relative error of any term, X, is

$$\frac{ex}{xx}$$

The relative errors for the four basic arithmetic operations above are

$$RE\,(X + Y) = \frac{xx}{xx + yy} \times \frac{ex}{xx} + \frac{yy}{xx + yy} \times \frac{ey}{yy}$$

$$RE(X - Y) = \frac{xx}{xx + yy} \times \frac{ex}{xx} - \frac{yy}{xx - yy} \times \frac{ey}{yy}$$

$$RE(X \times Y) = \frac{ex}{xx} + \frac{ey}{yy}$$

$$RE\left(\frac{X}{Y}\right) = \frac{ex}{xx} - \frac{ey}{yy}$$

An examination of the absolute error formulas above requires that particular attention be directed to three commonly encountered sources of unnecessary programmatic errors:

1. When two numbers of nearly identical magnitude are subtracted, the magnitude of the absolute error term may approach or exceed the magnitude of the difference. This cancellation effect can result in erroneous results that differ from the correct result by orders of magnitude.
2. When the denominator is small in relation to the numerator in a division, the magnitude of the absolute error term may render the quotient useless.
3. When comparing two floating-point quantities whose true infinite values are equal or near equal, the results of the comparison (=, >, <, =>, <=) will usually be determined solely by the absolute error term and will not reflect the true infinite values. Any program branch logic based on such a comparison will often be erroneous.

We close this discussion of roundoff errors by quoting John Palmer of the Intel Corporation (1980):

> Mathematical software is easy for the uninitiated to write but notoriously hard for the expert. This paradox exists because the beginner is satisfied if his code usually works in his own machine while the expert attempts, against overwhelming obstacles, to produce programs that always work on a large number of computers. The problem is that while standard formulas of mathematics are fairly easy to translate into FORTRAN they often are subject to instabilities due to roundoff error.

At least some of the generalized numerical solutions to common mathematical procedures have coding that is so involved and tricky in order to take care of all possible roundoff contingencies that they have been termed "pornographic algorithms."

Fortunately, the internal extended (temporary) real format implemented in the I8087 version of the IEEE Floating-Point Standard as well as the control of rounding and other features means that code written by programmers who are unfamiliar with analyzing their programs for roundoff errors and other problems will have a much greater chance of working correctly.

CHARACTERISTICS OF I8087 FLOATING-POINT ARITHMETIC

Rounding

A major contribution of the IEEE standard and of the I8087 to accurate numerical computation is the ability to control the rounding mode after computation and before storage of the result. Thus the programmer can specify how infinitely precise results are to be rounded to fit the designated storage format.

It is important to note that if the correct infinite precise result is exactly representable in the designated storage format, that exact result is stored regardless of any programmatic rounding orders. If storage of the exact result is impossible, that is, if roundoff must be employed, four modes are available under program control:

1. *Round to nearest* (in case of a tie, round to the one with a zero in the least significant bit): As noted earlier, this rounding mode will generally result in the smallest roundoff error and is the recommended mode for almost all cases.
2. *Truncation*: Round toward zero. Truncation is commonly implemented on floating-point processors in mini-/midi-/maxi-/supercomputers. In general, truncation introduces a roundoff bias toward results with a smaller magnitude.
3. *Round to next smaller* (less than or equal to true result).
4. *Round to next larger* (greater than or equal to true result).

The last two directed rounding modes are vital in implementing interval arithmetic, which we will describe shortly.

Recall that all data types (real, long real, extended real, word integer, double-precision integer, signed 18-digit packed BCD) are first converted to (temporary) extended real when pushed/loaded into the I8087 stack top with *no* roundoff error relative to their storage representation in system memory. Additionally, all arithmetic within the I8087 employs extended real (80-bit) and stores the result in internal registers as extended real. If storage of a precise infinite result is not possible, the indicated rounding mode is employed and the inexact flag is set (P for imprecise, not P for precise). The imprecise flag is also set when rounding occurs during a push or store to system memory. Thus *exact arithmetic* may be implemented via software.

Interval Arithmetic

Interval arithmetic is practical to implement using the round-to-next-smaller and round-to-next-larger rounding modes so that calculations within an algorithm can be programmed to include all possible roundoff error in both directions. This will ensure that the two answers delineate or bound the area where the infinite precise answer lies. In addition, interval arithmetic can be used to estimate the effects of noisy data (in a measurement sense). Thus if the yield of maize is recorded as 100 bushels per acre with a probable measurement error of 2½ bushels, the calculations involving this datum would proceed with both 97½ and 102½ bushels per acre.

In effect, the interval data type employs an ordered pair for each datum:

$$X = [X\ \text{low} : X\ \text{high}]$$

and uses the round down : round up modes as well as the signed zeros and signed infinities of the I8087 as specified in the IEEE Standard. In the usual case where X low is equal to or less than X high, the interval X includes all numbers within the interval. The other possible case where X low is greater than X high implies that the interval X includes all numbers not within the interval. The signs on zero and infinity permit open intervals (X low is greater than X high) or closed intervals (X low $< \pm$ X high) when zero or infinity is an endpoint with the sign signifying which case pertains. If an interval endpoint is neither zero nor infinity, the interval is closed (X low $>$ X high). A more complete discussion of interval arithmetic is not appropriate in this text. Students with a need for more complete information are referred to an article by R. E. Moore (1979).

Infinity

Infinity has a format with the exrad all 1 bits and the significand all 0 bits. Infinity is the default response to overflow and to divide by zero. Two modes of infinity arithmetic are implemented:

1. *Affine* with minus infinity, which is less than all other numbers, and plus infinity, which is greater than all other numbers. The affine infinity mode requires a minus zero and plus zero which are equal in comparison and in all arithmetic except division where

$$\frac{+1}{+0} = +\text{infinity} \qquad \frac{+1}{-0} = -\text{infinity}$$

   Signed zeros and signed infinities often represent underflowed or overflowed quantities. When computing in the affine mode, the rules of arithmetic preserve many of the relationships that would hold among underflowed or overflowed quantities. By selecting the nondefault affine mode, the programmer accepts full responsibility for determining that such arithmetic is valid for both the algorithm and for the data.
2. *Projective* with only one infinity and one zero. The infinity (with sign ignored) is larger in magnitude than other numbers. The projective mode of infinity is more conservative mathematically and thus is the default mode.

Not a Number

Not a number has a format with the exrad all 1 bits and the significand nonzero. Arithmetic operations involving NAN result in a NAN and the setting of the invalid operation flag. One obvious use of NAN is to start all floating-point data receptacles as NAN and thus cause a fault during any computation with an uninitialized datum. Additionally, if the significand field of array element NAN starting values contains the array element index, a reference to an uninitialized array element would not only indicate that it was uninitialized but also which element it was. This technique would be a powerful and very economical debugging aid, particularly for novice programmers.

EXCEPTIONS AND INTERRUPTS

As in all processors, exception detection allows the I8087 to report programming and/or data errors via an interrupt so as to allow specialized and responsive correction actions or to allow default corrective actions with subsequent resumption of execution. Additionally, the detection of exceptions can be employed to implement software extensions to the I8087 co-processor system.

As was noted earlier and as is shown in Figure 6.3, each type of I8087 exception has a flag and a flag mask. The occurrence of an exception causes the appropriate associated flag to be set, following which the subsequent action depends on the flag mask.

If the flag mask is off, then an interrupt is generated that is passed to the I8259A priority interrupt controller and then to the I8086/8088, where it is fielded either as a device interface event with an interrupt number ranging from 32 through

255 or as an Intel reserved interrupt with a vector table entry from 5 through 31. The exception-handling routine would be designed and coded in the normal manner employing both I8086/8088 host processor and I8087 co-processor (escape) instructions. By accessing the registers in the I8087 control registers, as shown in Figure 6.3, the exception interrupt servicing routine has available both the address in system memory of the escape instruction that caused the exception and the address of the referenced datum (if it was a system memory resident datum). Exception interrupt service routines require an exceptional knowledge of the underlying mathematics behind floating-point arithmetic and of numerical analysis to correctly design, write, debug, and maintain. For all but the deeply involved expert, it is not an advisable activity.

If the flag mask is set, then an on-chip microcoded default exception handler is invoked that performs the corrective action appropriate to the vast majority of cases, following which execution is resumed. The exception flag remains set until it is read and reset by an escape software instruction.

The *denormalized operand exception* sets the flags and as a default allows the operation to proceed as if the operand were unnormalized. If the interrupt is allowed, it occurs before processing.

The *inexact result exception* signifies that the true result cannot be exactly represented in the specified format. The true result is rounded as specified; the flag is set; and as a default, execution continues. If the interrupt is allowed, it occurs after result storage.

The *underflow exception* signifies that the result is nonzero but cannot be represented as a normalized number in the specified format. The flag is set and gradual underflow is allowed as the default. If the interrupt is allowed, it occurs after storage of the result.

The *overflow exception* signifies that the result is too large in magnitude to be represented in the specified format. The flag is set and infinity with the sign of the correct result is stored as the default. If the interrupt is allowed, it occurs after storage of the result.

The *zero divisor exception* signifies that the divisor was zero while the dividend was a finite nonzero number. The flag is set and infinity is stored with the sign derived as the exclusive-or (XOR) of the signs of the input operands as the default. If the interrupt is allowed, it occurs before processing.

The *invalid operation exception* can be caused by two entirely different conditions:

1. If the invalid operation exception is caused by the use of a not-a-number (NAN) as one or both of the input operands, the default result is either the input NAN or the "larger" of the two input NANs.
2. If the invalid operation exception is caused by the I8087 stack overflow, stack underflow, or by the specification of an indeterminate form such as 0/0, inf.-inf., and so on, the default result is an "indefinite" NAN with a special bit pattern in the significand. Indeterminate forms are usually fatal errors that

should abort the program immediately. Alternatively, more information may be obtained by allowing the indefinite NAN to propagate to the end of the program and then investigating how it contaminated the subsequent calculations. Stack underflow and stack overflow are also usually fatal errors, although a complicated exception interrupt service routine might extend the I8087 stack to system memory through software.

If the interrupt is allowed, it occurs before any processing.

It is *recommended* that novice or nonexpert floating-point data type programmers mask all exceptions except invalid operations. With the default exception handler results as described above, in conjunction with the reliable infinity arithmetic; invalid operation due to the use of indefinite forms or stack underflow/overflow are the only exceptions that are likely to be fatal to program execution producing useful results.

BINARY-CODED-DECIMAL DATA MANIPULATIONS

Many applications involving monetary quantities such as are commonly encountered in business data processing are stored and manipulated as binary-coded-decimal entities. The commonly employed procedural-level language for these applications, COBOL, employs BCD storage and manipulation for many data entities.

As you know from Chapter 4, the I8086/8088 has two instructions to adjust the results to BCD using the binary signed integer with carry addition and subtraction instructions using BCD input operands. Referring to the examples of BCD arithmetic employing these algorithms in Chapter 4, it is obvious that the programming is tedious and the operations slow. Multiplication and division present further difficulties.

If an I8087 co-processor is available, the use of the extended floating-point internal format can be used to manipulate 18-digit BCD numbers with a sign byte appended on the left (10-bytes) after conversion. Recall that the instruction

```
FBLD        Memory
```

will convert a memory-resident signed 18-digit packed BCD number to extended real without error and push it to the top of the I8087 stack. The BCD format is shown in Figure 6.1. Similarly, the instruction

```
FBSTP       Memory
```

will round, as specified, an I8087 top-of-stack resident extended real quantity, convert it to a signed 18-digit packed BCD number, and pop it to memory. Converted BCD numbers in the I8087 can be manipulated in a manner analogous to other extended real quantities. For business data processing purposes, exact mode arithmetic is strongly suggested.

MULTI-PRECISION INTEGER DATA MANIPULATIONS

One of the chief arguments against 8-bit machines is the restriction of direct manipulation of signed integer quantities to the range −128 through +127. Of course, multiprecision arithmetic may be employed through software, but it is tedious to program and is very slow during execution. The 16-bit microcomputers are a major improvement in this respect.

Analogously, one of the chief arguments against 16-bit machines is the restriction of direct manipulation of signed integer quantities to the range −32,384 through +32,383. Again, of course, multiprecision arithmetic may be employed through software. The I8087 co-processor numeric data processor provides an important improvement by allowing direct manipulation of floating-point coded 16-bit, 32-bit, and 64-bit integer quantities.

Recall that the instructions

```
FILD        Memory
```

will convert a memory-resident signed word (16-bit), double word (32-bit), or quad-word signed integer to extended real with no errors due to representation limitations and then push it to the top of the I8087 stack. Similarly, the instructions

```
FIST        Memory
FISTP       Memory
```

will convert the top-of-stack resident extended real quantity to the specified integer format and store or pop it to memory. It is extremely important to realize that the conversion can cause overflow and that, in this case, overflow should usually be considered a fatal program error. Therefore, it is suggested that the overflow interrupt be allowed during those sections of a program employing the I8087 for quasi-multiprecision integer data manipulations and that an appropriate integer overflow interrupt servicing routine be provided in the I8086/8088. Also, exact mode arithmetic is usually vital.

7

ASM 86: The Intel 8086/8087/8088 Assembly Language

Procedural-level languages such as Pascal or BASIC can decrease the time required to transliterate a problem-solution design into executable code when compared with the time required when an assembly language is used. Additionally, these higher-level languages have the advantage of a degree of machine independence that often allows relatively easy transfer of programs from one vendor's computer to those of another vendor. Finally, more people know and have facility in using these languages than have practice in using a lower-level language.

On the other hand, most procedural-level languages do not permit a programmer to access directly many of the unique features provided by the specific computer design. The compilers—the translators—for higher level languages tend to produce object machine code that is generalized to cover all possible situations, even those situations that are expected to occur very rarely. Additionally, most compilers produce object code consisting of a fairly small and restricted subset of the available operand addressing modes. Nevertheless, compilers for such relatively simple languages as FORTRAN and COBOL are available that generate code that usually executes almost as rapidly and occupies only a trifle more space than most assembly language programmers would produce when solving the same problem. For most situations, the optimal solution usually involves implementing most of the problem solution in a procedural-level language while using assembly language for the few lowest-level routines that must solve special strange data manipulations that are either time and/or space critical.

It must be noted that certain data manipulations that are cumbersome and difficult to accomplish in a procedural language are often straightforward and easy to implement using an assembly language. Additionally, the direct control of most peripherals via device drivers employing the interrupt system of the combined hardware–software interface is best accomplished using an assembly language. Finally, anyone who has the intellectual drive to understand the computer deeply must become intimately familiar with the machine at the instruction–register–memory–device level, a task that is only possible employing assembly language. It should be realized that this human–computer intimacy is not for everyone.

FEATURES OF THE ASM 86

The assembly language designed for the I8086 family that is available from the Intel Corporation is unusual in providing some of the features usually available only in modern higher-level languages. These advanced features can be interpreted as constituting extremely desirable and useful facilities. Alternatively, these features can be interpreted as being unnecessary but nice complications. A more usual and simpler assembly language is presented in Chapter 10 as a hypothetical example for the design and implementation of an assembler-linker system. Assembler processors following the more traditional design path are commercially available from various software houses. This chapter will present an overview of the assembly language syntax, semantics, and pragmatics of the Intel 8086/8087/8088 Macro Assembly Language (ASM 86) as available from the Intel Corporation.

The group of assembly language statements and comments that are presented to the assembler for transformation into corresponding machine language instructions is called a *module* (Figures 7.1 to 7.4). The assembler is a program that acts as a translation function for a named module:

$$\text{source module} \xrightarrow{f} \textit{object module}$$

In keeping with the memory segmentation design of the I8086/8088, in which memory is addressed as physical segments via a 16-bit segment register, the assembly language provides for segments. Although a module may contain as many segments as desired, only four are ever "current" at one time. Thus your ASM 86 module may define:

1. A segment for global data
2. A segment for local data
3. A segment for the stack
4. A segment for the main program
5. Segments for subprograms
6. A segment for interrupt serving routines
7. A segment for the interrupt vector, and so on

Four or fewer segments are active at any one time during execution:

1. The *current code segment,* whose physical starting address is the memory paragraph in the CS register. The 20-bit physical address of a segment starts at the contents of the segment register shifted left 4 bits, that is, at the start of a paragraph.
2. The *current data segment,* which is addressed via the DS register in a similar manner.
3. The *current stack segment,* which is similarly addressed via the SS register.
4. The *current extra segment,* which is addressed via the ES register, is usually needed only if string data are used, and often may not be needed.

It is the program implementor's duty to provide instructions to define segments and to load appropriate values into the segment registers before attempting to access the segment.

ASM 86 employs the procedure as the subroutine concept mechanism. A procedure is a programmer-defined block of code or data with no limitations regarding the data manipulations specified, that is, no limitations on the instructions and data containers employed to implement the manipulations. The use of the procedure mechanism in an assembly language is very unusual, if not unique. The somewhat simpler and more usual method employed by most assemblers is described in Chapter 10. Although it is highly recommended as "good programming practice" only to CALL procedures and RETurn, it is possible to conditionally/unconditionally branch to a procedure as well as to allow program control to "sequentially flow" into a procedure.

A macro definition and substitution facility is furnished by ASM 86. A macro consists of a programmer-defined and programmer-named block of code that is physically inserted into the assembly language module at each point where the macro name occurs as the operation code. This facility, common in almost all assemblers, allows a programmer to augment, as is desirable or necessary, the instruction set of the I8086/8087/8088 computer system with "extra" functionality. As discussed in Chapter 10, a macro may have arguments or parameters that allow the changing of any or all portions of any or all instructions within the macro, including labels, operations codes, operand addresses, and/or comments.

THE MODULE

An assembly language module is defined as the set of source statements that are presented as a file to the assembler as input (source module) and as the corresponding set of object code (object module) that results as a file from the successful assembly of a correct source module. The source module is presented to the assembler as an input file with a name—an identifier. The assembler output file—the object module—will have a default name consisting of the name of the source file unless a directive is issued to name it something else. The object file is normally one of the

```
LOC  OBJ                  LINE    SOURCE

                             1    ;**************************************************************************
                             2    ;*                                                                        *
                             3    ;*          PROGRAM FOR FLOATING POINT ADDITION WITH INTEL'S 8087         *
                             4    ;*                                                                        *
                             5    ;**************************************************************************
                             6    ;DEFINE INITIALIZATION ROUTINE
                             7    EXTRN INIT87:FAR
                             8    ;
                             9    ;
----                        10    DATA SEGMENT
0000 3E03                   11            CONTROL_87      DW      033EH    ;DEFINE CONTROL WORD
0002 9A191442               12            NUM             DD      37.025   ;DEFINE TWO FLOATING
0006 9A408245               13            NUM1            DD      4168.075;NUMBERS
000A ????????????????       14            ANS             DQ      ?        ;SPACE FOR ANSWER
     ??
----                        15    DATA ENDS
                            16    ;
                            17    ;
                            18    ;ALLOCATE CPU STACK SPACE
----                        19    STACK SEGMENT STACK 'STACK'
0000 (100                   20                            DW      100 DUP(?)
     ????
     )
00C8                        21            STACK_TOP       LABEL   WORD
----                        22    STACK ENDS
                            23    ;
                            24    ;
----                        25    CODE SEGMENT
0100                        26            ORG 100H
                            27            ASSUME CS:CODE,DS:DATA,SS:STACK,ES:NOTHING
0100 B8----          R      28            START:  MOV     AX,DATA          ;SET UP
0103 8ED8                   29                    MOV     DS,AX            ;SEGMENT
0105 B8----          R      30                    MOV     AX,STACK         ;REGISTERS
0108 8ED0                   31                    MOV     SS,AX            ;
010A BCC800          R      32                    MOV     SP,OFFSET STACK_TOP
010D 8BEC                   33                    MOV     BP,SP            ;
                            34    ;
                            35    ;
010F 9A0000----      E      36                    CALL INIT87              ;INITIALIZE
0114 9BD92E0000             37                    FLDCW   CONTROL_87       ;
                            38    ;
                            39    ;
0119 9BD9060200             40                    FLD     NUM              ;LOAD DATA ON STACK TOP
011E 9BD9060600             41                    FLD     NUM1             ;LOAD SECOND DATA VALUE ON TOP
0123 9BD8C1                 42                    FADD    ST,ST(1)         ;FLOATING POINT ADD NUM & NUM1
0126 9BDD160A00             43                    FST     ANS              ;STORE RESULT
012B F4                     44                    HLT
----                        45    CODE ENDS
                            46    END

ASSEMBLY COMPLETE, NO ERRORS FOUND
```

```
SDK-86 MONITOR, V1.2
.#
.D20:0,11
0000 3E 03 9A 19 14 42 9A 40 82 45 00 00 00 00 00 00   <-- MEMORY DUMP BEFORE EXECUTION
0010 00 00
.#
.#
.D32:0,2B
0000 B8 20 00 8E D8 B8 36 00 8E D0 BC C8 00 8B EC 9A
0010 00 00 35 00 9B D9 2E 00 00 9B D9 06 02 00 9B D9   <-- MEMORY DUMP OF PROGRAM
0020 06 06 00 9B D8 C1 9B DD 16 0A 00 F4
.#
.#
.G 0000- 48 32:0,2B

BR @0032:002B
.D20:0,11                                   ANS
0000 3E 03 9A 19 14 42 9A 40 82 45[00 00 80 A6 19 6D
0010 B0 40
.
```

BIAS EXP
04 B0 6D 19 A6 80

UN BIAS = 04B −3FF − C = 12

\# = 10000 0100 1101,0001 1001 1010 0110 1000

= 4096 + 64 + 32 + 12 + 1 = 4205

= 1/16 + 1/32 + 1/256 + 1/512 + 1/2048 + 1/16384 + 1/32768 + 1/131072 = .100

37,025 + 4168.075 = 4205.100

Figure 7.1 Example of an ASM86 module.

```
LOC  OBJ                  LINE    SOURCE

                             1    ;**************************************************************************
                             2    ;*                                                                        *
                             3    ;*         PROGRAM FOR FLOATING POINT MULTIPLICATION WITH INTEL'S 8087    *
                             4    ;*                                                                        *
                             5    ;**************************************************************************
                             6    ;DEFINE INITIALIZATION ROUTINE
                             7    EXTRN INIT87:FAR
                             8    ;
                             9    ;
----                        10    DATA SEGMENT
0000 3E03                   11            CONTROL_87      DW      033EH   ;DEFINE CONTROL WORD
0002 8096984B               12            NUM             DD      2E7     ;DEFINE TWO FLOATING
0006 00008040               13            NUM1            DD      4.0     ;NUMBERS
000A ??????????????         14            ANS             DQ      ?       ;SPACE FOR ANSWER LONG REAL FORMAT
     ??
0012 ??????????????         15            ANS1            DT      ?       ;  "    "     "   TEMP REAL   "
     ??????
001C ??????????????         16            ANS2            DT      ?       ;  "    "     "   BCD         "
     ??????
----                        17    DATA ENDS
                            18    ;
                            19    ;
                            20    ;ALLOCATE CPU STACK SPACE
----                        21    STACK SEGMENT STACK 'STACK'
0000 (100                   22                            DW      100 DUP(?)
     ????
     )
00C8                        23            STACK_TOP       LABEL   WORD
----                        24    STACK ENDS
                            25    ;
                            26    ;
----                        27    CODE SEGMENT
0100                        28            ORG 100H
                            29            ASSUME CS:CODE,DS:DATA,SS:STACK,ES:NOTHING
0100 B8----           R     30            START:  MOV     AX,DATA          ;SET UP
0103 8ED8                   31                    MOV     DS,AX            ;SEGMENT
0105 B8----           R     32                    MOV     AX,STACK         ;REGISTERS
0108 8ED0                   33                    MOV     SS,AX            ;
010A BCC800           R     34                    MOV     SP,OFFSET STACK_TOP
010D 8BEC                   35                    MOV     BP,SP            ;
                            36    ;
                            37    ;
010F 9A0000----       E     38                    CALL INIT87              ;INITIALIZE
0114 9BD92E0000             39                    FLDCW   CONTROL_87       ;
                            40    ;
                            41    ;
0119 9BD9060200             42                    FLD     NUM              ;LOAD DATA ON STACK TOP
011E 9BD9060600             43                    FLD     NUM1             ;LOAD SECOND DATA VALUE ON TOP
0123 9BD8C9                 44                    FMUL    ST,ST(1)         ;FLOATING POINT MULT NUM & NUM1
0126 9BDD160A00             45                    FST     ANS              ;STORE RESULT
012B 9BDDD1                 46                    FST     ST(1)            ;SAVE RESULT
012E 9BDB3E1200             47                    FSTP    ANS1             ;STORE RESULT IN TEMP REAL FORMAT
0133 9BDF361C00             48                    FBSTP   ANS2             ;STORE RESULT IN BCD FORMAT
0138 F4                     49            HLT
----                        50    CODE ENDS
                            51    END

ASSEMBLY COMPLETE, NO ERRORS FOUND
```

```
SDK-86 MONITOR, V1.2
.#
.D20:0,25
0000 3E 03 80 96 98 4B 00 00 80 40 00 00 00 00 00 00
0010 00 00 00 00 00 00 00 00 00 00 00 00 00 00 00 00
0020 00 00 00 00 00 00
.#
.#
.D33:0,38
0000 B8 20 00 8E D8 B8 38 00 8E D0 BC C8 00 8B EC 9A
0010 00 00 37 00 9B D9 2E 00 00 9B D9 06 02 00 9B D9
0020 06 06 00 9B D8 C9 9B DD 16 0A 00 9B DD D1 9B DB
0030 3E 12 00 9B DF 36 1C 00 F4
.#
.#
.G 0000- 48 33:0,38

BR @0033:0038
.D20:0,25
0000 3E 03 80 96 98 4B 00 00 80 40 00 00 00 00 D0 12
0010 93 41 [00 00 00 00 00 80 96 98 19 40 [00 00 00 80
0020 00 00 00 00 00 00
.
```

← MEMORY DUMP BEFORE EXECUTION

← MEMORY DUMP OF PROGRAM

LONG REAL 41 93 12 D0 (BIAS EXP)

EXP = 419 - 3FF = 1A = 26.

10011 0001 0010 1101 0000 0000 0000 (BINARY POINT)

= 80,000,000

TEMP REAL 0419 98 96 80 0000 (BIAS EXP)

EXP = 0419 - 3FFF = 1A = 26

1001 1000 1001 0110 1000 0000 0000 (BINARY POINT)

= 80,000,000

BCD 80 00 00 00 = 80,000,000

Figure 7.2 Example of an ASM86 module.

```
LOC  OBJ                 LINE     SOURCE

                            1     ;*******************************************************************************
                            2     ;*                                                                             *
                            3     ;*               PROGRAM TO FIND LOG n(X)   WITH INTEL'S 8087                 *
                            4     ;*                                                                             *
                            5     ;*******************************************************************************
                            6     ;DEFINE INITIALIZATION ROUTINE
                            7     EXTRN INIT87:FAR
                            8     ;
                            9     ;
----                       10     DATA SEGMENT
0000 3E03                  11             CONTROL_87      DW      033EH   ;DEFINE CONTROL WORD
0002 0A00                  12             n               DW        10    ;DEFINE n ;MUST BE INTEGER
0004 E803                  13             X               DW      1000    ;DEFINE X ;MUST BE INTEGER
0006 ????????              14             ANS             DD      ?       ;SPACE FOR ANSWER
----                       15     DATA ENDS
                           16     ;
                           17     ;
                           18     ;ALLOCATE CPU STACK SPACE
----                       19     STACK SEGMENT STACK 'STACK'
0000 (100                  20                             DW      100 DUP(?)
     ????
     )
00C8                       21             STACK_TOP       LABEL   WORD
----                       22     STACK ENDS
                           23     ;
                           24     ;
----                       25     CODE SEGMENT
0100                       26             ORG 100H
                           27             ASSUME CS:CODE,DS:DATA,SS:STACK,ES:NOTHING
0100 B8----          R     28             START:  MOV     AX,DATA         ;SET UP
0103 8ED8                  29                     MOV     DS,AX           ;SEGMENT
0105 B8----          R     30                     MOV     AX,STACK        ;REGISTERS
0108 8ED0                  31                     MOV     SS,AX           ;
010A BCC800          R     32                     MOV     SP,OFFSET STACK_TOP
010D 8BEC                  33                     MOV     BP,SP           ;
                           34     ;
                           35     ;
010F 9A0000----      E     36                     CALL INIT87             ;INITIALIZE
0114 9BD92E0000            37                     FLDCW   CONTROL_87      ;
                           38     ;
                           39     ;
0119 9BD9E8                40                     FLD1                    ;LOAD 1 ON TOS
011C 9BDF060200            41                     FILD    n               ;LOAD THE BASE
0121 9BD9F1                42                     FYL2X                   ;CALCULATE Y*LOG2X
0124 9BDB160600            43     FIST ANS
0129 9BDDD1                44                     FST     ST(1)           ;SAVE TOS
012C 9BD9E8                45                     FLD1                    ;LOAD 1 ON TOS
012F 9BD8F1                46                     FDIV    ST,ST(1)        ;DIVIDE 1/(Y*LOG2X)
0132 9BDB160600            47     FIST ANS
0137 9BDF060400            48                     FILD    X               ;LOAD ARGUMENT
013C 9BD9F1                49                     FYL2X                   ;CALCULATE Y*LOG2X
013F 9BDB160600            50     FIST ANS
0144 9BDB160600            51                     FIST    ANS             ;SAVE RESULT
0149 F4                    52                     HLT
----                       53     CODE ENDS
                           54     ;NOTE ....THIS PROGRAM WAS WRITTEN FOR INTEGERS IT CAN EASILY BE
                           55     ;         CHANGED TO HANDLE REALS
                           56     END
```

```
ASSEMBLY COMPLETE, NO ERRORS FOUND


SDK-86 MONITOR, V1.2
.#
.D20:0,9
0000 3E 03 0A 00 E8 03 00 00 00 00
.#
.#
.D31:0,49
0000 B8 20 00 8E D8 B8 37 00 8E D0 BC C8 00 8B EC 9A
0010 00 00 36 00 9B D9 2E 00 00 9B D9 E8 9B DF 06 02
0020 00 9B D9 F1 9B DB 16 06 00 9B DD D1 9B D9 E8 9B
0030 D8 F1 9B DB 16 06 00 9B DF 06 04 00 9B D9 F1 9B
0040 DB 16 06 00 9B DB 16 06 00 F4
.#
.#
.G 0000- 48 31:0,49

BR @0031:0049
.#
.D20:0,9
0000 3E 03 0A 00 E8 03 03 00 00 00
.
```

$\log_{10} 1000 = 3$

Figure 7.3 Example of an ASM86 module.

```
LOC  OBJ                    SOURCE

                            ;**************************************************************************
                            ;*                                                                        *
                            ;*              PROGRAM FOR BCD OPERATIONS WITH INTEL'S 8087              *
                            ;*                                                                        *
                            ;**************************************************************************
                            ;DEFINE INITIALIZATION ROUTINE
                            EXTRN INIT87:FAR
                            ;
                            ;
----                        DATA SEGMENT
0000 3E03                           CONTROL_87      DW       033EH     ;DEFINE CONTROL WORD
0002 89674523010000                 NUM             DT   123456789     ;DEFINE TWO BCD
     000000
000C 23010000000000                 NUM1            DT         123     ;NUMBERS
     000000
0016 ??????????????                 ANS             DT           ?     ;SPACE FOR ANSWER BCD FORMAT
     ??????
0020 ??????????????                 ANS1            DT           ?     ;  "    "    "   BCD  "
     ??????
002A ??????????????                 ANS2            DT           ?     ;  "    "    "   BCD  "
     ??????
0034 ??????????????                 ANS3            DT           ?     ;  "    "    "   BCD  "
     ??????
----                        DATA ENDS
                            ;
                            ;
                            ;ALLOCATE CPU STACK SPACE
----                        STACK SEGMENT STACK 'STACK'
0000 (100                                           DW       100 DUP(?)
     ????
     )
00C8                                STACK_TOP       LABEL    WORD
----                        STACK ENDS
                            ;
                            ;
----                        CODE SEGMENT
0100                                ORG 100H
                                    ASSUME CS:CODE,DS:DATA,SS:STACK,ES:NOTHING
0100 B8----           R             START:  MOV     AX,DATA            ;SET UP
0103 8ED8                                   MOV     DS,AX              ;SEGMENT
0105 B8----           R                     MOV     AX,STACK           ;REGISTERS
0108 8ED0                                   MOV     SS,AX              ;
010A BCC800           R                     MOV     SP,OFFSET STACK_TOP
010D 8BEC                                   MOV     BP,SP              ;
                            ;
                            ;
010F 9A0000----       E                     CALL INIT87                ;INITIALIZE
0114 9BD92E0000                             FLDCW   CONTROL_87         ;
                            ;
                            ;
```

```
0119 9BDF260200                    FBLD     NUM          ;LOAD DATA ON STACK TOP
011E 9BDF260C00                    FBLD     NUM1         ;LOAD SECOND DATA VALUE ON TOP
0123 9BDDD2                        FST      ST(2)        ;SAVE STACK TOP
0126 9BD8E1                        FSUB     ST,ST(1)     ; SUBTRACT (NUM1 - NUM)
0129 9BDF361600                    FBSTP    ANS          ;BCD STORE RESULT OF SUBTRACTION
012E 9BDDD2                        FST      ST(2)        ;SAVE STACK TOP
0131 9BD8C1                        FADD     ST,ST(1)     ; ADD (NUM+NUM1)
0134 9BDF362000                    FBSTP    ANS1         ;BCD STORE RESULT OF ADDITION
0139 9BDDD2                        FST      ST(2)        ;SAVE STACK TOP
013C 9BD8C9                        FMUL     ST,ST(1)     ; MULTIPLY (NUM1*NUM)
013F 9BDF362A00                    FBSTP    ANS2         ;BCD STORE RESULT OF MULTIPLICATION
0144 9BD8F1                        FDIV     ST,ST(1)     ; DIVIDE (NUM/NUM1)
0147 9BDF363400                    FBSTP    ANS3         ;BCD STORE RESULT OF DIVISION
014C F4                            HLT
----                      CODE ENDS
                          ;
                          ;NOTE IF ANSWER DOESN'T COME OUT AS AS INTEGER THEN NDP
                          ;ROUNDS TO FORM AN INTEGER AND THEN OUTPUTS AS BCD VALUE
                          END

ASSEMBLY COMPLETE, NO ERRORS FOUND


SDK-86 MONITOR, V1.2
.#
.D20:0,3D
0000 3E 03 89 67 45 23 01 00 00 00 00 00 23 01 00 00
0010 00 00 00 00 00 00 00 00 00 00 00 00 00 00 00 00
0020 00 00 00 00 00 00 00 00 00 00 00 00 00 00 00 00
0030 00 00 00 00 00 00 00 00 00 00 00 00 00 00
.#
.#
.D40:0,4C
0000 B8 20 00 8E D8 B8 46 00 8E D0 BC C8 00 8B EC 9A
0010 00 00 45 00 9B D9 2E 00 00 9B DF 26 02 00 9B DF
0020 26 0C 00 9B DD D2 9B D8 E1 9B DF 36 16 00 9B DD
0030 D2 9B D8 C1 9B DF 36 20 00 9B DD D2 9B D8 C9 9B
0040 DF 36 2A 00 9B D8 F1 9B DF 36 34 00 F4
.#
.#
.G 0000- 48 40:0,4C

BR @0040:004C
.#
.D20:0,3D
0000 3E 03 89 67 45 23 01 00 00 00 00 00 23 C1 00 00
0010 00 00 00 00 00 00 66 66 45 23 01 00 00 C0 00 80
0020 12 69 45 23 01 00 00 00 00 00 47 50 18 E5 51 01
0030 00 00 00 00 14 37 00 01 00 00 00 00 00 C0
.
```

← MEMORY DUMP BEFORE EXECUTION

← MEMORY DUMP OF PROGRAM

num, num1, Ans, Ans1, Ans2, Ans3

123456789 − 123 = 123456666
123456789 + 123 = 123456912
123456789 × 123 = 15185185047
123456789 ÷ 123 = 1003714

Figure 7.4 Example of an ASM86 module.

inputs to a program (LINK 86) that combines modules preparatory to loading into physical memory and execution.

The *NAME directive* assigns a programmer-chosen name to the object module output file generated by the assembly of the source module. The format is

```
NAME identifer          ; 1 to 31 characters
                        ; (letters, digits, and/or
                        ; underscore, sign, and
                        ; question mark) and starting
                        ; with a letter or one of the
                        ; special characters
```

The NAME directive may *not* have a label and the identifier may *not* consist of an instruction name, a macro name, a pseudo-operations keyword (such as PROC or MACRO), a global variable name, a label name, a variable name from the module itself, and so on. This rule is designed to avoid the double definition of names with a probable resultant mixup and eventual catastrophic happenings.

The *PUBLIC directive* specifies which of the variable names or labels are to be available to other modules for linking (via LINK 86). In effect, the PUBLIC directive orders the assembler to make the address of the specified data container labels available so that other modules can reference them for data access/storage or for program contol flow (i.e., CALL). A 17-bit integer that is defined through an EQU can also be made PUBLIC. An attempt to make register names, including the I8087 stack registers, PUBLIC either directly or via an EQU is *not* allowed. The format is

```
PUBLIC identifier, identifiers, . . .
```

In order for an identifier declared PUBLIC in one module to be referenced and used in another module, it must be declared external in the using module.

The *EXTRN directive* informs the assembler which of the variable names or labels referenced in this module are defined in other modules and are available via the PUBLIC directive in those other modules. The EXTRN directive will specify a type for the identifier as

1. BYTE, WORD, DWORD (for data containers)
2. NEAR or FAR (for labels or procedures)
3. ABS for constants (EQU) of size WORD (implied)

The format is

```
EXTRN identifier:type, identifier:type, . . .
```

The physical placement of EXTRN directives is important. Of the two possible placements, the first is preferable:

1. If the programmer knows the segment in which the external symbol is defined and declared PUBLIC, declare it EXTRN in a segment of the same name:

```
DATA        SEGMENT     PUBLIC
            EXTRN       BUFFER:WORD
DATA        ENDS
```

2. If the programmer does not know the segment in which the external symbol is defined and made PUBLIC, declare it EXTRN at the beginning of the module outside of all segments. This will require that the appropriate segment register be loaded with the segment base address *and* that this segment register be forced into use during access of the data container or label.

```
MOV         AX,SEG BUFFER
MOV         DS, AX
MOV         BX,DS:BUFFER
```

Alternatively, the last order above could have the segment register specified via the external directive (discussed later)

```
ASSUME ES:SEG BUFFER
```

The *END directive* informs the assembler that the end of the source module has been found. For a main program module, the format is

```
END label
```

The label reference is to the label of main program start, which will result in the code segment (CS) register and the program counter (IP) register being given correct values for the start of execution. For all modules not containing the main program, the format must be

```
END         ; no reference to a label allowed
```

SEGMENTS: ADDRESSABILITY AND CONTROL

THE SEGMENT DIRECTIVE

Every instruction and every data container of a program must be located within some segment during execution. This necessity results from the design of the I8086/8088 that requires all memory addressing to involve an offset from the base of a segment (pointed to by one of four segment registers—CS, DS, SS, or ES). An assembly language module can involve one complete segment, several complete segments, a portion of one segment, or portions of several segments.

The purpose of defining and specifying a segment is to allow the access of the instructions and/or data containers in that segment: that is, to establish addressability for the segment contents via a segment register. A segment is defined by employing the assembly directives (pseudo-operations)

```
label SEGMENT align combine "class"
        -
        -
        -
label ENDS
```

where the pseudo-operations (keywords) in uppercase are required while the information indicated in lowercase is optional. A segment will be either a code, a data, a stack, or an extra segment, with its contents being addressed via the corresponding segment register.

label

Although this information is optional, it is highly recommended that all segments be given a name, preferably a unique name within the segments that will be involved in the current program. As labels within a module must be unique, and as segment names within a module are labels, segment names within a module must be unique. If you neglect to name a segment, the assembly system will assign the name ??SEG. The segment name assembles as an offset address within the module.

align

If this optional information is omitted (the usual case in practice), the starting or base address of the segment will be divisible by 16 base 10 and thus agree with the usual contents of a segment register. The keyword PARA has the same effect. This parameter must be used or implied for segments that are completely specified in a single contiguous source block within a single module. If the segment definition constitutes a portion of a final linked segment, the starting address of the currently defined segment portion may not be a paragraph—an address divisible by 16—but may be a byte or a word. This can be indicated by the keywords BYTE or WORD.

combine

This optional information specifies how this segment may be combined with other segments during linking (via LINK 86) and loading into memory preparatory to execution. The possibilities are:

omit: (the default) the segment is complete unto itself and is not to be combined with any other segments during linking. The align parameter should be PARA or implied to be PARA by not being specified.

PUBLIC: specifies that this segment fragment will be combined with all other segment fragments with the same name during linking (with the order of concatenation specified to LINK 86). A common usage would involve global data containers (see the PUBLIC and EXTRN directive discussed previously under the heading of modules).

COMMON: specifies that this segment will start at the same address and completely overlap all other segments of the same name when linked together. This storage arrangement is exactly that of FORTRAN COMMON.

STACK: specifies that this segment is to be a portion of the run-time stack during execution. It will be referenced via the stack segment register (SS) and be accessed via CALL, PUSH, POP, RET, INT, and IRET instructions. Stack segments are concatenated by LINK 86, begin at "high-memory addresses," and "grow downwards." They would be adjacent to, but at lower memory addresses than, the COMMON segment (if it exists) after linking.

MEMORY: specifies that this segment will start at the highest memory address of all segments linked. If more than one segment is specified as MEMORY, LINK 86 will treat the first one encountered as MEMORY and treat all the rest as COMMON. The use of this parameter should normally be rare.

AT expression: specifies the absolute memory address at which this segment will be loaded into memory. The expression can be somewhat complicated as long as it evaluates to a constant and contains only currently known elements. This constant is multiplied by 16 to obtain the absolute memory load address (example: 1234h will result in the segment start or base address being 12340h). Segments of the operating system might employ this parameter to force their location at specific addresses. The interrupt vector should start at address 00000h, for example.

'class'

The concept of class can be employed as a directive at load time to force segments with the same class name to be collected together. Certain utility programs available from the Intel Corporation also can be used to manipulate the group of segments with the same class name. If assembly language routines are to be used as subprograms to procedural-level routines, all requirements of the specific compiler must be observed in the assembly module. For example, the PL/M-86 compiler uses the class names 'CODE', 'DATA', 'STACK', 'CONST', AND 'MEMORY'. In other cases where the source program is entirely assembly language, freedom exists relative to class names. All class name must be enclosed in single quotation marks.

Nesting Segments

Although source-level assembly language segments may be nested, the resultant object module will consist of unnested separate segments. During translation, the assembler will employ a separate offset address within the segment pointer which is sequentially incremented by the length of each instruction and/or data container. Thus if the assembler encounters the following two situations, the resulting object module will be the same.

```
CODE SEGMENT                   CODE SEGMENT
      -                              -
      -                              -
      -                              -
      DATA SEGMENT                   -
            -                        -
            -                  CODE ENDS
            -                  DATA SEGMENTS
      DATA ENDS                      -
      -                              -
      -                              -
CODE ENDS                      DATA ENDS
```

Nesting segments may often furnish an excellent method of structuring source code so as to indicate the logical relationships of segments. For instance, the left example above would indicate that the segment named DATA is owned and used by the segment named CODE.

THE ASSUME DIRECTIVE: ESTABLISHING ADDRESSABILITY

As you will recall, every instruction and data container of a program must be contained within some segment and is accessible by addressing via a segment register. The ASSUME pseudo-operation is used to specify which segment register should be used with which segment during execution. In effect, it specifies the mapping between the logical locations in the source module and the physical real memory addresses when the object module is executing. The format is

```
ASSUME seg-reg:seg-name, seg-reg:seg-name, . . .
```

where seg-reg is CS:, DS:, SS:, or ES: and seg-name is the name of a segment or the name of a group of segments (groups will be discussed shortly) or a label within a segment. An alternative form is

```
ASSUME NOTHING
```

which requires that every memory reference be a diad of the form

```
MOV     AX,DS:ANY_WORD
```

Although situations exist where the latter style of programming is "handy," it should be avoided.

Loading the CS Register

Although the code segment register can be loaded using the technique for loading any other segment register, this practice is unusual. Recall that all fetches of instructions must involve the CS register and that this reference pattern cannot be overridden. The physical address of the instruction to be fetched is derived as

(CS) + (IP) → address of instruction

An intrasegment conditional branch, absolute JMP, CALL, or RET will change the value in the program counter—the IP—while leaving the value in the code segment—CS—register intact. An intersegment (long) JMP, (long) CALL, interrupt INT n, a hardware RESET, a (long) RET, or an IRET will change the values of both the CS and IP registers.

JMP (long)	(CS) = target(CS); (IP) = offset of target
CALL (long)	(CS) = target(CS); (IP) = offset of target
INT n	(CS) = 4 × n; (IP) = (4 × n) + 2
RESET	(CS) = OFFFFh; (IP) = 0000h
RET(long)	(CS) from stack; (IP) from stack
IRET	(CS) from stack; (IP) from stack

In almost all sensible situations, the CS register will be set to the address in memory of the main program code segment by the loader (LOC 86), with the IP register being set to zero. Thus execution will start at the beginning of the main program code segment.

Loading the DS, SS, and ES Registers

Whereas the code segment register is somewhat automatically loaded, the other segment registers must explicitly be loaded by the program. To accomplish this, the assembler translates the SEGMENT pseudo-operation as an address that is altered during linking and loading to be the physical address of the segment base or start. Thus the use of the segment name as an operand will access the address of the segment base; that is, the content of this location in memory is its address. Recall also that a segment register is loaded from another register. The example below shows the suggested solution to this situation:

```
DATA      SEGMENT
ONE_BYT   DB        8
DATA      ENDS
STRING    SEGMENT
LONG_ST   DB        1000 DUP(' 'A) ; ASCII BLANKS
STRING    ENDS
STACK     SEGMENT
          DW        500DUP(0)
ST_TOP              ; STACK GROW DOWNWARD
STACK     ENDS
CODE      SEGMENT
;
; INITIALIZE SEGMENT REGISTERS
;
          ASSUME    CS:CODE
          MOV       AX,DATA
          MOV       DS,AX
          MOV       AX,STRING
          MOV       ES,AX
          MOV       AX,STACK
          MOV       SS,AX
          MOV       SP,OFFSET ST_TOP
          ASSUME    DS:DATA,ES:STRING,SS:STACK
;
; DATA CONTAINERS IN DATA, STRING, STACK
; SEGMENTS AVAILABLE TO INSTRUCTIONS IN
; CODE SEGMENT
```

The designers of the I8086/8088 provided an automatic "do not interrupt until after the next instruction" for segment register loads in order to assure that the stack pointer register was also loaded after the stack segment register. This "interrupt delay" is true for all MOV or POP instructions involving a segment register.

If a data container referenced as an operand in an instruction is not covered by an ASSUME directive, it can be addressed by prefixing the operand with the segment register designation

```
CS:ANY_THING
```

This temporary segment register designation is in effect only for the single instruction. Recall particularly that certain instructions assume specific segment registers with *no* provisions for overriding:

1. Implicit references to the stack *always* employ the SS (stack segment) register. These are PUSH, POP, CALL, RET, INT, and IRET.

2. String instructions *always* employ the ES (extra segment) register for the operand indirectly addressed (pointed to) by the DI register. The SI defaults to the DS register, but this can be overriden.

Register Indirect Memory References (Anonymous References)

Indirect references to memory with the data container address in a register, such as (BX), (BP), and so on, employ default segment registers or allow temporary segment register designation as above. The default segment registers are

(BX)	defaults to segment register DS
(BP)	defaults to segment register SS
(SI) or (DI)	used as index register without a base register defaults to DS
(BX) (DI)	defaults to segment register DS
(BP) (SI)	defaults to segment register SS

These default implicit segment register designations can be temporarily overriden as described above. For example,

ES:(BX)	uses the ES register
CS:(SI)	uses the CS register

The string instructions can use either byte- or word-length instructions. Normally, these instructions employ the SI register as an offset in the data segment (DS) of the source string and the DI register as an offset in the extra segment (ES) of the destination string. The construct

```
MOVS (DI),(SI) ; is it byte or word?
```

does not specify if the string move should involve bytes or words. The assembler provides alternative solution syntax as follows:

```
MOVSB       (DI),(SI)
MOVS        BYTE PTR(DI),(SI)
MOVSW       (DI,(SI)
MOVS        WORD PTR(DI),(SI)
```

The BYTE PTR and WORD PTR construct can be used in any indirect register memory reference situation where the context is not implied from the instruction or from either operand.

THE GROUP DIRECTIVE

The group directive allows a programmer to specify that certain segments must be contained within the same physical 64K-byte memory segment. The format is

```
LABEL GROUP SEG-NM, . . .
```

where the label must be a unique group name which can be used in almost all of the ways that segment names allow except in another group directive. Similarly to the SEGMENT pseudo-operation, the GROUP pseudo-operation is translated into an address that is altered during linking and loading to be the physical address of the group base or start. Thus the instructions

```
ALL_OF_IT    GROUP     CODE,DATA,STACK,STRING
             MOV       AX,ALL_OF_IT
             MOV       CS,AX
                -
                -
             ASSUME    CS:ALL_OF_IT, DS:ALL_OF_IT,
                       SS:ALL_OF_IT,ES:ALL_OF_IT
```

will load the group base into the code segment register, with the loader (LOC 86) calculating this base address to cover all four of the segments. The order of the segments in physical memory *may not* be as specified; therefore, the group directive must be used with care. For most purposes, the class parameter of the segment directive is a better choice to force segments together and allow a commonality.

THE LABEL DIRECTIVE

The label directive creates an addressable name with an associated address offset within the current segment that can be used as a branch address or as the address of a data container. The format is

```
NAME     LABEL     type
```

where the name must be unique and the type can be (if instructions follow) NEAR or FAR, which allows the label name to be used in unconditioned branches, conditional branches, or subprocedure calls; or (if data container declarations follow) BYTE, WORD, DWORD, or the name of a structure or record. The usual uses of the label directive are:

1. To define an alternative entry point into a routine. For example, the sine of an angle is equal to the cosine of the angle plus 90°. The subroutine to calculate these functions is often combined into a single routine with two entry points:

```
SIN     PROC    FAR
        FLD     ARG         ; FLOAT LOAD
        MOV     DEG,90.0
        FLD     DEG
        FADDP               ; FLOAT ADD & POP
        FSTP    ARG         ; FLOAT STORE & POP
COS     LABEL   FAR
        FLD     ARG
        -
        -
          calculate and return
        -
```

2. To allow the double definition of data containers with different data types. Note that the segment parameter COMMON will allow this between data segments, while the label pseudo-operation allows it within a segment in much the same manner as the FORTRAN EQUIVALENCE. For example,

```
                -
BYTE_ARRAY      LABEL   BYTE
WORD_ARRAY      DW      50DUP(0)
                -
                -
                ADD     AL, BYTE_ARRAY(17)
                ADD     AX,WORD_ARRAY(8)
                -
```

are accessing memory in the same data area.

PROCEDURES

The Intel ASM 86 assembly language uses the procedure to implement the subroutine concept. A procedure is a named block of code that is usually invoked by a CALL and provides for a RETurn. It is possible, but not recommended, for procedures to be branched to or to have control "fall through" sequentially to them. Even though an algorithmic solution to a problem may be implemented in ASM 86 assembly language without using the procedure concept, they assist by forming the basis for structured modular programming with the advantage of easier maintenance and documentation. A procedure is defined by

```
NAME        PROC        type
             -
             -
             -
            RET
             -
NAME        ENDP
```

where the type is NEAR (default) for procedures logically and physically in the same segment or FAR for procedures in a different segment that will require a change of the code segment (CS) register when called and when returning. Nested procedures are allowed to any depth. Although not highly recommended, "in-line" or "macrolike" procedures that are entered via sequential code "fall through" would allow a program to be broken up into logical named blocks of code in a manner supported by some procedural-level languages such as PL/1.

A procedure is allowed to invoke—to CALL.—itself and thus be a *recursive procedure.* As a general rule, recursive programming should be avoided when an iterative solution to the problem can be designed, although exceptions to this rule are not uncommon. A recursion procedure must:

1. Be implemented with reentrant code. All data containers for local variables must be declared, accessed, manipulated, and stored on the stack. The (BP) addressing mode is appropriate.
2. Discard (pop) all local data containers from the stack before RETurning.

As the stack will expand and grow larger with each recursive call, the size of the stack may become excessive fairly quickly and finally exceed the allowed memory space.

DATA CONTAINERS

Identifiers are used to name entities within programs such as procedures, segments, groups, modules, data containers, and so on. During the assembly process, these identifiers are given a relative—an offset—address that is modified during the linking process and again modified during the loading process to produce a 20-bit physical address using the appropriate segment register and offset. Identifiers usually appear in a source program as a label, although the name of a module is one exception. All data containers except immediate operands are explicitly identified via a label or an offset from a label.

DECLARATIONS

Constants

A constant is a value that names itself. ASM 86 allows the following types of constants:

Bit (append B)	110B; 10101010B
Octal (append O or Q)	76310; 01234567Q
Decimal (append D or nothing)	76D; 0123456789
Hexadecimal (append H, start with 0 to 9)	55H; 0ABH; 12FFH
Real decimal (exponential or point)	3.14; .0314E2; 9.459
Real hexadecimal (append R)	40490FDBR; 0C0000000R
ASCII (enclose in single quotes)	'A'; 'GEORGE', '123'

The permissible range for a constant follows from the context of its use. The use of constants is permitted in the following contexts:

1. Immediate values as the source operand in instructions. The value must be containable in either an 8-bit byte or a 16-bit word.

```
MOV BL,5
MOV AX,'XY'
```

2. As the right-hand side of an assembly time equivalence statement—a directive to the ASM 86 assembler to interpret an alias for an identifier as the identifier itself.

```
FIVE        EQU 5           ; same meaning as
            MOV   AL,FIVE   ; MOV AL,5
```

   The EQU directive has aliasing powers well beyond those indicated by this example. Registers may be assigned alias names, for example.

3. As the initial contents of a named memory area defined as a data container.

```
TEN     DB      10
TEN     DB      0AH
TEN     DB      00001010B
```

The declaration of data containers, as well as their initialization, will be investigated further when we discuss variables in the next section.

Variables

A variable is a named data container whose contents can be explicitly changed by the execution of instructions. A data container has an address in memory that is an offset within a specified segment and reserves a fixed-size memory storage cell—a type—such as a byte, a word, or more. The general format is

name type expression

where the data container name is an ASM 86 label without a colon suffix; type is DB, DW, DD, DQ, or DT (10 bytes); and expression is defined in various ways described in the following:

1. Initializing to a constant expression; allows any type that will "fit":

```
BYTE       DB 5          ;  8-bit value
WORD       DW 1234H      ; 16-bit value
DOUBLE     DD -3.4E38    ; 32-bit value
QUADE      DQ 2.3E       ; 64-bit value
TMP_REAL   DT -23456     ; 80-bit BCD or real value
```

2. No initialization; will contain "junk":

```
BYTE       DB   ?        ; one byte
WORD       DW   ?,?      ; two words
TENS       DT   ?,?,?    ; three 80-bit areas
```

3. Initialization of an array to same value or "junk":

```
BYTES      DB  123DUP(0)           ; 123 bytes, each 0
BYTES      DB  123DUP(?)           ; 123 bytes of "junk"
QUADE      DQ  50DUP(9)            ; 50 quades (eight bytes) = 9,9,..
FUNNY      DB  2DUP(0,3DUP(1))     ; eight bytes = 0,1,1,1,0,1,1,1
```

4. Initializing an array to a list of values (16 or fewer):

```
PRIMES     DW 2,3,5,7,11,13,17,19,23,29,31,37,41,43,47,53
SQUARES    DW 0,1,4,9,16,25,36,49,64
HI         DB 'HI FRIEND', ODH,OAH;carriage return and line feed
```

5. Initializing strings; bytes only, ASCII only, 3 to 255 bytes:

```
DIGITS     DB          '0-123456789'
HELLO      DB          'HELLO'
SINGLE_
QUOTE      DB          ''''          ; one byte—not a string
```

6. Initializing addresses; words or double-words only:

```
TBLE_OFFSET    DW    TABLE          ; offset of table
TBLE_PTR       DD    TABLE          ; offset and segment
                                    ; base address of table
TBLE_IN4       DW    TABLE+3        ; offset of fourth byte
TBLE_PREFIX    DW    TABLE-1        ; offset of byte before table
```

Records

A record is a *bit pattern* employed to allow bit packing into bytes or words. A template is defined for values in a DB or DW area declared elsewhere; that is, a record does not declare a data container: it does define the format of the data container of size 8 bits or 16 bits. The format is

```
name      RECORD      field:expression, . . .
```

where both the record name and the field name(s) must be unique within the module and the expression, which must be prefixed by a colon, and must evaluate to a positive nonzero constant of 8 or less for a byte or 16 or less for word declaration usage of a record format. This value is the field size in bits. If the record format is less than 8 for a byte of 16 for a word record, the values are right-justified in the data container, with the left-end bits being undefined "junk." It is highly recommended that this situation be avoided by defining a constant field to occupy this space with zero bits.

```
BYTE      RECORD      M_F:1,YR:3,DEPT:4
```

where the field M_F could have the value OB or 1B, the field YR could have values from 0 through 7, and the field DEPT could have values from 0 through 15. A data container for a record is declared:

```
STUDENTS      BYTE      500DUP(?)
```

Records may be initialized in two ways:

```
BYTE          RECORD      M_F:1=0, YR:3=0, DEPT:4=0
STUDENTS      BYTE        500DUP(0,0,0)
```

Although the manipulation of bit fields within bytes or words is obviously possible using the logical instructions (AND, OR, XOR, NOT), the use of records allows an easier and more understandable implementation. On the other hand, memory is inexpensive and as the main use of records is to save storage, the arguments for the use of records is somewhat weak except in special circumstances such as the construction of flag, status, exception, and control fields for devices and processors. As a last point, a record can be used as follows (using the last of the examples above):

```
MOV AL,STUDENTS(DI)<1,4,13>
```

Structures

A structure is a named template for a data area made up of a contiguous heterogeneous conglomeration of named subareas. Memory space is not allocated, only a data template. The subareas of a structure template may contain simple variables or arrays of any length initialized or not. Multiple structure arrays may be declared as will be shown. Thus the following terminology is appropriate: structures of arrays, arrays of structures, and arrays of structures with arrays. The format for defining a structure is

```
name            STRUC
     subname      type       expression
        -           -            -
        -           .            -
        -           -            -
                  type       expression
name              ENDS
```

where the structure name and subnames within the structure must be unique identifiers in the module; "type" is a data container declaration pseudo-operation (DB, DW, DD, DQ, or DT), and "expression" is as defined early for data container declarations including initialization. Similarly to records, a data container is declared for a structure by using the structure name in the operation field:

```
name        struc_name        expression
```

where "name" is a unique identifier within the module, "struct_name" is the identifier of a structure template defined in the module, and "expression" is as defined previously except that template-defined initialization of nonsimple subareas cannot be changed (initializations for arrays and lists are not overridable). The expression can contain a duplicate (DUP) specification allowing arrays of structures. In many ways, the structure facility of ASM 86 is equivalent to the structure facility of PL/1 and its equivalent in COBOL. An example should be helpful.

```
STUD                 STRUC
          SEX        DB        0
          YEAR       DB        0
          DEPT       DB        0
          MISC       DW        200DUP(?)
          MORE       DW        100DUP(0)
```

```
STUD          ENDS
ALL_STUDS     STUD      1000DUP(<,,,200DUP(0),)
```

Labels

A label is a named offset location address within a specific segment with a unique name within the domain of its usage. If a label is only used, and therefore known about, in a segment; it is termed NEAR and must have a unique name within its module. The value of a NEAR label is its offset from the segment start or base address. A near label may be implicitly defined by appending a colon to the label on a normal instruction or by using the label definition pseudo-operation with a near designation:

```
HERE          LABEL     NEAR      ; both labels have the
SAME_SPOT:    MOV       AX,BX     ; same offset value
```

If it is necessary for another segment to access a label—say by a CALL—it must be declared FAR and have a unique name among all the identifiers that will be known by the link routine (LINK 86), that is, all of the module, segment, procedure, public, and external names involved in the program. The value of a FAR label is the address diad—offset within segment : segment base address—a 32-bit value. A FAR label must be declared PUBLIC.

ACCESSING DATA CONTAINERS

The general format for instructions in a source module of ASM 86 is

```
label:    OPCODE    destin,source    ; comment
```

where the label (with colon) is an optional unique identifier among all the names in the module and, if present, defaults to have a NEAR offset value from the segment base address. The required opcode is any legal operations code, pseudo-operation, or macro name. The destination operand is a register or memory address derived by any of the various addressing modes, or it may be absent for certain instructions (example: POPF). The source operand is required for two operand instructions (example: MOV, ADD) and is prohibited for no operand and for one operand instructions (example: INC). The comment (with semicolon) is optional, although an entire line can consist of a comment. Two operand instructions can be any one of the types register-register; register-memory; memory-register; register-immediate; and memory-immediate, but not memory-memory except for string operations, where both addresses are register indirect.

Immediate operands: These are 8-bit or 16-bit immediate values in the source (second) operand position. The allowable types are bit, octal, decimal, hexadecimal, and ASCII. Real immediate values are not allowed.

Register operands: The I8086/8087/8088 registers available as operands are:

Segment registers: CS,DS,SS,ES

Address pointer and index register: BX,BP,SI,DI

Counter registers: CX,CL

General-purpose registers: AX,AH,AL,BX,BH,BL,CX,CH,CL,DX,DH,DL, SP,BP,SI,DI

Floating-pointer register: ST,ST(0) through ST(7)

Indicator registers: Flags, Exception, Status, Environment

Memory operands: These either (1) designate an address in memory of a byte, word, double-word, quad-word, or 10-byte data container; or (2) designate an address in memory of a jump, conditional jump, CALL, interrupt service, RETurn, or interrupt return.

Data container addressing is accomplished via three major methods: simple variable, indexed variable, and structured variable. Simple variables may be referenced directly by citing their identifier:

```
MOV     AL,DATUM
```

or indirectly by referencing the address pointer/index register that has been program loaded and controlled to contain the memory address of the desired datum:

```
MOV     AL,(BP)     ; use BX, BP, SI, or DI
```

An indexed variable may be referenced in the manner of a simple variable with an appended value specified as the content of a base/index register plus/minus a constant or expression:

```
MOV     AL,DATUM(5)
MOV     AL,DATUM(DI) ; use BX, BP, SI, or DI
MOV     AL,DATUM(DI+5)
MOV     AL,(BP+5)
MOV     AL,(BP) (DI)
MOV     AL,(BP+5) (DI+5)
MOV     AL,(BP+DI)
MOV     AL,(BP+DI-10)
```

The memory-resident stack of the I8086/8088 is available for variable data storage via the PUSH/POP instructions, which implicitly specify a stack pointer (SP) register memory indirect access. The SP register cannot be used as an explicit base or index register, although the effect can be obtained by

```
        MOV     BP,SP       ; byte stack operation with
        MOV     AL,SS:(BP)  ; NO SP INC/DEC
```

A named subarea within a structure may be referenced by appending, with a period, the subarea name after the structure name. Base address and index registers (limit = two registers), as well as constants or expressions, may be used to allow reference to arrays of structures and an array used as a subarea of a structure. Referring to the structure STUD example with the declaration ALL_STUDS used earlier, the following examples are given:

```
        MOV     AL,ALL_STUDS(SI).SEX
        MOV     AX,ALL_STUDS(BP).MISC(SI)
        MOV     AL,ALL_STUDS(BP).(2)          ; = .DEPT
```

The structure definition may be used to implement linked-list structures in the manner of SLIP (Weizenbaum, 1963) and Knuth (1973). Our example employs a doubly linked list with a pointer to the next cell, a pointer to the previous cell, and an information area. A template for each cell followed by the declaration of 500 cells could be

```
CELL        STRUC
    NEXT    DW 0            ; POINTER TO NEXT CELL
    LAST    DW 0            ; POINTER TO PREVIOUS CELL
    INFO    DB 51DUP(?)
CELL        ENDS
LIST        CELL 500DUP(< >)
```

To initialize the forward and backward pointer subareas to form a doubly linked circular list of available cells—a garbage list—the following code would be employed:

```
; INITIALIZE DOUBLY LINKED LIST
;
            MOV BX,OFFSET LIST      ; address cell (0)
            MOV SI,TYPE LIST        ; cell size
            MOV CX,LENGTH LIST-1    ; array size-1
            MOV AX,BX
            SUB AX,SI               ; address cell (n-1)
            MOV DX,BX
            ADD DX,SI               ; address cell (n+1)
FIX_PTR_LP: MOV (BX).LAST,AX
            MOV (BX).NEXT,DX
            ADD BX,SI
            ADD AX,SI
            ADD DX,SI
```

```
            LOOP FIX_PTR_LP
;
; MAKE LIST CIRCULAR ; FIX FIRST AND LAST CELL
;
            MOV BX,OFFSET LIST
            MOV SI,TYPE LIST
            MOV BP,LENGTH LIST-1
            MULT BP,SI
            ADD BP,BX
            MOV (BX).LAST,BP
            MOV (BP).NEXT,BX
```

This code illustrates the use of load-time value-returning operand operators. The five *value-returning* operators are:

SEG label: yields segment base address

OFFSET label: yields offset in bytes within segment

TYPE label: data container: size in bytes code: NEAR or FAR

LENGTH label: yields number of elements in an array

SIZE label: number of bytes in dimensional array

```
SIZE = TYPE * LENGTH
```

THIS: anonymous label of any type with offset at this location in this segment

The following operand operators are also available to override the implicit attributes of an operand.

1. *Type override*: TYPE PTR MEM_OPERAND, where TYPE can be BYTE, WORD, DWORD, QWORD, TBYTE, NEAR, FAR, or a structure name; and MEM_OPERAND is a variable name label, a code label, or a number. Possible uses are

```
INC     BYTE PTR(BX)
INC     WORD PTR(SI)
MOV     WORD PTR(DI),99
```

2. *Segment override*: SR:MEM_OPERAND, where SR can be CS, DS, SS, or ES, and where the override is in effect for the single instruction only.

```
CS:ANY
```

Remember that the implied segment register of operands for certain instructions cannot be overriden (example: PUSH, POP, CALL, RET, and strings).

3. *Very near branches*: SHORT label, where label is within +127 to −128 bytes of the branch instruction.

TARGETS OF JUMP AND CALL INSTRUCTIONS

The eventual final target of a JMP or CALL instruction must be a label in a code segment whose address can be derived directly or indirectly in the present code segment (NEAR) or in a different code segment (FAR). Thus the operand of JMP/CALL instruction can be a code label, a variable name label, a register, or an address expression.

JMP/CALL Direct

The operand of a direct JMP or CALL instruction is an explicit label occurring in the same segment or in a different segment. If the label target is in a different segment, a FAR label, the target label must be declared EXTRN. The format is

```
label:    JMP     TARGET ; comment
label:    CALL    TARGET ; comment
```

where the label: and comment are both optional. The ASM 86 assembler will generate an 8-bit offset (SHORT) if the intrasegment target is within −128 to +127 bytes; an 16-bit offset (NEAR) if the intrasegment target is not SHORT; or a (FAR) 32-bit offset (offset : segment start) if the target is declared EXTRN.

JMP/CALL Indirect

The operand of an indirect JMP or CALL instruction is either a base/index register previously loaded with the offset of the intrasegment target or a memory data container label (indexed or not) in this segment. The latter situation allows the construction of jump or call tables. A jump/call table for an indirect intrasegment target would consist of 16-bit words previously loaded with offsets in the current segment. A jump/call table for an indirect between segments target would consist of 32-bit double-words previously loaded with offset : segment bases. Examples are

```
JMP      WORD PTR (BX)          ; intrasegment
CALL     WORD PTR (SI)          ; intrasegment
JMP      WORD PTR TABLE(SI)     ; intrasegment
CALL     WORD PTR TABLE(BX)     ; intrasegment
CALL     DWORD PTR TABLE(DI)    ; intersegment
```

As the use of a jump for accessing a different segment or procedure is not recommended (it is very bad programming practice), the indirect intersegment JMP through a memory-resident table is not illustrated.

JMP/CALL Double Indirect

The operand of a double indirect JMP/CALL is a base/index register previously loaded with the offset of an intrasegment 16-bit word jump/call table or an intersegment 32-bit double-word call table previously loaded with the offsets or offsets : segment bases, respectively. Examples are

```
JMP     WORD PTR (BX)      ; intrasegment
CALL    WORD PTR (SI)      ; intrasegment
CALL    DWORD PTR (BP)     ; intersegment
```

8

I8089 Direct Memory Access and Channel-Oriented Input/Output

Employing FORTRAN, we are used to I/O statements such as

```
READ(5,99) A,B,C
WRITE(6,91) X,Y
```

In programming with procedural-level languages, we are depending on the compiler (the language translator) to transform such I/O statements into parameterized calls to the input/output control system (IOCS) of the operating system. In effect, the FORTRAN READ and WRITE statements request that the control software system perform a service. Usually, the programmer is not particularly concerned regarding the method employed.

Similarly, employing an assembly language, it would be extremely nice if we could parameterize our I/O needs in an analogous manner and use statements something like

```
INPUT      A,B,C,TTY,LABEL99
OUTPUT     X,Y,CRT,LABEL91
```

Again, we would be depending on the assembler (the language translator) to transform these fairly high level I/O orders to parameterized sections of code that accomplish the I/O. This code could either be inserted into the assembly procedure at each appropriate place macro style, or it could be referenced as a call-style out-of-line subroutine with only one copy existing.

As noted in Chapter 5, when programming the I8086/8088, all of the methods noted above would eventually result in a

```
INT     nnn
```

software interrupt (supervisory call) through the interrupt vector table to an appropriate routine to accomplish the actual physical data transfer. With a modern operating system, much of the noninteractive input would have been prefetched from the device into a memory-resident input buffer, from which the program would "read" data via MOV instructions. Similarly, the program would "output" data via MOV instructions to a memory-resident output buffer the contents of which would finally be written to the appropriate device by the operating system IOCS (input/output control system).

A TECHNOLOGICAL PERSPECTIVE

At the most elementary level, a microprocessor is forced to deal directly with the individual bits and these one at a time. First-generation microprocessors in the early 1970s and first-generation computers in the 1940s were "stuck" with this albatross-like performance limitation of very primitive input and output of each bit, requiring action by the computer.

Almost immediately after their introduction, provisions were provided in microprocessors that allowed the input or output of a nibble or byte in parallel. Unfortunately, this early nibble- or byte-oriented I/O required the detailed control and attention of the microprocessor in controlling the individual actions of the external device. Input and output was tedious to program and extremely slow during execution. Detailed knowledge of the device timings and line voltages was required. The I4004 and the I8008 were typical microprocessors of this era.

One important advance associated with second-generation microprocessors such as the I8080 was the availability of single-chip interface controllers such as those discussed in Chapter 5. Figures 5.11 to 5.14 will remind you of the functionality of the I8251A as an example of a single-chip device interface controller. These devices removed the lowest-level device control from the microprocessor and allowed the transfer of an entire byte to and from a device in parallel under microprocessor control.

A second important advance also associated with second-generation microprocessors, such as the I8080, and almost necessary with third-generation microcomputers, such as the I8086/8088, was the introduction and availability of direct memory access (DMA) controllers such as those discussed briefly in Chapter 5. DMA allowed a whole block of data to be input or output without microprocessor intervention beyond initiating and noting the termination of the transfer. Additionally, if register resident data were available, the microprocessor could continue data manipulation in parallel with the DMA transfer. A primitive form of compute-I/O multiprocessing became available using microcomputers. The twin availability of I/O device controllers and DMA allowed the application of microcomputers to problems that required moderate amounts and speeds of I/O.

The third generation of microcomputers, characterized by the I8086/8088, has also seen the development and introduction of the semiautonomous input/output processor into the world of the small. Originally conceived and implemented in the mid-1950s for "supercomputers" with the aid of federal development funds, the microcomputer version of interest to us is the I8089 Input/Output Processor (IOP). The I8089 continues the trend of removing yet another level of control from the microprocessor by assuming all device controller overhead, "soft-error" recovery, and block I/O data transfers. A further separation of processing responsibilities is achieved, resulting in a cleaner implementation of the compute function in the processor with I/O in a separate processor. This constitutes a viable form of multiprocessing with simultaneously executing specialized processors communicating via messages in a common system memory (mailbox fashion). The interrupt structure of the host I8086/8088 microprocessor is utilized to force attention to the message-in-system-memory mailbox.

When utilizing the IOP DMA facility, the I8086/8088 processor performs an I/O operation by building a message in system memory that defines the I/O function. The I8089 IOP reads the message, configures itself appropriately, carries out the I/O function, and notifies the I8086/8088 processor via a software interrupt when it is finished as well as an indication of any errors. All I/O devices appear to be transmitting or receiving entire blocks (buffers) of data to or from system memory. High-level logical input/output is facilitated using a separate modularized function in a manner that allows an intelligently and independently designed and maintained IOCS portion of an operating system.

DIRECT MEMORY ACCESS

Direct memory access is a special hardware data transfer path and control logic that allows a block of data to be rapidly transferred directly from a device interface to system memory, or vice versa, without intervention by the microprocessor during the transfer. The microprocessor must define, set up, and initiate the transfer as well as note its completion.

The transfer path for DMA is almost always via the system bus, including the data, the address, and the control lines. The control logic for DMA is usually a VLSI programmable DMA controller chip. The appropriate device to use with an I8086-8088 microcomputer is either an I8237 or an I8257. The I8237 programmable DMA controller is illustrated in Figure 8.1 and the I8257 is shown in Figure 5.28.

Essentially the same, the I8257 has 16-bit data paths (usable as 8-bit or 16-bit paths) whereas the I8237 has 8-bit data paths. Thus the I8257 is more suitable for use with the I8086. Additionally, the I8237 was designed for use with the older I8080/8085 microprocessors that allowed only 16 bits in an address and therefore

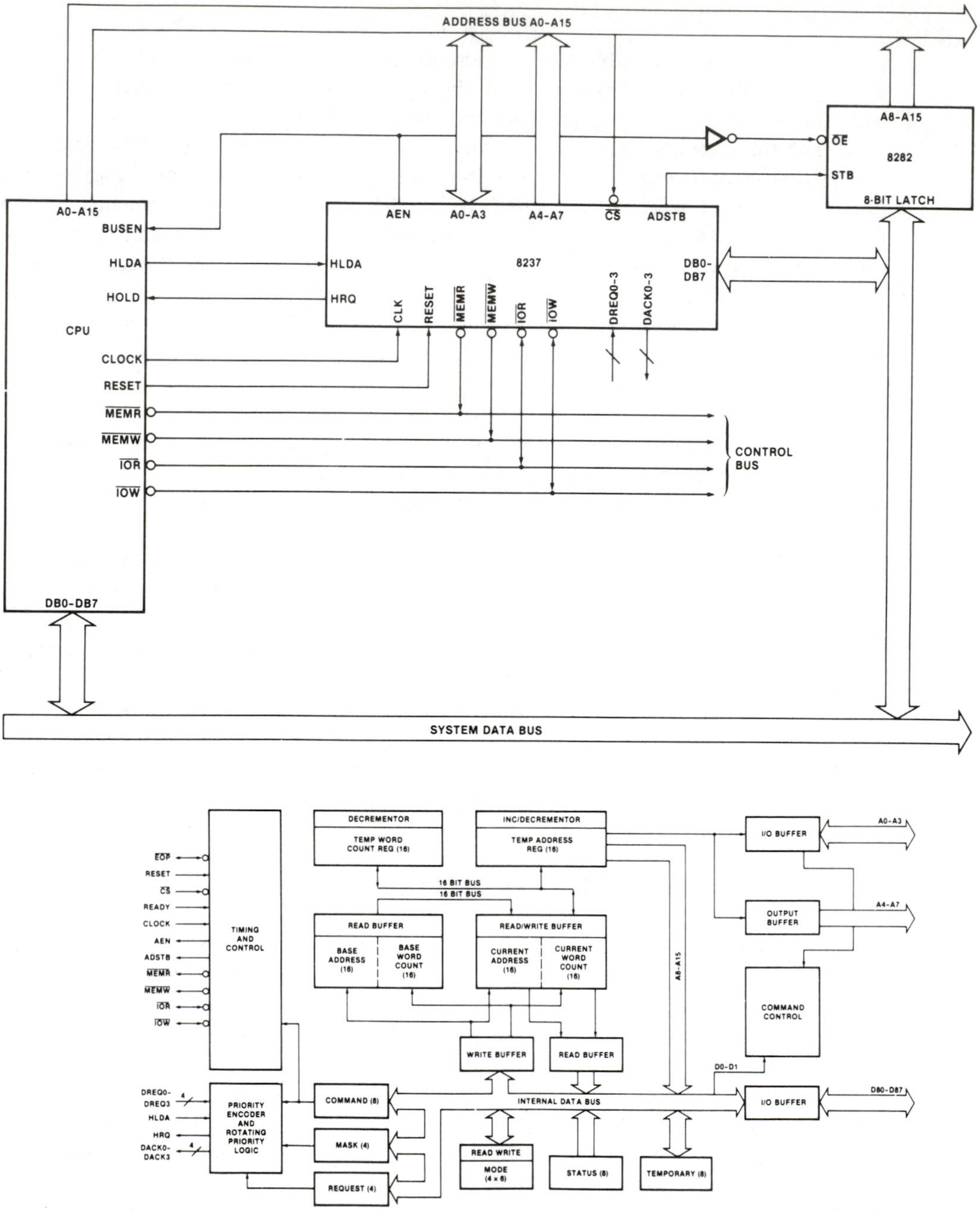

Figure 8.1 I8237 programmable DMA controller. (*Top*) The DMA controller's position in a system. (*Bottom*) I8237 block diagram. The I8237 should be compared to the I8257A programmable DMA controller illustrated in Figure 5.28. (Reprinted by permission of Intel Corporation. Copyright 1980.)

could only address 64K bytes of memory. Nevertheless, the I8237 is usable as a DMA controller with the I8088. This essentially allows the replacement of the CPU processor chip in an older I8080 or I8085 system with the newer, more capable I8088 processor (a clock chip must also be added and some rewiring done).

The I8237/8257 DMA controller is either "idle" or "active." When no DMA channel requires service, the device will be idle and execute a series of "S1 states," one for each clock cycle. During each clock cycle S1 state, a check will be made to see if any channel is requesting DMA service (by sampling the DREQ lines) and additionally check if the processor is attempting to write/read its interrupt registers (by sampling the CS line). As long as DREQ is low and CS is high (i.e., no service is required), the I8237/8257 will remain idle and cycle through a series of S1 states waiting for a service request. Thus four basic conditions exist:

DREQ	CS	Action in the DMA controller
Low	Low	Idle cycle—program condition
Low	High	Idle cycle
High	Low	Active cycle
High	High	Active cycle

When the DREQ lines and the CS line are both low, the microprocessor I8086/8088 can inspect and/or change the DMA I/O definitions of the I8237/8357 DMA controller by reading from or writing to the internal registers. Some of the address lines and the IOR/IOW signals determine the action, while the DMA controller can execute such commands as "CLEAR" or "CLEAR a portion of a register."

If the I8237/8257 is in the idle cycle and one of the four channels requests a DMA service, the controller will turn DREQ high and thus enter the active cycle. A *READ* transfers data from memory to an I/O device interface (MEMR and IOW are active), whereas a *WRITE* transfers data from an I/O device interface to memory (MEMW and IOR are active). The data transfer can be in:

1. *Single transfer mode*: This mode consists of one datum transfer (one byte or one word only). The count register will be decremented and when it is zero, the terminal count (TC) line will be activated. The address register(s) also will be incremented or decremented as appropriate.
2. *Block transfer mode*: The data transfer will continue with appropriate count and address register(s) decrementation or incrementation until the count becomes zero or the device interface sends an end-of-process signal.
3. *Demand transfer mode*: This is similar to block transfer mode except that the device may not be able to deliver or accept data fast enough. In this instance, the transfer will orderly-stop (allowing the I8086-8088 microprocessor to ac-

cess memory) and then resume when the device is again able to deliver or accept data. This is a form of "cycle stealing."

Programmable DMA controllers can be cascaded to allow more than four data channels. It is also possible to program the controller to "autoinitialize" a channel when it completes a transfer and thus automatically prepare itself for another transfer by restoring the original address and word count register values.

Besides providing data transfers from a device interface direct to memory (WRITE) and direct from memory to a device interface (READ), the I8237/8257 programmable DMA controllers allow *memory-to-memory* block data moves using channel 0 as the source and channel 1 as the destination. This programmatic style can facilitate the movement of blocks of data and programs from one area of memory to another with minimal programming effort and with a minimum expenditure of microprocessor time. Its employment with operating systems is of obvious utility. The external end-of-process signal can be employed to allow the data itself to terminate the transfer by placing an end-of-file character at the end of the source data block in memory.

DMA/PROGRAM SYNCHRONIZATION

As was mentioned in Chapter 5, a program employing a DMA channel to input or output data (or perhaps to move data within memory) can continue the execution of its non-I/O instructions quite independently of the DMA transfer. It is thus possible for program execution in the I8086-8088 to get "ahead" of the DMA transfer and use the contents of a memory location as "data" before the DMA controller has delivered the data to that memory location; or in the case of a DMA output, to change the contents of a memory location to a new value before the DMA controller has output the "data" from that memory location. Either situation would result in incorrect program action and would be disastrous. The program designer must be aware of these possibilities and insert "wait for DMA completion signal" instructions at appropriate places in the program. Compilers for languages such as FORTRAN must generate these synchronization "waits" where needed. You will recall that the generic name for this situation of independently executing interdependent procedures is *co-routines.* We will examine this concept in some depth, as synchronization of cooperating co-routines is vital to DMA input/output and fundamental to operating systems.

A Process

It is constructive to consider the concept of a process when discussing co-routines. *A process is a program in execution.* The current state of a process is a "snapshot" of all of the contents of its memory locations and registers. The state of a process changes over time as each instruction is executed. In an environment involving co-routines—and this involves any program in an interrupt environment—a program can be viewed as a nonempty set of processes that are activated, suspended, resumed, and terminated during the execution of the program.

An *active process* has one or more of its instructions executed and has one or more of its instructions yet to be executed. An active process is *awake* if its instructions are currently being executed; otherwise, an active process is *asleep.* An *inactive process* is *asleep* or *terminated.* An *asleep inactive process* may be activated only by an awake active process explicitly *awakening* it. An *asleep active process* may be awakened by an event or interrupt. The possible conditions of the process P can be summarized as a process that has started execution:

1. Active
   a. Awake: P's instructions are currently being executed.
   b. Asleep: Instructions of some other process are currently being executed and P is awaiting wakeup via an interrupt or event.
2. Inactive
   a. Asleep: Instructions of some other process are currently being executed and P cannot be awakened by an interrupt. P can be activated only by another process, such as the operating system, explicitly awakening it.
   b. Terminated: P is completely finished.

Figure 8.2 should be helpful in conceptualizing this scheme.

Concurrency

To achieve efficient use of computational system resources, computation and input/output should be overlapped and occur simultaneously via co-routines whenever feasible. The program roughly diagrammed in Figure 8.2 does this. The typical program is often of the general form:

1. Initialize
2. Read
3. Calculate
4. Print
5. If more data, then repeat from 2
   else, stop.

If these steps must all be accomplished in strict sequential order, an unnecessarily inefficient use of available resources will result. The situation illustrated in Figure 8.2 is much better. However, in many cases involving interactive computing with a one-user (uniprogramming) microcomputer, the efficient use of the time available to the computational system is of minor importance compared to the psychologically

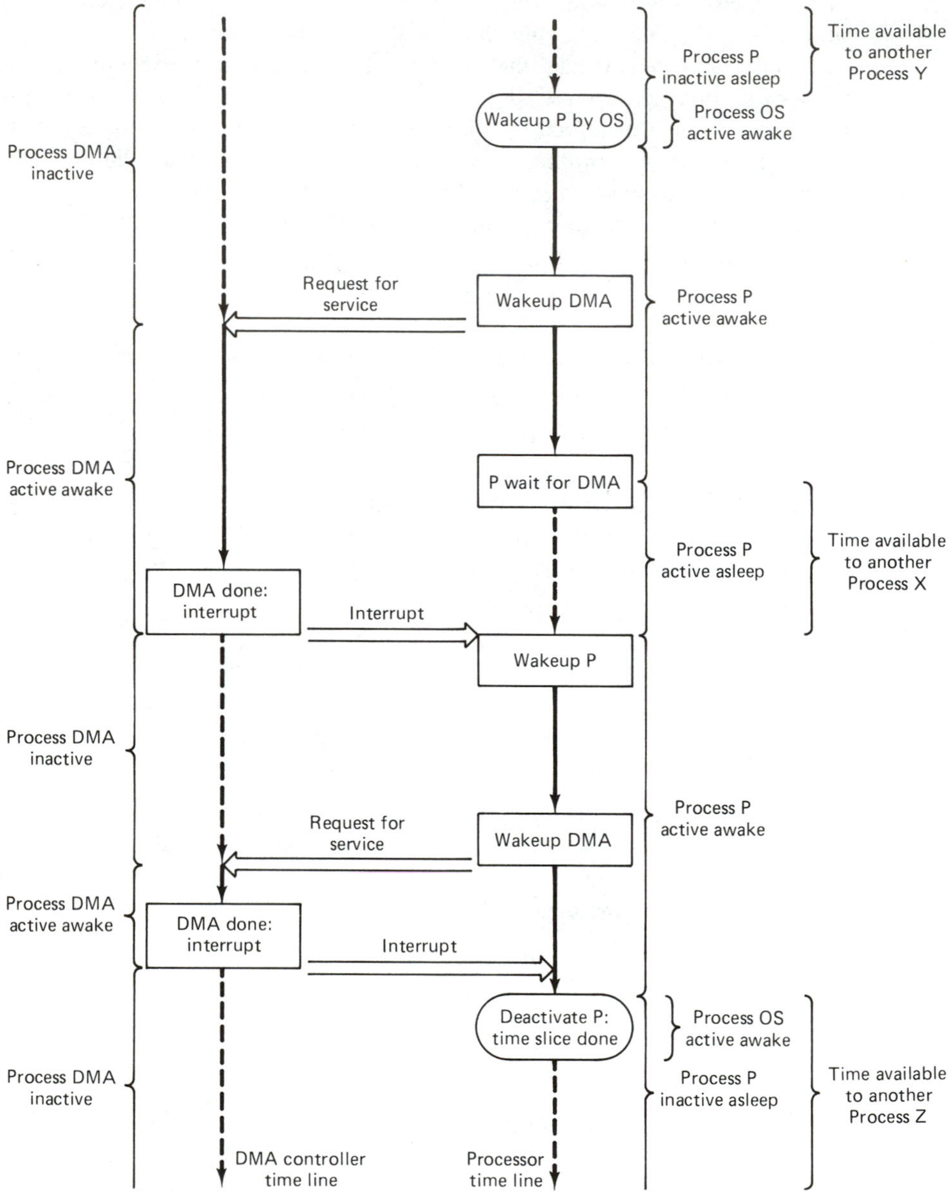

Figure 8.2 Co-routine process control diagram of DMA-processor cooperation.

satisfying use of the human user's time. In this common situation with single-user microcomputers, the strictly sequential order of execution illustrated above may be the most satisfactory plan for terminal I/O with DMA overlap execution for disk data being utilized for preexisting input data and for SPOOLing summary data to the printer after execution is complete.

In some realistic situations with multiuser high-ability microprocessor systems such as are easily possible with the I8086 or the iAPX 286, all of the data will be systems resident before the program is initiated. One possible situation will illustrate this not-so-rare situation: Consider a microcomputer system accepting inventory changes (materials bought and sold) from several stores after closing each day. After all the data from each store are transferred, the microcomputer will load and execute an inventory file update and materials ordering program. Input will consist of the old inventory file, the transaction files from each store, and the file of materials already ordered. Output will consist of a new (updated) inventory file, a stack of materials orders, and a new (updated) materials ordered file. We would expect, and therefore will assume, that this microcomputer system would be under the control of an operating system with an adequate concurrent process (co-routine) facility to allow fairly adequate simultaneous use of computational resources. It should also be noted that this example is very similar to the traditional "batch programming mode" of punched card/line printer maxi- and minicomputers.

During the period when output for the previous program is being SPOOLed to the printer from disk, we would expect the operating system also to be loading our example program and filling double-input buffers from the input sources. Thus when our program starts execution, its initial input is already in buffers in systems memory and no input time is expended. Anytime one of the input buffers is exhausted via MOVes by our program (pseudoinputs from buffers), the program will switch to the other buffer of the double-buffer pair for each device and the operating system will simultaneously invoke DMA to refill the empty buffer. The program never performs physical input but only MOVes input data from buffers kept full by the operating system. Any output is similarly moved to one of the double output buffers for each file. When one output buffer becomes full, the program will switch to the other buffer of the double-buffer pair for each device and the operating system will simultaneously invoke DMA to empty the full buffer to the disk output files—one of which is the printer SPOOL file which will be time-overlap-printed during the loading/execution of the subsequent program. Figures 8.3 and 8.4 may be helpful in understanding this concept.

Critical sections

The scheme shown in Figure 8.4 for suspending process "P" contains several important timing-dependent sequences of instructions. Examining Figure 8.4, note the labeled critical section on the left associated with input. Suppose that the new input buffer is not full; therefore, process P should immediately invoke process "IOCS in" and put itself to sleep. If this sequence of instructions is interrupted in any manner that does not allow return to that exact point with none of the control

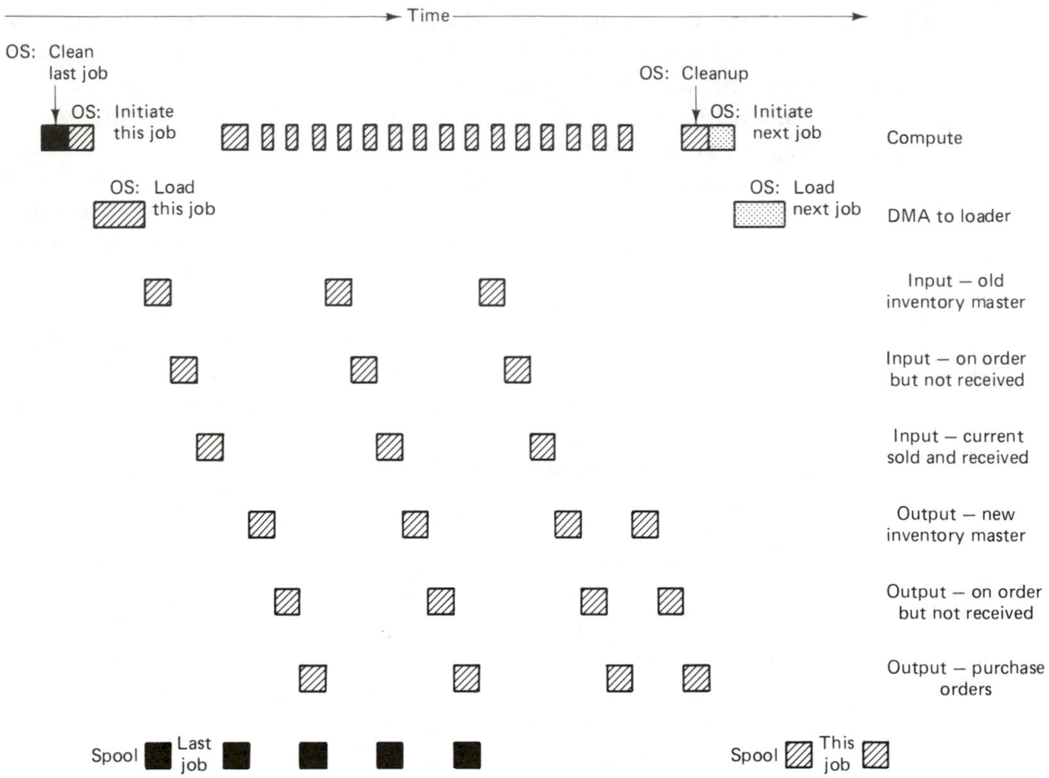

Figure 8.3 Resource utilization of an I/O-bound program using three input files with cooperating processes for DMA I/O with double-buffered prefetch/postput.

variables changed, there will be a real danger (a nonzero probability) that process "P" and process "IOCS in" will both be in the sleep state with each waiting for the other to awaken it and because each is asleep it cannot do anything, including awakening the other. Thus a *deadlock* might exist. Two processes are deadlocked if neither can continue until the other continues. A critical section encompasses that contiguous sequential group of instructions that cannot be separated in execution lest a deadlock result. To avoid timing-dependent errors, including deadlocks, a critical section must be allowed to execute to completion with no intervening instructions from the other process. The student is asked to determine under which conditions the two candidate critical sections noted in Figure 8.4 are really critical sections and when they are not critical sections. Implementation details and conditions can determine if a candidate critical code section is a truly critical section and must be individually executed without interruption. Thus general rules for detecting critical sections are not particularly helpful. A further discussion of critical sections will be necessary when we consider operating systems in Chapter 9. The *semaphore and locking* mechanism will be introduced in the next section, dealing with a more generalized input/output processor.

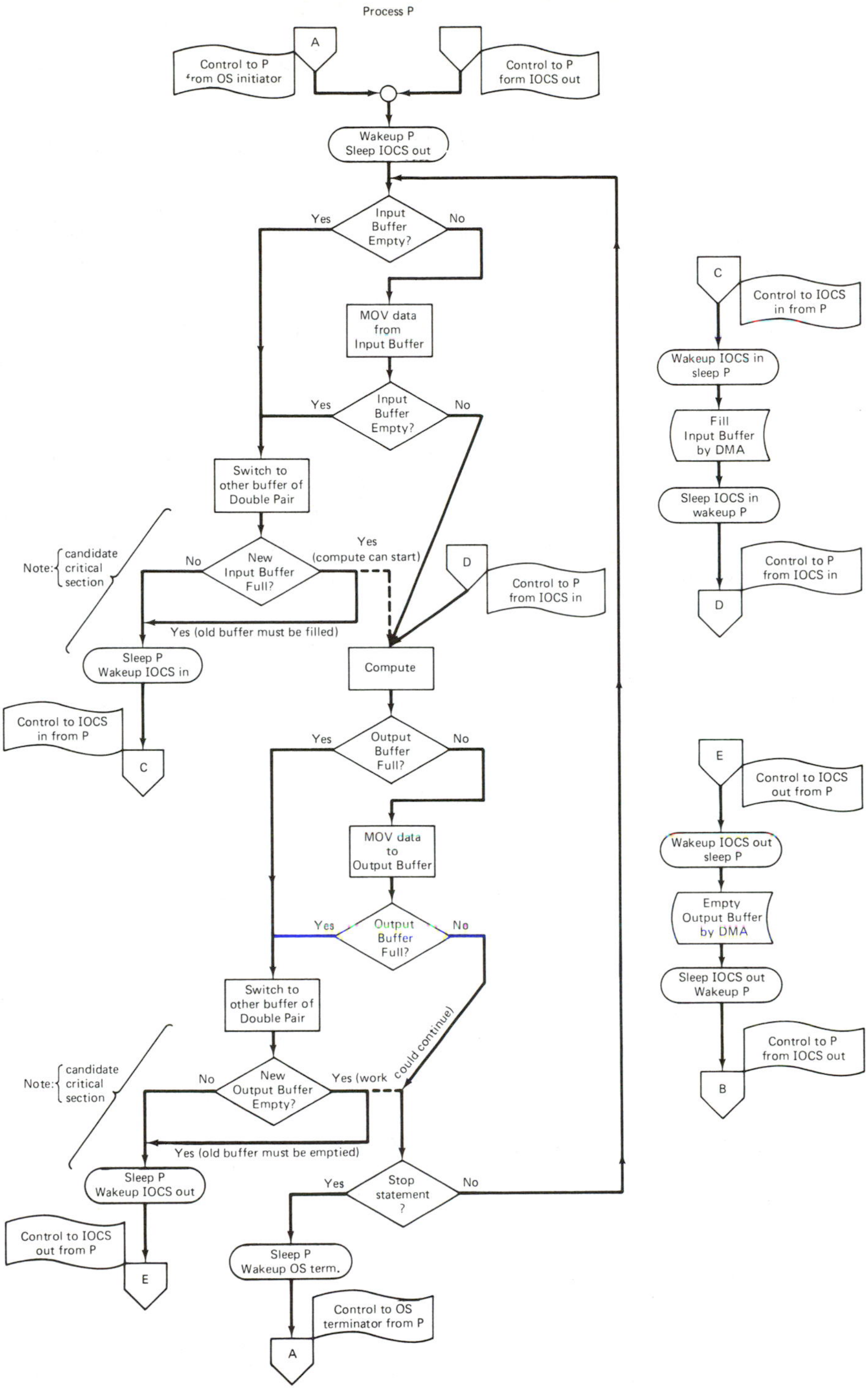

Figure 8.4 Logic control diagram of cooperating processes to accomplish the program execution timing shown if Figure 8.3. Some minor simplification is included; for example, I/O error interupts effects are ignored. One assumption is that one DMA block will fill/empty a complete buffer. Also, one "shot" of compute uses/fills an entire buffer.

THE I8089 INPUT/OUTPUT PROCESSOR

The I8089 IOP is a general-purpose single-chip system with two independent I/O channels controlled by a single time-shared special-purpose processor. The processor combines an instruction set specifically designed for efficient input/output processing, including high-speed DMA block data transfers. The Intel Corporation maintains that the IOP concept is a continuation of the trend of simplifying the interaction of program execution in the CPU with the I/O devices of the system.

An I8086/8088 program performs an I/O operation by building an I/O command message in system memory that completely describes the function that the I8089 IOP must carry out and notifies the IOP. The IOP then reads the I/O command message from system memory, executes the function described, and finally notifies the I8086/8088 upon completion. All device controller overhead, soft-error recovery, and DMA data block transfer functions of the I8089 IOP are accomplished without I8086/8088 intervention and, most important, with simultaneous co-routine compute-I/O execution.

Inter-processor communication is via a channel control block that points to an I/O task specific area called a parameter block for transmitting information and which points to the appropriate channel program known as a task block, that is, an I8089 program. These communication areas, which are defined in Figure 8.5, will be detailed shortly.

The I8086/8088 central processor must issue initialization commands to the I8089 input/output processor when the system is powered up and when the system

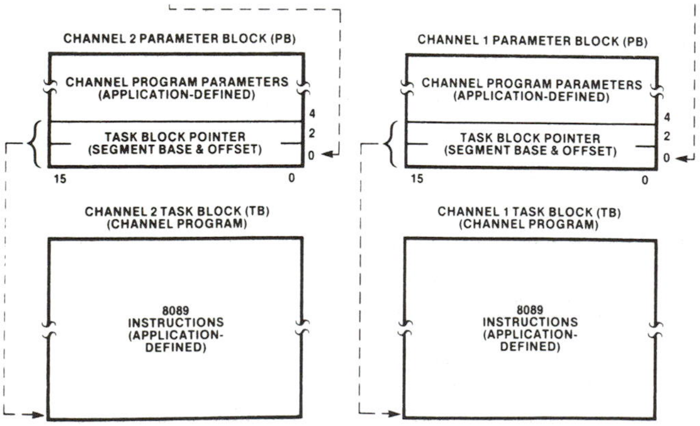

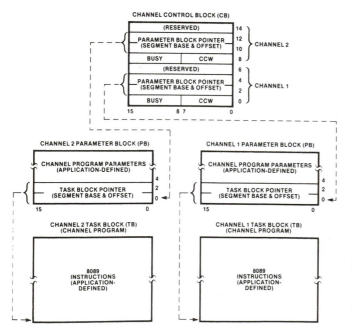

Figure 8.5 I/O command message areas employed to communicate input/output function descriptions and orders between the I8086/8088 and the I8089 IOP. (Reprinted by permission of Intel Corporation. Copyright 1980.)

is reset. This initialization is accomplished via a series of pointer-linked message blocks in system memory that are read by the IOP and used as parameters to its initialization program while configuring the data buses and the control access to them. Following initialization, and until another initialization is caused by reset or power-up, CPU-IOP communication is also via pointer-linked message blocks in system memory centered on the channel control block (CB).

As the channel control block (CB) is located in system memory as shown in the middle portion of Figure 8.6, it is available to both the I8086/8088 CPU and to the I8089 IOP after its address is passed to the IOP during initialization. As one consequence, the access of the channel control block must involve the system bus, as must all transfer of data to/from the I8086/8088 and all DMA input/output data. Thus the system bus and system memory are not only a vital resource, they are a resource that can easily become a limiting factor in system performance; they can easily become a bottleneck. Unnecessary use (access) of the system bus and system memory should be avoided when practical.

The Intel Corporation emphasizes that the I8089 IOP is a true general-purpose front-end input/output processor that can advantageously be employed for:

1. *Bus-width matching*: The IOP allows both 16-bit and 8-bit I/O components to be connected to 16-bit memory with odd–even byte banks (as is normal with the I8086) and also allows both 16-bit and 8-bit I/O devices to be connected to nonbanked 8-bit memory (as is necessary with the I8088).
2. *Winchester-style hard disks*: The IOP has the ability to meet the speed and data latency requirements of high-performance hard disks.
3. *Graphic displays*: The IOP has the data transfer bandwidth to support graphic displays and the data manipulation instructions to assume responsibility for display screen refresh, thus removing major overhead from the I8086/8088 system CPU processor. Additionally, the I8087 floating-point processor is often of extreme use in fast graphics processing.
4. *String processing*: The IOP has instructions for string processing, such as translate, scan-for-match/nonmatch, and block memory-to-memory moves that can be executed in parallel with the I8086/8088 CPU system processor.
5. *Operating system support*: A multitasking operating system can dispatch input/output tasks to the IOP with minimum overhead, including SPOOLing (Simultaneous Process—Output On Line) and preloading to disk of input data from slow devices. Additionally, the IOP has the instructions necessary to support disk directory search, update, and free-space mapping (including pointer following in data base searches).

Memory for the I8089 IOP exists in two separate and distinct address spaces as shown on the top and bottom of Figure 8.6:

1. System memory coincides with the I8086/8088 memory space and is accessed using the 20-bit address line system bus. System memory/bus cycles may be-

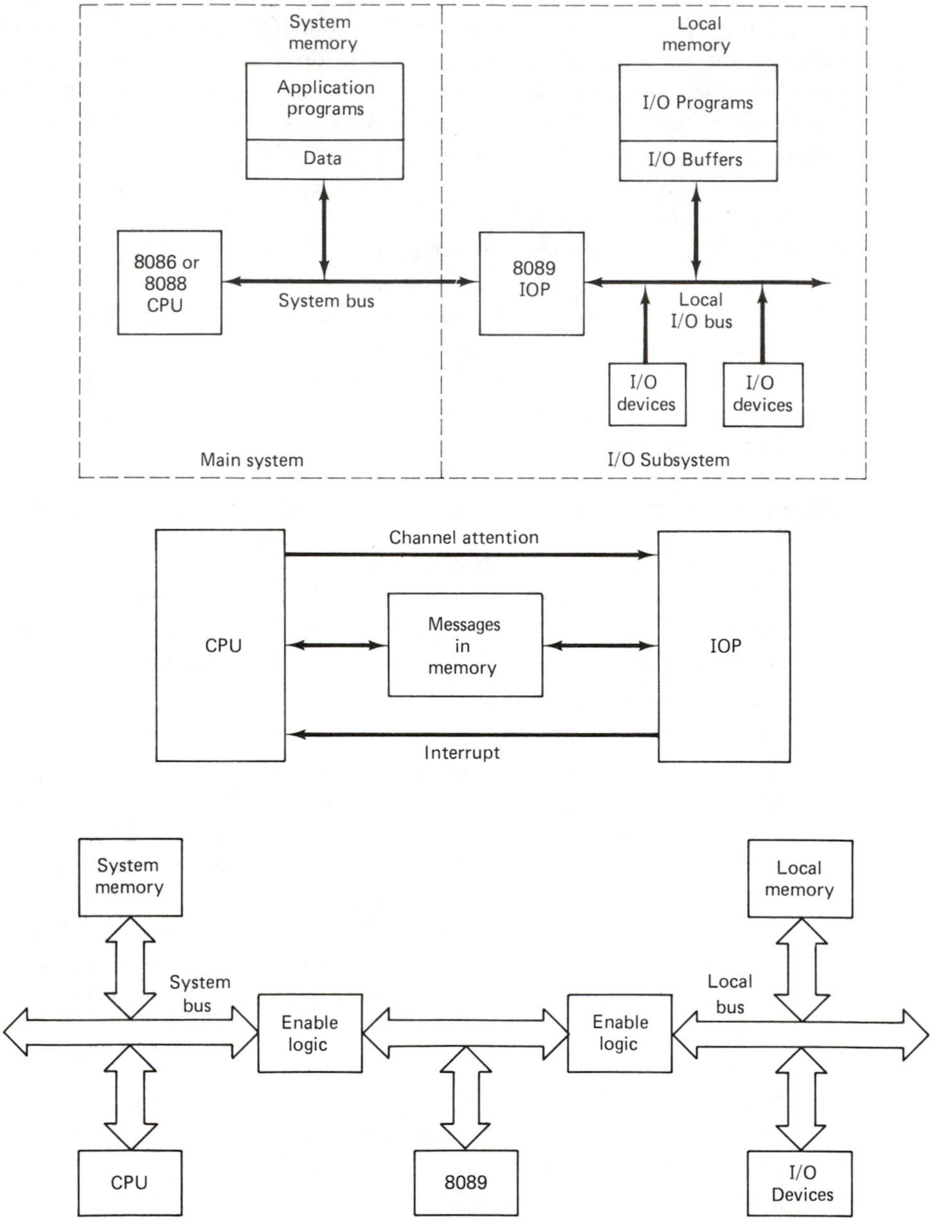

Figure 8.6 I8089 IOP-I8086/8088 CPU multiprocessing systems concept. (Reprinted by permission of Intel Corporation. Copyright 1980.)

come a critically short resource and can constitute a bottleneck. The IOP accesses system memory as an unsegmented array of 8-bit bytes without regard for address alignment or for the 64K-byte segments of the I8086/8088. A 20-bit address pointer register allows access to any and all of the possible 1,048,576 bytes directly by their physical address.

2. Local memory or I/O space is accessed using the 16-bit address line local bus. Thus the I8089 IOP is designed with *memory-mapped input/output.* Local memory is the I/O space but can (normally does) contain much of the IOP programs and buffers. Local memory and system memory may coincide; that is, local memory is not necessary and the I/O space and IOP program may be placed entirely in system memory. System performance would probably be downgraded, as system memory cycles and bus cycles both would be bottlenecks.

The organization or architecture of the IOP is shown in Figure 8.7. The *common control unit* allocates IOP cycles to the various processing units. All IOP operations, such as an instruction execution, a DMA data transfer, a response to a channel attention request, and so on, are a sequence of internal cycles each of which requires from two to eight clock cycles plus any possible wait states and bus transactions. As examples: a bus cycle requires one internal cycle, and the execution of an IOP instruction may require several internal cycles.

The *arithmetic-logic unit* (ALU) is capable of unsigned binary arithmetical and logical operations employing 8-bit, 16-bit, and 20-bit source operands, resulting in an 8-bit, 16-bit, or 20-bit result. The typical instructions are

Register ← Register + Memory
Memory ← Memory + Register

Note particularly that neither register-to-register nor memory-to-memory arithmetic-logic is allowed. Signed values in the standard two's-complement form may be employed, although no means of detecting a signed-value overflow into the high-order bit (the nonexistent "sign bit") is provided. Arithmetical operations involve 20 significant bits using the following rules:

Input operands
- Byte: bit 7 is propagated to the left through bit 19
- Word: bit 15 is propagated to the left through bit 19
- Pointer (24/32 bit): truncated on left to bit 19

Operations: 20-bit operations

Output operands
- Byte: truncated on left to bit 7
- Word: truncated on left to bit 15
- Pointer: bits 0–19 stored

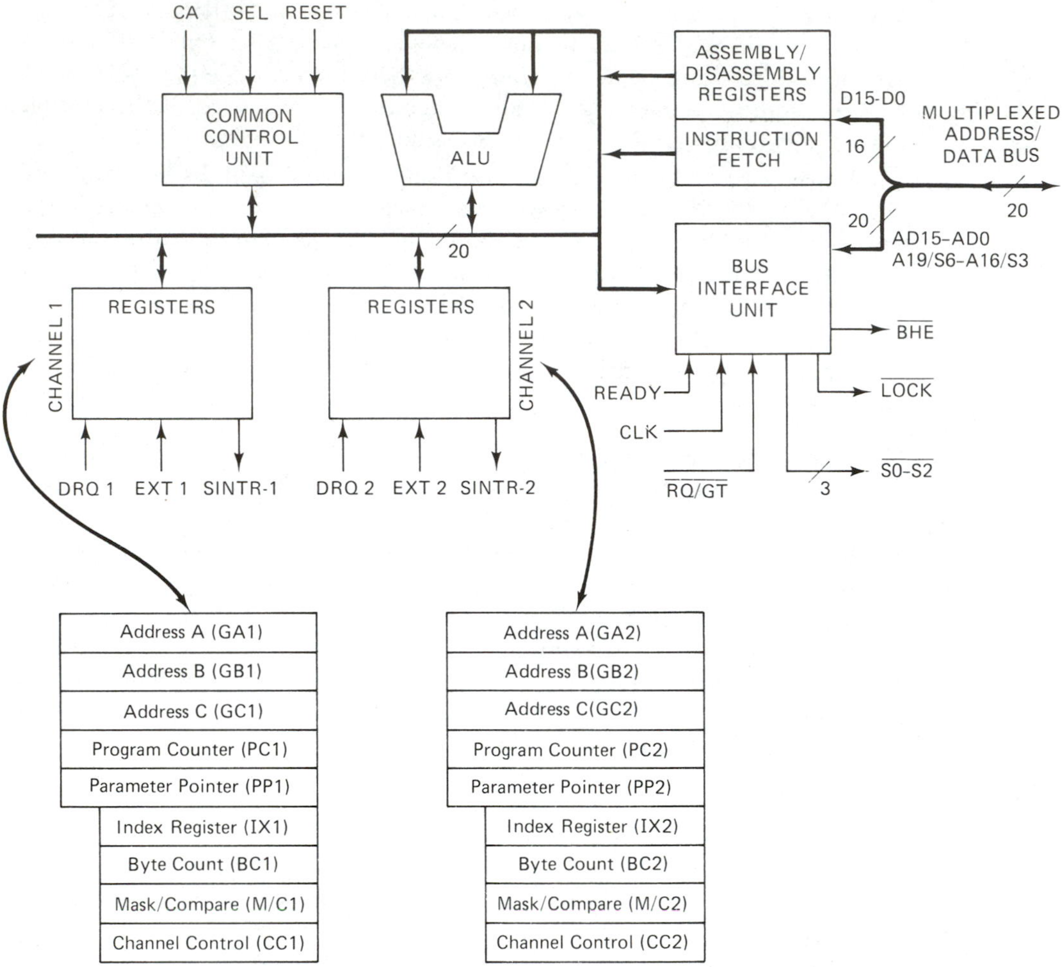

Figure 8.7 Architecture of the I8089 input/output processor (IOP). (Reprinted by permission of Intel Corporation. Copyright 1980.)

The instruction set of the I8089 IOP will be presented somewhat later.

All I8089 IOP data enters/leaves the chip through the *assembly/disassembly registers,* which are used to minimize the number of bus cycles when data are being transferred between different-width buses. For example, in transferring data from an 8-bit peripheral to the 16-bit memory of an I8086 system, the IOP would use two bus cycles to obtain the datum, assemble it, and then transmit the 16-bit assembled datum to memory in one bus cycle. Odd memory addresses may force a byte transfer to memory at the start and at the conclusion of a block transfer with the action being controlled by the microcode of the IOP without DMA channel program (task block) knowledge.

The *instruction fetch unit* fetches instructions for the executing channel DMA task block. Note that two channels may be dispatched at the same time but that only one execution unit exists so that only one channel task block (channel program) is actually executing at any one instant. In effect, the common control unit, the ALU, the assembly/disassembly registers, and the instruction fetch unit are shared in a time-multiplexed manner between the two channels, each with its private set of registers. As would be expected, one channel or the other can be given preemptive priority or they can alternate in their use of the shared resources.

The I8089 *bus interface unit* (*BIU*) performs all bus cycles for the input/output processor, including instructions/data and memory/peripherals bus usage. Referring to Figure 8.6, note that two buses are available to the IOP:

1. The *system bus* is shared with the central processor and can access up to 1 megabyte of memory using 20-bit addresses. If the central processor is an I8086, the system data bus will physically be 16 bits wide; if an I8088, 8 bits wide physically.
2. The *local bus* is private to the I8089 and can access up to 64K memory or memory-mapped I/O peripherals using a 16-bit address. The local data bus may physically be 8 bits or 16 bits wide, irrespective of the width or the system data bus if a "remote configuration" is chosen. Alternatively, if a "local configuration" is used, the system data bus and the local data bus must be of the same width. Figure 8.8 may be helpful.

As was mentioned before, it is possible to configure a system without a local bus; that is, the I/O memory-mapped space may be a portion of system memory space. Access to the system bus or to the local bus is determined by a tag bit associated with each address pointer register of each of the two channels.

CHANNELS

The instruction execution portions of the I8089 IOP can service either of two "independent" DMA channels but only one at any one instant. Each channel has the ability to execute channel programs (task blocks). Additionally, a channel may be idle. As shown in Figures 8.7 and 8.9, each channel has its own private set of 10 registers and associated control logic that govern channel operation during DMA block data transfers. Peripheral-device transfer timing control (synchronized transfer) allows the channel to wait for a signal on the DMA request line (DRQ) before performing the next fetch-and-store sequence of the data block transfer. The device may signal an end-of-block or termination error condition via the external terminate line (EXT). Between DMA data fetch and data store the data will be within the I8089 IOP, allowing the channel to execute channel program (task block) instructions to count bytes, translate data, and/or examine data for a bit pattern as well as terminate or continue the DMA transfer based on the manipulation results. For ex-

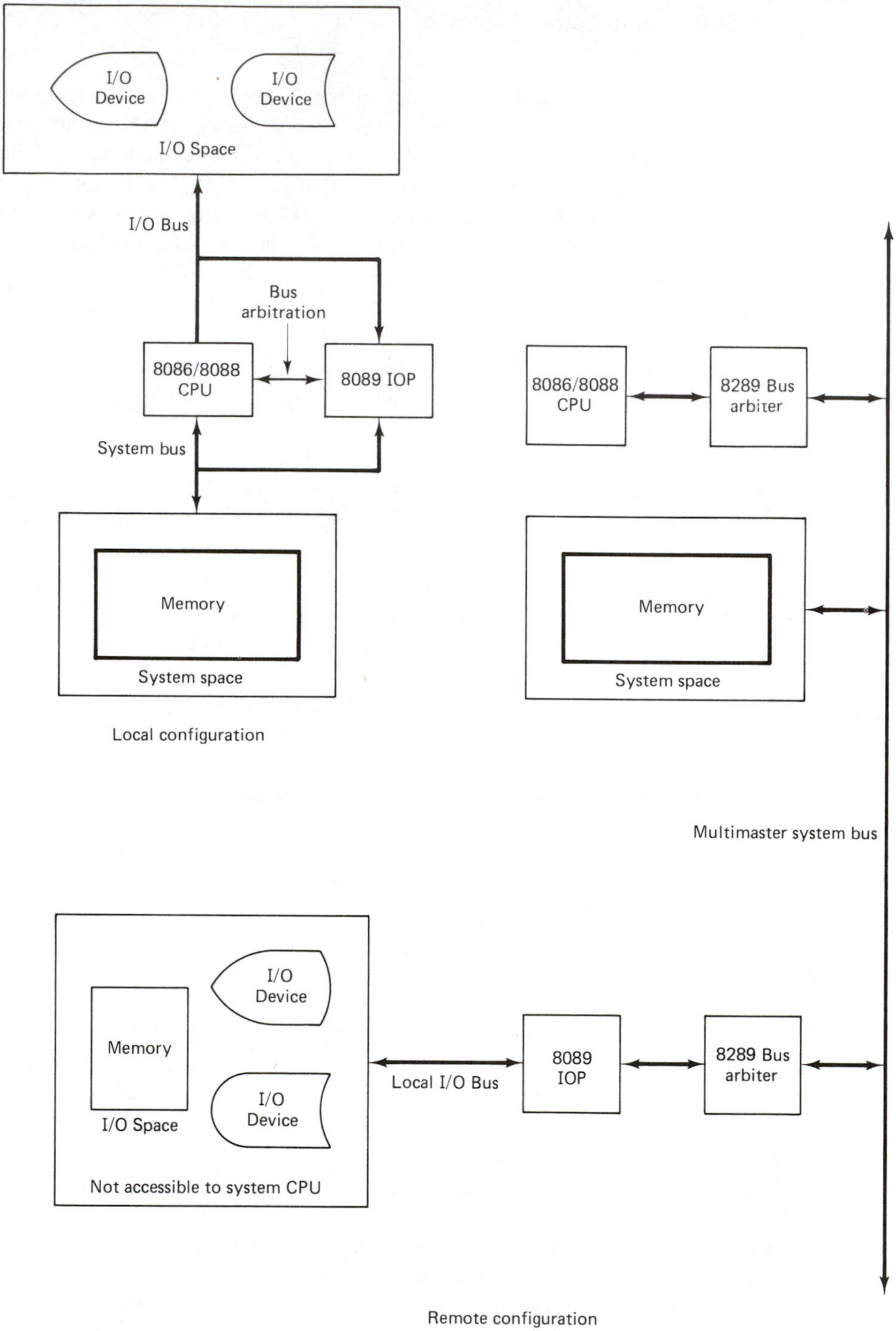

Figure 8.8 Possible I8086/8088 central processor-I8089 input/output processor configurations. (Reprinted by permission of Intel Corporation. Copyright 1980.)

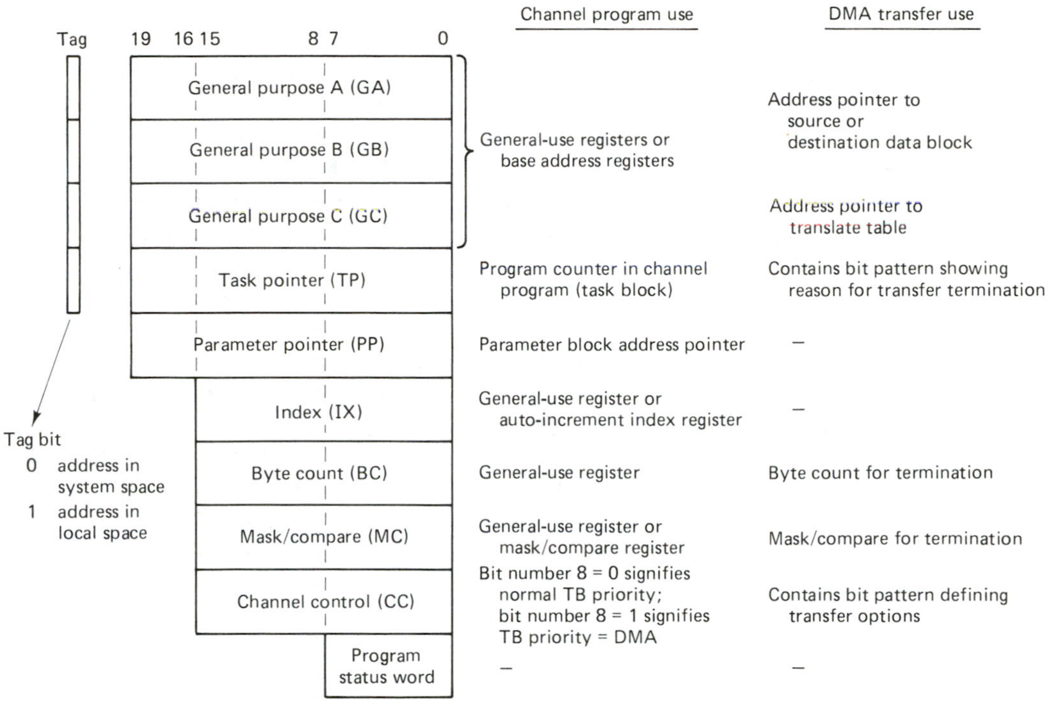

Figure 8.9 The I8089 IOP registers and their normal use. Two register sets exist, one set for each DMA channel.

ample, an end-of-line condition can be recognized and the appropriate action taken. Each channel can also cause, via task block channel program software, a software system interrupt to the I8086/8088 central processor by activating the system interrupt line (SINTR).

General-Purpose Registers

Each channel has three 20-bit registers that can be used for any programmatic purpose, including base address, by a task block channel program. During a DMA data block transfer, registers GA and GB hold the physical address of the source and destination data. These address registers can be indexed by the index register (IX). If the source datum byte is to be translated (i.e., if the source byte is to be used as a pointer to the destination datum byte in a translate table), register GC must point to entry byte zero of the 256-byte translate table. If the address contained in registers GA, GB, GC, or TP is to a location in system space, the corresponding tag bit will be set to zero. If the address in the register is a pointer in local (I/O) space, the corresponding tag bit will be set to 1.

Task Block Pointer Register

The TP register is employed as the program counter during execution of a task block channel program. When the IOP starts, or resumes, a channel program, the channel control units loads the TP register from the parameter block whose address in system memory is contained in register PP. The channel control unit increments or changes the value of the TP register during channel program execution in the normal manner expected for any program counter, including provisions for branches, conditional branches, subprogram CALLs, and subprogram RETurns. The use of this register for purposes other than as a program counter could produce strange and probably disastrous IOP program results.

Note that a task block channel program is implied for each peripheral device type. It must be designed to satisfy both the device's physical and electronic requirements through coding in the I8089 IOP language. We will examine the instruction set shortly. Also implied is the storage of this peripheral control DMA block data transfer routine in memory that is available to the IOP at a location whose address can be loaded into the parameter block during system initialization and subsequently be loaded into the PP register by the common control unit just before the start of a channel program.

Parameter Block Pointer Register

The PP register is not used during DMA transfer operations but is vital as an address pointer to the information necessary as parameters for task block channel program execution and for DMA block data transfers. Because a program executing in the I8086/8088 central processor specifies the contents of a parameter block and stores it in system memory, it is necessary and is assumed that the contents of the PP register is an address in system memory. Hence the PP register has no associated tag bit (a tag bit set to 0 is assumed).

Index Register

The 16-bit IX register is not used during DMA transfer operations but is necessary for accessing memory using some of the available I8089 input/output processor memory addressing modes in which the address of the operand is computed by adding the content of the index register (IX) to the content of a base register (GA, GB, or GC). The IX may be autoincremented as the last step in instruction execution in one memory addressing mode, providing a convenient method of processing arrays and strings.

Byte Count Register

The BC register may be used as a 16-bit general-purpose register during task block channel program execution. During DMA block data transfer operation, the BC register is decremented for each byte transfered. If a DMA transfer of a known length block of data is desired, the number of bytes should be loaded into the BC register and the byte-count-termination option specified. The decrementation of the BC register always occurs during DMA transfer in an unsigned 16-bit register modulus 10000 base 16 so that the next value after 0000 base 16 is FFFF base 16. Modular arithmetic is sometimes termed *circular arithmetic* because it "wraps around."

Programmers will recognize that using the BC register for purposes of task block channel program execution and simultaneously using the BC register for byte-count termination of a DMA data block can produce strange, erratic, and undesirable results both to the channel program results and for the DMA transfer.

Mask/Compare Register

Although the MC register can be employed as a general-use register by a task block channel program, the main use of this register is to perform a masked compare to an 8-bit value. The results of the masked comparison can be used to control program logic flow within a task block channel program through the use of conditional branch instructions. The results of the masked comparison are also useful in terminating a DMA block data transfer if the terminate-on-masked-compare option is specified.

The operation of the mask/compare register (MC) compares the bits specified by 1 bits in the mask (high-order byte of the MC register) of a DMA byte to the corresponding bits of the comparator (low-order byte of the MC register). This is logically equivalent to

(MASK & COMPARATOR) XOR DMA

Thus a "true condition" results if, and only if, the incoming DMA byte and the comparator byte are identical in all of the bit positions having a 1-value in the mask byte. Figure 8.10*a* gives two examples of "true conditions."

Channel Control Register

The CC register contains 10 fields that govern a DMA transfer. These 10 fields, as illustrated in Figure 8.10*b* and defined in Figure 8.15, are loaded by the task block channel program before initiating a DMA transfer. Note that bit 8, the "chained channel program execution" bit, increases the priority of a channel program to equal the priority of a DMA transfer. Again, although a task block channel program can employ the CC register as a general-use register, such a practice may inadvertently change bit 8 and thus result in unplanned and undesirable channel program execution priority changes. In some circumstances, the resulting effects on timing between channel program execution and DMA block data transfer may result in strange and unanticipated computational results.

Program Status Word

The programmer unavailable PSW records the state of the channel and thus allows channel operation to be orderly-suspended and subsequently resumed at a later time. A "suspend" order results in the first four words of the parameter block being used as a save area for the task address pointer, its tag bit, and the PSW. Figure 8.10*c* illustrates the PSW and Figure 8.10*d* shows the save area. A "resume" order results in the restoration of the information saved and the resumption of channel execution.

CONCURRENT CHANNEL OPERATION

Both channels can be active concurrently but only one can actually execute an instruction or transmit a datum at a time. In the technical terminology of concurrent processes discussed earlier in this chapter, each channel can be:

Active awake: executing an instruction or transmitting a datum

Active asleep: waiting for access to the channel control unit or to a data bus

Inactive asleep: idle and available for assignment

Only one channel at a time may be *active awake.* During this period, the other channel may be *active asleep* or *inactive asleep.* A little thought could convince you that if one channel is active asleep, the other should be active awake, but this may not be true, as the needed bus may be the system bus that is currently being used by the I8086/8088 CPU. On the other hand, both channels may be inactive asleep; that is, both channels may be idle and available for work assignment.

At the finish of each IOP internal cycle, the channel control unit assigns the next internal cycle on the following basis:

1. An inactive asleep channel does not receive a cycle. If both channels are inactive asleep, the next internal cycle does nothing except consume time.
2. If only one channel is active and it is awake, it will be assigned the internal cycle.
3. If both channels are active asleep, the next internal cycle does nothing but consume time. This can happen if both channels need the system bus and it is in use by the I8086/8088 CPU or by another processor.
4. If one channel is active awake and the other channel is active asleep and not blocked by nonavailability of the system bus due to use by the I8086/8088 CPU, the next internal cycle will be assigned to the other channel if it is involved in an activity of equal or higher priority. Otherwise, the active awake channel will be given the next internal cycle. Note that this rule can result in a

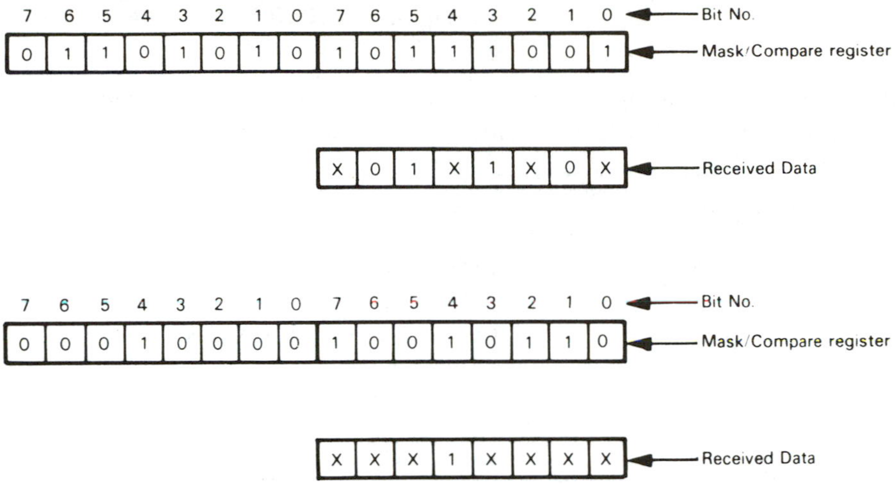

X can be 0 or 1

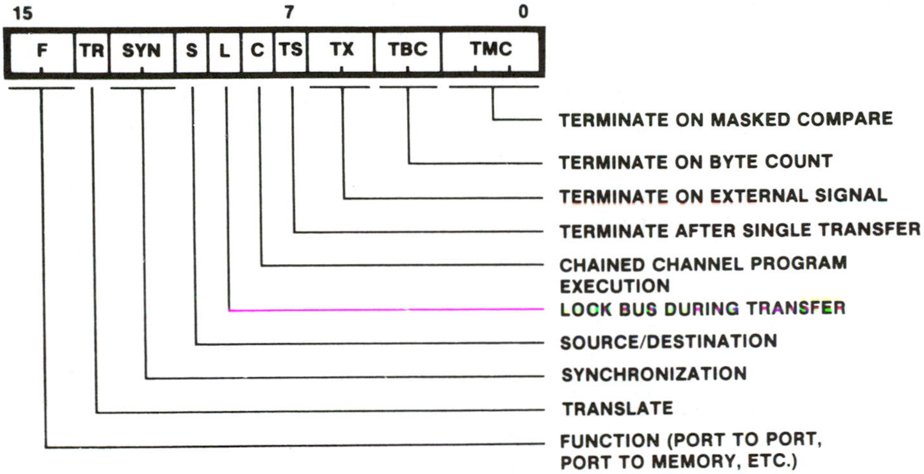

Channel Control Register

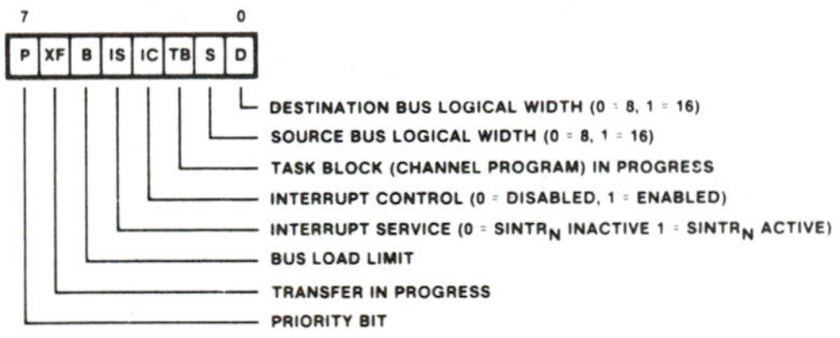

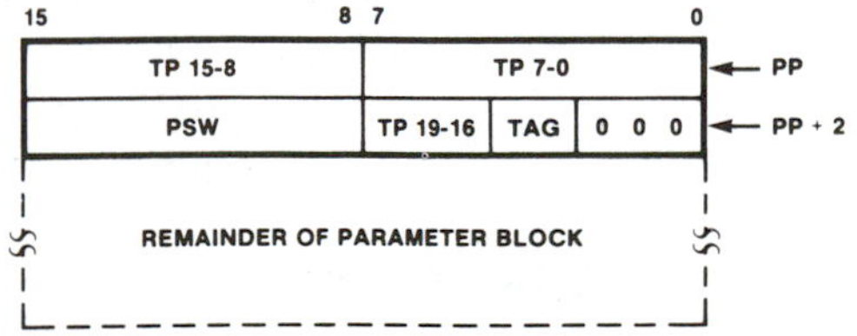

Figure 8.10 Details of the MC, CC, and PSW registers of the I8089 IOP. (Reprinted by permission of Intel Corporation. Copyright 1980.)

flip-flop of cycles between the two channels executing activities of equal priority with no resource blocking conditions. The activity priorities are:

Priority (1 = highest)	Activity
1	DMA transfer
1	DMA termination sequence
1	Chained channel program (bit 8 of CC register = 1)
2	Channel attention sequence
3	Channel program
4	Idle channel cycles

When a DMA block data transfer terminates for any one of four possible reasons (masked compare, byte count, external signal, single transfer), the channel will execute an internal to the I8089 chip ROM resident program to orderly-terminate the channel in a manner allowing correct channel resumption. This routine executes at priority 1.

When the I8089 IOP recognizes a channel attention request on the CA line to the channel control unit, the channel will execute an internal ROM resident routine at priority 2 to read and examine the channel command word in the channel control block placed in system memory by the I8086/8088 central processor. Note that the use of priority 2 does not allow this activity to interfere with DMA block data transfer, DMA termination, or (programmer judged important) chained channel program execution.

Two different conditions can override the channel priority scheme:

1. The I8089 IOP can have the LOCK signal activated, which will prevent a channel from giving up an internal cycle regardless of the relative priorities of the two channels. Thus in a multiprocessing system it is possible to guarantee exclusive use of a shared resource to a channel.
2. If one channel receives a channel attention request (priority 2) over the CA line while it is performing a DMA block data transfer (priority 1), the channel attention request will be serviced at the end of the next datum transfer within the block transfer. A DMA termination or a chained channel program activity will postpone but not prevent recognition of a channel attention request.

I8089 IOP INSTRUCTIONS

INSTRUCTION FORMAT

Instructions vary from two to six bytes in length, with the basic instruction occupying two bytes. One or more of the instruction bytes in positions 3 through 6 can contain immediate data and/or address offset values as well as other information.

Referring to Figure 8.11, in general, byte 1 contains in the three bit positions 13 to 15 the designation of the data register to be used as one of the source operands (which also may be the destination operand container). Bits 11 and 12 usually refer to the number of offset/datum information bytes following the main instruction word, although other information may be placed in this field with certain specific instructions. Bits 9 and 10 designate one of the four memory addressing modes, while bit 8 signifies if the operation involves byte or word operand data. The operation code is contained in bits 2 to 7 and thus implies a maximum of $2^6 = 64$ instructions (of course, many of these have four addressing modes). Bits 0 and 1 are employed to designate the register holding the memory address. Instructions can reference operand data as:

1. Contents of *one* register byte or word as a datum or as an address.
2. Contents of *one* memory byte or word as a datum; or a triple byte as an address; or four bytes as a segment/offset address.
3. Contents of *one* register byte or word.
4. In one case, byte or word data can be moved from memory to memory.

In other terms, some instructions reference a single datum; some reference two data, in which case one must be register resident and the other memory resident, with the exception that data can be moved memory to memory. It must be remembered that memory-resident data in the context of I8089 IOP can truly be memory resident, or it may be a memory-mapped peripheral device and thus be a DMA I/O datum.

OPERAND ADDRESSING

There are three types of operands:

1. *Register operands*: As discussed previously, registers are available for use as general computational value containers, as address pointer and modifier containers, as control information containers, and as count or compare information containers. Recall that the registers are identified by alphabetic diads and that a separate register set is available for each of the two channels.
2. *Immediate operands*: Both byte (8-bit)- and word (16-bit)-length unsigned immediate operands are allowed with the MOV, +, &, and | instructions. Recall that the ALU of the I8089 performs unsigned arithmetic-logic but that the addition of the two's complement of a value is correctly equivalent to a subtraction of that value with no (sign bit) overflow indication.
3. *Memory-resident operands*: It is extremely important to realize that I8089 IOP input/output is memory mapped. Thus memory-resident operands can actually be resident in systems or local memory space or, alternatively, may be derived from a device controller register that is a portion of the memory-mapped I/O

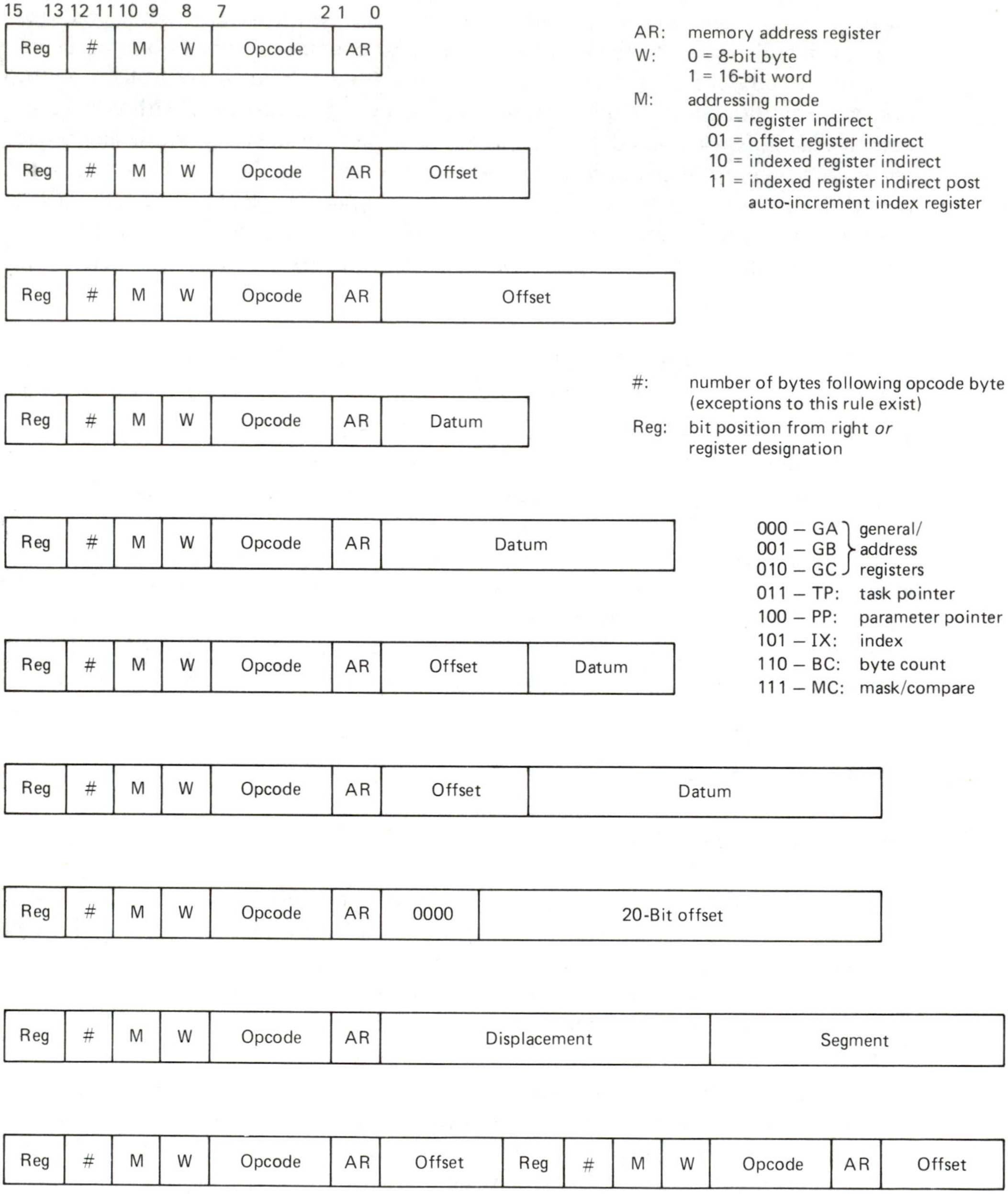

Figure 8.11 Instruction formats of I8089 IOP.

(local) space. Additionally, memory-resident operands must be transferred to/from the IOP via a bus which requires that an address be calculated. Recall that the effective address is the physical address in the I8089 with no segmentation such as exists with the I8086/8088.

All memory (and therefore, all I/O) addressing is of the general type *indirect through a register* with four variations. We emphasize that direct memory addressing is not available and also that indirect addressing through memory is not available on the I8089 IOP.

Address register indirect addressing (termed *based addressing* by Intel) signifies that the address of the datum to be employed as a source or as a destination operand is in one of the four address registers. These registers are the three general address registers (GA, GB, GC) that are tagged as being 20-bit to refer to system memory space or 16-bit to refer to local memory–I/O space, as well as the parameter pointer register (PP), which is assumed to be a 20-bit reference to system memory space. Additionally, the task pointer (TP) register is employed as the IOP program counter during task block channel program execution and necessarily always points to the current instruction in system or local memory as per its tag. The address in memory of the desired datum is derived as

$$\text{Physical Address} = [\text{Address Register}]$$

while the datum itself is

$$\text{Datum} \leftarrow [\text{Memory (Physical Address)}]$$

where (. . .) signifies indexing and [. . .] signifies contents of.

Offset register indirect addressing (termed *offset addressing* by Intel) signifies that the address of the datum is to be calculated as the contents of the designated address register plus the value of the offset in the instruction.

$$\text{Physical Address} = [\text{Address Register}] + \text{Offset}$$

The offset in the instruction can be an unsigned 8-bit, 16-bit, or 20-bit value. As shown in Figure 8.11, the 20-bit address occupies three bytes.

Indexed register indirect addressing (termed simply *indexed addressing* by Intel) derives the address of the datum as the contents of the designated address register plus the contents of the index register:

$$\text{Physical Address} = [\text{Address Register}] + [\text{Index Register}]$$

As the IX register contains only 16 bits, this form of coursing through an array can be used directly only with arrays of size 64K bytes or less.

Indexed register indirect address with auto-postincrement (termed *indexed auto-increment* by Intel) derives the address of the datum as above but also increments the IX register *after* address calculation and use (by one for byte data or by two for word data).

Physical Address = [Address Register + Index Register]
[Index Register] = [Index Register] + [Width Field] + 1

INSTRUCTIONS

We will consider the instructions of the I8089 input/output processor in four groups: data transfer/movement, arithmetic-logic, program control/transfer, and processor control.

Data Transfer/Data Movement Instructions

The instructions in this group move a datum between an IOP channel register and memory (in one case, memory to memory). The datum can be an 8-bit byte, a 16-bit word, a 16-bit address in local memory, a 20-bit address in system memory (stored as a three-byte value), or a 32-bit segment/offset diad system memory address. Immediate values are also allowed.

```
MOVB    MC,(GC + IX +)        ; move
MOVBI   (GA + 7),FFH          ;    byte
MOVB    (GA + IX),(GB + 1)    ;      datum
MOV     GA,(PP + 6)           ; move
MOV     (GA + IX +),MC        ;    word
MOVI    MC,FFOOH              ;      datum
MOVP    PP,(GA + IX)          ; move 20-bit pointer
MOVP    TP,(GB + 15)          ; to/from three bytes
LDP     TP,(BP + 6)           ; Load 20-bit pointer
LDPI    GA,12345689H          ; from 32-bit displacement + SEGMENT.
```

The LDP instruction employs a four-byte datum using the first two bytes as a displacement into the segment whose starting address is in the second two bytes. The physical address is calculated in the same manner as an I8086/8088 address:

Physical Address = [Displacement] + (Segment * 16)

It must be noted that the I8089 IOP employs seven instruction encodings to specify the four instruction mnemonics above and the Intel Corporation assembly language mnemonics follow these seven. A well-constructed and carefully designed assembler can correctly identify the intention of the programmer and thus minimize mnemonics.

Arithmetic/Logic Instructions

The arithmetic-logic instructions of the form

$$[\text{Destination}] \leftarrow [\text{Destination}] + [\text{Source}]$$

require that the destination or source operand, not both, be a register, although the source operand can be an immediate datum. (Memory/register and register/memory operations are allowed, but register/register and memory/memory operations are not allowed.) Arithmetic is unsigned binary and condition flags are not provided. As would be expected, a two's-complement input value results in a subtraction. All four memory addressing modes are allowed as well as immediate source operand data.

```
ADDB        X,Y
ADDBI       X,Immediate
ADD         X,Y
ADDI        X,Immediate
ANDB        X,Y
ANDBI       X,Immediate
AND         X,Y
ANDI        X,Immediate
ORB         X,Y
ORBI        X,Immediate
OR          X,Y
ORI         X,Immediate
NOTB        X,Y ; X = not (Y) ; Y unchanged
NOT         X,Y
```

If the result (destination) is a 20-bit register (GA, GB, GC, or TP), addition results will carry into the high-order bit positions for a word operation. Similarly, results of byte operations will propagate into the high-order bit positions of the 20-bit and the 16-bit registers. If the result (destination) is memory, the stored result will be truncated (chopped) on the high-order end.

The single-operand arithmetic-logic instructions follow the same general rules.

```
INCB      X       ; memory only
INC       X       ; register or memory
DECB      X       ; memory only
DEC       X       ; register or memory
NOTB      X       ; memory only
NOT       X       ; register or memory
CLR       X,n     ; memory byte only, #n is
SETB      X,n     ; bit position from right (0 – 7)
```

It must be emphasized that the single operand instructions that operate on a byte are restricted to memory-resident operand locations (register operand bytes are not allowed).

Program Control/Program Transfer Instructions

These instructions all cause a destructive change of the value of the task pointer register (the I8089 IOP program counter) that result in a program branch (a jump) with sequential execution resuming at the new label point. Although the Intel Corporation-furnished assembler has two forms of each instruction, corresponding to the two hardware forms, one for a jump/branch to a near label (within +127 to −128 bytes) or a far label (within +32767 to −32768 bytes), a decently designed assembler can determine which instruction form to generate (long or short jump) without programmer direction.

```
JMP       label
LJMP      label          ; unconditional branch
JZB       X,label
LJZB      X,label        ; branch on
JNZB      X,label
LJNZB     X,label        ; condition
JZ        X,label
LJZ       X,label        ; of X=
JNZ       X,label
LJNZ      X,label        ; zero/nonzero
JMCE      X,label        ; branch on memory byte X = or ≠ to
LJMCE     X,label
JMCNE     X,label        ; compare byte XORed mask byte of MC register
LJMCNE    X,label
JBT       X,N,label
LJBT      X,n,label      ; branch on bit #n=on/off in memory byte X
JNBT      X,n,label      ; #n is bit position 0–7
LJNBT     X,N,label
CALL      save,sub_id    ; store task pointer register and tag
LCALL     save,sub-id    ; in three-byte memory physical
                         ; location save; load TP register
                         ; and tag with physical address of
                         ; sub_id (address of subprocedure)
```

Note that the CALL, a subprogram instruction, has no corresponding return instruction and no hardware-supported stack as a receptacle for the return address. Rather, the programmer specifies a memory-resident three-byte receptacle for the return address when using the CALL and employs the MOVP (move 20-bit physical address with tag) instruction in the subprocedure to effect a return to the invoking routine. The lack of a hardware stack pointer register mechanism could be considered a serious programmatic shortcoming of the I8089 IOP if it was used for general computation tasks. Rather, the IOP is not employed as a general-purpose processor; does not possess an interrupt structure; is not expected to support recursive subprocedure calls; and has a separate, therefore private, register set for each channel, including the program counter (TP register). For these reasons, the usual problems of subroutine invocation/return encountered with the general-purpose computer case are not relevant. The following method will be satisfactory for all situations where the code is not placed in read-only memory (ROM):

```
                -
                -
        CALL SUB_ID+3,SUB_ID
                -
                -
                -
SUB_ID: LJMP START ; *+3 because jump-to-near instruction is three bytes long
                -
START:          -
                -
                -
        MOVP RETURN,TP ; return instruction
END_IT: END
```

The TSL instruction is used primarily with a semaphore variable to control access to a memory area shared between two or more co-routines that may be executing simultaneously in one or more processors.

```
TSL X,#b,label          ; branch on X ≠ zero to label,
                        ; X=#b on X=zero, lock bus
                        ; during execution
```

Our example will emphasize the timing of a data buffer usage situation where channel 1 of the I8089 IOP is reading data from a device and filling the input buffer; an applications program of the I8086/8088 CPU is obtaining these data from the input buffer, manipulating the data, and placing the results in an output buffer, whereupon channel 2 of the I8089 IOP will write the contents of the output buffer to a device. The entire process will be repeated many times. It is important that the filling of a buffer be completed before the use of that buffer starts.

In other terms, the input process, the calculation process, and the output process are executing on independent processors but accessing common data areas in a predetermined order. If the input buffer is accessed for data to use in calculation before it is input, the results will be wrong; if the output buffer is output before calculation is complete and placed in the output buffer, the results will be wrong. Therefore, the three processes executing in the three independent processors must be interleaved in a very specific order and not allowed to proceed prematurely. Note that our example requires time-synchronized access to shared data. Thus it is somewhat natural to provide a variable that controls such access. By accepted convention, such a variable is termed a *semaphore.* In terms of the TSL instruction, the first operand—a byte location in common memory—is the shared-data-area access-control semaphore. When the semaphore has a value of zero, access if allowed; when the semaphore has a nonzero value, access is prohibited. Figure 8.12 illustrates the program schema. Semaphore examination and control in the I8089 IOP is easily controlled by the single instruction loop

```
P_V_TEST: TSL SEMAPHORE,#1H,P_V_TEST
```

which will do a branch-to-itself cycle until the semaphore is made zero by the co-routine, then make the semaphore nonzero, and fall through to the DMA block data transfer. Similar semaphore examination and control in the I8086/8088 CPU requires three instructions plus both a preparation and a post-test instruction:

```
             MOV          AL,1d
P_V_TEST:    LOCK XCHG    SEMAPHORE,1d
             TEST         AL
             JNZ          P_V_TEST
AVAILABLE:   MOV          SEMAPHORE,1d
```

which will cycle until the semaphore is made zero by the co-routine executing in the I8089 IOP, then fall through to make the semaphore nonzero, and execute the buffer–CPU transfer.

Processor Control Instructions

The instructions in this group allow a channel program to control I8089 IOP hardware facilities.

```
NOP        ; no operation—two bytes long
HALT       ; terminates/concludes a channel program
```

The HALT instruction clears the busy byte in the channel control block and causes the channel to perform idle cycles and be available for assignment (inactive asleep).

```
SINTR ; causes a software interrupt to the I8086/8088 CPU
```

The SINTR software interrupt instruction sets the interrupt service bit (bit 4 from right) in the programs status word (PSW). Additionally, if the interrupt control bit (bit 3 from right) in the PSW is set, the channels SINTR line is activated; otherwise, the SINTR line is not activated. An IOP channel program can use the SINTR software interrupt instruction to gain attention from (to interrupt) the I8086/8088 CPU.

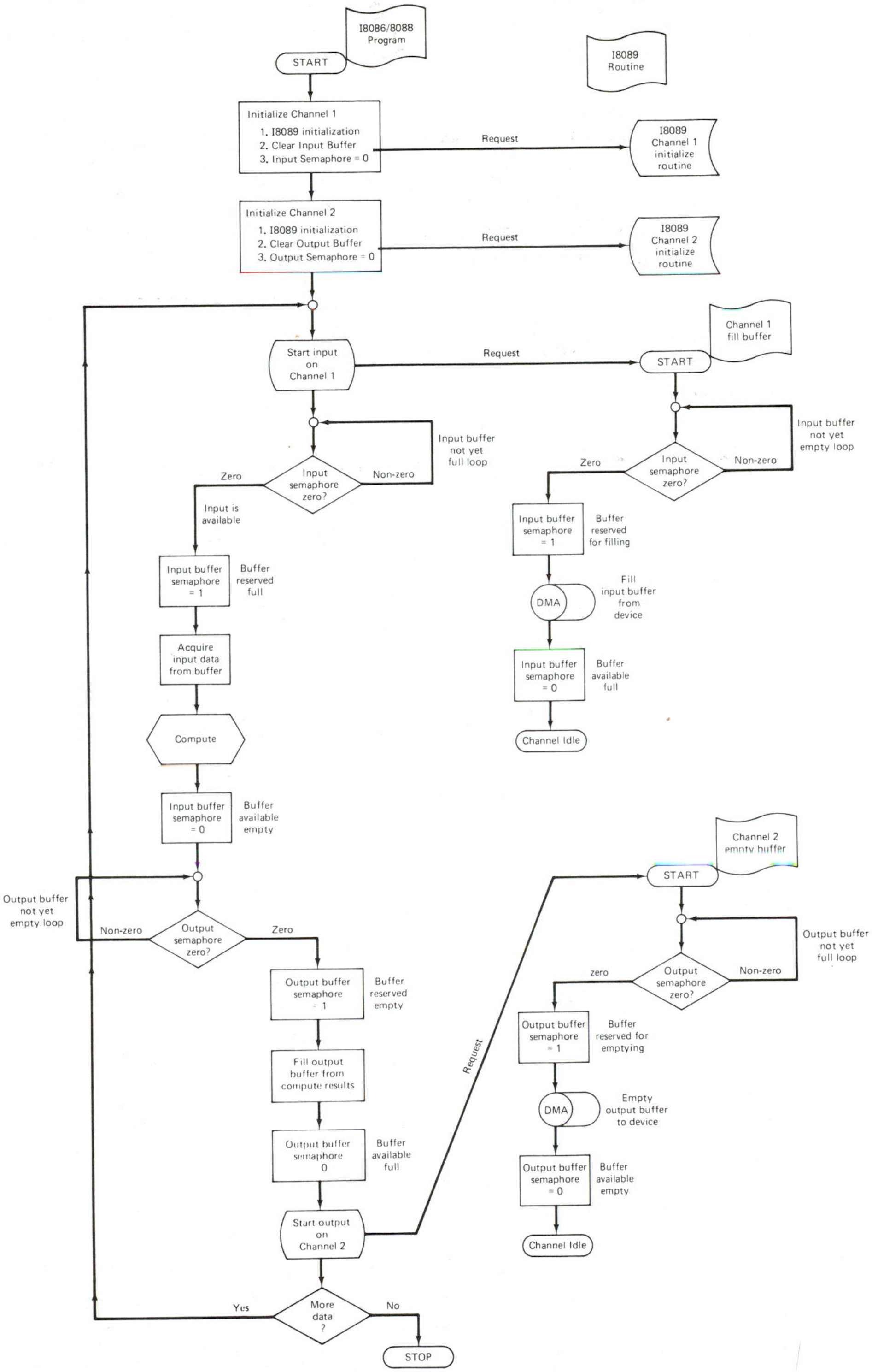

Figure 8.12 Schema for applications program/channel 1/channel 2 co-routines to use shared input buffer and shared output buffer using

```
WID        SRC.DEST        ; specifies the logical bus
                           ; widths for a DMA transfer
```

The WID instruction is used after every system reset to set the logical bus widths. The logical bus widths remain unchanged until reset by a subsequent WID instruction or a processor reset. This instruction alters bits 0 and 1 of the channel PSW:

```
PSW bit 0—destination bus logical width      ; 0 = 8 bits
PSW bit 1—source bus logical width           ; 1 = 16 bits
```

Logical bus width may not exceed physical bus width.

```
XFER        ; enter DMA block data transfer mode after next instruction
```

The XFER instruction prepares the channel for a data transfer during the period of its' and the next instruction's execution. Any instruction except one that alters the GA, GB, or GC register may follow XFER, including the NOP or WID. In a synchronized DMA block data transfer, the subsequent instruction may "ready" the device by sending the last parameter or a "start" command.

CPU–IOP COMMUNICATIONS

The I8086/8088 central processor and the I8089 input/output processor communicate information to each other via shared system memory. That is, the arrangement constitutes a multiprocessor computer system that employs the "mailbox" concept whereby one processor leaves a message in memory for the other processor to read.

In the preceding section we discussed the semaphore concept of controlling access to the shared "mailbox"—the shared data area. This solution strategy is based on two most important assumptions; both processors know about the mailbox and are attempting to access it. The possibility also exists that one processor places a message in memory for the other, but the other processor does not know about it and therefore does not receive it, in fact, does not even look for it. Therefore, we must solve the mailbox communication problem with one assumption: Both processors know about the mailbox, but the receiver may be unaware that the "mail person" has left a letter. We need a mechanism equivalent to the habit of the old-time neighborhood mailman who rang the doorbell just after he placed the mail in the mailbox. As you know, one mechanism for demanding the attention of a processor is the interrupt.

The SINTR instruction of the I8089 IOP can be used to demand the attention of the I8086/8088 CPU because the CPU was designed and implemented with a satisfactory interrupt system. On the other hand, the I8089 does not have an interrupt system, so another method must be employed to inform it that a message exists for it in memory. Further, as the I8089 is effectively two channel processors, two mailboxes exist and the notification method must be able to inform one channel of a message for it without disturbing the other channel.

The I8089 IOP design provides two signals that result in the necessary notification and, in effect, act like a single-purpose interrupt (even though they do not technically constitute an interrupt): (1) Channel Attention, CA (pin 23), and, (2) Select, SEL (pin 24). Select (SEL) "low" designates channel 1 and select (SEL) "high" designates channel 2. The I8086/8088 CPU can control signal pulses on these control lines by executing an OUT byte or OUT word instruction.

The only remaining problem is to inform the IOP of the system memory locations of the messages for each channel; that is, just where are the mailboxes? Additionally, the software of the CPU and the software of the I8089 must employ the same format for the messages. A double-tiered method is employed to communicate the necessary information from the CPU to the IOP:

1. The agreed-upon common message format consists of an address pointer—chained series of three message blocks—a channel control block, parameter blocks for each device, and task blocks (channel programs) for each device. We will be very specific about these blocks shortly.
2. The I8089 IOP executes in two modes:
   a. An initialization mode during which the IOP executes a chip-resistent ROM-based program that among other tasks obtains and stores the channel control block address in system memory
   b. The command mode or channel program (task block) execution, during which DMA block data transfers may occur

MESSAGE BLOCKS FOR COMMANDS

Channel Control Block

All I8086/8088 CPU-to-I8089 IOP communications center on the channel control block (CB) located in system memory and thus available to both processors. The address of the channel control block in system memory is passed to the IOP by the CPU during the IOP initialization process. The channel control block consists of two four-word areas, one for channel 1 and the other for channel 2. As illustrated in Figure 8.13, the channel control block for each channel contains

Word 0	
byte 0:	Channel command word
byte 1:	Channel busy semaphore (00H = free, FFH = busy)
Words 1 and 2	Address of parameter block in system memory using I8086/8088 segment/offset style
Word 3	Unused (reserved for possible future use by Intel for design expansion)

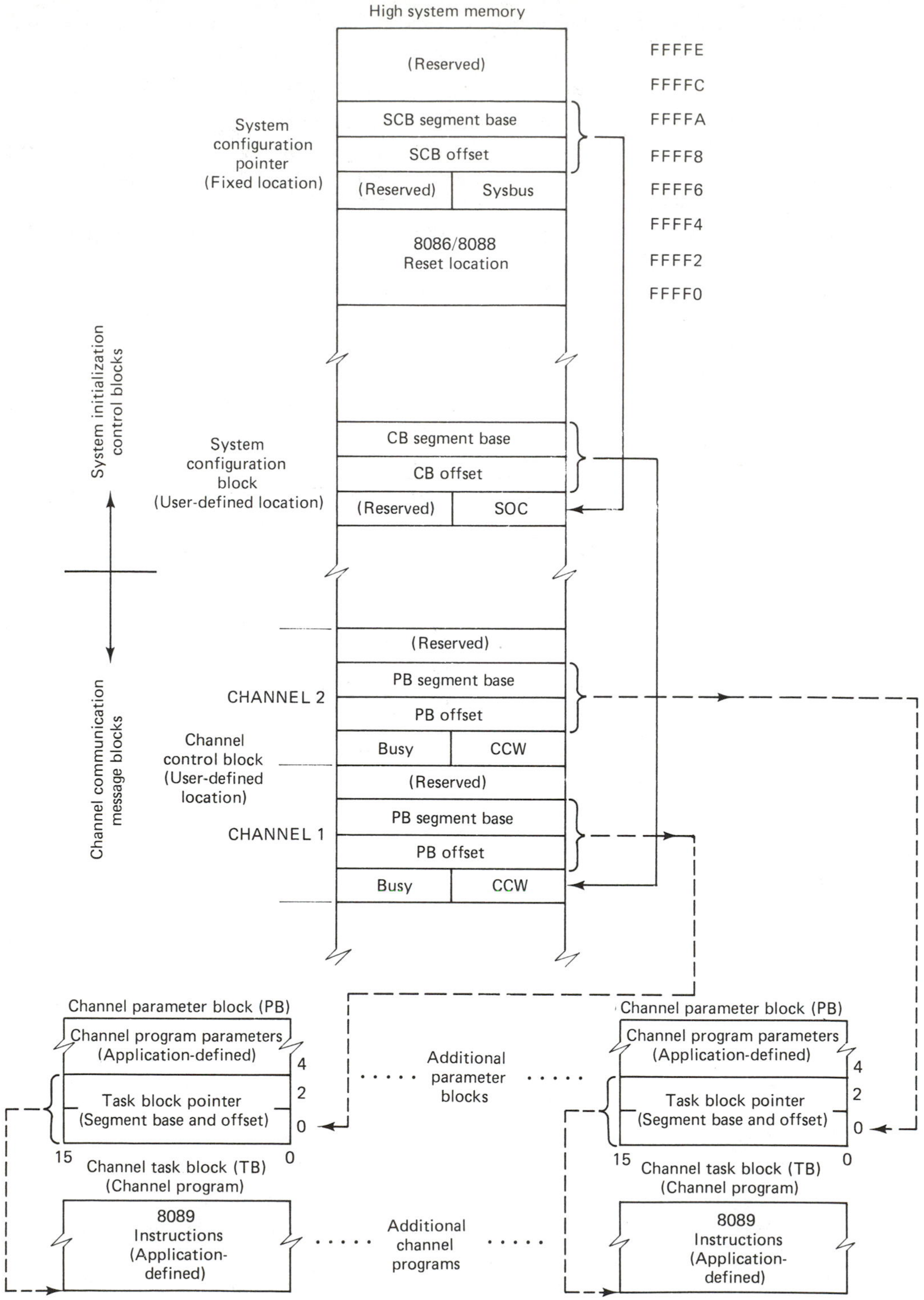

Figure 8.13 Multiprocessor communication blocks allowing I8086/8088 CPU-to-I8089 IOP messages. (Reprinted by permission of Intel Corporation. Copyright 1980.)

After I8089 initialization, any channel attention request results in the requested channel setting its busy semaphore flag to FF base 16 and then reading the CCW field and the parameter block address from the channel control block. Thus it is the responsibility of the I8086/8088 CPU program to fill in the CCW and the parameter block with the correct information necessary for the I8089 IOP to accomplish the desired function. The fields of the CCW are defined in Figure 8.14.

Parameter Block

Besides the address of the channel program task block, the parameter block must also specify the device (an address in I8089 local memory), the address of the data buffer, and any other pertinent information or directions concerning the DMA block data transfer or other channel program parameters. Two examples are shown in Figure 8.15.

The parameter block for a device action can often be preprepared and placed in I8089 IOP local memory, thus reducing transfer contention on the system bus. On the other hand, the information in the parameter block may be specific to the DMA block data transfer—such as the track/sector of a disk or which of two double buffers—and cannot be determined until just before the I/O request by the CPU. This situation would require that the parameter block be in memory shared by the CPU and the IOP, that is, in system memory. (To be very specific, only the variable information would necessarily be in system memory.) Note that the information to set the channel control register must be transmitted to the IOP in some manner. This information can be furnished by the CPU via the parameter block, or it can be specified as constants within the channel program task block, or as a combination of these methods.

Task Block (Channel Program)

A channel program is written specifically for each DMA block data transfer and other I8089 IOP task as appropriate to the device. It seems worthwhile again to note that the XFER instruction must have one instruction following it to allow time for the IOP to initiate the DMA block data transfer. From Figure 8.14, note that a value of 110 in the command field (CF) of the channel command word (CCW) of the channel control block (CB) will result in the suspension of IOP channel activity with the channel program counter (task pointer = TP), the TP tag, and the PSW being saved in the first two words of the parameter block and the busy byte semaphore of the control block being set to zero. A suspended channel program can be resumed by setting the CF to 101, but as the task block pointer in the parameter block has been stored over by the save, the channel program cannot be started over from the beginning without resetting the task block double-word (segment-offset) pointer. It is important to realize that starting another channel program during the suspension of a channel program may, and probably will, destroy the register contents of the suspended channel program and result in unwanted, strange,

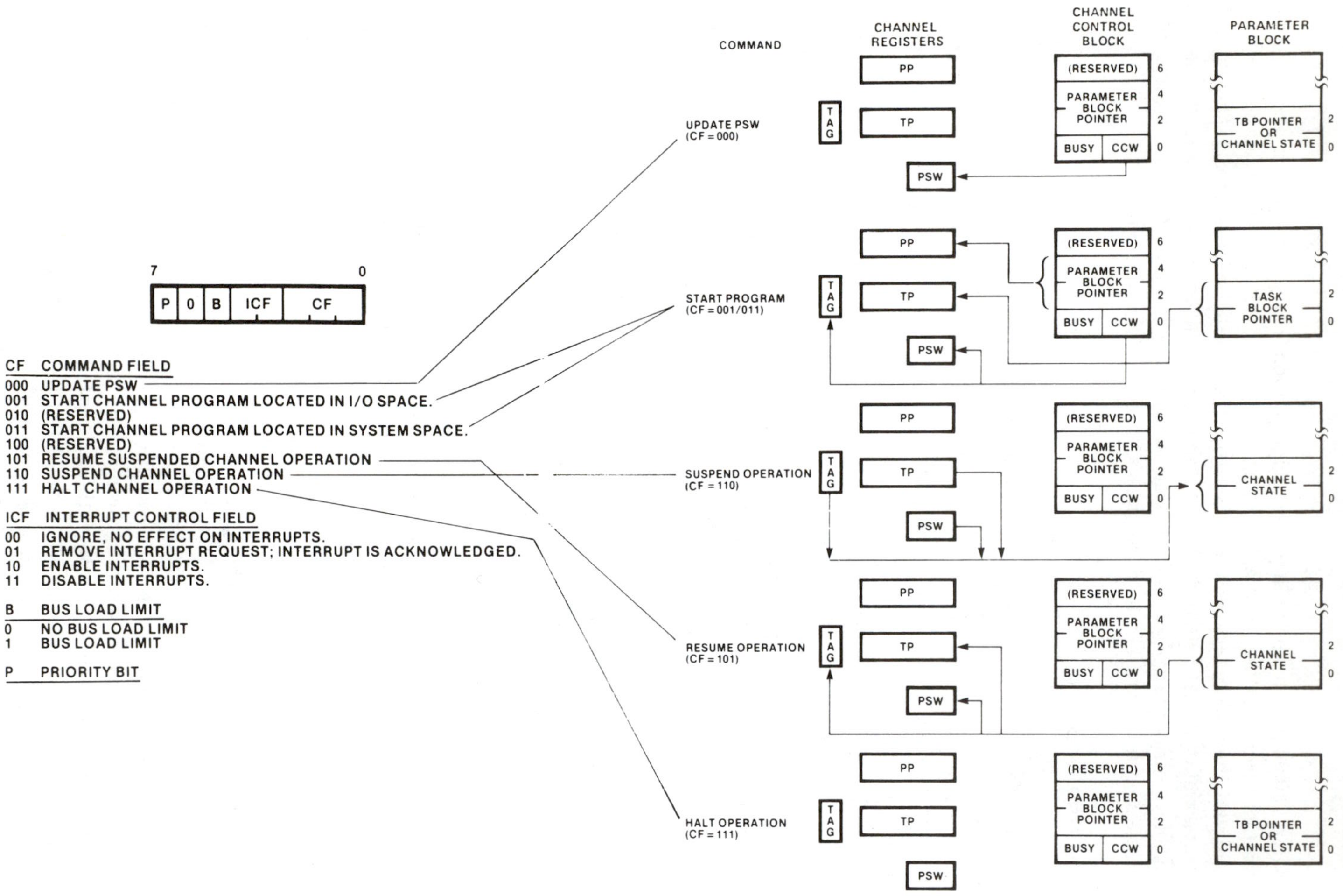

Figure 8.14 Coding of bits in channel command work (CCW) of channel control block (CB) in system memory. (Reprinted by permission of Intel Corporation. Copyright 1980.)

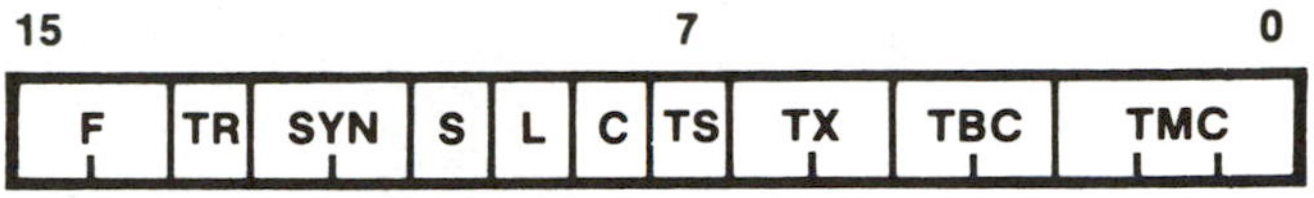

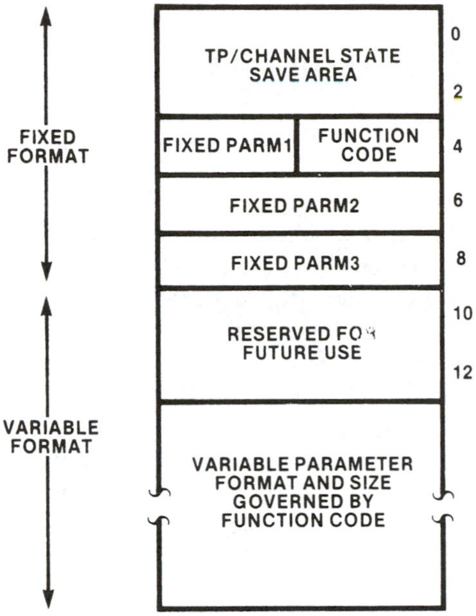

F	FUNCTION
00	PORT TO PORT
01	MEMORY TO PORT
10	PORT TO MEMORY
11	MEMORY TO MEMORY

TR	TRANSLATE
0	NO TRANSLATE
1	TRANSLATE

SYN	SYNCHRONIZATION
00	NO SYNCHRONIZATION
01	SYNCHRONIZE ON SOURCE
10	SYNCHRONIZE ON DESTINATION
11	RESERVED BY INTEL

S	SOURCE
0	GA POINTS TO SOURCE
1	GB POINTS TO SOURCE

L	LOCK
0	NO LOCK
1	ACTUATE LOCK DURING TRANSFER

C	CHAIN
0	NO CHAINING
1	CHAINED: RAISE TB TO PRIORITY 1

TS	TERMINATE ON SINGLE TRANSFER
0	NO SINGLE TRANSFER TERMINATION
1	TERMINATE AFTER SINGLE TRANSFER

TX	TERMINATE ON EXTERNAL SIGNAL
00	NO EXTERNAL TERMINATION
01	TERMINATE ON EXT ACTIVE; OFFSET = 0
10	TERMINATE ON EXT ACTIVE; OFFSET = 4
11	TERMINATE ON EXT ACTIVE; OFFSET = 8

TBC	TERMINATE ON BYTE COUNT
00	NO BYTE COUNT TERMINATION
01	TERMINATE ON BC = 0; OFFSET = 0
10	TERMINATE ON BC = 0; OFFSET = 4
11	TERMINATE ON BC = 0; OFFSET = 8

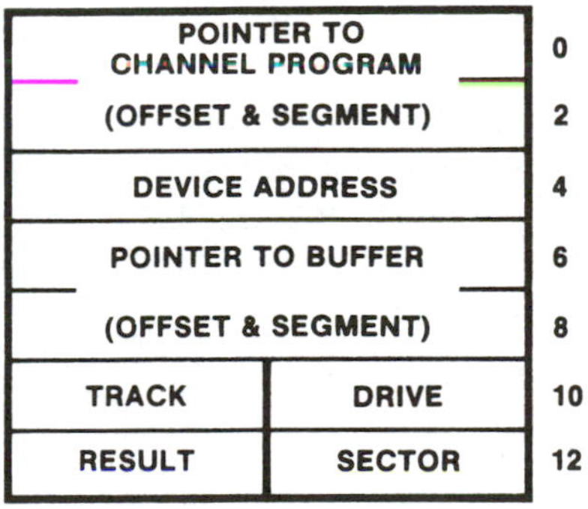

TMC	TERMINATE ON MASKED COMPARE
000	NO MASK/COMPARE TERMINATION
001	TERMINATE ON MATCH; OFFSET = 0
010	TERMINATE ON MATCH; OFFSET = 4
011	TERMINATE ON MATCH; OFFSET = 8
100	(NO EFFECT)
101	TERMINATE ON NON-MATCH; OFFSET = 0
110	TERMINATE ON NON-MATCH; OFFSET = 4
111	TERMINATE ON NON-MATCH; OFFSET = 8

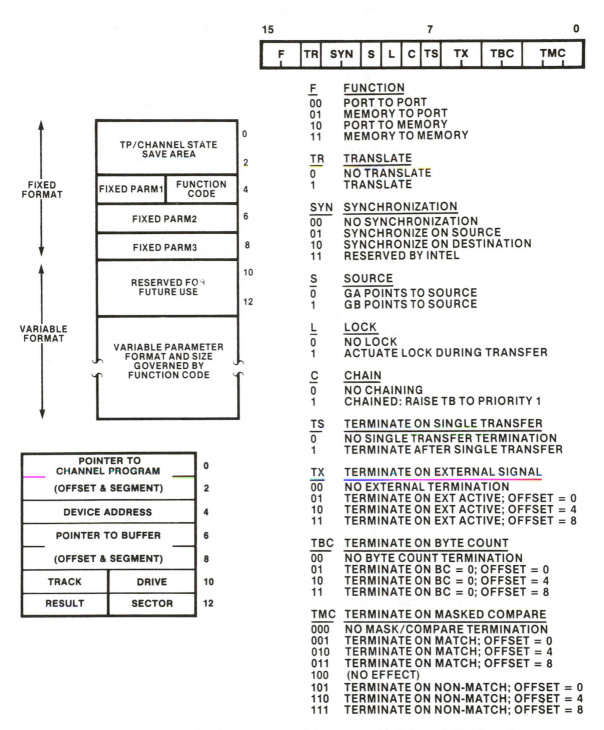

Figure 8.15 Possible formats and contents of the parameter block. Some of this information is used to set the values of the various fields in the channel control register. (Reprinted by permission of Intel Corporation. Copyright 1980.)

and unforeseen results. The suspension of a channel program during a DMA block data transfer has no effect on the I/O device. Therefore, extreme care must be taken and detailed knowledge of the device must exist for channel suspension to be "safe."

PROGRAMMING THE I8089 IOP

INITIALIZATION

Before the IOP channels can perform I/O tasks, the device must be informed of the address in system memory of the channel control block (already known by the I8086/8088), the physical width of the system bus (8-bit for I8088; 16-bit for I8086), and which processor is master of the system bus [I8086/8088 is master if in local mode; lone I8089 is master in remote configuration (if two, then one of them is bus master); refer to Figure 8.8].

The initialization sequence begins when the IOP has its RESET line (pin 21) activated. This halts any operation in progress, does not change the contents of any registers, but clears the chain bit in the channel control register (CC). The IOP initialization sequence is accomplished via an on-chip ROM program as shown in Figure 8.16, with the 20-bit address of the channel control block being kept in a register unavailable to the programmer (which we will term the *CCB register*).

CHANNEL INITIALIZATION

Although Figure 8.17 is a fairly good overview of the interaction of the I8086/8088 CPU and the I8089 IOP before, during, and after the DMA block data transfer, we will concentrate on the actions of the IOP. When the CPU requests action of the IOP through the CA and SEL lines via an OUT byte or OUT word instruction, the IOP must start a channel program by executing an on-chip ROM resident series of instructions:

```
;    Channel initialization routine (on-chip ROM) assumes that
;    I8089 IOP has been initialized; therefore,
;    CCB register contains address of channel control block.
;
;    Assumes that I8086/8088 CPU has set semaphore of channel to zero.
;
     LDP       PP, (CCB+OFFSET)        ; Load pointer to parameter block
                                       ; Channel 1 OFFSET=2
                                       ; Channel 2 OFFSET=10
     MOVB      (CCB+OFFSET),FFH        ; Set semaphore to Busy
                                       ; Channel 1 OFFSET=1
                                       ; Channel 2 OFFSET=9
     LDP       TP,(PP)                 ; Load pointer to channel program
                                       ; TP register is program counter
```

```
;  I8089 IOP Initialization Routine (on-chip ROM)
;  Assume system bus is 8 bits wide
;  CCB is channel control block address register

LDPA    GA, #FFFF6H       ;  Load system bus byte
MOVB    Reg, @ GA         ;  and set system bus
                          ;  width bit (16-bit if
                          ;  bit 0 = zero)
INCW    GA                ;  Load address of system
LDPA    CCB, @ GA         ;  configuration block
                          ;  from 32 bit pointer
MOVB    Reg, @ CCB        ;  Load system
                          ;  command byte and
                          ;  set I/O bus width
                          ;  (16-bit if bit 0 = zero)
                          ;  set Req/Grant (using
                          ;  bit 1)
LDPA    CCB, @ CCB + 2    ;  Load address of channel
                          ;  control block (CB)
                          ;  from 32-bit pointer
MOVB    @ CCB + 1, #00H   ;  Clear channel 1 semaphore
MOVB    @ CCB + 9, #00H   ;  Clear channel 2 semaphore
HALT                      ;  Idle IOP — inactive asleep

;  Reg can be any register.
;
;  CCB register not available to channel programs.
;  Channel control block cannot be moved after
;  initialization, as CCB cannot be changed
```

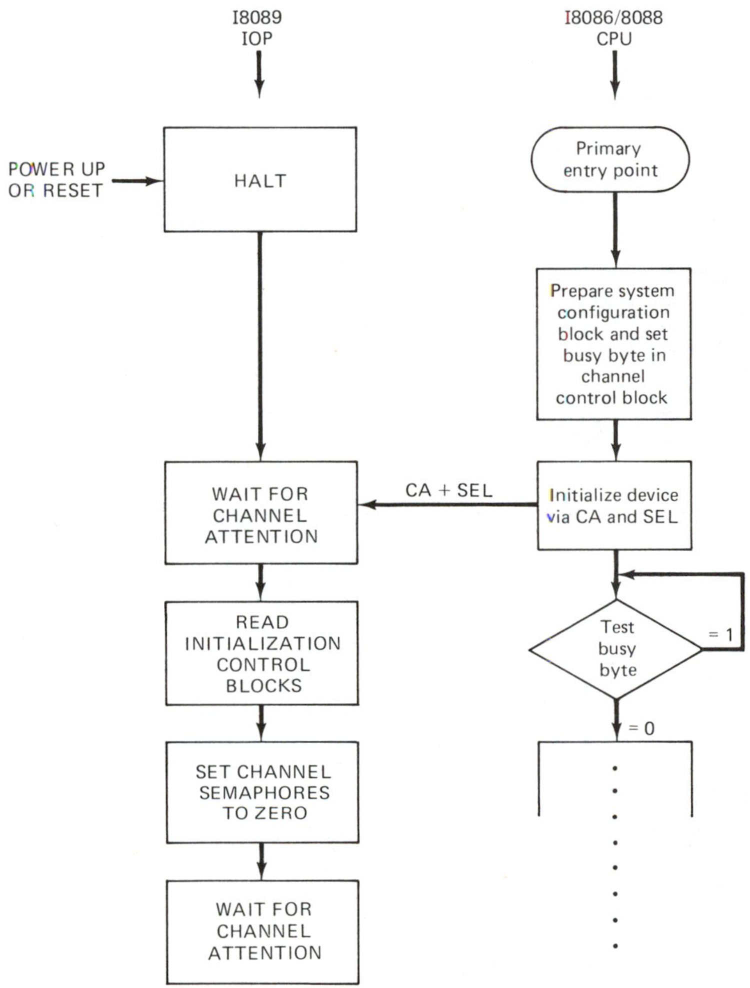

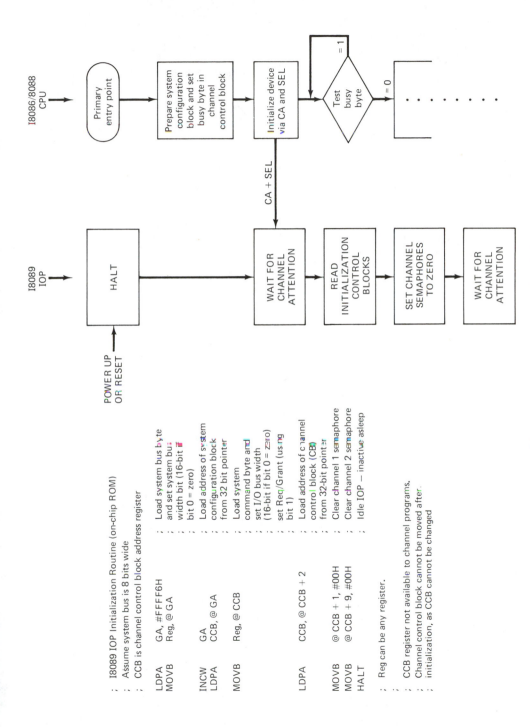

Figure 8.16 I8089 IOP initialization sequence provides the IOP with the physical bus width, the address of the channel control block in system memory, and bus master identification (is IOP master of slave). Refer to Figure 8.13 while considering program. (Reprinted by permission of Intel Corporation. Copyright 1980.)

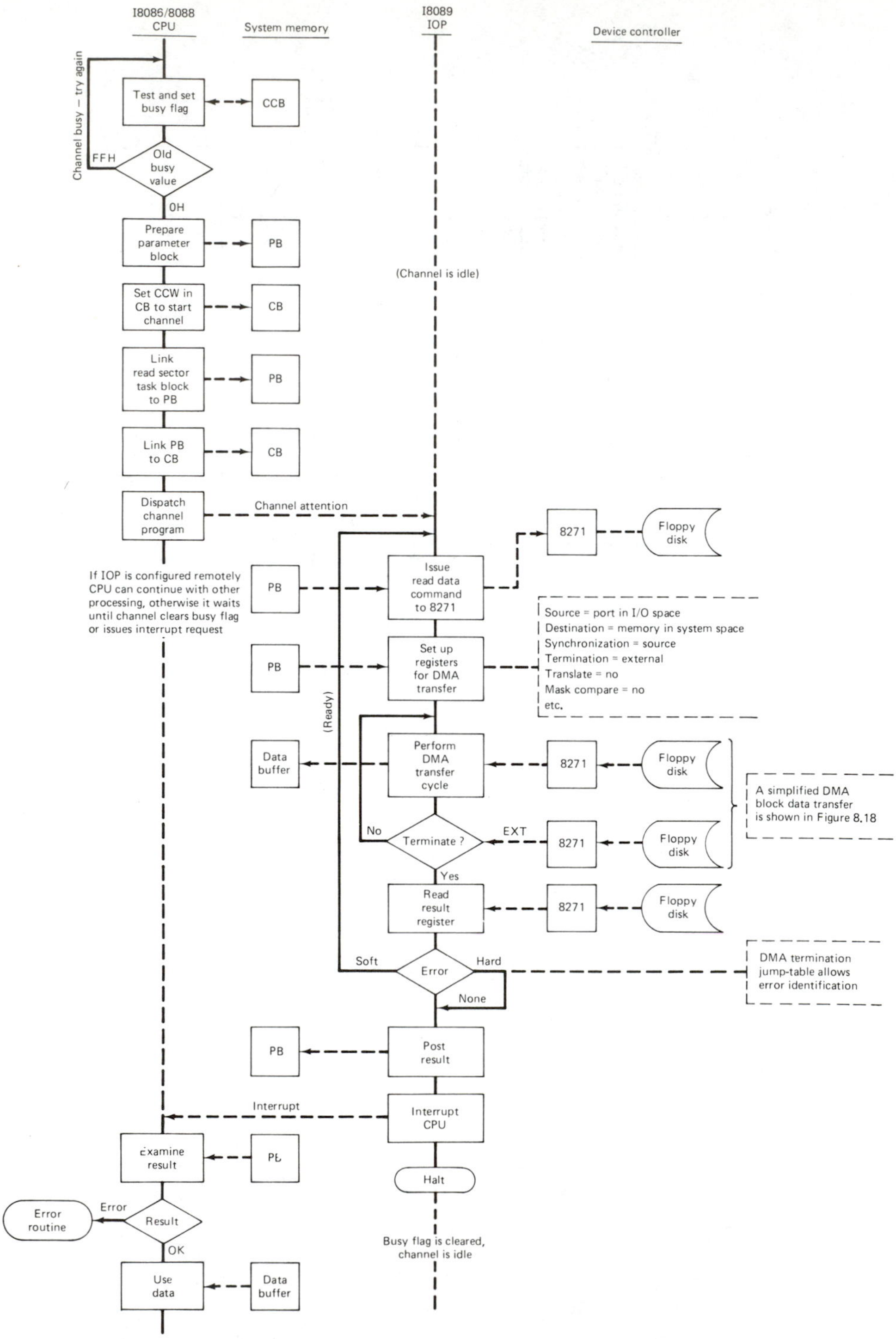

Figure 8.17 Illustration of an I8086/8088 CPU-I8089 IOP transaction. (Reprinted by permission of Intel Corporation. Copyright 1980).

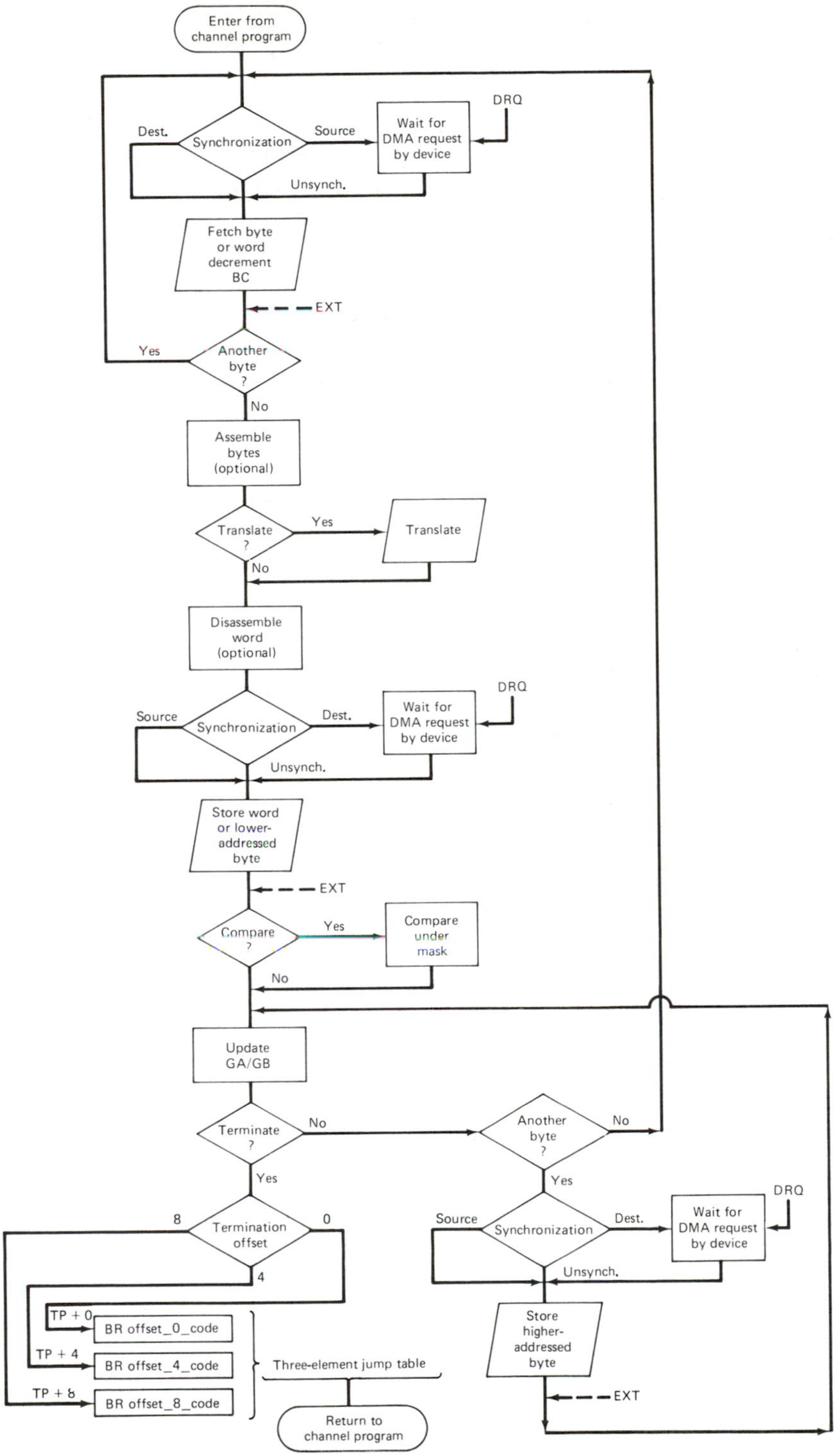

Figure 8.18 Illustration of an I8089 IOP DMA block data transfer with minor simplifications. Note that the termination offset jump table allows reaction to error conditions. (Reprinted by permission of Intel Corporation. Copyright 1980).

Note that this channel initialization routine will start a channel program (task block) in either channel as ordered by the CPU via the SEL line and that the routine will not distinguish (will work as well) between a task block resident in system memory as in local I/O memory.

The suspension of a task block channel program causes the program counter (TP register) and the program status word (PSW register) to be stored in the parameter block. It is possible to restart a channel after suspension:

```
; Channel restart routine (on-chip ROM)
;
        MOVB    PSW, (PP+3) ; Load PSW and
        LDP     TP, (PP)    ; load program counter (TP) from
                            ; save area of parameter block
```

THE DMA DATA TRANSFER PROCESS

A DMA single datum transfer cycle is shown in action flow form in Figure 8.18. A complete block data transfer is a series of these single datum transfers, as is also shown. In general, the information encoded into the fields of the channel control register (CC) directs the flow of logic during the transfer (refer to Figure 8.15 for a definition of the fields). Note that an unending (infinite length) data transfer can be initiated if no termination condition is specified.

If a designated termination condition occurs during a DMA single datum transfer cycle, the channel logic will use the appropriate contents of the channel control register field corresponding to the termination condition (see Figure 8.15) to add an offset value of 0, 4, or 8 to reflect the reason for termination to the channel program counter (the TP register) before exiting to the channel program. In effect, this action of offsetting the TP register (the PC) forms a three-element termination jump table that can be used within the channel program to react correctly to termination caused by one of three possible causes:

1. DMA transfer termination caused by a signal from the device or the interface (external signal)
2. DMA transfer termination caused by having completed the transfer of the specified number of bytes (byte count)
3. DMA transfer termination caused by finding/not finding a byte with a specified bit pattern (masked compare)

9

Operating Systems

An operating system consists of all the programs that control the equipment and software resources of the computer system, such as processors, main memory, I/O devices, secondary storage, files, libraries, and so on. These program modules simplify the use of the system, resolve conflicts in resource usage, and attempt to optimize the performance of the system under a given set of restraints. In effect, the operating system acts as an interface between the applications program and the actual physical computer. In a broader sense, it is a buffer that smooths the interface of the user with the harsh realities of the bare hardware.

An operating system is a program, usually quite complicated and large with many modules, that controls the operation of the computer. In most, if not all, cases, the operating system accomplishes this function by being the resident main program executing in the computer hardware with an application program being treated as a subprogram that is CALLed at the appropriate time, and allowed to execute, with the RETurn being made to the "main program," the operating system. In this philosophical viewpoint, errors in the applications program with requests for help or services are merely CALLs to existing submodules of the operating system.

Thus the operating system constitutes and provides a predefined environment in which any of a myriad of software packages can execute or run. As an example, a Pascal compiler is a program that translates a *source program* in the syntax and semantics—the grammar and associated meaning of Pascal—to the corresponding I8086/8088 machine language *object program.* We would expect this compiler to mesh closely with the facilities and modules of the operating system both during the translations and during the subsequent execution of the resultant object code. During compilation, modules of the operating system will be used to read characters from the terminal, allow editing of the Pascal statements, to compile and print the listing, and to store the object program in a file on disk. During execution, object code produced by the compiler of sophisticated languages such as Pascal requires a fairly large set of support modules constituting a run-time environment. Errors during execution will need interrupt-handler modules, which also are provided by the operating system.

This example implies that *all* the support services provided by the computational system that are not hardware are a portion of the operating system. Such a viewpoint is just a trifle extreme. It would imply that a program purchased to accomplish heat control in a home (a realistic application for an I8086/8088), which is invoked and executed once every minute for years on end, would be a portion of the operating system. Most computer users and experts would not agree but would prefer to class this program as an application that is invoked by and executes under the control of an operating system.

So just what is an operating system? What constitutes an operating system? How can we tell if program "X" is a portion of the operating system or not? We suggest the following criteria:

1. If a program module controls a hardware or software resource of the computational system, it is an operating system module.
2. If a program module controls noncomputer equipment or manipulates nonsystem data, it is an applications module.

Thus we define an operating system as an organized coherent collection of program modules designed to manage and control the computational system's resources. These resources may be classified as memory, processors, devices, and information (programs and data). The operating system must keep track of each and every resource, decide which program is to get which resource, allocate the resource, monitor its use, and eventually reclaim the resource for reallocation to another program.

THE CONCEPT OF A PROCESS

In Chapters 5 and 8 we discussed the idea of a process as a program in execution. It was specified that a process may be active awake, active asleep, or inactive asleep. When dealing with operating systems, it is almost necessary to employ the concept of a program being a set of processes that are activated, suspended, resumed, and terminated during the program's execution.

Recall from Chapter 8 that a process is *active* if at least one of its instructions has been executed and at least one of its instructions remains to be executed; otherwise, it is inactive. This definition implies that an inactive process either has not yet started, has been temporarily suspended, or has completely finished. It also implies that a process can be activated (e.g., be started), then suspended (e.g., be put to sleep), later resumed (e.g., awakened), and finally finished (terminated). Thus a process has a sort of life cycle in which the process is always initially in the inactive state before execution starts and progresses to the active state through various stages of execution until its termination, when it again becomes inactive. During its active state, a process may be suspended or temporarily put to sleep to await some necessary or desirable action (such as I/O), after which it will wake up and again be in the active awake state with instructions being executed.

But what precisely is a process? Is it really sufficient to specify a process as "a program in execution?" Being very technical, the answer is yes. Being a trifle less technical, we are alluding to a manner of thinking, a philosophical concept of viewing a program during its execution by the processor of a computer, particularly the viewing of the interplay of different programs during their execution and how they interact with each other. Thus the concept of a process implies action; the concept of a process implies the dynamic invocation of different programs that interact with each other during the manipulation of data to obtain answers.

Recall from Chapter 6, when we were considering the I8087 floating-point processor, how the I8086/8088 could possibly continue executing instructions at the same time that the I8087 was executing a floating-point instruction. To allow this parallelism, there has to be a degree of *independence* between the two sets of data and instructions, one set for the control of the I8086/8088 processor and the other set for the I8087 processor. Also recall from Chapters 5 and 8, when we were considering DMA, how the I/O processor could be executing instructions for filling or emptying a buffer at the same time that the I8086/8088 CPU was executing program instructions. To allow this parallelism, there had to be a degree of *independence* between the two sets of data and instructions, one set for the DMA processor and one set for CPU. To complete this viewpoint, let us consider an applications program that is prosaically calculating a payroll when it encounters a CALL instruction to a subprogram to sort the employees' names into alphabetical order. To allow a valid sorting of the names, the calling program must be suspended while the sort program is executing lest it access the common data (the names). To allow for this noninterference, there had to be a degree of *independence* between the two sets of data and instructions, one set for the payroll program and the other set for the sort subprogram.

Thus the concept of a process must include not only a program in execution but the idea of independence with a high degree of interaction. Also note that a process must have a processor on which to execute. Now, a processor can only be executing one process at any one instant. Thus truly concurrent processing requires multiple processors. A single processor can execute many processes, but only one at a time. Nevertheless, even on a single processor a process may start (become active awake), be suspended (become active asleep as the payroll program did when the sort was called), be resumed (become active awake again as the payroll program did when the sort returned), and finally be terminated (become inactive). A multiple-processor can, but does not necessarily have to, execute many processes with one active on each processor at any one time. Thus an I8086/8087/8089 system could have up to three processes simultaneously active awake. Figure 9.1 will assist understanding. It is strongly suggested that the section on DMA/program synchronization in Chapter 8 be reviewed at this point.

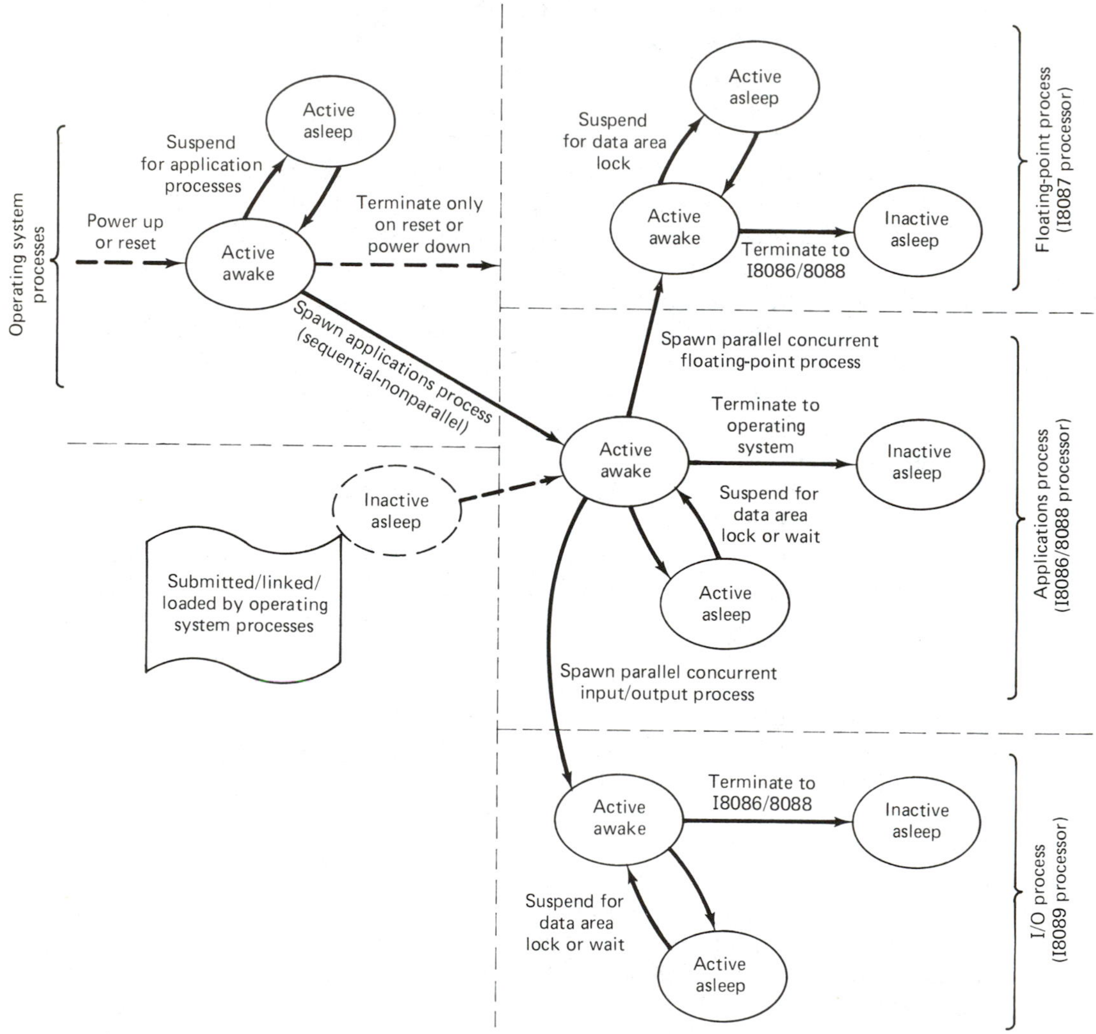

Figure 9.1 Process viewpoint of Applications Program in I8086/8088-I8087-I8089 multiprocessor system with operating system resident in I8086/8088.

A HISTORICAL PERSPECTIVE AND A PHILOSOPHY

Although many authors maintain that the ENIAC machine of J. Presper Eckert and John Mauchly of the University of Pennsylvania was the first electronic digital computer, there were numerous other developmental efforts that are serious contenders for the honor, such as Konrad Zusc in Germany, the Turing group in Great Britain, and John V. Atanosoff of Iowa State College (now University) at Ames. Perhaps we are too close to the events and to the people themselves to truly sort it all out; perhaps the records will indicate almost true simultaneity; or perhaps the concepts were so elegant and self-evident that many people found them without intellectual cross-fertilization.

Similarly, it is almost impossible to assign definitive credit for the organization of the vital computer control ideas and their implementation into complete operating systems. Among these developments were assemblers, compilers, relocation, I/O subsystems, libraries of both programs and data, and so on. Without any intent to precipitate an argument regarding specific credit, I hasten to mention Captain (Dr.) Grace Murray Hopper, USNR, and Professor Maurice Wilkes of Great Britain as two of the truly inventive and influential pioneers.

For our purposes it is not necessary to give credit and accolades to the people; rather, a brief account of the trends is appropriate. In the beginning, as we should all recall once in a while, there were a few physically large, very expensive, relatively slow, logically small, almost unique computers without software that were programmed in absolute binary. In effect, the computer was the personal property of the designer guru, who ungraciously allowed a privileged few acolytes to test the circuits while calculating exotic but useful results.

In 1951 the first commercially available computer, the UNIVAC I, became available, followed by the IBM 701, the IBM 650, and a literal host of other entries into the promising but infant entrepreneurial information processing world. In these early systems, each programmer personally operated the computer—loading paper tape or decks of cards, punching buttons, examining the contents of storage via banks of lights, and so on—that is, actually spending more time getting the computer ready for a job than was spent in the useful execution of the job. Additionally, those early systems constituted a scarce resource. There was not nearly enough time to satisfy the demand; people waited in line in the dark of night to "get time" on "the computer." The computer guru and the lesser priests become salespeople extolling the use of the system. Wilkes (and others) "invented" the system subprograms which grew into program libraries; Hopper (and others) "invented" the assembler and the compiler. Job-by-job processing came into vogue and persisted until the mid-1950s.

Then someone (actually quite a few people in many places) automated the process of cleaning up from one job and starting the next job. With the availability of both ingenuity and hardware, the batch-processing executive came into being and was widely adopted. From our present standpoint, it is important to remember that the batch-processing executive systems of the latter half of the 1950s and the early 1960s were implemented on the "giant" computers of that era and were aimed primarily at "scientific" applications. In the context of processing ability, I would guess that the earlier batch systems (implemented on pretransistor vacuum-tube-based machines) had about the power of the present-day I8086/8087/8089 system. Of course, the later transistor-based systems [such as the CDC 1604, the IBM 7090, the UNIVAC (ERA) 1103] possessed significantly more processing power. Additionally, with the use of transistors in implementing computers becoming fairly standard in about 1959, a class of relatively small and slow character-oriented machines for business data processing became available.

Some genius someplace (more likely quite a few semigeniuses at many places) dreamed of combining the available hardware into a "distributed system" for fast sequential processing of jobs one at a time. Using the more common IBM line of products, these early batch systems could be distributed as shown in Figure 9.2. Es-

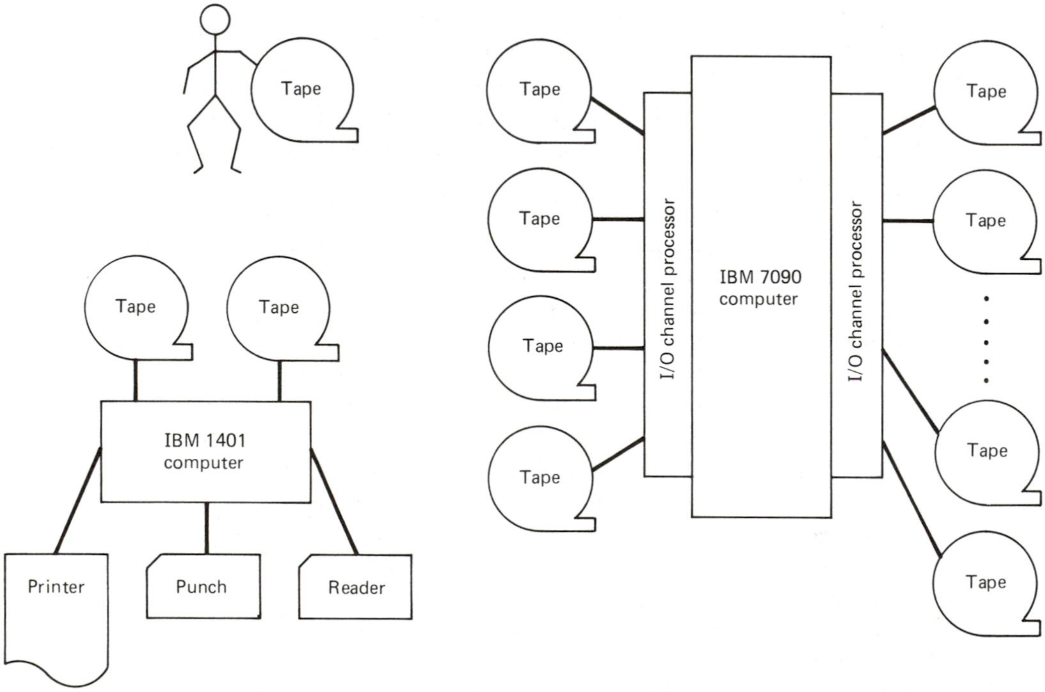

Figure 9.2 Example of "batch processing" circa 1960. An operator would build a "batch" of jobs sequentially on a tape using the card reader of the 1401; dismount, carry, and mount the tape on the 7090 as input; dismount, carry, and mount another output from the preceding batch from the 7090 to the 1401, where it was printed/punched while the current batch was processing and building another output tape.

sentially, the IBM 1401 was a dedicated input/output computer under the control of a fairly simple "executive" program that read cards from the card reader and built an input tape as well as reading an output tape and print/punching it as directed. Although to the user it appeared to be accomplishing two tasks, in reality the resident single program was executing straightforward input/output. The IBM 7090 was under the control of an adequate but fairly straightforward sequentially scheduled uniprogramming executive or operating system. This operating system (the IBM version was called IBSYS, the SHARE version was called SOS) would execute one program from the input tape, producing results on the output tape, then proceed to the next program on the input tape, and so forth. Note that only one program was in memory and executing at any one time—hence the term *uniprogramming*—and that programs were executed strictly sequentially in the order of their occurrence on the input tape. In many ways, the modern microcomputer operating system CP/M, to be discussed on page 318, is equivalent to these early batch uniprogrammed executives.

As we shall consider in some detail momentarily, uniprogramming a comparatively large, very expensive, fairly rare system still resulted in less than optimum performance both from the user standpoint and from the standpoint of the utilization of available resources. For example, the single program most often did not fully occupy memory—thus it was maintained that the memory resource was being wasted; the single program very often had to wait for an input or an output to be completed before proceeding—thus it was maintained that the arithmetic-logic resource was being wasted. Of course, it was possible to maintain that this waste was a necessary penalty while using the computer, but the computer was a scarce, very valuable, and necessary piece of equipment and work was available and waiting. Additionally, at times a very long running job "captured" the machine for hours while literally hordes of users awaited their turn—and they did not wait patiently or quietly. They complained, they "screamed," they got people fired.

Because the tautology that "necessity is the mother of invention" is at least partially valid, the idea of multiprogramming was implemented at a number of universities and by a number of commercial computer vendors. Just who had the idea first will probably never be known; just who had a system implemented and successfully operating is still a matter of interesting argument. Be that as it may, the consequences have been manifold. Now we could "fill" memory with programs and, when one program was waiting for I/O, "give" the ALU to another program. Thus, in one brillant stroke, the problem of wasted memory and wasted time was solved. But was it?

In a very real sense, multiprogramming did solve many of the resource utilization problems while causing other problems. As one example, there was a particularly brillant user (who shall remain unidentified) at one installation (which shall also be unidentified) who immediately rearranged a massive arithmetic-oriented program to do all input at the beginning, calculate for long periods, and only then do all output—thus capturing the computer for hours and effectively "shutting out" and alienating other users. Of course, the solution is simple: If the computer had a time-out clock interrupt, give one person the ALU for a few seconds, and then give it to the next person for a few seconds, and then the next, and so on in a round-robin sort of arrangement. Did this strategy solve the "user wait situation"? Well partially, at least. Note that this time-out (time slicing, really) allowed a priority scheme so that preferential service could be given to certain important (affluent is a more correct term) users. Also note that the complexity of the operating system increased—dramatically increased—in both memory needs and in running time. Some users complained that the operating system used much too much memory and "hogged" up to half the time (or more). At about this time (1963–1964), the minicomputer became available and underwent, over the years, the same software trend of development, job-by-job processing through uniprogramming to multiprogramming. That is, the minicomputer vendors and users did not seem to profit from the previous experience of the maxicomputer area; rather, they had to undergo the same path of learning all over again. Unfortunately, the advent of the microcomputer in the 1970s has shown the same intellectual development trends.

Returning to the multiprogrammed systems, note that the ALU could now be busy almost all the time and that memory is full. But this "perfect" situation in fact did not occur. What we found was that computer memory was too small to hold enough programs to keep the ALU busy during the I/O. The solution: obviously, larger memories; but memories of the required size just did not exist and if they were to be developed and become available in the then current technology, they would have been too expensive. Again, human ingenuity came to the rescue. So there were 3 or 7 or 15 or even 127 programs in memory, each taking its turn with a short time slice of the ALU to execute a few hundred or even several thousand instructions and then relinquish control for a while before getting another time slice. But recall that each of these many programs is executing only a relatively small portion of its total instructions during any one time slice and that only the executing instructions and associated data must be in memory at that time. The rest of each program could be elsewhere—say, on a disk.

Thus the concept of paging, segmentation, and virtual memory was derived for the Atlas machine in Great Britain in 1959 and introduced to America in 1963 with the Burroughs B5000. In this scheme the system divides a program up into "chunks," sometimes called pages (equal-sized chunks) and sometimes called segments (unequal module-sized chunks). Only those pages (or segments, as the case may be) that are currently necessary for program execution are placed in memory at any one time; the rest are kept on disk. Pages/segments are shuffled into and out of memory from disk as needed during program execution. In this manner, memory needs for each program are minimized and more programs can be serviced in these *virtual memory* multiprogrammed operating systems. Note that this process involves a cost—sometimes a large cost—in facilities and time overhead. First, logic must be available to recognize when a new page or segment is needed, which one is needed, and which one can be removed from memory (replaced) to make room for the new one. This logic often involves additional hardware that costs money and usually involves additional operating system modules that occupy memory space. Additionally, the data paths (buses) to and from the necessary additional disks will be kept fairly busy and often may become overloaded. The trite comment that "nothing is really free" is true.

TYPES OF OPERATING SYSTEMS

UNIPROGRAMMING OPERATING SYSTEMS

Uniprogramming operating systems tend to be smaller in size, simpler in design, materially easier to understand, and easier to maintain correctly, as well as cheaper to purchase. Implied is a need for less memory and less disk space. As the previous discussion has indicated, the chief disadvantage is the sequential nature of executing one program to completion before starting the next.

It must be pointed out that a uniprogramming environment is eminently suited for many applications of microcomputers such as I8086/8088 systems. Most personal computers, almost by definition, are used by one person at a time. This one-user environment is naturally and most satisfactorily serviced by a relatively clean and simple uniprogrammed operated system. If there is no need for servicing two (or more) users at once, there is no advantage to having the ability to do so. In some cases, it may be truly economical to purchase and use a second system rather than purchase a second terminal and multiprogram the microcomputer. In other cases the reverse may be true.

Figure 9.3 illustrates the normal and traditional assignment of memory areas when employing a uniprogrammed operating system. Almost invariably, some memory space is not utilized. Although this seems wasteful, it must be remembered that sufficient memory must be available to accommodate the largest program that will be executed. If only one program at a time is required to be executed, this "waste" of memory may be the most satisfactory and economical compromise.

Figure 9.4 illustrates two of the infinitely possible resource utilization situations employing a uniprogrammed operating system. Although it is possible to have DMA input/output time exactly match and mesh (interplay on a wall clock basis), it is almost certain that this perfect match will never occur and that computer resources will be wasted. Again, note that "wasting" resources is of absolutely no importance and should be completely ignored if those resources are not needed at that time for other purposes. As an example in another context, most people own three or four ensembles of clothing, of which only one set is used at a time and during sleep none at all. We do not usually consider hanging a jacket in the closet as wasting that jacket. If you will, an idle resource is wasteful only if some useful purpose exists for it and the resource is not usable—is not currently capturable.

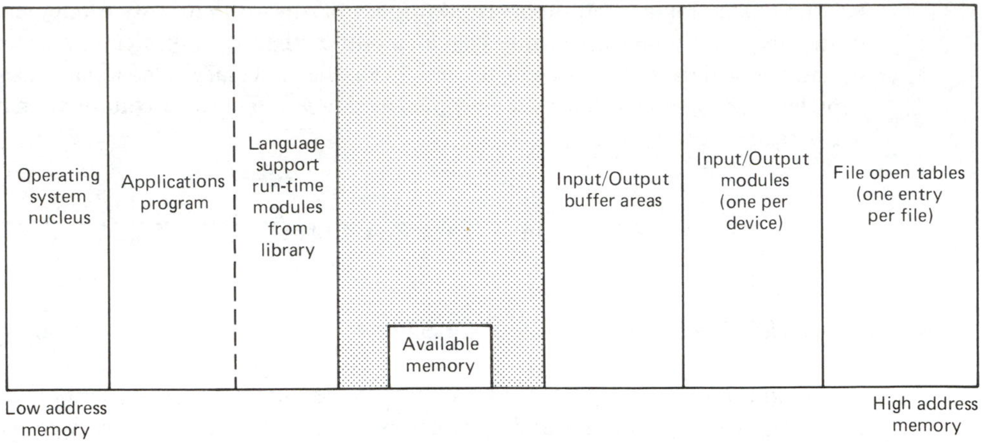

Figure 9.3 When using a uniprogramming operating system, memory is traditionally allocated with the applications program and any unused area in the middle addresses. The operating system resident nucleus and interrupt vector table are placed in low-address memory, while the I/O modules, tables, and buffers are placed in high-address memory.

MULTIPROGRAMMING OPERATING SYSTEMS

Multiprogramming operating systems tend to be larger in size, more complicated in design, often difficult to understand and maintain, as well as more expensive to purchase. A need for more memory and more disk space is implied. The chief advantages are the possibility of more efficient CPU and DMA channel usage, the possibility of priority processing of certain jobs resulting in the possibility of nonsequential job processing, and the possibility of two or more interactive terminal users "thinking" that they have the entire system for their private use.

A multiprogramming environment is practical employing the I8086 microcomputer, particularly if the CPU is augmented by an I8089 IOP and sufficient memory is available. With the Intel Corporation's multitasking operating system, the Bell Laboratory UNIX operating system, or Western Digital's MP/M operating system, such a system should have at least the throughput capacity of many of the minicomputer systems currently available. If the I8086/8089 memory-rich system also had the I8087 floating-point processor and sufficient "hard" Winchester-type disks, it is probable that it would have about one-fifth the production ability of the DEC VAX 11/780 midicomputer. This throughput capacity could be almost assured by supplementing the Intel system with the recently announced I80130 operating system firmware VLSI chip, which provides 35 instructions specifically designed to support the kernel of the Intel real-time multitasking operating system.

Such an augmented I8086/I8089/I8087/I80130 memory-rich Winchester-disk-supported system could be employed to provide up to an eight-terminal system for office automation, medium-size to small business accounting/inventory applications,

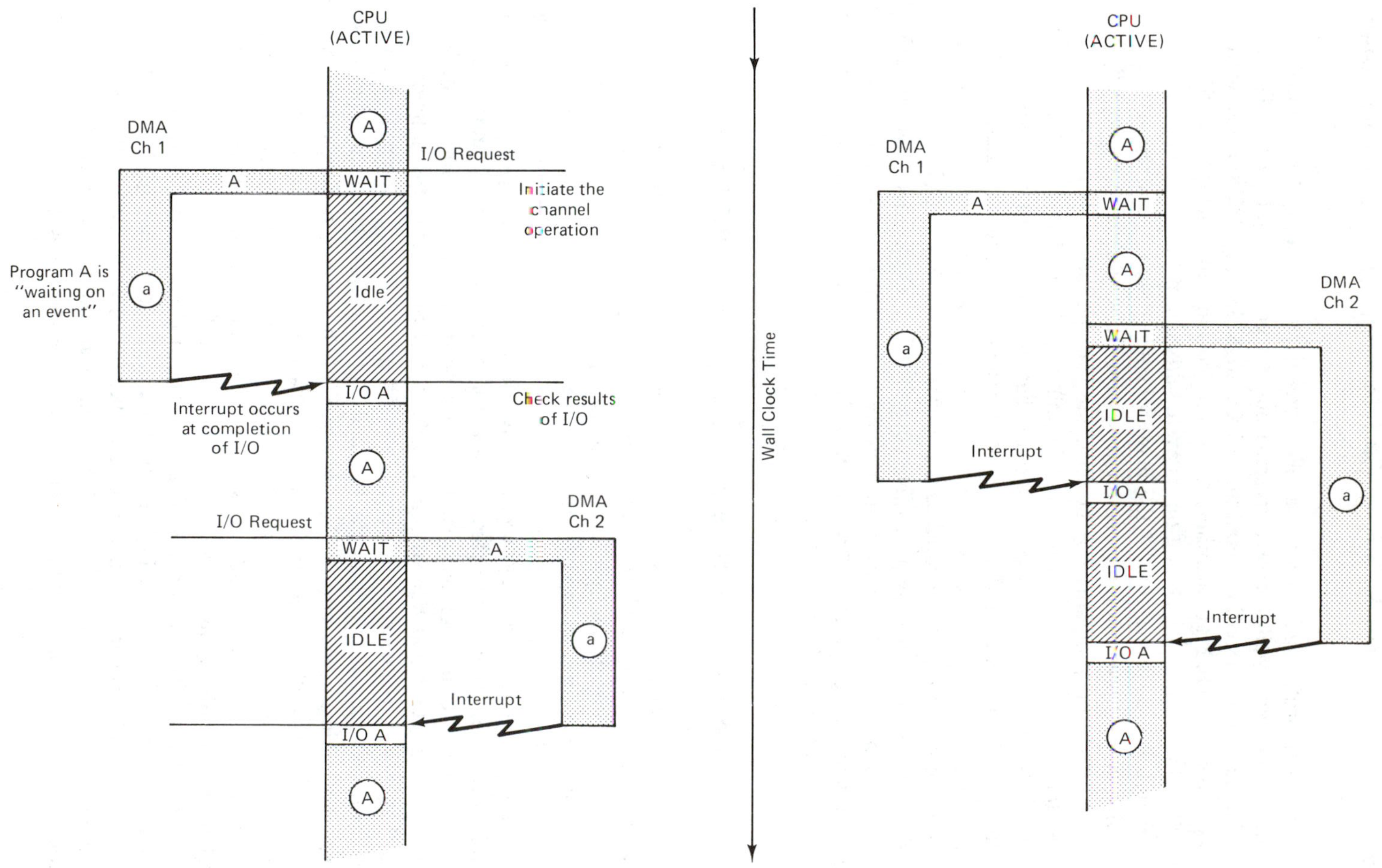

Figure 9.4 System hardware resource utilization under a uniprogramming operating system. (*Left*) The situation when the CPU, DMA channel 1, and DMA channel 2 all must access the same identical memory area for data. (*Right*) The situation when there is some but not complete independence of data area access in memory.

medical-dental professional records applications, instructional systems, small engineering calculations, building security–environment control, and so on. The hardware for such systems could retail for $5000 to $15,000 (1983 prices), with the software (systems and applications) probably costing anywhere from $5000 to $25,000 or much more, depending on its availability and necessity to customize it.

Figure 9.5 illustrates two of the many possible resource utilization situations employing a multiprogramming operating system. It would be most unlikely that the needs of several programs for the CPU and for the DMA channels would ever time-match as perfectly as is indicated in the right-hand diagram of Figure 9.5. Rather, it is very probable (almost certain) that at least one of the resources will constitute a "bottleneck" and that the other resources, and consequently the programs, would have to wait for service. If the critical resource bottleneck is always memory, more memory is indicated as a possible "cure"; if it is CPU cycles, an additional CPU is implicated as a possible cure; if it is I/O channels, another DMA channel is indicated. The performance analysis for bottlenecks of even a small multiprogrammed computer system can be difficult, with the true situation often being counterintuitive and nonobvious.

MANAGING SYSTEM RESOURCES

The one most fundamental and important viewpoint of a computational system views it as a *tool* being used by a human as an aid in problem solving. This conceptual view is so important that it bears repeating in different words: A computer with auxilary memory, an input/output terminal, and software is a device that may be used by a human being as a tool to assist in solving a problem. This philosophy places the person at center stage and relegates the computational system to its proper role—the same role as occupied by an automobile, as a hammer and nails, as a stove, or as any other tool: as a vital aid to a person in accomplishing a desirable task. It is important that human beings never forget that they—the individual person, that is—are the centrally necessary portion of the extended computational system. You—the person sitting at the terminal—are the only reason that the system exists. The ultimate measure of the usefulness of the system is fundamentally the measure of how well (or badly) the system assists you in solving your very specific problems without unnecessary effort or undue travail. The computational systems should serve you—you should not serve the system. (At the same time, a good worker understands the use of, and maintains, his or her tools.)

Let us consider the process of a user approaching a computational system with a problem to solve using Figure 9.6 as a guide in our thinking. First, note that there are several terminals available so that the system is implied to be a multiprogramming system. One way of considering this situation is that more than one person can each be solving a problem simultaneously without really knowing or caring

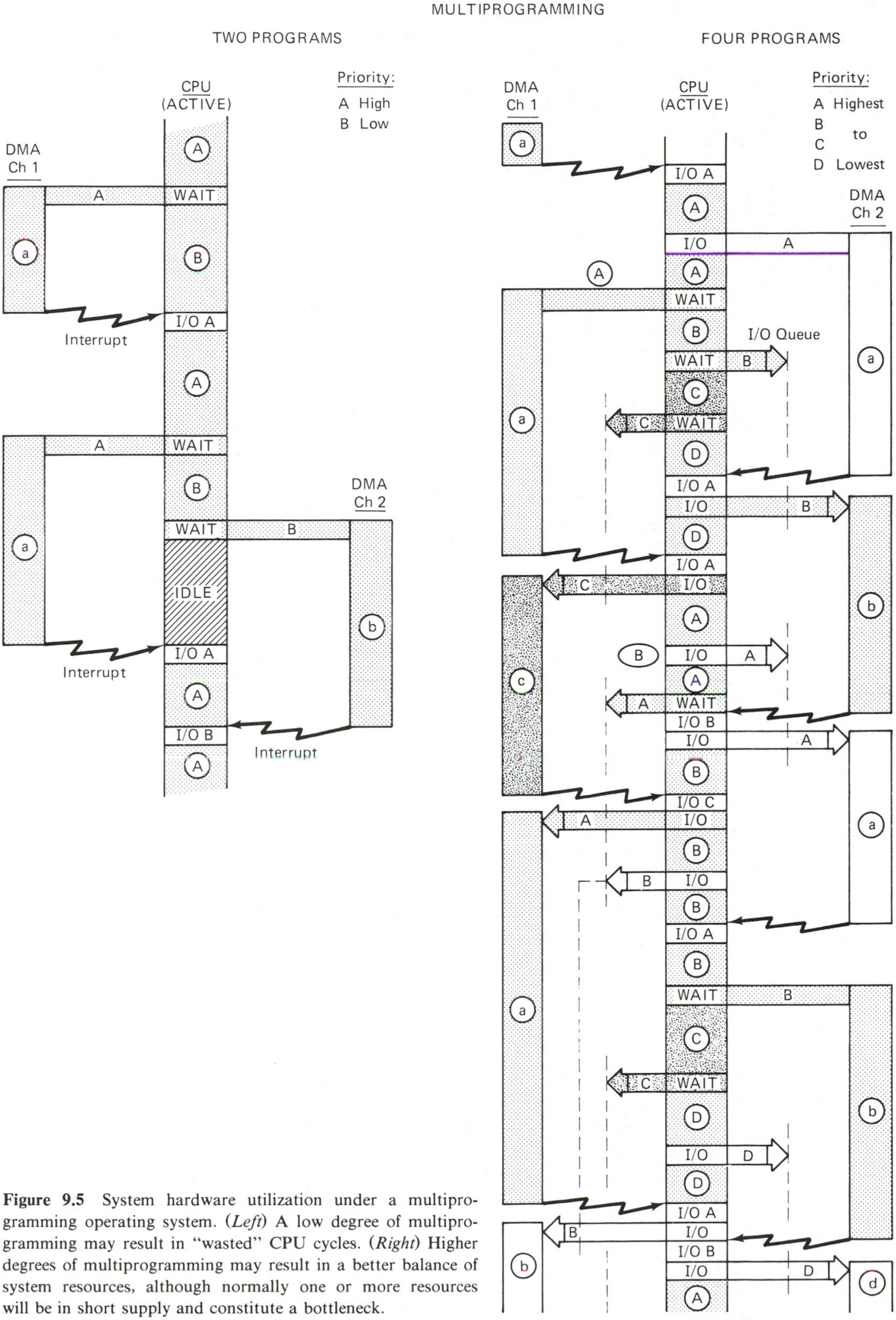

Figure 9.5 System hardware utilization under a multiprogramming operating system. (*Left*) A low degree of multiprogramming may result in "wasted" CPU cycles. (*Right*) Higher degrees of multiprogramming may result in a better balance of system resources, although normally one or more resources will be in short supply and constitute a bottleneck.

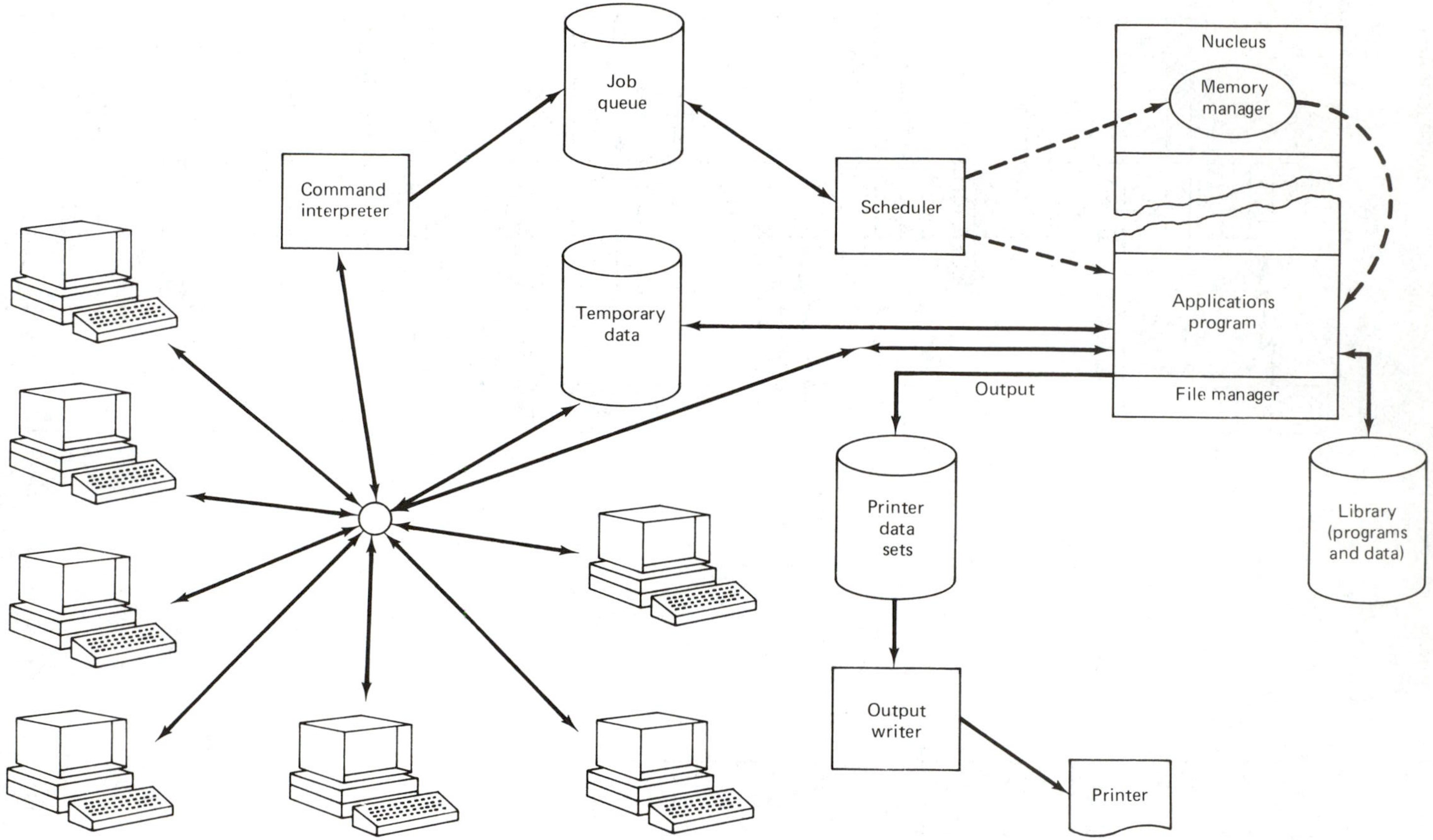

Figure 9.6 Job flow in a relatively simple computationed system involves several portions (modules) of the operating system. The command interpreter decodes the imperatives (orders), while the scheduler queues tasks for the system. Also illustrated are the memory manager, the file manager, and the SPOOLing (simultaneous processing-output on line) output writer.

about the other people and their problems. Alternatively, if you wish, you can mentally destroy or unhook all the terminals but one (your own personal private terminal) and transform the system of Figure 9.6 into a smaller, cheaper uniprogrammed system. For our purposes, either viewpoint is satisfactory at the present level of detail.

In our scheme, the computer user would key-in his or her identification and desire to use a particular software package. The imperatives would be recognized, interpreted, and passed to the appropriate module of the operating system by the command interpreter module. In most systems, the scheduler will reserve devices, memory, files, and other resources for each task and then request the appropriate module to initiate services as needed. The main task of the memory manager is to allocate and reclaim main (primary) memory as necessary to load and execute the requested work. Similarly, the main task of the processor manager is to allocate and assign the necessary processor (CPU–I/O) to the executing work as necessary as well as to reclaim them for other work as needed. As would be expected, the management of memory and processor is somewhat simple in a uniprogrammed system, more complicated in multiprogrammed system, and very involved in a time-sharing virtual memory system with "rich" abilities. Additionally, the management of program-data libraries, files, and devices will be involved. The interrelationships of various operating system models is roughly sketched in Figure 9.7. These modules are processes when loaded into memory and executing.

MEMORY MANAGEMENT

The memory management modules of an operating system are concerned with the management of main (primary) memory. Four functions are important:

1. Keeping track of the current status of each location of primary memory. A location is either allocated to a specific use or "free" and available for allocation. Allocation is usually made in blocks.
2. Deciding which memory requestee will be assigned how much memory. In multiprogramming systems, this decision process may necessitate conflict resolution and attention to priority. An allocation policy is thus implemented.
3. Deciding exactly which group of locations will be assigned to which requestee. In virtual memory systems, this decision process may necessitate reclaiming a page/segment from another requestee.
4. Deciding when to deallocate and reclaim which memory block.

In all cases, the bookkeeping implied above must be kept current. The policies implemented by the memory management modules may reflect a desire to keep the

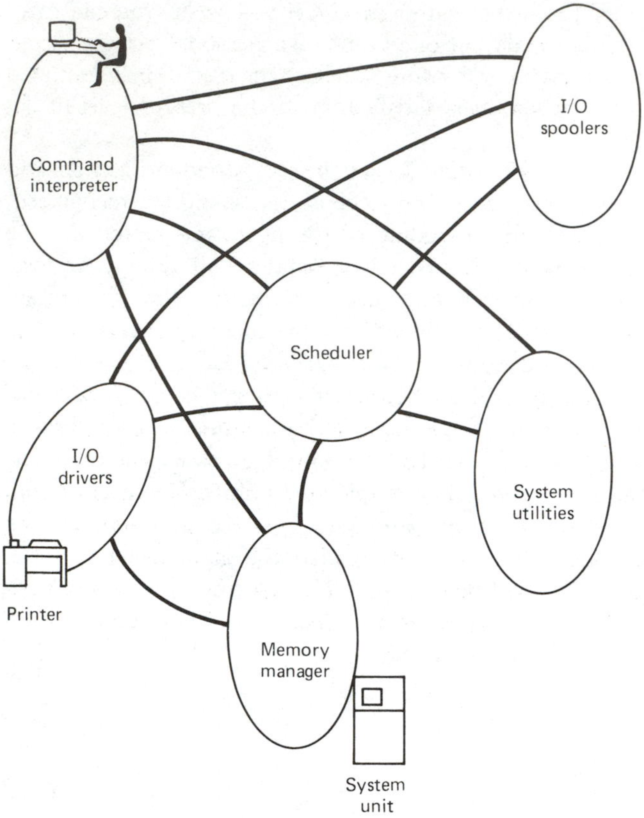

Figure 9.7 An operating system can profitably be considered as a set of parallel processes which interact in well-defined ways but are basically independent. Many of these processes are cyclic and never terminate; that is, they may be active awake or active asleep but cannot be inactive.

modules small and simple, by the need to increase system flexibility, by the desire to maximize system efficiency, or (usually) by some combination of these and other factors.

PROCESSOR MANAGEMENT

The processor management modules of an operating system are concerned with the assignment of processors to processes. It is usual to identify the following three divisions in processor management:

1. Job scheduling, which creates the processes and which decides, in multiprogrammed systems, which of the ready processes will receive the processor or, in a multiprocessor, which ready process will be assigned which processor.
2. Processor scheduling, which, in multiprogramming/multiprocessing, decides which process gets which processor now and for how long. Often, this decision involves a priority policy.
3. Traffic control or the recording of the status of each process and processor.

In this viewpoint the computer user considers his or her job as a collection of tasks which he or she wishes the system to perform. The operating system creates processes to accomplish the tasks. Job scheduling is concerned with the management of jobs and thus is a macro scheduler; choosing which jobs to run when. Processor scheduling is concerned with the management of processes and thus is a micro scheduler, assigning processors to the processes of already scheduled jobs. In a uniprogram operating system, job scheduling is usually very simple (often sequential) and processor scheduling directly follows as a simple sequential expansion of the job—compile, link, load, and execute.

DEVICE MANAGEMENT

The device management modules of an operating system are concerned with the management of input/out devices such as terminals, printers, disks, and so on, as well as the supporting logic, such as control units and DMA channel controllers. Although many designs choose to include the management of files with the management of the repository devices, we choose to separate the two in our present discussion. It is usual to identify four divisions in device management that parallel those treated in memory management (in point of fact, memory is often treated as a device by hardware and sometimes by software):

1. Keeping track of the current status of all I/O devices and their control units. In general, a device can be allocated to a specific use or be "free" for allocation.
2. Deciding which device requestee will be assigned the device, when the assignment will take place, and for how long. Devices can be *dedicated* to a single process while that process is active, *shared* by two or more processes, or be a *virtual device* whereby one physical device is simulated using another physical device (usually a disk).
3. Allocating or physically assigning a device/control unit/DMA channel to a process.
4. Deallocating or reclaiming a device/control unit/DMA channel from a process.

A satisfactorily mnemonic name for the module that keeps track of the allocation states of I/O devices could be "I/O traffic controller." Recall that the modules that are associated with the operation of the device itself are called "I/O device handlers."

INFORMATION MANAGEMENT

The information management modules of an operating system are concerned with the storage and retrieval of information within the computational system. By common tradition, information is held as a file, that is, a named collection of records.

The contents of each file can be either data or program (and a program is data to another program, such as a compiler or loader). Thus it is common to speak of program libraries, of data collections, and of directories or indexes. Note that the IBM term "data set" is completely synonymous with our use of the term "file." Again, in small uniprogrammed systems, device management and information management are often enclosed into one common set of modules. Such simplification in design is often justified because information must be stored on devices. It follows that the same four somewhat parallel functional decisions are involved in information management as were involved in device management:

1. Keep track of all the information (all the files) in the system via various tables, such as a file directory that contains the name, location, and accessing rights of each and every file. Note that every user who can write, and thus change, the file directory can allow himself or herself the power to read, change, and/or destroy any and all files in the system, including the modules of the operating system itself.
2. Deciding which file access requestee process (and thus which user) will be allowed to store/retrieve information in what form and location on/from which devices. The policy governing these decisions should reflect efficient disk space utilization, efficient access time (minimal head movement and interdisk interference), file protection, information security, and flexibility of use.
3. The allocation modules must locate the desired information and allow access within the appropriate access rules.
4. When the information is no longer needed by the process, the file must be deallocated. Any temporary table entries and pointers must be destroyed. If the file was changed (updated), the original may, or, may not, exist and may or may not be preserved as the backup version (the father file).

Note that we are not considering a data base management system (DBMS) at this time.

CP/M-86: A CONTROL PROGRAM FOR MICROCOMPUTERS

CP/M is a commonly available disk-based operating system for microcomputers commercially produced and marketed by Digital Research, P.O. Box 579, Pacific Grove, California 93950. The terms CP/M, CP/M-86, Digital Research, the internal source language statements, and the documentation are protected under the applicable copyright laws with all rights reserved to Digital Research. CP/M was developed for the I8080 by Gary Kildall, working as a software consultant for the Intel Corporation. In 1981 it was reported that there were more than 250,000 CP/M systems for over 350 different microcomputer models encompassing over 3000 different hardware configurations. At the present time, CP/M is a family of portable uniprogramming operating systems, programming languages, and applications programs that are easy to use with relatively complete and clear documentation.

In 1972, the predecessor of Digital Research (Microcomputer Applications Associates), as a consultant to Intel Corporation, defined and implemented PL/M as a higher-level systems programming language intended to replace assembly language as the implementation tool for systems on the Intel 8-bit microprocessors. PL/M (Programming Language for Microcomputers) is a refinement of the XPL compiler-writing language that borrows syntax and semantics from both ALGOL and PL/I. Unfortunately, a PL/M compiler is not generally available to the microcomputer user community because of copyright, licensing, and other legal considerations. The CP/M program editor known as ED traces its beginnings to the first substantial PL/M program—a paper-tape-based editor for the I8008.

A *systems programming language* is a relatively machine-dependent high-level language used to implement system software, such as operating systems, text editors, compilers, and so on. Thus PL/M "matches" the architectures of the Intel 8-bit and 16-bit microcomputers as well as closely allied machines. All of the facilities of the computer are accessible and no nontrivial extensions exist beyond the basic capabilities of the machines. Additionally, PL/M and other systems languages require minimal "run-time support" (software routines to accomplish a task not available in the actual computer design) since application facilities such as extensive I/O are not a portion of the language. It is considered essential that the compiler for a systems language translate the source statements into efficient machine language code from both a space-used and an execution-time standpoint. As a systems programming language, PL/M is easier to understand and use, much more concise, and results in modules that are more amenable to maintenance and enhancement. All in all, PL/M is a major improvement over assembly language for implementing operating systems.

MAA also proposed an operating system for the 8-bit I8080 microcomputer for the Intel Corporation, but this proposal was rejected. CP/M was, nevertheless, completed by the predecessor of Digital Research in 1974 as a single-user file system. The design largely eliminated data loss and employed a directory to control storage allocation, resulting in a very simple and reliable file system that gave excellent access to the relatively slow floppy disks. Because CP/M was used by a myriad of non-computer-expert users, it was important that the system allow changing disks without file loss or data record mixup.

CP/M has undergone at least two major redesign-reimplementation efforts. The first of these, in the mid-1970s, decomposed CP/M into two parts: the disk operating system itself, coded in PL/M that remains invariant from computer model to model, and a small variant assembly language interface portion that "marries" the system to the particular microcomputer model. This allowed system implementers and end users to adapt their own physical I/O drivers to the standard CP/M. The second major redesign took place in 1979 as a result of the proliferation of different recording densities and sizes of floppy disks as well as Winchester hard disks for microcomputers. In response to these technological advances, CP/M was redesigned as a table-driven system by removing all disk-type dependent parameters from the PL/M-coded invariant disk operating system to tables in the assembly language-coded variant I/O portion. Thus CP/M became a very general uniprogramming multifunction operating system whose exact configuration is defined by the system implementer through tables and I/O subroutines at generation time.

It must be noted that Digital Research has extended the functionality of their software product to encompass multiterminal multiprogramming time sharing in the product they term MP/M (Multiprogramming Monitor for Microcomputers). Additionally, in 1980, the firm introduced CP/NET to manage a network of nonhomogeneous microcomputers. CP/NET connects microcomputers of any brand operating under CP/M to other microcomputers under MP/M via a well-defined but arbitrary communications protocol (message syntax).

INTERNALS

The overall design as well as the user interface of CP/M-86 is almost identical to CP/M for the 8-bit I8080, I8085, and Z-80-based systems. CP/M-86 consists of three systems modules:

1. The *console command processor* (CCP) is the human–system interface that receives, parses, interprets, and executes commands, as well as performing any other communication with the user that is necessary.
2. The *basic disk operating system* (BDOS) module is the invariant portion that performs system services, such as managing files and directories.
3. The *basic input/output system* (BIOS) module provides the logical-to-physical mapping of files and directories and contains the device drivers for those peripherals present in the specific user configuration. Thus the BIOS module is variant, being different for each system.

An important design goal of Digital Research was to isolate all code to a single module that would change as devices were added or removed from a user configuration. Therefore, the console command processor module and the basic disk operating system module are standard across all copies of CP/M-86, whereas the basic input/output system is tailored to each individual user's configuration. This tailoring is accomplished via the use of a BIOS-created jump vector table that must reside in the code segment (CS). The BDOS module searches this jump table and then branches to the BIOS entry points of the appropriate routine also in the code segment (CS). Note that the CCP module and the BDOS module are completely relocatable and may reside at any address of any of the segments (CS, DS, ES, or SS) other than those memory locations occupied by the BIOS module in CS or in physical low memory addresses (the so-called *base memory page*). Thus CP/M-86 loads user programs starting at location 100 hexadecimal and places the default buffers and file control blocks in low-address memory identical with the 8-bit CP/M system. Figure 9.8 may be helpful.

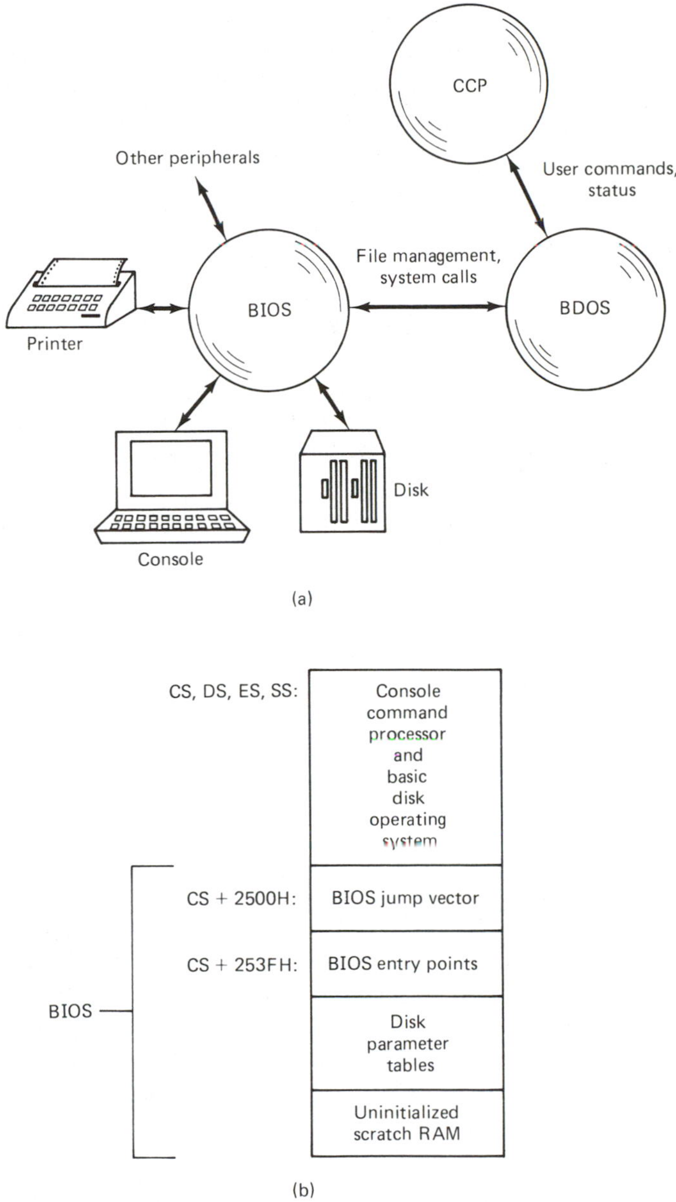

Figure 9.8 Memory allocation and module relationships for CP/M 86. Note that the console command processor (CCP) and the basic disk operating system (BDOS) can be located anywhere in memory in any of the four segments. The basic input/output system (BIOS) must start at 2500h in the code segment (CS).

Because I8086/8088 programs are extremely easy to relocate in physical memory by altering the segment start address in the CS register, dependence on absolute addresses is almost unnecessary within CP/M-86. To accomplish a CALL for CP/M-86 service, an application program must first place the required parameter (arguments) in the appropriate registers and then invoke interrupt number 224 using the instruction

```
INT 224
```

The utilities supplied by Digital Research with CP/M-86 include:

PIP: Peripheral Interchange Program, which allows file transfer between devices and disk units, including reformatting and file concatenation/extraction. Disk-to-disk, keyboard-to-disk, disk-to-printer, and so on, operations are provided.

ED: A text editor that allows creation and modification of ASCII files using such commands as string substitutions, search, insert, delete, block move, and so on.

ASM 86: A macro assembler using standard Intel Corporation syntax for operation codes and addressing.

DDT 86: Dynamic Debugging Tool, allows interactive program test under single-instruction trace with register and status display. Users are permitted to display (and patch) memory in Intel assembler mnemonic syntax.

SUBMIT: Allows the user to form new commands to CP/M-86 by grouping together prototype commands with parameters in a sort of "command procedure."

STAT: Alters and displays I/O device and file status such as free space, online diskette status, physical-to-logical device mappings, and so on.

The standard CP/M-86 BIOS includes the following standard primitive device command routines:

Console status

Console in/console out

List out

Select drive/set track/set sector

Read sector/write sector

The CP/M-86 program interface is unchanged from that of CP/M in that system services retain the same function numbers. A sample of these function numbers is shown in Figure 9.9.

Function number	Function description	Entry parameters	Returned value
1	Read a character from the console.	None	ASCII character
2	Write a character to the console.	ASCII character	None
3	Read a character from the reader device.	None	ASCII character
4	Write a character to the punch device.	ASCII character	None
5	Write a character to the list device (usually a printer).	ASCII character	None
7	Get I/O status.[a]	None	I/O status byte
8	Set I/O status.[a]	I/O status byte	None
9	Output print buffer to console.	Address of a print buffer	None
10	Input a character string from the console.	Address of a read buffer	The read buffer is filled to its maximum length or until a <CR> is typed.
11	Interrogate console for a character ready.	None	01 if a character is ready.
12	Lift head.	None	None—head is lifted from currently logged disk.
13	Initialize CP/M disk access.	None	None—disk drive A is "logged in" for access. The DMA address is set to 0080H.
14	Select and log in disk.	Value corresponding to the desired disk: A = 0, B = 1, etc.	None—specified disk is selected for subsequent file operations.
15	Open file.	Address of FCB for the file to be opened	Byte address of the FCB in the disk-directory, or 225H if file is not found—the disk map (DM) bytes in the FCB are filled by CP/M.

Figure 9.9 Available functions of the CP/M 86 operating system.

Function number	Function description	Entry parameters	Returned value
16	Close file.	Address of FCB for the file to be closed	Byte address of the FCB in the disk directory, or 255 if not found—the disk map of the FCB is written to the directory, replacing any existing data for that file.
17	Search for file.	Address of FCB containing name and type of file to search for; "?" matches any character	Byte address of first FCB in directory that matches the name and type in the input FCB. If no match, 225H is returned.
18	Search for next occurrence.	Address of FCB as in 17, but called after 17 before any other disk access	Byte address of next match. 225H if no additional match.
19	Delete file.	Address of FCB of file to be deleted	None—FCB in directory is marked as deleted. (E5H is placed in ET field.)
20	Read record.	Address of FCB containing a disk map; normally as a result of opening the file (15) and setting NR to the record to be read	0 = successful read 1 = read past logical end of file (^Z) 2 = reading unwritten data Data read is placed in memory at the DMA address (function 26).
21	Write record.	Same as read, but NR is set to the record to be written	0 = successful write 1 = error in extending file 2 = error of disk data 255H = no more directory space—data written is taken from memory starting at the DMA address.
22	Create file.	Address of FCB of new file, all data set to 0 except name and type	Byte address of directory entry of new file or 255H if directory is full.

Figure 9.9 (*continued*)

Function number	Function description	Entry parameters	Returned value
23	Rename file.	Address of FCB with old file name and type in first 16 bytes and the new file name in the next 16 bytes	Directory address of old file, or 255H if not found. The file name and type are changed to that specified.
24	Interrogate disk log-in.	None	Byte with 1 bit set for each disk logged in. LSB = disk A, etc.
25	Interrogate drive number.	None	Number of disk to be used for next access.
26	Set DMA address.	Address of 128-byte buffer	None—subsequent reads and writes take data to/from memory beginning at this address.
27	Interrogate allocation.	None	Address of the current disk-allocation data. (Used by STAT—not well documented.)

Note: NTRY is the CP/M entry point.

[a] If implemented.

Figure 9.9 *(continued)*

In January 1983, the Intel Corporation announced the availability of the I80150. This single chip combines the CP/M-86 operating system with essential hardware facilities as an OS processor extension to the I8086/8088 family.

UNIX

UNIX is a commonly available disk-based operating system commercially marketed under various acronyms by several firms under licensing agreements with Bell Laboratories, Murray Hill, New Jersey 07974. The term UNIX is a protected trademark of Bell Laboratories; additionally, the internal source language statements, the documentation, and the names of the different versions are all protected by the applicable copyright laws with all rights reserved to the developing and/or marketing firm. UNIX was developed starting in 1969 by Ken Thompson and Dennis Ritchie as an aid for conducting research relative to computer software. In 1981, it was reported that there were more than 2000 UNIX installations supported by over 100 commercial suppliers employing most of the important 32-bit and 16-bit available midicomputers, such as the DEC VAX and minicomputers such as the PDP 11, as well as microcomputers such as I8086, the Z8000, and the MSC 68000. At the present time, UNIX is a family of compatible multiprogramming operating systems, programming languages, programming-aid packages, and applications programs that are extremely popular in universities, research installations, and professional programming houses. Although the documentation and system protection could be improved, the system does provide a superior environment for program development and package transport to other systems. Just as CP/M promises to become, or is, the "standard" uniprogramming operating system for microcomputers; UNIX promises to become the "standard" multiprogramming time-sharing system for the more capable microcomputer and minicomputer systems.

In 1969, the story goes, Ken Thompson, who was employed to accomplish various programming research projects by Bell Labs with somewhat inadequate resources, found an abandoned DEC PDP 7 with no software and decided to produce a set of programs for it that would aid him in his programming. In effect, he envisaged a group of programming tools. Over time, with the collaboration of another software researcher, Dennis Ritchie, these programs evolved into a full operating system of a type that was extremely useful in software research and development. Employing hindsight, this development and result seem natural. After all, they were developing a tool to help themselves in their own research and development and the tool they developed should end up being fairly good for that task. On the other hand, remember that there were several dozen (or hundreds of) other people around the United States, Great Britain, and the world with almost the same needs and oportunities. Only Ken Thompson and Dennis Ritchie actually followed through on the task of solving their own problem, and in the process created a useful tool for thousands of others. To the Ken Thompsons and Dennis Ritchies of our field—credit and accolades. Would that there were more of this ilk.

In February 1971, the transfer of UNIX to the DEC PDP 11 was complete and by some time in 1972 it was recoded in a newly designed high-level system programming language known as C which was also the product of Dennis Ritchie. One long-time benefit of this transfer to C as the implementation language is that UNIX can be implemented with minimal effort on any computer with a C compiler. Conversely, the popularity of UNIX has resulted in a proliferation of efforts to produce C compilers for a myriad of computers, including the I8086-8088. Whether the chicken or the egg came first is never clear, although I favor the proposition that the quality of UNIX forced the acceptance and implementation of C. This is not to say that the language C is deficient as a system language, as that would be wrong. C is very satisfactory and compares favorably with the other system languages, such as PL/M, BLISS, BCPL, PL/I, ALGOL, Concurrent Pascal, and so on, and is vastly superior to employing assembly language.

Word of the quality of UNIX spread extremely rapidly through Bell Labs and its parent company, Western Electric, as well as to research universities. In 1973, Western Electric agreed to distribute UNIX to nonprofit organizations, with the result that a user's group was formed (currently named USENIX). Version 5 of

UNIX, distributed in 1973 to many universities, was replaced in 1975 by Version 6—still in use by many installations. In January 1979, Version 7 was distributed, incorporating several hundred person-years of effort and extensive feedback from many user installations.

Because the design of UNIX was, and is, simple to understand and extremely easy to change, there are probably many different versions of UNIX currently in existence as a result of each installation tailoring UNIX to their specific needs. Additionally, several "UNIX-like" products are currently being marketed that contain some major incompatibilities and, unfortunately, are not really UNIX (*caveat emptor*). Because UNIX was created in a few person-years by two people who were also the major users of the system, it has a coherent and consistent design that could be termed "polished."

DESIGN GOALS

At least in retrospect, it seems that the designers of UNIX (Thompson and Ritchie) had three goals in mind:

1. To support only very basic levels of functions while allowing user applications programs to furnish sophistication
2. To have a single general service method serve a number of related purposes
3. To accomplish a complicated task by combining several small tasks

On the other hand, most computer types have at least been exposed to the common complaint that UNIX is not a casual user-friendly system in that its human interface is deficient. Even experienced computer users have raised serious questions concerning the nonmeaningfulness and inconsistency of the names and syntax of commands, languages, and functions. Happily, the creation of private alias names is extremely easy, but this feature has contributed to the proliferation of different private versions of UNIX and must result in difficulties in transferring programs from system to system. Additionally, UNIX has been termed a recluse that is hidden from the user and is silent in operation, with so little feedback that it is difficult to tell what the system is currently doing. Again, the design of UNIX allows a user to construct private functions that provide this feedback, but this very feature has contributed to the proliferation of very unique versions of UNIX.

INTERNALS

The UNIX design incorporates few, if any, new concepts but is a superior blend of the better features of previous systems. Numerous features were borrowed from the MULTICS and the AOS operating systems, and the system implementation language C is modeled after BCPL. Thompson and Ritchie deserve great credit for the coherence and simplicity with which these features were blended in an unusually elegant design. UNIX supports a multiuser, multitasking environment in which each user has access to the full resources of the computer on a time-sharing basis. Scheduling and swapping algorithms are implemented that allow the processor and memory to service more tasks effectively than is usually practical, while protecting each user from inadvertent or purposeful intrusion by other users. Nevertheless, it must be stressed that the UNIX is not user proof in that deliberate knowledgeable attempts to circumvent the protection schemes have been successful. This last statement is almost a general rule for all operating systems.

At this point it is appropriate to recall that a computer is an information-manipulating machine and that a named collection of information is called a file. Thus it is natural to note that a computer uses files as input and produces files as output and may, during this process, create and consume one or more intermediate files. UNIX employs this concept by generalizing the concept of a file to include all possible information sources, such as a keyboard, a port to a network, a buffer, a disk, and so on, and all possible information destinations, such as a CRT, a printer, a network port, a memory buffer, a disk, and so on. In the UNIX system, programs communicate with their environment through read and write commands to a set of open files. A program can open any file (an existing named collection of information or its generalization as an I/O device) for which it has the appropriate access permission. Each program starts with three already opened files: standard input, standard output, and error output—all connected with the user's terminal. These default device assigned standard open files may be fairly easily reassigned to different devices when desirable.

Each and every operating system must provide facilities for running programs and some sort of a file system for managing information. The basic structure of the UNIX file system is fairly conventional—a rooted tree in which each nonterminal (interior) mode is a directory and each terminal (leaf) node is either a file or a directory as shown in Figure 9.10. Additionally, a directory is simply a file and a file is just a linear sequence of bytes and, as far as the file system is concerned, has no internal structure. Thus a user "sees" no disk tracks or cylinders; there are no physical or logical records; there are no fixed or variable records and no blocking; there are no sequential, indexed sequential, or random access files; and there is no user-controlled buffering. The file system does all of the work connected with the idiosyncracies of each device for the applications program and all files look alike. This allows any file produced by a human being or by a program to be input to any other program. This last statement has extremely important and far-reaching implications. The standard byte-stream file structure allows the UNIX user to specify a file as input to a sequence of programs with intermediate results being passed to the next program without user worry regarding file structure or record layout. In the parlance of UNIX, these intermediate files are termed "pipes" and allow concurrent processing of the procedures in the sequence of programs if the hardware is available and the logic allows it. Figure 9.11 employs the class registration process of a school or college to illustrate this facility.

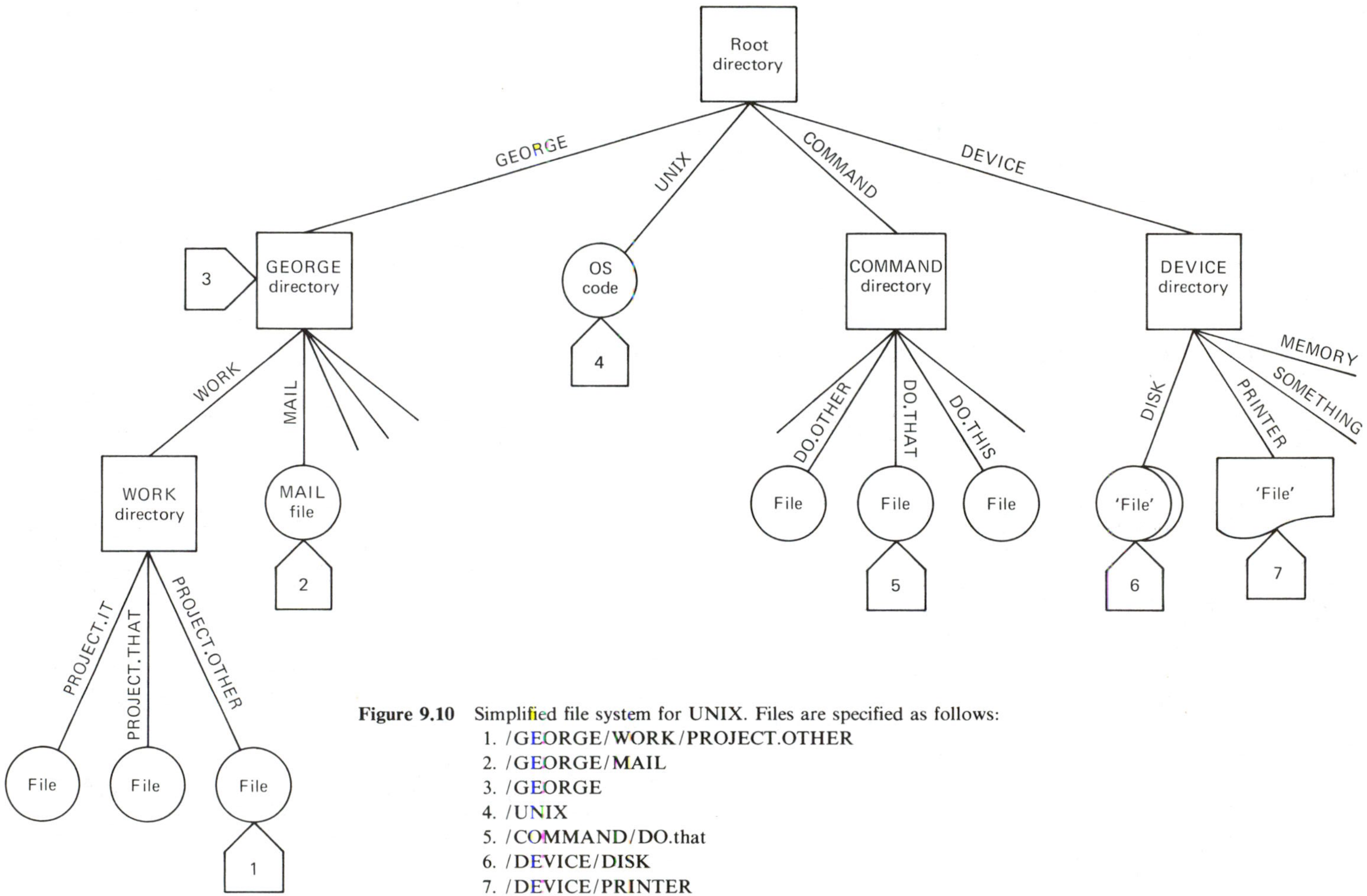

Figure 9.10 Simplified file system for UNIX. Files are specified as follows:

1. /GEORGE/WORK/PROJECT.OTHER
2. /GEORGE/MAIL
3. /GEORGE
4. /UNIX
5. /COMMAND/DO.that
6. /DEVICE/DISK
7. /DEVICE/PRINTER

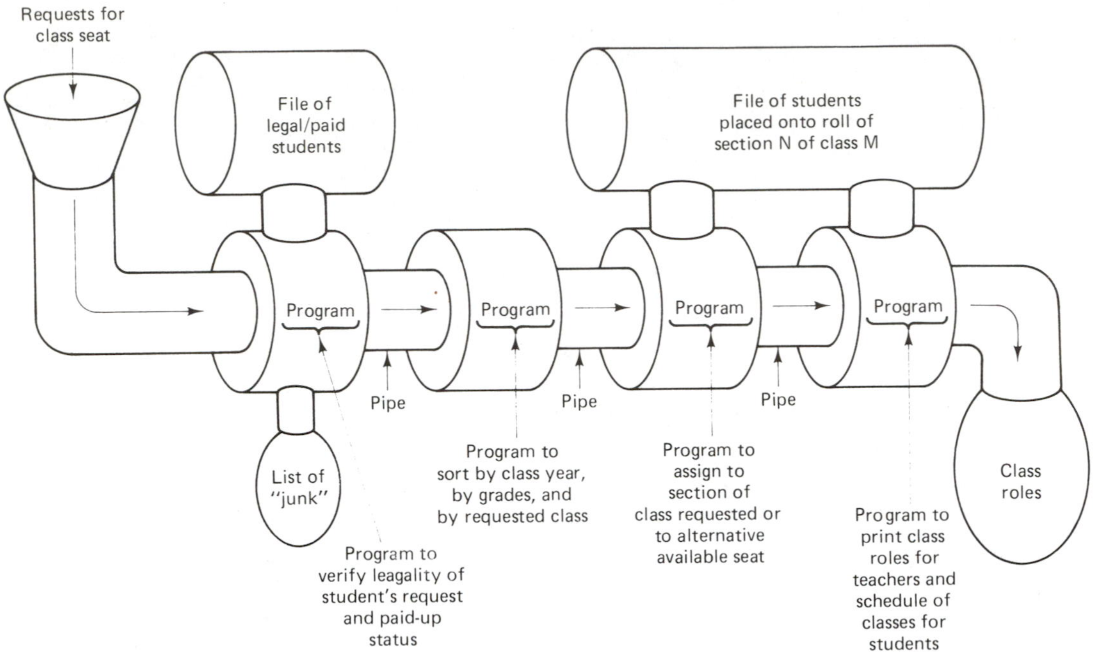

Figure 9.11 UNIX concept of temporary files, or *pipes*, communicating information from one program, or *filter*, to the next program.

This view of a file (an "object" in UNIX terminology) as a pure byte stream without internal structure and which is generalized to include all I/O devices implies that the file itself includes only data with no specified records, end-of-file, or other information. This amorphous structural characteristic means that any file–I/O device has the "correct format" to be the input or output of any process (program) and thus completely circumvents the concepts of direct-access or indexed sequential access modules. Although this characteristic vastly simplifies the passing of files from process to process and thus allows the pipe concept as a practical implementation, it must be emphasized that it also means that files contain no self-identifying information. This results in data being presented to the user on a terminal or printer with no identifying or header information. This is one aspect of the common charge of UNIX being non-user-friendly. On the other hand, it is this very characteristic of a file not containing "header" information that allows the "pipe" concept of interprocess file movement. Additionally, the user process must accomplish all internal file structure manipulations and simulate indexed sequential or direct-access characteristics and record/block structure on a sequential stream of bytes. Again, this is another aspect of the nonfriendly change against UNIX. On the other hand, it allows the "piping" of objects between processes (programs).

Why are nonstructured, information-only, byte-stream objects that allow interprocess pipe communication and make files and I/O devices identical of such importance? After all, anyone who has ever used a computer knows that it is possible to input data from a device, output data to a device, and to create a file that is usable by another program. But remember how you had to describe the record size, the blocking size, the internal structure, the end of file, and so on. Remember how this description was accomplished in a "command language"—a job control language. Recall how the data description portions of JCL were almost impossible to write correctly and how many data/device definition-related errors crept into your programs. UNIX bypasses all of these difficulties through its concept of an object. In effect, by doing less for you, it simplifies and unifies (see Figure 9.12). For the

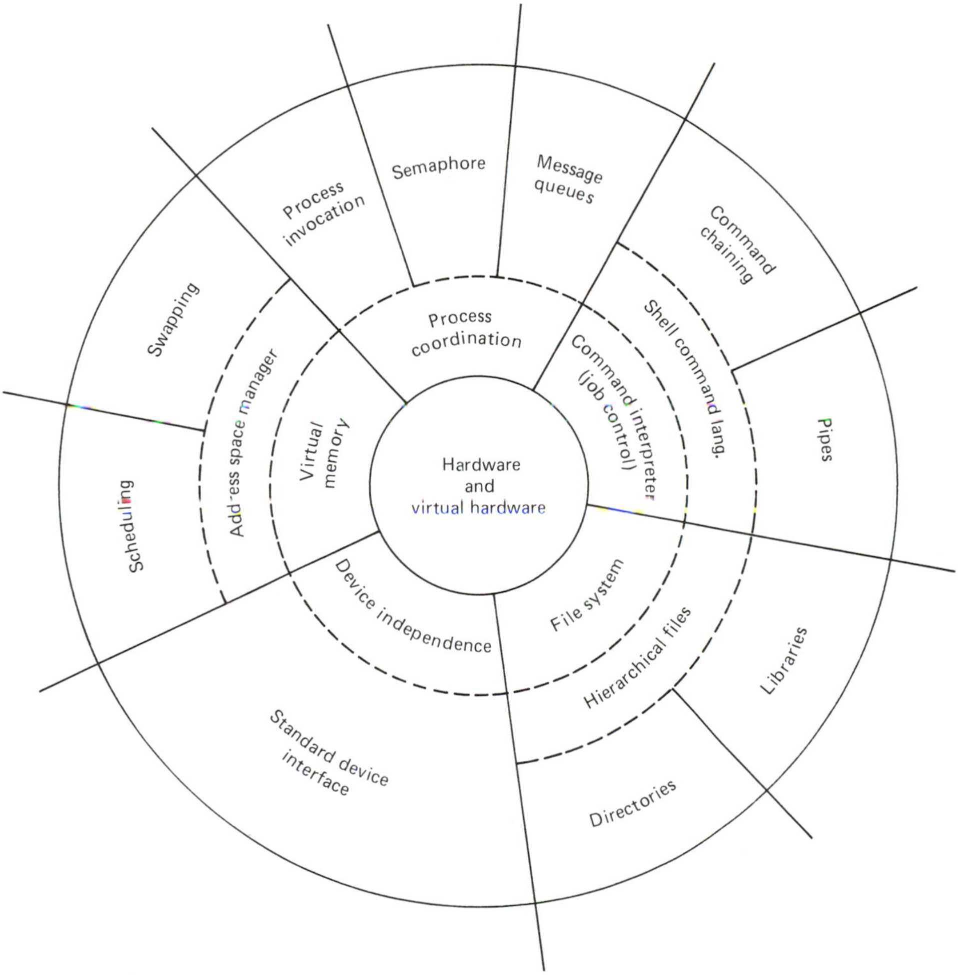

Figure 9.12 The UNIX operating system can be viewed as a software enhancement or extension of the hardware. In this viewpoint, an operating system implements a virtual computing machine as a high-level problem-solving (programming) environment by controlling and allocating resources among competing tasks.

sophisticated user, UNIX is extremely nice; for the novice, UNIX may not provide enough help during execution and thus be somewhat frustrating.

COMMAND LANGUAGE

It is imperative to realize fully that the basic philosophy of UNIX maintains that special-purpose functions can and should be allowed by the clever combined use of a relatively small set of system primative functions. Agreement or disagreement with this philosophy is relatively unimportant, as each user or each installation can easily create (and store as an object) any new complicated or desirable function as a "command procedure" combination of other commands.

Files (*objects*) contain whatever information and only the information that the user deliberately places in it. No internal structuring is expected by UNIX itself, although certain programs (application or system) may expect certain structures. Text files may contain new-line characters and the output of the assembler or a compiler conforms to the expected input format of the linking loader. Thus any structure within a file is necessitated by the receiving program and is not needed or seen by UNIX. UNIX only sees a sequential series of characters—a byte stream.

Directory files (objects) are ordinary files that provide the mapping (the path) between the file name and the file itself. Files are accessed via a path name such as

```
/GEORGE/WORK/PROJECT.OTHER
```

as illustrated in Figure 9.10. All information to be manipulated by the computer executing under the control of UNIX exists in a file. This concept is generalized so that the user program must be a file before linking loading. In fact, UNIX itself is a file.

Shell commands normally consist of a key character followed by a command name followed by an argument or arguments:

```
% Command Arg Arg . . . Arg
```

where the command is the name of a program that really is a file name given as a path name. Some of the available commands are

LS	list files in current directory on device (usually CRT)
PR	list on printer
CAT	concatenate files
CP	copy file
MV	move file
RM	remove file
DATE	furnish current date
WC	furnish count of words in file
WHO	furnish list of current UNIX users

GREP	search file for pattern of characters
ED	editor
LN	link
CHDIR	change directory
PASSWD	change password

Some users of UNIX complain that the command names are inconsistent and nonmnemonic. They further complain that UNIX lacks interaction with the user, making it difficult to determine what the system is currently doing. In spite of their vocal objections, it must be noted that most of those objecting continue to use and prefer UNIX. UNIX assumes that the user is primarily interactive and uses the keyboard as the default input file and the CRT as the default output file. Any other files must be specified (before use they must be opened). Examples of possible shell commands are

% LS > ANYDEVICE	list files in current directory on device (> means to)
% CAT < ANYFILE	list on CRT the contents of ANYFILE (< means from)
% CP < FILE1 > FILE2	copy file
% DATE ; LS	list current date and files in current directory on CRT
% (DATE ; LS) > ANYFILE	put date and file in current directory in file ANYFILE
% DATE > > ANYFILE	append date on end of ANYFILE

Interprocess temporary files (pipes) are designated by a vertical bar:

% LS | COPY | WC

A process can often be made faster in execution by the use of pipes as well as being somewhat simpler to invoke. Following Kernighan and Mashey, (1981), we present

% PROG < IN > OUT

which instructs the shell of UNIX to supply PROG with input from file IN and place the output in file OUT.

% LS > FILELIST

which copies the names of the files from the current directory to the file FILELIST.

% WC < FILELIST

which additionally counts the entries in FILELIST and places this number on the CRT (with *no* explanation).

% PR-4 < FILELIST > TEMP

which alternately formats the file names in FILELIST into four columns and places this in TEMP.

```
% PR-4 < FILELIST > TEMP % LPR > TEMP
```

which additionally SPOOL-prints the formatted file names on the printer while other work can proceed. Note that the files FILELIST and TEMP still exist and consume space.

```
% LS > FILELIST
% PR-4 < FILELIST > TEMP
% RM > FILELIST
% LPR > TEMP
% RM > TEMP
```

would also remove these files and prevent using disk space permanently.

```
% LS | PR-4 | LPR
```

would accomplish exactly the same task as the five preceding commands employing the pipe facility. Additionally, it is very probable that the process would execute faster, as the second command could start and use available computer time before the first command completed. A similar overlay of the third command with both the second and first can often occur automatically.

No attempt has been made to be complete in this overview of UNIX. Rather, an attempt has been made to present the philosophy and "flavor" of this productive environment for multiprogramming by nonnovice users.

THE iRMX 86 OPERATING SYSTEM

The iRMX 86 Operating System is marketed by the Intel Corporation as a real time system with an event-driven scheduler. As in most operating systems, the design can be viewed as a series of layers around the hardware, with each layer taking advantage of the mechanisms and facilities furnished by the layer below it. Figure 9.13 illustrates this gross design philosophy that is somewhat typical of all operating systems, including CP/M and UNIX. In most instances, including the iRMX 86, the operating system extends the instructions and data types of the central processor (the I8086/8088) by adding a number of new data types and functions (OS pseudo-instructions) to operate on the additional data types.

In keeping with modern usage, the operating system data types of the iRMX 86 operating system are known as *objects*. The objects provided by the system are given below with the functions (pseudo-instructions) available to manipulate them.

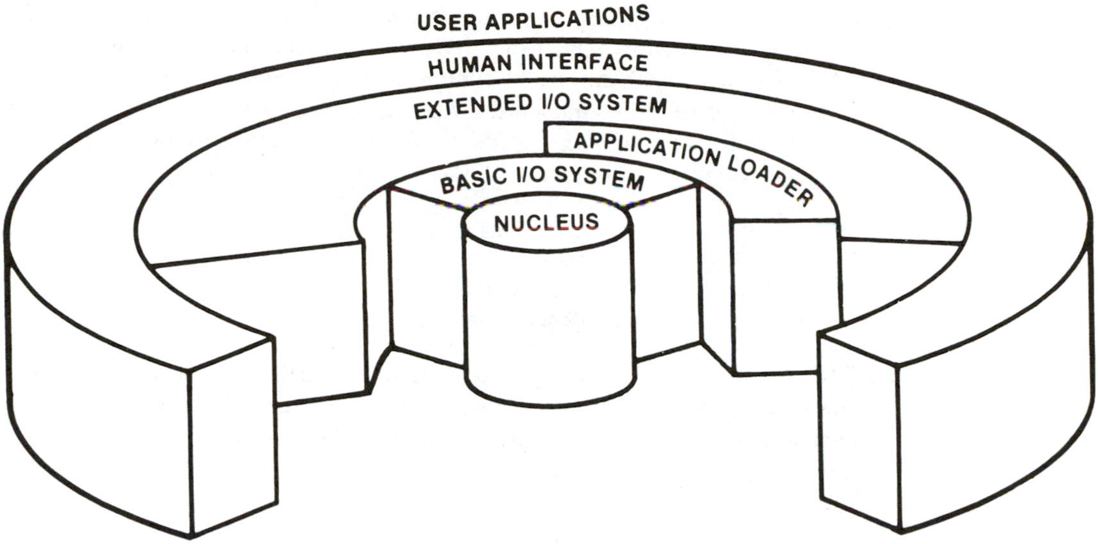

Figure 9.13 Layer design of the iRMX86 operating system. (Reprinted by permission of Intel Corporation. Copyright 1982).

JOBs: the means of organizing resources. Jobs are independent but may share resources. A job consists of one or more tasks. Each job is assigned a pool of memory. The available function to manipulate this object is

Create Job

TASKs: a portion of a job with an instruction stream, an execution stack, and private data. Task execution is based on an event-driven, priority-based scheduling algorithm. The available functions to manipulate the task objects are

Create Task
Delete Task
Suspend Task
Resume Task
Sleep Task
Set Task Priority

SEGMENTs: a contiguous block of RAM primary memory allocated in 16-byte portions called paragraphs with a maximum size of 64K. Segments are dynamically created from free memory space to which they are returned when deleted. The functions provided to manipulate segment objects are

Create Segment
Delete Segment

MAILBOXes: provide a mechanism for intertask and interjob data transfer via message segments. The usual iRMX 86 implementation provides two queues for each mailbox: one to contain message segments sent but not yet received, the other to contain tasks waiting to receive a message segment. It is common for one or both queues to be empty. The functions available to manipulate mailbox objects are

Create Mailbox
Delete Mailbox
Send Message
Receive Message

REGIONs: the means employed to accomplish mutual exclusion from "critical code regions" and to control the serialization of access to shared data. This concept was discussed in Chapters 6 and 8. The functions available to manipulate region objects (a queue of tasks) are

Create Region
Delete Region
Receive Control
Accept Control
Send Control

TOKENs: the 16-bit identifiers of the individual operating system objects. Each object has its own unique token. When an operating system primitive procedure is invoked (or CALLed), it is passed the tokens of the data structures that it will use via parameters on the operating system stack. The functions available to manipulate token objects are

Enable Deletion of Object
Disable Deletion of Object
Get Type of Objects
Get Tokens of Objects of Task

Interrupts require that operating system primitive functions be available with which to construct interrupt handlers and the resulting interrupt tasks. The functions available to the designer of interrupt servers are

Enable Interrupt Level #
Disable Interrupt Level #
Set (Assign) Interrupt Level # to service routine
Reset (Reassign) Interrupt Level # to new service routine
Get Interrupt Level #
Enter Interrupt Level #
Exit Interrupt Level #
Signal (Activate) Interrupt Level #
Wait (suspend) Interrupt Level # until signal

An operating system must be able to report and react to errors in the CALL parameters to its primitive functions. The iRMX 86 system provides two functions that allow the construction and use of such *exception* handlers:

Set (assign) Address of Task Exception Server
Get Address of Task Exception Server

Additionally, the design of the Intel OS Nucleus allows the designer to add operating system data types (i.e., objects) and thenceforth to access and manipulate these user-defined objects. In effect, provision is made for extensibility action through data type : function assignment of composite objects. The functions that allow this include

Set OS Extension

which modifies one of the interrupt vector entries (reserved by the Intel Corporation for such use) to point to the extension procedure defining the object and its manipulation, and

Signal (Invoke) OS Extension

which invokes the predefined OS object : function extension.

CAPABILITIES

The Intel Corporation presents this operating system as "an easy to use, comprehensive multiprogramming software system based on a real time, event driven scheduler." Facilities are provided for executing programs concurrently, sharing information and resources, servicing events, and interactively controlling the system and its resources. The I/O system (IOS) provides for a tree-organized file structure where the terminal (file) leaves can each be a named data file or a named directory file containing information about other data files and directory files. Physical files provide the connection mechanism between named files and storage devices. The IOS also provides *stream files* for data communication between tasks and jobs as if the data were first written to and then read from a first in–first out file.

THE I80130 OPERATING SYSTEM FIRMWARE PROCESSOR

This component provides 35 operating system kernel primitive instructions and supports five system data types (objects) through microprogramming. These instructions and objects are those previously described for job and task management, interrupt servicing, management, intertask communication and synchronization, and memory management.

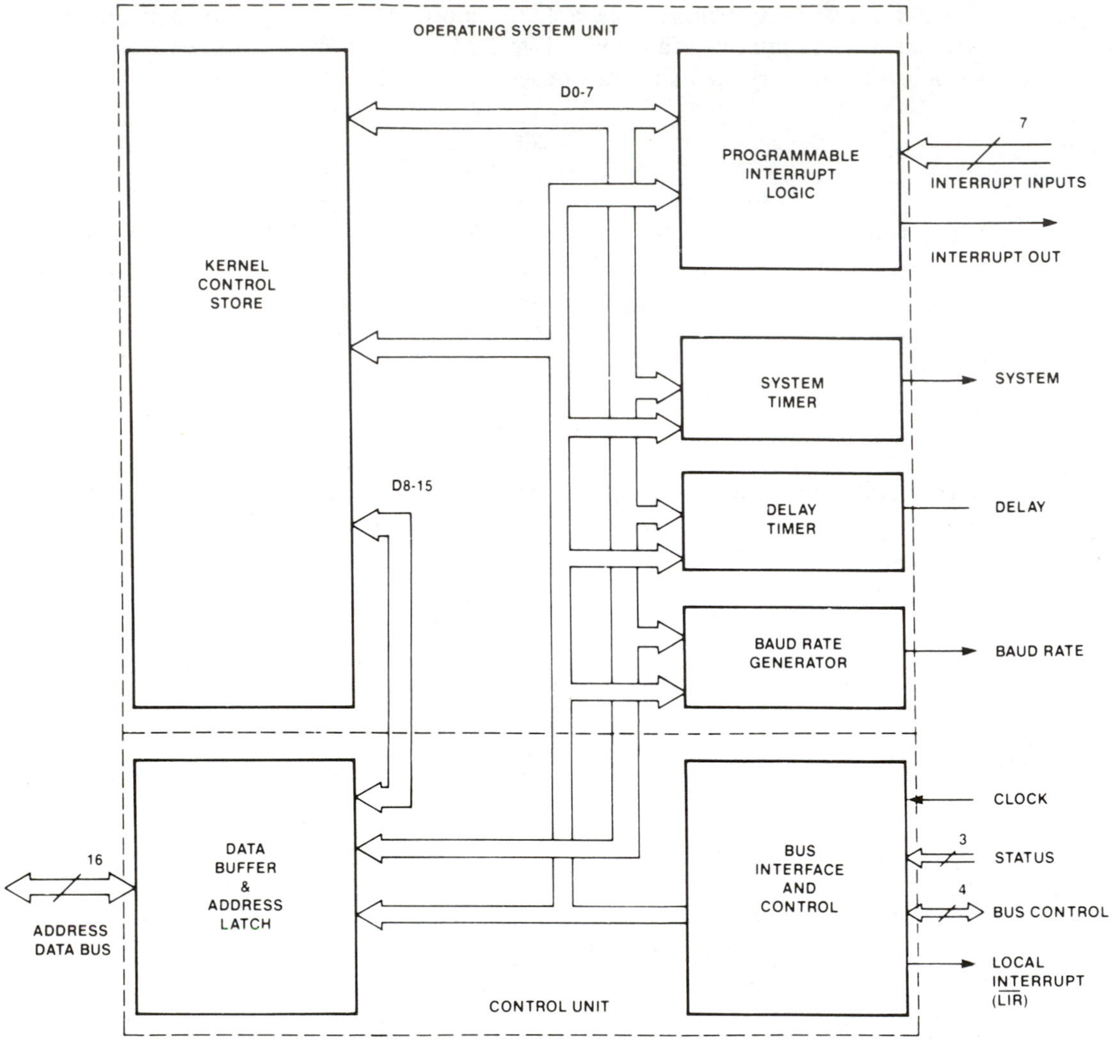

Figure 9.14 Internal organization of the I80130 operating system firmware processor (OSP), which furnishes 35 operating system primitive kernel instructions that manipulate five systems data types. (Reprinted by permission of Intel Corporation. Copyright 1981.)

The internal architecture of the I80130 OSP is shown in Figure 9.14 and an example of its integration into a relatively simple system is shown in Figure 9.15. The use of the I80130 OSP should result in four clear advantages when compared to the alternative software implementation:

1. Relieving the implementor of the operating system of the enormous task of designing and testing the kernal instructions

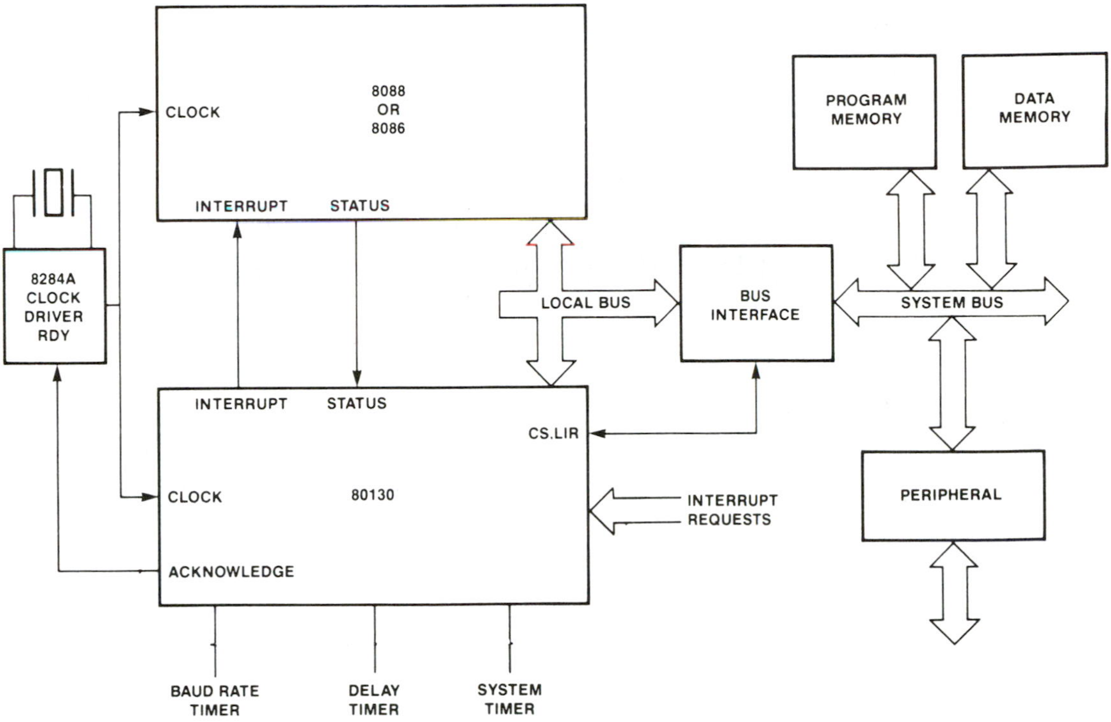

Figure 9.15 Example of the possible integration of the I80130 operating system firmware processor into a simple system. (Reprinted by permission of Intel Corporation. Copyright 1981.)

2. Better protection from deliberate or inadvertent change or "clobbering" of the kernel portion of the operating system
3. Faster execution of the operating system modules and thus reduced system overhead
4. Cleaner modularization of the system

It must be noted that the implementation of the operating system function in a separate processor was pioneered by the Control Data Corporation via the peripheral processor concept for control and for I/O in the CDC 6600. The first delivery of this system in October 1964 followed intense work by Seymour Cray and James E. Thornton starting in the summer of 1960. The off-loading from the CPU of operating system pseudo-instructions should materially increase the throughput of a multiprogrammed system.

10

Assemblers and Linkers

In Chapter 3 we gave the following code fragment for an IF-THEN-ELSE construct in both procedural-level language code and in I8086/8088 assembly language:

```
IF A > B                          IF:     CMP     AX,BX
    THEN DO;                              BLE     ELSE
         -
                                  THEN:   -
         - /* Some things */
         -                                - ; some things
       END;                               -
    ELSE DO;
                                          JMP     NEXT
         -                        ELSE:   -
         -/* Other things */              -
         -                                - ; other things
       END;                               -
NEXT:                             NEXT:
```

Although we noted in Chapter 3 that the I8086/8088 does not actually execute either of the foregoing versions of the program fragment, at this point it is again necessary to emphasize that all conventional computers (including the I8086/8088) can execute only programs presented to them as binary machine code entities. That is, the circuits of the computer are designed and implemented to recognize, interpret, and execute operations codes expressed as bit patterns as well as operand addresses expressed as binary numbers. Thus the code segment above would be executed in the following form:

Program/data location (hex)	Operation code/ operand address	Notes
31	39	CMP opcode
32	01	Operands registers AX and BX
33	7E	JLE opcode
34	OA	Displace to location 3E
35		
36		
37		Instructions in the
38		THEN clause
39		
3A		
3B		
3C	EB	JMP opcode
3D	O6	Displace to location 46
3E		
3F		
40		Instructions in the
41		ELSE clause
42		
43		
44		
45		
46		Instructions following
47		IF-THEN-ELSE
48		

Note that there is a one-to-many relationship between the statements of a procedural-level language (such as Pascal or PL/I) and assembly language and that the statements in a procedural-level language do not directly correspond on a one-to-one basis with the statements in the assembly language equivalent. On the other hand, there is a one-to-one direct correspondence between the statements of assembly language and the equivalent binary machine code, with two bytes being occupied by the operation code/mode information and one or more bytes being occupied by the operand memory address (in the example, a displacement).

Now it is perfectly possible to compose programs in binary machine language even though it is tedious, error prone, time consuming, and an unnecessary waste of intellectual powers. Very early in this age of the computer (1950 or before), someone (probably several geniuses in many places) made the now obvious inference: Why not write a program to convert mnemonic operation code–symbolic operand name combinations to binary operations code–binary numeric operand address combinations? It was tried; it worked; and the symbolic assembler process was born. At the present point in the development of computers, an assembler seems obvious; when the idea was new, it was not obvious and was not universally accepted. Many journeymen programmers resisted the idea and employed a myriad of "reasons" to continue coding in binary. Such reasoning seems archaic at present. Happily, it resulted in essentially no slowdown of progress. Nevertheless, it should be noted that the Vanguard rocket (America's answer to the Sputnik in 1957) was controlled by a program coded in binary machine language and contained a single simple mistake that resulted in a spectacular and expensive fiasco.

The "automatic programming systems" provided by an assembly language translator for each computer naturally led to the idea of also converting more mathematical and business English-oriented syntax to binary machine code. Thus by the mid-1950s the compiler was born, and by 1957 the first popular procedural-level language—FORTRAN—existed. Again, many journeymen programmers resisted for a variety of reasons. Happily, this intellectual tempest is almost dead. Lest I be completely misunderstood, at this time and probably for some time to come, several somewhat special situations for which assembly language coding is justified exist. The number and diversity of these situations is rather rapidly diminishing, however. The justification for employing assembly language must be an economic justification; that is, the savings in memory space and execution time must more than offset the increased programming effort and cost. Thus the usual case would involve a situation where several hundred thousand uses of the program would be expected. An obvious example involves the microcomputers currently employed to control carburetion and timing in automobiles, where millions of copies are involved.

It is extremely important to realize that the foregoing reasoning depends entirely on the assumption that a good assembly language programmer can code a specific algorithm so that it is smaller and/or executes faster than the code output by the compiler of an available procedural-oriented language. For most situations in the past, this was true; for many situations at present, this is true; for a few situations in the future, this will continue to be true. However, it is also true that newer languages and their associated compilers are getting better and better, so that the use of assembly language is diminishing and presently is relatively minor. At the same time serious programmers and all educated people should have an understanding and appreciation of what goes on behind the obvious. One method of guaranteeing this knowledge relative to computers is to learn and use an assembly language for at least a few programs.

THE COMPUTATIONAL PROCESS

Each and every time a new computer is designed and produced, it presents the same problem to the producing company and through them to the intended user. Imagine, if you will, that one of your brillant computer architects working with several designers has just informed you that they have evolved a breakthrough in chip design that will allow the capture of a significant portion of the word processing/

office automation market. This could mean millions of dollars of profit for your company and thousands of dollars in your personal paycheck.

Attractive—you bet. But wait; they propose to design, implement, and deliver an excellent computer that will interpret and execute binary machine language! Binary machine language! Nobody, but nobody, programs in binary machine language. For this new computer to be useful and to sell, you must design, implement, and deliver with the hardware such things as an operating system, compilers, editors, and in this specific case, a "turn-key" applications system for word-processing/office automation. Without these, and probably more, the product will not sell, the profits will not materialize, and your personal paycheck and future is doomed. Additionally, you cannot wait until the new computer is designed and a prototype implemented before you start work on the software. If you do, your competition will "beat" you to the market. You must develop the hardware and its software in parallel. Both must be ready at about the same time.

An impossible technical management task? No! Recall that computers are really somewhat general-purpose information-manipulating machines. You can use one of your present computers to produce the software for your new computer. The critical requirement is that you know exactly and precisely what the binary machine code of the new computer will be. Is this requirement realistic? Can your architect and designer define the binary machine code well enough? Probably not exactly, but probably good enough.

You decide to go ahead. Among the software you need is an assembler and among your resources is an existing computer that has a procedural-level language available. Unfortunately, the textbook coverage and professional literature regarding the design and implementation of an assembler are somewhat sparse. This is in contrast to the copious literature available regarding compilers and operating systems. At this time, I am able to cite only three texts on assemblers that might be helpful: Barron (1972), Calingaert (1979), and Donovan (1972).

Almost invariably, the process of preparing a program for execution consists of a series of steps somewhat like those illustrated in Figure 10.1 and reviewed in the following list:

1. *Algorithm design* After a problem is defined, it is usual to break it into logical and independent subproblems (modules) each of whose solutions is somewhat easy and constitutes an independent function with well-specified inputs, a defined manipulation, and the desired output. This is a human intellectual task of high order.
2. *Code into computer language*: Each of the modules defined above is translated into the correct and legal syntax of the chosen computer languages. It is important to identify and correct any coding errors at this point. It is also important to test each module by itself in order to find and correct any logic errors in the problem solution strategy.
3. *Translate (assemble or compile)*: The translation system of programs transforms (transliterates in the case of assembly language, translates in the case of

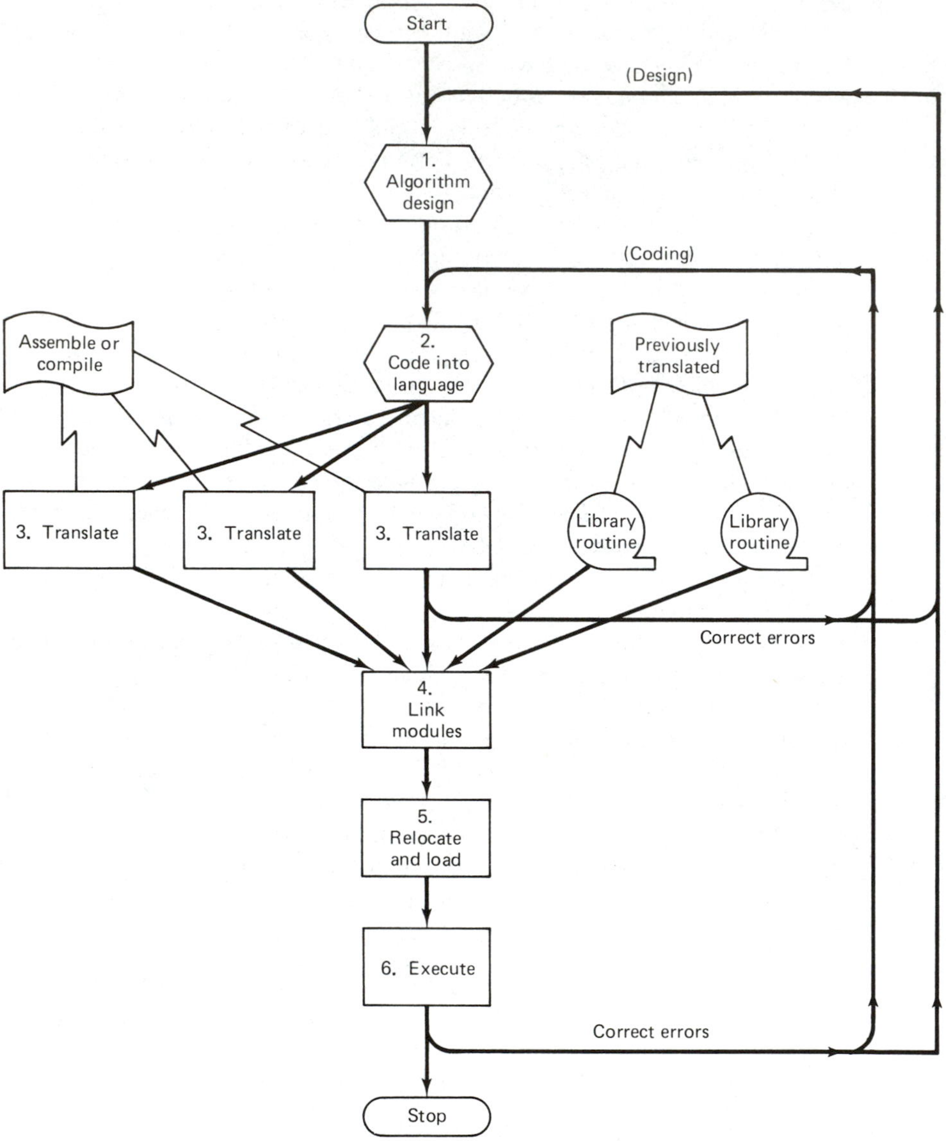

Figure 10.1 A possible view of the computer-based problem solving process. In this chapter, we concentrate on the translation step with emphasis on assembly, on the module linking step, and on the relocation/load step.

a procedural-level language) the source code statements from step 2 to binary machine code for the target computer (usually termed "object code"). If the translation system is correct (the assembler and/or compiler is correct), the syntax of the module will be transformed while the semantics will not be altered. Syntax errors are often identified during compilation or assembly. An overall design for the assembly process will be detailed shortly.

4. *Link modules*: If the design and coding of the problem solution strategy involves any subordinate modules (subroutines and/or functions), as is usual, it is necessary to combine the separately translated modules into a single coordinated whole. It is usual for each module to be translated into binary machine code, with the address of the code beginning at zero and, in the case of the I8086/8088, the beginning address of the data segment, the stack segment, and any strings in the extra segment also beginning at zero. Linking is the concatenation of the code from the different modules into a single "load module" whose beginning address is zero and involves the resolution of intermodule address references caused by such instructions as CALL. All code addresses will be byte offsets within the code segment. Similarly, the defined areas within the data segment, the stack segment, and the extra (string) segment must be concatenated and the relative addresses resolved. Object code (translated) modules may be derived directly from the compiler/assembler or may be obtained from libraries of previously translated modules.
5. *Relocate and load into main memory*: The movement of each byte of the code, the data, the stack, and the extra (string) segment into main memory is termed "loading" and is usually accomplished via disk-to-memory I/O instructions. Additionally, the addresses of the beginning of the code, the data, the stack, and the extra (string) segment must be loaded into the CS, the DS, the SS, and the ES registers. In the I8086/8088, this constitutes relocation and allows the different segments to be loaded into main memory at any address divisible by hexadecimal 10 (16 base 10). The relocation process in computer architectures not processing segment registers is somewhat more complicated but straightforward. Note that code/data relocation precludes the use of absolute addresses (nonrelocatable addresses) except in special circumstances such as the interrupt vector situation. It is somewhat common for the linking step and the relocating loader step to be combined into a single operating system functional module known as a linking loader.
6. *Execute*: After loading is completed, execution of the linked/relocated/main-memory-resident program is started by the operating system initializing the instruction pointer register (IP)—that is, the program counter—to the offset of the initial executable instruction of the main program in the code segment. As the main program is commonly the physically first module in the user program, this offset is most commonly, but not necessarily, zero. The setting of the IP is usually accomplished by the operating system executing a CALL instruction (or equivalent) to the user program, so that it is, in effect, a subpro-

gram of the operating system. The user program is terminated, in the normal nonerror case, via a RETurn instruction (or equivalent) to the operating system. Alternatively, this program initiation/termination process may be implemented as "software interrupts" employing specific interrupt vector numbers in the range 32 through 255 base 10. Interrupts were discussed in Chapter 5.

DESIGNING AN ASSEMBLER

A symbolic assembler system must have the ability to:

1. Map or transform symbolic (alphabetic) operation codes into the corresponding and equivalent binary code.
2. Assign addresses relative to the module start for each instruction and datum.
3. Record references to other modules (CALL and RETurn instructions) and to data not defined within the module (external data) in order for the link process to be carried out correctly.
4. Record and report any syntactical errors in the module.

It is almost certain that several hundred production/commercial assembly systems have been designed, implemented, and marketed over the last 35 or so years (at least one for each different computer). Additionally, it is probable that many thousand additional assemblers for simplified versions of real and imaginary computers have been designed and implemented as class projects by as many long-suffering computer science sophmore/junior-level students in literally scores of academic institutions around the world. My point is that the problem of designing and implementing a symbolic assembly system has been accomplished so often by so many people for so many computers using so many languages that the design is well defined and the choices available during implementation are clear.

Almost invariably, the design of a symbolic assembler consists of two first-level modules or passes:

PASS 1: Assign numeric addresses to each instruction and to each datum using location counters. This will involve looking up the length, in bytes, of each instruction in an OP_CODE table. Illegal and misspelled operation codes will often be found at this stage and reported as errors. If an instruction contains a memory displacement that can vary in length (such as the JMP instruction that can have a target displacement of 8 bits, 16 bits, or 32 bits), a serious problem arises. How much should the location counter be incremented—one byte, two bytes, or four bytes? Possible solutions to this dilemma will be cited shortly. Similarly, data segment, stack segment, and extra segment relative address location counters must be initialized and incremented for each data area reservation pseudoinstruction, such as

WORDS. References to external data and to other modules involve addresses that are a combination of a 16-bit segment registers and a 16-bit displacement and thus require four bytes of address space in the binary machine code object module that will ultimately be supplied and filled in by the linker.

PASS 2: Complete the assembly process by generating the binary machine code equivalent for each instruction via information obtained from the OP_CODE table and the various addresses of code and data calculated during PASS 1. During this process, various syntax errors may be found and recorded for eventual reporting. At the conclusion of PASS 2, it is necessary to output, if no errors were found (usually to a disk), the object module in binary machine code for use by the linker and/or to output a listing of the source module with associated object code annotated with any errors.

Note that the fundamental purpose of PASS 1 is to calculate addresses for use by PASS 2 in generating binary machine code. PASS 1 would be unnecessary if "forward references" were prohibited—that is, if labels or data identifiers to places in the module not yet encountered were prohibited. This programmatic restriction would prevent the use of program clauses such as the IF-THEN-ELSE, as illustrated at the beginning of this chapter. Such a restriction is not acceptable, and thus a two-pass assembler is usual.

In our example I8086/8088 symbolic assembly processor, we will employ the somewhat common microprocessor systems programming dialect G of the procedural-oriented language PL/1-PL/IG. If a PL/G compiler is available on our I8086/8088 computational system, we will use it to implement an assembler; if a PL/G compiler is available only in another system, say an IBM/370, we will employ it on that computer to implement a cross-assembler. A cross-assembler, then, is an assembler that executes on a computer of "type A" and outputs legal binary machine code for a computer of "type B." Note that there is essentially no difference between an assembler and a cross-assembler.

It is also necessary for us to define the syntax and other characteristics of our example assembly language. In the interest of helping comprehension of the underlying process of translation (for assembly code, it is really transliteration), we keep the syntax fairly simple and uniform but somewhat realistic and useful.

1. An assembly language statement shall consist of one instruction that shall occupy one record that is terminated by an "end-of-line" (EOL) ASCII character.
2. Each statement shall be "free-format," except that, if a label occurs it shall start in column 1 and be terminated by a colon (:). The operations code shall be surrounded by one or more blanks and shall precede the operand(s), which shall be separated by commas and contain no blanks. An EOL or semicolon (;) character shall delimit (end) a statement.

3. A comment shall begin with a semicolon (;) and be terminated by an EOL character. Thus a semicolon in column 1 of a record defines the entire record (line) as a comment. Additionally, a statement may be followed by a comment.
4. An assembly language module shall consist of two main portions:
   a. The first portion shall define the container areas of the data, stack, and extra segments, as well as record external references; and
   b. The second portion shall contain the code segment.
5. The first portion shall have the first statement be the pseudo-operation/operand diad

   DATA AREAS

   followed by the appropriate data area definitions. The pseudo-operation used will identify the segment involved. The end of the data definition section and the start of the code area will be signified by the pseudo-operation

   CODE SEGMENT

   The physical end of the module shall be signified by the pseudo-operation

   END PROCEDURE

   For purposes of our illustration, we specify that no segment can be larger than hex 10000 = 65536 base 10 bytes = 2^{16}.
6. References to other modules (i.e., CALL) and references to external data areas shall be specified in the first portion by the pseudo-operation

   EXTERNAL

   Data areas that will be made available as externals to other modules will be declared as

   GLOBAL

7. The assembler shall accept only "pure code," that is, the contents of the code segment shall be "read only" and self-altering code will not be allowed.
8. Identifiers or labels (and thus code branch destinations, data, stacks, and strings) must start with an alphabetic ASCII character, be 10 characters or less in length, and may not include any embedded blanks.

Thus the overall format of a source module for entry into the I8086/8088 assembler whose design we are discussing is given in Figure 10.2.

```
        PROCEDURE        ANY_NAME
;
;                    Example of source module format of
;                    assembly language being used as
;                    example for assembling
;
        DATA             AREAS
          .
          .
          .
        CODE             SEGMENT
          .
          .
          .
        END              ANY_NAME
```

Figure 10.2 Overall format of the source assembly language module for input into the assembler described in the text.

DATA CONTAINERS

Remembering that the vital task of PASS 1 is the determination of addresses (the forward-reference problem) and that PASS 2 will generate the memory addresses (at least of forward-branch code), we have chosen to accomplish as much of the assembly task as convenient in PASS 1. As the I8086/8088 provides three independently addressed data areas and as we choose to also allow access to data defined and addressed in other modules (external data), it is convenient to require that all data symbols (names) be defined at the beginning of the program. Thus all noncode labels (data labels) could be assigned an address in their segment before the code segment is encountered. This would allow the generation during PASS 1 of the binary machine code for all instructions except forward-reference branch instructions. We have chosen not to generate binary machine code operand addresses until PASS 2, even though we do move the binary version of the operations code to the machine code area during PASS 1. It is worth noting that all of the assembly processing for a syntax that requires all data definitions to precede the code could be accomplished in PASS 1 except for the addresses of forward-reference branches and that these could be resolved in a very brief type of PASS 2, almost an afterthought. On the other hand, it is as justifiable to minimize the work of PASS 1 and delay as much processing as possible for PASS 2. The usual approach is a compromise.

Our example assembler will have two inputs:

1. The source assembly module to be translated
2. A table of legal operations codes and pseudo-operations in source language form, in machine language form, their associated instruction lengths, and their associated segment

This assembler will output two files:

1. An annotated listing of the module giving the source version, the binary machine code version (in hexadecimal), the associated relative addresses in the four segments, and any error messages.
2. A file of 80 character records containing the relocatable binary machine code version of the module with sufficient note information to allow linking, relocation, and loading. The format of this file will be that given in Figure 10.3.

Record 1			
	Columns	1–4	'PROC'
		7–16	Module name
		20–29	'CODE' size (in four hexadecimal digits)
		30–39	'DATA' size
		40–49	'Stack' size
		50–59	'EXTRA' size
		76–80	'00001' (record sequence number)
Records 2 to N			
	Columns	1–5	'Extrn' or 'GLOBL'
		7–16	Symbolic name
		18–22 24–28 30–34 36–40 42–46 48–52 54–58 60–64 66–70	Segment number and location in segment one plus four hexadecimal digits (up to nine references per card)
		76–80	Sequence number
Records N+1 to M			
	Columns	1–5	'DATA' or 'STACK' or 'EXTRA'
		7–10	Location in segment of constant
		11–70	Hexadecimal digit pairs giving value of constant (30 hexadecimal pairs per record allowed)
		76–80	Sequence number
Record M+1 to K			
	Columns	1–4	'CODE'
		7–10	Location in segment of start
		12–13	Number of bytes in this record (28 allowed)
		15–70	Binary machine code in hexadecimal pairs
		76–80	Sequence number
Record K+1			
	Columns	1–3	'END'
		7–16	Module name
		76–80	Sequence number

Figure 10.3 Object Code syntax and associated semantics for the assembler and linker discussed in the text.

Note that the start and the end of the binary machine code file is indicated by a unique record and that the body of the file consists of six types of records: EXTRN—one record for each external data container or procedure referenced with the reference location in the code segment given to allow the link routine to insert addresses during the linking process; GLOBL—one record for each global data container with the segment number and reference location within the segment to allow the link routine to resolve external references of other modules; DATA, STACK, and EXTRA—one record for each defined container with the value and starting location in the appropriate segment [a constant longer than 30 bytes will require extra record(s)]; and CODE—one record for every 28 bytes, with the starting location number of bytes in the code segment (locations to have external addresses supplied by the link routine should be set to zero). The requirement is to supply all information that will be needed by the link routine for it to function correctly.

In our assembler, we have chosen to combine many of the traditional internal working data areas into a single fairly large combined table. Thus, we require three internal data areas (Figure 10.4):

1. A symbol table that has a large enough capacity to contain the identification (name) of each unique label occurring in the module as well as its relative location within one of the four segments (data, stack, extra, or code). As each symbol is encountered during PASS 1, it is placed in the symbol table together with its segment type and relative location. External symbols are also entered with a location of zero. As all languages prohibit duplicate labels (all languages that I know of, anyway), it is necessary to search the table for the possible existence of a label before it is entered. This search occurs during a period (PASS 1) when the table is being added to. Additionally, during PASS 2, the symbol table must be searched to determine the location within which segment of each operand. As a search of the symbol table must be accomplished repeatedly, it is important that the search operation be fast.
2. A master table in which to store almost all of the information about the module being assembled, such as the source statement, the segment, the line number, the statement number, the binary machine code, and the relative location, as well as the extracted symbolic label, operation code, and operands.
3. A small group of miscellaneous variables such as a container for the line counter, the statement counter, the relative location within each segment counter, and so on.

We have chosen to combine many data containers usually encountered in an assembler into one comprehensive table, called the *master table.* If the implementation language supports relatively complicated data structures, they can somewhat simplify the logical design of an assembler. We assume an implementation language with this facility in our design and thus are contemplating a language for implementation such as PL/G. If the implementation language is lacking this ability, it would

```
DECLARE
  SOURCE_FILE(500) CHAR(80),
  OP_CODE_TABLE 1(256),            /* This table is initialized to the */
    2 NAME CHAR(10),               /* correct values via an */
    2 TYPE FIXED DEC(1),           /* INITIAL clause */
    2 LENGTH FIXED DEC(1),
    2 BINARY_CODE BIT(6);
DECLARE
  SYMBOL_TABLE 1(250),
    2 NAME CHAR(10),
    2 TYPE FIXED DEC(1)            /* Segment */
    2 LOCATION CHAR(10);           /* Hexadecimal digits */
DECLARE
  MASTER_TABLE 1(999),
    2 LINE_NO FIXED DEC(3),
    2 STMNT_NO FIXED DEC(3),
    2 KEY FIXED DEC(1),            /* Segment */
    2 LOCATION CHAR(10),           /* Hexadecimal digits */
    2 BINARY_CODE CHAR(10),        /* Hexadecimal digits */
    2 SOURCE_STMNT CHAR(80),
    2 LABEL CHAR(10),
    2 OP_CODE CHAR(10),
    2 FIRST_OPERAND CHAR(10),
    2 SECOND_OPERAND CHAR(10),
    2 REPEAT_CODE CHAR(10);
DECLARE
  OBJECT_FILE(400) CHAR(80);
DECLARE
  LINE_COUNTER FIXED DEC(3),
  STMNT_COUNTER FIXED DEC(3),
  LOCATION_COUNTER(5) FIXED DEC(5);
```

Figure 10.4 Necessary data areas for the assembler discussed in the text.

be necessary to break the master table of this design into several data areas. A little thought should allow the student to incorporate this complication into the design of an assembler.

Let us further consider the proposition of searching a table. In general, there are three types of table search: linear (sometimes known as *sequential*), binary (sometimes known as *logarithmic*), and hash coding.

Linear/Sequential Table Insertion and Search

The table is searched sequentially from its start to its finish. New items are added at the end; thus the table is ordered in the order that labels are encountered in the module. This method is suitable for tables that change size (grow) between searches. The average search time is the time required to search one-half the table.

For a very large table, the sequential search method is usually considered too slow. As a general rule of thumb, this method should be employed only on tables of 100 entries or less.

Binary (Logarithmic) Insertion and Search

The table must be in sorted order before search and thus the binary search method is not considered suitable for tables that change size (grow) between searches because of the difficulty and time required to add new labels in their lexicographical sort position. A sorted table may be probed at its midpoint to see if the desired item is in the fore half or the back half. The indicated half is then treated similarly, until the item is found or a "not found" is indicated. The average search time is rounded up to log base 2 of the table size, which is the power-of-2 number above the table size. As a general rule, this method is not suitable for symbol table searches, although a linked-list method may alleviate the objection noted above.

Hash Table Search and Insertion

Hash table techniques are eminently suited to symbol table use, as they are fast and work for tables that change in size. The idea is to use a function to transform the symbol (the label) into an index or position in the table; that is,

table_index ← hash (symbol_ID)

As a rule of thumb, the table should be about one-half larger than the size expected to be needed. The major difficulty with hash table techniques is finding a function that will distribute the symbols (the labels) evenly over the table, with a minimum number of them being indexed to the same position, called a *collision.* Collisions are often "solved" by placing or searching for "symbol" (the label) in the next available sequential table location. Collisions are a real problem due to the traditional habit of programmers to use such data names as I, X, STACK1, and so on, and in this way, limit their variable names' vocabulary. In the absence of collisions, the search time (the "probe" time) for a hash table consists of the calculation time for the hash function, plus the indexing time. Various more advanced schemes for designing hash tables have been developed (such as two-level hashing); the literature on searching is very large, sometimes interesting, and often reveals valuable programming techniques that are useful in other contexts.

Cook and Oldehoeft (1982) give a heuristic for the Cichelli (1980) method of constructing a minimal perfect hash table—minimal space with minimal collisions—for small static sets of words such as an opcode table. Cichelli used the function:

index ← length of word + value of first letter + value of last letter

Under many conditions, a solution requires much time. We give the algorithm of Cook and Oldehoeft as a useful tool.

1. Compute the frequency of letters occurring at either end of words in the set. If a letter appears as both the first and last letter of the same word, assign it a large value.
2. Order the letters by decreasing frequency, resolving ties arbitrarily.
3. Let each word be represented by a triple: (letter 1, letter 2, length) where letter 1 is the first letter and letter 2 is the last letter. For each triple (word), interchange letter 1 and letter 2 if letter 2 precedes letter 1 in the letter ordering.
4. Using letter 2 as the key, sort the list of triples in descending order.
5. Assign letter values. Begin with the first triple. For each group of triples with the same letter 2, attempt to find a letter value assignment for letter 2. Note that for this group of triples, either letter 2 = letter 1 or letter 1 precedes letter 2 in the letter ordering and letter 1 has previously been assigned a value. Thus only letter 2 needs to be assigned a value to place the group of triples (words) in the hash table. Beginning with 0, search for a value for letter 2 that maps the group of triples to distinct empty table slots. If it finds a value, it assigns the value to letter 2 and places the group of triples (words) in the table. If it does not find a value, it backs up, depending on the reason for its failure. One reason for failure is that two triples in the group have the same value of letter 1 and length sums. Hence the two triples will have identical hash values for any value assignment to letter 2. In this case the algorithm backs up to the nearest group that computes a value assignment for a letter 1 of one of the two triples. For all other failures, the algorithm backs up to the previous group of triples. Note that when the algorithm backs up it unassigns letter values and removes the associated hash table entries along the way.

PASS 1

PASS 1 must process the source module one input record at a time after first initializing the data areas discussed above. All input records, including comments, are stored without change in the master table with the appropriate line and statement count. The statement is then subjected to lexical analysis, as shown in the flowchart of Figure 10.5*a*.

Lexical analysis is the process of assembling and extracting lexical elements from the character string constituting the statement. *Syntactical analysis* is the process of identifying the extracted elements. If a higher-level language, such as PL/G, is employed for implementation that offers suitable character string primitives for finding the next blank, lexical analysis becomes trivial. The restricted syntax of an assembly language also trivializes syntactical analysis. If the first element starts in column 1, it is a label; if column 1 is blank, the label does not exist. The first nonla-

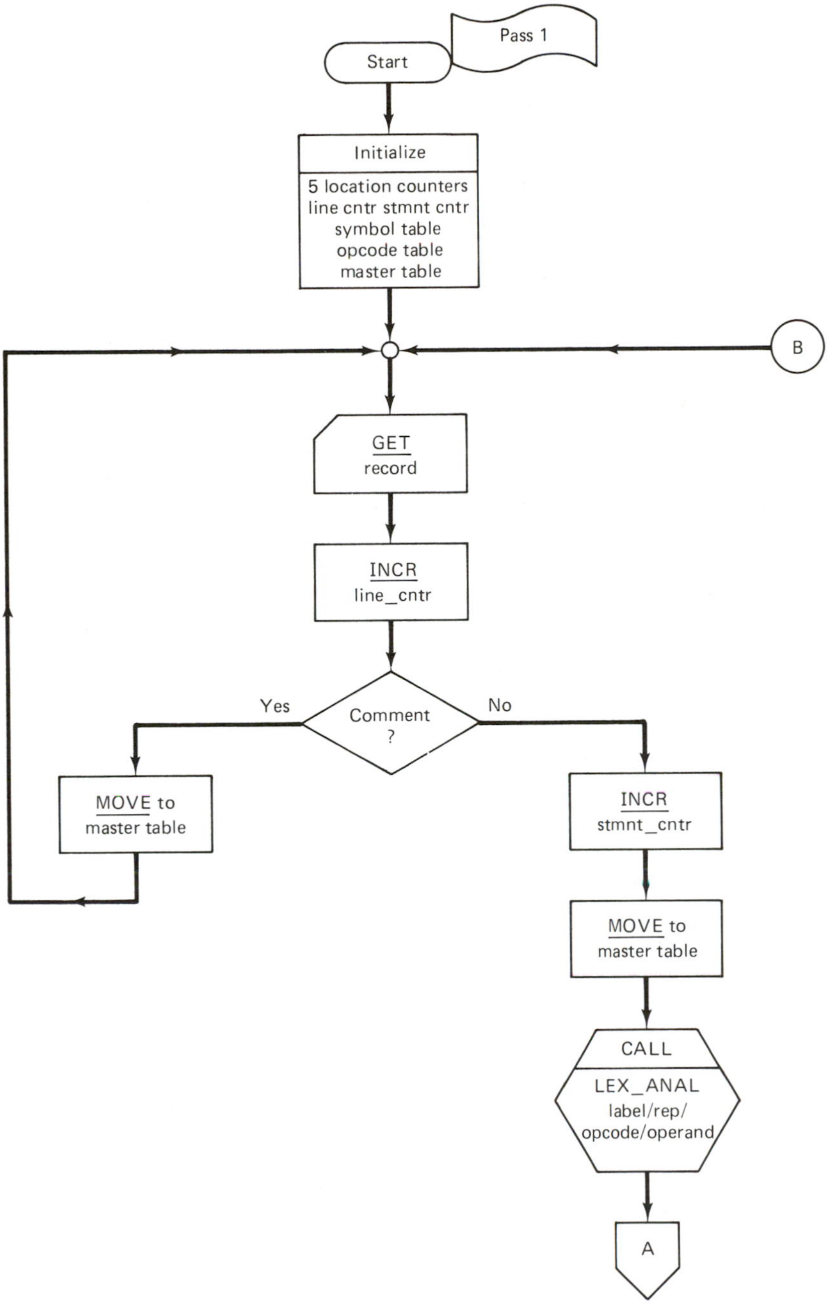

(a)

Figure 10.5 PASS 1 of assembler as discussed in the text.

bel element will be the operations/pseudo-operations code followed by one or two operand addresses, register designations, or immediate value. As these syntactical elements are extracted and identified by the subprocedure shown at the bottom-right of the flowchart in Figure 10.5*a.*, they are moved to the master table for later use. The symbolic operations code is immediately used as the search key into the operations code table.

As we have previously discussed the three methods of table search, it will suffice to note that the opcode table is completely initialized and does not grow during the assembly process; thus it could be stored in sorted order and a binary (logarithmic) search employed. Alternatively, it is often possible to identify a function that allows hash searching of the opcode table with almost no collisions and with a minimum of extra space consumed, as discussed earlier. When the opcode is identified as either a pseudo-operation code (the key is moved to the master table) or an operations code (the key of 6 and the binary machine version is moved to the master table), the length is found (from the opcode table for operations codes, from the operand field for pseudo-operations). Finally, the appropriate relative location counter within the data, stack, extra, or code segment is incremented accordingly.

The key, just identified, is used in a decision block to direct further processing, as shown near the top of the flowchart in Figure 10.5*b*. If available in the implementation language, a CASE statement would be suitable for this multiway branch; if not, a series of nested conditional branches will suffice. Referring back to our definition of the source language syntax of an input module to our assembler, recall that the first record encountered must be a PROCEDURE name (kind = 0) record. This record will generate the initial record of the output binary machine code file.

The next input source code record will identify that the following records, until a CODE record is encountered, will specify an external module name, or data areas (external or internal). The specific pseudo-operation found in the record will indicate the segment involved. The appropriate key will be used to control which relative location counter is incremented (which segment is currently involved). If a reference to an external module (subprocedure) is involved in the code segment, the specifications of our example assembly language syntax require the programmer to furnish an EXT pseudo-operation for each such unique procedure referenced. Similarly, references to external data areas also require that an EXT pseudo-operation be the references to external data, stack, or extra segment data containers for variable or for constant data. Each external reference input record will cause an entry in the symbol table with key = 1 and a relative location of zero. Additionally, each external reference input record will cause an EXTRN output record to be generated. Note that references to external data areas and procedures must have the relative location in the appropriate segment recorded in the EXTRN output record during the symbol table search of PASS 2. The programmer can allow data areas in the module to be accessed via EXT references in other modules by specifying them using the GLOBAL pseudo-operation.

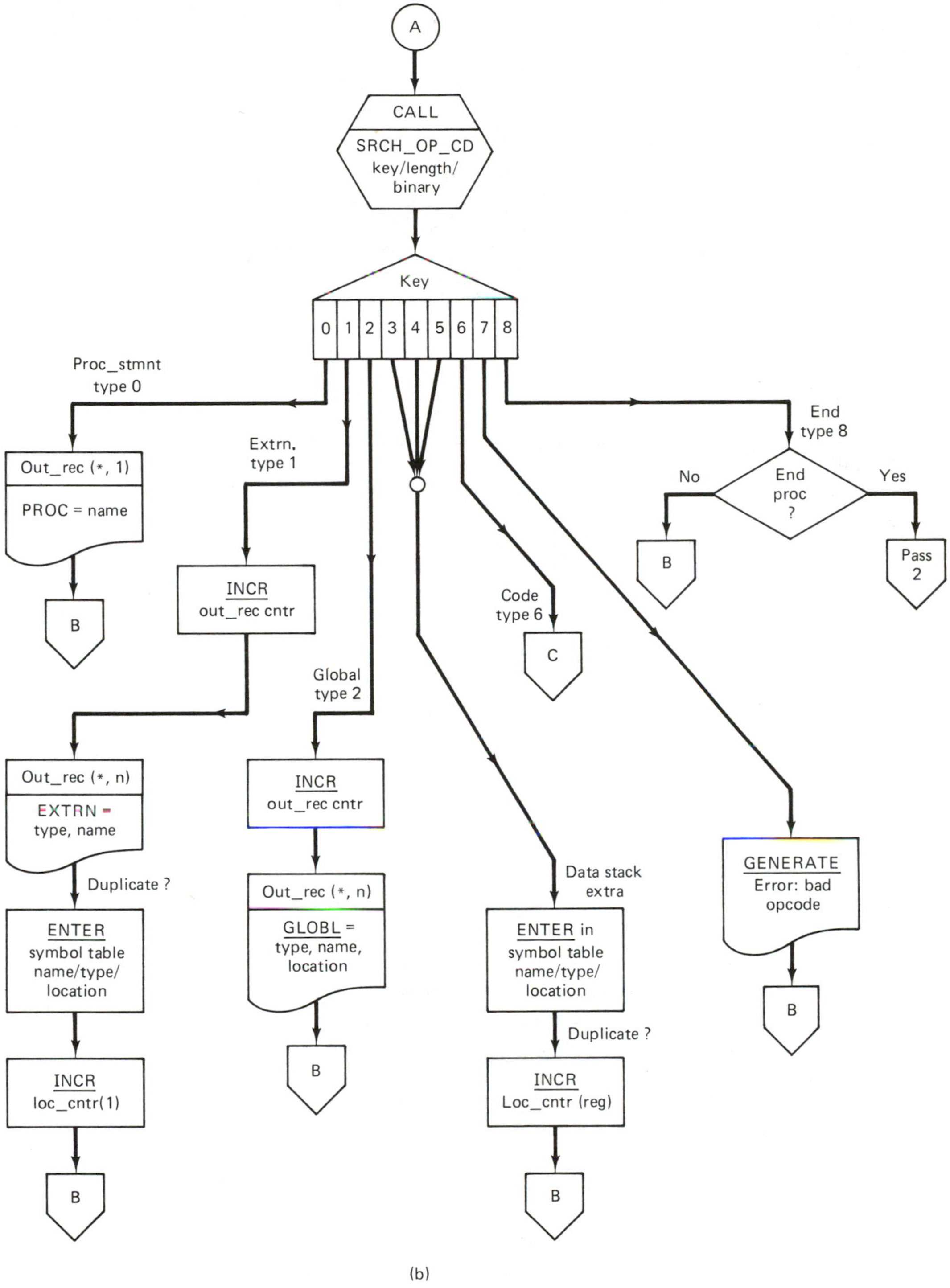

(b)

Figure 10.5 *(continued)*

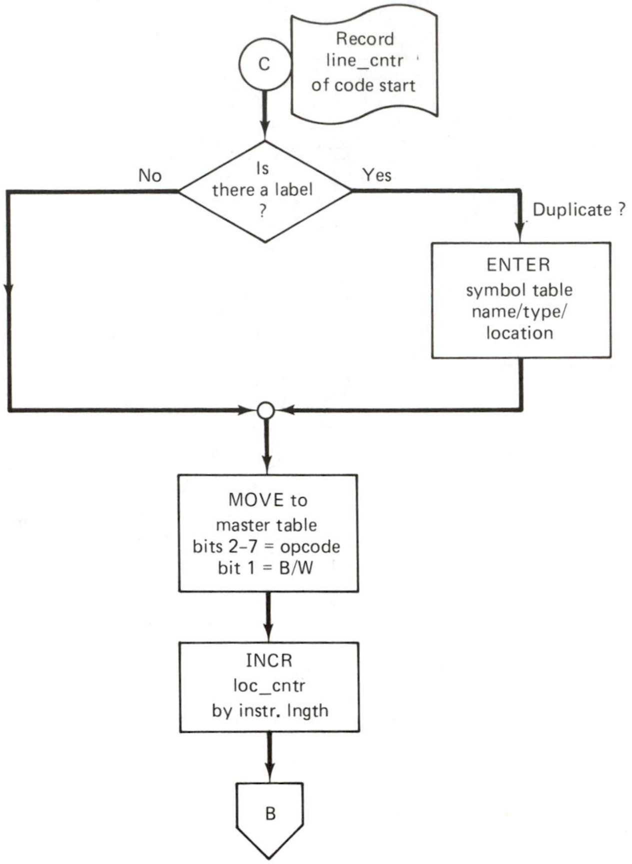

(c)

Figure 10.5 (*continued*)

References via labels to data containers for variables and for constants can be defined via pseudo-operations in the data segment and the extra (string) segment, while word-width variable areas can be defined for the stack. In our example assembly language, we specify that a data container must have a label, one of the following pseudo-operation mnemonics, and a length in the case of a variable or a value in the case of a constant. The pseudo-operation available to specify data segment containers are:

label:	WORDS	number of words
label:	BYTES	number of bytes
label:	CONSTANT	value followed by the letter B for bit, D for decimal, H for hexadecimal, or C for ASCII

Stack segment data containers are limited to word-size variable data containers whose addresses always start at the high-address end of the area and progress downward.

label:	STACK	size in words

Extra segment data containers are limited to word- or byte-indexed string containers for constant or variable data.

label:	WORDSTRG	length in words
label:	BYTESTRG	length in bytes
label:	STRGCONST	value followed by the letter indicating coding as above

Good coding practice might suggest that data containers be specified in some particular order, say external, global, data, stack, extra (string). Nevertheless, our assembler should possess the ability to interpret correctly data container definitions that occur in any order. The end of the data container definitions and the start of the code segment is signaled by the pseudo-operation CODE as shown in Figure 10.2.

Each source language input record in the CODE section consists of an optional label, an operations code, and one or two operands (with an intervening comma). The main task of PASS 1 is to assign a relative location to each label. This task requires that the length of each instruction be determined by looking up the operation code in the opcode table and then incrementing the code segment location counter appropriately. As this process makes the binary machine code version of the operations code available, it is moved to the master table at this time. Any labels are recorded in the symbol table with their relative location and a type = 6. This process continues, statement by statement, until the pseudo-operation END is found which will cause a branch to PASS 2.

PASS 2

At the conclusion of PASS 1, all processing is completed relative to label addresses and operation codes. The main tasks remaining to be accomplished in PASS 2 are the resolution of operand addresses, the output of a suitable listing, and the output of the binary machine code object file in the format expected by the link routine.

When examining the flowchart of PASS 2 shown in Figure 10.6, it should be realized that we are examining assembly language in which the syntax

Operation A,B

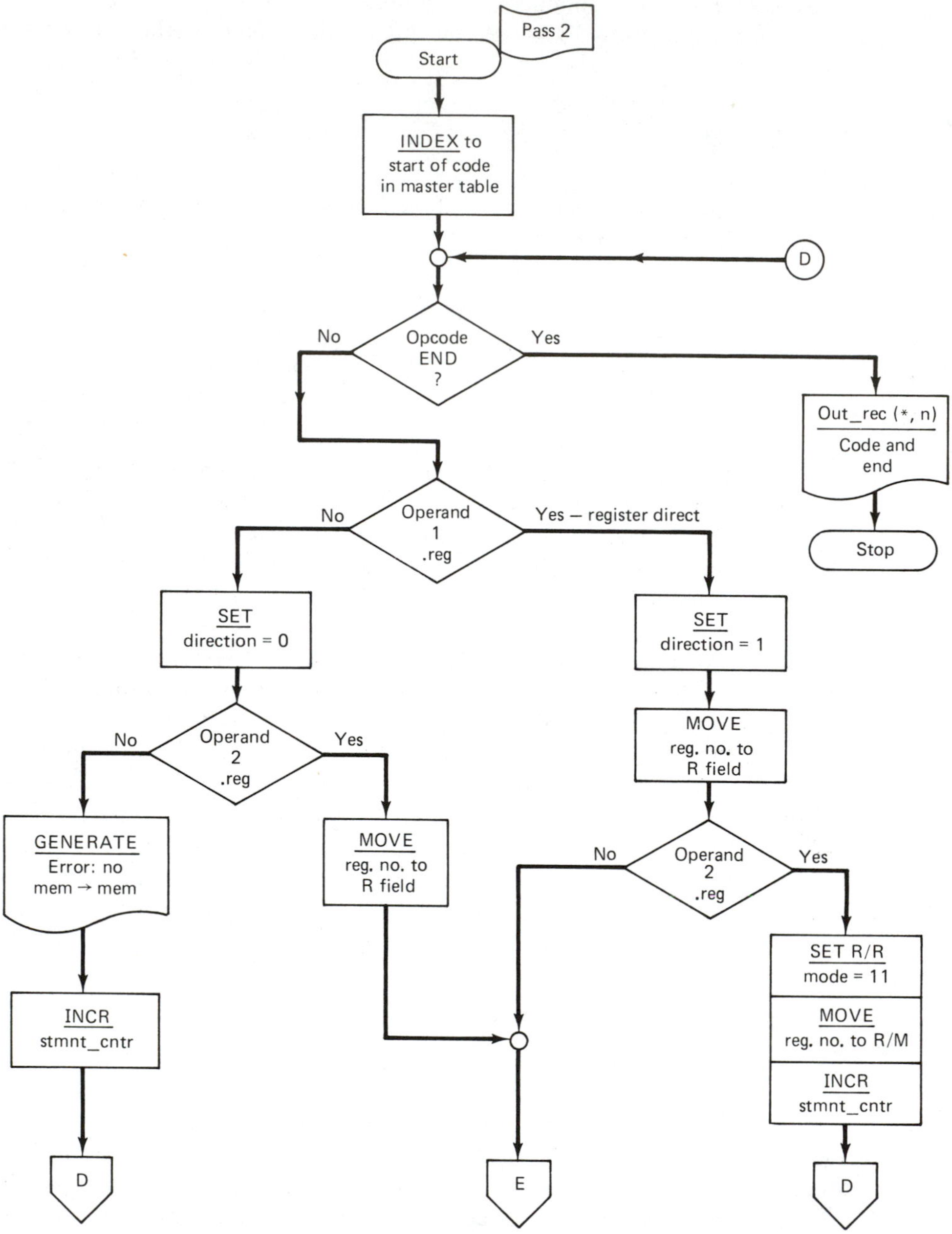

Figure 10.6 PASS 2 of assembler as discussed in the text.

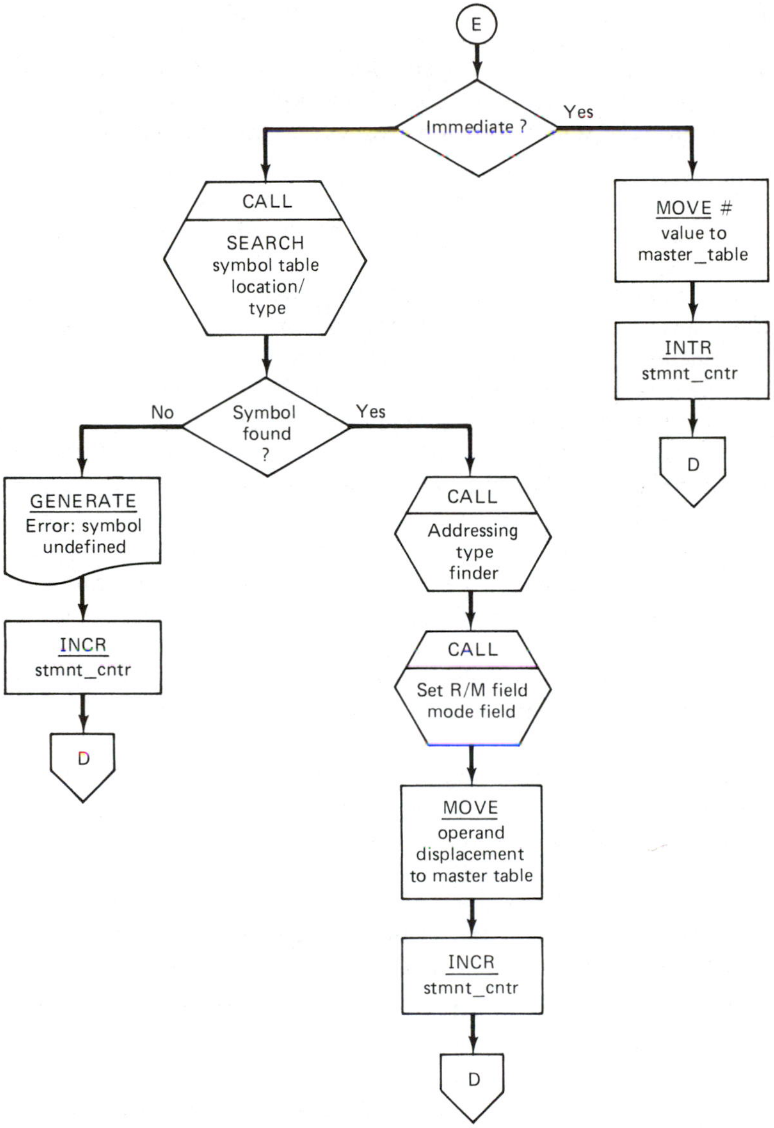

Figure 10.6 (*continued*)

has the semantics

$$A \leftarrow A + B$$

The final value of the first operand is determined by the initial value of the first operand plus the value of the second operand with no change to the second operand occurring. The source-level format must be transformed to the binary machine code format

operation, register designation, other operand designation

As only one of the operands may directly refer to memory, the other operand must specify a register (or both operands may designate registers). Note that the requirements that a register be noted first in the machine code may require a reversal of operands if source operand 1 is specified as a memory addresses. This would also require that the direction bit (following the opcode in byte 1 of the instruction) be set to zero instead of one. The most involved portion of PASS 2 is outlined in Figure 10.6*b* and involves the derivation of a memory location/displacement based on the addressing type.

When an external symbol is encountered while resolving memory addresses in PASS 2, it is necessary to record the segment relative location of the reference in the appropriate EXTRN record of the binary machine code file for use by the link routine.

When the END symbolic pseudo-operation is encountered, it is still necessary to write the binary machine object code file to an appropriate device—probably a floppy or Winchester disk—while recording the file name (procedure ID), file type (object file), physical address, and length in the library directory.

Additionally, it is also necessary to display a listing of the assembly source code with its associated relative locations, segments, and binary machine code in hexadecimal notation. Any error notations should be interspersed in this listing so that they immediately follow the statement in question. Presumably, the existence of an error would preclude the writing of the binary machine object code file to a disk-based library. On the other hand, it is often desirable to store the assembly source language version of a procedure on a disk-based library for later use and possible change.

DESIGNING A LINKER

A LINK routine must have the ability to form a single loadable object file from one or more binary machine object code files of separately assembled and/or compiled procedures. It must:

1. Transform all addresses of subprocedure reference instructions to the offset location within the concatenated code segment assigned to the subprocedure.

2. Transform all operand address references (including external references) to the offset location within the correct segment—data, stack, or extra (string)—as assigned during concatenation of the operand areas.
3. Copy the binary machine instructions and constant data into the correct locations within the correct segments of the load module binary machine code file that is ready for loading and execution.

Recall that the assembler produces as output an object file for each procedure that consists of up to eight different kinds of records (refer to Figure 10.3 to refresh your memory). One or more of these assembly-output single-procedure binary machine code object files will constitute the input to the link routine. The user of the link routine will name the main program and the system will follow the external subprocedure references in finding and incorporating the additional object files needed. The output of the link routine will be a single binary machine code load-module file.

The general design of our example link routine consists of two first-level modules: PASS 1 and PASS 2 (following traditional terminology). PASS 1 will assign addresses to the start of the code segment for each procedure and copy the object code with new offsets from the load-module start addresses. Similarly, it will assign addresses to the constants, if any, in the data and extra (string) segments and copy the values into these locations. Additionally, it will construct and maintain a symbol table containing the names of all needed procedure and external data container references, with notes as to the locations needing address information amendment later. As procedures are found (the binary machine code file is located) and as global data references within these procedures occur, the symbol table entry will be marked (global data containers will correspond to external references).

When all external references are satisfied, PASS 2 will amend the address information of the load module with the relative location of the external references as calculated in PASS 1. The linked binary machine object code file will then be cataloged and written to a floppy or Winchester disk for later loading and execution.

DATA CONTAINERS

Again, as with the assembler, the main task of PASS 1 of the linker is to resolve the addresses of data areas and of instructions, while the main task of PASS 2 is to enter these addresses into the concatenated load module. Our link routine will have one or more binary machine object code files with identical formats as input, each with multiple records as defined in Figure 10.3. The first of these files—the main program—is identified by the user when invoking the link routine. The link routine will have one binary machine code load module and an indication of successful completion or an error message as output. The format of the load module is specified in Figure 10.7. Several internal work data containers are also necessary, including a symbol table, location within segment counters, and containers to save references to external references. These are specified in Figure 10.8.

Columns 1–5	'DATA' or 'STACK' or 'EXTRA' or 'CODE'
Columns 7–11	Starting address within segment of object bytes or constant data in hexadecimal digit notation
Columns 13 and 14	Number of bytes (hexadecimal pairs) noted on this record
Columns 17–76	Hexadecimal digit pairs representing bytes of object code or constant data—30 bytes (hexadecimal pairs) allowed
Columns 78–80	Sequence number (0 to n) of record within file

Figure 10.7 Format of record within the load module file output by the link routine discussed in the text as an example.

THE LINK ROUTINE

Referring to the flowchart of the link routine in Figure 10.9, after initializing the data areas to character blanks, numeric zeros, or bit zero depending on the data type, the first processing task is initiated by the programmer via a request to execute the link routine while furnishing the name of the main program. This name is then entered into line 1 of the symbol table and a search initiated for the binary machine code object file in the catalog. Later, this search point will be returned to for each subprocedure specified by an external reference record. If the needed object file is not found, an error message is written and processing is immediately terminated.

Records from each binary machine code object file are input one by one and examined for type—one of eight PROC, EXTRN, GLOBL, DATA, STACK, EXTRA (string), CODE, or END. The first record of each object file will be a PROC

```
Declare
  SYMBOL_TABLE(999) 1,
    2 NAME CHAR(10),                  /* Procedure or external/global */
    2 TYPE FIXED DEC(1),
    2 LOCATION CHAR(4),               /* Hexadecimal within segment */
    2 FOUND BIT(1),
    2 REFERENCES CHAR(2,18);          /* Hexadecimal within */
                                      /* procedure */
Declare
  SYM_TAB_LINE_CNTR FIXED DEC(3),     /* Hexadecimal within */
  LOCATION_CNTR(2,4) CHAR(4),         /* each of four segments */
  INPUT_RECORD CHAR(80),
  OUTPUT_RECORD CHAR(999,80);
```

Figure 10.8 Necessary data areas for the link routine discussed in the text.

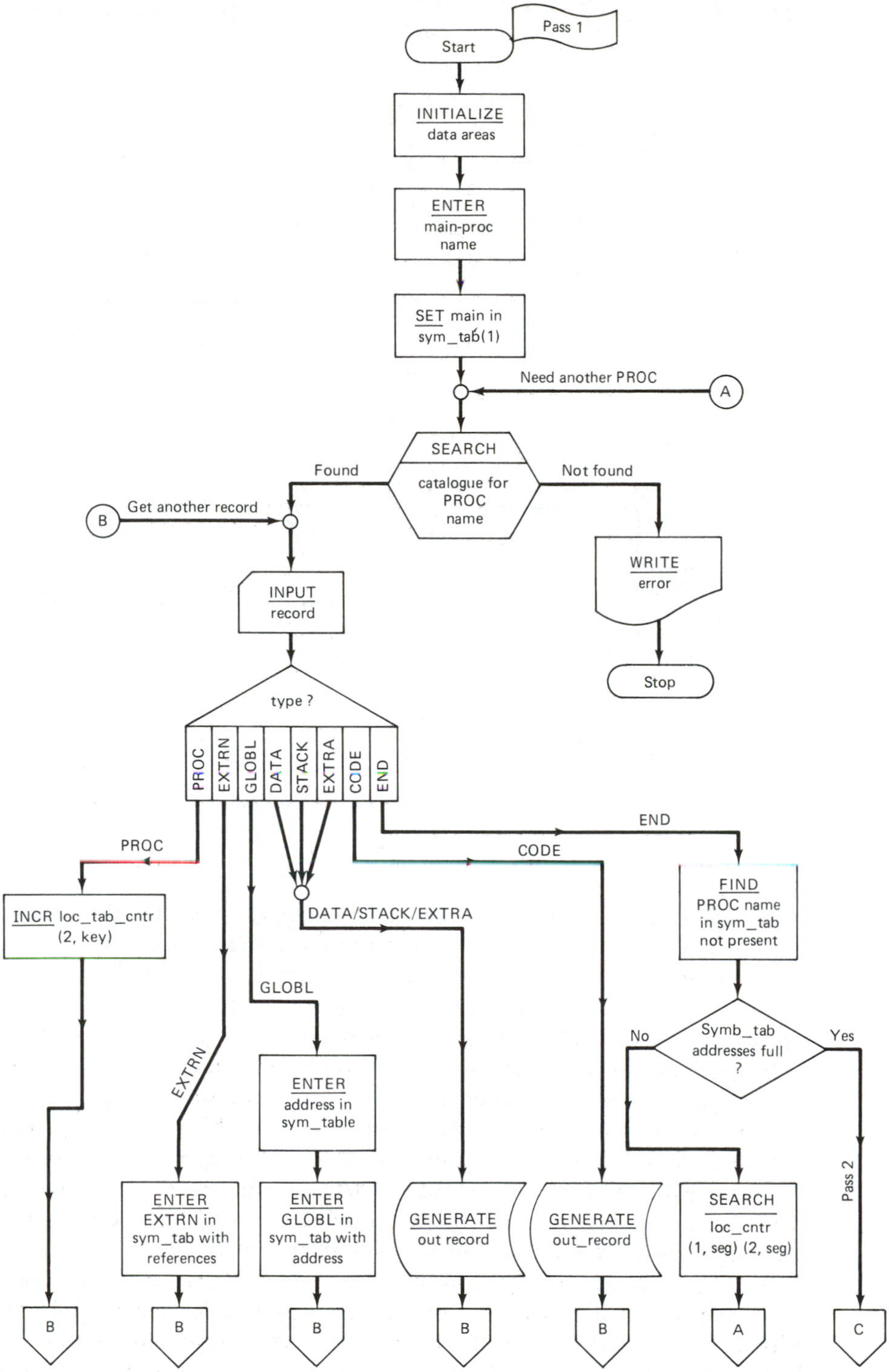

Figure 10.9 Logic of the link routine described in the text.

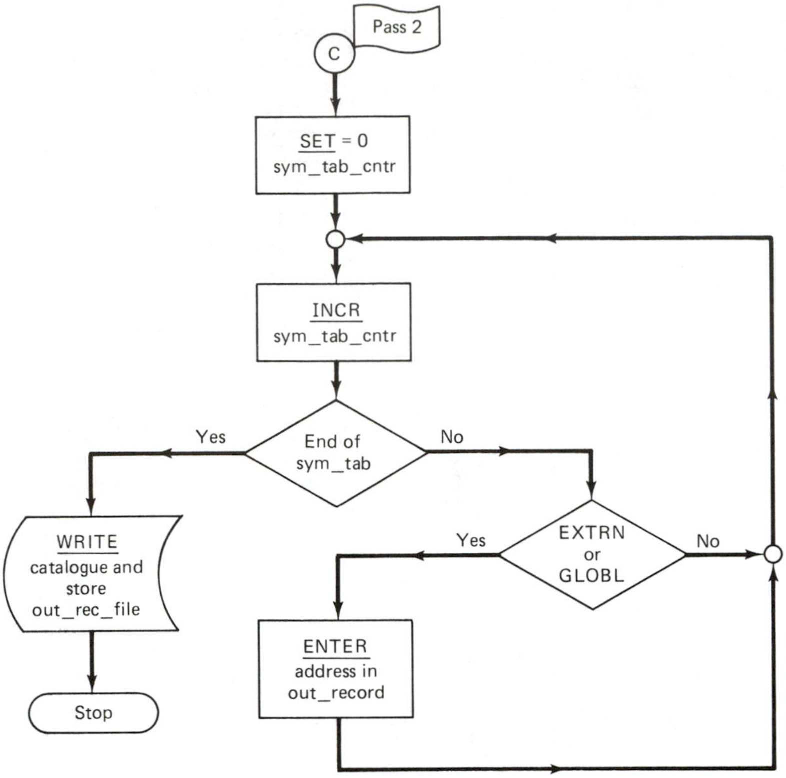

Figure 10.9 (*continued*)

record, while the last record will be an END record. The CODE records will follow the other records and immediately precede the END record. The first record (type 1 = PROC) contains the size of each segment in the procedure. These sizes are placed in the second portion of the location counters for each segment. When the procedure END (type 8) record is encountered, these segment sizes within the procedure will be added to the current start-of-segment addresses for the procedure in the first portion of the location counters to give the start of each segment for the next procedure to be linked. The next record of the current procedure is then obtained. We will briefly discuss the actions taken for each of the record types.

An EXTRN (external = type 2) record indicates that a subprocedure or a data area in another procedure is referenced as an operand by one or more instructions (and therefore locations) in the code section of this procedure. The referenced external name must be entered in the symbol table (if a reference to a data container, it may be present as a GLOBL in the symbol table) and the relative locations within the procedure segment of the references changed to locations within the linked load module segment, as well as recorded in the symbol table for use in PASS 2.

A GLOBL (global = type 3) record indicates that a data container in this procedure is being made available for reference by another procedure via an EXTRN record in another procedure. The referenced global data container name must be found in the symbol table (or entered into it, if the external reference has not yet been encountered). The relative location within the procedure segment is changed to the location within the load module segment and also recorded as the location in the symbol table for use in PASS 2.

A DATA (type 4), a STACK (type 5), or an EXTRA (type 6) record will contain the hexadecimal coding of a constant at a procedure segment location. This within-procedure load address must be changed to the correct location within the load module segment and the information placed in the output record format and thence into the load module file. Similarly, a CODE (type 7) record will have its within-procedure-segment start location transformed to a load module segment location and the code information placed in the load module file.

An END (type 8) record signifies the end of the current-procedure binary machine code object file and causes the symbol table to be searched for an external procedure name not yet linked into the load module. If such a not-yet-linked reference is found, the addresses of the start of its segments within the load module are calculated by adding the second portions of the location counters to the first portions and then transferring to the search-the-file catalog routine for the needed procedure binary machine code object file (point A in Figure 10.9). If all external procedure references have been satisfied, a branch to PASS 2 of the link routine is made.

The entire task of PASS 2 (shown in Figure 10.9*b*) is to insert linked load module locations of external references into the operand address locations of instructions referencing subprocedures or global/external data areas. This is accomplished by sequencing through the symbol table and using the load module segment reference addresses for each external reference (as recorded in the symbol table) as repositories for the load module segment addresses of the external symbol (as recorded in the symbol table).

When the entire symbol table has been processed—all external reference addresses resolved—the completely linked load module object file is ready for loading and execution. It is cataloged and stored in the file system of the I8086/8088 on a floppy or Winchester device.

MACROS AND CONDITIONAL ASSEMBLY

A programmer implementing an algorithm in assembly language often is forced to use the same fragment of code in several places within a procedure; that is, some blocks of code are repeated many times in the program. This code block may save register contents in the memory stack, perform a particular set of operations such as string reversal, invoke an operating system's I/O operation, and so on. The task of entering these repeated code fragments into the source version of a program is often faciliated by a good editor system, although excellent editors are somewhat rare. One viewpoint of a macro holds that it is a method whereby a programmer can define and use instructions that the computer designer did not include in the instruction set because of economic considerations, technical limitations, lack of programming experience, oversight, ignorance, or stupidity. Additionally, the purpose of the code block is usually not self-evident; the mnemonics of the instructions do not readily reveal the algorithmic-level task. For example, the use of the instruction

```
INT        nnn
```

invokes an interrupt that causes the interrupt server routine to perform some desirable action as indicated by the interrupt number. For this discussion, let us imagine that nnn is 47 and that the action will be the transfer of a line (with EOL) of ASCII characters from the keyboard to the input buffer in the program. Program clarity would be vastly improved by using the action mnemonics

```
GET_LINE
```

A MACRO facility is an adjunct to a basic assembler that allows the programmer to order the macro processor to substitute predefined code blocks in the place of the macro name. Thus the use of the macro name GET_LINE would cause the macro processor to substitute INT 47 into the code of the assembly procedure at that place before PASS 1 of the assembler is invoked. This process is termed *expansion* because (usually) a block of code is substituted for a macro name, with the result that the assembly procedure is expanded and enlarged.

Note that macro processing occurs before assembly and must result in assembly source code that constitutes legal input to PASS 1 of the assembler. In essence, then, a macro assembler (an assembler with the ability to expand macros) is an assembler with an appended macro processor as PASS 0. As the code block consisting of the instructions to be substituted for the macro name must be available at the time needed, it is universally required that they physically occur at the start of the procedure. Thus the overall format of the input for our example assembler, as given in Figure 10.2, must be changed to include a section for macro definitions, as shown in Figure 10.10. If the definition of a referenced macro is not found in this area, the systems library file catalog should be searched for the name and the definition added. The contents of the MACRO DEFINITION area will be ignored (but copied into the master table) during PASS 1 of the assembler. It may facilitate macro processing to remove this task to the macro processor. Our example macro assembler will follow this plan. We will insert the character "%" into column 1 of these source statements to signal PASS 1 to copy and ignore them—to treat them similarly to comments. If a label occurs in the macro definition, as is possible, the label will be moved one column to the right so that the label has the format % LABEL: . Thus the decision block in the middle of the PASS 1 flowchart of Figure 10.5*a* must also recognize the "%" character as well as the ";" character. This is the only change necessary to the assembler, although it will sometimes facilitate processing to have the master table constructed by the macroprocessor (PASS 0), as we will illustrate in our example processor.

The definition of our example macro will have the format

```
&label:MACRO    NAME(arg1,arg2,...)
     -                                  ; body of macro
     -                                  ; to be expanded
     -                                  ; and substituted
     MEND       NAME
```

where the items in lowercase letters are optional. Note that labels and/or arguments may or may not occur. (The subject of arguments will be treated soon.) A reference to a macro and thus an order to expand the definition and substitute the results at this place in the assembly source code will consist of the use of the macro name in the assembly operation code field with the arguments (if any) occurring in the operand address field (separated by commas and with no blanks; the arguments must correspond to the definition arguments in type, precision, and position):

```
label:      NAME (arg1, arg2, . . . , argn)
```

again, where the items in lowercase letters are optional.

SUBSTITUTION MACRO PROGRAMMING

We will approach the problem of communicating an understanding of the power of macro-assembly programming via examples. In its very simplest form, the use of a macro name in an assembly procedure is the use of an alias for a block of code and thus is an order to replace the macro name with the block of code. Suppose that we wish to use the following exact sequence of instructions at several points in our procedure:

```
MOV     AX,DATUM
MOV     BX,DATUM+2
MOV     CS, DATUM+4
MOV     DX,DATUM+6
```

where the data container is defined in the data segment via the pseudoinstruction

```
DATUM:      WORDS       4
```

if we defined macro as follows:

```
MACRO   LOAD_4           ; start of definition
MOV     AX,DATUM         ; body
MOV     BX,DATUM+2       ; of
MOV     CX,DATUM+4       ; macro
MOV     DX,DATUM+6       ; definition
MEND    LOAD_4           ; end of macro definition
```

we could employ the macro name as follows:

```
LOAD_4
```

as the operations code at any point in the code segment of our procedure, with the result that this macro reference (or macro call) will be expanded into and replaced by the four instructions constituting the body of the macro.

Macro Arguments

Further suppose that when our LOAD_4 macro is expanded the first time, we wish it to refer the data container named DATUM and that we require that the second use refer to THAT. This can be accomplished by employing an argument:

```
MACRO   LOAD_4(&THIS)
MOV     AX,&THIS
MOV     BX,&THIS+2
MOV     CX,&THIS+4
MOV     DX,&THIS+6
MEND    LOAD_4
```

To expand this macro with the memory operand referring to DATUM, we would use

```
LOAD_4   DATUM
```

while reference to the data container THIS would be

```
LOAD_4   THIS
```

resulting in the substitution of code in the two references placed as follows:

First Reference		Second Reference	
MOV	AX,DATUM	MOV	AX,THIS
MOV	BX,DATUM+2	MOV	BX,THIS+2
MOV	CX,DATUM+4	MOV	CX,THIS+4
MOV	DX,DATUM+6	MOV	DX,THIS+6

Multiple arguments are sometimes useful:

```
MACRO   LOAD_4(&HERE,&THERE,&HOME,&AWAY)
MOV     AX,&HERE
MOV     BX,&THERE
MOV     CX,&HOME
MOV     DX,&AWAY
MEND    LOAD_4
```

In this case, also note that the addressing-mode portion of the memory resident operand data container may be specified in the macro reference:

```
LOAD_4    DATA 1,(BX),123H,(DI)
```

Additionally, note that a register reference may be specified in an argument.

Labels may be specified in an argument as follows:

```
          MACRO    STORE_4 (&LABEL,&SAVE)
&LABEL:   MOV      &SAVE+0,AX
          MOV      &SAVE+2,BX
          MOV      &SAVE+4,CX
          MOV      &SAVE+6,DX
          MEND     &STORE_4
```

The expansion reference in the program could be

```
STORE_4        LOOP,DATA_AREA
```

Label arguments are often necessary to overcome the problem of duplicate labels being forwarded in the expanded source code as input to PASS 1. Also note that arguments may occur in either or both operand positions, the first (the to) operand or the second (the from) operand. The problem of duplicate labels within the several expanded versions of a multiply referenced macro with internal labels is often very bothersome. Some macro processors provide a facility for *generating unique labels.* This can be illustrated as

```
          MACRO    STORE_4(&LABEL#,&SAVE)
&LABEL#:  MOVW     &SAVE+0,AX
          MOVW     &SAVE+2,BX
          MOVW     &SAVE+4,CX
          MOVW     &SAVE+6,DX
          MEND     STORE_4
```

where the '#' character appended to the label argument causes a system-incremented number to be inserted during each expansion of the macro. Thus the first reference,

```
STORE_4      LOOP#,DATA_AREA
```

will expand with the label LOOP1, while the next call,

```
STORE_4      LOOP#,THERE
```

will have the label LOOP2, and so on.

Macro References within Macros

In some programming situations, it is highly desirable to allow one macro to refer to another macro within its body. As an example, in the Intel 8086/8088, which is somewhat limited in numbers of data registers, it may often be desirable to save the contents of certain registers to allow their alternative use for other purposes. Later, it may be desirable to restore or load the initial contents back while saving the (then) current contents. A macro to exchange register contents can be constructed using the previously defined two macros: LOAD_4 and STORE_4.

```
MACRO      EXCH_4 (&NEW_SAVE,&OLD_SAVE)
STORE_4    &NEW_SAVE
LOAD_4     &OLD_SAVE
MEND       EXCH_4
```

This macro would be referenced in the assembly language source code as

```
EXCH_4      OLD_REG_AREA,NEW_REG_AREA
```

and would generate eight instructions and substitute them into the source code for input into PASS 1 of the assembler.

Instruction Variation with Macros

It is usually possible to control the length specifier of the registers operands within a macro so as to have word or byte instructions generated into the expanded version. We will use the LOAD_4 example employed previously:

```
MACRO      LOAD_4(&WHICH,&DATA)
MOV        A&WHICH,&DATA
MOV        B&WHICH,&DATA+2
MOV        C&WHICH,&DATA+4
MOV        D&WHICH,&DATA+6
MEND       STORE_4
```

If this macro is called

```
LOAD_4     'X',FROM_AREA
```

the expanded version substituted into the assembly code for input by PASS 1 of the assembler would be exactly as illustrated previously. On the other hand, if this macro is called

```
LOAD_4     'L',.FROM_AREA
```

the expanded version will be

```
MOV        AL,FROM_AREA
MOV        BL,FROM_AREA+2
MOV        CL,FROM_AREA+4
MOV        DL,FROM_AREA+6
```

Note that the AH, BH, CH, and DH byte registers are not changed and that the FROM_AREA+1, . . . +3, . . . +5, and . . . +7 bytes of the memory resident data are not involved.

Thus it is true that a macro assembler could allow any and all portions of a macro to be varied during expansion through the use of appropriate arguments. This could include the whole operations code or the necessary portions of any or all instruction. Similarly, this expansion variation via arguments could include the entire symbolic operand reference, only the addressing mode portion, or only the length specifier of any or all instructions. Although most macro processors do not provide for this extreme argument substitution freedom during expansion, the usual limitations are not normally onerous or particularly limiting for program composition.

CONDITIONAL ASSEMBLY PROGRAMMING

Conditional macro expansion provides a powerful tool to control which instructions are generated by the macro processor into the expanded code that is input to PASS 1 of the assembler. Although there is no processing reason why conditional assembly could not be allowed within non-macro-assembly source code, it often has been limited to macro generation. The macro assembler for the IBM/360, the IBM/370, the IBM 434X, and the IBM 303X extended computer family allows many aspects of conditional assembly in nonmacro contexts. The usual limitation of conditional assembly to the macro processor does provide a convenient, but not necessary location for the translation process and does prevent the "cluttering up" of PASS 1 of the assembler. Additionally, no real program composition limitation results, as any portion of an assembly program can be presented by the programmer to the macro assembler as a macro. Indeed, the entire procedure may be defined as a macro.

Conditional Directives

With your attention focused on the fact that conditional assembly occurs during the generation of code that will later be processed by PASS 1 of the assembler, we emphasize that the two basic conditional directives are AIF and AGO. By using these two directives, it is possible to construct loops that repeat blocks of code (identical repeats or repeats with variations), that skip blocks of code, that choose between alternate blocks of code, and so on. That is, the conditional branch and the absolute branch provide the means to build an arbitrarily complex flow of statement expansion during macro processing. The latter generalization is not unexpected, as it is also true of all algorithmic processes. Note that we are pointing out that although such conditional assembly directives as ACASE, ALOOP, AREPEAT, ASTOP, and so on, may exist in some macro assembler systems, they are unnecessary—but nice. As the usage of such additional directives is somewhat obvious from their mnemonic name, we will restrict our discussion to the AGO and AIF as well as the associated syntax for specifying expansion-time labels (which will not appear in the generated code), the expansion-time conditional operations, and the creation/use of expansion-time constants and variables. Although the AGO expansion-time directive is simpler, its use is easier to comprehend after an understanding of the AIF. Therefore, we treat the AIF first.

The AIF Conditional Assembly Directive

The generalized format of this conditional branch expansion-time directive is

```
Label:  AIF (condition) action
```

where

1. The label starts in column 1, and may consist of a "permanent" label that will occur in the code passed to PASS 1 of the assembler or may be an expansion-time label of the form .LABEL (starting with a period and alphabetic character and not longer than 10 characters in total).
2. The AIF occupies the operations code field.
3. The condition is enclosed in parentheses and always explicitly specifies a comparison: EQ, NE, LT, GT, LE, or GE, with the usual meaning. The operands of this expansion-time conditional can involve the macro arguments, expansion-time variables, or expansion-time constants. Depending on the type of the conditional operands, the operations +, −, *, /, & (and), | (or), and | | (concatenate or join end to end) may be employed within an operand to be evaluated at expansion time.

4. The action is performed if, and only if, the conditional expression evalutes to true. Only one action is allowed and thus the AIF resembles the FORTRAN logical IF and *does not resemble* the more powerful IF-THEN-ELSE. In effect, the AIF specifies a "do the action if true" or "skip the action if false" expansion-time operation. Two general actions are possible:
   a. Conditional branch to a label within the macro of the permanent or expansion-time type. In this case the AIF becomes an AIF (true) go-to or AIF (false) continue.
   b. Perform the single action specified, such as increment a variable. The action would be of the form

      &Variable = expression

      and can only involve an expansion-time variable on the left-hand side. The right-hand-side expression can include the operation/operand complications allowed within a conditional expression operand (see rule 3).

The AGO Conditional Assembly Directive

The generalized format of this unconditional branch expansion-time directive is

```
Label:      AGO      Label of branch target
```

where the label and the AGO follow rules 1 and 2 of the AIF, while the branch target label follows rule 4a of the AIF for labels.

Expansion-Time Conditional Assembly Labels

Expansion-time labels are signified by the first character being a period, the second character being a letter, and the entire label being 10 or fewer characters in length. The entire purpose of expansion-time labels is to serve as branch targets for the AIF and AGO conditional assembly directives. In some programming situations, algorithm construction is facilitated by branching to an expansion-time label of a dummy statement. This could be accomplished by the use of the operation code NOP (no operation), but this solution would result in one byte of useless code appearing in the final binary object machine code. For this reason, some macro processors furnish the conditional assembly directive ANOP for use in these circumstances.

```
.Label:      ANOP
```

The ANOP conditional assembly directive fully corresponds to the CONTINUE statement in FORTRAN.

Algorithm construction also is sometimes facilitated by the ability to branch (AIF or AGO) directly to the MEND statement and thus terminate expansion of the macro immediately. The use of a labeled ANOP immediately preceding the MEND statement will allow this. Alternatively, some macro processors make available the conditional assembly directive MEXIT. It can be used with either the AIF or AGO:

```
AGO     MEXIT
AIF     (condition) MEXIT
```

and results in the immediate termination of the expansion of the macro.

Expansion-Time Conditional Assembly Data

Constant values for use only at expansion time are specified by the occurrence of the constant value. In other words, as in almost all computer languages, constants are self-naming. The coding of the value is indicated by a letter appended on the right—B = binary; D = decimal; F = floating point; H = hexadecimal—enclosed in quotes with an appended B for bit; or in the case of ASCII, by enclosing the character string in single or double quotation marks. The following are examples of legal macro expansion-time constant values:

```
1001B      = 9 decimal numeric
987D       = 987 decimal numeric
7.3F       = 7.3 floating-point numeric
7AH        = 122 decimal numeric
'0'B       = logical false
'GEORGE'   = ASCII string
```

Variable data containers are usually, but not always, restricted to scalar-size areas, and thus the use of arrays or structures is not commonly provided for. All variable data containers are declared by setting them equal to an appropriate constant using an expansion-time directive, as in the following three examples:

```
&Variable:   SET     1001B
&FALSE:      SET     '0'B
&NAME:       SET     'GEORGE'
```

Changes to the contents of a variable data container are also accomplished by the SET assembly time directive:

```
&COUNTER:   SET     &COUNTER+1
&ALPHA:     SET     &NAME| | 'b'| | 'GORSLINE'
```

All of the operations allowed within the AIF condition operand evaluation (see rule 3 in that section) are normally allowed. Thus we would expect the operations +, −, *, /, &, | , and | | as well as parentheses to be valid. The right-hand-side expression of a SET directive statement can contain expansion-time constants, expansion-time variables, and/or macro arguments.

Example

```
             MACRO    LOAD_REGS(&NUM,&SAV)
             AIF      (&NUM LT 0d).ERROR
             AIF      (&NUM GT 14d).ERROR
             AIF      (&NUM EQ 0d)MEXIT
&COUNT:      SET      0d
&REGS:       SET      'AX','BX','CX','DX','SP','BP',
                      'SI','DI','CS','DS','SS','ES',
                      'IP','FLAGS'
.LOOP:       MOV      &REGS(&COUNT),&DATA+
                      &COUNT
&COUNT:      SET      &COUNT+1d
             AIF      (&COUNT GE &NUM)MEXIT
             AGO      .LOOP
.ERROR:      ANOTE    '*****'
             ANOTE    'MACRO ARGUMENT WRONG'
             ANOTE    '*****'
&SYSERROR:   SET      '1'b
             MEND     LOAD_REGS
```

This example contains two new constructs available in many macro processors: (1) the use of the conditional assembly directive ANOTE to cause a single line consisting of the alphanumeric constant in the operand field to be placed in the assembly listing, and (2) the use of a systems variable to communicate a condition to the macro-assembler system (in this case, we choose &SYSERROR as the vehicle to inform the assembly system that the object file should not be stored, so that loading and execution would not be attempted).

This example conditional assembly macro could be called using

```
LOAD_REGS      NUMBER,SAVE_AREA
```

provided that the data container NUMBER had previously been given a value between zero and 14, indicating the number of registers to be loaded from the data container SAVE_AREA consisting of the same number of words.

DESIGNING A MACRO PROCESSOR

The four tasks that a macro processor must accomplish are:

1. *Recognize the macro definition* by the word delimiters MACRO and MEND. In our example, this task is simplified by the requirement that all macro definitions immediately follow the PROCEDURE statement and precede the DATA areas. Intervening comments are allowed as shown in Figure 10.10. Note that our example processor will not correctly process nested macro definitions, although it will allow macro references (calls) within macro definitions to an arbitrary depth.
2. *Save the definition* for use during the expansion process. In our example, the definitions will be placed in the master table together with all of the source program statements, comments, and expanded references. Thus this task is being removed from PASS 1 of the assembler and accomplished by the macro processor—PASS 0. The assembler flowchart in Figure 10.5 will be affected. A table of macro names must also be constructed. We will allow macro definitions to occur in the systems library and be incorporated into the macro source code by defining a macro pseudo-operation

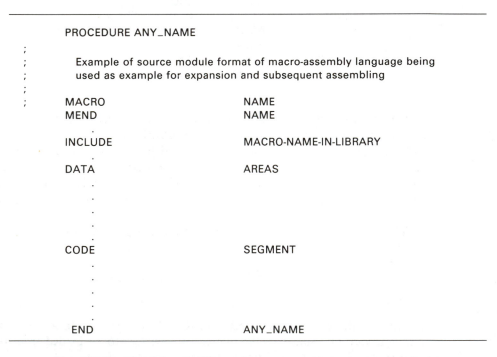

```
      PROCEDURE ANY_NAME
;
;       Example of source module format of macro-assembly language being
;       used as example for expansion and subsequent assembling
;
;     MACRO                    NAME
      MEND                     NAME
        .
      INCLUDE                  MACRO-NAME-IN-LIBRARY
        .
      DATA                     AREAS
        .
        .
        .
        .
        .
      CODE                     SEGMENT
        .
        .
        .
        .
        .
       END                     ANY_NAME
```

Figure 10.10 Overall format of the source macro-assembly language module for input into the macro assembler described in the text.

INCLUDE NAME

that will cause the system program library to be searched and the referenced macro definition to be inserted into the procedures.

3. *Recognize macro references* (calls) within the DATA areas and within the CODE segment. This will require that the symbolic contents of the operations code field of every statement be searched for in the macro names table constructed in task 2. As our example macro processor allows macro references within macro definitions, this search will also be required for each expanded statement generated in task 4.
4. *Expand macro references* (calls) while following the conditional assembly directives and substituting symbolic values for dummy macro arguments found within the body of the definition. As each expanded statement is generated, it must be entered into the master table as a sequential portion of the source code that will be assembled by PASS 1.

A careful examination of the tasks of macro processer (PASS 0) and of the assembler PASS 1 of our example should reveal that no incompatible tasks exist. Thus it would be possible to combine the macro processer (PASS 0) into the assembler PASS 1 and perhaps shorten total assembly time at the expense of clarity. We will not follow this approach but will keep the macro processor functionally separated from our basic assembler.

DATA CONTAINERS

Recalling that the vital task of PASS 0—the macro processor—is to substitute the conditionally expanded macro definitions into the assembly source program at the macro reference (call) points, we will require input data containers, temporary work data areas, and output data containers. Our example macro processor will need two inputs:

1. The assembly language source code module.
2. If any library resident macros are referenced, these macro definitions are required to be in the program library.

Our assembler will produce as output:

1. An augmented version of the source code in the master table with the INCLUDED library resident macro definitions, the conditionally expanded macro references, and any notes encountered via ANOTE directives. The definition and reference (call) statements will be marked with a "%" in column 1.
2. A bit variable indicating success or failure of the macro processor.

Our example PASS 0 (macro processor) will use two data containers as work areas during processing:

1. A macro name table that will be dynamically built as macro definitions and INCLUDE directives are encountered. This table of macro names will be used in task 3 to allow recognition of macro references (calls).
2. An argument list table that will be built from the macro reference (call) and used to facilitate substitution of actual for dummy arguments during macro expansion. If nested macro references (a call within a definition) are encountered, this table will be augmented using a special character to separate the different argument groups. These groups will be created and destroyed using a stack discipline.

PASS 0 MACRO PROCESSING

Although it is usual to divide a macro processor into PASS 1 and PASS 2, our source language requirement that all macro definitions occur before the data areas and the code segment, together with our use of the master table for storing the bulk of the information, have allowed us to consider the macro processor as a single processor—PASS 0. This design also allows us to relax completely the usual restriction that macro definitions that are referenced within a macro definition must physically precede the referencing macro definition. In essence, the traditional PASS 1 is contained in Figure 10-11*a* and the traditional PASS 2 (the expansion phase) occupies Figure 10.11*b* and *c*.

Figure 10.11*a* gives the logic of PASS 0A of our example macro processor. The main task of this portion is to identify macro definitions whether they be library resident (INCLUDE) or occur in the source file. All macro definitions are transferred *in toto* to the master table for later use during the expansion phase, with column 1 being made a "%" character as a signal for the assembler routine (PASS 1 and PASS 2) to ignore them. Additionally, the macro name is entered into the macro name table together with the line number of the definition in the master table to aid the expansion phase in locating the definition when needed. The end-of-procedure statement is also found (presumably after the expansion phase) and serves as the signal that macro processing is complete. A transfer to PASS 1 of the assembler then occurs.

An important element of the traditional two-pass macro processor will occur after all macro definitions have been found and copied to the master table as determined by encountering a DATA AREA or CODE SEGMENT statement. Each operations code must be identified as a macro reference (call) or as a symbolic assembly opcode of a normal instruction for the I8086/8088. Our design searches the (now complete) macro name table for this purpose. A failure of this search is assumed to indicate a normal assembly statement, which is then copied *in toto* to the master table for later assembly by PASS 1 and PASS 2. A search success indicates a

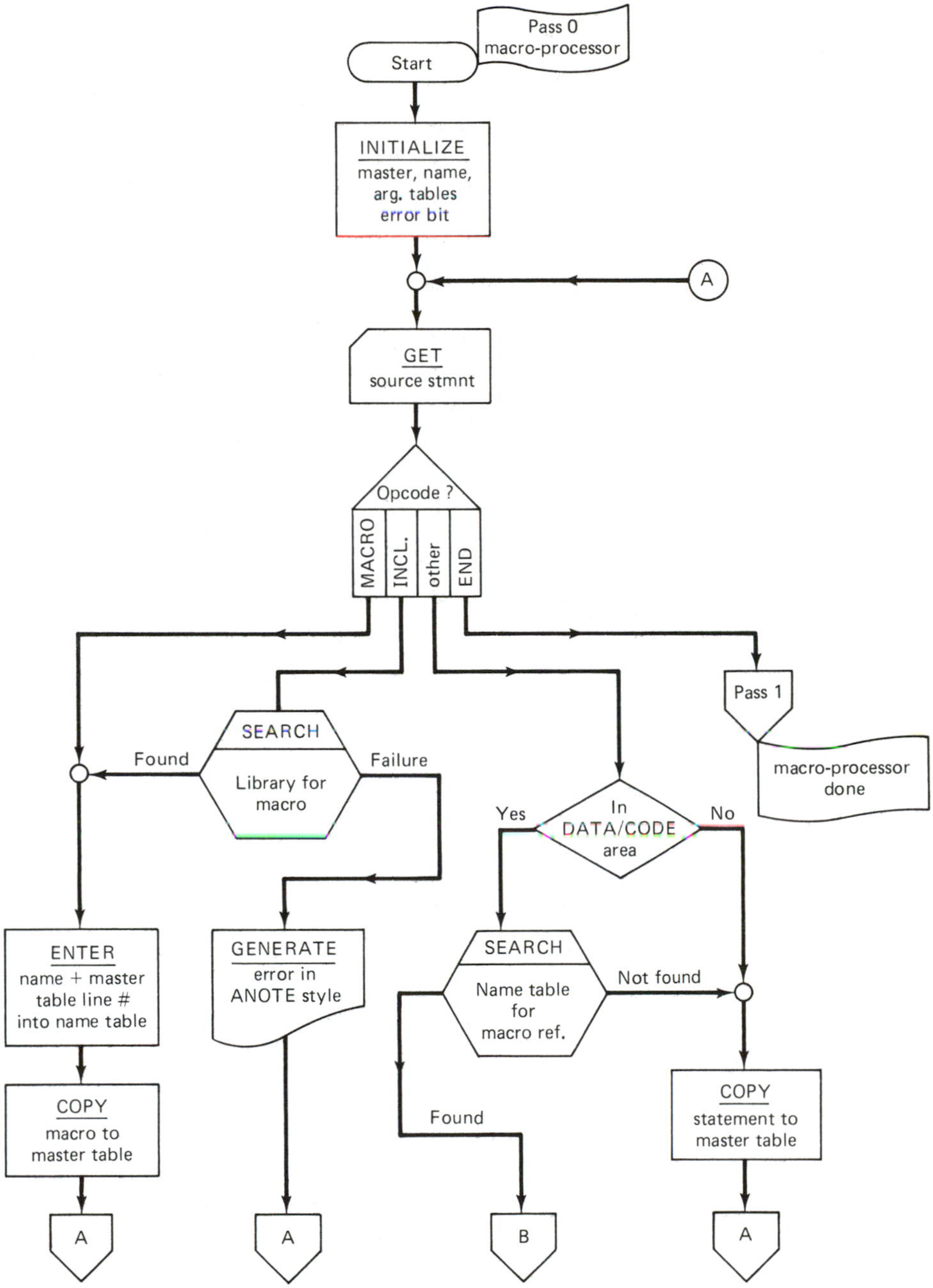

Figure 10.11 Flow diagram of the macroprocessor (PASS 0) discussed in the text.

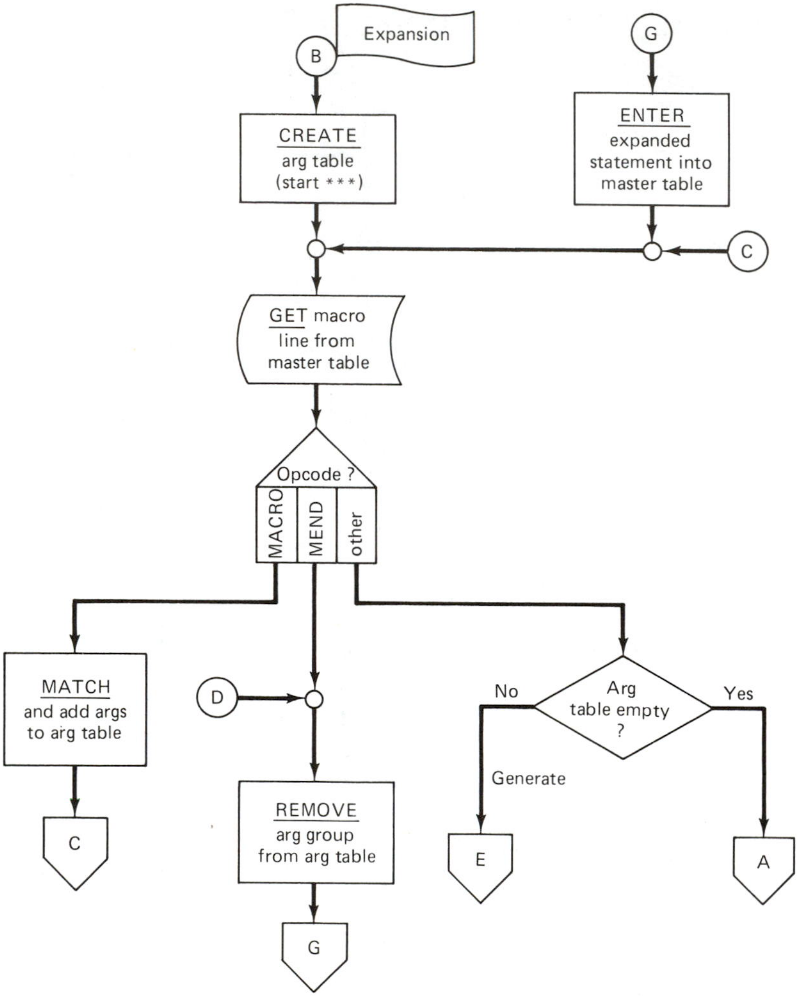

(b)

Figure 10.11 *(continued)*

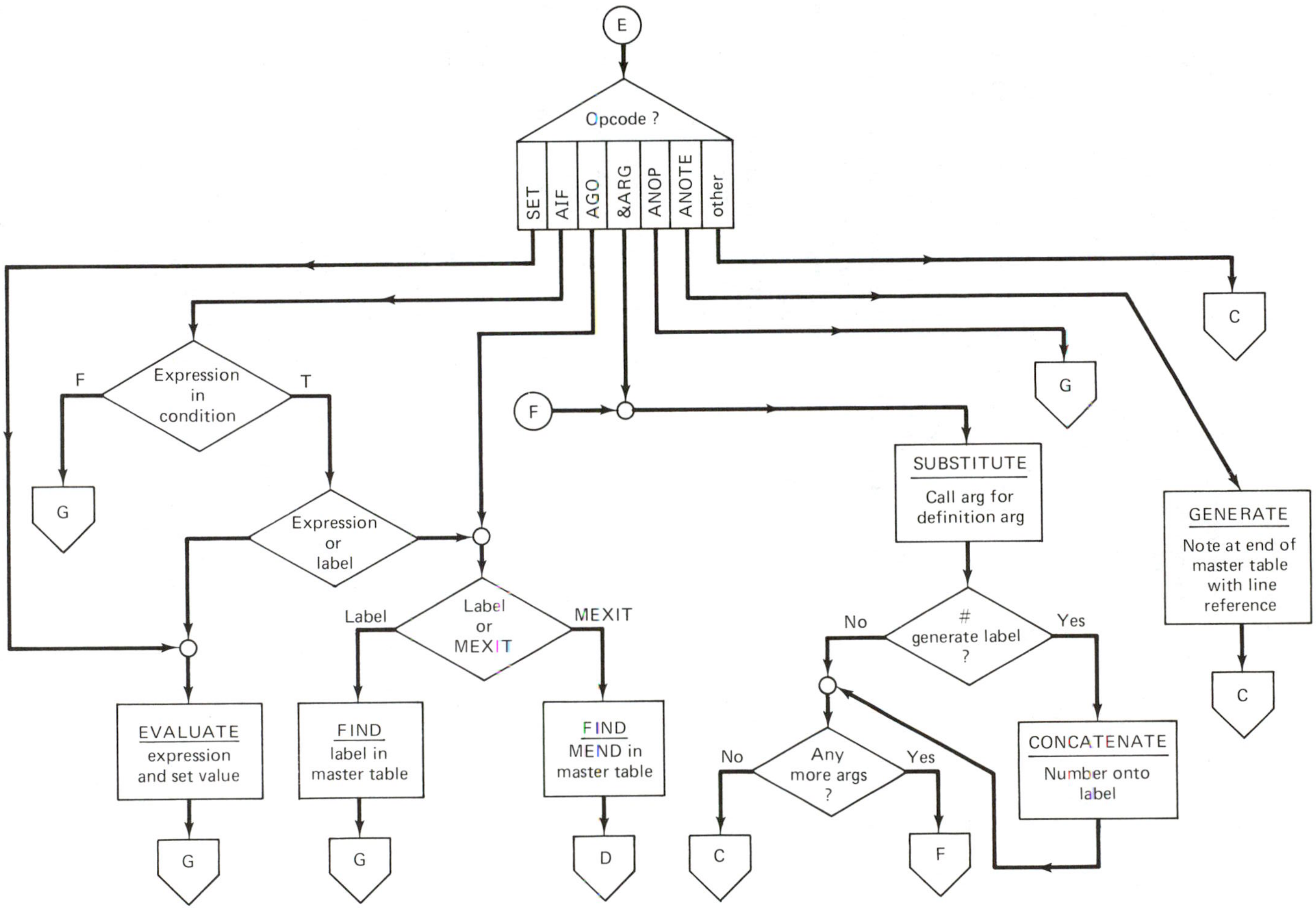

(c)

Figure 10.11 *(continued)*

macro reference (call) and therefore invokes the expansion phase, as shown in Figure 10.11*b* and *c*.

The first task of the expansion phase is the construction of an argument table with one entry for each argument of the macro reference in occurrence order and indexed by position. As our design allows macro references within macro definitions, this table may contain, at any instant, arguments from more than one macro. Therefore, the end of argument group for a macro is marked by a series of asterisks for identification purposes. Note that these argument names are those employed by the programmer in the reference (call) and are different from the dummy argument names used in the macro definition. These dummy names are also entered into the argument table in their respective positions during expansion processing of the MACRO statement of the definition (left-hand side of Figure 10.11*b*).

The argument groups in the argument table with embedded macro references form a sort of stack. Therefore, when a MEND (end of macro definition) statement is found, an argument group is removed from the table (up to an asterisk line) as shown in the center bottom of Figure 10.11*b*. The occurrence of an asterisk group as the last entry in the argument table is used as the test (right-hand side of Figure 10.11*b*) to determine if another macro definition statement should be obtained from the master table (transfer to point E in Figure 10.11*c*) or if another statement should be input from the programmer-furnished assembly source code (transfer to point A in Figure 10.11*a*).

The actual macro expansion is illustrated in Figure 10.11*c*. Each expanded statement is entered into the master table at point C in Figure 10.11*b* just before the next line of the current macro definition is obtained for expansion. The actions that are processed by the different macro definition directives are given from left to right in Figure 10.11*c*.

The *SET* directive invokes a routine to evaluate the expression in the operand field. This interpretive routine must recognize parentheses and initiate evaluation at the point of deepest nesting. Arithmetic expression evaluation in our example will follow the rules of FORTRAN, BASIC, Pascal, and PL/I arithmetic expressions, with the limitations that macro references are not allowed and all constants and variables must be of the same type (all integer or all floating point and all of the same precision). The operations allowed are +, −, *, /, and ( ). The storage receptacle in the label position must also agree in type and precision. Logical expression evaluation also follows the same rules, with the operators allowed being &, | , XOR, NOT, and ( ) (and, or, exclusive or, not, parentheses). ASCII character string expressions may contain the concatenate operator "| | ." It is important to note that we are allowing one-dimensional data containers as defined earlier. A reference to a specific array element is accomplished as

```
&ARRAY(subscript)
```

where the subscript can be constant or an &variable derived from a SET statement or from an argument. For processing simplicity—to disallow the evaluate routine from invoking the evaluate routine (a recursive routine invocation)—we are not allowing expression subscripts.

The *AIF* directive first invokes the expression evaluation routine to evaluate a TRUE (do the right-hand-side operand) or a FALSE (proceed to the next macro definition line) condition. If the AIF condition expression is true, the operand can be either an expression (equivalent and treated exactly like a SET directive) or a label. In the case of a label, an expansion-time go-to is implied that results in a search within the macro definition in the master table for the label and subsequent expansion of that statement. Note that the branch target may be MEXIT, signifying a branch to the MEND statement.

The *AGO* directive results in a search for the label and subsequent expansion of the target macro definition statement. Again, the branch may be to the MEND statement.

The *&ARG* directive directs the expansion phase to search the argument table for the dummy macro definition argument and replace it with the reference (call) actual argument. Additionally, any LABEL# generation situations will result in appending an incremented systems number in the place of the # directive. Note that the &ARG directive may repeatedly be invoked for any one macro definition statement (point F in Figure 10.11*c*).

The *ANOTE* directive causes this macro definition line to be appended at the end of the master table with a reference to the line number involved. As the position of the end of the master table is not known at this time (expansion is not completed), temporary storage with subsequent appending is necessary.

All other macro definition statements are copied *in toto* directly into the master table.

11

Procedural-Level Languages

One of the many definitions of a language is: any method of communicating ideas, as by a system of signs, symbols, gestures, or the like. This very broad definition seems to include a written and oral message between human beings, a fist fight, the depression of the accelerator of an automobile, the release of a specific pheromone by an animal, as well as the set of computer commands that we term a program. Some of these examples involve natural systems that developed over time without plan or direction. Some of these examples involve human-made systems where the communication method and its parameters received thought and design effort. Some of these examples involve elements of unplanned development constrained by elements of social acceptability or technological limitations.

As you have recognized, this extremely broad view of languages is not particularly helpful when considering the immediate question of communicating with a computing machine regarding what actions to accomplish in what order with what data and how to report the results—be it a printout, the opening of a valve, or some other presumably desirable result. Programming languages, however, do have several distinguishing characteristics that are worth noting:

1. They are artificial languages that were deliberately designed to fulfill a need to communicate an algorithm and data to a computer.
2. They are subject to change and augmentation as the result of experience; that is, currently used computer languages are "live" languages. This is not to say that "dead" computer languages do not exist in the sense that Latin is a "dead" language; they do exist, as is shown by the IT language for the IBM 650 computer.

3. Programming languages have dialects associated with each translator for each computer model. On the other hand, there is (usually) an accepted "standard" syntax and associated semantics as well as a preferred pragmatics for each language.
4. Although programming languages are designed to facilitate human-to-machine communications, the universal need for program modification and correction has resulted in a common and continued use of them for human-to-human communication. Thus the modern pragmatics of programming emphasizes clarity and human understandability.

LEVELS OF PROGRAMMING LANGUAGES

In Chapter 1 we presented the concept of micro control and showed how each instruction consists of a number of instruction steps. Figures 1.12 and 1.13 gave the sequence of instruction steps for the add immediate instruction of a hypothetical simple microcomputer ignoring interrupts. It is common to implement the microcontrol sequencing of instruction steps in pure hardware. Alternatively, it is common to implement these instruction steps as a small routine programmed on a more primitive "host" computer. This lowest level of programming is termed *microprogramming* and the languages employed are known as *microprogramming languages.* At least some of the instructions and other functions of the I8086/8088 are implemented via microprogramming.

We have discussed *binary machine code* and the impracticability of human beings employing it to communicate algorithms to a computer. In Chapter 10, we presented a *symbolic assembly language,* an example two-pass assembly routine, the concept of a *macro assembly language,* and conditional assembly, together with the design of a macro processor.

At the beginning and throughout Chapter 3, we presented fragments of a *procedural-level language* as a vehicle for learning the flow-of-program-control instructions of the I8086/8088. In using this teaching technique, we were following the maxim of building on already known material in presenting new material. Thus we were assuming that the IF-THEN-ELSE, DO WHILE, and so on, were either already known or so naturally understandable that they would be clear. A procedural language allows the programmer to concentrate on the solution steps of the problem while largely ignoring the computing machine itself, that is, to concentrate on the task of problem solving while allowing a translator (a compiler) to assign registers, memory locations, and so on.

In the very last few years, the idea of *functional languages* (Backus, 1978) has generated a good deal of interest, work, and publicity. At least one of my respected fellow workers (Earl Schweppe, University of Kansas, personal communication) has termed it the third and most important contribution of John Backus, the first two being FORTRAN and the Backus–Naur form. Functional programming is still experimental and lacks available languages for solving real-world problems. We must therefore ignore it in this text.

In summary, the levels of computer languages that we have noted are:

Language level	Language statements		Computer instructions
Microprogramming	Many	to	One
Binary machine code	One	to	One
Assembly language	One	to	One
Macro assembly language	One	to	Many
Procedural language	One	to	Many

PROCEDURAL-LEVEL LANGUAGES

Sammet (1969) has defined what we are terming a procedural language as having four characteristics:

1. The programmer need have no knowledge of the binary machine code or of the assembly language of the computer, although such knowledge may be helpful in producing efficient programs.
2. The procedural language must be largely machine independent; that is, a given source form of a program must be able to be compiled and executed successfully on two different vendor or model computers with a minimum of changes.
3. The source form of a procedural language is close to and very similar to the notation of the applications area, in contrast to assembly language. Middle school, secondary school, and college students have little difficulty with the meaning of the statement

   ```
   A ← (B + C) * D
   ```

   but find the following I8086/8088 assembly code more difficult:

   ```
   MOV     AX,B
   ADD     AX,C
   MULT    AX,D
   MOV     A,AX
   ```

4. The compilation—the translation—of the source form of a procedural language normally results in the generation of several binary machine code instructions, as illustrated in point 3.

Ease of learning is the primary advantage of procedural languages. This follows from the somewhat "natural" and "applications-oriented" notation. On the other hand, some procedural languages are quite complex, whereas others are quite wordy. Nevertheless, more attention can be given to the problem itself than to the idiosyncrasies of the physical hardware.

The second important advantage of procedural languages follows from the somewhat natural and brief notation. As the program is smaller and easier to understand in its more natural source form, it is easier to compose correct programs, to debug incorrect ones, to change and enhance them, and to transfer them to new computers. Additionally, the probability of locating, obtaining, and using a program from someone else is enhanced. Programmer-to-programmer communication is vastly improved.

In summary, the advantages of procedural languages amount to large savings in programmer costs, implementation time, and maintenance effort—all equivalent to significant reductions in total costs and schedules. Alternatively, compilers may be slow, produce binary machine code that is large and slow, be error prone, not provide execution time error help for debugging, and be expensive. As none of these disadvantages are necessary, or common, for a popular language compiler for a popular computer such as the I8086/8088, they should be discounted. (If your compiler has two or more of these characteristics, you should replace the compiler and place your supplier on a "suspect list.")

Procedural-level computer languages are commonly classed by the applications areas of their chief use. Thus there are languages designed for numerical scientific applications, for business applications, for strings-of-symbols manipulation, and for systems programming as well as a few somewhat general-purpose languages. During our discussion of the basics of procedural languages, we will refer to features of the following languages:

Numerical scientific-oriented procedural languages: BASIC, FORTRAN, APL,

Business-oriented procedural language: COBOL

String-oriented procedural language: SNOBOL

Systems programming languages: PL/G, PL/M-86, Concurrent Pascal, C

General-purpose languages: Pascal, PL/I, Ada

EXAMINING LANGUAGES

SYNTAX–SEMANTICS–PRAGMATICS

Syntax is defined as the way in which words are put together to form phrases and sentences; *semantics* as the meaning; and *pragmatics* as the relationship of these to the user in practical occurrences. In different words: Syntax is a set of rules specifying which forms of the language are grammatically acceptable, while semantics is the meaning associated with the specific form used. Of course it is possible, and often probable, that the meaning intended by the composer of the program statement is different from the meaning assigned by the compiler or by the human reader. It is the task of the language designer to present the language specifications so clearly that compiler designers and textbook authors can help programmers to minimize misunderstandings of the syntax–semantics diadic relationship.

LEXICAL ELEMENTS

The *available symbols* that can be combined to form the lexical elements—the vocabulary—of a procedural language are well-specified subsets of the ASCII character set. Thus the standard FORTRAN language does not allow lowercase alphabetic letters, while Pascal allows the use of uppercase and lowercase. In fact, some systems convert all lowercase letters in the source text into uppercase; other systems merely treat uppercase and lowercase letters as identical; while other systems treat them as different.

The *vocabulary* of procedural language usually encompasses several different elements that are used to name, or identify, some element of the program:

Keywords. Those combinations of symbols whose use is reserved to indicate some specific action within the program. Examples include PROGRAM, PROCEDURE, PROC, IF, GOTO, GO TO, THEN, ELSE, WHILE, DO, READ, PUT, END, and so on. Each keyword in a language has an associated specific semantics (a meaning) in that language. In general, the symbol combination constituting a keyword is not allowed in other contexts (i.e., it is a reserved word).

Labels. Those program elements that mark, or flag, a specific spot or location within the program that presumably will be the target of a branch. Additionally, labels (identifiers) are used to allow the naming (identification) of blocks of code, procedures, or data containers.

Data Containers. Those program elements that identify or name the logical program container for a datum or a collection of data. Thus the logical program data container possesses a name and a value. If the value of a data container is allowed to change during the execution of a program (if the identifier appears in an input statement or in the left-hand side of an assignment statement), it is known as a *variable.* The rules for naming variables are different for each procedural language but, in general, they must start with an alphabetic letter and not exceed a specified length. If the value of a data container is also the name (self-naming), references to it can appear only on the right-hand side of assignment statements or in an output statement and it is termed a *constant.* As the name of a constant is also its value, the contents of such a data container cannot be changed during program execution.

(The use of a constant as the argument to a subprogram in a FORTRAN CALL can circumvent this rule, often with strange and undesirable results.) Some procedural languages (termed *strongly typed*) require that all logical data containers be explicitly specified in DECLARE statements before use, giving the characteristics of the "logical" contents, such as type, size/precision, dimensionality/shape, and so on. Some procedural languages allow a reference to an identifier implicitly to cause the creation of a logical data container. The pragmatics of programming strongly suggests that explicit declaration of all logical data containers is "good programming practice" that will result in fewer errors. It must be noted that reference to a data container identifier during actual execution of the referencing instruction is a reference to the contents of the data container—to the value stored at that physical memory address at that instant in time. All data containers are considered to be memory resident. Registers are assumed not to exist in these languages.

Operations. First, it must be noted that many of the language keywords are aliases for operations. Obvious examples include READ, WRITE, PUT, and GET. Additionally, procedural-level languages provide only for the manipulation of values within the computer memory itself. Thus the current value contained in one datum container may be moved to another datum container or to itself without change or with change during the movement. Various operations are available for these actions: + (plus), – (minus), * (multiply), / (divide), ** (exponentiate), & .AND., | .OR., .NOT., = .EQ. (also = or ← as replacement), < .LT., > .GT., <= .LE., => .GE., | | concatenate, and so on. The rules concerning priority of expression evaluation and parenthesizing vary among languages, although the rules of FORTRAN apply generally to BASIC, Pascal, and PL/I. APL evaluation is right to left.

THE CONCEPTS OF BINDING AND BINDING TIME

The terms *binding* and *binding time* refer to concepts of the mapping association of an identified program object—often a data container—with a specific spot or location within entities of the program, such as logical procedure space, logical program space, virtual memory address (page/displacement), physical storage address, and so on. In general, the earlier that objects are bound, the easier the translation/linking/loading/execution tasks, with the concomitant result of fewer freedoms for making decisions during the later tasks. The six relatively common and straightforward binding times for procedural-level languages are program composition time, compilation time, linkage time, loading time, procedure invocation time, and execution reference time.

Program composition time binding maps the identifier (the name) of a program element to (1) a procedure, (2) a block of code, (3) a specific statement, or (4) a data container. This program composition logical reference binding has no implications regarding location or address or value (except for constants). Ordering implication most usually results. In certain languages, program composition time binding implies limitations—loss of freedom—concerning legal data container contents, legal reference times, and possibly even transient existence times during execution.

Compilation time binding maps the identifier—the name—to a relative location within the routine or results in an unresolved identifier reference to a program element of another separately translated routine. Loss of freedom occurs relative to addition or deletion of labels and data objects as well as to the size and shape of compound data objects. Freedom remains regarding the composition and relative ordering of external objects, such as separately compiled routines as well as variable data—often within strict limitations.

Linkage time binding maps the objects to relative locations within the load module while resolving the external references by mapping the unresolved compile-time identifier references to the correct load module relative locations. Freedom remains regarding the storage address of the load module and the values of variable data—again, often within strict limitations. The composition and ordering of procedures and their relative locations has been determined; that is, they are bound.

Load time binding moves and maps the object module to real memory locations from which the instructions and data are available via actual addresses. In the Intel I8086/8088, these main memory addresses of length 20 bits are derived as the contents of the appropriate 16-bit segment register multiplied by "10" hexadecimal plus the 16-bit offset (displacement) within the segment. Thus, after loading, the binding of program elements to main (real) memory addresses is complete. The values of variable data are not bound until they are input or calculated during execution.

As discussed in Chapter 9, the loading process may involve directly loading the object module *in toto* into main memory with immediate load time binding. Alternatively, with virtual memory systems, portions of the program and data areas known as pages or segments may be dynamically loaded as needed into real memory with load-time binding for each portion occurring at that time during execution. As a corollary, certain pages or segments may be "unloaded" and "unbound" during execution, as the real memory space they occupy is needed for other program portions.

Procedures invocation time binding maps the association between arguments (actual parameters) in the invocation statement (CALL or function reference) and the corresponding arguments (formal parameter or dummy argument) in the invoked (subprocedure) routine. Five basic techniques exist for transferring arguments: pass by value, pass by result, pass by value-result, pass by location (reference or address), and pass by name.

1. ***Pass by value.*** The invocation statement in the calling routine furnishes the *value* of the argument. The receiving routine places this value in its own local data container created as the result of the existence of the call by value formal parameter. Common languages that employ this technique include Pascal and SNOBOL. It should be noted that changes to the value of a pass by value dummy

argument in the receiving routine have no effect on the value of the actual parameter in the invoking routine.

2. ***Pass by result.*** The actual parameter in the invocation statement of the calling routine receives the value assigned to the formal parameter in the subordinate routine. This relatively rare technique is available in Ada. Note that a local data container is created in the subordinate routine as a result of the call by result formal parameter. The value is transferrred during the return phase and thus a value for the actual parameter in the invocation statement of the calling routine is not available until return time during execution.

3. ***Pass by value-result.*** The formal parameter in the subordinate routine corresponds to a local data container that is initialized to the value of the actual parameter in the invoking routine in a manner and at a time fully equivalent to the pass by value technique. Similarly, the result value is furnished via the actual-formal parameter pair during the return process and is fully equivalent to the pass by result technique. Pass by value-result is rarely employed in language design and is not a feature of the more popular languages mentioned in this chapter.

4. ***Pass by location/Pass by address/Pass by reference.*** The actual parameter in the invoking statement of the calling routine is the address of the named data container. This address is employed as the address of the formal parameter in the subordinate routine. Thus any change within the subordinate routine to the value within the data container will be a simultaneous change to the identical data container in the invoking routine; in point of fact, they are a single identical data container. In effect, the formal parameter identifier is an alias for the actual parameter identifier. The pass by location technique is employed in FORTRAN, COBOL, Pascal, and PL/I. In some dialects of FORTRAN, the passing of the address of a constant is allowed; the changing of this value in the subordinate routine will result in violation of the rule that the value of a constant is also its name. Strange and disastrous results are to be expected when this happens.

5. ***Pass by name.*** Although this technique has historically received much attention, its use is extremely rare (none of our example common languages employ it). Pass by name delays the evaluation of the actual-formal parameter diad until *each* time it is referenced in the subordinate routine. Multiple references can and usually do, employ different values.

Execution time binding maps the value into the identifier (name) specified data container in main memory. This value–address association is accomplished for obtaining contents via identifier references in assignment statement right-hand expressions, in output statements, and via actual parameters in procedure invocation statements. The value address association for setting contents is accomplished via an identifier reference on the left-hand side of an assignment statement, in an input statement, and via actual parameter setting on the return from or during the execution of a subordinate procedure.

DATA TYPES

It is a commonly stated and universal truism that the art and science of programming consists of finding or developing an algorithmic model of the real-world problem and then describing that model using a programming language. This process requires the programmer to choose a computer-language-supported representation of the objects (the data) in the algorithmic model. This choice of object representation has considerable effects on both the correctness and the clarity of the problem solution. The single most overriding consequence of the choice of a particular object representation is the set of manipulations—the operations—that can be performed on the object. The allowable operations should have a corresponding valid meaning in the real-world problem environment. Being formal, a data type is a collection of data objects and operations that can be validly performed on the objects. *Primitive data types* include Boolean, numeric, and character. We will first discuss these and then describe and discuss the aggregation of data into primitive data structures supported directly by the common procedural languages.

The *Boolean-bit-logical* primitive data type has only two values: true or false. These are expressed in various languages as .TRUE., TRUE, '1'B, etc.; and .FALSE., FALSE, '0'B, etc. A few languages, such as COBOL, do not have a Boolean data type, although they do provide for the evaluation of conditional expressions and thus in effect have a temporary receptacle of this type unavailable to the programmer. The operators for Boolean data include the diadic & (also expressed as .AND. or AND) and the | (also expressed as .OR. or OR) operators and the monadic ¬ (also expressed as .NOT. or NOT). Operators are also provided for mapping non-Boolean values into true or false Boolean values. These include the = (.EQ), < (.LT.), > (.GT.), <= (.LE.), and the => (.GE.). Movement of Boolean values from one data container to another is allowed via the assignment statement. Input and output are also allowed.

The *bit string* primitive data type is allowed in the PL/I language and in some dialects of FORTRAN. The allowable values are the concatenation of a specified number of Boolean values into a string that is considered and treated like a single entity. The accessing of individual bits within the bit string is allowed via functions such as substring:

```
SUBSTR (name, starting-position, length)
```

which will extract the portion of the string with name as an identifier starting at the character position specified (counting starts at one) for the number of positions specified by the length argument. Input, output, movement via replacement statements, and concatenation (| |) are also allowed. We will delay discussing fixed- and variable-length strings until the section on character strings.

The *character* primitive data type has values in the ASCII character set. The common languages Pascal and Ada possess this type and do not allow the concatenation of characters into strings. Rather, they allow arrays of single-character elements. Although the point is arguable, in my opinion this restriction constitutes a severe and undesirable limitation. The operations allowed are replacement, input, output, and comparison.

The *character string* primitive data type allows values that are a specified length of the concatenation of ASCII characters. The length may assume values from zero (for a null string) through n (where n is implementation dependent but is commonly 255 or 16383) and may be of varying length as determined by the contents. In the latter case, right-hand trailing blank characters are considered not to be a portion of the string. Some languages, such as SNOBOL, treat all character strings as dynamically varying in length with no programmer-supplied length directives. PL/I and BASIC require the programmer to specify a maximum length for each string when the identifier-data container diad is declared. Again, it is important to remember that the character string is a single nondivisible scalar entity that can be input, output, moved, built via the concatenation operator (| |), be an operand of comparison operations, and be subject to extraction via the substring function with the extracted substring subject to the same operations.

The operations appropriate to strings of characters (or bits) are:

1. Create a string of character text.
2. Concatenate two or more strings to form a string.
3. Extract a portion of a string to form a string without changing the original string.
4. Search a string for the occurrence of a specified substring.
5. Compare two strings or substrings.
6. Find the length (number of characters) of a string.
7. Delete a substring (replace with a null string).
8. Replace a substring with another substring.
9. Insert a string into another string at a specified point.

Pascal, C, APL, and many older dialects of FORTRAN do not support the string primitive data type. In these languages, somewhat convoluted code fragments must be composed to simulate some of the nine string operations above.

The *numeric* data types are present in all programming languages. Even SNOBOL, designed for manipulating character strings, needs numeric-data-type containers to act as counters, string lengths, control values, and so on. The numeric data types commonly available include the integer, the fixed-point, and the floating-point primitive data types, with coding often in binary or decimal and sometimes with a provision for specifying allowable ranges and precision.

The *integer* primitive data type is used for exact arithmetic on whole numbers within a fixed value range, usually including zero and negative values. The input, output, movement, comparison, and arithmetic operations seem always to be allowed. It should be emphasized that division results in the quotient being truncated (chopped) at the radix point so that 3 / 2 → 1 and 2 / 3 → 0. Some languages, such as Pascal and Ada, require the programmer to specify the range within the declaration statement; other languages imply the range as the maximum/minimum capacity of the implementation-dependent data container. Some languages such as PL/I allow the programmer to specify the number base encoding (binary or decimal) even though this is unnecessary with integer numeric quantities, as all allowable values can be exactly represented in any number base.

The *fixed-point* primitive data type is used for noninteger numeric values with a specified number of digits or bits both before and after the radix point (thus explicitly specifying the range). The usual operations of input, output, movement, comparison, and arithmetic are allowed, with truncation occurring on the right-hand side of the fractional portion. This data type is not available in FORTRAN, APL, or SNOBOL. PL/I requires the programmer to specify the number base encoding within the declaration, with decimal encoding being the default. Note that the values of fixed-point numbers are uniformly spaced over the range that is specified via two parameters: the total number of digits or bits used to represent the maximum/minimum value, and the number of digits or bits to the right of the radix point in the fractional portion.

The *floating-point or real* primitive data type is used for noninteger numeric values with a specified number of significant digits or bits and a widely varying magnitude. Recall the encoding and operations allowed with floating-point numbers as discussed in Chapter 6. From a practical programmer point of view, the most important characteristics of floating-point quantities are:

1. Employing binary coding, they do *not* contain the integers as a subset (decimal-coded real numbers do include the integral values within the allowed range).
2. There are only a finite set of exactly representable values, with "gaps" between each two neighboring values.
3. They are not uniformly distributed; that is, the "gaps" are smaller between neighbors closer to zero and wider between neighbors farther from zero.

Conversion between data types is often necessary during program composition (Pascal uses the term *coercion*). Implied conversion just prior to value assignment is usually allowed between numeric data types but is prohibited between all others. Implied conversion within an expression involving different numeric data types (mixed-mode arithmetic) is allowed in some dialects of some languages and prohibited in others. Conversion functions are either available or can be implemented via assembly language for explicit primitive data type to primitive data type for all meaningful situations.

DATA AGGREGATES

The term *data aggregate* is used to specify the logical joining of individual datum containers into an aggregate with a group identifier (name). Human beings generally have no difficulty with the concept, as they are used to thinking of a specific person as one of a group of people. Data aggregates in computer language almost always imply an ordering. This usually causes no difficulty, as human beings are used to seat number–row number entities in a theater or house numbers on a street. Thus the identifier of a data aggregate in procedural computer languages conforms to the natural language concept of collective nouns with a hierarchical ordering of zero to N named or numbered classification levels to arrive at the individual (scalar, element, or atomic) datum.

Arrays

We specified the possibility of zero levels of classification to allow us to include the degenerate aggregate, consisting of a single atomic or scalar datum. If we add atoms in a single linear direction and/or its exact opposite, we would construct a single-dimensional array. If we now add an equal number of atoms to each element of the one-dimensional array at 90°, we arrive at a two-dimensional array. (The terms *vector* and *matrix* are sometimes employed; they should be suppressed because of their implications regarding vector and matrix arithmetic operations, which are rarely available except through procedure calls: APL is an exception, in that true vector/matrix operators are available.) Similarly, three-dimensional arrays, four-dimensional arrays, . . . , *n*-dimensional arrays can be constructed. BASIC, FORTRAN, Pascal, PL/I, and Ada all allow the declaration of arrays of specified dimensionality with the extent (number of elements) specified for each dimension. The allowed dimensionality is dialect and language dependent.

Limitation on the concept and actuality of arrays in available common procedural-level languages are:

1. The shape must be a regular polygon with "square corners"—triangular, trapezoidal, and so on, shapes are not supported in commonly available languages.
2. The dimensionality is often limited and must be declared before compilation (as must the size).
3. Each element or atom of an array must be of the same primitive data type.
4. Although vector/matrix operations are available in APL, the usual operations are applied in an element-by-element fashion. Thus the PL/I code

```
DECLARE A(4,4), B(4,4), C(4,4) . . . ;
   -
   -
   -
A = B * C ;
   -
   -
```

implies

```
A(1,1) = B(1,1) * C(1,1)
A(1,2) = B(1,2) * C(1,2)
A(1,3) = B(1,3) * C(1,3)
   -
   -
A(4,4) = B(4,4) * C(4,4)
```

and not the matrix multiplication of rows by columns. It is for this reason that I personally avoid the row/column and vector/matrix terminology for arrays. Some dialects of BASIC also allow array operations that, similarly to PL/I, imply element-by-element execution.

Structures–Records

A programmer must often manipulate data objects that logically consist of a number of different primitive data types. Additionally, the data objects often involve arrays of differing dimensionality and sizes, to say nothing of strings of differing maximum length. As an example, we offer (using PL/I-like pseudocode)

```
DCL 1 STUDENT_REC,
      2 NAME,
            3 LAST CHAR(34) VARY,
            3 MIDDLE CHAR(10) VARY,
            3 FIRST CHAR(10) VARY,
            3 GENERATION CHAR(5) VARY,
      2 STUDENT_NUM FIXED DEC(9,0)
      2 ADDRESS(2),
            3 NUMBER CHAR(6) VARY,
            3 STREET CHAR(20) VARY,
            3 TOWN CHAR(20) VARY,
            3 STATE CHAR(2),
            3 ZIP FIXED DEC(5,0),
            -
            -
            -
```

Note that we can refer to the entire record (perhaps for input from a file) as STUDENT_REC; we can access the student number as an integer via STUDENT_REC.STUDENT_NUM; we can access the home address zip code as STUDENT_REC.ADDRESS(2).ZIP. This qualified name techniques via a "." is employed in Pascal, PL/I, and Ada. COBOL employs "FIRST in NAME in STUDENT_REC" as its qualified name technique. Note that there may be arrays of structures, structures of arrays, and so on, to an implementation-dependent arbitrary complexity.

Arrays of structures and arrays within structures are subject to the usual and normal limitations of arrays regarding regularity in shape, size, subsumed types, and element-by-element processing. Structures have relaxed the rules of data aggregates in that:

1. The shape may be arbitrary.
2. The elements or atoms may be of mixed primitive data types and sizes.
3. The elements may be other structures, or arrays, or arrays of structures.

It must be emphasized that APL, FORTRAN, and BASIC do not provide the structure facility.

Data structures in the more generic sense are not normally directly provided by the commonly available procedural languages. This implies that the program composer must provide suitable definitions of data containers and the corresponding necessary operations for such data structures as stacks, queues, dequeues, trees, lists, and so on. One early very successful package of FORTRAN subprograms for manipulating doubly linked circular branched lists was designed and implemented as SLIP by Weizenbaum (1963).

User-Defined Data Types and Operations

User-defined data types and operations are sometimes referred to as abstract data types or are included in the meaning of the term *extensible languages.* It is true that the existence of the square-root function in FORTRAN and BASIC constitutes an additional operator for real/floating-point data and that the programmer can define other functions and, in this sense, extend the language. The creation of the SLIP system by Weizenbaum, which allows the definition of a new data type—the cell—and its dynamic aggregation into a doubly linked list via a coherent set of newly defined functions (operations) certainly does enlarge the problem-solving domain of FORTRAN and, in this sense, extends the language. Nevertheless, the field of computer science does not include these commonly available language abilities in its use of the terms: user-defined data types, abstract data types, and extensible languages.

The macro preprocessor ability of many dialects of PL/I allows the recognition of programmer-defined data types, data aggregates, and operators; the generation of appropriate PL/I source code, and the substitution of that code into the program at specified places before passing the expanded program to PASS 1 of the compiler for lexical and syntactic analysis. Sammet and her coworkers (Tobey et al., 1967) used this facility to transfer with extensions the symbolic algebraic system called FORMAC from IBM 7094 FORTRAN to IBM 360 PL/I. Although the PL/I macro ability is a form of language extensibility and does allow a form of abstract data types, this facility is somewhat primitive, limited, and unnatural from a modern language viewpoint. For example, the production of intermediate *legal* PL/I source code severely limits the abilities of the macro processor as well as forcing the programmer to debug at that level—a level at which he or she did not compose the program.

The data type user-defining language extension abilities of the Pascal, Ada, APL, C, and so on, languages more truly reflect the modern viewpoint of clarity, information-hiding requirements, and execution-time checking. We draw your attention to two data type declaration statements in Pascal as examples:

1. *Enumeration* (scalar in Pascal) type declarations are simply an exhaustive list of the values that are primitive for the type. For example

```
TYPE
        units = (inches, feet, yards, miles);
```

   after which the actual variable identifier could be declared:

```
VAR
        distance : units ;
```

   Alternatively, the two declarations can be combined:

```
VAR
        distance : (inches, feet, yards, miles);
```

2. *Set* type declarations allow a programmer to progress one step further:

```
TYPE
        units = (inches, feet, yards, miles);
        measures = SET of units;
VAR
        size, distance, depth : measures;
```

CONTROL STRUCTURES

The power of the computer that allows us to compose solutions to problems is rooted in the branch-on-condition or continue instruction implemented in the circuits that execute the binary machine code. Procedural-level languages provide a variety of program-flow-of-control constructs. The science of programming (if the terms *sci-*

ence and *programming* are not antithetical) has progressed to the point of accepting (with a growing body of positive evidence) the hypothesis that limiting the context of the use of a limited set of control structures enhances the clarity and probability of correctness of a program while increasing the ease of understanding during modifications and enhancements. The paper by Elshoff and Marcotty (1982) is highly recommended as an introduction to this type of reasoning at a very pragmatic level. It is important, but hopefully unnecessary, to note that control structures are often used as basic actions within other control structures. That is, control structures can appear within control structures to an arbitrary (implementation-dependent) nesting depth. The control structures likely to be encountered in common procedural-level languages are given below, roughly following the classification scheme of Ledgard and Marcotty (1981):

D-Structure (named for Edsger W. Dijkstra)

Sequence: The normal sequential execution of statements following from the incrementation of the program counter just after instruction fetch.

Conditional Branch (IF-THEN-ELSE)

Loops (DO WHILE condition/REPEAT WHILE condition): The termination test is implied at the loop start.

D Prime-Structures

Conditional Branch: Single-Way IF (IF-THEN/FORTRAN logical IF); Multi-Way Branch (CASE/SELECT/FORTRAN arithmetic IF/FORTRAN-computed GOTO).

Loops: DO UNTIL condition/REPEAT UNTIL condition—The exit test is implied at the loop foot.

For loops (Do index count): The exit test can be implied at loop start or foot, depending on dialect and language.

RE (Repeat Exit) Structures

RE1 Exit (EXIT/LEAVE): Immediately exit and leave the presently executing loop through the foot and advance outward one nesting level.

REn Exit (EXIT(N)/LEAVE label): Immediately exit and leave the presently executing loop and advance outward through the loop feet N nesting levels or through the foot of the loop with the specific label.

L-Structures

An L-structure is any control structure without restrictions on the branch target (i.e., the unrestricted use of labels and GOTO commands).

GOTO label: The strongest and most dangerous control structure. All modern texts strongly argue against the use of the unconditional branch or completely ignore it (if a programmer is unaware of the GOTO, it will not be used). Although procedure invocation is equivalent to an unconditional branch (*with an implied return*), the CALL/PERFORM and function reference are fully accepted in modern programming.

BLOCK STRUCTURING AND THE SCOPE OF IDENTIFIERS

In the more modern procedural-level languages, the idea of blocks of code, the nesting of these blocks, and the concomitant scope restriction on the knowledge of an identifier only within the block of its declaration is common. We must approach the problem of separately composed and separately translated (separately compiled or assembled) procedures which are only then linked into one load module versus procedures that are composed and occur internally to other procedures (physically within). The former are often termed *external subprocedures* to distinguish them from the latter-termed *internal subprocedures.* We are avoiding the additional problems attendant with co-routines.

External subprocedures imply that the compiler (or assembler) knows little or nothing about the identifiers used in other procedures and thus the labels and the data container names are all private to the procedure. Knowledge of the identifiers used in other procedures is unknown, although they may be referenced via the argument/parameter mechanism. Additionally, a few languages provide one or another type of EXTERNAL reference facility that may almost correspond to the assembly language directive of that name. FORTRAN furnishes a COMMON data area accessible by program-private names on a positional/data container size basis that opens the door to Pandora's mythical box of disasters.

Internal subprocedures imply that the compiler is fully aware of all of the identifiers and their implications during translation and that a single integrated object file will be produced. Because other separately compiled external subprocedures may be referenced, the link routine must still be employed and the implications of externals is true for these situations. Identifiers declared (implicitly or explicitly) within a nested subprocedure or block are known only within that subprocedure or block and within any subprocedure or blocks nested within it. Thus in the example shown in Figure 11.1, the following scope of identifiers holds:

Variable Z is known:
- Locally by block A
- Globally by block B
- Globally by block C
- Globally by block D

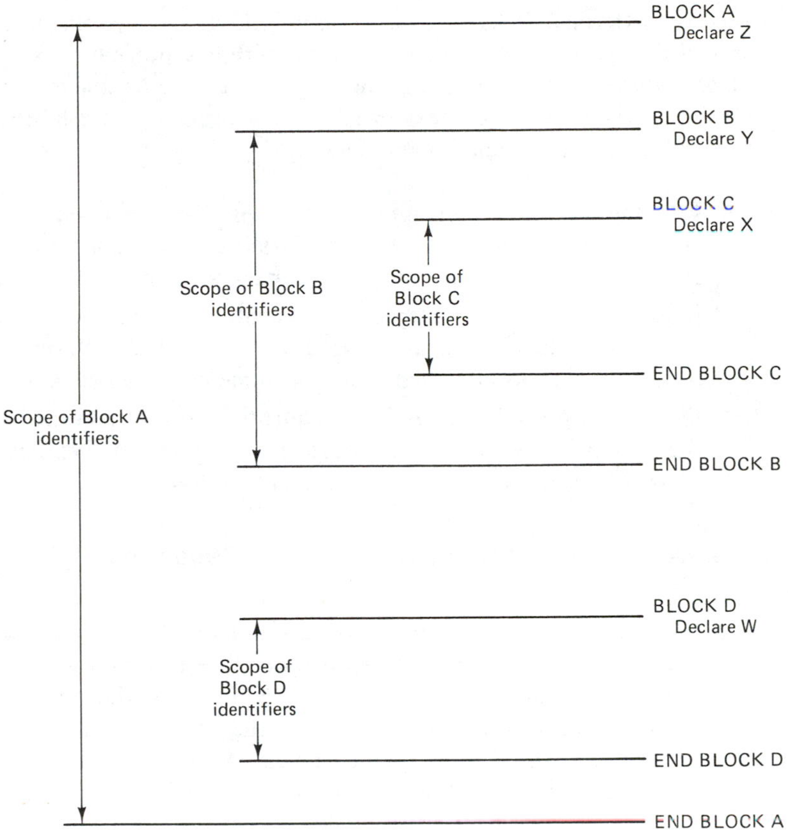

Figure 11.1 Scope of the identifier in relation to the logical placement of blocks or internal procedures in a "block-structured" language.

Variable Y is known:	And is unknown by:
Locally by block B	Block A
Globally by block C	Block D
Variable X is known:	And is unknown by:
Locally by block C	Block A
	Block B
	Block D
Variable W is known:	And is unknown by:
Locally by block D	Block A
	Block B
	Block C

As our example we will use PL/I in which the concept of external procedures coexists with the block-structured concepts of internal procedures, blocks within procedures (termed BEGIN blocks), and code groups within procedures or blocks (termed DO groups). Although the labels within a procedure with subsumed internal procedures, begin blocks, and do groups must be unique, as they are all known at compile time, in the context of serving as branch target labels, they follow the scope rules of data container identifiers.

1. Internal procedures must be invoked via CALL or via a function reference and thus are "out-of-line" blocks. Variable declarations are permitted with local-global scope. Argument/parameter pairs are normally used.
2. Begin blocks must be entered via sequential flow of control or via a branch to the optional label of their keyword initial statement. Variable declarations are permitted with local/global scope. Arguments/parameters are not allowed.
3. Do groups must be entered via sequential flow of control or via a branch to the optional label of their keyword initial statement. Neither variable declarations nor argument/parameter pairs are allowed.

Pure Code, Reentrant Procedures, and Recursion

By definition, pure code—*a pure procedure*—is code that never modifies any portion of itself during execution. Thus, a pure code procedure contains only instructions (some of which may contain immediate operands; that is, constants). The data container areas for a pure code procedure—the variables—must be elsewhere. Note that the code segment (CS), the data segment (DS), the stack segment (SS), and the extra or string segment (ES) addressing plan of the I8086/8088 naturally and easily support the pure code concept, although it can be violated if necessary. Although historically, the ability of a program to alter itself was considered important—even vital—modern programming practices that emphasize clarity and modifiability of the source code severely discourage—to the point of prohibition—self-modifying code. SNOBOL does provide the ability for a program to modify itself at the source statement level.

In multiprogramming systems, several different and distinct user jobs may "simultaneously" require the execution of the same subprocedure, say the SQRT function. One obvious and commonly used solution is to link this subprocedure into each and every load module referencing it. Thus several copies of the same subprocedure may occupy memory space simultaneously. This can be considered wasteful and expensive, particularly if memory is in short supply and constitutes a system bottleneck. Two other possible solutions would have only one copy of the "common" subprocedure in memory but usable by any and all programs that need its services. One of these latter solutions would require that the "common" subprocedure complete execution once started (invoked) by any user job. This requirement can result in quite serious scheduling problems and is not possible with the scheduler of those multiprogramming systems which reallocate the ALU processor on the occurrence of certain critical conditions. Thus this solution is not considered very practical. The other possible solution, which requires only one copy of the "common" subprocedure in main memory, is termed *reentrant code.*

For a procedure to be a *reentrant procedure,* it must satisfy two requirements: first, it must be a pure procedure, and second, all of the data containers that are used by it must be in the data areas of the invoking (calling) procedure. The realities of time slicing and interrupts, together with the possible loss of control of the ALU processor at the end of executing any instruction, forces the second requirement to be extremely severe, to the point that all register contents must be saved for eventual restoration each and every time that control of the ALU processor is lost. The save area must be in the private memory area of the user job that is losing control.

When composing programs, it is often convenient to have a procedure invoke itself as a subprocedure. A procedure that invokes itself is termed a *recursive procedure.* The traditional examples employed by a myriad of instructors in attempting to convey the concepts and the utility of recursion in programming include (for positive integers)

$$\text{Factorial—N!} = \begin{cases} 1 & \text{if } n = 0 \\ n \times (n-1)! & \text{if } n > 0 \end{cases}$$

$$\text{Powers—}X^n = \begin{cases} 1 & \text{if } n = 0 \\ X \times X^{n-1} & \text{if } n > 0 \end{cases}$$

$$\text{Tower of Hanoi—Han(N)} = \begin{cases} 1 & \text{if } n = 1 \\ 2 \times \text{HAN}(N-1)+1 & \text{if } N > 1 \end{cases}$$

$$\text{Fibonacci—Fib(N)} = \begin{cases} N - 1 & \text{if } n = 2 \\ \text{Fib}(N-1)+\text{Fib}(N-2) & \text{if } n > 2 \end{cases}$$

Advocates of FORTRAN or BASIC, languages that do not allow recursive procedures, have been known to claim that all "useful and practical" problems that are defined in handbooks via recursive functions (see the four examples just above) can be restated as iterative solutions, often with savings in memory required and execution time. The truth of these claims is dependent on the definition of "useful and practical." As one example of their flavor, we present, in pseudocode, the factorial in both styles:

```
PROC FACT(N) RETURNS(INTEGER); /* Iterative */
     IF N = 0 |  N = 1
        THEN RETURN(1);
        ELSE DO;
             ANSWER = 1;
             DO I = 2 TO N;
                  ANSWER = ANSWER * I;
                  END;
             RETURN(ANSWER);
             END;
```

```
    END FACT;
PROC FACT(N) RETURNS(INTEGER) RECURSIVE;
    IF N < 3
        THEN RETURN(N);
        ELSE RETURN (N * FACT (N-1));
    END FACT;
```

As a last point, many of the data manipulations necessary to process strings and trees are naturally defined and most clearly coded as recursive procedures.

INPUT/OUTPUT AND FILES

Input and output are perhaps the most unsatisfactory aspect of programming languages. Although every programming language must support I/O, a standard method is notably lacking. Perhaps at least a portion of the trouble can be blamed on the attempt to use a single set of constructs to accomplish two different tasks with very dissimilar requirements:

1. Communication between human beings and the computer, as well as
2. Supplementary storage of data whose physical size is too large or whose time length of storage is too long to allow residence in main memory.

At least one commercial system, the IBM System 38, has successfully attempted a unification of these concepts by considering all nonintermediate calculation data to be permanent and global to the simulated main memory. The UNIX operating system, briefly discussed in Chapter 9, also uses a variant of this approach by treating human–computer interaction information identically with the more permanent file data. *Files* are usually defined as named collations of data not resident in main memory; that is, files are data aggregates. Perhaps the chief difference between files, as data aggregates, and other data aggregates that were discussed earlier in this chapter, is a result of the creation and destruction lifetime global/local nature of different data items.

The usual view of a complete and linked program is based on its linguistic autonomy: it is the largest unit of execution, it is the largest unit over which identifiers are known, and it is the largest unit (in both memory space and time) over which program main memory data storage persists. Within the program, declarations of data identifiers have local/global scope characteristics, as was shown in Figure 11.1. A valid, if somewhat unusual view, of a computational system emphasizes the fact that the operating system is the only "main" program and that the invocation of a compiler, of the link routine, of the loader, of the scheduler, and of a user's program is really the "calling" of a subprogram. This viewpoint allows us to define a file as a data aggregate known to the operating system—to view the file as the most global data of the computational system. Contrary to the normal procedural-level language definition of global data, we do not want the file known by all of the user programs subsumed under the operating system (the main program). If we use the concept of separately compiled programs, which also necessitates the idea of external subprocedures (a truism in this instance), we force communication establishment and knowledge of a file to be transmitted via some kind of argument or parameter. In procedural-level languages, special statements exist just for this purpose.

Even if we reject this view, we must still accept the fact that a file is a named data aggregate that is known to the operating system. This unifying concept, though, raises unpleasant spectors of data privacy violations. Some mechanism must be defined to disallow unauthorized access to these global data aggregates—these files. Happily, the "external" concept and implementation results in these global files being unavailable to subsumed procedures. But the file—the global data aggregate—must be made available to a particular program. Procedural-level languages use the parameter/argument diad for this task. The equivalent mechanism is used to transmit file information through the use of statements such as OPEN file, CLOSE file, READ file, WRITE file, and so on. Additionally, the operating system (in whose global scope the file is defined, exists, and is known) can check file access rights and thus refuse or grant access under conditions specified by the file owner. The term *capability* is often used.

In summary, our view of a file equates it with a global data aggregate of the "main" (operating system) program that can, but need not be, made available via parameters to (separately compiled) external (user programs) "subprograms." Computer programming languages provide special statements for the communication of these file parameters requests to, and access response from, the operating system.

Human–computer communication, on the other hand, has the necessity of transliterating program internal opaque data encoding into humanly decipherable form, and vice versa. Three somewhat different techniques are used in procedural languages to specify this message formatting information:

1. Remote format specification, specifying the identifiers, the order, the spacing, and other information. Because remote formats are labeled statements (or data areas) it is possible to employ them for many I/O statements or to alter, construct, and input them. FORTRAN and PL/I employ this method, although the PL/I format is normally a portion of the I/O statement itself. The remoteness of the format information from the I/O statement and from the declaration statement can be a problem for program clarity and understanding. Free format specifies the identifiers and order, with the system furnishing an implied spacing, layout, and other information.
2. Picture specification places the I/O description of the data in the data declaration statement. This method is used in COBOL and in PL/I. The remoteness of the picture description from the I/O statements is not usually a problem for program clarity. The incorporation of the I/O description into the data container declaration unifies the design-time considerations of almost all aspects of each data item and should minimize some errors due to design negligence.

3. I/O procedures are employed by Pascal, C, and Ada, in which the identifier, spacing, and so on, are furnished as arguments and the procedure invoked is specific to the data type, which implicitly specifies most of the layout. Some I/O procedures may be somewhat generalized and require an argument(s) to specify type and other details.

It should be noted that the differences between these three methods of I/O are more syntactical than real; all three methods finally invoke subprocedures to accomplish the I/O task, including formatting.

The difficulty most students have in learning I/O, as experienced by generations of instructors, is mute testimony to the relative opaqueness of these constructs in computer languages. In many cases, the I/O portion of a language seems to be an afterthought that received little deep design effort and was considered uninteresting. Nevertheless, despite their seeming awkwardness, the necessary commands exist. On the other hand, in all instances where it is appropriate, but only where appropriate, I highly recommend free-format I/O.

THE EXECUTION ENVIRONMENT: THE RUN-TIME PACKAGE

Recall that we have used the term *load module* in its usual sense of referring to the linked set of all referenced object modules with all external identifier references resolved (with the possible exception of files and perhaps a few other very special cases of execution-time dynamic loading and linking). Imagine, for a moment, that our load module contains the binary machine code equivalent of the PL/I statement

```
A = B + C / D ;
```

where A is declared as float binary, B is declared as fixed decimal, C is declared as fixed binary, and D is declared as float decimal. The compiler designer may have decided to insert the necessary code to convert the data types in line as necessary in the code. This strategy would probably result in a larger load module (as the conversion routines would presumably appear many times in many places) that would execute fairly fast (as no invocation of the conversion procedures occurs that would require time). Alternatively, the compiler designer may have decided to insert calls to single copies of conversion routines. This alternative strategy would probably result in a small load module with slower execution. Let us further suppose that the value contained in the data area with the identifier "D" is zero when the division operation is attempted. Division by zero is not defined in mathematics or in the ALU of computers; thus an interrupt is posted whose hardware-defined default result is usually immediate program termination. An exception has occurred and some procedural-level languages allow the program composer to specify actions to be taken if a specific exception occurs. Thus if the PL/I block

```
ON ZERODIVIDE BEGIN;
                -
                -
                -
            END;
```

had preceded the exception in the scope, or global to the scope, of the exception, the "fix-up" specified in the begin block would have been executed, with execution returning to the point of interruption. Many (most) programming languages provide a set of "standard fix-ups" for commonly occurring exceptions. These routines are often automatically linked into the load module or, alternatively, dynamically loaded and linked during execution as needed.

The set of routines to accomplish data type conversions, to accomplish exception fix-ups or handling, and to accomplish I/O formatting, as well as to accomplish other necessary execution-time work, is quite large and may require several thousand bytes of memory. Collectively, these routines constitute the language environment and often are termed the *run-time package.* Students are often shocked to discover that their 20-line PL/I program, which would be expressed as 100 assembly statements, requires 48 kilobytes of memory because a large run-time package was linked into their load module.

12

The Intel I186/I188 and the Intel I286

In a dynamic field such as the microprocessor-integrated circuit industry, advancements and improvements are announced at fairly short time intervals with amazing regularity. The Intel Corporation delivered production quantities of two new members of the I8086/8088 family in 1982 and 1983. The iAPX 186/iAPX 188 are augmented versions of the I8086/8088 that reduce the need for supporting integrated-circuit chips and also add new instructions. The iAPX 286 increases the size of maximum real memory while adding hardware virtual memory support as well as augmenting the instruction set with the 10 new iAPX 186 instructions and 16 additional instructions to support protection of code and data areas in the virtual memory logical address space. Additionally, the iAPX 286 can execute programs in the "real address" mode or in the "virtual address" mode.

THE iAPX 186/iAPX 188

Increases in ci:cuit density on a single silicon integrated-circuit chip have allowed the packaging of the circuits previously requiring at least 5 and often 15 or 20 chips. Thus the normal I8086 CPU with an augmented instruction set, a clock generator, a programmable interrupt controller, a memory chip-select subsystem, and a two-channel direct memory access (DMA) subsystem is all packed onto a single chip. The 8-MHz iAPX 186 should be capable of higher program throughput than the 8-MHz I8086, be over 160% as fast as the 5-MHz I8086, and be more than 80% as fast as the 10-MHz I8086. A valid comparison of the iAPX 188 with the I8088 should give similar results; but in general, the 8-bit data path to and from memory for both data and instructions will limit the throughput of both the I8088 and the iAPX 188 somewhat severely. Additionally, the 10 new instructions will allow the construction of operating systems with lower overhead and thus extra clock cycles will be available to user programs.

Figure 12.1 shows a block diagram of the iAPX 186 and emphasizes it as a logical proper superset of the I8086. Additionally, the iAPX 186 must be considered a logical subset of the iAPX 286. That is, the iAPX 186 adds 10 instructions to the repertoire of the I8086, and the iAPX 286 adds 16 more instructions beyond those of the iAPX 186, as well as virtual memory. All in all, there are serious reasons to question the economics of designing and marketing new products using the I8086/8088 now that the iAPX 186 and iAPX 188 are available (see Figures 12.2 and 12.3). This is not saying that currently marketed products using the I8086 are obsolete. It is saying that new designs should use the iAPX 186 or the iAPX 188. A smaller, simpler, and more economical product should result with enhanced abilities. It must be noted that the use of the I8089 input-output processor with an iAPX 186/188-based system seems somewhat superfluous. The I8087 floating-point co-processor is a natural augmentation for the iAPX 186/188 for those applications requiring such abilities. The I80130 operating systems' primitive chip may also be a justifiable augmentation.

ADDITIONAL INSTRUCTIONS

The additional arithmetic instruction is the *signed integer multiply immediate*:

```
IMULB       AL,OFFH ; AX ← AL * immediate byte
IMULW       AX,OFFFFH ; AX ← AX * immediate word
```

In the latter case, note that the result value from the multiplication occupies a 16-bit word and not twice the space of the input values.

Three additional stack data movement instructions are provided. The *PUSH immediate* instruction can have a word or byte immediate datum as an operand that is pushed onto the stack as a word:

```
PUSH OFFFFH
```

with the stack pointer (SP) register being decremented by 2 in both cases. Recall that the stack grows downward toward lower addresses. The *PUSHA* and *POPA* (A for all) pushes or pops all eight word-size general-purpose registers onto the stack with appropriate decrementation or augmentation of the stack pointer (SP) register by 16. The operands are implied as the eight registers (in order):

```
PUSHA
POPA
```

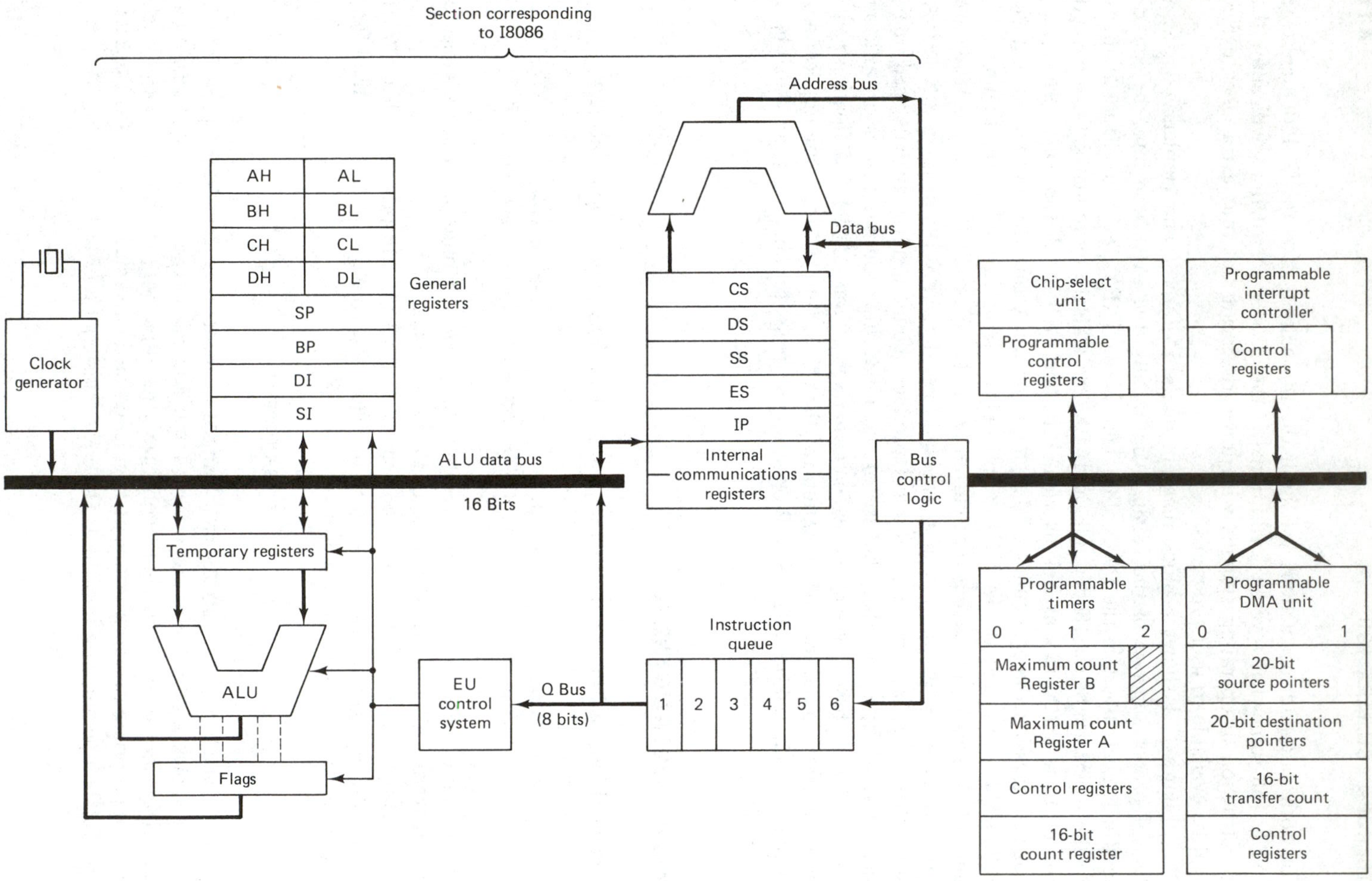

Figure 12.1 Block diagram of iAPX 186. Note that five additional functional units augment the basic I8086 portion (with 10 additional instructions) to allow the 186 chip to function as a microcomputer. (Reprinted by permission of Intel Corporation. Copyright 1982.)

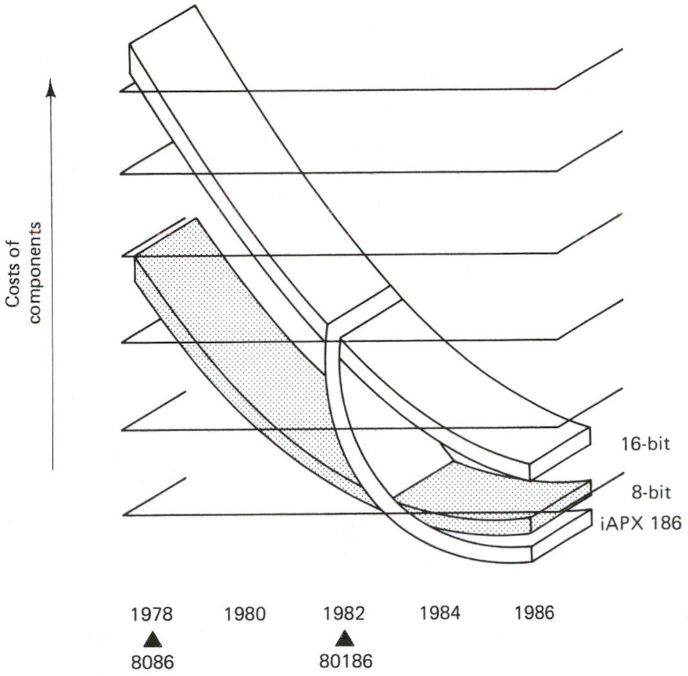

Figure 12.2 Generalized costs of computer-board components over time for microcomputers. Keyboard, CRT, disk storage, and other external devices are not included, as they should be equivalent. Note that the I8086 was introduced in 1978 and the iAPX 186 in 1982. (Reprinted by permission of Intel Corporation. Copyright 1982.)

These three stack instructions are extremely useful in subroutine invocation and return macros, particularly when compilers for procedural-level languages are involved.

Both byte- and word-oriented *block input/output* instructions have been added:

```
WORD PTR    INS
BYTE PTR    INS
WORD PTR    OUTS
BYTE PTR    OUTS
```

where the input or output physical port number is implied to have been previously placed in the DX register by the programmer. Note the close similarity to the string instructions of the I8086, in that the starting address of the input data destination in memory must have been placed in the DI register previously or the starting address of output data placed in memory in the SI register. As with the I8086 string instructions, the repeat prefix may be used to form a single instruction loop to allow

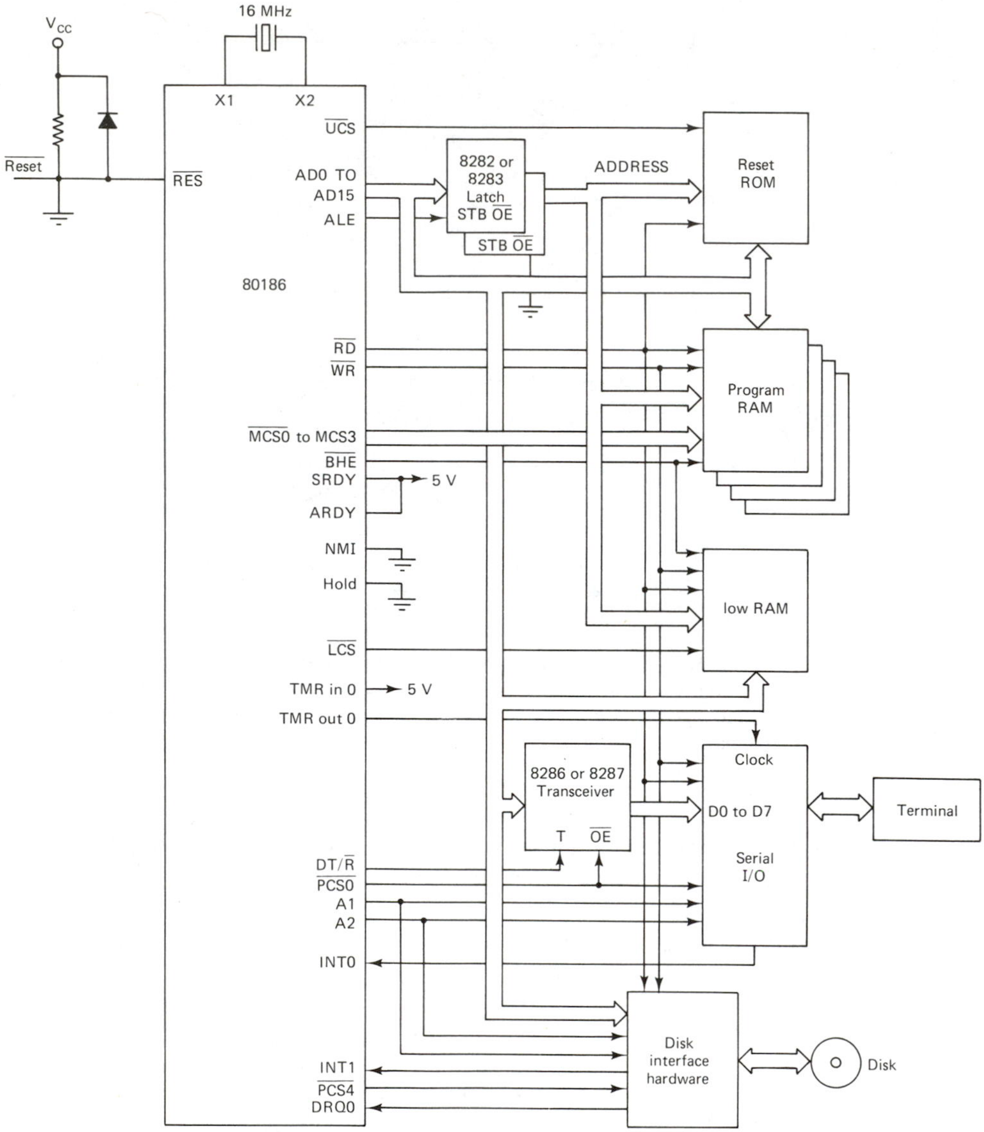

Figure 12.3 iAPX 186-based microcomputer block digram. The addition of an I8087 floating-point processor would result in additional capabilities. (Reprinted by permission of Intel Corporation. Copyright 1982.)

the input or output of a data block of length 1 to 64K bytes or 32K words by placing the count of the number of transfers needed in the CX register. For example, the following instruction will input the block of data bytes of the length specified in the CX register from the port specified in the DX register to the area of memory specified by the DI register:

```
REP BYTE PTR INS
```

The shift and rotate instructions of the I8086 are augmented to allow an immediate value to specify the amount of shift/rotate instead of requiring that the amount be programmer-preloaded into the CL (the count) register. In effect, the shift/rotate immediate instructions of the iAPX 186/188 first load the immediate-amount-of-shift operand into the CL register and then perform the operation in the manner of the I8086. Included in the *shift/rotate immediate* instruction augmentations are shift and rotate right or left logical:

```
SHL    XB,OFH
SHL    XW,OFFH
SHR    XB,OFH
SHR    XW,OFFH
ROL    XB,OFH
ROL    XW,OFFH
ROR    XB,OFH
ROR    XW,OFFH
```

the shift right arithmetic:

```
SAR    XB,OFH
SAR    XW,OFFH
```

and the rotate right or left through the carry bit:

```
RCL    XB,OFH
RCL    XW,OFFH
RCR    XB,OFH
RCR    XW,OFFH
```

The *check index for array bounds instruction* is particularly useful for compiler-generated procedural-level language code for applications involving data arrays because it allows a program to check the array limits before it attempts to access an element supposedly within the array.

```
BOUND    IndexReg,Memory
```

where the first operand is the register containing the array index and the second operand is the memory-resident array bounds value. If the index value violates the array bounds, an exception is posted as maskable interrupt 5. The interrupt service routine for this index out-of-bounds interrupt (5) should be designed to cause the graceful termination of the program with appropriate error messages. Alternatively, this exception may be employed to allocate additional space to the array, although this approach requires caution lest other data be overwritten and destroyed. As most neophyte programmers have experienced (to their chagrin), an index-out-of-bounds error is extremely common, easy to inadvertently cause, and often difficult to identify and correct. The use of the BOUND instruction by checkout compilers would be a major help to programmers.

Almost all block-structured procedural-level languages with local–global data area characteristics (see Chapter 11) such as Ada, Pascal, and PL/I employ a temporary data area to contain all data local to the procedure and pointers to the similar areas of calling procedures that contain data containers global to the procedure. These dynamically created "stack frames" are destroyed upon exiting (returning from) the procedure. A stack discipline of a push stack frame and a pop stack frame is suitable for implementing this local–global data characteristic of block-structured languages. The iAPX 186/188 furnishes the instructions.

```
ENTER          size,level
LEAVE
```

where the first operand specifies the total memory area occupied by the local variables data area, which may be of size 0 to 64K bytes. The level of the procedure can be zero for the main program to N depending on the nesting (this parameter is used to force pointers to be included in more global areas for stack frames of nested procedures). The LEAVE has no operands and results in the subsequent unavailability of the local variable data containers.

THE iAPX 286

The Intel I80286 is a four-stage pipelined central processor that can execute in two modes: (1) a real address mode in which it presents the architecture of the iAPX 186; that is, it is program-code compatible with the I8086/8088 and offers the extra 10 instruction groups of the I80186; and (2) a virtual address mode which is supported by 16 additional instructions for manipulating task and data description areas. To achieve these functions, the I80286 incorporates 130,000 circuits on the chip. This is in contrast to the first microprocessor, the I4004 of 1971, with 2300 circuits on the chip. The 56.5 circuits/chip ratio in 11 years is equivalent to an average fivefold increase in circuits per chip per year. A more realistic trend over time in the immediate past suggests a doubling of circuit numbers each year. An extrapolation of this doubling trend over time would suggest that a processor chip should become commercially available in 1983 with 250,000 circuits, and another processor chip in 1984 with over half a million circuits—occurrences that I fully expect and which may be conservative.

Referring to Figure 12.4, note that the iAPX 286 processor chip is designed as four independent processing subunits that act in parallel to increase CPU throughput while reducing bus requirements and contention. Because these four subunit functional areas are separate and distinct from each other, simultaneous action is possible and usual, with a consequent twofold speedup over the two concurrent subunits of the I8086.

1. The *bus subunit* implements a demultiplexed bus interface between the I80286 chip and system memory–I/O subsystems as well as monitoring for bus cycle requests from the chip address subunit and other system processors. If there is a pause in bus use, the prefetch portion of the subunit prefetches the next instruction into the six-byte instruction queue as in the I8086.
2. The *instruction subunit* accepts, decodes, formats, and queues up to three instructions transferred from the six-byte prefetch queue of the bus subunit.
3. The *execution subunit* implements the eight central processor registers, the arithmetic-logic unit, and the microprogrammable control logic to execute the instructions obtained from the three-instruction queue of the instruction subunit. The read-only memory (ROM) containing the microcode is within the control portion of the execution subunit. Because of prefetching and predecoding, instruction execution is usually near maximum. Conditions that can reduce instruction execution rate include (a) branches in the code that nullify the instruction prefetch/decode of instructions in the branch; and (b) extreme use of the bus by instructions such as string movement or use by other processors, including DMA; as well as (c) contention for memory access often associated with high bus usage.
4. The *address subunit* includes the four segment registers that implement real memory 20-bit addresses that are used directly when the I80286 is running in I8086/80186 real address mode. Additional logic is implemented that converts these 20-bit addresses into 24-bit real memory addresses when the I80286 is running in virtual memory mode. The latter process will be discussed shortly.

It is important to note that the I80286 furnishes the central processor instructions of the I8086/8088 plus the additional instructions of the iAPX 186, as well as additional instructions and addressing logic to support virtual memory with an address space of 16K (16,384), 64K segments per user (1024 megabytes = 1 gigabyte), that is mapped into a maximum of 16 megabytes of real memory. On the other hand, the iAPX 286 does not include the clock generator, chip select, timer, interrupt, or DMA logic of the iAPX 186. Rather, the I80286 must be configured into a system employing separate chips for these functions, somewhat in the fashion of the I8086/8088, as illustrated in Figures 12.5 and 12.6. Note that the I80287 ver-

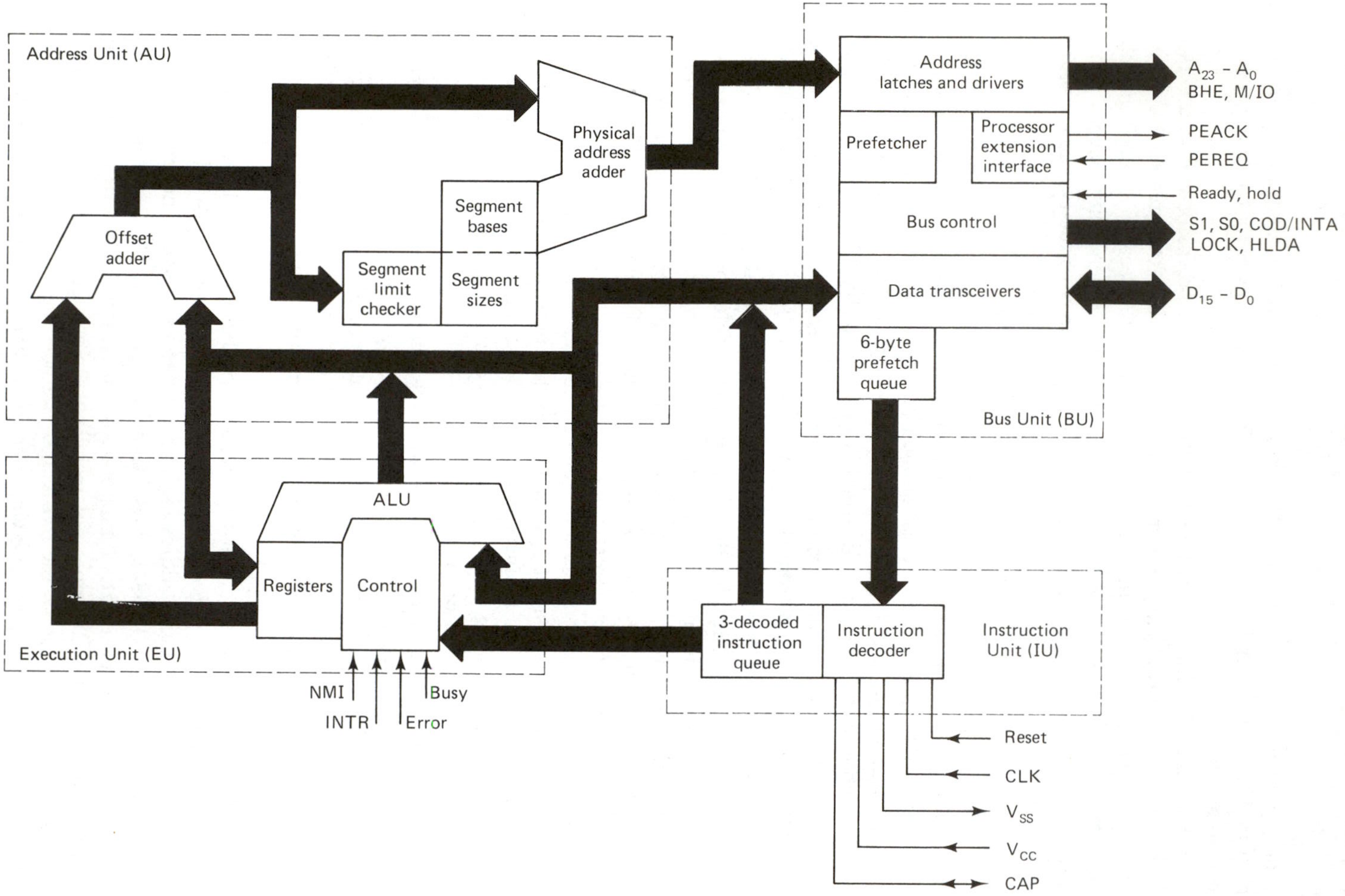

Figure 12.4 Block diagram of iAPX 286. Note the four subunits that normally execute portions of the same, or sequential, instructions simultaneously, resulting in a measure of pipelined concurrency. (Reprinted by permission of Intel Corporation. Copyright 1982.)

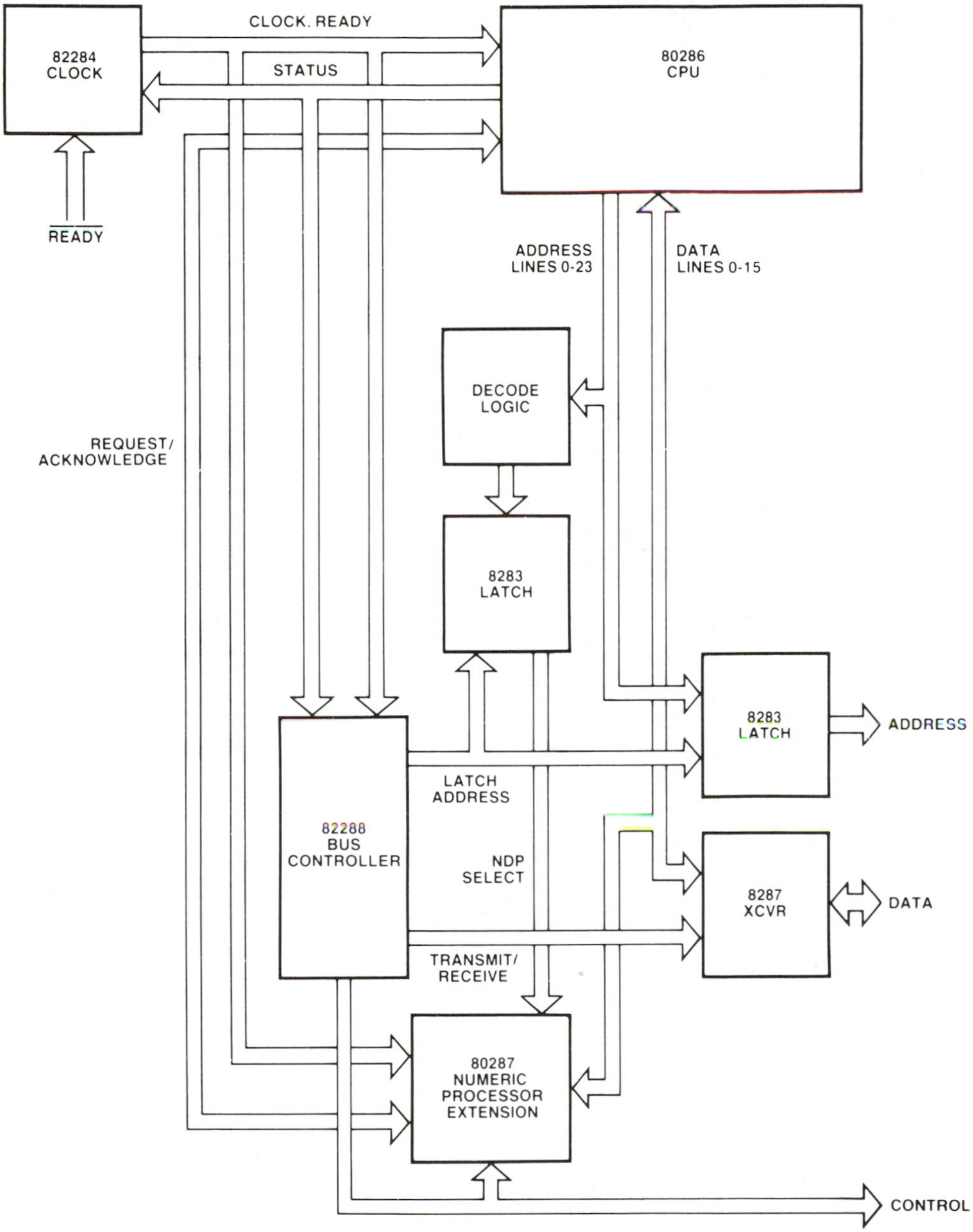

Figure 12.5 iAPX 286-based system including the I80287 numeric data processor employing only a local bus. (Reprinted by permission of Intel Corporation. Copyright 1982.)

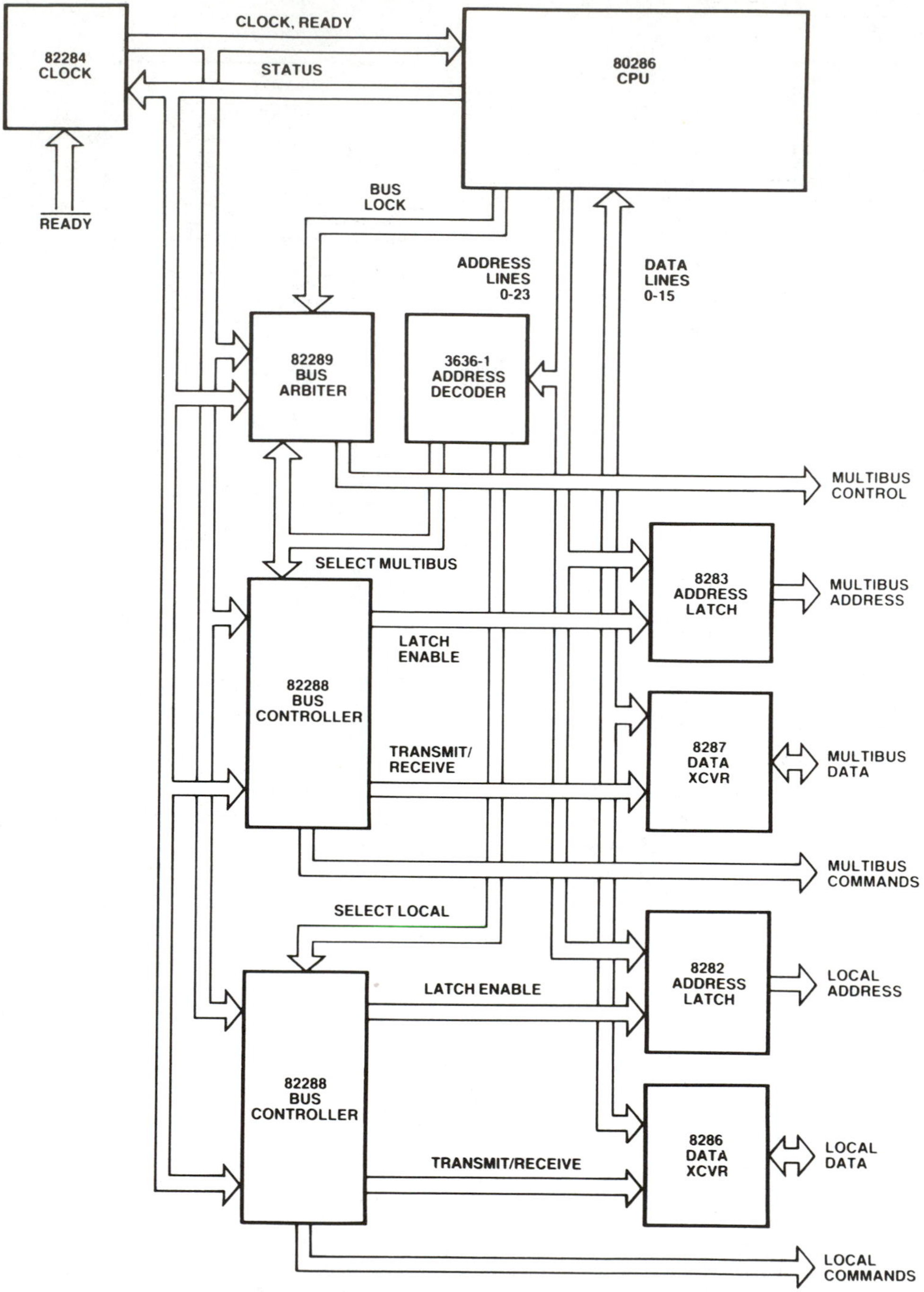

Figure 12.6 iAPX 286-based system configured with a local bus and a global bus (the multibus). (Reprinted by permission of Intel Corporation. Copyright 1982.)

sion of the floating-point numeric data processor is compatible and available. It is expected that a compatible I80130 operating system instruction chip will be available in the near future.

THE REAL ADDRESS MODE

The I80286 can address up to 1 megabyte of memory in the real address mode while executing the instructions with the operand addressing modes of the iAPX 186. That is, the I80286 in the real address mode is compatible with I80186. Additionally, programs written for the I8086/8088 will execute correctly on the iAPX 286 in the real address mode, although the advantages of the additional available instructions will not be realized.

As you recall from a previous discussion, I8088 programs will execute faster employing an I8086 because the 8-bit local bus limitation of the I8088 is alleviated by the 16-bit bus of the I8086. I8086 programs will execute on the iAPX 186 or on the iAPX 286 in the real address mode at a rate determined by the ratio of the chip clock rates with the following two caveats. First, the one-chip functions of the I80186 drastically reduce chip-to-chip information transfers, with the likely result that program execution on the 8-MHz I80186 processor would be slightly faster than on the 8-MHz I8086 processor even though the internal organization of the CPU is identical. Second, the division of the I80286 CPU into four concurrent subunits should allow programs to execute faster than on the I8086 CPU, which has only two concurrent subunits. For both 8-MHz and 10-MHz versions of the two processors, the Intel Corporation reports a speedup ratio of 3.3, although the program itself could have important effects. Actual measurements reported by D. A. Patterson of the University of California at Berkeley (1982) with four programs gave speedup ratios that can be interpreted as ranging from 2.8 to 3.3 for similar-speed (8-MHz) processors. This work also suggests that the iAPX 286 in the real memory mode approaches the execution speed of the DEC VAX 11/780, although the comparison involves different compilers and is somewhat questionable.

THE PROTECTED VIRTUAL ADDRESS MODE

First, it must be emphasized that the I80286 in protected virtual address mode with sufficient main memory (up to 16 M, but probably at least 1 M), with an I80287 numeric processor and with one or more I80289 I/O processors on a nonlocal bus, is not in the same performance class as the usual 8-bit or 16-bit microcomputer. This is particularly true if the system is configured with the I80130 operating system instruction chip. It definitely is well beyond the class of personal computers and most business-oriented microcomputer-based small systems. The "loaded" iAPX 286 in protected virtual address mode is fully as capable as most 16-bit minicomputers and with the I80287 is probably in the performance class of the lower-end 32-bit midicomputers. Additionally, the numerical characteristics of the floating-point processor may result in such superior iteration convergence characteristics compared to many midicomputer processors that faster-than-expected execution may be obtained for numerous numerical algorithms.

Second, the very characteristics mentioned above result in a virtual memory iAPX 286 normally operating as a multiprogrammed time-sliced system with the modern mode being interactive time sharing. Although special circumstances rarely may necessitate a single very high priority critical program "capturing" all of the cycles, this eventuality can be accommodated by manipulating job priorities within the capabilities of available multiprogramming and/or time-sharing operating systems.

Third, the cost of acquiring a computational system in this performance class is dominated by the cost of disk storage, terminals, communications lines, printers, and other I/O equipment, with the cost of memory being relatively cheap and the cost of the central processor being almost insignificant.

Fourth, the cost of designing, coding, documenting, debugging, and maintaining programs far exceeds the cost of the computational system itself. These original and continuing software expenses probably consume well over three-fourths of the total computing budget. Various reports place them at about 80%, with a range from over 50% to nearly 90%, with the central tendency on the high side.

Virtual Memory

When we were considering operating systems in Chapter 9, we deliberately neglected virtual memory because the I8086/8088 is not designed to host such a system gracefully or efficiently. The I80186 and the I80286 in the real addess mode similarly are not conducive to hosting a virtual memory system. On the other hand, the iAPX 286 in the protected virtual memory mode is eminently suitable for this computational mode.

With real memory multiprogramming, it is usual to have more than one program completely resident in real memory at any one time. The CPU is given to one program for a while (for a time slice) or until it cannot use the arithmetic-logic unit (often because of I/O requirements), and then the CPU is given to another program, and then another, in some priority scheme. Virtual memory uses time slices and priority scheduling of the ALU in the same manner. The difference is that only those portions (segments or pages) of programs and data currently or almost currently being accessed are kept in real memory, with the rest residing on disk (in virtual memory) until needed. Then they are shuffled into real memory, replacing those not used for the longest period. If the portions of programs and data that are moved back and fourth between real and virtual memory as needed are all the same size, they are called *pages;* if they are of unequal size, they are called *segments.* The iAPX 286 employs segments, with each procedure being a segment (or more than one if it is larger than 64K) and its data being another segment (or more as necessary). Figure 12.7 covers these ideas in the general sense.

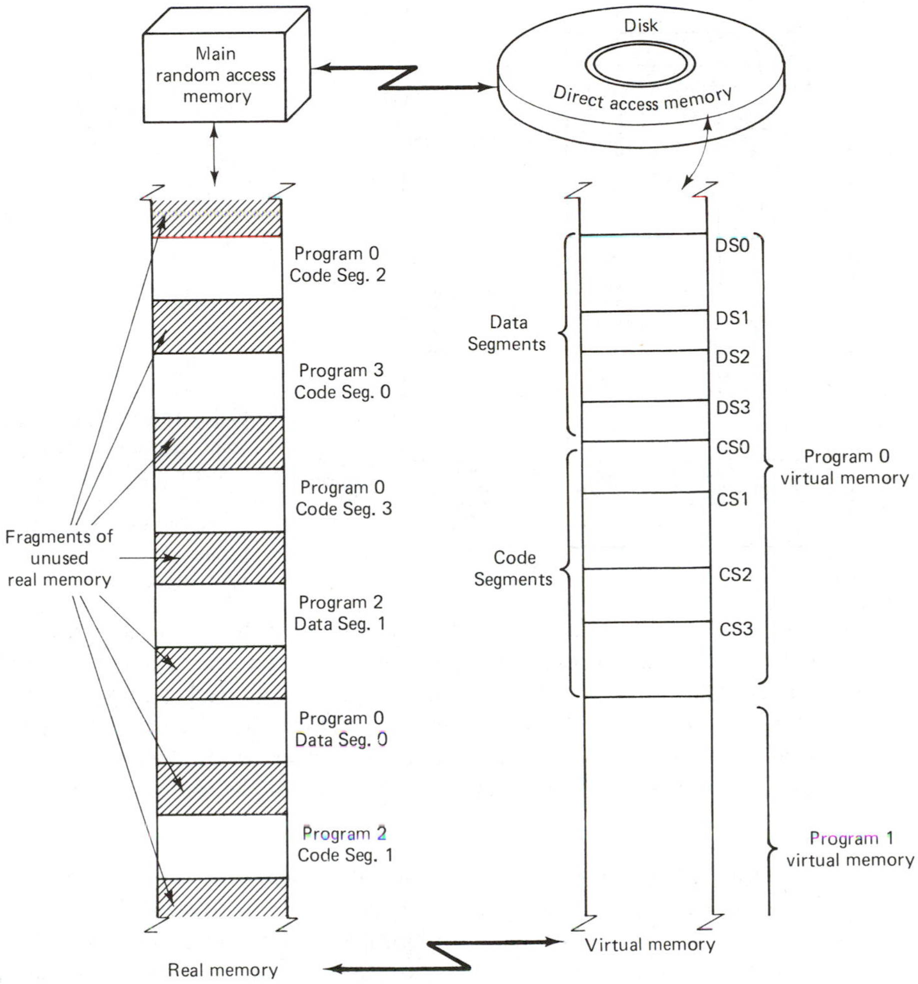

Figure 12.7 The general concept of virtual memory involves movement of those code and data portions from the disk to the main memory as they are needed. Other portions of the same or other program may need to be moved to the disk to create space as new portions are needed. As the segments are of unequal sizes, main memory fragments may be unused.

An address of an instruction and of a datum on the iAPX 286 in the virtual memory mode consists of two portions, (1) a segment identifier, and (2) an offset within the segment, in a manner reminiscent of addressing in the I80286 real mode or the scheme of the I8086/8088 and the I80186. From Figure 12.8 it is apparent that the segment-identifier portion of an I80286 virtual address is basically different from the segment real address held in one of the four segment registers of the nonvirtual address machines. Note that the offset-within segment retains the same

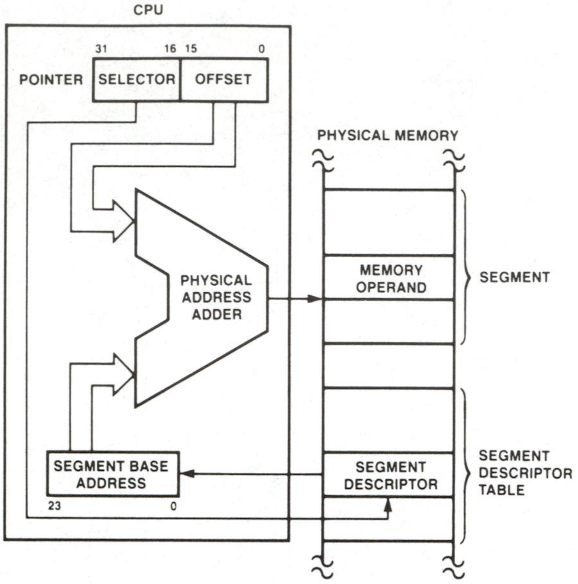

Figure 12.8 Virtual address (logical program address) transformation to real memory address mechanism of the iAPX 286. The segment description table format is detailed in Figure 12.12. (Reprinted by permission of Intel Corporation. Copyright 1982.)

general syntax and function. The segment identifier—the segment selector—is a pointer to the appropriate entry of a memory-resident segment table (Figure 12.9) that contains, among other information, the 24-bit real memory beginning address of the segment. The 24-bit real memory address of the desired datum is then derived as the sum of the segment start and offset within the segment. The following characteristics of the virtual and real addresses of the iAPX 286 are worthy of note:

1. There can be up to 16K segments, each of a maximum size of 64K bytes, in the virtual (logical) address space of a program, giving a maximum program size of 16K $\times$ 64K $= 2^{30} =$ 1 gigabyte $=$ 1,073,741,824 bytes (base 10). A virtual memory address is an example of a pointer data type.
2. There can be up to $2^{24} =$ 16 megabytes $=$ 16,777,216 bytes of real main memory. A physical real memory address is also an example of a pointer data type.
3. The 16-bit segment identifier in the program logical address is a pointer to a 24-bit start of segment in real memory. That is, the address of the segment is an indirect address through the segment description table. Thus a mapping function from logical (virtual) program addresses to real memory addresses is implemented using the logic of the address subunit of the I80286, as shown in Figure 12.4.
4. It will sometimes be true that the code or data segment needed will not currently be resident in real memory but instead will be resident on the segmenting virtual memory disk. Before the contents of a nonresident segment can be accessed, it must be transferred to real memory. This process is illustrated in Figure 12.10.

Segment ID number	0 = segment in main memory 1 = segment on disk	Starting address of segment in main memory or on disk	Size of segment (bytes)	0 = code segment 1 = data segment
0	0	0DF700	0319	1
1	1	Disk addresses	011E	1
2	1	Spindle:	01F8	1
3	1	Side:	00F9	1
4	1	Track:	020C	0
5	1	Sector:	041D	0
6	0	001700	0210	0
7	0	089A00	044A	0

Figure 12.9 Possible segment table for program zero of Figure 12.7. Each access of memory checks this table to determine its presence in main memory or not. If present, the starting location is employed for address calculation. If absent, the segment is loaded, the table updated, and then the starting address used for address calculation.

If the nine steps given in Figure 12.10 for "paging" a nonresident segment into real memory were implemented using software or if they involved too many memory/disk accesses, the amount of time consumed for each virtual-to-real segment transfer would become excessive, resulting in unacceptably high overhead and low system throughput. For these important economic reasons, much of the needed logic is supported by specialized instructions and much of the necessary information is retained in fast specialized registers and/or fast scratch pad (cache) memory. In the next few pages we will explain these hardware facilities and their use during program execution in the I80286 in the virtual memory mode.

The *segment registers* of the I80286 are pointers into a main memory table of *segment descriptors* that are copied to and maintained in fast cache by operating system special instructions during virtual-to-real memory segment transfer. As shown in Figure 12.11, the 48-bit cache resident descriptor includes the real memory starting address and size of the variable-length segment, as well as information concerning who can access the segment for what purposes. A fuller explanation of these three fields is given in Figure 12.12. Remember that the four quickly accessible extended 64-bit segment registers (16-bit segment register plus 8-bit access right plus 24-bit real memory address plus 16-bit segment size) refer to a currently executing real memory resident code segment and the three associated data, stack, and extra (string) segments. Similar information for nonactive segments is maintained in the corresponding segment description tables. Addressing within active segments is thus much faster than addressing to a nonactive segment. Program designers can cooperate with the system in speeding execution by restricting intersegment program branches or off-segment data accesses as much as possible. Academicians would use the terms *restrict the locality of addressing* and *increase the density of addressing* of

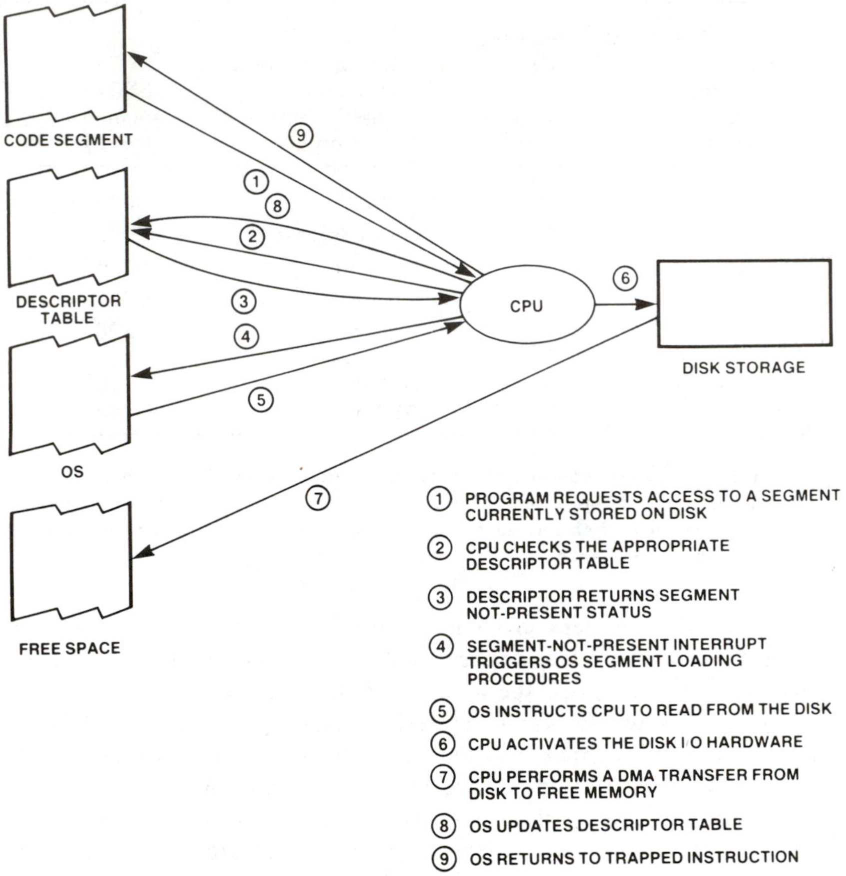
CODE SEGMENT
DESCRIPTOR TABLE
OS
FREE SPACE
CPU
DISK STORAGE
1 PROGRAM REQUESTS ACCESS TO A SEGMENT CURRENTLY STORED ON DISK
2 CPU CHECKS THE APPROPRIATE DESCRIPTOR TABLE
3 DESCRIPTOR RETURNS SEGMENT NOT-PRESENT STATUS
4 SEGMENT-NOT-PRESENT INTERRUPT TRIGGERS OS SEGMENT LOADING PROCEDURES
5 OS INSTRUCTS CPU TO READ FROM THE DISK
6 CPU ACTIVATES THE DISK I/O HARDWARE
7 CPU PERFORMS A DMA TRANSFER FROM DISK TO FREE MEMORY
8 OS UPDATES DESCRIPTOR TABLE
9 OS RETURNS TO TRAPPED INSTRUCTION

Figure 12.10 iAPX 286 actions actuated when a needed segment is not resident in real memory. (Reprinted by permission of Intel Corporation. Copyright 1982.)

both code and data. The accessing of non-real-memory resident segments will slow execution even more drastically by forcing the nine-step process shown in Figure 12.10.

It must be noted that the design of the iAPX 286 in the virtual memory mode was conceived so as to support, somewhat adequately, block-structured procedural-level languages such as Ada, Pascal, C, and PL/I. Thus the implementation of pure code, reentrant code, and recursion, as well as the concepts of local/global data as discussed in Chapter 11, are supported through additional descriptor tables and associated instructions to manipulate the contents of them. The execution of compiled code for a block-structured language procedure with local/global data requires that the ideas of a generalized process stack be supported. Efficiency considerations suggest special fairly fast memory registers for task data that are used repeatedly, with other noncurrently used data being kept in main memory. These data areas are

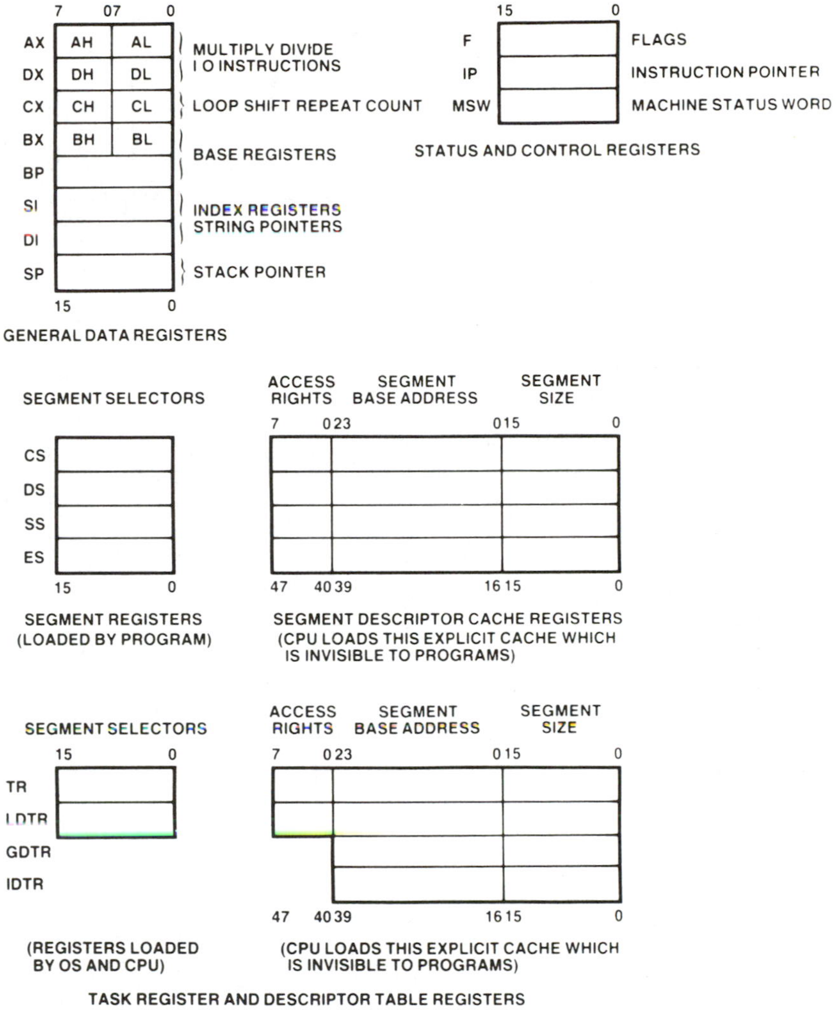

Figure 12.11 Extended register set of the iAPX 286 when executing in protected virtual memory mode. (Reprinted by permission of Intel Corporation. Copyright 1982.)

termed *descriptor tables.* From the bottom of Figure 12.11, note that the fast cache is employed to speed access to the current descriptor information.

The *task register* (TR at the bottom of Figure 12.11) contains the address of the *system segment descriptor,* as shown in Figure 12.13. The system segment descriptor, in turn, contains the address of—points to—the task state segment, which contains current information about the task and thus allows the task to be suspended for later resumption. Included are pointers to higher privilege levels (to be discussed later), to the local descriptor table, and a back link to the next task in a

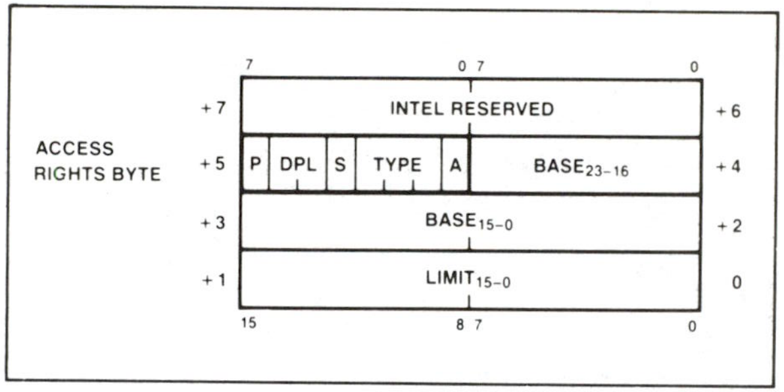

Access Rights Byte Definition

Bit Position	Name	Function	
7	Present (P)	P = 1 Segment is mapped into physical memory. P = 0 No mapping to physical memory exists, base and limit are not used.	
6–5	Descriptor Privilege Level (DPL)	Segment privilege attribute used in privilege tests.	
4	Segment Descriptor (S)	S = 1 Code or Data segment descriptor S = 0 Non-segment descriptor	
3	Executable (E)	E = 0 Data segment descriptor type is:	Data Segment
2	Expansion Direction (ED)	ED = 0 Grow up segment, offsets must be ≤ limit. ED = 1 Grow down segment, offsets must be > limit.	Data Segment
1	Writeable (W)	W = 0 Data segment may not be written into. W = 1 Data segment may be written into.	Data Segment
3	Executable (E)	E = 1 Code Segment Descriptor type is:	Code Segment
2	Conforming (C)	C = 0 Code segment may only be executed when CPL ≥ DPL.	Code Segment
1	Readable (R)	R = 0 Code segment may not be read. R = 1 Code segment may be read.	Code Segment
0	Accessed (A)	A = 0 Segment has not been accessed. A = 1 Segment selector has been loaded into segment register or used by selector test instructions.	

Type Field Definition (bits 3–1)

Figure 12.12 Format and semantics of the code and data segment descriptor table registers. (Reprinted by permission of Intel Corporation. Copyright 1982.)

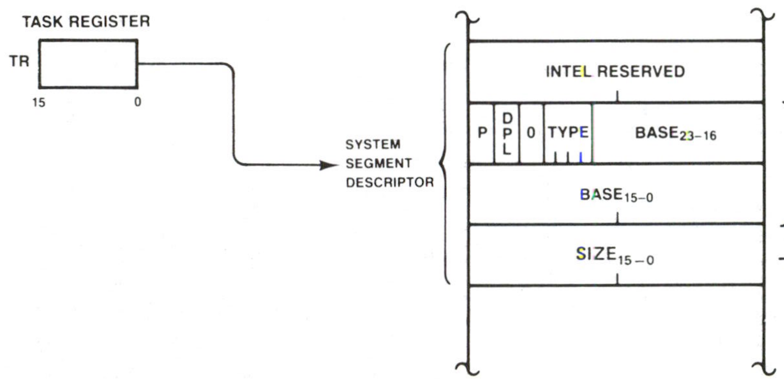

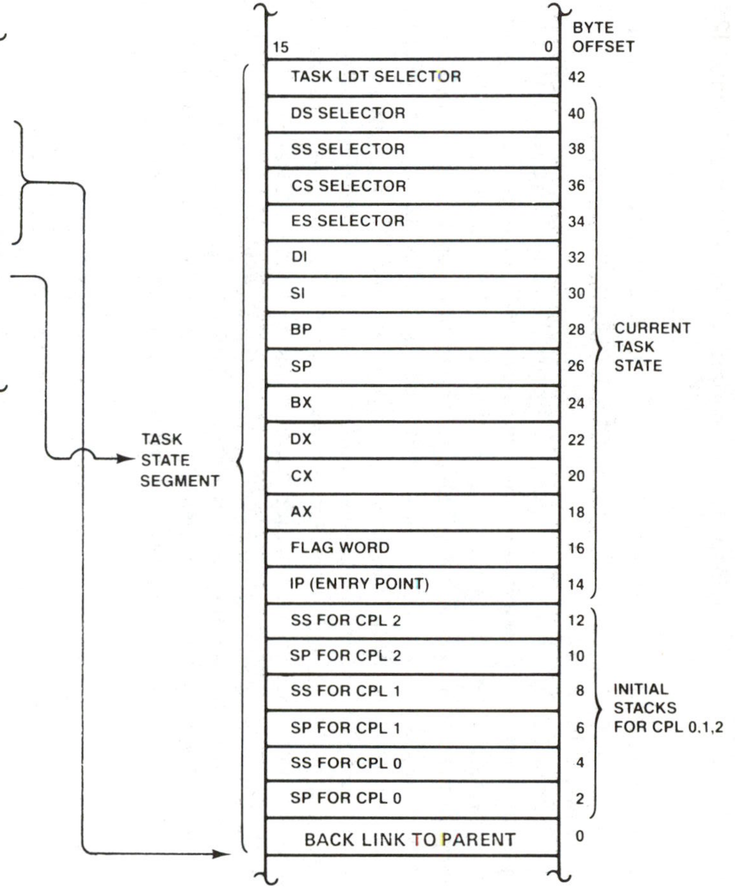

P	DESCRIPTION
1	BASE AND LIMIT FIELDS ARE VALID
O	SEGMENT IS NOT PRESENT IN MEMORY, BASE AND LIMIT ARE NOT DEFINED

TYPE	DESCRIPTION
1	AVAILABLE TASK STATE SEGMENT. MAY BE USED AS THE DESTINATION OF A TASK SWITCH OPERATION.
3	BUSY TASK STATE SEGMENT. CANNOT BE USED AS THE DESTINATION OF A TASK SWITCH.

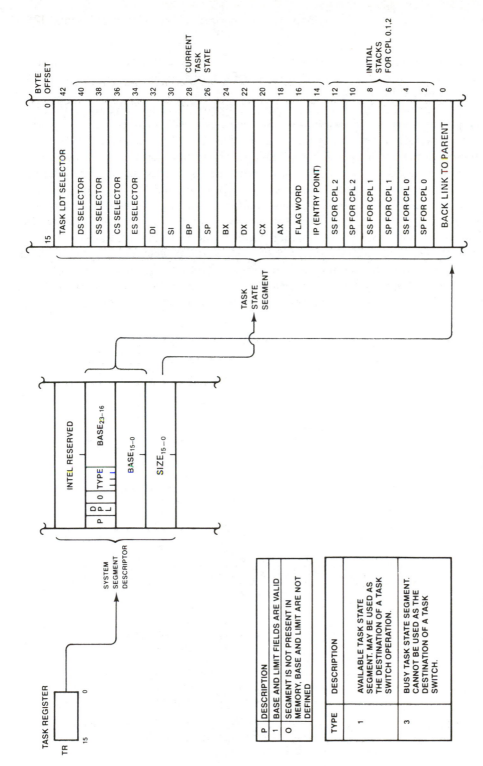

Figure 12.13 Formats and linkage pointers of the task register, system segment descriptor, and task state segment triad of the iAPX 286 in virtual memory mode. (Reprinted by permission of Intel Corporation. Copyright 1982.)

chain of nested task invocations. An extension to the flags register assists the operating system to invoke the routines necessary for task switching. The machine status word is shown in Figure 12.14.

As indicated in the bottom portions of Figure 12.11 and Figure 12.15, three other pointer registers to descriptor tables exist: a local descriptor table, a global descriptor table, and an interrupt descriptor table. The *global descriptor table* is used by the operating system and is unavailable to applications programs, allowing it to be placed in a known location in fast cache memory; thus no pointer or access rights information is needed. The interrupt vector of the iAPX 286 in the protected mode is known as the *interrupt descriptor table.* Only a single copy at a known location is necessary; thus no pointer or access rights information is needed. On the other hand, each task requires information local to the task and unavailable to other tasks, including data, access rights, size, etc. Thus a *local descriptor table* is required for each task. This situation regarding description tables is shown in Figure 12.16.

A *protection mechanism* is implemented in the I80286 in the virtual memory mode to prevent an applications program from modifying the operating system or

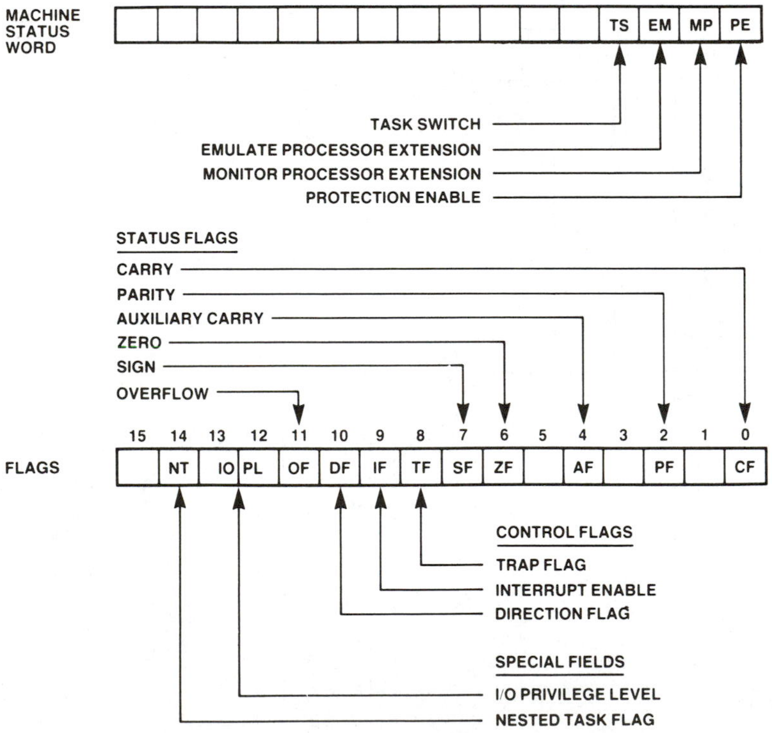

Figure 12.14 The flag and machine status registers of the iAPX 286 form a proper superset of the flag register of the iAPX 186 and the iAPX 86/88. (Reprinted by permission of Intel Corporation. Copyright 1982.)

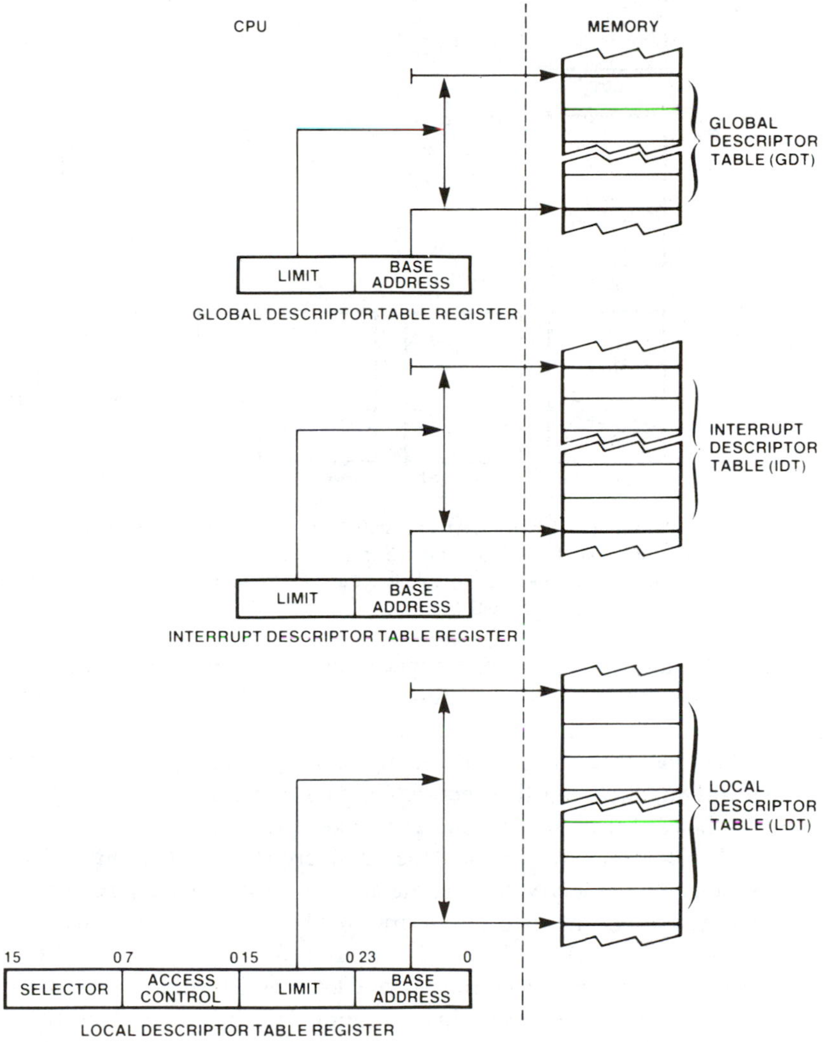

Figure 12.15 Linkages between the descriptor table registers and the corresponding descriptor tables of the I80286 in virtual memory mode. (Reprinted by permission of Intel Corporation. Copyright 1982.)

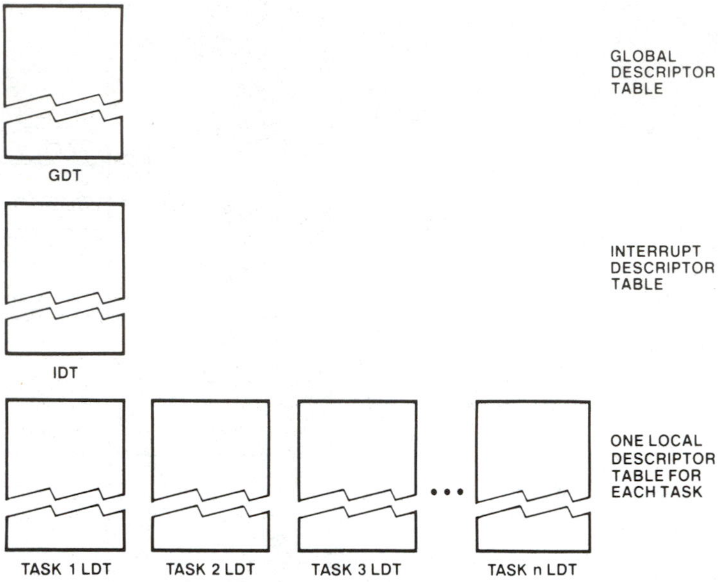

Figure 12.16 Because each executing task requires a private descriptor table, there are numerous local descriptor tables in the iAPX 286. Only a single global and a single interrupt descriptor table is required. (Reprinted by permission of Intel Corporation. Copyright 1982.)

its tables and to prevent one applications program from accessing the data or code of another applications program in the normal multiprogramming environment of this system. The design approach used incorporates the operating system into the applications program so that the addressing space of any one program includes its own private area and the operating system area. This use of a global address space allows an applications program to invoke operating system's services via a fairly fast CALL instruction rather than the relatively slow and traditional context switching mechanism necessary with separate address spaces. To assure protection of the operating system and its data tables from deliberate or inadvertent change by the applications program through illegal actions following such a CALL for services, the system supports four hierarchical privilege levels within each user's virtual address space—applications space plus operating system space. This scheme is shown in Figure 12.17. The protection level of each segment is defined within the appropriate descriptor table.

The segment is the natural unit for protection implementation; thus four segment access privileges are available: (1) execute-only, (2) execute and read, (3) read-only, and (4) read-and-write. These access privileges are checked during segment register loading and as each instruction is executed. The hardware-enforced protection privilege levels constitute rigid firewalls that prevent bugs or deliberate tampering from propagating to the more privileged operating system levels or to other tasks. A program can access data at only the same or a lower privilege level: it can

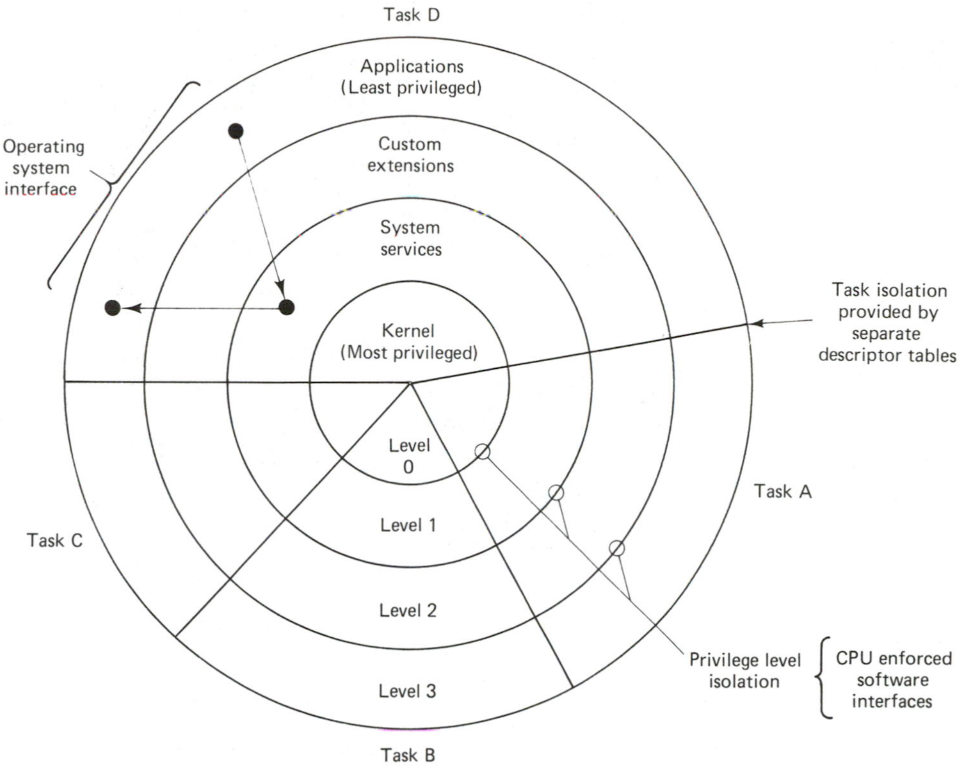

Figure 12.17 Four protection/privilege levels of the iAPX 286 in virtual memory mode. (Reprinted by permission of Intel Corporation. Copyright 1982.)

CALL services only at the same or a more privileged level. A separate stack/stack pointer diad is maintained for each privilege level to prevent unauthorized access via stack manipulation.

When a procedure invokes (CALLs) another procedure, a set (possibly null) of parameters or arguments is passed. These are automatically copied from the caller's stack to the stack of the invoked procedure. In this way, communication between privilege levels is restricted to a single mechanism and protection can be enforced. This enforcement mechanism is termed a *gate* and is employed in all interprotection-level privilege and intertask transfers, including interrupt services. (The interrupt descriptor table consists of a series of gates to the service routines.) The gate format and semantics is given in Figure 12.18. In this fashion, excellent protection is afforded through different types of CALLs, or transfers of control between tasks, as illustrated in Figure 12.19. In effect, a call gate provides an additional level of indirectness that enables verification of the legality of the invocation of the privilege levels of the invoking procedure/invoked procedure.

Name	Value	Description
TYPE	4 5 6 7	–Call Gate –Task Gate –Interrupt Gate –Trap Gate
P	0 1	–Descriptor Contents are not valid –Descriptor Contents are valid
DPL	0–3	Descriptor Privilege Level
WORD COUNT	0–31	Number of words to copy from callers stack to called procedures stack. Only used with call gate.
DESTINATION SELECTOR	16-bit selector	Selector to the target code segment (Call, Interrupt or Trap Gate) Selector to the target task state segment (Task Gate)
DESTINATION OFFSET	16-bit offset	Entry point within the target code segment

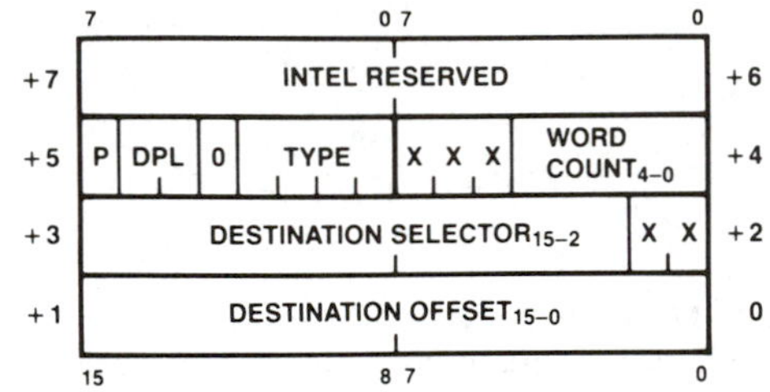

SELECTOR

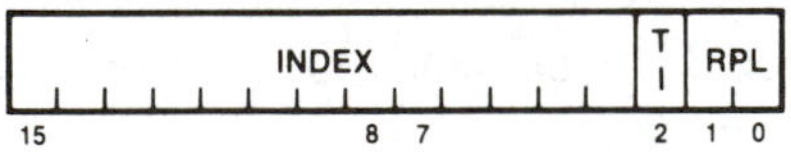

BITS	NAME	FUNCTION
1–0	REQUESTED PRIVILEGE LEVEL (RPL)	INDICATES SELECTOR PRIVILEGE LEVEL DESIRED
2	TABLE INDICATOR (TI)	TI = 0 USE GLOBAL DESCRIPTOR TABLE (GDT) TI = 1 USE LOCAL DESCRIPTOR TABLE (LDT)
15–3	INDEX	SELECT DESCRIPTOR ENTRY IN TABLE

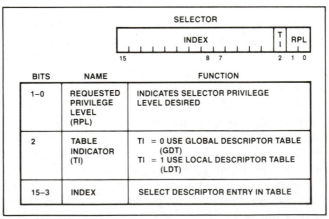

Figure 12.18 Format and semantics of the gate descriptor areas that allow implementation of the four protection/privilege levels of the iAPX 286. (Reprinted by permission of Intel Corporation. Copyright 1982.)

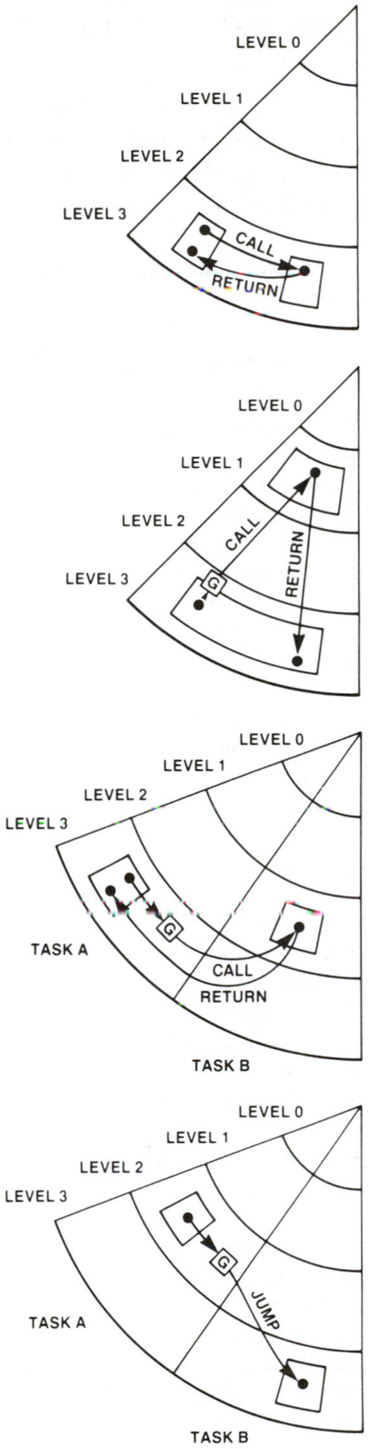

(a) Unrestricted procedure invocation within a privilege level of a task is allowed with no gate usage.

(b) Interprivilege level procedure invocation within a task is checked for legality by the use of a gate.

(c) Procedure invocation between tasks of the same or different privilege levels is checked for legality by the use of a gate.

(d) All intertask and interprivilege level transfer-of-control operations require the use of a gate.

Figure 12.19 The use of gate descriptor areas (see Figure 12.18 for the semantics) to enforce inter-task protection and inter-privilege level protection in the iAPX 286. (Reprinted by permission of Intel Corporation. Copyright 1982.)

With these mechanisms, the iAPX 286 furnishes a satisfactory and safe multiprogramming environment with variable-size segmented virtual memory for execution of programs coded in block-structured procedural-level languages while protecting the system, other programs, and data from inadvertent or malicious tampering.

Sixteen additional instructions are provided to allow manipulation of the added registers, the gates, and the various descriptor tables:

```
LTR    Memory/Register   ; Load or store the 16-bit
STR    Memory/Register   ; selector that chooses one of
                         ; the task state segments.
LLDT   Memory/Register   ; Load or store the 16-bit
SLDT   Memory/Register   ; selector that points to the
                         ; local descriptor table.
LGDT   Memory            ; Load or store the six-byte
SGDT   Memory            ; base address and size of the
                         ; global descriptor table.
LIDT   Memory            ; Load or store the six-byte
SIDT   Memory            ; base address of the interrupt
                         ; table.
LAR    Memory/Register   ; Load the segment access byte
                         ; of the descriptor table and
                         ; set the zero flag ON.
LSL    Memory/Register   ; Load the segment size
                         ; of the descriptor table and
                         ; set the zero flag ON.
LMSW   Memory/Register   ; Load or store the machine
SMSW   Memory/Register   ; status flag to enter virtual
                         ; memory mode. The SMSW
                         ; instruction does not "leave"
                         ; the virtual memory mode—only
                         ; a reset or power up allows
                         ; entry into the real memory mode.
ARPL   Memory/Reg        ; Adjust the privilege level of
                         ; a segment to the maximum
                         ; of the original value and the
                         ; value specified. If value is
                         ; changed, set the zero flag ON.
VERR   Segment ID        ; Verify that the segment specified
VERW   Segment ID        ; is read-accessible or write-
                         ; accessible. Set the zero flag to
                         ; 0 if true, to 1 if false.
CTS                      ; Clear the machine state byte
                         ; task switch flag, which was set
                         ; by a previous task switch.
```

13

Computer-to-Computer Communication

NETWORKS: WHAT AND WHY

It often facilitates, and is sometime necessary for the accomplishment of a task to be able to access data or programs that are resident on a computer somewhere else. For such cases there are three general solution strategies; either (1) go to the remote computer and use the data or programs at that location, (2) have the data or programs sent to you for installation and use on your local computer, or (3) establish a computer-to-computer communication line. The time, effort, and expense of traveling to a remote computer is not extremely attractive, at least to some people, and tends to result in less than optimal profit figures for the business. The acquisition and installation of programs via the mail or the local computer dealer store is often difficult, time consuming, and frustrating due to language dialect differences, documentation deficiencies, I/O incapabilities, and so on. The transport of data may involve legal difficulties of ownership, of privacy, of copyright, of timeliness, of sheer bulk, or of cost.

The single most widely used technique that most often allows the circumvention or complete solution to those problems is computer-to-computer communication. Such communication may be as rudimentary as the user of a small personal computer temporarily acting as an intelligent terminal via a dial-up line to another computer. Such communication may imply that your computer is a station in a local network serving an office or a building. Such communication may imply regional, national, or international abilities for data sharing, for specialized program use, and for more mundane business contacts. The possibility of dispersing much "white-collar work" to the home—forming a new kind of "cottage industry"—may be involved with the consequent complete reshaping of the workplace, of family life, and commuting. Tanenbaum (1981) uses the phrases "to end the tyranny of geography" and "to have alternate sources of supply" for computer processing.

It is important to recall that the relative cost of communication versus the cost of computer processing has undergone a dramatic change over the past several years. The advent of the minicomputer in the mid-1960s, coupled with the wide availability of the microcomputer in the mid-1970s, has resulted in fundamentally different approaches to data capture and processing. In many applications, data are generated at diverse and scattered locations such as checkout stations in different locations in many stores, each with multiple receiving docks each served by diverse suppliers. The inventory control problem, the ordering of supplies problem, the pricing process, the whole management situation was complicated, slow, and error prone prior to the 1970s. The data were gathered and transmitted for processing to an expensive centralized computer. The cost of communicating the raw data was economically justified by the high cost of the computer and data processing. Now that computers with significant power can be obtained for an almost negligible cost, it is economically attractive to automate the data collection and distribute the initial processing to the work sites with only summary data being passed upward to control management via relatively expensive communication facilities. This mode of business is presently common and will soon become almost universal. In this treatment, we deliberately ignore the broad sociological effects of very rapid data availability, analysis, and use.

The purpose of allowing one computer to communicate with another computer is to facilitate the accomplishment of one or more of three objectives:

1. To allow the transfer of programs and/or data
2. To allow the remote use of unique computational power, programs, and/or data collections
3. To allow users at remote locations to interact in a unique nonoral way at speeds not possible using alternative methods

NETWORK STRUCTURE AND TOPOLOGY

Various terminologies have evolved to identify the components involved in networks, that is, in computer-to-computer communication. The computers that communicate are termed *hosts* or *nodes.* The host computers are connected by a *transport system,* a *transmission system,* or a *communication subnet.* In most cases the transport system will consist of transmission lines and switching elements. The switching elements are often termed *intermessage processors, IMPs, nodes,* or other descriptive terms. The transmission lines can be broadly grouped into (1) point-to-point channels, and (2) broadcast channels. In a network using point-to-point channels, any two nodes may be connected via a cable or a telephone line. If not so connected, they would communicate through an intermediate *store-and-forward node.* In a network using broadcast channels, nodes are connected to the single communications channel and compete for its use as well as having access to all messages.

Figure 13.1 illustrates some of the topologies possible when nodes are connected via a transmission system. Point-to-point channels by their very nature are static, although the store-and-forward IMPs may dynamically switch messages via different routes in some networks. Broadcast channels may be allocated in a static scheme; for example, the available time may be allocated in slices on a round-robin basis, allowing a node to send only when its time slot comes up. Channel capacity is usually wasted as a result. In many circumstances, this waste of channel capacity is not important; in other circumstances, this waste cannot be tolerated. Dynamic

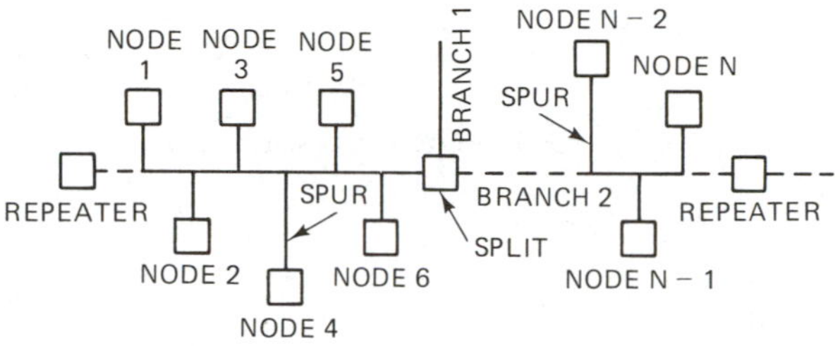

(a) Network with bus topology. Note the possible existence of branches (spurs) through the use of splitters.

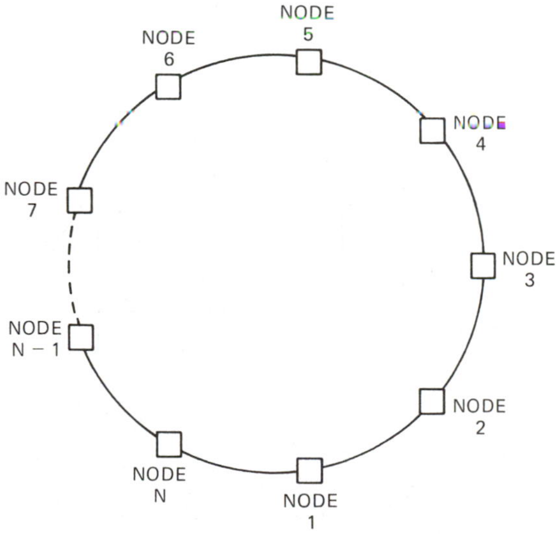

(b) Network with ring topology. The failure of any one node will cause the failure of the network unless some form of bypass exists.

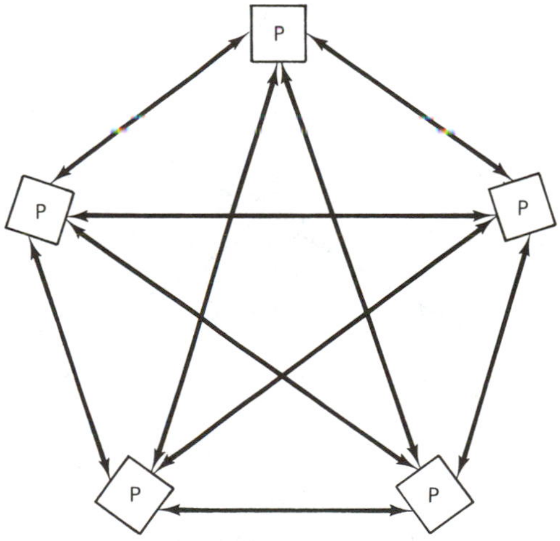

(c) A fully connected network topology is expensive but fail soft. It can be considered as elaboration of a ring.

Figure 13.1 Possible network topologies. (Adapted with permission from G.W. Gorsline, *Computer Organization: Hardware/Software*, Prentice-Hall, Englewood Cliffs, N.J., 1980.)

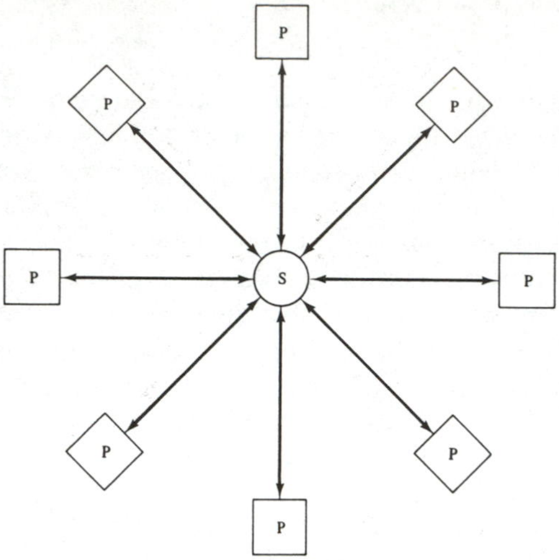

(d) Network with star topology.

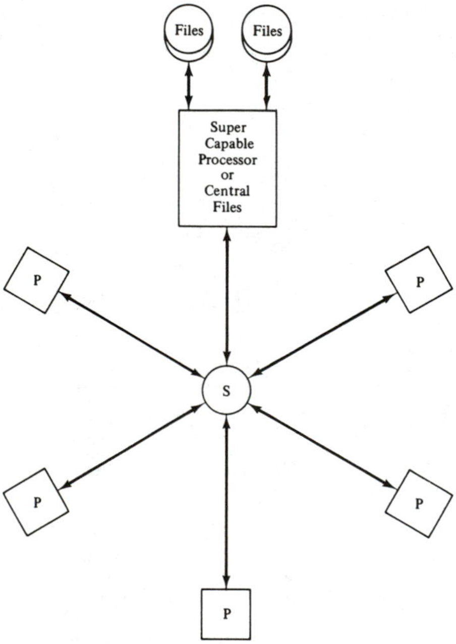

(e) Network with star topology dominated by a master node.

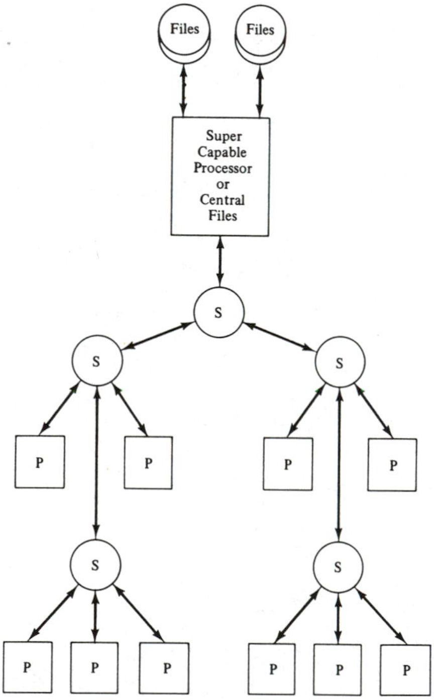

(f) Network with tree topology. It can be considered an elaboration of a star with concentrator (switch) modes reducing communication lines.

Figure 13.1 (*continued*)

allocation of a broadcast channel may be centralized in an arbitration unit or decentralized, with each switching IMP containing a priority algorithm. Alternatively, for example in Ethernet, sending nodes simply contend for channel use by noting lack of activity.

It has become common to distinguish between *wide-area networks* and *local-area networks* (LANs). Local-area networks include computer-to-computer communication within an office, a building, or a small complex with distances of 1 kilometer or less involved. Although wide-area networks can involve communication within an office or building, the ability to communicate over long distances is the vital criterion, with city-to-city links implied and worldwide computer-to-computer data transfer not uncommon.

In our discussion we concentrate on four situations while largely ignoring the general case:

1. A microcomputer communicating directly with another microcomputer using a dial-up connection over ordinary telephone lines
2. A microcomputer communicating directly with a relatively large host computer, with the microcomputer assuming the role of a terminal, either "dumb" or "intelligent"
3. A microcomputer communicating with another computer (of any capacity), with the microcomputer becoming a node in a public or private wide-area network such as SNA or DECNET
4. A microcomputer communicating with other computers, usually small, via a private local area network such as Ethernet or WangNet

THE ISO NETWORK PROTOCOL REFERENCE MODEL

As a direct result of the necessity for the software and hardware of two communicating computers to recognize the start of a message, the contents of a message, and the end of a message, a widely accepted standard has evolved in an effort to prevent the development of hundreds of different methodologies, with resultant chaos. The International Standards Organization has adopted a seven-layer protocol as an answer to the need for commonality of terms and methods, as well as providing clean functional separation for ease of implementation and maintenance. The software engineering principles of program design that are used in this methodology can be summerized as follows (Zimmerman, 1980):

1. A protocol layer exists for each different level of abstraction.
2. Each protocol layer performs one and only one well-defined function.
3. Information flow across the interface from layer to layer is minimal.
4. The number of protocol layers should be small to minimize complexity but large enough to assure the single-function-per-layer requirement.

5. The functionality of each layer should facilitate the adoption of the standard by not grossly violating preexisting network implementations.

The overall function of a network protocol is to allow any program in any computer to send a message to, or receive a message from, any program in any other computer without regard to the exact process of sending or receiving. In other words, the details of message sending and receiving is not only abstracted away from the applications program (in the manner of a CALL to system I/O routines in Pascal and BASIC) but is also abstracted away from the operating system to the network itself. In effect, the applications program requests the operating system to send "message X" to program A and is allowed to ignore the details. The operating system performs some formatting services and presents the formatted message to the network for transmission and then is allowed to ignore the details. Further formatting is accomplished by the network and sending occurs. The reverse process occurs at the receiving node, which, because of the abstractions, may be a different vendor computer with a different operating system, file structure, character encoding scheme, and so on. Thus the layered protocol allows communication program to program with the same ease that exists for I/O of any other type.

Figure 13.2 illustrates the concept of this separation of function by abstraction from the gross three levels—application program, operating system, network—to the seven-layer abstractions of the ISO protocol model. Although actual physical communication occurs only at the lowest level, a form of "virtual communication" exists at each of the other six layers, with the highest-level applications-to-applications program virtual communication being the object of everything.

The *physical layer* (layer 1) is concerned with correctly transmitting raw bits. Definitions of the voltages to represent a 0 and 1, the time a bit occupies, whether the line is half-duplex or full-duplex (one way at a time or both ways simultaneously), initial hookup–final unhook convention, how many and which pins are used for what, multiplexing, and so on.

The *data link layer* (layer 2) is concerned with the recognition of the message "frames" or "packets" by appending unique bit patterns, creating and checking error-detecting codes, acknowledging correct message reception or requesting resending, controlling message flow, and assuring proper sequencing of the frames. Usually implemented in hardware.

The *network layer* (layer 3), often termed the *communication subnet layer,* is concerned with message addresses, the breaking of messages into "frames" or "packets" and their reassembly, the route used for transmission, and the flow of messages. Often implemented as an I/O driver module.

The *transport layer* (layer 4) is lowest-level true source-to-destination layer, so that virtual communication in this level is not aware of any intermediate IMPs that may have been involved in the lower-level physical, data link, and network layers. Figure 13.2 attempts to illustrate this point. The transport layer is concerned with system-independent data communication in a reliable manner with correct frame sequencing. It is often implemented as a module of the operating system.

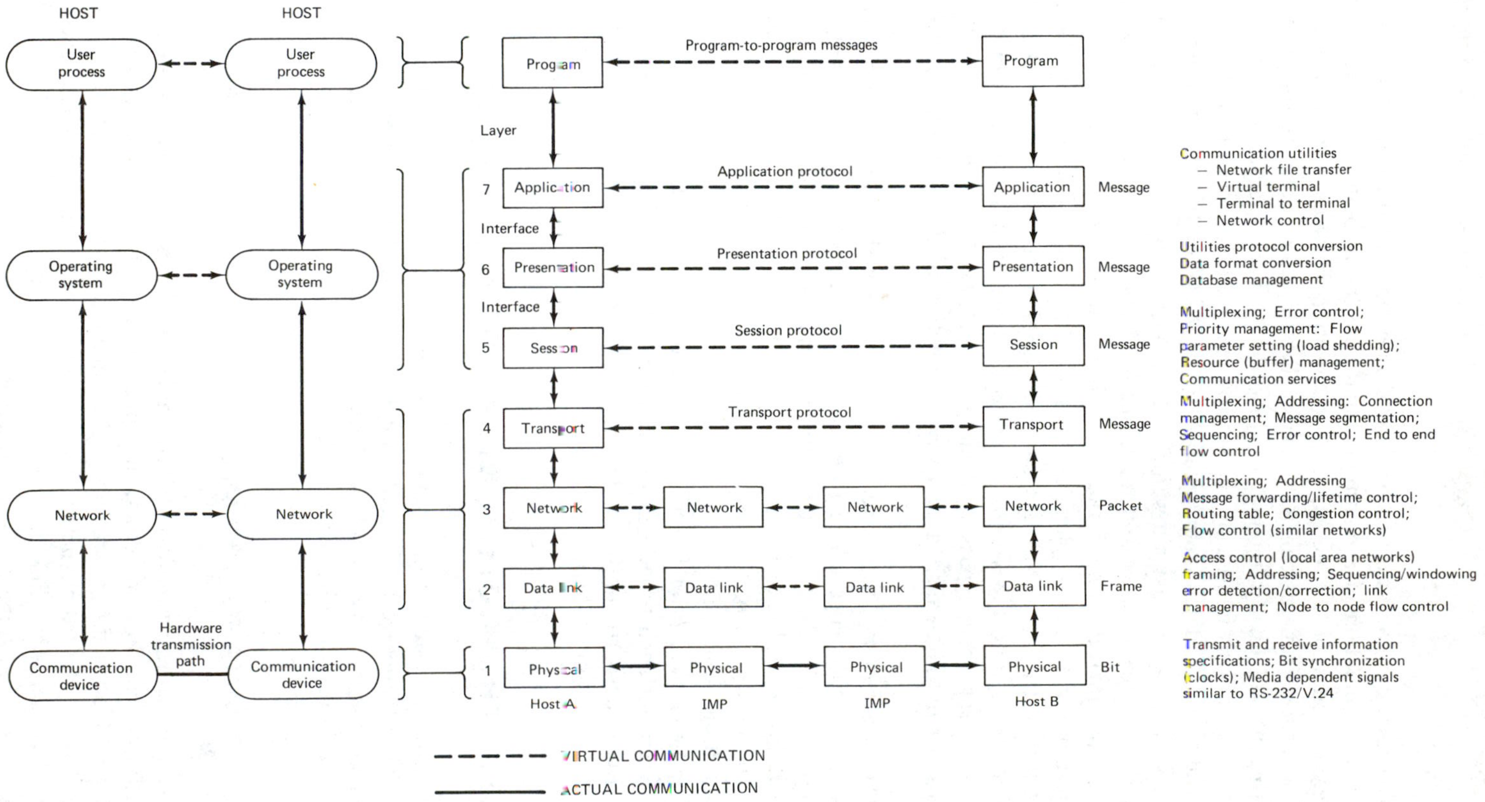

Figure 13.2 Conceptual view of the ISO network protocol reference model. (Adapted with permission from A.S. Tanenbaum, *Computer Networks*, Prentice-Hall, Englewood Cliffs, N.J., 1981.)

The *session control layer* (layer 5) is concerned with the establishment, maintenance, and termination of a communication connection between software processes in different nodes of the network. A connection between two user processes is termed a *session.* It might consist of a user logging onto a remote time-sharing system, using it, and finally logging off. In order to initiate a session, the user must give an address. This is used by the session control layer to authenticate communication rights, to validate communication mode, to allow billing for services, and so on. The session layer must allow for, and recover from, inadvertent and unwanted broken communications, as well as protecting both end nodes (the sender and the receiver) from logical damage caused by interrupted and broken communications. Thus, in many data base application, it is absolutely vital that a transaction not be aborted in midstream lest the data base be left in an inconsistent state. This requirement may necessitate the session layer to completely buffer a transaction request and data message before passing it along to the next layer for action. The session layer is normally implemented as a service function of the host node operating system.

The *presentation layer* (layer 6) is concerned with reformatting messages for presentation to the network and received from the network, such as changing character codes (ASCII-EBCDIC), text compression, encryption/decryption, and changing or adding needed control information, such as end-of-line, cursor address, and so on. The separation of these functions into a module of the operating system is the usual design solution.

The *application layer* (layer 7) is concerned with directly interacting with the user program for such services as file transfer, data base management, network control, and terminal virtualization. This layer is normally implemented as service modules of the operating system.

THE COMMUNICATIONS CHANNEL

Communications channels in a network are the links that connect the nodes (hosts and IMPs) of the network. The links are implemented using a physical medium with a capacity—the maximum amount of traffic accommodatable at one instant—that is measured in hertz or bits per second.

THE PHYSICAL TRANSMISSION MEDIA

Media can be either *bounded*—wires, cables, etc.—or *unbounded*—radio, microwave, infrared, etc. In some cases, the apparent exclusive use of a bounded medium may involve hidden use of an unbounded medium during the actual transmission. Thus the use of the telephone system (apparently consisting of wires) may involve the use of a microwave link without the necessity or even desirability of the user knowing it. In fact, some of the intermediate links may be via radio signals to and from a communications satellite, and other links may involve fiber optics carrying the message as visible light waves, as well as coaxial cables.

Twisted-pair wires of copper (usually) are the original and often the cheapest medium for local telephone message transmission. The ubiquitous telephone network switching and linkage system, with fairly good service and repair characteristics, allows the user to concentrate on the connectivity problems. Data can be transmitted in a digital form of current for a 1-bit and no current for a 0-bit, with the term *hertz* (Hz) signifying changes per second; or alternatively and more commonly, data can be transmitted in an analog form of sound employing different tones (frequencies), loudness (amplitude), and/or phase (chopped frequency) modulations to increase the capacity. In general, telephone switched lines can allow the detection of 1200 changes per second of analog signal—technically, 1200 BAUD. The use of various modulations can increase the data rate to about 4800 bits per second (4.8 kbps) and often to 9600 bps = 9.6 kbps. Leased lines may allow an additional modulation resulting in a capacity of 19,200 bps = 19.2 kbps. Twisted-pair wire is commonly used for connections of low-speed equipment such as terminals and lower-performance printers. Because the clock in the sending node often is not exactly matched in cycle speed to the clock in the receiving node of analog transmission, messages of more than a few bits in length may result in nonrecognition of a bit. Therefore, messages are often restricted to be one character in length and are termed *asynchronous communication.* If clock synchronization can be accomplished, longer messages are possible through the use of *synchronous communication.* Figures 13.3 and 13.4 should be helpful. The standards for analog twisted-wire pairs include Electronic Industries Association (EIA) RS-232-C and CCITT V.24.

Coaxial cables are expensive but have the ability to support high data rates with good immunity to electrical interference as well as a low error rate. Coaxial cables are normally $3/8$ or $1/2$ inch in diameter and consist of a control wire surrounded by a positioning insulator of plastic surrounded by copper wire mesh or extruded aluminum shield, with everything again protected by an outer shield. A *baseband coaxial cable* network employs a single-frequency signal at very high data rates, about 10 to 12 megabits per second (10 to 12 Mbps). A *broadband coaxial cable* network employs a large number of frequency subchannels to allow simultaneous transmission of many signals of high through low data rates. It is practical for a cable TV enterprise to carry over 50 standard color TV channels and thousands of low-speed data signals simultaneously, a fact that is economically encouraging to stockholders in these firms, who foresee their possible bright profit future as local computer communication utilities.

The *fiber optics* currently available can support data rates at least 1000 times greater than those of coaxial cables, with extremely low error rates and complete immunity to electrical interference. Although it is probable that line-tapping methods will be developed to breach security without detection, currently such methods seem remote, if not impossible. The physical size and weight compared to many twisted-wire pairs and multiple coaxial cables of similar capacity assures continued development and increased use of fiber optics in the near future.

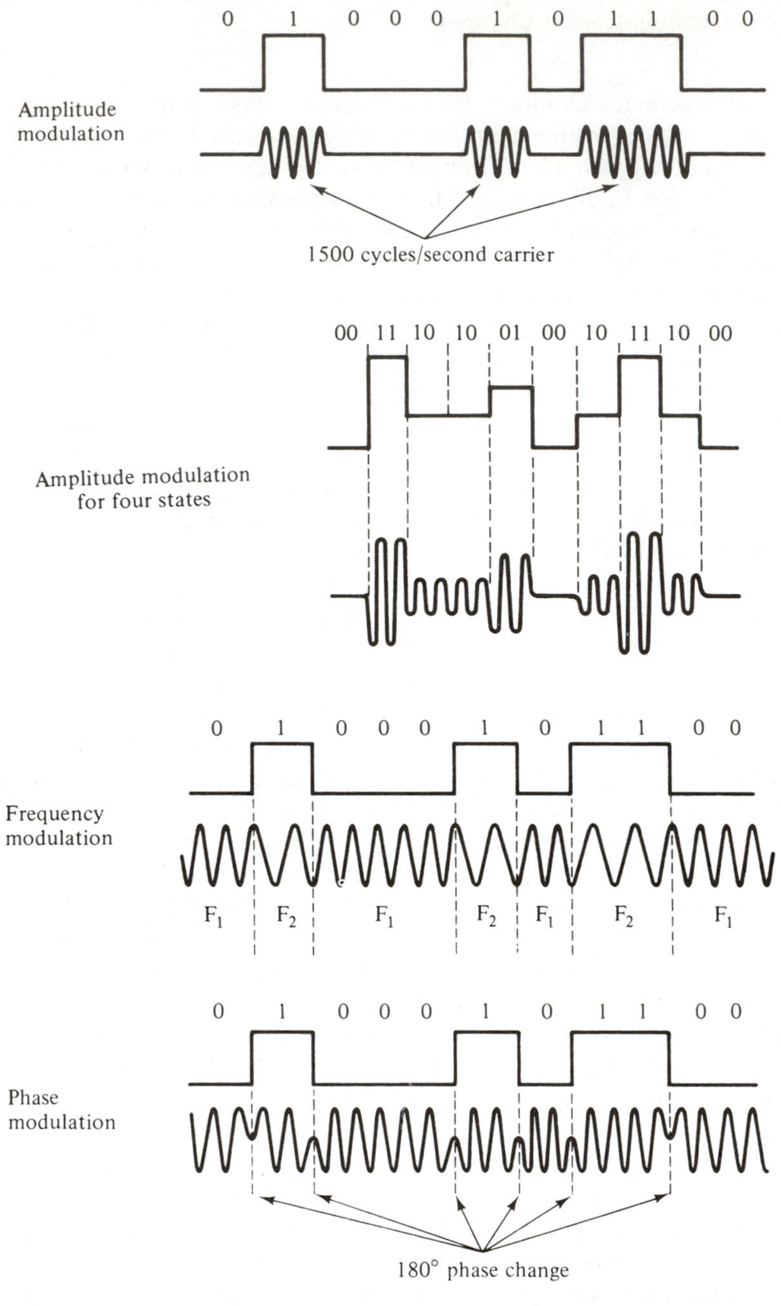

Figure 13.3 Modulation techniques commonly employed with analog message transmission to allow increased carrying capacity (bps--bits per second) as multiples of the baud rate (changes of state per second). Although only 1200 baud is currently practical, modulation may allow 9600 bps or even 19,200 bps. (Reprinted with permission from G.W. Gorsline, *Computer Organization: Hardware/Software*, Prentice-Hall, Englewood Cliffs, N.J., 1980.)

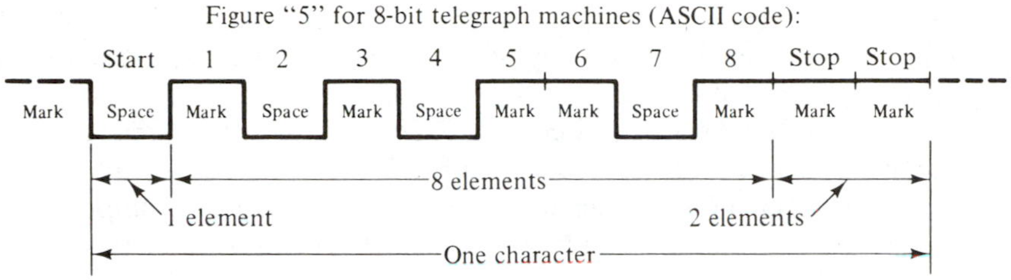

Asynchronous transmission with start-stop structures.

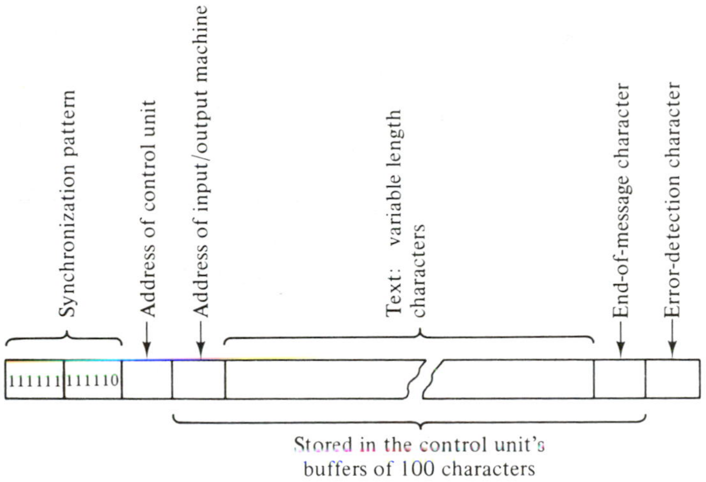

Synchronous transmission with synchronizing pattern.

Figure 13.4 Synchronous and asynchronous message transmission techniques. (Reprinted with permission from G.W. Gorsline, *Computer Organization: Hardware/Software*, Prentice-Hall, Englewood Cliffs, N.J., 1980.)

Unbounded media include such technologies as radio as used in the ALOHANET in Hawaii. For our present purposes, we will ignore it and other possible unbounded media.

MULTIPLEXING

With many computer nodes each attempting to use the network, the capacity or bandwidth of the physical communication channel may result in contention for access. It therefore often becomes economically attractive to divide or allocate the channel among multiple users. *Multiplexing* is a method for accomplishing such allocation. In general, two types of channel multiplexing will be found, although a few people class the clustering of many twisted-wire pairs together in a cable as space-division multiplexing.

Frequency-division multiplexing (FDM) assigns a different restricted frequency bandwidth to each channel in a wide-bandwidth very capable physical medium such as a coaxial cable or a fiber optics cable. As a possible example, the human voice has a frequency range of only about 4000 Hz (4 kHz), and this bandwidth can be modulated, as described earlier, to allow up to about 19.2 kbps. If a wide-width medium is employed, such as a coaxial cable, many messages could be multiplexed in different 4-kHz areas simultaneously. Figure 13.5 illustrates the idea. MODEMS

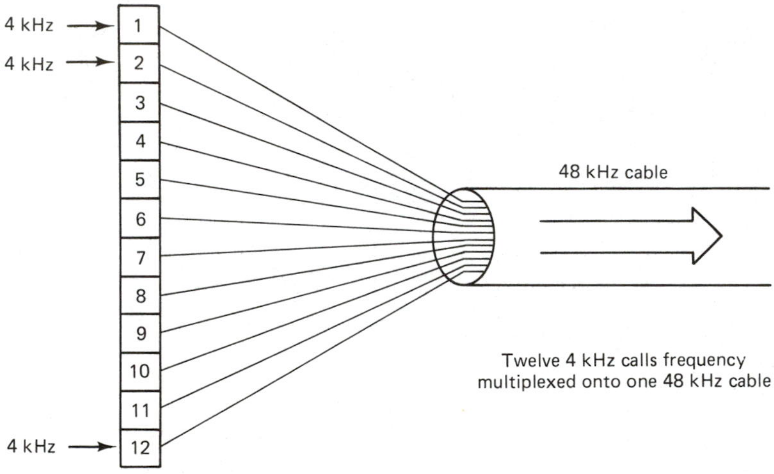

(a) Frequency division multiplexing

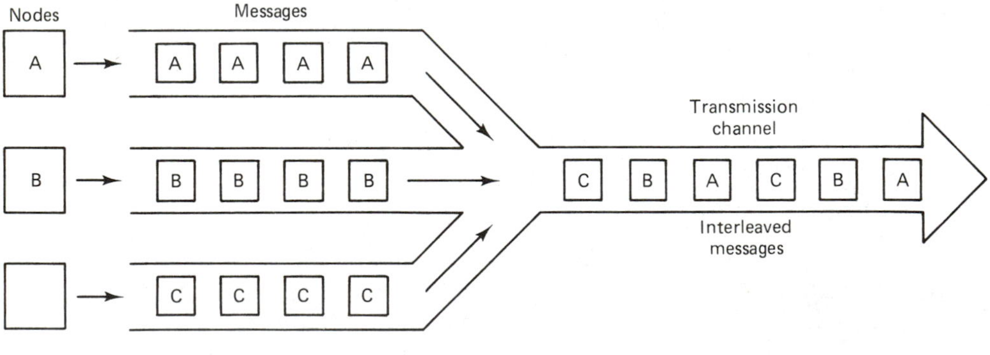

(b) Time-division multiplexing

Figure 13.5 Two main types of message multiplexing. (Adapted with permission from material copyrighted by Digital Equipment Corporation, 1982.)

(modulators/demodulators) commonly exist to allow frequency-division multiplexing. FDM techniques actually are employed with unbounded radio-wave media that allow a receiver to be tuned to a unique radio or TV channel. This last example can be used to argue that FDM is very similar to space-division multiplexing.

Time-division multiplexing (TDM) can be employed with either analog or digital transmission over a single channel. Figure 13.5 illustrates the concept of interleaving packets onto the single channel. Each TDM subchannel to or from a node is assigned a time slice either in exact round-robin order, or alternatively, each frame can carry a destination address. It is possible and somewhat common to combine TDM and FDM so that the frequency-division subchannels are time-division multiplexed.

CHANNEL ACCESS

Access techniques determine which node acquires the use of a channel next. These techniques mediate between nodes that are competing for a channel. In general, access techniques are either of the polling type or of the contention type.

Polling techniques of channel access determine the order of channel use so that conflicts or message collisions are avoided. *Centralized polling* involves the network master node querying each node in turn relative to its need to use the channel and granting usage rights in round-robin order. Note that time-division multiplexing can be considered a form of centralized polling. *Token passing* is common with ring networks and has been used with bus networks. Token passing is accomplished by passing a unique bit pattern token signifying access privilege from node to node. A node receiving the token can transmit a message and then pass the token on, or if it has no message to send, it promptly passes the token on. The *slotted ring* network continually circulates slots of uniform size frames containing source, destination, control, error codes, and a data area with a bit specifying use or not. Each node needing to send a message waits for an empty slot and, when one is found, uses it. Each slot is checked for incoming data addressed to the node which it removes—freeing the slot for another use. If a slot arrives back at the sending node, an error condition is indicated; either the destination address was incorrect or the destination node was "sick." In both cases, the originating node is expected to free the slot and initiate some corrective action, at least delay sending to the sick node for a period of time.

Contention techniques of channel access are based on the probable existence of internode contention for channel use and use message collisions as a portion of the channel allocation algorithm. The *carrier-sense multiple access with collision detect* (CSMA/CD) technique will be explained as our example using Figure 13.6. Carrier sensing is the ability of each node to detect channel use (traffic), called *listen-before-talking.* Nodes will not attempt to use a busy channel but will wait for a nonbusy channel. Because of the time that is required for a signal—a message—to travel across the network (small but significant and known as *propagation delay*), it is pos-

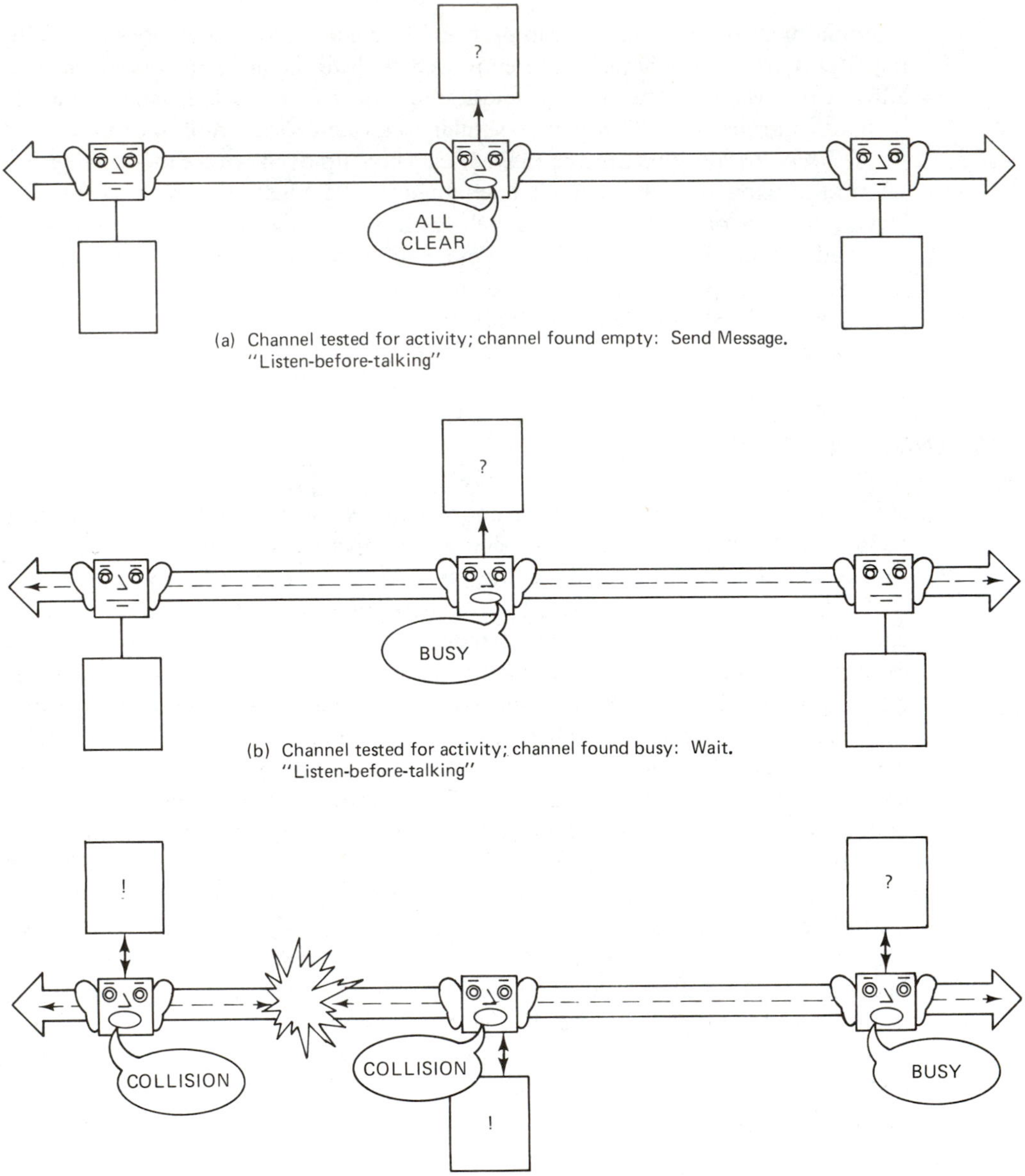

(a) Channel tested for activity; channel found empty: Send Message. "Listen-before-talking"

(b) Channel tested for activity; channel found busy: Wait. "Listen-before-talking"

(c) Channel found empty by two (or more) nodes who each transmit; collision results: both stop sending and wait random time before trying again. "Listen-while-talking"

Figure 13.6 Carrier-sense multiple access with collision detect technique of distributed contention channel sharing (CSMA/CD). (Adapted with permission from material copyrighted by Digital Equipment Corporation, 1982).

sible for two nodes both to detect a free channel and both to start sending almost simultaneously. This results in the collision of two messages and their mutual destruction. Collision detection is sensed by the nodes while they are transmitting via changes in the channel energy level (*listen-while-talking*). A collision causes both sending nodes to stop sending, wait a random time, check for a free channel, and finally send again.

Acquiring a Communication Channel

In order for a message from one computer to be received by another computer, a transmission path—a physical media connection—must be established. In general, two techniques are used to establish the communication route: circuit switching and packet switching.

Circuit switching is the common method used for initiating and completing telephone connections. Each time a call is "dialed," an electrical path is established by switches in the telephone network to form an end-to-end connection and form a physical linkage. The initial switching consumes a significant time (in terms of computer processing) known as the *call setup time.* After the connection is established, the use of the circuit is continuous and exclusive for the entire connection time. When the call is completed, the circuit is terminated through switching caused by the callers "hanging up" the receivers.

The telephone circuit-switched network is widely and commonly used for the transmission of data between host computers and terminals (both "dumb" terminals and microcomputer systems being used as "intelligent" or "smart" terminals). As the use of telephones increased for both voice and computer communication, commensurate localization of switching evolved so that presently it is common to encounter:

PBX: The private branch exchange allows calls between phones within the same premises without external switching into the local phone company's system, while providing access to "outside" lines. The newer version is termed PABX, private automated branch exchange, and is microprocessor based. All signals are of an analog form, requiring that computer communications be converted from and to digital signals via a modem. Figure 13.7 illustrates the process.

CBX: The computerized branch exchange employs time-division multiplexing to allocate channels. Input to the CBX must be analog, so computer communications must be converted from digital to analog via a modem. Output from the CBX is digital; that is, the analog voice signal and the just-converted analog computer signal are converted to digital via time-slice sampling and then sent over the established telephone circuits to the receiver, where the reverse conversions occur. Note particularly that a computer digital message is converted to analog, back to digital, transmitted, converted to analog, and finally converted back to digital. Figure 13.7 may help in un-

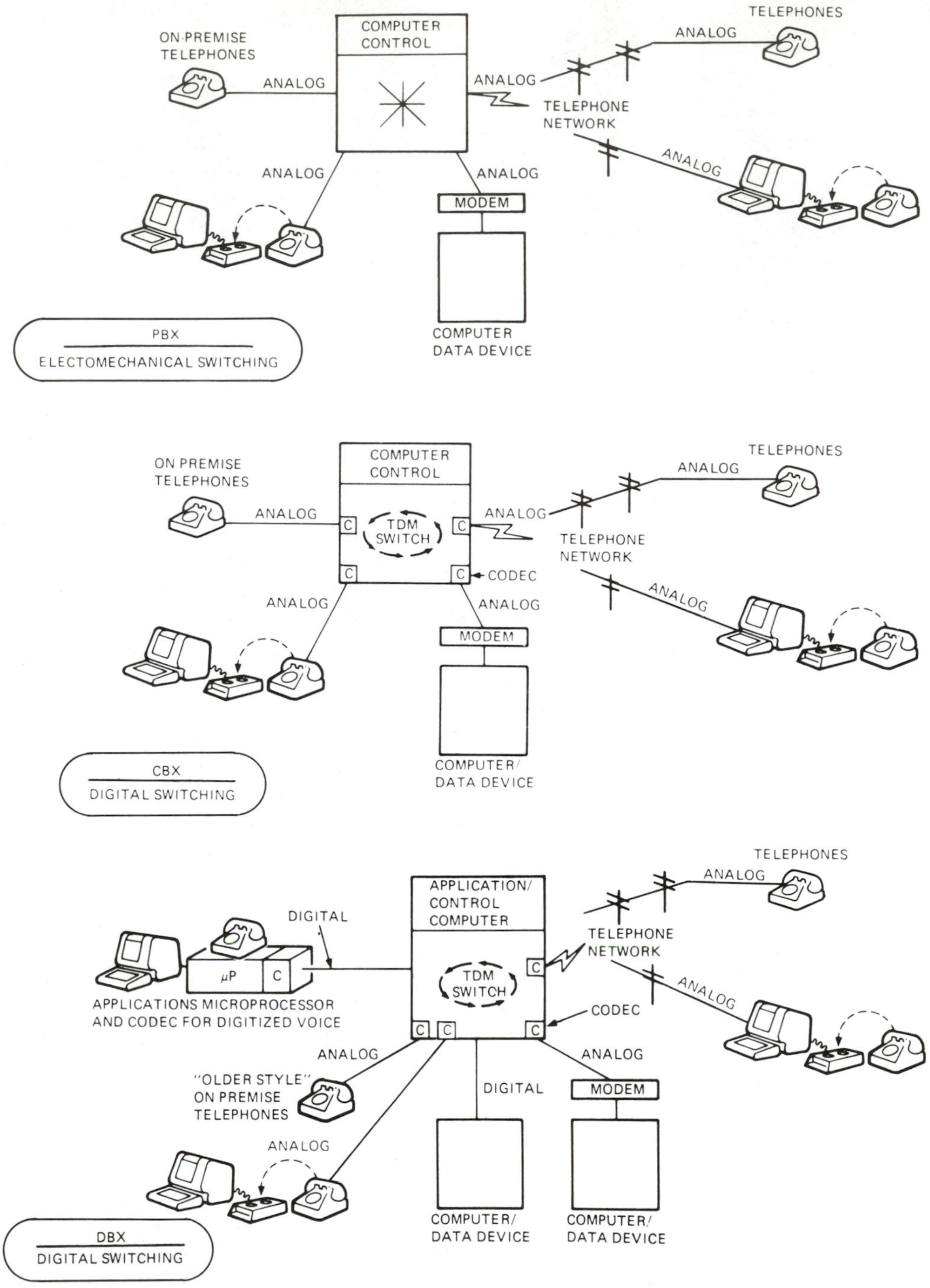

Figure 13.7 Three common on-premises telephone system local switching and nonlocal access methods. In all three cases, the long-distance transmission may be statistically sampled with time-division multiplexing. (Adapted with permission from material copyrighted by Digital Equipment Corporation, 1982).

derstanding this process. Note that the CBX has a superset of the PBX/PABX abilities.

DBX: The digital branch exchange is relatively new and presently somewhat expensive. Similarly to the CBX, time-division multiplexing is used to allocate channels. As shown in Figure 13.7, the DBX can be employed in the manner of a CBX. Additionally, the DBX allows computer-originated digital signals to be sent directly to other computers without the double conversion to analog and back to digital at both nodes. Additional abilities, such as least-cost routing, voice storage and forwarding, call forwarding, and conference calls, are becoming common features of the DBX.

Circuit switching using the telephone system remains a viable methodology for data transmission using rates up to 2.4 kbps (kilobits per second) for "long-haul" switched lines, 4.8 kbps for long-haul leased lines, and perhaps 9.6 kbps for localized lines. The current upper limit of 56 Kbps will probably remain into the 1990s. In terms of characters or bytes per second, these rates vary from the low end of 10 Bps (bytes per second), through 300 Bps, 600 Bps, 1200 Bps, 2400 Bps, to a possible 7000 Bps depending on the use of synchronous versus asynchronous and frequency-division multiplexing together with time-division multiplexing.

Packet switching is the computer-oriented solution to the need for transmitting brief bursts of data employing the total capacity of a high-bandwidth (high capacity) channel. A packet is a discrete portion of a message of fixed or variable length with (usually) a maximum length that is constructed by the network system. A packet can contain bits for synchronization, control, message number, current packet number, number of packets in message, destination address, source address, acknowledgment, error control, and data. The previously discussed ISO Network Protocol Reference Standard provides an example. Figure 13.2 is a good summary. Packet transmission techniques can be used with circuit-switched methods but are more common in store-and-forward IMP-based dynamic switched routing networks and in broadcast-bus-based networks.

POINT-TO-POINT COMPUTER COMMUNICATION

The very simplest means of allowing one computer to transmit data to another computer uses the public circuit-switched telephone network in passing data converted to analog form via a modem. In its most elementary form, the originator first lifts the telephone off the hook, dials the number desired, talks to the answering party, and then orally arranges for both to switch their respective modems into the circuit for data exchange using an agreed-upon character set, baud rate, multiplexing, asynchronous–synchronous node, and so on. After data transmission is complete, both parties switch back to voice mode, congratulate each other, and terminate the call by hanging up their telephones. The scheme is illustrated in Figure 13.8. This method is practical and common in at least three situations:

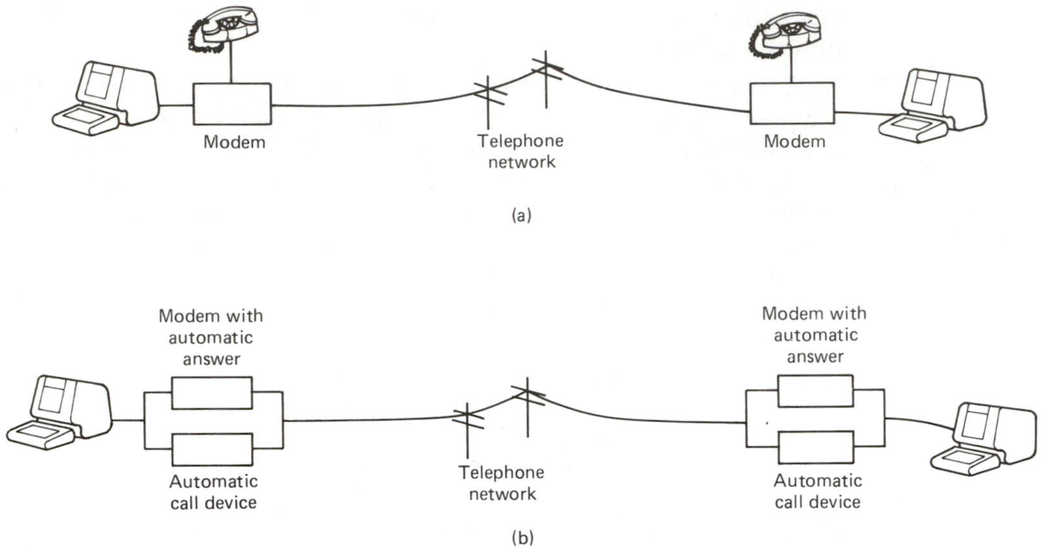

Figure 13.8 Point-to-point circuit-switched communication over the public telephone network. (*Top*) Manual human intervention for establishing and releasing the channel. (*Bottom*) Automatic call and automatic answer system for establishing and releasing the channel.

1. A dumb terminal conversing with a remote host computer
2. A microcomputer or intelligent terminal interacting with a remote computer with superior capabilities, such as unique programs, specialized data bases, or additional arithmetic abilities
3. A microcomputer interacting with a remote microcomputer in order to allow two human users to solve a common problem, such as joint authorship of a paper, remote business dealings, and so on.

The *automatic answering modem* can often facilitate this process of computer-to-computer communication. The augmented modem itself senses the ring of the telephone, "picks up the receiver," switches in the receiving computer, allows data to flow, and finally "hangs up the phone" when the originating party terminates the call connection. The automatic answering modem is somewhat common in the service-oriented time-sharing and data base query environment. Note that the originating party must be aware of and use the specified character set, baud rate, multiplexing method, synchronous-asynchronous node, and so on, of the service-oriented host equipment in addition to having made satisfactory arrangements before the call for access permission, security codes, billings, and so on.

The addition of an *automatic calling device* in the originating node together with an automatic answering modem in the receiving node can fully automate the data transmission process. A call can be initiated by almost any preprogrammed event, such as a wall-clock-timed interrupt, a smoke or burglar alarm, or a keyboard command. The automatic calling device reacts to a command by electrically "taking the phone off the hook," waiting for a dial tone, sequentially generating the tones for the desired destination, waiting for an answer, allowing data to flow, and finally "hanging up the phone" when the data exchange is completed. Note that the automatic calling device must be able to wait for and recognize a dial tone, recognize and "hang up" if the destination phone transmits a busy signal, and transfer control to data transmission if and only if a successful connection is accomplished. Additionally, many automatic calling devices include circuitry for automatic redial/retry at preprogrammed intervals if a busy signal was detected. Again, prearrangements regarding communication permission, security, billing, and message protocol must have been accomplished by the parties involved.

MICRO-TO-MICRO COMMUNICATION

Concentrating our discussion on the case where one microcomputer is desirous of communicating with another microcomputer allows us to ignore the important cases where rigid communication protocols must be observed, as established for a relatively large host computer service center employing a predefined network. Small computers currently have a simple single communications port, usually configured for standard EIA RS-232-C-type communication. The RS-232-C standard provides facilities for housekeeping functions, network control, and a single two-way path for data exchange. As our discussion is limited to circuit-switched telephone-system-based microcomputer-to-microcomputer communications, we can assume ASCII character coding serial data transmission. In some cases, asynchronous character-by-character with acknowledgment transmission will be involved; in other cases synchronous packet with acknowledgment will be used. Half-duplex node with two-way but only one-way-at-a-time transmission will be most common, although full-duplex node with simultaneous two-way transmission is sometimes employed.

Our description of events will follow Figure 13.8. In the no-traffic-between-calls state, the automatic calling device is idling and the microcomputer is either idling or occupied in some other task. The telephone is "on the hook." At a time determined by an event—a keyboard command, a timer interrupt, a programmed command, or an alarm—the microcomputer will cause the automatic calling device to recognize a telephone number by sending a unique bit pattern. If the modem is currently being used, it will prevent the recognition of this prenumber bit pattern. If the modem is not in use, the automatic calling device will recognize the "a call number will follow" unique bit pattern, send a signal to the modem to stay out of the circuit, and prepare to accept the telephone number that it is to call. This mutual lockout hardware feature of the modem–automatic calling device is necessary to prevent interdevice interference, resulting in chaos.

The ASCII-coded dial digits are then sent from the microcomputer to the automatic calling device, where they are saved in registers together with optional command codes. When the end-of-number command is received, the automatic calling device will seize the line, wait for the dial tone, place the call, and wait for the answer-back tone from the automatic answering modem at the remote microcomputer. It will then transfer line control to the modem, drop out of the circuit, and go to an idle state. The modem–microcomputer diad pair will carry out the data transmission and eventually complete the process, with phone "hangup" being accomplished by the modem just before it enters the idle state.

Unfortunately, no accepted standard exists for communication involving an automatic answering modem or an automatic calling device, although the RS-232-C EIA standard does specify pin usage, voltages, and timing. Options may be available with an automatic calling device, such as recognition of different modems at the originating microcomputer; abortion of a dial attempt before connection; variation in character format in asynchronous mode (7-bit/8-bit ASCII, parity/no parity bit, one or two stop bits); redial if busy; rotary dial or touch tone; and the desire of the dialer to send only as requested.

MICRO-TO-NETWORK COMMUNICATION

Consideration of the case where it is necessary for a microcomputer to communicate within an established wide-area computer network or by using the message protocols of an established wide-area network require a knowledge of the network communication requirements. We will briefly consider the IBM SNA (System Network Architecture) and Bisynchronous Communication (Bisync) as well as the DEC DECNET situations, all of which employ synchronous communication of packets of data enclosed within various header and trailer information blocks.

COMMUNICATION PROTOCOLS

ASYNCHRONOUS COMPUTER-TO-COMPUTER COMMUNICATION

Asynchronous computer-to-computer circuit-switched asynchronous communication is the normal communication mode used for a small computer to communicate with another small computer or terminal when they are not a portion of a preplanned "permanent" network and massive amounts of data are not involved. Normally, the physical communication will be the telephone system via a modem using frequency modulation, with the connection preestablished either manually or by automated dialing. Transmission speeds will probably be in the range of 10 to 30 characters per second, with each character being returned (echoed back) to the sender for verification of correctness. A PBX may, or may not, be involved at either end of the circuit.

It should be noted that it is possible to design and construct modems that can identify, react to, and correctly receive different forms of modulation (frequency, amplitude, phase), different line speeds, and so on. Nevertheless, it is currently most common for the sender and receiver to have agreed beforehand on these matters. Additionally, although not common, it is also possible to design and implement a switching network using character-by-character asynchronous communication by having the intermediate IMP (intermessage processor) build a "packet" within a buffer before it extracts the routing information and then forward the "packet" as necessary. This technique is somewhat rare.

WIDE-AREA NETWORKS

Binary synchronous protocol (BSP or Bisynch) is currently a very popular communication protocol developed by the International Business Machine Corporation for the exchange of data between a host and devices at a distance. Bisynch is a character-oriented protocol usable with various character encodings, including the almost universal ASCII and the EBCDIC common with large IBM equipment as well as plug-compatible computers such as Amdahl, Nixdorf, and so on.

A data link consists of a master computer and a slave station as well as modems, phone lines, and so on. The master node controls message flow by polling and selecting a slave station. A slave station can respond only to the master computer; it cannot itself initiate communication. In many cases the data link will be attached to the microcomputer system (DMA or I8089) through a USART (univeral synchronous/asynchronous receiver/transmitter), which supports all common asynchronous and synchronous protocols as well as serial-to-parallel and parallel-to-serial conversions. The use of an I8089 I/O processor with a USART and a programmable interrupt controller will allow program logic to provide formats, synchronization, and validation for Bisynch data from or to the channel.

The basic unit of the Bisynch protocol is the message block, consisting of a header, a body, and a trailer (Figure 13.9):

1. Header
   a. Two (or more) synchronization characters
   b. One start-of-header character
   c. Addressing and control information for the particular slave station
2. Text
   a. One start-of-text character
   b. N information characters, each of which can be;
      (1) 7-bit ASCII code with the eighth bit being used for parity error detection, or
      (2) 8-bit byte data using EBCDIC or microcomputer internal binary with no parity error detection possible

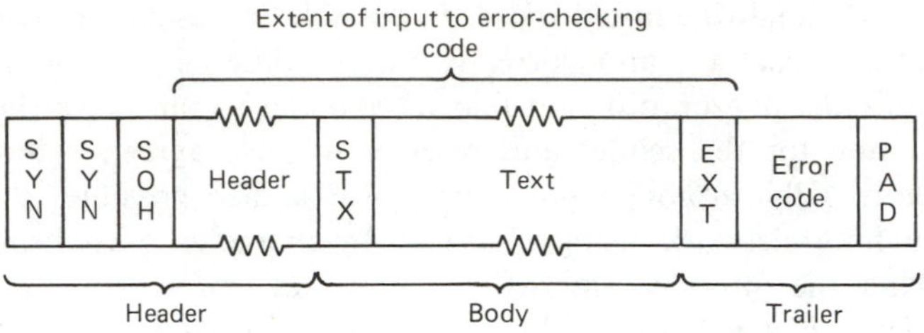

(a) 7-bit Bisynch format allowing parity within each byte

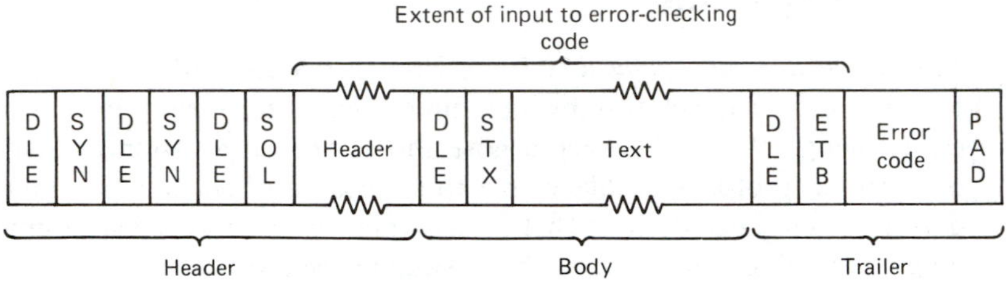

(b) 8-bit Bisynch (Transparent Mode) — all bit patterns are meaningful

SYN: Synchronization Byte
SOL: Start-of-Header Byte
STX: Start-of-Text Byte
EXT: End-of-Text Byte
ETB: End-of-Transparent-Text Byte
DLE: Data-Link-Escape Byte
PAD: Packet Assembler/Disassembler Parameter Byte

Figure 13.9 Bisynchronous communication block formats.

3. Trailer
   a. One end-of-text character
   b. One or more error-detection/correction characters usually one of the following:
      (1) Longitudinal parity character derived via a modulo 2 addition (XOR) of the positional bits of each byte over the text, or
      (2) A checksum character derived via modulo 256 addition of the bytes of the text, or
      (3) A two-or-more-character cyclic redundancy code calculated using an error-checking polynomial
   c. One or more message block "pad" characters

Bisynchronous communication transmits information as a block of characters, the time interval of character sending/reception being

2400 bps:	3333.3 microseconds
4800 bps:	1666.7 microseconds
9600 bps:	833.3 microseconds
19,200 bps:	416.7 microseconds

Therefore, normally, sufficient time exists between character reception for movement to and from storage in memory as well as for the calculation of a checksum subtotal or error-checking polynomial subresult.

Bisynchronous communication was originally intended for a point-to-point data transmission and was designed assuming that a physical transmission line had been previously established. This could have been accomplished either by "hard wiring" or by "dial-up" methods. In any case, no provision was made for address or line-switching information. Point-to-point message block transmission is still the most common Bisynch method. The need for some installations to allow multiple-terminal or multicomputer access to a single physical transmission line—the situation would be a multidrop line or a concentrator—has resulted in the Bisynch protocol being extended in a primitive manner to at least allow such use. In this situation, an idle line or idle concentrator is sent a normal Bisynch block with the text containing address information that is used by the receiver to establish a "permanent" point-to-point line that then acts in the normal Bisynch node. It is my opinion that communication protocols specifically designed for such use (SDLC, X.25, Ethernet, etc.) are far superior to "stretching" Bisynch into uses for which it was not designed. On the other hand, if it is necessary for one computer to communicate with another computer, it is necessary that the sender and receiver employ a single mutually understandable method. Thus you may be forced to implement a communications protocol not of your liking or choice.

System Network Architecture/Synchronous Data Link Control (SNA/SDLC) was released by IBM in 1974 to allow centralized star-shaped or tree-shaped networks with a single large host computer and numerous terminals. In 1976, SNA was extended to allow multiple host computers, each with their own treelike network, to intercommunicate host to host. The design was extended to allow more general node-to-node communication in 1979. The concept and implementation of SNA continues to evolve, with additional freedoms, abilities, and features being announced as they become available or as competition demands. It is important to note that SNA was developed before the ISO seven-layer network standard, and thus a one-to-one correspondence does not exist, although the functionality is similar. Figures 13.10 and 13.11 should be examined when considering SNA techniques.

SDLC is a bit-oriented physical-level protocol that is used for half-duplex or full-duplex synchronous message exchanges between a "primary" sending station and a "secondary" receiving or responding station via "frames." Each frame is enclosed within frame synchronization flags (01111110 base 2 = 7E base 16 = 126 base 10) that mark the beginning of the destination address and control fields as well as the error-checking CRC field. The unique 7E base 16 value of the flag does

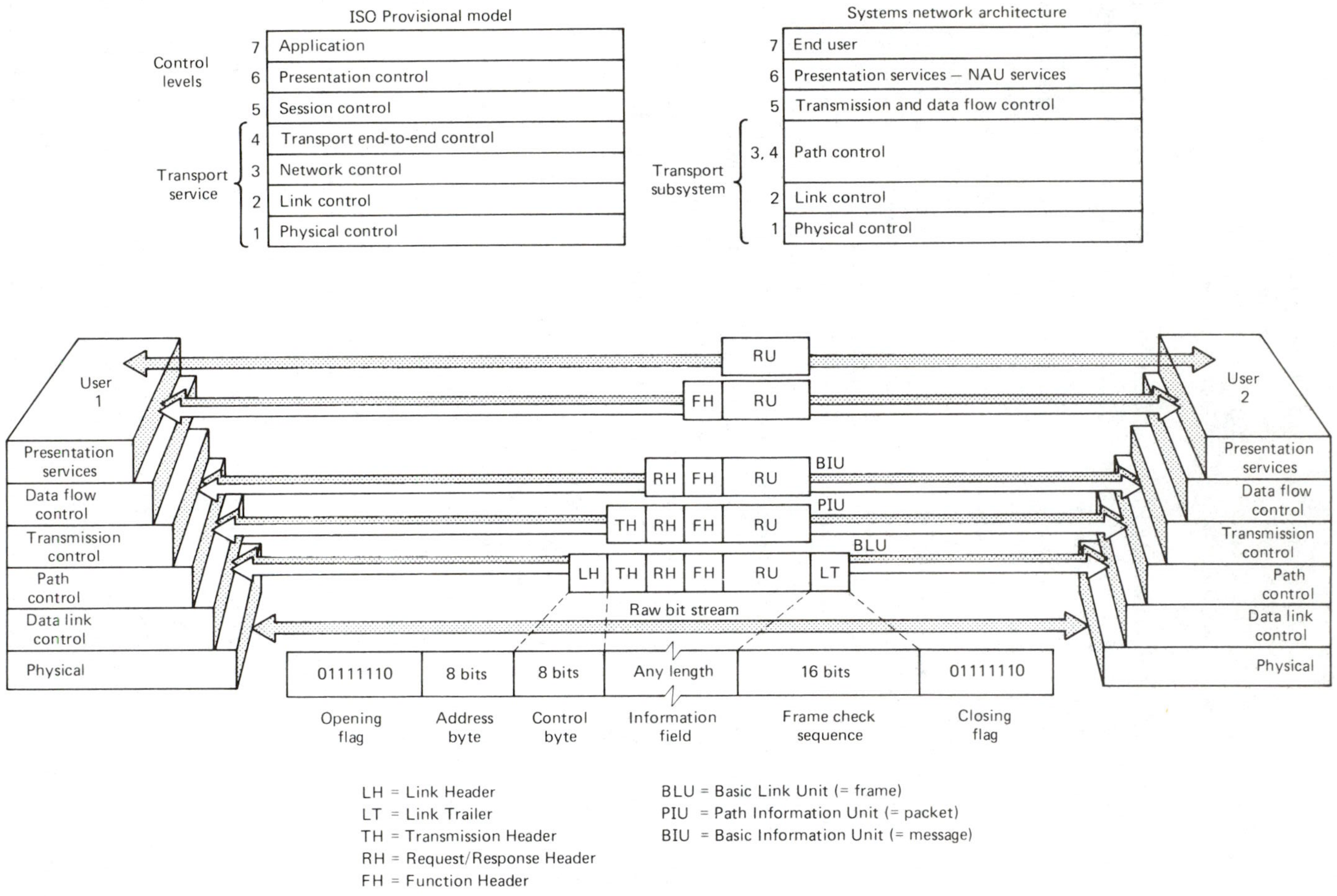

Figure 13.10 Architecture of the SDLC (Synchronous Data Link Control) portion of SNA (System Network Architecture)as defined by IBM. (Adapted with permission from *IBM Syst. J. 15*(1):24-38, 1976.)

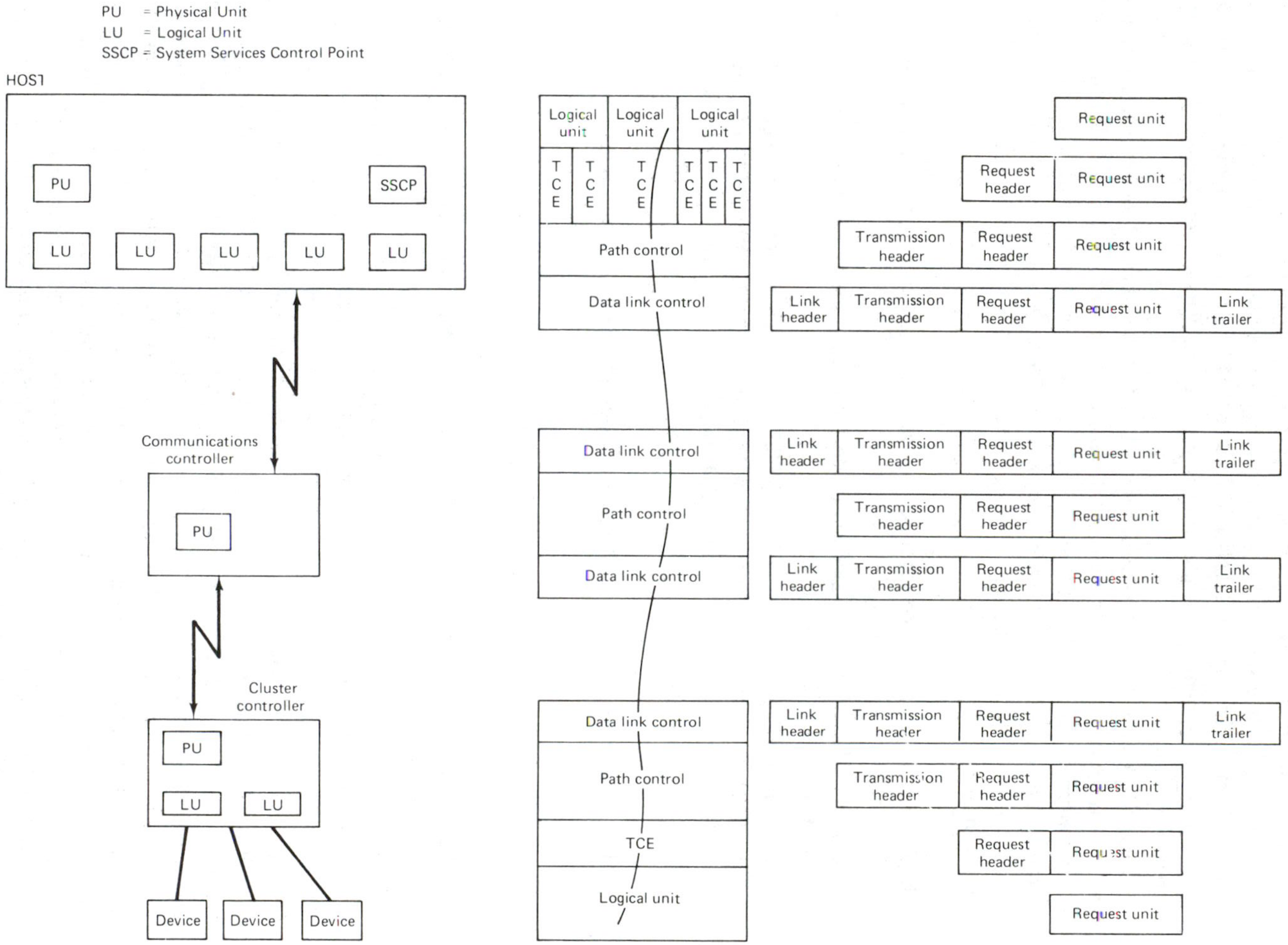

Figure 13.11 SNA message transmission-reception with an intermediate switching IMP. (Adapted with permission from *IBM Syst. J. 21*(2):179-210, 1982.)

not restrict the bit patterns used in the frame as the modem inserts a binary zero after all contiguous five binary 1's when sending, and similarly strips the inserted zero when receiving. The various levels involved in SNA are shown in Figure 13.10 and the technique of appending header information at the various levels and its stripping is shown in Figure 13.11.

An SNA network consists of *nodes* of four types: type 1 nodes are terminals, type 2 nodes are terminal or peripheral cluster controllers, type 4 nodes are front-end communication processors, and type 5 nodes are host computers. Each node contains one or more *network-addressable units* (NAU) consisting of software modules allowing a computational process to use the SNA network. Three types of NAU can exist:

1. *Logical Unit (LU)*: the interface between an executing process and the SNA network.
2. *Physical Unit (PU)*: the one-per node logic that brings the node on-line, takes it off-line, tests it, and so on.
3. *System Services Control Points (SSCP)*: the one-per-host computer (type 5) node that contains complete knowledge of and controls the front ends, controllers, and terminals in the SNA network. This collection of resources is termed a domain.

The System Network Architecture divides the necessary tasks into three functional areas:

1. *Link-control functions*: dynamic switchable communication path scheduling and error control
2. *Path-control functions*: dynamically selecting the physical communications link within the network
3. *Transmission control functions*: identifying the message origin and destination both physically and as an executing software process in a physical node

The link-control and path-control functions are performed at every node, including intermediate dynamic path-switching intermessage processor (IMP) nodes employed during frame transmission. The transmission control function is performed only at the message origin and message destination nodes—at the "ends." Messages are termed *request units* and are shuttled from station to station along their dynamically selected path within the network to their final destination. To allow this process, the various SNA levels append and strip "header" information each time the frame encounters a hardware node component. This is illustrated in Figure 13.11.

Digital Network Architecture/Digital Data Communications Message Protocol/DECNET (DNA/DDCMP/DECNET) was first released by the Digital Equipment Corporation as specifications for DDCMP in 1973 as a character (byte)-oriented protocol allowing full-duplex or half-duplex synchronous or asynchronous communication. DNA was introduced in 1975, and full-blown dynamic packet switching was available in DECNET phase III in early 1980. Further developments are to be expected. It must be emphasized that a DECNET is merely a collection of machines or nodes; some nodes may execute applications programs, some nodes may perform dynamic packet switching, and some nodes may do both. In general, the communication tasks possible with DECNET correspond to those tasks possible with SNA/SDLC and the tasks suggested by the ISO model. The division of the overall communication task into hierarchical functions differs between the protocols. An overall view of the DNA layers is shown in Figure 13.12.

LOCAL-AREA NETWORKS

A local-area network (LAN) is a data communication system for the interconnection of terminals and computers that are within a short physical distance of each other. In each local network there are control mechanisms that allow the capacity of the communications channel to be shared. Local area networks may possess different topologies such as star, ring, or bus and use different communication media, such as twisted pair. We will concentrate our attention on the bus topology and will employ the *Ethernet* implementation as our example.

A bus-based LAN has the advantage of easy reconfiguration, in that nodes can be added or deleted at almost any location. Bus-based networks have the inherent characteristic of soft failure; that is, the failure of a node does not result in complete network failure but affects only the failed node and any work for which the features of that node are vital. Thus a bus-oriented LAN has attractive reliability characteristics if bus access control is distributed to each node. Unfortunately, this very feature results in the need for a complex communication protocol and difficulties in network monitoring. Stated very baldly, there is a nonzero probability of two or more nodes simultaneously using the bus and thereby mutually destroying each other's messages. A bus network is typically implemented of coaxial cable with or without branches and/or signal-boosting amplifiers. Figure 13.13 conveys the distance limitations and interconnection possibilities. Cable-based LANs commonly employ either (1) CATV broadband coaxial cable with multiple-frequency multiplexed channels, or (2) baseband coaxial cable with a single channel that must be shared.

As mentioned earlier (also, see Figure 13.6), contention techniques for channel access anticipate conflicts for bus usage and employ such conflicts to control and allocate access to the channel. *Carrier-sense multiple access with collision detect* (CSMA/CD) techniques are a common and practical contention method for allowing many nodes access to one channel, with access control completely distributed to the individual nodes. As shown in Figure 13.6, when a node wishes to send a message over the common bus, it first tests the channel for the presence or absence of a carrier signal. If the channel is empty, the message is sent; if the channel is busy, the message is delayed. A random time later the node again tests the bus for activity. The term *listen-before-talking* is employed.

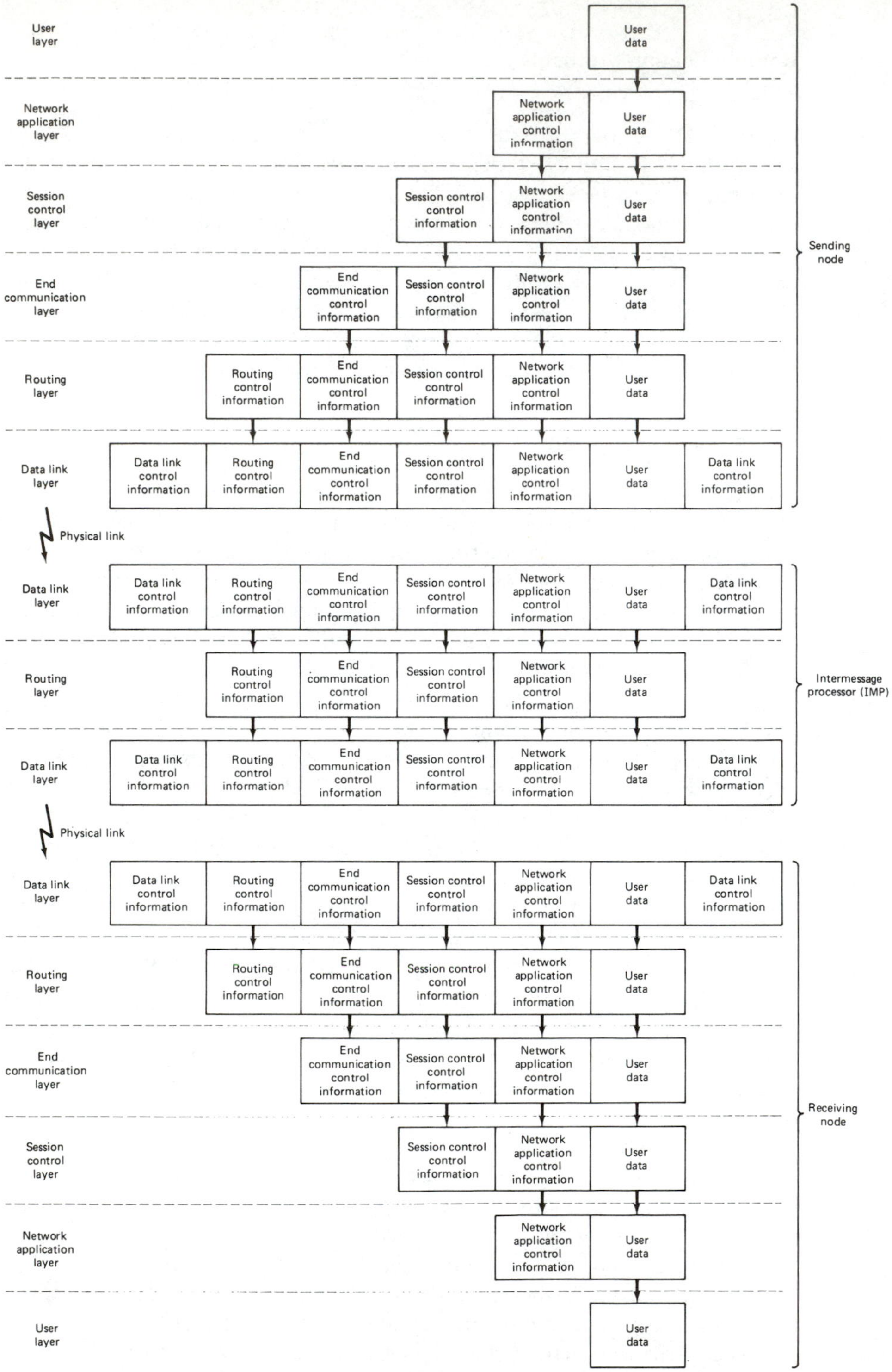

Figure 13.12 Architecture of the DECNET packet switching message transmission-reception network including the actions of an intermediate IMP. (Adapted with permission from material copyrighted by Digital Equipment Corportion, 1981.)

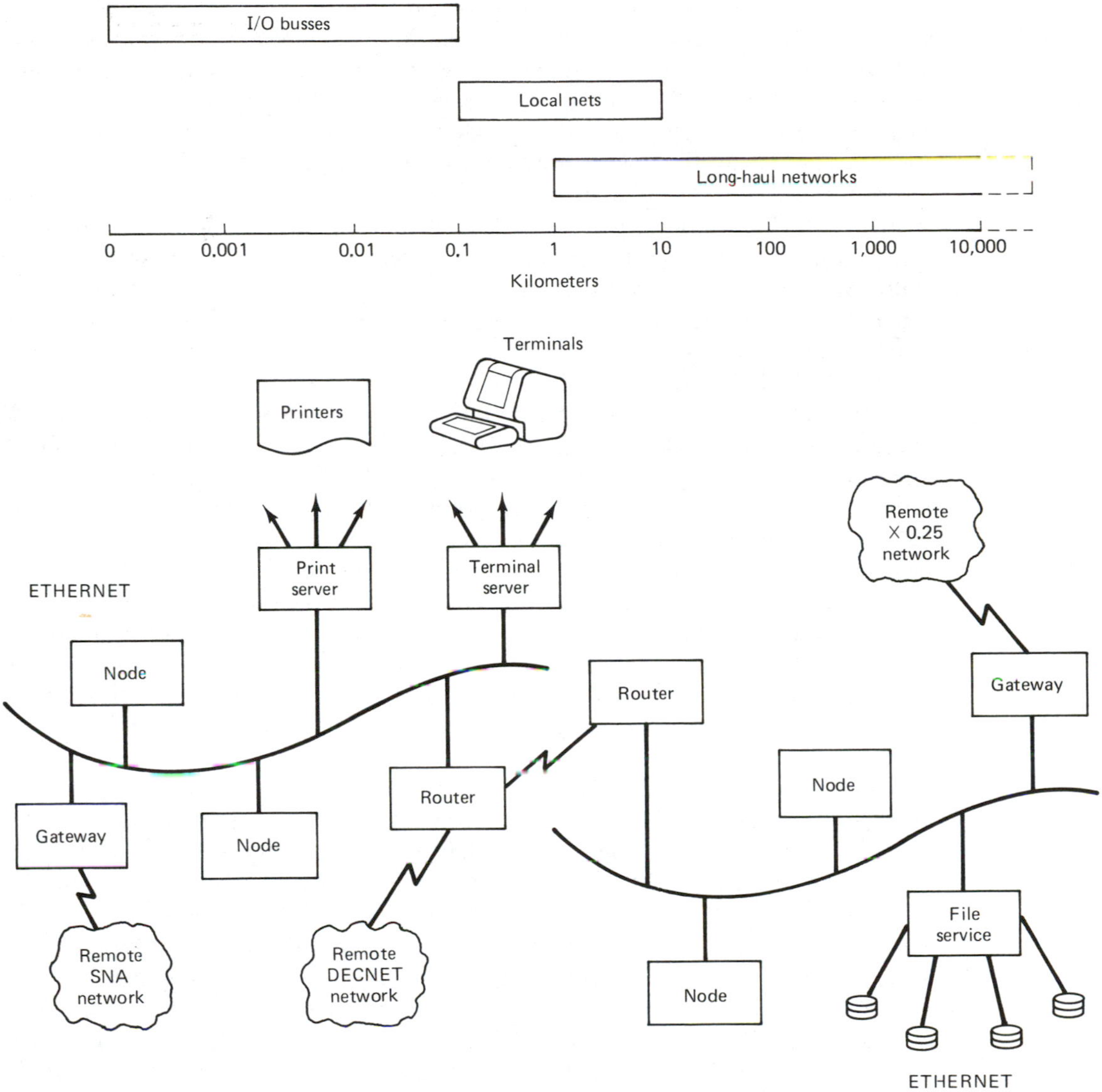

Figure 13.13 Local-area networks (LANs) satisfy the needs for shorter distance communication. The bottom portion illustrates the possibility of interconnecting two or more LANs and also allowing access to wide-area or long-haul networks. (Adapted with permission from material copyrighted by Digital Equipment Corportion, 1982.)

Additionally, because of the time it takes a signal to travel across the network, termed *propagation* delay, it is possible for a node to detect a free channel that almost immediately becomes busy as the signal from another node arrives. The result will be two, or more, nodes simultaneously transmitting with mutual message destruction and a detectable change in the energy level of the channel. Thus collision detect is the ability of a transmitting node to detect a message collision via *listen-while-talking.* Upon detecting a collision, each node sends a short burst of noise to assure that other nodes also detect the collision, then both stop transmitting for a short time period (of random or unique-per-station length), and then reinitiates message transmission by the listen-before-talking technique. Successive collisions normally cause longer wait-before-again-attempting periods. To assure that all nodes detect a collision, message packets must be of at least some minimum length. All stations accept packets addressed to them and discard any not addressed to them or that are found to be in error.

It is obvious that the fewer the collisions, the more efficient the network. It follows that larger packets are most efficient. Because of the listen-before-talking technique, the number of collisions is usually very low and successive collisions very rare. Thus CSMA/CD is a very efficient form of distributed access control to a contention-based network. On the other hand, there is no absolute maximum access time, although excellent statistical statements can be made.

Ethernet is a distributed-control, multiaccess, packet communication system for transmitting digital data among localized computing systems, intelligent terminals, mass storage nodes, terminal concentrators, and so on. The shared single communication bus is passive and broadcast in nature, with each node using packet address recognition to accept or ignore packets. Security and privacy may, therefore, be a problem. As a node may serve as a repeater to another Ethernet or as a gateway to a long-haul network, Ethernet must be viewed as a packet-switched local-area network. Figure 13.13 is pertinent. CSMA/CD access procedures can use coaxial cable, twisted-pair, fiber optics, and other transmission media.

The Experimental Ethernet system was developed at the Xerox Palo Alto Research Center starting in 1972. Starting in 1980, a cooperative effort involving Xerox, Intel, and DEC has produced an updated version known as the "Ethernet Specifications." As of late 1981, several computer vendors were committed to support Ethernet with commercially available hardware and software products. These included ICL, HP, DEC, Nixdorf, Intel, Thompson, CSF, and Xerox. Intel markets the two-board iSBC 550 Ethernet Communications Controller that implements the physical and data link levels.

A *station*—a mode—is the basic addressable device connected to an Ethernet. Within a station, an interface exists between layers two and three of the ISO model —between the data link layer and the network layer as shown in Figure 13.14. The *controller* for a station is a set of functions and algorithms that control access to the Ethernet channel. These functions include signaling conventions, encoding/decoding, serial/parallel conversion, address recognition, error detection, buffering, CSMA/CD channel access management, and packet formatting. A *transceiver* con-

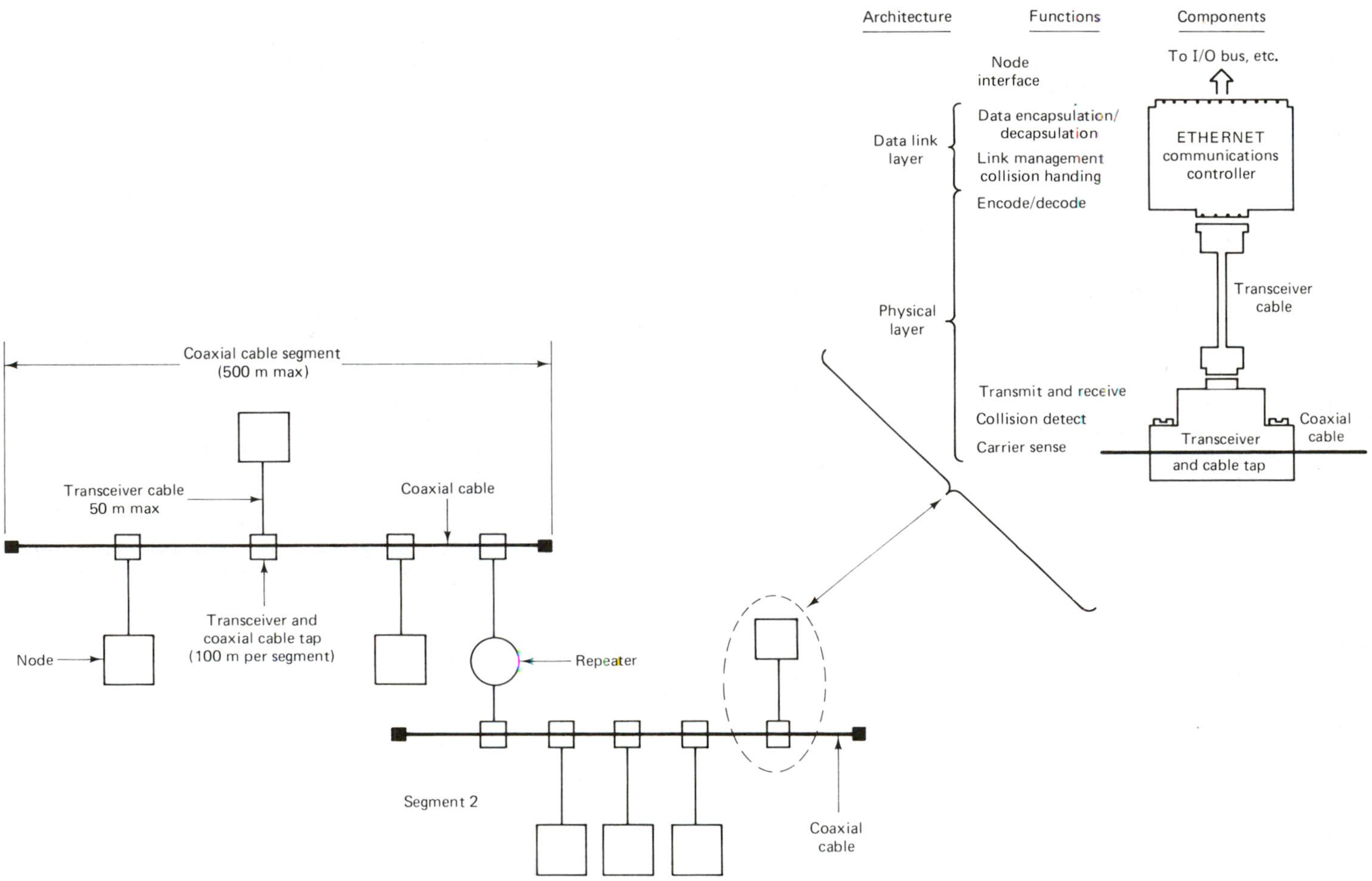

Figure 13.14 Two Ethernet segments connected via a repeater and a "blow-up" of a node connector. (Adapted with permission from material copyrighted by Digital Equipment Corporation, 1982.)

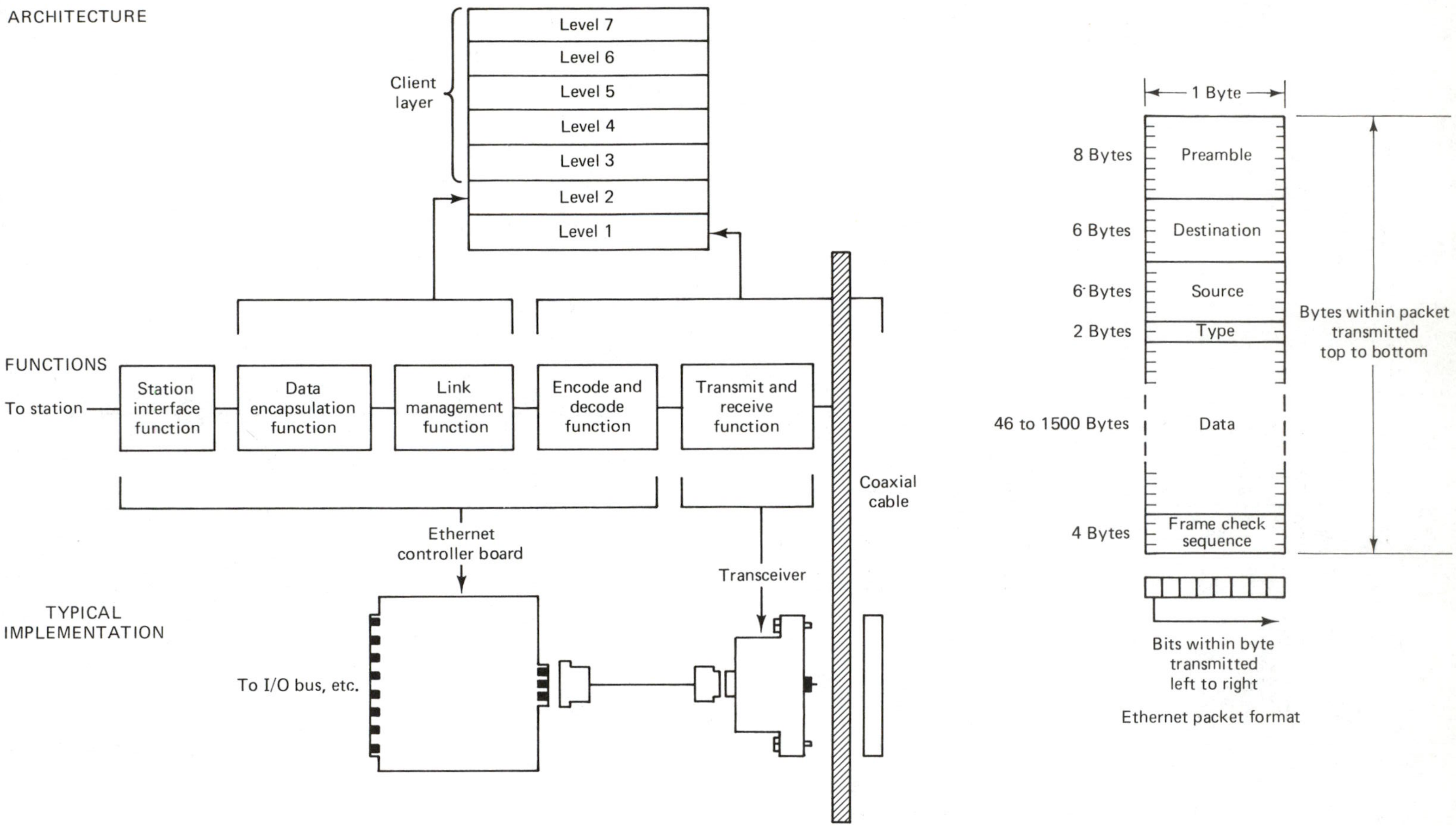

Figure 13.15 Ethernet node showing the packet format and the assignment of responsibility for the lower-level communication layers. (Adapted with permission from material copyrighted by Digital Equipment Corporation, 1982.)

tains the electronics necessary to transmit/receive signals on the channel, recognize the carrier wave when another station is transmitting, and recognize a collision via energy changes in the channel.

The Ethernet *packet* contains six fields, as shown in Figure 13.15. The minimum packet size is 72 bytes; the maximum is 1526 bytes, with the variation being in the data field, which can vary from 46 to 1500 bytes in length.

1. *Preamble*: 8 bytes = 64 bits, starting with a 1 bit and alternating—10101 . . . 101011—as well as ending with two 1 bits.
2. *Destination address*: 6 bytes = 48 bits; if the leading bit is zero, the address is to a unique station; if one, to a logical group of recipients. A completely zero address signifies all nodes, that is, a broadcast packet.
3. *Source address*: 6 bytes = 48 bits.
4. *Type*: 2 bytes = 16 bits; identifies the protocol used at the network layer and above. Thus it specifies how the data field information will be interpreted. This interpretation is not a portion of the Ethernet format.
5. *Data*: 46 (minimum) to 1500 (maximum) bytes. The minimum 46-byte size assures that a valid packet will be distinguished from a collision fragment.
6. *Frame check sequence (CRC)*: 4 bytes = 32 bits generated by a polynomial covering the destination address, the source address, the type, and the data fields. The polynomial is

$$\begin{aligned} G(x) = X = X^{32} &+ X^{26} + X^{23} + X^{22} + X^{16} \\ &+ X^{12} + X^{11} + X^{10} + X^{8} + X^{7} \\ &+ X^{5} + X^{4} + X^{2} + X + 1 \end{aligned}$$

Packets must be spaced by a quiescent period of 9.6 microseconds or more. The delay-after-a-collision-is-detected before retransmission is attempted uses a uniformly distributed random number from the interval 0 to $2m - 1$, where m is the number of the retransmission attempts and is limited to be 10 or less multiplied by 51.2 microseconds (512 bit times).

As for *reliability,* an Ethernet is probabilistic. Packets may be lost due to collisions, transmission noise, an inactive receiver node, or discard (accidental or purposeful). High-level communication protocols must be designed and implemented to allow for and recover from lost packets. It is the responsibility of the source and destination processes to take the algorithmic precautions necessary to assure reliable communication of the quality they deem necessary.

Bibliography

ANONYMOUS. *The 8086 Family User's Manual.* Santa Clara, Calif.: Intel Corporation, 1979.

ANONYMOUS. *iAPX 86/30–iAPX 88/30 Operating System Processors.* Santa Clara, Calif.: Intel Corporation, 1981.

ANONYMOUS. *iAPX 286/10 High Performance Microprocessor with Memory Management and Protection.* Santa Clara, Calif.: Intel Corporation, 1982.

ANONYMOUS. *Introduction to Local Area Networks.* Maynard, Mass.: Digital Equipment Corporation, 1982.

ANONYMOUS. *Introduction to the iAPX 286.* Santa Clara, Calif.: Intel Corporation, February 1982.

BACKUS, J. Can Programming Be Liberated from the von Neumann Style? A Functional Style and Its Algebra of Programs, *Commun. ACM 21*(8):613–641, 1978.

BARRON, D. W. *Assemblers and Loaders,* 2nd ed. New York: Elsevier, 1972.

BRAUN, E., and S. MACDONALD. *Revolution in Miniature.* New York: Cambridge University Press, 1978.

CALINGAERT, P. *Assemblers, Compilers, and Program Translation.* Rockville, Md.: Computer Science Press, 1979.

CICHELLI, R. J. Minimal Perfect Hash Functions Made Simple, *Commun. ACM 23*(1):17–19, 1980.

CLARK, W. A. From Electron Mobility to Logical Structures: A View of Integrated Circuits, *Comput. Surv. 12*(3):325–356, 1980.

COOK, C. R., and R. R. OLDEHOEFT. A Letter Oriented Minimal Perfect Hashing Function, *SIGPLAN Notic. (ACM) 17*(19):18–27, 1982.

COONEN, J. T. Underflow and Denormalized Numbers, *Computer 14*:75–87, March 1981.

COONEN, J. T., W. KAHAN, J. PALMER, T. PITTMAN, and D. STEVENSON. A Proposal Standard for Binary Floating Point Arithmetic, *SIGNUM Newslett. (ACM),* Special Issue, pp. 4–12, October 1979.

CULLUM, P. G. The Transmission Subsystem in Systems Network Architecture, *IBM Syst. J. 15*(1):24–38, 1976.

DONOVAN, J. J. *Systems Programming.* New York: McGraw-Hill, 1972.

ELSHOFF, J. L., and M. MARCOTTY. Improving Computer Program Readibility to Aid Modification, *Commun. ACM 25*(8):512–521, 1982.

FOSTER, C. C. *Real Time Programming: Neglected Topics.* Reading, Mass.: Addison-Wesley, 1981.

GEORGE, F. D., and G. E. YOUNG. SNA Flow Control: Architecture and Implementation, *IBM Syst. J. 21*(2):179–210, 1982.

GIBSON, G., and Y. LIU. *Microcomputers for Engineers and Scientists.* Englewood Cliffs, N.J.: Prentice-Hall, 1980.

GORSLINE, G. W. *Computer Organization: Hardware/Software.* Englewood Cliffs, N.J.: Prentice-Hall, 1980.

GREENFIELD, S. E. *The Architecture of Microcomputers.* Cambridge, Mass.: Winthrop, 1980.

KERNIGHAN, B. W., and J. R. MASHEY. The UNIX Programming Environment, *Computer 14*: 12–24, April 1981.

KNUTH, D. E. *The Art of Computer Programming,* Vol. 1: *Fundamental Algorithms,* 2nd ed. Reading, Mass.: Addison-Wesley, 1973, Chapter 1.

KORNERUP, P., and D. M. MATULA. *A Feasibility Analysis of Fixed-Slash Rational Arithmetic.* Tech. Rep. CS7810, Computer Science Department, Southern Methodist University, Dallas, July 1976. (Also presented at the 4th IEEE Symp. Comput. Arith., Santa Monica, Calif., October 1978.)

LEDGARD, H., and M. MARCOTTY. *The Programming Language Landscape.* Chicago: Science Research Associates, 1981.

LEVENTHAL, L. A. *Introduction to Microcomputers: Software, Hardware, Programming.* Englewood Cliffs, N.J.: Prentice-Hall, 1978.

MCWHORTER, E. W. The Small Electronic Calculator, *Sci. Am.,* pp. 86–98, May 1976.

METCALFE, R. M., and D. R. BOGGS. Ethernet: Distributed Packet Switching for Local Computer Networks, *Commun. ACM 19*(7):395–403, 1976. [Reprinted in *Commun. ACM 26* (1):90–95, 1983.]

MOORE, R. E. *Methods and Applications of Interval Analysis.* SIAM Studies in Applied Mathematics. Philadelphia: SIAM, 1979.

NASSI, I., and B. SCHNEIDERMAN. Flowchart Techniques for Structured Programming, *SIGPLAM Notic. (ACM) 8*:12–16, August 1973.

OSBORNE, A. *8089 I/O Processor Handbook.* Berkeley, Calif.: Osborne/McGraw-Hill, 1980.

PALMER, J. F. *The INTEL 8087 Numeric Data Processor.* AFIPS Conf. Proc., 1980, Nat. Comput. Conf., Anaheim, Calif., May 1980, pp. 997–893.

PATTERSON, D. A. A Performance Evaluation of the Intel 80286, Comput. Arch. News (ACM) 10(5):16–18, 1982. [Comment by H. M. Levi and D. W. Clark, On the Use of Benchmarks for Measuring System Performance, *Comput. Arch. News 10*(6):5–8, 1982.]

RECTOR, R., and G. ALEXY. *The 8086 Book.* Berkeley, Calif.: Osborne/McGraw-Hill, 1980.

RITCHIE, D. M., and K. THOMPSON. The UNIX Time-Sharing System, *Commun. ACM 17* (7):365–375, 1974. [Reprinted in *Commun. ACM 26*(1):84–89, 1983.]

ROSIN, R. F. Contemporary Concepts of Microprogramming and Emulation, *Comput. Surv. 1* (4):197–212, 1969.

SAMMET, J. *Programming Languages: History and Fundamentals.* Englewood Cliffs, N.J.: Prentice-Hall, 1969.

STEVENSON, D. A Proposed Standard for Binary Floating Point Arithmetic: Draft 8.0 IEEE Task P754, *Computer 14*:51–62, March 1981.

STONE, H. S. *Microcomputer Interfacing.* Reading, Mass.: Addison-Wesley, 1982.

TANENBAUM, A. S. *Computer Networks.* Englewood Cliffs, N.J.: Prentice-Hall, 1981.

THACKER, W. I. Rational as an Alternative to Floating-Point Arithmetic. Unpublished M.S. thesis, Virginia Polytechnic Institute and State University, May 1978. (Also reported in the 17th Annu. Natl. Bur. Standards Symp., *Tools for Improving Computing in the 80's,* June 1978, p. 242.

TOBEY, R., J. BAKER, R. CREWS, P. MARKS, and K. VICTOR. *PL/I-FORMAC Interpretor User's Reference Manual.* SHARE Contributed Program Library 360D-03.3.004., October 1967.

WEIZENBAUM, J. Symmetric List Processor, *Commun. ACM 6*:524–544, 1963.

ZIMMERMAN, H. OSI Reference Model: The ISO Model of Architecture for Open System Interconnection, *IEEE Trans. Commun. COM-28*:425–432, April 1980.

Instruction Set*

INTEL 8086 AND 8088; INTEL 8087 NDP

Effective Address Calculation Time

EA Components		Clocks*
Displacement Only		6
Base or Index Only (BX,BP,SI,DI)		5
Displacement + Base or Index	(BX,BP,SI,DI)	9
Base + Index	BP+DI,BX+SI	7
	BP+SI,BX+DI	8
Displacement + Base + Index	BP+DI+DISP BX+SI+DISP	11
	BP+SI+DISP BX+DI+DISP	12

*Add 2 clocks for segment override

Key to 8087 Exception Codes:

I = invalid operation
Z = zero divide
D = denormalized
O = overflow
U = underflow
P = precision

Key to Flag Codes:

1 = unconditionally set
0 = unconditionally cleared
X = altered to reflect operation result
U = undefined (mask it out)
R = replaced from memory (e.g., SAHF)
b = (blank) unaffected

Many instructions allow their operands to be coded in more than one way. For example, FADD (add real) may be written without operands, with only a source, or with a destination and a source. The instruction descriptions in this section employ the simple convention of separating alternative operand forms with slashes; the slashes, however, are not coded. Consecutive slashes indicate an option of no explicit operands. The operands for FADD are thus described as:

```
//source/destination, source
```

This means that FADD may be written in any of three ways:

```
FADD
FADD source
FADD destination, source
```

AAA

AAA (no operands)
ASCII adjust for addition

Flags: O D I T S Z A P C — U, U U X U X

Operands	Clocks	Transfers*	Bytes	Coding Example
(no operands)	4	—	1	AAA

AAD

AAD (no operands)
ASCII adjust for division

Flags: O D I T S Z A P C — U, X X U X U

Operands	Clocks	Transfers*	Bytes	Coding Example
(no operands)	60	—	2	AAD

AAM

AAM (no operands)
ASCII adjust for multiply

Flags: O D I T S Z A P C — U, X X U X U

Operands	Clocks	Transfers*	Bytes	Coding Example
(no operands)	83	—	1	AAM

AAS

AAS (no operands)
ASCII adjust for subtraction

Flags: O D I T S Z A P C — U, U U X U X

Operands	Clocks	Transfers*	Bytes	Coding Example
(no operands)	4	—	1	AAS

ADC

ADC destination,source
Add with carry

Flags: O D I T S Z A P C — X, X X X X X

Operands	Clocks	Transfers*	Bytes	Coding Example
register, register	3	—	2	ADC AX, SI
register, memory	9+EA	1	2-4	ADC DX, BETA [SI]
memory, register	16+EA	2	2-4	ADC ALPHA [BX] [SI], DI
register, immediate	4	—	3-4	ADC BX, 256
memory, immediate	17+EA	2	3-6	ADC GAMMA, 30H
accumulator, immediate	4	—	2-3	ADC AL, 5

ADD

ADD destination,source
Addition

Flags: O D I T S Z A P C — X, X X X X X

Operands	Clocks	Transfers*	Bytes	Coding Example
register, register	3	—	2	ADD CX, DX
register, memory	9+EA	1	2-4	ADD DI, [BX].ALPHA
memory, register	16+EA	2	2-4	ADD TEMP, CL
register, immediate	4	—	3-4	ADD CL, 2
memory, immediate	17+EA	2	3-6	ADD ALPHA, 2
accumulator, immediate	4	—	2-3	ADD AX, 200

*For the 8086, add 4 clocks for each 16-bit word transfer with an odd address.

AND	**AND** destination,source Logical and	Flags: O D I T S Z A P C 0 X X U X 0 (O=0, S=X, Z=X, A=U, P=X, C=0)

Operands	Clocks	Transfers*	Bytes	Coding Example
register, register	3	—	2	AND AL,BL
register, memory	9+EA	1	2-4	AND CX,FLAG_WORD
memory, register	16+EA	2	2-4	AND ASCII [DI],AL
register, immediate	4	—	3-4	AND CX,0F0H
memory, immediate	17+EA	2	3-6	AND BETA, 01H
accumulator, immediate	4	—	2-3	AND AX, 01010000B

CALL	**CALL** target Call a procedure	Flags: O D I T S Z A P C

Operands	Clocks	Transfers*	Bytes	Coding Examples
near-proc	19	1	3	CALL NEAR_PROC
far-proc	28	2	5	CALL FAR_PROC
memptr 16	21+EA	2	2-4	CALL PROC_TABLE [SI]
regptr 16	16	1	2	CALL AX
memptr 32	37+EA	4	2-4	CALL [BX].TASK [SI]

CBW	**CBW** (no operands) Convert byte to word	Flags: O D I T S Z A P C

Operands	Clocks	Transfers*	Bytes	Coding Example
(no operands)	2	—	1	CBW

CLC	**CLC** (no operands) Clear carry flag	Flags: O D I T S Z A P C 0 (C=0)

Operands	Clocks	Transfers*	Bytes	Coding Example
(no operands)	2	—	1	CLC

CLD	**CLD** (no operands) Clear direction flag	Flags: O D I T S Z A P C 0 (D=0)

Operands	Clocks	Transfers*	Bytes	Coding Example
(no operands)	2	—	1	CLD

CLI	**CLI** (no operands) Clear interrupt flag	Flags: O D I T S Z A P C 0 (I=0)

Operands	Clocks	Transfers*	Bytes	Coding Example
(no operands)	2	—	1	CLI

CMC	**CMC** (no operands) Complement carry flag	Flags: O D I T S Z A P C X (C=X)

Operands	Clocks	Transfers*	Bytes	Coding Example
(no operands)	2	—	1	CMC

*All mnemonics copyright Intel Corporation 1980.

CMP

CMP destination,source
Compare destination to source

Flags	O	D	I	T	S	Z	A	P	C
	X				X	X	X	X	X

Operands	Clocks	Transfers*	Bytes	Coding Example
register, register	3	—	2	CMP BX, CX
register, memory	9+EA	1	2-4	CMP DH, ALPHA
memory, register	9+EA	1	2-4	CMP [BP+2], SI
register, immediate	4	—	3-4	CMP BL, 02H
memory, immediate	10+EA	1	3-6	CMP [BX].RADAR [DI], 3420H
accumulator, immediate	4	—	2-3	CMP AL, 00010000B

CMPS

CMPS dest-string,source-string
Compare string

Flags	O	D	I	T	S	Z	A	P	C
	X				X	X	X	X	X

Operands	Clocks	Transfers*	Bytes	Coding Example
dest-string, source-string	22	2	1	CMPS BUFF1, BUFF2
(repeat) dest-string, source-string	9+22/rep	2/rep	1	REPE CMPS ID, KEY

CWD

CWD (no operands)
Convert word to doubleword

Flags	O	D	I	T	S	Z	A	P	C

Operands	Clocks	Transfers*	Bytes	Coding Example
(no operands)	5	—	1	CWD

DAA

DAA (no operands)
Decimal adjust for addition

Flags	O	D	I	T	S	Z	A	P	C
	X				X	X	X	X	X

Operands	Clocks	Transfers*	Bytes	Coding Example
(no operands)	4	—	1	DAA

DAS

DAS (no operands)
Decimal adjust for subtraction

Flags	O	D	I	T	S	Z	A	P	C
	U				X	X	X	X	X

Operands	Clocks	Transfers*	Bytes	Coding Example
(no operands)	4	—	1	DAS

DEC

DEC destination
Decrement by 1

Flags	O	D	I	T	S	Z	A	P	C
	X				X	X	X	X	

Operands	Clocks	Transfers*	Bytes	Coding Example
reg16	2	—	1	DEC AX
reg8	3	—	2	DEC AL
memory	15+EA	2	2-4	DEC ARRAY [SI]

DIV

DIV source
Division, unsigned

Flags	O	D	I	T	S	Z	A	P	C
	U				U	U	U	U	U

Operands	Clocks	Transfers*	Bytes	Coding Example
reg8	80-90	—	2	DIV CL
reg16	144-162	—	2	DIV BX
mem8	(86-96) +EA	1	2-4	DIV ALPHA
mem16	(150-168) +EA	1	2-4	DIV TABLE [SI]

ESC	ESC external-opcode,source Escape			Flags O D I T S Z A P C
Operands	**Clocks**	**Transfers***	**Bytes**	**Coding Example**
immediate, memory	8+EA	1	2-4	ESC 6,ARRAY [SI]
immediate, register	2	—	2	ESC 20,AL

FABS	FABS (no operands) Absolute value				Exceptions: I	
Operands	Execution Clocks		Transfers		Bytes	Coding Example
	Typical	Range	8086	8088		
(no operands)	14	10-17	0	0	2	FABS

FADD	FADD //source/destination,source Add real				Exceptions: I, D, O, U, P	
Operands	Execution Clocks		Transfers		Bytes	Coding Example
	Typical	Range	8086	8088		
//ST,ST(i)/ST(i),ST	85	70-100	0	0	2	FADD ST,ST(4)
short-real	105+EA	90-120+EA	2/4	4	2-4	FADD AIR_TEMP [SI]
long-real	110+EA	95-125+EA	4/6	8	2-4	FADD [BX].MEAN

FADDP	FADDP destination, source Add real and pop				Exceptions: I, D, O, U, P	
Operands	Execution Clocks		Transfers		Bytes	Coding Example
	Typical	Range	8086	8088		
ST(i),ST	90	75-105	0	0	2	FADDP ST(2),ST

FBLD	FBLD source Packed decimal (BCD) load				Exceptions: I	
Operands	Execution Clocks		Transfers		Bytes	Coding Example
	Typical	Range	8086	8088		
packed-decimal	300+EA	290-310+EA	5/7	10	2-4	FBLD YTD_SALES

FBSTP	FBSTP destination Packed decimal (BCD) store and pop				Exceptions: I	
Operands	Execution Clocks		Transfers		Bytes	Coding Example
	Typical	Range	8086	8088		
packed-decimal	530+EA	520-540+EA	6/8	12	2-4	FBSTP [BX].FORECAST

FCHS

FCHS (no operands)
Change sign

Exceptions: I

Operands	Execution Clocks		Transfers		Bytes	Coding Example
	Typical	Range	8086	8088		
(no operands)	15	10-17	0	0	2	FCHS

FCLEX/FNCLEX

FCLEX (no operands)
Clear exceptions

Exceptions: None

Operands	Execution Clocks		Transfers		Bytes	Coding Example
	Typical	Range	8086	8088		
(no operands)	5	2-8	0	0	2	FNCLEX

FCOM

FCOM //source
Compare real

Exceptions: I, D

Operands	Execution Clocks		Transfers		Bytes	Coding Example
	Typical	Range	8086	8088		
//ST(i)	45	40-50	0	0	2	FCOM ST(1)
short-real	65+EA	60-70+EA	2/4	4	2-4	FCOM [BP].UPPER_LIMIT
long-real	70+EA	65-75+EA	4/6	8	2-4	FCOM WAVELENGTH

FCOMP

FCOMP //source
Compare real and pop

Exceptions: I, D

Operands	Execution Clocks		Transfers		Bytes	Coding Example
	Typical	Range	8086	8088		
//ST(i)	47	42-52	0	0	2	FCOMP ST(2)
short-real	68+EA	63-73+EA	2/4	4	2-4	FCOMP [BP+2].N_READINGS
long-real	72+EA	67-77+EA	4/6	8	2-4	FCOMP DENSITY

FCOMPP

FCOMPP (no operands)
Compare real and pop twice

Exceptions: I, D

Operands	Execution Clocks		Transfers		Bytes	Coding Example
	Typical	Range	8086	8088		
(no operands)	50	45-55	0	0	2	FCOMPP

FDECSTP

FDECSTP (no operands)
Decrement stack pointer

Exceptions: None

Operands	Execution Clocks		Transfers		Bytes	Coding Example
	Typical	Range	8086	8088		
(no operands)	9	6-12	0	0	2	FDECSTP

FDISI/FNDISI	FDISI (no operands) Disable interrupts				Exceptions: None		
Operands	Execution Clocks		Transfers		Bytes	Coding Example
	Typical	Range	8086	8088		
(no operands)	5	2-8	0	0	2	FDISI

FDIV	FDIV //source/destination, source Divide real				Exceptions: I, D, Z, O, U, P	
Operands	Execution Clocks		Transfers		Bytes	Coding Example
	Typical	Range	8086	8088		
//ST(i),ST short-real long-real	198 220+EA 225+EA	193-203 215-225+EA 220-230+EA	0 2/4 4/6	0 4 8	2 2-4 2-4	FDIV FDIV DISTANCE FDIV ARC [DI]

FDIVP	FDIVP destination, source Divide real and pop				Exceptions: I, D, Z, O, U, P	
Operands	Execution Clocks		Transfers		Bytes	Coding Example
	Typical	Range	8086	8088		
ST(i),ST	202	197-207	0	0	2	FDIVP ST(4),ST

FDIVR	FDIVR //source/destination,source Divide real reversed				Exceptions: I, D, Z, O, U, P	
Operands	Execution Clocks		Transfers		Bytes	Coding Example
	Typical	Range	8086	8088		
//ST,ST(i)/ST(i),ST short-real long-real	199 221+EA 226+EA	194-204 216-226+EA 221-231+EA	0 2/4 4/6	0 6 8	2 2-4 2-4	FDIVR ST(2),ST FDIVR [BX].PULSE, RATE FDIVR RECORDER. FREQUENCY

FDIVRP	FDIVRP destination,source Divide real reversed and pop				Exceptions: I, D, Z, O, U, P	
Operands	Execution Clocks		Transfers		Bytes	Coding Example
	Typical	Range	8086	8088		
ST(i),ST	203	198-208	0	0	2	FDIVRP ST(1),ST

FENI/FNENI	FENI (no operands) Enable interrupts				Exceptions: None	
Operands	Execution Clocks		Transfers		Bytes	Coding Example
	Typical	Range	8086	8088		
(no operands)	5	2-8	0	0	2	FNENI

FFREE	FFREE destination Free register				Exceptions: None	
Operands	Execution Clocks		Transfers		Bytes	Coding Example
	Typical	Range	8086	8088		
ST(i)	11	9-16	0	0	2	FFREE ST(1)

FIADD	FIADD source Integer add				Exceptions: I, D, O, P	
Operands	Execution Clocks		Transfers		Bytes	Coding Example
	Typical	Range	8086	8088		
word-integer	120+EA	102-137+EA	1/2	2	2-4	FIADD DISTANCE TRAVELLED
short-integer	125+EA	108-143+EA	2/4	4	2-4	FIADD PULSE COUNT (SI)

FICOM	FICOM source Integer compare				Exceptions: I, D	
Operands	Execution Clocks		Transfers		Bytes	Coding Example
	Typical	Range	8086	8088		
word-integer	80+EA	72-86+EA	1/2	2	2-4	FICOM TOOL.N PASSES
short-integer	85+EA	78-91+EA	2/4	4	2-4	FICOM [BP+4].PARM COUNT

FICOMP	FICOMP source Integer compare and pop				Exceptions: I, D	
Operands	Execution Clocks		Transfers		Bytes	Coding Example
	Typical	Range	8086	8088		
word-integer	82+EA	74-88+EA	1/2	2	2-4	FICOMP [BP].LIMIT [SI]
short-integer	87+EA	80-93+EA	2/4	4	2-4	FICOMP N_SAMPLES

FIDIV	FIDIV source Integer divide				Exceptions: I, D, Z, O, U, P	
Operands	Execution Clocks		Transfers		Bytes	Coding Example
	Typical	Range	8086	8088		
word-integer	230+EA	224-238+EA	1/2	2	2-4	FIDIV SURVEY.OBSERVATIONS
short-integer	236+EA	230-243+EA	2/4	4	2-4	FIDIV RELATIVE_ANGLE [DI]

FIDIVR	FIDIVR source Integer divide reversed				Exceptions: I, D, Z, O, U, P	
Operands	Execution Clocks		Transfers		Bytes	Coding Example
	Typical	Range	8086	8088		
word-integer	230+EA	225-239+EA	1/2	2	2-4	FIDIVR [BP].X_COORD
short-integer	237+EA	231-245+EA	2/4	4	2-4	FIDIVR FREQUENCY

FILD	FILD source Integer load				Exception: I	
Operands	Execution Clocks		Transfers		Bytes	Coding Example
	Typical	Range	8086	8088		
word-integer	50+EA	46-54+EA	1/2	2	2-4	FILD [BX].SEQUENCE
short-integer	56+EA	52-60+EA	2/4	4	2-4	FILD STANDOFF [DI]
long-integer	64+EA	60-68+EA	4/6	8	2-4	FILD RESPONSE.COUNT

FIMUL	FIMUL source Integer multiply				Exceptions: I, D, O, P	
Operands	Execution Clocks		Transfers		Bytes	Coding Example
	Typical	Range	8086	8088		
word-integer	130+EA	124-138+EA	1/2	2	2-4	FIMUL BEARING
short-integer	136+EA	130-144+EA	2/4	4	2-4	FIMUL POSITION.Z_AXIS

FINCSTP	FINCSTP (no operands) Increment stack pointer				Exceptions: None	
Operands	Execution Clocks		Transfers		Bytes	Coding Example
	Typical	Range	8086	8088		
(no operands)	9	6-12	0	0	2	FINCSTP

FINIT/FNINIT	FINIT (no operands) Initialize processor				Exceptions: None	
Operands	Execution Clocks		Transfers		Bytes	Coding Example
	Typical	Range	8086	8088		
(no operands)	5	2-8	0	0	2	FINIT

FIST	FIST destination Integer store				Exceptions: I, P	
Operands	Execution Clocks		Transfers		Bytes	Coding Example
	Typical	Range	8086	8088		
word-integer short-integer	86+EA 88+EA	80-90+EA 82-92+EA	2/4 3/5	4 6	2-4 2-4	FIST OBS.COUNT [SI] FIST [BP].FACTORED_PULSES

FISTP	FISTP destination Integer store and pop				Exceptions: I, P	
Operands	Execution Clocks		Transfers		Bytes	Coding Example
	Typical	Range	8086	8088		
word-integer short-integer long-integer	88+EA 90+EA 100+EA	82-92+EA 84-94+EA 94-105+EA	2/4 3/5 5/7	4 6 10	2-4 2-4 2-4	FISTP [BX].ALPHA_COUNT [SI] FISTP CORRECTED_TIME FISTP PANEL.N_READINGS

FISUB	FISUB source Integer subtract				Exceptions: I, D, O, P	
Operands	Execution Clocks		Transfers		Bytes	Coding Example
	Typical	Range	8086	8088		
word-integer short-integer	120+EA 125+EA	102-137+EA 108-143+EA	1/2 2/4	2 4	2-4 2-4	FISUB BASE_FREQUENCY FISUB TRAIN_SIZE[DI]

FISUBR	FISUBR source Integer subtract reversed				Exceptions: I, D, O, P	
Operands	Execution Clocks		Transfers		Bytes	Coding Example
	Typical	Range	8086	8088		
word-integer short-integer	120+EA 125+EA	103-139+EA 109-144+EA	1/2 2/4	2 4	2-4 2-4	FISUBR FLOOR [BX][SI] FISUBR BALANCE

FLD	FLD source Load real				Exceptions: I, D	
Operands	Execution Clocks		Transfers		Bytes	Coding Example
	Typical	Range	8086	8088		
ST(i) short-real long-real temp-real	20 43+EA 46+EA 57+EA	17-22 38-56+EA 40-60+EA 53-65+EA	0 2/4 4/6 5/7	0 4 8 10	2 2-4 2-4 2-4	FLD ST(0) FLD READING [SI].PRESSURE FLD [BP].TEMPERATURE FLD SAVEREADING

FLDCW	FLDCW source Load control word				Exceptions: None	
Operands	Execution Clocks		Transfers		Bytes	Coding Example
	Typical	Range	8086	8088		
2-bytes	10+EA	7-14+EA	1/2	2	2-4	FLDCW CONTROL WORD

FLDENV	FLDENV source Load environment				Exceptions: None	
Operands	Execution Clocks		Transfers		Bytes	Coding Example
	Typical	Range	8086	8088		
14-bytes	40+EA	35-45+EA	7/9	14	2-4	FLDENV [BP+6]

FLDLG2	FLDLG2 (no operands) Load $\log_{10}2$				Exceptions: I	
Operands	Execution Clocks		Transfers		Bytes	Coding Example
	Typical	Range	8086	8088		
(no operands)	21	18-24	0	0	2	FLDLG2

FLDLN2	FLDLN2 (no operands) Load $\log_e 2$				Exceptions: I	
Operands	Execution Clocks		Transfers		Bytes	Coding Example
	Typical	Range	8086	8088		
(no operands)	20	17-23	0	0	2	FLDLN2

FLDL2E	FLDL2E (no operands) Load $\log_2 e$				Exceptions: I	
Operands	Execution Clocks		Transfers		Bytes	Coding Example
	Typical	Range	8086	8088		
(no operands)	18	15-21	0	0	2	FLDL2E

FLDL2T	FLDL2T (no operands) Load $\log_2 10$				Exceptions: I	
Operands	Execution Clocks		Transfers		Bytes	Coding Example
	Typical	Range	8086	8088		
(no operands)	19	16-22	0	0	2	FLDL2T

FLDPI	FLDPI (no operands) Load π				Exceptions: I	
Operands	Execution Clocks		Transfers		Bytes	Coding Example
	Typical	Range	8086	8088		
(no operands)	19	16-22	0	0	2	FLDPI

FLDZ	FLDZ (no operands) Load + 0.0				Exceptions: I	
Operands	Execution Clocks		Transfers		Bytes	Coding Example
	Typical	Range	8086	8088		
(no operands)	14	11-17	0	0	2	FLDZ

FLD1	FLD1 (no operands) Load + 1.0				Exceptions: I	
Operands	Execution Clocks		Transfers		Bytes	Coding Example
	Typical	Range	8086	8088		
(no operands)	18	15-21	0	0	2	FLD1

FMUL	FMUL //source/destination,source Multiply real				Exceptions: I, D, O, U, P	
Operands	Execution Clocks		Transfers		Bytes	Coding Example
	Typical	Range	8086	8088		
//ST(i),ST/ST,ST(i)	97*	90-105	0	0	2	FMUL ST,ST(3)
//ST(i),ST/ST,ST(i)	138	130-145	0	0	2	FMUL ST,ST(3)
short-real	118+EA	110-125+EA	2/4	4	2-4	FMUL SPEED_FACTOR
long-real	120+EA	112-126+EA	4/6	8	2-4	FMUL [BP].HEIGHT
long-real	161+EA	154-168+EA	4/6	8	2-4	FMUL [BP].HEIGHT

*occurs when one or both operands is "short"—it has 40 trailing zeros in its fraction (e.g., it was loaded from a short-real memory operand).

FMULP	FMULP destination,source Multiply real and pop				Exceptions: I, D, O, U, P	
Operands	Execution Clocks		Transfers		Bytes	Coding Example
	Typical	Range	8086	8088		
ST(i),ST	100*	94-108	0	0	2	FMULP ST(1),ST
ST(i),ST	142	134-148	0	0	2	FMULP ST(1),ST

*occurs when one or both operands is "short"—it has 40 trailing zeros in its fraction (e.g., it was loaded from a short-real memory operand).

FNOP	FNOP (no operands) No operation				Exceptions: None	
Operands	Execution Clocks		Transfers		Bytes	Coding Example
	Typical	Range	8086	8088		
(no operands)	13	10-16	0	0	2	FNOP

FPATAN	FPATAN (no operands) Partial arctangent				Exceptions: U, P (operands not checked)	
Operands	Execution Clocks		Transfers		Bytes	Coding Example
	Typical	Range	8086	8088		
(no operands)	650	250-800	0	0	2	FPATAN

FPREM	FPREM (no operands) Partial remainder				Exceptions: I, D, U	
Operands	Execution Clocks		Transfers		Bytes	Coding Example
	Typical	Range	8086	8088		
(no operands)	125	15-190	0	0	2	FPREM

FPTAN	FPTAN (no operands) Partial tangent				Exceptions: I, P (operands not checked)	
Operands	Execution Clocks		Transfers		Bytes	Coding Example
	Typical	Range	8086	8088		
(no operands)	450	30-540	0	0	2	FPTAN

FRNDINT	FRNDINT (no operands) Round to integer				Exceptions: I, P	
Operands	Execution Clocks		Transfers		Bytes	Coding Example
	Typical	Range	8086	8088		
(no operands)	45	16-50	0	0	2	FRNDINT

FRSTOR	FRSTOR source Restore saved state				Exceptions: None	
Operands	Execution Clocks		Transfers		Bytes	Coding Example
	Typical	Range	8086	8088		
94-bytes	210+EA	205-215+EA	47/49	94	2-4	FRSTOR [BP]

FSAVE/FNSAVE	FSAVE destination Save state				Exceptions: None	
Operands	Execution Clocks		Transfers		Bytes	Coding Example
	Typical	Range	8086	8088		
94-bytes	210+EA	205-215+EA	48/50	94	2-4	FSAVE [BP]

FSCALE	FSCALE (no operands) Scale				Exceptions: I, O, U	
Operands	Execution Clocks		Transfers		Bytes	Coding Example
	Typical	Range	8086	8088		
(no operands)	35	32-38	0	0	2	FSCALE

FSQRT	FSQRT (no operands) Square root				Exceptions: I, D, P	
Operands	Execution Clocks		Transfers		Bytes	Coding Example
	Typical	Range	8086	8088		
(no operands)	183	180-186	0	0	2	FSQRT

FST	FST destination Store real				Exceptions: I, O, U, P	
Operands	Execution Clocks		Transfers		Bytes	Coding Example
	Typical	Range	8086	8088		
ST(i)	18	15-22	0	0	2	FST ST(3)
short-real	87+EA	84-90+EA	3/5	6	2-4	FST CORRELATION [DI]
long-real	100+EA	96-104+EA	5/7	10	2-4	FST MEAN READING

FSTCW/ FNSTCW	FSTCW destination Store control word				Exceptions: None	
Operands	Execution Clocks		Transfers		Bytes	Coding Example
	Typical	Range	8086	8088		
2-bytes	15+EA	12-18+EA	2/4	4	2-4	FSTCW SAVE CONTROL

FSTENV/ FNSTENV	FSTENV destination Store environment				Exceptions: None	
Operands	Execution Clocks		Transfers		Bytes	Coding Example
	Typical	Range	8086	8088		
14-bytes	45+EA	40-50+EA	8/10	14	2-4	FSTENV [BP]

FSTP	FSTP destination Store real and pop				Exceptions: I, O, U, P	
Operands	Execution Clocks		Transfers		Bytes	Coding Example
	Typical	Range	8086	8088		
ST(i)	20	17-24	0	0	2	FSTP ST(2)
short-real	89+EA	86-92+EA	3/5	6	2-4	FSTP [BX].ADJUSTED RPM
long-real	102+EA	98-106+EA	5/7	10	2-4	FSTP TOTAL DOSAGE
temp-real	55+EA	52-58+EA	6/8	12	2-4	FSTP REG SAVE [SI]

FSTSW/ FNSTSW	FSTSW destination Store status word				Exceptions: None	
Operands	Execution Clocks		Transfers		Bytes	Coding Example
	Typical	Range	8086	8088		
2-bytes	15+EA	12-18+EA	2/4	4	2-4	FSTSW SAVE_STATUS

FSUB	FSUB //source/destination,source Subtract real				Exceptions: I,D,O,U,P	
Operands	Execution Clocks		Transfers		Bytes	Coding Example
	Typical	Range	8086	8088		
//ST,ST(i)/ST(i),ST	85	70-100	0	0	2	FSUB ST,ST(2)
short-real	105+EA	90-120+EA	2/4	4	2-4	FSUB BASE_VALUE
long-real	110+EA	95-125+EA	4/6	8	2-4	FSUB COORDINATE.X

FSUBP	FSUBP destination,source Subtract real and pop				Exceptions: I,D,O,U,P	
Operands	Execution Clocks		Transfers		Bytes	Coding Example
	Typical	Range	8086	8088		
ST(i),ST	90	75-105	0	0	2	FSUBP ST(2),ST

FSUBR	FSUBR //source/destination,source Subtract real reversed				Exceptions: I,D,O,U,P	
Operands	Execution Clocks		Transfers		Bytes	Coding Example
	Typical	Range	8086	8088		
//ST,ST(i)/ST(i),ST	87	70-100	0	0	2	FSUBR ST,ST(1)
short-real	105+EA	90-120+EA	2/4	4	2-4	FSUBR VECTOR[SI]
long-real	110+EA	95-125+EA	4/6	8	2-4	FSUBR [BX].INDEX

FSUBRP	FSUBRP desination,source Subtract real reversed and pop				Exceptions: I,D,O,U,P	
Operands	Execution Clocks		Transfers		Bytes	Coding Example
	Typical	Range	8086	8088		
ST(i),ST	90	75-105	0	0	2	FSUBRP ST(1),ST

FTST	FTST (no operands) Test stack top against +0.0				Exceptions: I, D	
Operands	Execution Clocks		Transfers		Bytes	Coding Example
	Typical	Range	8086	8088		
(no operands)	42	38-48	0	0	2	FTST

FWAIT	FWAIT (no operands) (CPU) Wait while 8087 is busy				Exceptions: None (CPU instruction)	
Operands	Execution Clocks		Transfers		Bytes	Coding Example
	Typical	Range	8086	8088		
(no operands)	3+5n*	3+5n*	0	0	1	FWAIT

FXAM	FXAM (no operands) Examine stack top				Exceptions: None	
Operands	Execution Clocks		Transfers		Bytes	Coding Example
	Typical	Range	8086	8088		
(no operands)	17	12-23	0	0	2	FXAM

FXCH	FXCH //destination Exchange registers				Exceptions: I	
Operands	Execution Clocks		Transfers		Bytes	Coding Example
	Typical	Range	8086	8088		
//ST(i)	12	10-15	0	0	2	FXCH ST(2)

FXTRACT	FXTRACT (no operands) Extract exponent and significand				Exceptions: I	
Operands	Execution Clocks		Transfers		Bytes	Coding Example
	Typical	Range	8086	8088		
(no operands)	50	27-55	0	0	2	FXTRACT

*n = number of times CPU examines $\overline{\text{TEST}}$ line before 8087 lowers BUSY.

FYL2X	FYL2X (no operands) Y · Log_2X				Exceptions: P (operands not checked)	
Operands	Execution Clocks		Transfers		Bytes	Coding Example
	Typical	Range	8086	8088		
(no operands)	950	900-1100	0	0	2	FYL2X

FYL2XP1	FYL2XP1 (no operands) Y · $log_2(X+1)$				Exceptions: P (operands not checked)	
Operands	Execution Clocks		Transfers		Bytes	Coding Example
	Typical	Range	8086	8088		
(no operands)	850	700-1000	0	0	2	FYL2XP1

HLT	**HLT** (no operands) Halt			Flags O D I T S Z A P C
Operands	**Clocks**	**Transfers***	**Bytes**	**Coding Example**
(no operands)	2	—	1	HLT

IDIV	**IDIV** source Integer division			Flags O D I T S Z A P C U U U U U U
Operands	**Clocks**	**Transfers***	**Bytes**	**Coding Example**
reg8	101-112	—	2	IDIV BL
reg16	165-184	—	2	IDIV CX
mem8	(107-118) + EA	1	2-4	IDIV DIVISOR_BYTE [SI]
mem16	(171-190) + EA	1	2-4	IDIV [BX].DIVISOR_WORD

IMUL	**IMUL** source Integer multiplication			Flags O D I T S Z A P C X U U U U X
Operands	**Clocks**	**Transfers***	**Bytes**	**Coding Example**
reg8	80-98	—	2	IMUL CL
reg16	128-154	—	2	IMUL BX
mem8	(86-104) + EA	1	2-4	IMUL RATE_BYTE
mem16	(134-160) + EA	1	2-4	IMUL RATE_WORD [BP] [DI]

IN	**IN** accumulator,port Input byte or word			Flags O D I T S Z A P C
Operands	**Clocks**	**Transfers***	**Bytes**	**Coding Example**
accumulator, immed8	10	1	2	IN AL, 0FFEAH
accumulator, DX	8	1	1	IN AX, DX

INC

INC destination
Increment by 1

Flags	O	D	I	T	S	Z	A	P	C
	X				X	X	X	X	

Operands	Clocks	Transfers*	Bytes	Coding Example
reg16	2	—	1	INC CX
reg8	3	—	2	INC BL
memory	15+EA	2	2-4	INC ALPHA [DI] [BX]

INT

INT interrupt-type
Interrupt

Flags	O	D	I	T	S	Z	A	P	C
			0	0					

Operands	Clocks	Transfers*	Bytes	Coding Example
immed8 (type = 3)	52	5	1	INT 3
immed8 (type ≠ 3)	51	5	2	INT 67

INTR

INTR (external maskable interrupt)
Interrupt if INTR and IF=1

Flags	O	D	I	T	S	Z	A	P	C
			0	0					

Operands	Clocks	Transfers*	Bytes	Coding Example
(no operands)	61	7	N/A	N/A

INTO

INTO (no operands)
Interrupt if overflow

Flags	O	D	I	T	S	Z	A	P	C
			0	0					

Operands	Clocks	Transfers*	Bytes	Coding Example
(no operands)	53 or 4	5	1	INTO

IRET

IRET (no operands)
Interrupt Return

Flags	O	D	I	T	S	Z	A	P	C
	R	R	R	R	R	R	R	R	R

Operands	Clocks	Transfers*	Bytes	Coding Example
(no operands)	24	3	1	IRET

JA/JNBE

JA/JNBE short-label
Jump if above/Jump if not below nor equal

Flags	O	D	I	T	S	Z	A	P	C

Operands	Clocks	Transfers*	Bytes	Coding Example
short-label	16 or 4	—	2	JA ABOVE

JAE/JNB

JAE/JNB short-label
Jump if above or equal/Jump if not below

Flags	O	D	I	T	S	Z	A	P	C

Operands	Clocks	Transfers*	Bytes	Coding Example
short-label	16 or 4	—	2	JAE ABOVE_EQUAL

JB/JNAE

JB/JNAE short-label
Jump if below/Jump if not above nor equal

Flags	O	D	I	T	S	Z	A	P	C

Operands	Clocks	Transfers*	Bytes	Coding Example
short-label	16 or 4	—	2	JB BELOW

JBE/JNA	**JBE/JNA** short-label Jump if below or equal/Jump if not above			Flags O D I T S Z A P C
Operands	**Clocks**	**Transfers***	**Bytes**	**Coding Example**
short-label	16 or 4	—	2	JNA NOT_ABOVE

JC	**JC** short-label Jump if carry			Flags O D I T S Z A P C
Operands	**Clocks**	**Transfers***	**Bytes**	**Coding Example**
short-label	16 or 4	—	2	JC CARRY_SET

JCXZ	**JCXZ** short-label Jump if CX is zero			Flags O D I T S Z A P C
Operands	**Clocks**	**Transfers***	**Bytes**	**Coding Example**
short-label	18 or 6	—	2	JCXZ COUNT_DONE

JE/JZ	**JE/JZ** short-label Jump if equal/Jump if zero			Flags O D I T S Z A P C
Operands	**Clocks**	**Transfers***	**Bytes**	**Coding Example**
short-label	16 or 4	—	2	JZ ZERO

JG/JNLE	**JG/JNLE** short-label Jump if greater/Jump if not less nor equal			Flags O D I T S Z A P C
Operands	**Clocks**	**Transfers***	**Bytes**	**Coding Example**
short-label	16 or 4	—	2	JG GREATER

JGE/JNL	**JGE/JNL** short-label Jump if greater or equal/Jump if not less			Flags O D I T S Z A P C
Operands	**Clocks**	**Transfers***	**Bytes**	**Coding Example**
short-label	16 or 4	—	2	JGE GREATER_EQUAL

JL/JNGE	**JL/JNGE** short-label Jump if less/Jump if not greater nor equal			Flags O D I T S Z A P C
Operands	**Clocks**	**Transfers***	**Bytes**	**Coding Example**
short-label	16 or 4	—	2	JL LESS

JLE/JNG	**JLE/JNG** short-label Jump if less or equal/Jump if not greater			Flags O D I T S Z A P C
Operands	**Clocks**	**Transfers***	**Bytes**	**Coding Example**
short-label	16 or 4	—	2	JNG NOT_GREATER

JMP	**JMP** target Jump			Flags O D I T S Z A P C
Operands	**Clocks**	**Transfers***	**Bytes**	**Coding Example**
short-label	15	—	2	JMP SHORT
near-label	15	—	3	JMP WITHIN_SEGMENT
far-label	15	—	5	JMP FAR_LABEL
memptr16	18+EA	1	2-4	JMP [BX].TARGET
regptr16	11	—	2	JMP CX
memptr32	24+EA	2	2-4	JMP OTHER.SEG [SI]

JNC	**JNC** short-label Jump if not carry			Flags O D I T S Z A P C
Operands	**Clocks**	**Transfers***	**Bytes**	**Coding Example**
short-label	16 or 4	—	2	JNC NOT_CARRY

JNE/JNZ	**JNE/JNZ** short-label Jump if not equal/Jump if not zero			Flags O D I T S Z A P C
Operands	**Clocks**	**Transfers***	**Bytes**	**Coding Example**
short-label	16 or 4	—	2	JNE NOT_EQUAL

JNO	**JNO** short-label Jump if not overflow			Flags O D I T S Z A P C
Operands	**Clocks**	**Transfers***	**Bytes**	**Coding Example**
short-label	16 or 4	—	2	JNO NO_OVERFLOW

JNP/JPO	**JNP/JPO** short-label Jump if not parity/Jump if parity odd			Flags O D I T S Z A P C
Operands	**Clocks**	**Transfers***	**Bytes**	**Coding Example**
short-label	16 or 4	—	2	JPO ODD_PARITY

JNS	**JNS** short-label Jump if not sign			Flags O D I T S Z A P C
Operands	**Clocks**	**Transfers***	**Bytes**	**Coding Example**
short-label	16 or 4	—	2	JNS POSITIVE

JO	**JO** short-label Jump if overflow			Flags O D I T S Z A P C
Operands	**Clocks**	**Transfers***	**Bytes**	**Coding Example**
short-label	16 or 4	—	2	JO SIGNED_OVRFLW

*All mnemonics copyright Intel Corporation 1980.

JP/JPE	JP/JPE short-label Jump if parity/Jump if parity even	Flags O D I T S Z A P C

Operands	Clocks	Transfers*	Bytes	Coding Example
short-label	16 or 4	—	2	JPE EVEN_PARITY

JS	JS short-label Jump if sign	Flags O D I T S Z A P C

Operands	Clocks	Transfers*	Bytes	Coding Example
short-label	16 or 4	—	2	JS NEGATIVE

LAHF	LAHF (no operands) Load AH from flags	Flags O D I T S Z A P C

Operands	Clocks	Transfers*	Bytes	Coding Example
(no operands)	4	—	1	LAHF

LDS	LDS destination,source Load pointer using DS	Flags O D I T S Z A P C

Operands	Clocks	Transfers	Bytes	Coding Example
reg16, mem32	16+EA	2	2-4	LDS SI,DATA.SEG [DI]

LOCK	LOCK (no operands) Lock bus	Flags O D I T S Z A P C

Operands	Clocks	Transfers*	Bytes	Coding Example
(no operands)	2	—	1	LOCK XCHG FLAG,AL

LODS	LODS source-string Load string	Flags O D I T S Z A P C

Operands	Clocks	Transfers*	Bytes	Coding Example
source-string	12	1	1	LODS CUSTOMER_NAME
(repeat) source-string	9+13/rep	1/rep	1	REP LODS NAME

LOOP	LOOP short-label Loop	Flags O D I T S Z A P C

Operands	Clocks	Transfers*	Bytes	Coding Example
short-label	17/5	—	2	LOOP AGAIN

LOOPE/LOOPZ	LOOPE/LOOPZ short-label Loop if equal/Loop if zero	Flags O D I T S Z A P C

Operands	Clocks	Transfers*	Bytes	Coding Example
short-label	18 or 6	—	2	LOOPE AGAIN

*All mnemonics copyright Intel Corporation 1980.

LOOPNE/LOOPNZ

LOOPNE/LOOPNZ short-label
Loop if not equal/Loop if not zero

Flags: O D I T S Z A P C

Operands	Clocks	Transfers*	Bytes	Coding Example
short-label	19 or 5	—	2	LOOPNE AGAIN

LEA

LEA destination,source
Load effective address

Flags: O D I T S Z A P C

Operands	Clocks	Transfers*	Bytes	Coding Example
reg16, mem16	2+EA	—	2-4	LEA BX, [BP] [DI]

LES

LES destination,source
Load pointer using ES

Flags: O D I T S Z A P C

Operands	Clocks	Transfers*	Bytes	Coding Example
reg16, mem32	16+EA	2	2-4	LES DI, [BX].TEXT_BUFF

NMI†

NMI (external nonmaskable interrupt)
Interrupt if NMI = 1

Flags:

O	S	I	T	S	Z	A	P	C
		0	0					

Operands	Clocks	Transfers*	Bytes	Coding Example
(no operands)	50	5	N/A	N/A

MOV

MOV destination,source
Move

Flags: O D I T S Z A P C

Operands	Clocks	Transfers*	Bytes	Coding Example
memory, accumulator	10	1	3	MOV ARRAY [SI], AL
accumulator, memory	10	1	3	MOV AX, TEMP_RESULT
register, register	2	—	2	MOV AX,CX
register, memory	8+EA	1	2-4	MOV BP, STACK_TOP
memory, register	9+EA	1	2-4	MOV COUNT [DI], CX
register, immediate	4	—	2-3	MOV CL, 2
memory, immediate	10+EA	1	3-6	MOV MASK [BX] [SI], 2CH
seg-reg, reg16	2	—	2	MOV ES, CX
seg-reg, mem16	8+EA	1	2-4	MOV DS, SEGMENT_BASE
reg16, seg-reg	2	—	2	MOV BP, SS
memory, seg-reg	9+EA	1	2-4	MOV [BX].SEG_SAVE, CS

MOVS

MOVS dest-string,source-string
Move string

Flags: O D I T S Z A P C

Operands	Clocks	Transfers*	Bytes	Coding Example
dest-string, source-string	18	2	1	MOVS LINE EDIT_DATA
(repeat) dest-string, source-string	9+17/rep	2/rep	1	REP MOVS SCREEN, BUFFER

MOVSB/MOVSW

MOVSB/MOVSW (no operands)
Move string (byte/word)

Flags: O D I T S Z A P C

Operands	Clocks	Transfers*	Bytes	Coding Example
(no operands)	18	2	1	MOVSB
(repeat) (no operands)	9+17/rep	2/rep	1	REP MOVSW

MUL	MUL source Multiplication, unsigned	Flags O D I T S Z A P C X U U U U X

Operands	Clocks	Transfers*	Bytes	Coding Example
reg8	70-77	—	2	MUL BL
reg16	118-133	—	2	MUL CX
mem8	(76-83) + EA	1	2-4	MUL MONTH [SI]
mem16	(124-139) + EA	1	2-4	MUL BAUD_RATE

NEG	NEG destination Negate	Flags O D I T S Z A P C X X X X X 1

Operands	Clocks	Transfers*	Bytes	Coding Example
register	3	—	2	NEG AL
memory	16 + EA	2	2-4	NEG MULTIPLIER

NOP	NOP (no operands) No Operation	Flags O D I T S Z A P C

Operands	Clocks	Transfers*	Bytes	Coding Example
(no operands)	3	—	1	NOP

NOT	NOT destination Logical not	Flags O D I T S Z A P C

Operands	Clocks	Transfers*	Bytes	Coding Example
register	3	—	2	NOT AX
memory	16 + EA	2	2-4	NOT CHARACTER

OR	OR destination,source Logical inclusive or	Flags O D I T S Z A P C 0 X X U X 0

Operands	Clocks	Transfers*	Bytes	Coding Example
register, register	3	—	2	OR AL, BL
register, memory	9 + EA	1	2-4	OR DX, PORT_ID [DI]
memory, register	16 + EA	2	2-4	OR FLAG_BYTE, CL
accumulator, immediate	4	—	2-3	OR AL, 01101100B
register, immediate	4	—	3-4	OR CX,01H
memory, immediate	17 + EA	2	3-6	OR [BX].CMD_WORD,0CFH

OUT	OUT port,accumulator Output byte or word	Flags O D I T S Z A P C

Operands	Clocks	Transfers*	Bytes	Coding Example
immed8, accumulator	10	1	2	OUT 44, AX
DX, accumulator	8	1	1	OUT DX, AL

POP

POP destination
Pop word off stack

Flags:

O	D	I	T	S	Z	A	P	C

Operands	Clocks	Transfers*	Bytes	Coding Example
register	8	1	1	POP DX
seg-reg (CS illegal)	8	1	1	POP DS
memory	17+EA	2	2-4	POP PARAMETER

POPF

POPF (no operands)
Pop flags off stack

Flags:

O	D	I	T	S	Z	A	P	C
R	R	R	R	R	R	R	R	R

Operands	Clocks	Transfers*	Bytes	Coding Example
(no operands)	8	1	1	POPF

PUSH

PUSH source
Push word onto stack

Flags:

O	D	I	T	S	Z	A	P	C

Operands	Clocks	Transfers*	Bytes	Coding Example
register	11	1	1	PUSH SI
seg-reg (CS legal)	10	1	1	PUSH ES
memory	16+EA	2	2-4	PUSH RETURN_CODE [SI]

PUSHF

PUSHF (no operands)
Push flags onto stack

Flags:

O	D	I	T	S	Z	A	P	C

Operands	Clocks	Transfers*	Bytes	Coding Example
(no operands)	10	1	1	PUSHF

RCL

RCL destination,count
Rotate left through carry

Flags:

O	D	I	T	S	Z	A	P	C
X								X

Operands	Clocks	Transfers*	Bytes	Coding Example
register, 1	2	—	2	RCL CX, 1
register, CL	8+4/bit	—	2	RCL AL, CL
memory, 1	15+EA	2	2-4	RCL ALPHA, 1
memory, CL	20+EA+ 4/bit	2	2-4	RCL [BP].PARM, CL

RCR

RCR designation,count
Rotate right through carry

Flags:

O	D	I	T	S	Z	A	P	C
X								X

Operands	Clocks	Transfers*	Bytes	Coding Example
register, 1	2	—	2	RCR BX, 1
register, CL	8+4/bit	—	2	RCR BL, CL
memory, 1	15+EA	2	2-4	RCR [BX].STATUS, 1
memory, CL	20+EA+ 4/bit	2	2-4	RCR ARRAY [DI], CL

REP

REP (no operands)
Repeat string operation

Flags:

O	D	I	T	S	Z	A	P	C

Operands	Clocks	Transfers*	Bytes	Coding Example
(no operands)	2	—	1	REP MOVS DEST, SRCE

REPE/REPZ

REPE/REPZ (no operands)
Repeat string operation while equal/while zero

Flags O D I T S Z A P C

Operands	Clocks	Transfers*	Bytes	Coding Example
(no operands)	2	—	1	REPE CMPS DATA, KEY

REPNE/REPNZ

REPNE/REPNZ (no operands)
Repeat string operation while not equal/not zero

Flags O D I T S Z A P C

Operands	Clocks	Transfers*	Bytes	Coding Example
(no operands)	2	—	1	REPNE SCAS INPUT_LINE

RET

RET optional-pop-value
Return from procedure

Flags O D I T S Z A P C

Operands	Clocks	Transfers*	Bytes	Coding Example
(intra-segment, no pop)	8	1	1	RET
(intra-segment, pop)	12	1	3	RET 4
(inter-segment, no pop)	18	2	1	RET
(inter-segment, pop)	17	2	3	RET 2

ROL

ROL destination,count
Rotate left

Flags O D I T S Z A P C
X X (O and C)

Operands	Clocks	Transfers	Bytes	Coding Examples
register, 1	2	—	2	ROL BX, 1
register, CL	8 + 4/bit	—	2	ROL DI, CL
memory, 1	15 + EA	2	2-4	ROL FLAG_BYTE [DI],1
memory, CL	20 + EA + 4/bit	2	2-4	ROL ALPHA , CL

ROR

ROR destination,count
Rotate right

Flags O D I T S Z A P C
X X (O and C)

Operand	Clocks	Transfers*	Bytes	Coding Example
register, 1	2	—	2	ROR AL, 1
register, CL	8 + 4/bit	—	2	ROR BX, CL
memory, 1	15 + EA	2	2-4	ROR PORT_STATUS, 1
memory, CL	20 + EA + 4/bit	2	2-4	ROR CMD_WORD, CL

SAHF

SAHF (no operands)
Store AH into flags

Flags O D I T S Z A P C
R R R R R (S Z A P C)

Operands	Clocks	Transfers*	Bytes	Coding Example
(no operands)	4	—	1	SAHF

SAL/SHL

SAL/SHL destination,count
Shift arithmetic left/Shift logical left

Flags	O	D	I	T	S	Z	A	P	C
	X								X

Operands	Clocks	Transfers*	Bytes	Coding Examples
register,1	2	—	2	SAL AL,1
register, CL	8+4/bit	—	2	SHL DI, CL
memory,1	15+EA	2	2-4	SHL [BX].OVERDRAW, 1
memory, CL	20+EA+ 4/bit	2	2-4	SAL STORE_COUNT, CL

SAR

SAR destination,source
Shift arithmetic right

Flags	O	D	I	T	S	Z	A	P	C
	X				X	X	U	X	X

Operands	Clocks	Transfers*	Bytes	Coding Example
register, 1	2	—	2	SAR DX, 1
register, CL	8+4/bit	—	2	SAR DI, CL
memory, 1	15+EA	2	2-4	SAR N_BLOCKS, 1
memory, CL	20+EA+ 4/bit	2	2-4	SAR N_BLOCKS, CL

SBB

SBB destination,source
Subtract with borrow

Flags	O	D	I	T	S	Z	A	P	C
	X				X	X	X	X	X

Operands	Clocks	Transfers*	Bytes	Coding Example
register, register	3	—	2	SBB BX, CX
register, memory	9+EA	1	2-4	SBB DI, [BX].PAYMENT
memory, register	16+EA	2	2-4	SBB BALANCE, AX
accumulator, immediate	4	—	2-3	SBB AX, 2
register, immediate	4	—	3-4	SBB CL, 1
memory, immediate	17+EA	2	3-6	SBB COUNT [SI], 10

SCAS

SCAS dest-string
Scan string

Flags	O	D	I	T	S	Z	A	P	C
	X				X	X	X	X	X

Operands	Clocks	Transfers*	Bytes	Coding Example
dest-string	15	1	1	SCAS INPUT_LINE
(repeat) dest-string	9+15/rep	1/rep	1	REPNE SCAS BUFFER

SHR

SHR destination,count
Shift logical right

Flags	O	D	I	T	S	Z	A	P	C
	X								X

Operands	Clocks	Transfers*	Bytes	Coding Example
register, 1	2	—	2	SHR SI, 1
register, CL	8+4/bit	—	2	SHR SI, CL
memory, 1	15+EA	2	2-4	SHR ID_BYTE [SI] [BX], 1
memory, CL	20+EA+ 4/bit	2	2-4	SHR INPUT_WORD, CL

SINGLE STEP

SINGLE STEP (Trap flag interrupt)
Interrupt if TF = 1

Flags	O	D	I	T	S	Z	A	P	C
			0	0					

Operands	Clocks	Transfers*	Bytes	Coding Example
(no operands)	50	5	N/A	N/A

STC

STC (no operands)
Set carry flag

Flags	O	D	I	T	S	Z	A	P	C
									1

Operands	Clocks	Transfers*	Bytes	Coding Example
(no operands)	2	—	1	STC

STD

STD (no operands)
Set direction flag

Flags	O	D	I	T	S	Z	A	P	C
		1							

Operands	Clocks	Transfers*	Bytes	Coding Example
(no operands)	2	—	1	STD

STI

STI (no operands)
Set interrupt enable flag

Flags	O	D	I	T	S	Z	A	P	C
			1						

Operands	Clocks	Transfers*	Bytes	Coding Example
(no operands)	2	—	1	STI

STOS

STOS dest-string
Store byte or word string

Flags	O	D	I	T	S	Z	A	P	C

Operands	Clocks	Transfers*	Bytes	Coding Example
dest-string	11	1	1	STOS PRINT_LINE
(repeat) dest-string	9+10/rep	1/rep	1	REP STOS DISPLAY

SUB

SUB destination,source
Subtraction

Flags	O	D	I	T	S	Z	A	P	C
	X				X	X	X	X	X

Operands	Clocks	Transfers*	Bytes	Coding Example
register, register	3	—	2	SUB CX, BX
register, memory	9+EA	1	2-4	SUB DX, MATH_TOTAL [SI]
memory, register	16+EA	2	2-4	SUB [BP+2], CL
accumulator, immediate	4	—	2-3	SUB AL, 10
register, immediate	4	—	3-4	SUB SI, 5280
memory, immediate	17+EA	2	3-6	SUB [BP].BALANCE, 1000

TEST

TEST destination,source
Test or non-destructive logical and

Flags	O	D	I	T	S	Z	A	P	C
	0				X	X	U	X	0

Operands	Clocks	Transfers*	Bytes	Coding Example
register, register	3	—	2	TEST SI, DI
register, memory	9+EA	1	2-4	TEST SI, END_COUNT
accumulator, immediate	4	—	2-3	TEST AL, 00100000B
register, immediate	5	—	3-4	TEST BX, 0CC4H
memory, immediate	11+EA	—	3-6	TEST RETURN_CODE, 01H

WAIT

WAIT (no operands)
Wait while $\overline{TEST}$ pin not asserted

Flags	O	D	I	T	S	Z	A	P	C

Operands	Clocks	Transfers*	Bytes	Coding Example
(no operands)	3 + 5n	—	1	WAIT

XCHG	XCHG destination,source Exchange			Flags O D I T S Z A P C
Operands	**Clocks**	**Transfers***	**Bytes**	**Coding Example**
accumulator, reg16	3	—	1	XCHG AX, BX
memory, register	17+EA	2	2-4	XCHG SEMAPHORE, AX
register, register	4	—	2	XCHG AL, BL

XLAT	XLAT source-table Translate			Flags O D I T S Z A P C
Operands	**Clocks**	**Transfers***	**Bytes**	**Coding Example**
source-table	11	1	1	XLAT ASCII_TAB

XOR	XOR destination,source Logical exclusive or			Flags O D I T S Z A P C 0 X X U X 0
Operands	**Clocks**	**Transfers***	**Bytes**	**Coding Example**
register, register	3	—	2	XOR CX, BX
register, memory	9+EA	1	2-4	XOR CL, MASK_BYTE
memory, register	16+EA	2	2-4	XOR ALPHA [SI], DX
accumulator, immediate	4	—	2-3	XOR AL, 01000010B
register, immediate	4	—	3-4	XOR SI, 00C2H
memory, immediate	17+EA	2	3-6	XOR RETURN_CODE, 0D2H

INTEL 80186 AND INTEL 80286 REAL ADDRESS MODE INTEL 80286 PROTECTED VIRTUAL ADDRESS MODE†

BOUND	Detect Index Out-of-Bounds		Interrupt #5
Operands	Clocks	Bytes	Coding Example
index-register-memory	13	2	BOUND SI, ARRAY

ENTER	Create Stack Frame		—
Operands	Clocks	Bytes	Coding Example
memory-immediate	11–16*(L-1)	4	ENTER AREA,3

IMUL	Signed Integer Multiply Immediate		Same Flags as IMUL
Operands	Clocks	Bytes	Coding Example
register-immediate	21–24	3–4	IMUL AL,126 IMUL AX,16473

*All mnemonics copyright Intel Corporation 1980.

†Additional instructions for the protected virtual address mode are given in the following section.

INS	Input String			Device Interrupts
Operands		Clocks	Bytes	Coding Example
(no operands)	port = DX address = SI count = CX	5 + 4 * N	1 + 1 (REP)	INS INS WORD PTR

LEAVE	Destroy Stack Frame			—
Operands		Clocks	Bytes	Coding Example
(no operands)		5	1	LEAVE

OUTS	Output String			Device Interrupts
Operands		Clocks	Bytes	Coding Example
(no operands)	port = DX address = DI count = CX	5 + 4 * N	1 + 1 (REP)	OUTS OUTS WORD PTR

POPA	Pop All Registers from Stack			Same Flags as POP
Operands		Clocks	Bytes	Coding Example
(no operands)		19	1	POPA

PUSH	Push Immediate to Stack			Same Flags as PUSH
Operands		Clocks	Bytes	Coding Example
immediate		3	2–3	PUSH 17 PUSH 18417

PUSHA	Push All Registers to Stack			Same Flags as PUSH
Operands		Clocks	Bytes	Coding Example
(no operands)		17	1	PUSHA

RCL	Rotate through Carry Left Immediate			Same Flags as RCL
Operands		Clocks	Bytes	Coding Example
register, immediate memory, immediate		5 + N 8 + N	3	RCL AX,7 RCL ANY,3

RCR	Rotate through Carry Right Immediate		Same Flags as RCR
Operands	Clocks	Bytes	Coding Example
register, immediate memory, immediate	5 + N 8 + N	3	RCR AX,3 RCR ANY,4

ROL	Rotate Left Immediate		Same Flags as ROL
Operands	Clocks	Bytes	Coding Example
register, immediate memory, immediate	5 + N 8 + N	3	ROL AL,2 ROL ANY,7

ROR	Rotate Right Immediate		Same Flags as ROR
Operands	Clocks	Bytes	Coding Example
register, immediate memory, immediate	5 + N 8 + N	3	ROR BH,5 ROR ANY,2

SAL/SHL	Shift Left Immediate		Same Flags as SAL/SHL
Operands	Clocks	Bytes	Coding Example
register, immediate memory, immediate	5 + N 8 + N	3	SAL CL,2 SHL ANY,5

SAR	Shift Right Arithmetic Immediate		Same Flags as SAR
Operands	Clocks	Bytes	Coding Example
register, immediate memory, immediate	5 + N 8 + N	3	SAR AX,4 SAR ANY,3

SHR	Shift Right Logical Immediate		Same Flags as SHR
Operands	Clocks	Bytes	Coding Example
register, immediate memory, immediate	5 + N 8 + N	3	SHR CX,2 SHR ANY,7

INTEL 80286 PROTECTED VIRTUAL ADDRESS MODE†

ARPL	Adjust Requested Privilege Level			If Change, ZF = 1
Operands		Clocks	Bytes	Coding Example
register memory		10–11	2	ARPL AX ARPL ANY

CALL	Task Gate Protected Call			Interrupts Possible
Operands		Clocks	Bytes	Coding Example
offset/segment address table of four-byte addresses		?	5 2	CALL DWORD PTR ANY CALL DWORD PTR TBL[DI]

CTS	Clear Task Switched Flag			TS Flag = 0
Operands		Clocks	Bytes	Coding Example
(no operands)		2	2	CTS

INT	Task Gate Protected Interrupt			—
Operands		Clocks	Bytes	Coding Example
(no operands) immediate		?	1 2	INT 3 INT 27

INTO	Task Gate Interrupt on Overflow			—
Operands		Clocks	Bytes	Coding Example
(no operands)		27 24 + M	1	INTO

IRET	Task Gate Return from Interrupt			—
Operands		Clocks	Bytes	Coding Example
(no operands)		?	1	IRET

†Additional instructions are given in the preceding section.

JMP	Task Gate Protected Jump		Interrupt Possible
Operands	Clocks	Bytes	Coding Example
offset/segment address table of four-byte addresses	?	5 2	JMP DWORD PTR THERE JMP DWORD PTR TBL[DI]

LAR	Load Access Rights Byte		Protection Exception Possible
Operands	Clocks	Bytes	Coding Example
register memory	14–16	3	LAR AX LAR ANY

LGDT	Load Global Descriptor Table Register		Protection Exception Possible
Operands	Clocks	Bytes	Coding Example
memory (six bytes)	11	3	LGDT ANY

LIDT	Load Interrupt Descriptor Table Register		—
Operands	Clocks	Bytes	Coding Example
memory (six bytes)	12	3	LIDT ANY

LLDT	Load Local Descriptor Table Word Pointer		Protection Exception Possible
Operands	Clocks	Bytes	Coding Example
register memory	17–19	3	LLDT BX LLDT WORD PTR ANY

LMSW	Load Machine Status Word		Protection Exception Possible
Operands	Clocks	Bytes	Coding Example
register memory	3–6	3	LMSW DX LMSW WORD PTR ANY

LSL	Load Segment Size		Protection Exception Possible
Operands	Clocks	Bytes	Coding Example
register memory	14–16	3	LSL AX LSL WORD PTR ANY

LTR	Load Task Register		Protection Exception Possible
Operands	Clocks	Bytes	Coding Example
register memory	17–19	3	LTR BX LTR WORD PTR ANY

RET	Task Gate Protected Return		Interrupts Possible
Operands	Clocks	Bytes	Coding Example
(no operands)	55 + M	1	RET

SGDT	Store Global Descriptor Table Register		Protection Exception Possible
Operands	Clocks	Bytes	Coding Example
memory (six bytes)	11	3	SGDT ANY

SIDT	Store Interrupt Descriptor Table Register		Protection Exception Possible
Operands	Clocks	Bytes	Coding Example
memory (six bytes)	12	3	SIDT ANY

SLDT	Store Local Descriptor Table Word Pointer		Protection Exception Possible
Operands	Clocks	Bytes	Coding Example
register memory	17–19	3	SLDT AX SLDT WORD PTR ANY

SMSW	Store Machine Status Word		Protection Exception Possible
Operands	Clocks	Bytes	Coding Example
register memory	2–3	3	SMSW BX SMSW WORD PTR ANY

STR	Store Task Pointer		Protection Exception Possible
Operands	Clocks	Bytes	Coding Example
register memory	2–3	3	LTR AX LTR WORD PTR ANY

VERR	Verify Read Access		ZF flag = 0 if true = 1 if false
Operands	Clocks	Bytes	Coding Example
segment identifier	14–16	3	VERR SEG_NAME

VERW	Verify Write Access		ZF flag = 0 if true = 1 if false
Operands	Clocks	Bytes	Coding Example
segment identifier	14–16	3	VERW SEG_NAME

8089 INPUT/OUTPUT PROCESSOR

IDENTIFIER	EXPLANATION
(no operands)	No operands are written
register	Any general register
ptr-reg	A pointer register
immed8	A constant in the range 0-FFH
immed16	A constant in the range 0-FFFFH
mem8	An 8-bit memory location (byte)
mem16	A 16-bit memory location (word)
mem24	A 24-bit memory location (physical address pointer)
mem32	A 32-bit memory location (doubleword pointer)
label	A label within −32,768 to +32,767 bytes of the end of the instruction
short-label	A label within −128 to +127 bytes of the end of the instruction
0-7	A constant in the range: 0-7
8/16	The constant 8 or the constant 16

ADD destination, source		Add Word Variable	
Operands	**Clocks**	**Bytes**	**Coding Example**
register, mem16	11/15	2-3	ADD BC, [GA].LENGTH
mem16, register	16/26	2-3	ADD [GB], GC

ADDB destination, source		Add Byte Variable	
Operands	**Clocks**	**Bytes**	**Coding Example**
register, mem8	11	2-3	ADDB GC, [GA].N_CHARS
mem8, register	16	2-3	ADDB [PP].ERRORS, MC

ADDBI destination, source		Add Byte Immediate	
Operands	**Clocks**	**Bytes**	**Coding Example**
register, immed8	3	3	ADDBI MC,10
mem8, immed8	16	3-4	ADDBI [PP+IX+].RECORDS, 2CH

ADDI destination, source		Add Word Immediate	
Operands	**Clocks**	**Bytes**	**Coding Example**
register, immed16	3	4	ADDI GB, 0C25BH
mem16, immed16	16/26	4-5	ADDI [GB].POINTER, 5899

AND destination, source		Logical AND Word Variable	
Operands	**Clocks**	**Bytes**	**Coding Example**
register, mem16	11/15	2-3	AND MC, [GA].FLAG__WORD
mem16, register	16/26	2-3	AND [GC].STATUS, BC

ANDB destination, source		Logical AND Byte Variable	
Operands	**Clocks**	**Bytes**	**Coding Example**
register, mem8	11	2-3	AND BC, [GC]
mem8, register	16	2-3	AND [GA+IX].RESULT, GA

ANDBI destination, source		Logical AND Byte Immediate	
Operands	**Clocks**	**Bytes**	**Coding Example**
register, immed8	3	3	GA, 01100000B
mem8, immed8	10	3 4	[GC+IX], 2CH

ANDI destination, source		Logical AND Word Immediate	
Operands	**Clocks**	**Bytes**	**Coding Example**
register, immed16	3	4	IX, 0H
mem16, immed16	16/26	4-5	[GB+IX].TAB, 40H

CALL TPsave, target		Call	
Operands	**Clocks**	**Bytes**	**Coding Example**
mem24, label	17/23	3-5	CALL [GC+IX].SAVE, GET__NEXT

CLR destination, bit select		Clear Bit To Zero	
Operands	**Clocks**	**Bytes**	**Coding Example**
mem8, 0-7	16	2-3	CLR [GA], 3

DEC destination		Decrement Word By 1	
Operands	**Clocks**	**Bytes**	**Coding Example**
register mem16	3 16/26	2 2-3	 DEC [PP].RETRY

DECB destination		Decrement Byte By 1	
Operands	**Clocks**	**Bytes**	**Coding Example**
mem8	16	2-3	DECB [GA+IX+].TAB

HLT (no operands)		Halt Channel Program	
Operands	**Clocks**	**Bytes**	**Coding Example**
(no operands)	11	2	HLT

INC destination		Increment Word by 1	
Operands	**Clocks**	**Bytes**	**Coding Example**
register mem16	3 16/26	2 2-3	INC GA INC [GA].COUNT

INCB destination		Increment Byte by 1	
Operands	**Clocks**	**Bytes**	**Coding Example**
mem8	16	2-3	INCB [GB].POINTER

JBT source, bit-select, target		Jump if Bit True (1)	
Operands	**Clocks**	**Bytes**	**Coding Example**
mem8, 0-7, label	14	3-5	JBT [GA].RESULT_REG, 3, DATA_VALID

JMCE source, target		Jump if Masked Compare Equal	
Operands	**Clocks**	**Bytes**	**Coding Example**
mem8, label	14	3-5	JMCE [GB].FLAG, STOP_SEARCH

JMCNE source, target		Jump if Masked Compare Not Equal	
Operands	**Clocks**	**Bytes**	**Coding Example**
mem8, label	14	3-5	JMCNE [GB+IX], NEXT_ITEM

JMP target		Jump Unconditionally	
Operands	**Clocks**	**Bytes**	**Coding Example**
label	3	3-4	JMP READ_SECTOR

JNBT source, bit-select, target		Jump if Bit Not True (0)	
Operands	**Clocks**	**Bytes**	**Coding Example**
mem8, 0-7, label	14	3-5	JNBT [GC], 3, RE_READ

JNZ source, target		Jump if Word Not Zero	
Operands	**Clocks**	**Bytes**	**Coding Example**
register, label	5	3-4	JNZ BC, WRITE_LINE
mem16, label	12/16	3-5	JNZ [PP].NUM_CHARS, PUT_BYTE

JNZB source, target		Jump if Byte Not Zero	
Operands	**Clocks**	**Bytes**	**Coding Example**
mem8, label	12	3-5	JNZB [GA], MORE_DATA

JZ source, target		Jump if Word is Zero	
Operands	**Clocks**	**Bytes**	**Coding Example**
register, label	5	3-4	JZ BC, NEXT_LINE
mem16, label	12/16	3-5	JZ [GC+IX].INDEX, BUF_EMPTY

JZB source, target		Jump if Byte Zero	
Operands	**Clocks**	**Bytes**	**Coding Example**
mem8, label	12	3-5	JZB [PP].LINES_LEFT, RETURN

LCALL TPsave, target		Long Call	
Operands	**Clocks**	**Bytes**	**Coding Example**
mem24, label	17/23	4-5	LCALL [GC].RETURN_SAVE, INIT_8279

LJBT source, bit-select, target		Long Jump if Bit True (1)	
Operands	**Clocks**	**Bytes**	**Coding Example**
mem8, 0-7, label	14	4-5	LJBT [GA].RESULT, 1, DATA_OK

LJMCE source, target		Long jump if Masked Compare Equal	
Operands	**Clocks**	**Bytes**	**Coding Example**
mem8, label	14	4-5	LJMCE [GB], BYTE_FOUND

LJMCNE source, target		Long jump if Masked Compare Not Equal	
Operands	**Clocks**	**Bytes**	**Coding Example**
mem8, label	14	4-5	LJMCNE [GC+IX+], SCAN_NEXT

LJMP target		Long Jump Unconditional	
Operands	**Clocks**	**Bytes**	**Coding Example**
label	3	4	LJMP GET_CURSOR

LJNBT source, bit-select, target		Long Jump if Bit Not True (0)	
Operands	**Clocks**	**Bytes**	**Coding Example**
mem8, 0-7, label	14	4-5	LJNBT [GC], 6, CRCC_ERROR

LJNZ source, target		Long Jump if Word Not Zero	
Operands	**Clocks**	**Bytes**	**Coding Example**
register, label	5	4	LJNZ BC, PARTIAL_XMIT
mem16, label	12/16	4-5	LJNZ [GA+IX].N_LEFT, PUT_DATA

LJNZB source, target		Long Jump if Byte Not Zero	
Operands	**Clocks**	**Bytes**	**Coding Example**
mem8, label	12	4-5	LJNZB [GB+IX+].ITEM, BUMP_COUNT

LJZ source, target		Long Jump if Word Zero	
Operands	**Clocks**	**Bytes**	**Coding Example**
register, label	5	4	LJZ IX, FIRST_ELEMENT
mem16, label	12/16	4-5	LJZ [GB].XMIT_COUNT, NO_DATA

LJZB source, target		Long Jump if Byte Zero	
Operands	**Clocks**	**Bytes**	**Coding Example**
mem8, label	12	4-5	LJZB [GA], RETURN_LINE

LPD destination, source		Load Pointer With Doubleword Variable	
Operands	**Clocks**	**Bytes**	**Coding Example**
ptr-reg, mem32	20/28	2-3	LPD GA, [PP].BUF_START

LPDI destination, source		Load Pointer With Doubleword Immediate	
Operands	**Clocks**	**Bytes**	**Coding Example**
ptr-reg, immed32	12/16	6	LPDI GB, DISK_ADDRESS

MOV destination, source		Move Word	
Operands	**Clocks**	**Bytes**	**Coding Example**
register, mem16	8/12	2-3	MOV IX, [GC]
mem16, register	10/16	2-3	MOV [GA].COUNT, BC
mem16, mem16	18/28	4-6	MOV [GA].READING, [GB]

MOVB destination, source		Move Byte	
Operands	**Clocks**	**Bytes**	**Coding Example**
register, mem8	8	2-3	MOVB BC, [PP].TRAN_COUNT
mem8, register	10	2-3	MOVB [PP].RETURN_CODE, GC
mem8, mem8	18	4-6	MOVB [GB+IX+], [GA+IX+]

MOVBI destination, source		Move Byte Immediate	
Operands	**Clocks**	**Bytes**	**Coding Example**
register, immed8	3	3	MOVBI MC, 'A'
mem8, immed8	12	3-4	MOVBI [PP].RESULT, 0

MOVI destination, source		Move Word Immediate	
Operands	**Clocks**	**Bytes**	**Coding Example**
register, immed16	3	4	MOVI BC, 0
mem16, immed16	12/18	4-5	MOVI [GB], 0FFFFH

MOVP destination, source		Move Pointer	
Operands	**Clocks**	**Bytes**	**Coding Example**
ptr-reg, mem24	19/27*	2-3	MOVP TP, [GC+IX]
mem24, ptr-reg	16/22*	2-3	MOVP [GB].SAVE_ADDR, GC

NOP (no operands)		No Operation	
Operands	**Clocks**	**Bytes**	**Coding Example**
(no operands)	4	2	NOP

NOT destination/destination, source		Logical NOT Word	
Operands	**Clocks**	**Bytes**	**Coding Example**
register	3	2	NOT MC
mem16	16/26	2-3	NOT [GA].PARM
register, mem16	11/15	2-3	NOT BC, [GA+IX].LINES_LEFT

NOTB destination/destination, source		Logical NOT Byte	
Operands	**Clocks**	**Bytes**	**Coding Example**
mem8	16	2-3	NOTB [GA].PARM_REG
register, mem8	11	2-3	NOTB IX, [GB].STATUS

OR destination, source		Logical OR Word	
Operands	**Clocks**	**Bytes**	**Coding Example**
register, mem16	11/15	2-3	OR MC, [GC].MASK
mem16, register	16/26	2-3	OR [GC], BC

ORB destination, source		Logical OR Byte	
Operands	**Clocks**	**Bytes**	**Coding Example**
register, mem8 mem8, register	11 16	2-3 2-3	ORB IX, [PP].POINTER ORB [GA+IX+], GB

ORBI destination, source		Logical OR Byte Immediate	
Operands	**Clocks**	**Bytes**	**Coding Example**
register, immed8 mem8, immed8	3 16	3 3-4	ORBI IX, 00010001B ORBI [GB].COMMAND, 0CH

ORI destination, source		Logical OR Word Immediate	
Operands	**Clocks**	**Bytes**	**Coding Example**
register, immed16 mem16,immed16	3 16/26	4 4-5	ORI MC, 0FF0DH ORI [GA], 1000H

SETB destination, bit-select		Set Bit to 1	
Operands	**Clocks**	**Bytes**	**Coding Example**
mem8, 0-7	16	2-3	SETB [GA].PARM_REG, 2

SINTR (no operands)		Set Interrupt Service Bit	
Operands	**Clocks**	**Bytes**	**Coding Example**
(no operands)	4	2	SINTR

TSL destination, set-value, target		Test and Set While Locked	
Operands	**Clocks**	**Bytes**	**Coding Example**
mem8, immed8, short-label	14/16	4-5	TSL [GA].FLAG, 0FFH, NOT_READY

WID source-width, dest-width		Set Logical Bus Widths	
Operands	**Clocks**	**Bytes**	**Coding Example**
8/16, 8/16	4	2	WID 8, 8

XFER (no operands)		Enter DMA Transfer Mode After Next Instruction	
Operands	**Clocks**	**Bytes**	**Coding Example**
(no operands)	4	2	XFER

Index